HIGH COURT CASE SUMMARIES

CIVIL PROCEDURE

Keyed to Friedenthal, Miller, Sexton
and Hershkoff's Casebook
on Civil Procedure,
10th Edition

WEST.

A Thomson Reuters business

Mat #41039019

© West, a Thomson business, 2006
© 2010 Thomson Reuters
    610 Opperman Drive
    St. Paul, MN 55123
    1–800–313–9378
Printed in the United States of America

ISBN: 978–0–314–26564–7

Table of Contents

Alphabetical Table of Cases

CHAPTER ONE

A Survey of the Civil Action

Capron v. Van Noorden

Instant Facts: Supreme Court dismissed case because the trial court did not originally have subject matter jurisdiction.

Black Letter Rule: In the Federal Courts, a case will be thrown out for lack of subject matter jurisdiction even if it has already made it to the appellate stage by the time the problem is discovered.

Tickle v. Barton

Instant Facts: Tickle's (P) attorney called Barton (D) anonymously and invited him to a banquet in WV, and while Barton (D) was there, served him with process.

Black Letter Rule: Service of process on a person who has been enticed into a jurisdiction by fraud is not valid.

Case v. State Farm Mutual Automobile Insurance Co.

Instant Facts: Insurance companies terminated contract with their agent when he entered local politics, and he sued them for it, but lost because what he accused them of doing wasn't prohibited.

Black Letter Rule: A complaint should not be dismissed if it alleges facts upon which a court could possibly grant relief, but this doesn't mean that the court should invent a basis for relief when the complaint does not state one.

Temple v. Synthes Corp.

Instant Facts: Temple (P) sued his doctor, the hospital, and a medical manufacturer in separate proceedings, for injuries sustained when a metal plate and screw device malfunctioned.

Black Letter Rule: It is not always necessary to make all joint tortfeasors parties to the same lawsuit.

DiMichel v. South Buffalo Ry. Co.

Instant Facts: Employee suing employer for injuries suffered in work-related fall sought discovery of employer's surveillance tapes and was granted right to view all tapes employer planned to introduce at trial.

Black Letter Rule: Surveillance films are material prepared for litigation and are thus subject to a qualified privilege that can be overcome only by a showing of substantial need and undue hardship; however, personal injury plaintiffs will have no difficulty showing that they have a substantial need to view the films before trial.

Alderman v. Baltimore & Ohio R. Co.

Instant Facts: Alderman (P), a passenger riding with a free pass on a train, sued the Railroad (D) for injuries suffered following a derailment.

Black Letter Rule: Summary judgment is appropriate where the plaintiff fails to demonstrate sufficient factual support for her claims.

Alexander v. Kramer Bros. Freight Lines, Inc.

Instant Facts: In a lawsuit resulting from the collision of two trucks the judge incorrectly charged the jury, which was held not to be reversible error since no objection to the charge had been made.

Black Letter Rule: When the trial judge has erroneously instructed the jury, judgment should usually not be reversed if no objection was made at the time the charge was given.

Diniero v. United States Lines Co.

Instant Facts: The judge gave the jury written questions regarding Diniero's (P) claims to have injured his back while working on U.S.L.'s ship, then withdrew the questions when the jury couldn't reach an agreement.

Black Letter Rule: The withdrawal of written interrogatories that have already been submitted to the jury is not an abuse of discretion by the trial judge.

Texas Employers' Ins. Assn. v. Price

Instant Facts: In an action for insurance benefits, the insurer appealed a jury verdict for an employee on grounds of juror misconduct.

Black Letter Rule: Jurors may not relate special knowledge as original evidence to be considered in jury deliberations.

Lavender v. Kurn

Instant Facts: Haney, a railroad employee, was found dead next to the tracks after being struck in the head, either by a hobo or by something protruding from a train, and the jury decided it had been the train.

Black Letter Rule: An appellate court cannot reverse a jury's decision for lack of evidence to support the verdict, when probative facts exist to support the jury's conclusion.

Hicks v. United States

Instant Facts: The doctor whose misdiagnosis of a woman led to her death was found not to have been negligent at trial, but negligent on appeal.

Black Letter Rule: The general rule that a trial judge's findings of fact should not be disturbed unless clearly erroneous does not apply when the judge's conclusions are based on undisputed testimony and evidence.

Des Moines Navigation & R. Co. v. Iowa Homestead Co.

Instant Facts: Iowa Homestead Co. (P) sued for back taxes and lost, then tried a second time because the first suit had been tried in federal courts, which had not had proper jurisdiction over the case.

Black Letter Rule: Even cases that have been decided without proper jurisdiction have res judicata value, at least until they are judicially annulled, vacated, or set aside.

Capron v. Van Noorden

(Victim) v. *(Negligent Injurer)*
6 U.S. (2 Cranch) 126 (1804)

U.S. SUPREME COURT THROWS OUT CASE FOR LACK OF SUBJECT MATTER JURISDICTION

■ **INSTANT FACTS** Supreme Court dismissed case because the trial court did not originally have subject matter jurisdiction.

■ **BLACK LETTER RULE** In the Federal Courts, a case will be thrown out for lack of subject matter jurisdiction even if it has already made it to the appellate stage by the time the problem is discovered.

■ PROCEDURAL BASIS

Writ of error to the United States Circuit Court of North Carolina for its judgment in action for damages for trespass on the case [i.e., negligence].

■ FACTS

Capron (P) sued Van Noorden (D) for "trespass on the case," an old form of negligence, in the federal circuit court of North Carolina. Although Capron (P) alleged in his complaint that Van Noorden (D) was a resident of North Carolina, he did not allege that he himself was a resident of some other state, or of a foreign country. Since the case did not involve any issues of federal law, the case could only have been heard in federal court if there was diversity jurisdiction—that is, if the parties were not both residents of the same state. Thus, since Capron (P) did not allege the necessary elements of diversity jurisdiction, the circuit court should have dismissed the case. However, the circuit court went ahead and heard the case, and Capron (P) lost. Capron (P) then appealed to the Supreme Court, but not on the grounds that he should have won in the trial court. Instead, Capron (P) argued that his own complaint had been defective, and that he should never have been allowed to go to trial at all The Supreme Court agreed, and overturned the verdict in favor of Van Noorden (D). Of course, this doesn't mean that Capron (P) ended up winning; instead, it's legally as if the entire trial never really happened.

■ ISSUE

Will the federal courts throw out a case on appeal for lack of proper subject matter jurisdiction?

■ DECISION AND RATIONALE

(Justice Not Named) Yes. The federal courts are courts of limited jurisdiction, which means that they cannot hear just any case that is brought before them. In fact, the issue of jurisdiction is so important that, even if it is not discovered that proper subject matter jurisdiction is lacking in a case until after a long, expensive trial which reached a correct result on the substantive issues involved, that case must still be tossed out. Certain areas of jurisdiction were granted to the Federal Courts by the U.S. Constitution, so overstepping these bounds and trying a case properly left to the state courts is a serious breach of the essential compromise at the heart of the American system of government, and an infringement of state sovereignty. Judgment reversed.

Analysis:

This case underscores the extreme importance of subject matter jurisdiction for the Federal Courts. If it is ever discovered, even after a case has gone through a trial and the complete appellate process, that proper subject matter jurisdiction was lacking, that case will be thrown out. There are several other reasons why a case might not be allowed to proceed to trial in a Federal District Court—such as lack of personal jurisdiction—but once a case has gone to trial, such objections, unlike subject matter jurisdiction, are deemed to have been waived, and cannot be re-opened on appeal. *Capron* went up to the Supreme Court of the United States, after having had a full trial, and it was still thrown out. And making this case an even stronger statement of the importance of subject matter jurisdiction is the fact that Capron (P), the party responsible for filing a deficient complaint in the first place, was the one to bring the question up on appeal. This sounds bizarre, but it actually works to Capron's (P) advantage. Normally, once a case has been decided, the same issue/event cannot be retried. But since the case has now been thrown out, it does not serve as a bar to a future action. So long as the statute of limitations has not run out. Capron can now bring his case in state court, or even in federal court again, if he can show proper jurisdiction this time around.

■ **CASE VOCABULARY**

TRESPASS ON THE CASE: Form of action for damages for an injury to a party because of the wrongful act of another which is not accompanied by a direct or immediate force.

WRIT OF ERROR: An order of an appellate court directed at the trial court to deliver the record to the appellate court so that the judgment can be reversed.

Tickle v. Barton

(Victim) v. *(Owner of Car)*
142 W.Va. 188, 95 S.E.2d 427 (1956)

WEST VIRGINIA COURT DECLINES TO EXERCISE JURISDICTION OVER INDIVIDUALS ENTICED INTO THE JURISDICTION BY FRAUD

■ **INSTANT FACTS** Tickle's (P) attorney called Barton (D) anonymously and invited him to a banquet in WV, and while Barton (D) was there, served him with process.

■ **BLACK LETTER RULE** Service of process on a person who has been enticed into a jurisdiction by fraud is not valid.

■ **PROCEDURAL BASIS**

Question certified to appeals court from denial of demurrer to plea in abatement challenging validity of service of process.

■ **FACTS**

Tickle (P) was injured in West Virginia by a car owned by Barton (D), a resident of Virginia. Tickle (P) sued Barton (D) in West Virginia court and served notice on him in Virginia. Barton (D) challenged this service, so Tickle (P) tried to find another way to serve notice. Therefore, when Barton (D) was in West Virginia attending a banquet. Tickle (P) served him notice again. Of course, Barton (D) challenged this too, claiming that Tickle's (P) lawyer had enticed him into West Virginia by fraud, by calling him up and inviting him to the banquet. Tickle's (P) attorney denied this claim, yet Tickle (P) demurred to this plea, so the court had to take Barton's (D) claim at face value. Therefore, the question was whether or not the alleged actions of Tickle's (P) attorney constituted fraud, which would make the service of process invalid.

■ **ISSUE**

If a person is enticed by fraud into a jurisdiction for service of process, is that service of process valid?

■ **DECISION AND RATIONALE**

(Haymond) No. The rule is clear: service of process is not valid if the person served has been enticed into the jurisdiction by fraud. The question really is whether or not the actions alleged here, which are assumed to be true because the issue has arisen on a demurrer, constitute fraud. As Tickle's (P) attorney did not have the authority to invite Barton (D) to the banquet, and did so with the intent of tricking him into coming to West Virginia in order to serve him with process, these actions do constitute misrepresentation or fraud. Barton (D) would not have come into West Virginia but for this unauthorized invitation, and though he knew that Tickle (P) was trying to serve him with process, he did not suspect that the invitation was in any way related to the lawsuit. Ruling affirmed.

■ **DISSENT**

(Given) No. It is true that the rule is clear. Service of process is not valid when the person served has been enticed into the jurisdiction by fraud. However, the actions alleged here, even if they are all true and capable of being proved, do not constitute fraud. At most, all the attorney did that was wrong was fail to identify himself when he called Barton (D). He didn't lie about the banquet—it really was going to happen. Plus, Barton (D) already knew about the lawsuit, and knew that Tickle (P) was trying to serve him with process, since there had already been one attempt to do so, so he should have realized that going into West Virginia might be dangerous. Therefore, Tickle's (P) demurrer should be upheld, and Barton (D) should be deemed to have been properly served.

Analysis:

The court in this case, which really does not give persuasive reasoning for why it believes that the alleged actions would constitute fraud, certainly gives the impression that it doesn't quite believe Barton's (D) story. It seems to imply that Barton (D) probably won't be able to prove his story, which he will now have to try to do. However, there are reasons for restricting a court's jurisdiction, after all, so letting clever lawyers circumvent the system through deceit and trickery probably isn't good public policy. So Barton (D) should at least get the chance to try to prove his allegations, as such actions are not the kind of behavior the court wants to encourage in attorneys. The most important aspect of this case, however, at least in this part of the course, is primarily to point out the difference between subject matter jurisdiction and personal jurisdiction, a distinction which confuses many beginning students of civil procedure. Subject matter jurisdiction affects whether a court can hear the *type* of case presented—here, there is no problem, since state courts are usually courts of general jurisdiction and can hear just about any type of case. Personal jurisdiction, on the other hand, involves the question of whether a court can exercise power over the particular individuals involved in the case. Here, the question is whether, and under what circumstances, a West Virginia court has personal jurisdiction over a resident of Virginia.

■ CASE VOCABULARY

DEMURRER: Formal objection which asserts, without disputing the facts, that a pleading does not state a cause of action.

PLEA IN ABATEMENT: Plea which objects to place, mode or time of asserting the plaintiff's claim; does not address any underlying merits.

Case v. State Farm Mutual Automobile Insurance Co.

(Agent) v. *(Insurance Companies)*
294 F.2d 676 (5th Cir. 1961)

APPEALS COURT RULES THAT LOWER COURT CANNOT ASSUME WORDS TO BE IN PLAINTIFF'S COMPLAINT

■ **INSTANT FACTS** Insurance companies terminated contract with their agent when he entered local politics, and he sued them for it, but lost because what he accused them of doing wasn't prohibited.

■ **BLACK LETTER RULE** A complaint should not be dismissed if it alleges facts upon which a court could possibly grant relief, but this doesn't mean that the court should invent a basis for relief when the complaint does not state one.

■ PROCEDURAL BASIS

Appeal from granting of motion to dismiss complaint for damages for breach of contract.

■ FACTS

Case (P), an insurance agent who represented three insurance companies (D) in his area, entered the race for County Supervisor of Adams County, Mississippi, in 1959. The insurance companies (D) then began to threaten that they would terminate his contract with them unless he dropped out of the race. Case (P) sued the insurance companies (D) for what he called "malicious" "meddl[ing] and interfer[ing]" with his work. The court interpreted this to mean that Case (P) was suing for wrongful termination, but the contract that existed between Case (P) and the insurance companies (D) gave the insurance companies (D) the right to terminate Case (P) without cause—that is, for any, or no, reason at all. Therefore, what Case (P) was accusing them of doing was perfectly within their rights, so Case's (P) complaint was dismissed for failure to state a claim upon which relief could be granted.

■ ISSUE

Will a complaint be dismissed if it fails to set forth facts upon which a court could possibly grant relief?

■ DECISION AND RATIONALE

(Cameron) Yes. A complaint will be dismissed if it fails to set forth facts upon which a court could possibly grant relief. This is true even if the court could imagine some other claim that the plaintiff might have made, but didn't. In this case, the plaintiff alleged in his complaint that the insurance companies (D) had effectively terminated his contract. There is nothing that can be said to this, except: So what? The insurance companies had every right to terminate his contract. There is no relief to be had. So there is nothing the court can do. Case (P) did argue in support of his complaint that the insurance companies (D) might have interfered with his civil rights, but there is nothing in the complaint itself to support this. Case (P) could have amended his complaint to reflect this argument, or others, and the outcome might have been different, but he did not. Therefore, the complaint as it stands does not set forth facts upon which a court might grant relief and must be dismissed. Judgment affirmed.

Analysis:

This case illustrates the importance and complexity of correct pleading. One of the first steps in any lawsuit is the filing of a complaint. If the complaint is not extremely carefully drafted, a case can be thrown out for a variety of reasons, as was shown in Case. This is less true under the Federal Rules, but was certainly the case before they were adopted, and to this day in many state court systems. Often, a case will be dismissed regardless of the ultimate merits of a plaintiff's claim, based simply on procedural problems with the complaint. This demonstrates just how important a thorough knowledge of procedure really is and the huge impact that procedural matters have on the resolution of substantive issues of law.

Temple v. Synthes Corp.

(Patient) v. *(Implant Manufacturer)*
498 U.S. 5, 111 S.Ct. 315 (1990)

IT IS NOT NECESSARY TO MAKE ALL JOINT TORTFEASORS PARTIES TO THE SAME LAWSUIT

■ **INSTANT FACTS** Temple (P) sued his doctor, the hospital, and a medical manufacturer in separate proceedings, for injuries sustained when a metal plate and screw device malfunctioned.

■ **BLACK LETTER RULE** It is not always necessary to make all joint tortfeasors parties to the same lawsuit.

■ **PROCEDURAL BASIS**

Writ of certiorari reviewing affirmance of dismissal of claim for failure to join necessary parties.

■ **FACTS**

Temple (P) underwent a surgery in which a plate and screw device, manufactured by Synthes, Ltd. (D), was inserted in Temple's (P) spine. Following the surgery, the device's screws broke off inside Temple's (P) back. Temple (P) sued Synthes (D) in a Louisiana federal district court based on diversity jurisdiction, alleging that the design and manufacture of the device were defective. In addition, Temple (P) initiated a state administrative proceeding against the surgeon and the hospital in which the surgery was performed. [Why didn't Temple bring only one action? Did he have a screw loose?] At the conclusion of the administrative proceeding, Temple (P) sued the doctor and hospital in a state court in Louisiana. Synthes (D) filed a motion to dismiss the original claim for failure to join the doctor and hospital in the suit. The District Court ordered Temple (P) to join those parties. However, Temple (P) refused, and the District Court dismissed the action with prejudice. The Fifth Circuit Court of Appeals affirmed the dismissal, on the grounds that Synthes (D) was prejudiced by not having the doctor and the hospital present in the original litigation, since one of Synthes' (D) defenses might be that the doctor and hospital were negligent. The Supreme Court granted certiorari.

■ **ISSUE**

Must all interested entities always be made parties to a lawsuit?

■ **DECISION AND RATIONALE**

(Per Curiam) No. All interested entities do not necessarily have to be made parties to a lawsuit. Rule 19 of the Federal Rules of Civil Procedure governs the joinder of parties. Rule 19(a) dictates when parties must be joined, and Rule 19(b) allows a court to dismiss a suit if such joinder is not feasible. In the case at hand, the Court of Appeals held that the doctor and hospital should have been joined pursuant to Rule 19(a). However, we agree with Temple (P) that it was error to label the joint tortfeasors as indispensable parties and dismiss the lawsuit under Rule 19(b). As stated in the Advisory Committee Notes to Rule 19(a), it is not necessary that all joint tortfeasors be named as defendants to a lawsuit. Rather, the doctor and the hospital were merely permissive parties, whose joinder is not required. We reverse the judgment of the Court of Appeals and remand for further proceedings consistent with this opinion. Reversed and remanded.

Analysis:

This case provides an early glimpse into the complex rules of joinder in federal courts. Basically, the Federal Rules of Civil Procedure detail the circumstances under which a party must be joined to a pending lawsuit. For example, if complete relief cannot be afforded without the presence of a certain party, he must be made a party to the lawsuit. This rule accomplishes the overriding goal of judicial efficiency, as it is in the public interest to have all related claims tried in the same lawsuit. While it is not yet necessary to understand all of the workings of joinder at this point in the course, close attention should be paid to the recurring theme of judicial efficiency. Often judicial efficiency, in itself, mandates certain steps in a civil trial. However, these policy considerations are balanced by the rights of the parties. In the case at hand, Temple (P) was not required to bring suit against all of the defendants in the same action, although this certainly would have been more efficient. Notice that Temple (P) benefits from not having to sue the manufacturer, doctor and hospital in the same proceeding, since the parties cannot argue that the other's negligence actually caused the injury.

■ CASE VOCABULARY

ADMINISTRATIVE PROCEEDING: A form of litigation before administrative agencies, rather than before a court.

DIVERSITY JURISDICTION: A means of federal subject-matter jurisdiction based on parties residing in different states.

JOINDER: The addition of persons or entities as parties to a lawsuit.

PER CURIAM: A phrase meaning "by the court," used to distinguish opinions written by the entire panel of judges rather than by a single judge.

WITH PREJUDICE: The dismissal of a claim which results in precluding the claim from being brought at a later time.

DiMichel v. South Buffalo Ry. Co.

(Employee) v. *(Employer)*

80 N.Y.2d 184, 604 N.E.2d 63 (1992)

NEW YORK COURT OF APPEALS DECIDES TO ALLOW DISCOVERY OF SURVEILLANCE FILMS

■ **INSTANT FACTS** Employee suing employer for injuries suffered in work-related fall sought discovery of employer's surveillance tapes and was granted right to view all tapes employer planned to introduce at trial.

■ **BLACK LETTER RULE** Surveillance films are material prepared for litigation and are thus subject to a qualified privilege that can be overcome only by a showing of substantial need and undue hardship; however, personal injury plaintiffs will have no difficulty showing that they have a substantial need to view the films before trial.

■ **PROCEDURAL BASIS**

Appeal from modification of order granting motion to compel disclosure of surveillance tapes in personal injury litigation.

■ **FACTS**

DiMichel (P), an employee of South Buffalo Railway Co. (D), was injured in a fall at work. He sued South Buffalo (D) for damages and during pretrial discovery asked South Buffalo (D) to make available to him any and all surveillance tapes they might have made of him. In personal injury suits surveillance tapes are usually the result of investigative work by the defense, which hopes to show somehow that the plaintiff's injuries are not as serious as he claims—imagine, for instance, the PI that follows the supposedly wheelchair-bound plaintiff until he catches him out dancing with his girlfriend. Obviously, not all tapes are this dramatic, but nevertheless it is to the plaintiff's advantage to know whether the defendant has produced anything that he might have to defend against. In this case, South Buffalo (D) refused to disclose any such material, and DiMichel (P) then moved to compel disclosure. The trial court granted this motion and ordered South Buffalo (D) to turn over all surveillance materials. The Appellate Division modified this order slightly, however, and ordered South Buffalo (D) to turn over all surveillance materials that it intended to use at trial, and not necessarily everything it had in its possession. Any materials that South Buffalo (D) had not turned over within 60 days of the Appellate Division's order it would be barred from introducing at trial. South Buffalo (D) appealed this order to the Court of Appeals, which is the highest state court in New York.

■ **ISSUE**

Are surveillance films material considered to be "prepared for litigation," and thus subject to a qualified privilege?

■ **DECISION AND RATIONALE**

(Wachtler) Yes. Surveillance films should be considered material prepared for litigation and so subject to a qualified privilege. The defendant has expended time and resources in preparing these films, exclusively in preparation for trial, and therefore cannot be compelled to release all such films it might have made. However, this does not leave the plaintiff without recourse. The privilege protecting these films is qualified and can be overcome by a factual showing of substantial need and undue hardship. Given the potential impact of surveillance films on a personal injury trial, showing substantial need should not be hard to do and has certainly been done in this case. Film, as an apparently objective and unbiased witness, can have an enormous impact on a jury. Yet films can obviously be altered, edited, and spliced to show a version of the "truth" that doesn't quite correspond to reality, as anyone who's been to the movies lately would agree. Even film that has not been altered can be shown removed from a context that would explain suspicious behavior or actions. If the plaintiff were not allowed to view before trial any tapes the defense intended to present as evidence, he could be caught totally unprepared to explain why the video should not be believed. Access to the films before trial would allow the plaintiff to have an expert verify or call into question their authenticity. Since this process can be time-consuming, it could be very prejudicial to make the plaintiff wait to authenticate a film until after it had been shown to the jury. Even if the plaintiff were able to show that the film had been tampered with, it would be hard to erase the images from the jurors' minds—especially if days or weeks had passed. In addition, New York has a long history of open and far-reaching pre-trial discovery, and it would run counter to that history to deny plaintiffs the right to view in advance those films that the defendants intended to show at trial. Order affirmed.

Analysis:

This case Illustrates, for one thing, the increased importance of pretrial discovery in recent years, and not just in federal courts. Many state systems have been greatly influenced by the Federal Rules of Civil Procedure, which encourage reliance on discovery, rather than the pleadings, as the best method of developing a case for trial. Of course, while extended skirmishes over the sufficiency of the pleadings have greatly diminished in number, contests over what is discoverable have increased dramatically, as *DiMichel* clearly demonstrates. This case also gives a clear indication of the philosophy behind the switch to emphasizing discovery over the pleadings. Discovery aims to help both sides be as prepared for trial as they can be, so that the outcome of the trial depends less on last-minute "Perry Mason" surprise evidence and the ability of the attorneys, and more on the actual merits of a party's case.

Alderman v. Baltimore & Ohio R. Co.

(Passenger) v. *(Railroad)*

113 F.Supp. 881 (S.D.W.V. 1953)

SUMMARY JUDGMENT IS APPROPRIATE WHERE NO MATERIAL ISSUES ARE IN DISPUTE

■ **INSTANT FACTS** Alderman (P), a passenger riding with a free pass on a train, sued the Railroad (D) for injuries suffered following a derailment.

■ **BLACK LETTER RULE** Summary judgment is appropriate where the plaintiff fails to demonstrate sufficient factual support for her claims.

■ **PROCEDURAL BASIS**

Ruling on motion for summary judgment on action for damages for willful and wanton conduct.

■ **FACTS**

Alderman (P) was injured while riding on a Baltimore & Ohio R. Co. (Railroad) (D) train when the railroad cars derailed. Alderman (P) was traveling on a free transportation pass, on which was printed that the passenger assumed the risk of all personal injury and relieved the Railroad (D) of liability. Alderman (P) sued the Railroad (D) for negligence in the maintenance of its tracks, later amending the complaint to charge the Railroad (D) with willful or wanton conduct. The Railroad (D) moved for summary judgment, contending that Alderman (P) could not prove that the Railroad's (D) conduct was willful or wanton.

■ **ISSUE**

In order to avoid summary judgment, must a plaintiff demonstrate that the facts forming the basis for the cause of action can be established?

■ **DECISION AND RATIONALE**

(Moore, J.) Yes. In order to avoid summary judgment, a plaintiff must demonstrate that the facts forming the basis for the cause of action can be established. In the instant action, West Virginia law supplies no precedent governing purported releases from liability contained on a railroad pass. However, the Supreme Court has held that this limitation of liability protects a railroad against liability for negligence, but that it does not amount to a release of liability for willful or wanton acts [No, it is not a coincidence that Alderman (D) amended her complaint to allege such conduct!]. In order for an act to be considered willful or wanton, the actor must have been conscious of his conduct and must have known that an injury would likely result from his conduct. In the case at hand, Alderman's (P) complaint failed to state facts sufficient to demonstrate that the Railroad (D) acted willfully. In order to establish willfulness, Alderman (P) must have shown that the Railroad (D) knew of the defect in the rail, that the defect would probably result in a break if a train ran over it, and that the Railroad (D) intentionally drove its train over the rail with an indifference to the consequences. The facts at hand demonstrate that the accident was likely caused by a transverse fissure in the rail, that a visual inspection was made of this particular rail the day proceeding the accident, and that such fissures could not be discovered upon visual examination. Alderman (P) will, therefore, be unable to prove that the Railroad (D) acted willfully and wantonly after having knowledge of the rail defect. The Railroad's (D) motion for summary judgment will be sustained.

Analysis:

The overriding policy consideration of judicial efficiency once again surfaces, this time in the context of a motion for summary judgment. As you will discover later in the course, a motion for summary judgment essentially dismisses a complaint at the very early stages of litigation. Where a complaint fails to state sufficient facts on which relief can be granted, and where the plaintiff fails to demonstrate additional facts in support of her claim, it is in the best interests of the judicial system to dismiss the complaint before precious judicial resources are expended. If a plaintiff has no chance of winning, why allow a case to go all the way to a jury? This efficiency consideration must, of course, be balanced against fairness. Where the facts indicate even a slight chance of a party prevailing on her claim, that claim should go to trial rather than being summarily dismissed. It is important to note the difference between a motion for summary judgment and a motion to dismiss. A motion to dismiss (also known as a demurrer) may be granted following the initial pleadings, where a claim fails to state sufficient grounds for relief even if all of the factual allegations are presumed to be true. A motion for summary judgment, on the other hand, is typically granted following the discovery process. If discovery fails to reveal any genuine issues of material fact in dispute, then Rule 56 allows the court to enter judgment as a matter of law in favor of the moving party.

■ CASE VOCABULARY

MOTION FOR SUMMARY JUDGMENT: Procedural device allowing for prompt resolution of a suit when no material issues are in dispute.

Alexander v. Kramer Bros. Freight Lines, Inc.

(Driver of Following Truck) v. *(Owner of Leading Truck)*

273 F.2d 373 (2d Cir. 1959)

COURT HOLDS CASE SHOULD NOT BE DISMISSED EVEN THOUGH TRIAL JUDGE GAVE INCORRECT JURY INSTRUCTION

■ **INSTANT FACTS** In a lawsuit resulting from the collision of two trucks the judge incorrectly charged the jury, which was held not to be reversible error since no objection to the charge had been made.

■ **BLACK LETTER RULE** When the trial judge has erroneously instructed the jury, judgment should usually not be reversed if no objection was made at the time the charge was given.

■ **PROCEDURAL BASIS**

Appeal from judgment for plaintiffs in action for damages for negligence.

■ **FACTS**

Two tractor-trailer trucks, one driven by Alexander (P), the other owned by Kramer Bros. Freight Lines, Inc. ("Kramer") (D), collided early one foggy morning on the Pennsylvania Turnpike. Alexander (P) was seriously injured, and his truck badly damaged. So, naturally, he sued Kramer (D) for damages. Alexander (P) claimed that Kramer's (D) truck had suddenly cut in ahead of him from the right, while the driver of Kramer's (D) truck claimed that he did not come in from the right, but that Alexander (P) had been following him closely for some time, and eventually hit him from behind. Kramer (D) thus claimed as a defense that Alexander (P) had been contributorily negligent, and therefore that the accident was at least partly his fault. When the judge instructed the jury on the issue of who bears the burden of proof with respect to contributory negligence, he got it wrong. Normally, the plaintiff has the burden of proving that he was not contributorily negligent, but the judge here told the jury that the defendant had to prove that the plaintiff was contributorily negligent. Kramer (D) should have objected at this point, but did not. The jury eventually returned a verdict for Alexander (P), and Kramer (D) appealed, claiming that the erroneous instruction on contributory negligence was reversible error. However, Federal Rule 51 ("Instructions to Jury: Objection") requires that an objection to the charge be clearly made before the jury retires, so where this is not done—except in rare circumstances—an erroneous charge will not be grounds for a reversal.

■ **ISSUE**

When the trial judge has erroneously instructed the jury, should judgment be reversed even though no objection was made to the charge at the time?

■ **DECISION AND RATIONALE**

(Swan) No. Or at least, not usually, and certainly not here. It is required by Federal Rule 51 that, when the trial judge incorrectly charges the jury with respect to any part of the law, that charge must be objected to before the jury retires for deliberations. Without this rule, there would obviously be a danger of too many frivolous appeals being filed, after the party who ended up losing had a chance to go over the judge's charge with a fine-tooth comb looking for anything that might arguably be wrong or even ambiguous. Rule 51 limits appeals based on error in the jury instructions to those cases where the charge was actually objected to, and the judge had time to correct the mistake. Of course, there are cases where the judge is so egregiously wrong, and the mistake so central to the outcome of the case, that an exception will be made and the error corrected on appeal regardless. But this is not one of those situations. Likewise, there are sometimes situations in which a party does express disagreement with a charge, but there is some question as to whether it was sufficiently explicit. Kramer (D) argues that it did take exception to the charge at one point in the proceedings, and so should be treated as one of these cases and allowed the benefit of the doubt, so to speak. However, the discussion to which Kramer (D) refers took place before Kramer (D) even presented its case, so was too far in advance of the actual charge to fall within the Rule 51 requirements. Judgment affirmed.

Analysis:

To understand this case fully, it is necessary to understand the breakdown in functions between judge and jury in a jury trial. As it is often put, the judge is the trier of law, and the jury is the trier of fact. This means that the judge is responsible for deciding what law should be applied in a particular case, and the jury must decide what the true facts are, i.e., which witnesses to believe, etc. What usually happens is that the judge will decide what law should apply and instructs the jury on this point. This is the "charge," or the "jury instruction." Of course, as with everything else in the adversary system, lawyers from both sides have a hand in the charge as well. Often each side will submit to the judge a list of which laws they believe should apply, as well as the particular phrasing of the charge, and the judge will review these submissions in deciding on the charge. The lawyers for each side are supposed to instruct the judge on the law that applies and bring to his or her attention any cases that are on point. In some state courts, any error in the charge to the jury is deemed to be automatic grounds for reversal. However, in federal court (and in state courts which follow the lead of the Federal Rules). Federal Rule 51 requires that when a trial judge errs in the charge to the jury with respect to any part of the law, that charge must be objected to by a party's lawyer before the jury retires for deliberations. Since Kramer's (D) attorney did not object at the appropriate time to the judge's charge, the judgment was not reversed. Thus it seems that silence isn't always golden!

■ CASE VOCABULARY

COLLOQUY: A high-level serious discussion; conference.

Diniero v. United States Lines Co.

(Sailor) v. *(Ship Owner)*

288 F.2d 595 (2d Cir. 1961), *cert. denied*, 368 U.S. 831, 82 S.Ct. 54

COURT HOLDS IT TO BE NO ABUSE OF DISCRETION FOR JUDGE TO ISSUE AND THEN WITHDRAW WRITTEN INTERROGATORIES TO THE JURY

■ **INSTANT FACTS** The judge gave the jury written questions regarding Diniero's (P) claims to have injured his back while working on U.S.L.'s ship, then withdrew the questions when the jury couldn't reach an agreement.

■ **BLACK LETTER RULE** The withdrawal of written interrogatories that have already been submitted to the jury is not an abuse of discretion by the trial judge.

■ **PROCEDURAL BASIS**

Appeal from judgment for plaintiff in action for damages for negligence.

■ **FACTS**

Diniero (P), a sailor aboard a ship operated by United States Lines Co. ("U.S.L.") (D), filed suit against U.S.L. (D) alleging that he had suffered permanent injury to his back as a result of his shipboard duties. After a long, complicated trial the judge submitted the case to the jury in the form of 8 written interrogatories. The jury deliberated for several hours and sent the judge several notes asking for clarification of the first question. The judge attempted to explain the question, but the jury was still unable to reach a verdict. After the jury had deliberated for almost 4 hours, they sent the judge a note saying that they did not think agreement would be possible, and he then withdrew all the interrogatories and asked them if they could reach a general verdict. After another 4 hours or so, they did, finding for Diniero (P). U.S.L. (D) appealed, claiming that, though the submission of written interrogatories is authorized, the withdrawal of such interrogatories, once submitted, is not authorized and is an abuse of discretion on the part of the judge.

■ **ISSUE**

Is the withdrawal of written interrogatories that have already been submitted to the jury an abuse of discretion by the trial judge?

■ **DECISION AND RATIONALE**

(Medina) No. It is not an abuse of discretion to withdraw from the jury previously submitted written interrogatories. Here, the judge submitted 8 questions to the jury, over which they deliberated for several hours, and of which they asked for clarification. The problem centered around question number 1, which was a truly ambiguous and confusing question. Withdrawing all the questions was an attempt to eliminate the confusion that the improperly worded question had caused, not an attempt to bias the jury, or to encourage the jury to ignore the law and decide for whichever party they liked better. The alternative to withdrawing the questions would probably have been to declare a mistrial and start over again—a course not to be recommended if it can be avoided, considering the extra expense involved and the extra burden on the courts. And it is certainly also relevant that the jury deliberated for almost as long a time after the questions were withdrawn as before. Of course, there have been and will be cases where written interrogatories are withdrawn from consideration for improper reasons or in improper ways, but in this case it was properly done and not an abuse of discretion. Judgment affirmed.

Analysis:

This case introduces the concepts of "general" and "specific" verdicts. It is still most common for judges to ask for a general verdict, which is basically just the jury finding in favor of one side over another. A special verdict, however, requires the jury to answer a series of specific questions about the facts of the case. The judge will then take these answers and apply the law himself to reach a general verdict. Another variation is for the jury to be asked to declare a general verdict, but in addition to answering interrogatories. This enables the judge to determine whether the jury's findings of fact are consistent with its general verdict. Both of these methods are used to control the jury, and to keep them from ignoring the law and deciding cases based on emotion, or prejudice.

Texas Employers' Ins. Assn. v. Price

(*Insurance Company*) v. (*Injured Worker*)
336 S.W.2d 304 (Tex. Civ. App. 1960)

JURORS MAY NOT RELATE THEIR OWN SPECIAL KNOWLEDGE AS EVIDENCE TO BE CONSIDERED IN JURY DELIBERATIONS

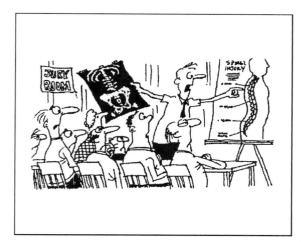

■ **INSTANT FACTS** In an action for insurance benefits, the insurer appealed a jury verdict for an employee on grounds of juror misconduct.

■ **BLACK LETTER RULE** Jurors may not relate special knowledge as original evidence to be considered in jury deliberations.

■ **PROCEDURAL BASIS**

Appeal seeking new trial following jury verdict awarding insurance benefits for injury.

■ **FACTS**

Loyal Grant Price (P) sued the Texas Employers' Ins. Assn. (D) to set aside an award in favor of Texas Employers (D). Alleging that he suffered total and permanent disability while working for the Port Houston Iron Works, Price (P) sought to recover insurance benefits. Texas Employers (D) contended that the injury resulted in only partial and temporary incapacity. Price's (P) own doctor testified that Price's (P) injury was twenty percent partial and, therefore, not completely permanent. However, the jury concluded that the disability was total and permanent, entering a judgment for Price (P) for over $13,000. Texas Employers (D) appealed on grounds of juror misconduct, arguing that one juror related to other jurors his own personal experience with permanent injuries. The juror opined that few companies would hire Price (P) with his history of back problems, and that Price (P) should be considered permanently disabled. Furthermore, Texas Employers (D) contended that the jury verdict was against the preponderance of the evidence. Texas Employers (D) sought a new trial on both grounds.

■ **ISSUE**

May a juror relate to other jurors his personal experiences as original evidence of material facts to be considered in their deliberation?

■ **DECISION AND RATIONALE**

(Collings, J.) No. A juror may not relate to other jurors his personal experiences as original evidence of material facts to be considered in their deliberation. In the case at hand, a juror related his personal experiences to the jury concerning the practices of employers in hiring workmen. He contended that Price (P) could not get a job in any company that had a union contract or employee benefits. The purpose of such statements was to show that Price (P) was totally incapacitated. We hold that the jury verdict was not necessarily against the weight of the evidence, even though the verdict conflicted with the testimony of Price's (P) doctor. However, the juror's use of his personal experiences in arguing that Price (P) should be considered permanently disabled constitutes material misconduct. The judgment of the trial court is reversed and the case is remanded for new trial.

Analysis:

This case presents an extremely narrow approach to the application of a juror's personal knowledge in jury deliberations. On one hand, trial by jury requires ordinary citizens to decide a case based solely on the facts and law at issue. On the other hand, jurors necessarily must utilize their own general personal experiences in arriving at a verdict. Therefore, a line must be drawn between general experience and special knowledge. In the case at hand, the juror presumably persuaded other jurors to find Price (P) permanently disabled, based on the juror's special knowledge of employment of disabled persons. The court held that this juror overstepped the permissible bounds of jury deliberation. Perhaps application of the knowledge would not have amounted to jury misconduct if the juror simply kept the knowledge to himself, or if he opined regarding more general considerations of total disability. Nevertheless, this restrictive holding can be criticized for infringing into the normally private arena of jury deliberation. Jurors are typically encouraged to utilize their own general experiences, and to communicate such experiences to other jurors in order to arrive at unanimous consent to a verdict.

Lavender v. Kurn

(*Administrator of Deceased's Estate*) v. (*Trustee of Deceased's Employer*)
327 U.S. 645, 66 S.Ct. 740 (1946)

U.S. SUPREME COURT REBUKES MISSOURI SUPREME COURT FOR WRONGLY OVERTURNING A JURY'S VERDICT WHEN THERE WAS EVIDENCE TO SUPPORT VERDICT

■ **INSTANT FACTS** Haney, a railroad employee, was found dead next to the tracks after being struck in the head, either by a hobo or by something protruding from a train, and the jury decided it had been the train.

■ **BLACK LETTER RULE** An appellate court cannot reverse a jury's decision for lack of evidence to support the verdict, when probative facts exist to support the jury's conclusion.

■ **PROCEDURAL BASIS**

Writ of Certiorari to the Supreme Court after Missouri Supreme Court reversed judgment for plaintiff in action for negligence.

■ **FACTS**

Lavender (P), the administrator of the estate of Mr. L.E. Haney, brought suit for the death of Mr. Haney against his employers, the St. Louis-San Francisco Railway Company (Frisco), and the Illinois Central Railroad Company. One dark December night in 1939, Haney was working as usual in the railyards outside Grand Central Station in Memphis, Tennessee, when a Frisco train pulled into the station. Haney opened a switch to permit the train to enter on the correct track, but did not close the switch after the train had passed, as he was required to do. When station personnel went to investigate, they found Haney lying dead, face-down near the track. He had been struck in the back of the head by some fast-moving, small, round object. At trial, Lavender (P) contended that Haney had been struck by a mail-hook attached to the train that had passed him, while the railroad companies (D) contended that Haney had been killed by a hobo. There was extensive evidence for and against both possible explanations, but the jury found that Haney had been killed by the mail-hook, and awarded damages accordingly. The Missouri Supreme Court reversed, however, ruling that the case should never have been allowed to go to the jury in the first place, as the "plaintiff failed to make a submissible case on that question." Lavender (P) appealed to the U.S. Supreme Court, which was possible since the suit was brought under the Federal Employers' Liability Act, rather than just common-law negligence.

■ **ISSUE**

Can an appellate court reverse a jury's decision for lack of evidence to support the verdict, when probative facts do, in fact, exist to support the jury's conclusion?

■ **DECISION AND RATIONALE**

(Murphy) No. "Only when there is a complete absence of probative facts to support the conclusion reached does a reversible error occur." Here, it is just not possible to say that there was a complete absence of facts to support the jury's decision. Obviously, there was evidence to support the other possible conclusion as well, but the entire purpose that a jury is supposed to serve is to evaluate and choose which set of facts to believe. The fact that the jury disbelieves some testimony in reaching a decision is almost inevitable. There was plenty of evidence for the jury here to decide that Haney was struck and killed by a mail-hook rather than a hobo. It was shown to be well within the realm of possibility for the mail-hook to have swung out from the train at the exact height of Haney's head. There was no evidence of a fight or struggle, which would have lent credit to the murder hypothesis. Also, had he been murdered, his gold watch and diamond ring would probably have been taken, which they were not. Therefore, the jury was well within its rights to decide that Haney was killed by the mail-hook, and this finding should not have been disturbed merely because the reviewing judges might have decided the case differently had they been on the jury. Reversed and remanded.

Analysis:

The opinion in this case gives a very clear explanation of the function and purpose of the jury, as well as how a jury's verdict should be regarded. The jury is supposed to review conflicting opinions, testimony, and evidence, and come to a conclusion about which facts should be accepted as true in a given case. Once a jury has come to a decision, "it would be an undue invasion of the jury's historic function for an appellate court to weigh the conflicting evidence, judge the credibility of witnesses and arrive at a conclusion opposite from the one reached by the jury." But the implications reach even deeper. The institution of the jury is firmly established in the U.S. Constitution, so ignoring a proper jury verdict is, in effect, denying the parties to that action a Constitutionally protected right. Therefore, a jury's verdict should always receive an extreme amount of deference, and once the reviewing court has discovered that there is any evidentiary basis to support that verdict, its review of that verdict is at an end.

■ CASE VOCABULARY

HEARSAY: A statement by other than the witness testifying at a hearing, which statement is offered into evidence to prove the truth of the matter stated.

RES GESTAE: Literally, things done; an exception to the hearsay rule, which may include as admissible, statements made by parties (and possibly by bystanders and strangers) when they are illustrative of a particular litigated act.

Hicks v. United States

(*Administrator of Deceased's Estate*) v. (*Navy Doctor's Ultimate Employer*)

368 F.2d 626 (4th Cir. 1966)

COURT RULES THAT FACTUAL DETERMINATION OF WHETHER CERTAIN CONDUCT CONSTITUTES NEGLIGENCE IS SOMETIMES QUESTION OF LAW, NOT FACT

■ **INSTANT FACTS** The doctor whose misdiagnosis of a woman led to her death was found not to have been negligent at trial, but negligent on appeal.

■ **BLACK LETTER RULE** The general rule that a trial judge's findings of fact should not be disturbed unless clearly erroneous does not apply when the judge's conclusions are based on undisputed testimony and evidence.

■ **PROCEDURAL BASIS**

Appeal from judgment for defendant in action for damages for medical malpractice.

■ **FACTS**

When Carol Greitens became suddenly ill with intense abdominal pain and continuous vomiting, she sought emergency treatment at the dispensary of the U.S. Naval Amphibious Base in Little Creek, Virginia. She was examined by a doctor, given some pain pills, and sent home. Several hours later, she fell unconscious, and was rushed back to the dispensary, but to no avail. She was declared dead shortly after her arrival, from a "high obstruction" in her intestines. Hicks (P), the administrator of Mrs. Greitens' estate, brought suit against the doctor who had examined Mrs. Greitens at the dispensary, charging that he had negligently misdiagnosed and treated her, and that he did not meet the requisite standard of care and skill required by the law of Virginia. Various expert witnesses testified, and all of them seemed to agree that the doctor had not used ordinary care in making his diagnosis, and had not followed locally standard procedures. Nevertheless, the trial judge, sitting without a jury, held that the doctor had not been negligent. Hicks (P) appealed.

■ **ISSUE**

Does the general rule that a judge's findings should not be disturbed unless they are clearly erroneous apply when the judge's conclusions are based on undisputed testimony and evidence?

■ **DECISION AND RATIONALE**

(Sobeloff) No. The general rule that a judge's findings should not be disturbed unless they are clearly erroneous does not apply when the judge's conclusions are based on undisputed testimony and evidence. This rule (embodied in Federal Rule 52(a): "Findings of fact ... shall not be set aside unless clearly erroneous....") stems from an appreciation of the fact that the trial judge is in a unique position with respect to his or her ability to evaluate the credibility of conflicting witnesses. The trial judge is actually there, watching and listening to the witnesses, and can get a much better sense of which witness(es) to believe or disbelieve than appellate judges can from the written record. In a case with conflicting witnesses, the appellate court should give a lot of weight to the trial judge's decisions. In this case, however, the witnesses were all in agreement about basic facts. There is thus no question of what those facts are (i.e., what the doctor did in his examination), but rather, whether those facts constitute negligence. This is really a question of law, not of fact. Thus the appellate court does not have to give the same deference to the trial court's findings. The testimony clearly shows that the doctor did not conform to the required standard of care, and was therefore negligent as a matter of law. Judgment reversed, and remanded to determine damages.

Analysis:

This case introduces one of the great secrets of the first year in law school: that is, that judges do not always do what they say they are doing in their opinions. It is well-known that appellate courts must give great deference to the trial court's findings of fact, but can review their findings of law at will. (Sometimes this will be referred to as "de novo" review, which basically means "anew," or sort of "from the beginning, with no preconceived notions.") So if you really don't like the way the case came out, call it a matter of law and go right ahead and review it. Well, it's not always that easy, of course, but it does seem to be what happened here. The appellate court, in declaring that all the testimony was basically in agreement, was right there changing the facts from what the trial court had found. The government's expert witness testified that the doctor had exercised "average judgment," and this is obviously what the trial court chose to believe. Believing a different witness, or that the witness really meant something else, is exactly what the reviewing court is supposed to avoid. It is obvious that the appellate court felt that this trial judge was just plain wrong in his decision. Perhaps they felt that going this route to overturn it would be easier then arguing that his findings of fact had been "clearly erroneous," but it seems as if that is really what they were doing.

■ **CASE VOCABULARY**

PROXIMATE CAUSE: That which, in a natural and continuous sequence unbroken by any independent intervening cause, produces an injury, without which the injury would not have occurred.

Des Moines Navigation & R. Co. v. Iowa Homestead Co.

(Taxpayer) v. *(Tax Collector)*
123 U.S. 552, 8 S.Ct. 217 (1887)

SUPREME COURT RULES THAT ITS JUDGMENTS ARE FINAL, EVEN IN CASES WHERE IT DID NOT PROPERLY HAVE JURISDICTION

■ **INSTANT FACTS** Iowa Homestead Co. (P) sued for back taxes and lost, then tried a second time because the first suit had been tried in federal courts, which had not had proper jurisdiction over the case.

■ **BLACK LETTER RULE** Even cases that have been decided without proper jurisdiction have res judicata value, at least until they are judicially annulled, vacated, or set aside.

■ **PROCEDURAL BASIS**

Writ of Error to the Supreme Court of Iowa.

■ **FACTS**

The Iowa Homestead Co. (P), a citizen of Iowa, originally brought suit for unpaid taxes against the Des Moines Navigation & Railroad Co. (D), another citizen of Iowa, along with quite a few other defendants, in a state court. Some of those other defendants were citizens of New York, and they moved to remove the suit to federal court. Apparently the whole suit got moved into federal court, even though there wasn't complete diversity. Nobody brought this up, though, and the case went to the U.S. Supreme Court with no discussion of jurisdiction. When the Iowa Homestead Co. (P) lost, they tried to give it another shot by bringing another action in Iowa state court against at least the Iowa defendant, claiming that the federal verdict was null and void due to the lack of proper subject matter jurisdiction. Well, the Iowa courts bought it, even the Iowa Supreme Court, but the U.S. Supreme Court got a little angry that anyone would call their verdicts "nullities," and said that the question of jurisdiction was settled and could not be attacked in a separate, additional lawsuit.

■ **ISSUE**

Do cases that have been decided without proper jurisdiction, but are still in force, still have res judicata value?

■ **DECISION AND RATIONALE**

(Waite) Yes. Until a case is judicially annulled, vacated, or set aside, it still has the power to bar future cases involving the same claim or cause of action, under the doctrine of res judicata. It is true that the federal courts did not properly have jurisdiction over this matter when it was first litigated, or at least over those parts of it as between the Iowa Homestead Co. (P) and the Des Moines Navigation & Railroad Co. (D), both being citizens of Iowa. However, the Iowa Homestead Co. (P) had every opportunity to object to the jurisdiction on appeal, and did not do so. If the jurisdiction had been attacked, the judgment could have been set aside as erroneously entered into, but Iowa (P) did not attack it; it has thus lost the ability to challenge the jurisdiction in another court. Since the jurisdictional matter was not challenged at any stage of the proceedings, all the way up to the Supreme Court, it was effectively settled. Thus all other courts are required to accept that decision, and give the required "full faith and credit" to the federal court's decision. Reversed.

Analysis:

This case is useful for introducing the idea of res judicata, an extremely important concept to learn. Yet this case is otherwise rather confusing to introduce at this stage of a Civil Procedure course. By far the most important thing to remember at this point, at least with respect to federal subject matter jurisdiction, is that it can be brought up and challenged at any time, even on appeal, by any party or the court itself. This distinguishes it from personal jurisdiction, which is waived if not objected to right away, at the very beginning of a case. Subject matter jurisdiction is extremely important. The fact that it can't be attacked collaterally (i.e., in a separate, subsequent lawsuit) has actually not been addressed that often, and not recently. And it just isn't likely to be as big an issue when you study subject matter jurisdiction in depth. What you should remember from this case, however, is the idea of resjudicata. Literally, this means something like "thing judged," but what it means is that, once a final judgment has been reached in a case, the parties involved in that case are prohibited from trying again, at least for the same cause of action.

■ CASE VOCABULARY

RES JUDICATA: Rule that final judgment on merits by court of competent jurisdiction is conclusive of rights of parties in all later suits involving the same cause of action.

CHAPTER TWO

Jurisdiction Over the Parties or Their Property

Pennoyer v. Neff

Instant Facts: Neff (P) sought to recover possession of land which had been seized and sold to pay off a default judgment against him, claiming that the judgment was invalid, as the court involved had not had personal jurisdiction over him.

Black Letter Rule: Every state possesses exclusive jurisdiction and sovereignty over persons and property within its territory; therefore, the courts of that state may enter a binding judgment against a non-resident only if he is personally served with process while within the state, or, if he has property within the state, if that property is attached before litigation begins.

Hess v. Pawloski

Instant Facts: Hess (D), a driver from Pennsylvania, negligently struck and injured Pawloski (P) on a Massachusetts public highway.

Black Letter Rule: A state has the power to declare that all non-residents who use its highways have impliedly consented to submit to the state's jurisdiction for all actions arising from that highway usage.

International Shoe Co. v. Washington

Instant Facts: A shoe company with salesmen in Washington State claimed not to be subject to Washington's jurisdiction when the state tried to collect unemployment taxes.

Black Letter Rule: A corporation will be subject to the jurisdiction of any state with which it has "minimum contacts" that make the exercise of jurisdiction consistent with "traditional notions of fair play and substantial justice."

Gray v. American Radiator & Standard Sanitary Corp.

Instant Facts: An Ohio company made a defective water valve and sold it to a company that used it in manufacturing a water heater in Pennsylvania, which it sold in Illinois, where it blew up.

Black Letter Rule: The International Shoe minimum contacts requirement is satisfied even when a corporation conducts no business within a state, so long as the act giving rise to the lawsuit has a "substantial connection" to the state.

McGee v. International Life Insurance Co.

Instant Facts: McGee (P), the beneficiary of a life insurance policy held by International Life (D), a Texas company, brought suit in California when International Life (D) refused to pay.

Black Letter Rule: A state may exercise jurisdiction over a defendant whose contacts with that state consist of only a single act, provided that that act is what gave rise to the claim for which jurisdiction is being sought, and was deliberately directed toward the state.

Hanson v. Denckla

Instant Facts: Various claimants to a Delaware trust filed suit against the trustee in Florida, claiming that the trust was invalid under Florida law.

Black Letter Rule: A state may not exercise jurisdiction over a defendant if the defendant's contacts with the state are negligible and non-deliberate, and the claim does not arise from those contacts.

World–Wide Volkswagen v. Woodson

Instant Facts: A New York family passing through Oklahoma was in a car accident, and tried to bring suit there against the dealer who sold them the car in New York.

Black Letter Rule: In order to be subject to a state's jurisdiction, a defendant must have chosen to have some contact with that state; considerations of fairness, convenience, and the interests of the state in overseeing the litigation are otherwise irrelevant.

Kulko v. Superior Court

Instant Facts: California woman sued New York ex-husband in California for additional child support payments.

Black Letter Rule: A state may not exercise jurisdiction over a defendant who has not purposefully availed himself of the benefits of that state, even if the state has a strong interest in the litigation.

Burger King Corp. v. Rudzewicz

Instant Facts: Rudzewicz (D) contracted with Burger King (D), a Florida corporation, to operate a Burger King restaurant in Michigan, then defaulted on payments, so Burger King (P) sued him in Florida.

Black Letter Rule: Once it has been established that the defendant has minimum contacts with a state, it is up to the defendant to prove that being required to defend a suit there would be "fundamentally unfair."

Asahi Metal Industry Co. v. Superior Court

Instant Facts: Victim of motorcycle accident brought suit in California court against Taiwanese tire-tube maker, who cross-claimed against Japanese manufacturer of the tire tube valve assembly.

Black Letter Rule: The defendant must purposefully avail himself of the forum by more than just putting a product into the stream of commerce with the expectation that it will reach the forum state, however, such conduct is enough to satisfy the minimum contacts requirement. Nonetheless, once it has been established that minimum contacts exist, the fairness requirement must still be met as well, which will be much harder to do in the case of a non-U.S. resident.

Perkins v. Benguet Consolidated Mining Co.

Instant Facts: Stockholder sued Philippine mining company in Ohio, based on that company's president's presence and activities there.

Black Letter Rule: When there are sufficient minimum contacts, a state may assert jurisdiction over a defendant even for causes of action arising outside the jurisdiction.

Helicopteros Nacionales De Colombia, S.A. v. Hall

Instant Facts: The representatives of several decedents sued Helicol (D), the owner of a helicopter that crashed in Peru, alleging that Helicol (D) had sufficient contacts with Texas to render it subject to in personam jurisdiction in that State.

Black Letter Rule: Personal jurisdiction may be satisfied by sufficient minimum contacts with the forum state so that maintenance of the suit does not offend the traditional notions of fair play and substantial justice.

Pebble Beach Co. v. Caddy

Instant Facts: Pebble Beach Co. (P) appealed from the district court's dismissal of its trademark infringement claim against Caddy (D), the owner of the "Pebble Beach" bed and breakfast, for lack of personal jurisdiction over Caddy (D), a resident of England.

Black Letter Rule: Due process is satisfied when (1) the defendant has performed some act or consummated some transaction within the forum or has otherwise purposefully availed himself of the privileges of conducting business in the forum, (2) the claim arises out of or results from these forum-related activities, and (3) the exercise of jurisdiction is reasonable.

Bellino v. Simon

Instant Facts: A baseball memorabilia seller sued two men in the trade for allegedly defaming the seller, resulting in lost sales and reputation damage.

Black Letter Rule: The exercise of personal jurisdiction over a nonresident defendant satisfies due process when (1) the defendant has purposefully availed himself of the benefits and protections of the forum state by establishing "minimum contacts" with that state; and (2) the exercise of jurisdiction over the defendant comports with "traditional notions of fair play and substantial justice."

Pennington v. Fourth National Bank

Instant Facts: Pennington (P) objected to the exercise of in rem jurisdiction over his personal intangible property.

Black Letter Rule: In rem proceedings require seizure of a res within the forum state's jurisdiction, as well as an opportunity for the owner to be heard.

Harris v. Balk

Instant Facts: Balk (P) instituted a suit against Harris (D) in North Carolina for payment of a $180 debt, and Harris (D) claimed that the debt had already been satisfied in a prior proceeding in Maryland.

Black Letter Rule: Courts may assert jurisdiction over debts provided personal jurisdiction over the debtor can be attained.

Shaffer v. Heitner

Instant Facts: Heitner (P) brought a shareholder's derivative suit against several officers and directors of Greyhound, a Delaware corporation, gaining in rem jurisdiction by attaching their stock in Greyhound.

Black Letter Rule: Minimum contacts must exist in order for in rem jurisdiction to attach.

Burnham v. Superior Court

Instant Facts: While visiting California for business and vacation, Dennis Burnham (D) was served with process for a divorce proceeding, and Burnham (D) contends that California jurisdiction violates due process.

Black Letter Rule: Jurisdiction based on physical presence comports with due process, regardless of the defendant's contacts with the forum State.

Insurance Corp. of Ireland v. Compagnie Des Bauxites De Guinee

Instant Facts: Compagnie des Bauxites de Guinee (CBG) (P) sued for the non-payment of insurance benefits, and the insurers failed to comply with the court's discovery order.

Black Letter Rule: The failure to comply with jurisdictional-related discovery may constitute implied consent to jurisdiction.

Pennoyer v. Neff

(*Current Occupier of Land*) v. (*Rightful Owner of Land*)

95 U.S. (5 Otto) 714 (1877)

SUPREME COURT SPELLS OUT THEORY OF PERSONAL JURISDICTION

■ **INSTANT FACTS** Neff (P) sought to recover possession of land which had been seized and sold to pay off a default judgment against him, claiming that the judgment was invalid, as the court involved had not had personal jurisdiction over him.

■ **BLACK LETTER RULE** Every state possesses exclusive jurisdiction and sovereignty over persons and property within its territory; therefore, the courts of that state may enter a binding judgment against a non-resident only if he is personally served with process while within the state, or, if he has property within the state, if that property is attached before litigation begins.

■ **PROCEDURAL BASIS**

Writ of Error to the Circuit Court of the United States for the District of Oregon, for its judgment in action to recover the possession of land.

■ **FACTS**

In the years prior to the Civil War, as America pursued its Manifest Destiny ever Westward, a young man named Marcus Neff (P) set out for the Oregon frontier—thus setting in motion a chain of events that would eventually culminate in one of the most famous Supreme Court cases ever—as well as the bane of law students everywhere for more than a hundred years. Neff (P) staked a claim for land from the federal government and in 1862 sought advice from a well-known Portland attorney (and future U.S. Senator) named John Mitchell, who specialized in land litigation. Whatever Mitchell did for Neff (P), Neff (P) apparently never paid him for it. Mitchell waited until late 1865, and then brought suit against Neff (P) in Oregon state court to recover the unpaid legal fees. As was totally proper under Oregon law at the time, Mitchell did not serve Neff (P) personally with notice of the suit, but published notice in a local newspaper (so-called "service by publication"). Neff (P), not being an Oregon resident at the time, somehow failed to see this notice, and did not show up to defend his rights in court. Mitchell thus easily obtained a default judgment against Neff (P) in 1866. Coincidentally enough, this happened to be the same year that Neff's (P) land patent arrived, which enabled Mitchell to have the land seized and sold at auction by the local sheriff to satisfy the judgment. At the auction, Mitchell himself was the lucky bidder. One can only assume that he got a fair price from himself for the land! Anyway, a few days after the auction Mitchell assigned the land to Sylvester Pennoyer (D), future Mayor of Portland and Governor of Oregon. Pennoyer (D) spent nine years and quite a bit of money improving the property, only to have Neff (P) show back up, claiming the land was still his. Neff (P) then sued Pennoyer (D) in federal court for possession of the property, claiming that the original judgment against him had not been valid, because the Oregon court had not had jurisdiction over him or the land. The Federal Circuit Court agreed that the other judgment was invalid and that the land really did belong to Neff (P), although not for the reasons that the Supreme Court later found persuasive. Apparently, the Circuit Court's decision was based on some technicality related to how the notice had been published. Of course, it's possible to suspect ulterior motives for the Circuit Court's judgment, since Judge Deady, the judge involved, seemed to be just as immersed in local politics as Mitchell and Pennoyer (D). In fact, Deady was later instrumental in exposing Mitchell for the lying, bigamous, adulterer that he was. (Not that this had a negative impact on his career as a Senator!) Pennoyer (D) appealed Deady's decision to the Supreme Court, but lost there too. So Neff (P) got his land back, and the country got a new-and-improved theory of personal jurisdiction. Well, the personal jurisdiction theory lived on for years, but Mitchell's career was eventually brought to a halt, when he was indicted and convicted for—of all things—land fraud in Alaska.

■ ISSUE

Can a state court exercise personal jurisdiction over a non-resident who has not been personally served with process while within the state, and whose property within the state was not attached before the litigation began?

■ DECISION AND RATIONALE

(Field) No. A state can obtain *in personam* jurisdiction over a non-resident only if that non-resident is personally served with process while within the territory of the state. *In rem* jurisdiction can be obtained if the non-resident owns property within the state, and that property is attached at the very outset of the trial. *In personam* jurisdiction means that the state has complete power over an individual, and stems from the notion that a state has exclusive control over all people within its borders; *in rem* jurisdiction stems from the idea that a state has exclusive control over all land within its territory, and means that the state can adjudicate disputes over the status of such property, but only up to the value of the property. In the case before us, the original action was initiated by publication of service. The Oregon state court which heard that case did not exercise either *in personam* or *in rem* jurisdiction—nor could it have. Neff (P), the defendant in that action, was not within the state of Oregon at the time, and so could not be personally served with process. Service of process is basically a command by a court to appear before it, or suffer the consequences. It dates back to a time when lawsuits were initiated not by a command to appear before the court, but by the sheriff actually taking the defendant into custody and physically bringing him before the court. But an Oregon sheriff could not go into another state—say California—and start hauling California residents back to Oregon to appear before an Oregon court. This would be an infringement of California's sovereignty. Thus, those same California residents could not be commanded to appear before an Oregon court either—unless, of course, they came into Oregon, in which case they came under Oregon's power, and could be seized or served with process while there. As Neff (P) was not within Oregon, he was not within Oregon's power, and could not be made to appear before an Oregon court. Period. Certainly not by publication in some obscure local newspaper, but not even if he had been tracked down and served with process personally wherever he was at the time. If he had come into Oregon and been served with process while there, then the Oregon courts would have had *in personam* jurisdiction over him. But he did not, and they did not. End of *(in personam)* story. *In rem*, however, still remains to be dealt with. While Oregon courts cannot exercise power over non-residents not found within the state, they do have power over any property the non-residents might own within Oregon. Originally, "property" in this context meant land, and dated back to the idea that a state should and did have ultimate power over all land within its borders. If there is a dispute over land, it makes sense that the state where that land is located should be able to mediate and resolve the dispute. And it also makes some sense that anyone who claims an interest in that particular piece of land should keep an eye on it—or at least check on it every so often. Ideally, an out-of-state landowner will appoint an agent of some kind to look after the land in his absence. It's not good public policy to encourage people to just abandon land for years at a time. Therefore, it is reasonable to assume that if land is attached by a court prior to a lawsuit, the owner of the land will—or should—find out about the lawsuit. (Attachment here simply means that the court forbids the land from being sold, etc., while the suit is pending. Practically speaking, the sheriff will go out to the land and post notices announcing the suit, so anyone living there or going by to check it out will see them and know what's going on.) If the owner of that land does not check on it at least occasionally, he doesn't really deserve to own it, and it will be forfeit to the other party. While this type of proceeding was originally limited to pure *in rem* actions actually relating to the land itself, the doctrine of *quasi in rem* jurisdiction developed to allow the attachment of land as a means of initiating an action that had absolutely nothing to do with the land. But the same theory was involved—anyone really taking care of his land would find out what was going on. However, this was not done in the case at issue. If Mitchell had attached Neff's (P) land at the very beginning of his suit, then the court would have been able to issue a valid judgment in the case. However, Mitchell did not attach Neff's (P) land at the beginning of the suit. In fact, there's no way that he could have done so, since Neff (P) did not own the land at the time Mitchell instituted the action. Neff's (P) land patent did not arrive until after Mitchell had already obtained a judgment. Thus the court had no basis for exercising jurisdiction over Neff (P) at all, so the default judgment must be declared invalid. Since the sheriff therefore had no power to auction the land, Neff (P) must still legally own it. Judgment affirmed.

Analysis:

Pennoyer represents the first time the U.S. Supreme Court enunciated a coherent, national standard for the exercise of jurisdiction by states over non-residents. The idea that a sovereign state had exclusive and complete power over everything and everyone within its borders, but not outside them, wasn't new, and was similar to how the international law worked at the time. What was different, of course, was that the various states of the United States were not independent and fully sovereign nation-states. The states were bound by the Constitution to give "full faith and credit" to the judgments of the courts of its sister states, which put some limitations on state power. These limitations were increased by the passage of the 14th Amendment after the Civil War, which allowed the direct challenge of judgments that had been rendered without proper jurisdiction. More mobility of people could be expected between the states than between countries, which increased the chances that one state's citizen would come under the jurisdiction of another state. A standard needed to be found that would allow states some power over non-residents without offending the power of other states. *Pennoyer* was the Supreme Court's answer to this problem, but as it turned out it was probably well on its way to being obsolete even at the time it was announced.

■ **CASE VOCABULARY**

EX PARTE: With the presence of one party only.

Hess v. Pawloski

(*Negligent Pennsylvania Driver*) v. (*Massachusetts Victim*)

274 U.S. 352, 47 S.Ct. 632 (1927)

SUPREME COURT APPROVES SCHEME TO GIVE STATES JURISDICTION OVER NON–RESIDENT DRIVERS INVOLVED IN ACCIDENTS ON PUBLIC ROADS

■ **INSTANT FACTS** Hess (D), a driver from Pennsylvania, negligently struck and injured Pawloski (P) on a Massachusetts public highway.

■ **BLACK LETTER RULE** A state has the power to declare that all non-residents who use its highways have impliedly consented to submit to the state's jurisdiction for all actions arising from that highway usage.

■ **PROCEDURAL BASIS**

Writ of Error to the Superior Court of Worcester County, Massachusetts, from its judgment in action for negligence.

■ **FACTS**

While driving in Massachusetts, Hess (D), a resident of Pennsylvania, negligently struck and injured Pawloski (P). (It is important to note that Pawloski (P) was the original plaintiff, and Hess (D) the original defendant, although the opinion refers to Pawloski (P) as the "defendant in error," and Hess (D) as the "plaintiff in error.") Pawloski (P) filed suit against Hess (D) in Massachusetts, under a statute which conditioned the use of public roads in Massachusetts by nonresidents on their implied agreement to consent to the jurisdiction of Massachusetts courts if they were involved in a accident while using those roads. The statute provided that any non-resident using Massachusetts roads would be assumed to have designated the registrar as his agent, for purposes of receiving service of process, provided that the non-resident thereafter received actual notice of any such service from the registrar. Hess (D) did receive actual notice of Pawloski's (P) suit, and made a special appearance to contest jurisdiction. When jurisdiction was upheld by both the trial court and the Supreme Judicial Court, Hess (D) appeared and defended the case at trial, where the jury found for Pawloski (P). Hess (D) appealed, claiming that the Massachusetts courts lacked jurisdiction over him and that the provision for service of process on the registrar was a violation of his 14th Amendment Due Process rights.

■ **ISSUE**

Does a state have the power to declare that all non-residents who use its highways have impliedly consented to submit to the state's jurisdiction for all actions arising from that highway usage?

■ **DECISION AND RATIONALE**

(Butler) Yes. A state does have the power to declare that all non-residents who use its highways have impliedly consented to submit to the state's jurisdiction for all actions arising from that highway usage. Motor vehicles can be extremely dangerous, and the state therefore has a powerful interest both in regulating their usage, and in making sure that those who choose to drive within the state shall be accountable for their actions, also within the state. The statute involved here does not discriminate against non-residents, or treat them unfairly. Rather, it ensures that litigation will only proceed when the non-resident has *actual* notice of the suit, and time to prepare a defense. The non-resident has already demonstrated, by choosing to drive within the state, that the forum is not so completely inaccessible or remote that subjecting him to jurisdiction there would be totally unfair. It has already been decided that a state may legitimately condition use of its highways by non-residents on the non-resident's explicit consent to that state's jurisdiction, and explicit designation of an in-state agent to receive service of process. [*Kane v. New Jersey*, 242 U.S. 160 (1916). New Jersey could require nonresident drivers, before allowing them to use its roads, to file a document designating a New Jersey agent for service of process.] The difference between this being done explicitly and implicitly is immaterial, at least with respect to whether a non-resident's due process rights are infringed—which they are not, in either case. Judgment affirmed.

Analysis:

As technology progressed, interstate travel became easier, which certainly increased the opportunities for interstate litigation. Nowhere was this more evident than in the development of the automobile. Not only did the automobile make traveling to another state much easier, it also undoubtedly caused more accidents to occur. Ergo, more accidents occurred involving out-of-state residents. Obviously, problems arose when the non-resident driver went back to his home state after causing an accident and possible injury to state residents. The state where the accident occurred could not exercise jurisdiction over the out-of-state driver, often leaving its injured residents in the lurch. So states began to explicitly condition the use of their roads on a driver's consent to submit to the state's jurisdiction if an accident occurred Gradually, this expanded to a form of implied consent, where any out-of-stater using the state's roads was "assumed" to have consented to jurisdiction. This lovely fiction preserved the letter of *Pennoyer* for a while longer, but was certainly the beginning of the end for that case's strict territory-based theory of jurisdiction. Once these types of laws were approved by the courts, states effectively had the power to exercise jurisdiction over non-residents not found within the state. A valid in personam judgment could be obtained, which the driver's home state was obliged to honor under the full faith and credit clause.

International Shoe Co. v. Washington

(Delinquent Taxpayer) v. *(Tax Assessor)*
326 U.S. 310, 66 S.Ct. 154 (1945)

SUPREME COURT REVOLUTIONIZES PERSONAL JURISDICTION

■ **INSTANT FACTS** A shoe company with salesmen in Washington State claimed not to be subject to Washington's jurisdiction when the state tried to collect unemployment taxes.

■ **BLACK LETTER RULE** A corporation will be subject to the jurisdiction of any state with which it has "minimum contacts" that make the exercise of jurisdiction consistent with "traditional notions of fair play and substantial justice."

■ **PROCEDURAL BASIS**

Appeal from sustaining of denial of motion to dismiss notice of assessment of unpaid unemployment contributions.

■ **FACTS**

International Shoe Co. (D) was incorporated in Delaware, and had its primary place of business in St. Louis, Missouri. It made and sold shoes in several states. In Washington State it did not maintain any offices or manufacturing facilities, but did employ some 11 to 13 salesmen during the years at issue (1937–1940). These salesmen were under the direct supervision of sales managers in St. Louis but lived and worked entirely within the state of Washington. The salesmen received samples from the company and showed these samples to potential customers to solicit orders. Sometimes the salesmen rented showrooms for the samples. Orders were filled from St. Louis, and the merchandise was sent straight to the customer, not to the salesman. The salesmen operated on commission and averaged around $31,000 per year (not bad during the Great Depression!). The State of Washington (P), in accordance with its laws on unemployment insurance, assessed International Shoe Co. (D) for its contribution and served notice both personally on one of the salesmen within the state and by mail to the St. Louis headquarters. International Shoe (D) challenged the service, claiming that the salesman was not a proper agent for service of process, and that it was not "present" or "doing business" within the state of Washington so as to be subject to that state's jurisdiction. The unemployment office, the Commissioner, the Superior Court, and the Supreme Court of Washington all held that service had been proper, and that jurisdiction did exist. International Shoe (D) appealed to the U.S. Supreme Court, claiming that its due process rights had been violated.

■ **ISSUE**

Is a corporation not chartered within a state subject to that state's jurisdiction if it has certain "minimum contacts" with the state?

■ **DECISION AND RATIONALE**

(Stone) Yes. A corporation is subject to the jurisdiction of a state so long as it has certain "minimum contacts" with that state. Many previous decisions have based jurisdiction over corporations on whether they are "present" within the state. Since it is much harder to determine whether a corporation—which is after all merely a fiction—is to be found within a state's borders for exercise of its territorial power than it is with an actual human defendant, there has been a lot of debate over what it means for a corporation to be "present" within a state. Discussions of "presence" have centered around the extent of a corporation's activities within a state necessary to make subjecting it to jurisdiction there consistent with due process. Generally, systematic and continuous activities within a state have been held to be enough to subject a corporation to jurisdiction there—especially when the cause of action arises from those activities, but even in some cases where the cause of action does not arise from those activities. In some cases even a single, isolated contact with a state has been enough, when that contact gives rise to the cause of action. Obviously, a corporation that has no contacts at all with a state should not be subject to that state's jurisdiction. But a corporation that does conduct activities within a state also enjoys the benefits and protections of the state's laws and should therefore be held subject as well to those laws, and to actions brought to enforce those laws. There is no mechanical way to decide whether, in a particular case, a corporation's contacts with a state have reached the level necessary for the exercise of jurisdiction; instead, the nature and extent of those contacts must be evaluated under traditional concepts of fairness and justice to determine whether it would be reasonable to require the corporation to defend a suit in that state. In this case, International Shoe (D) has benefitted from the laws of Washington, which protected its numerous sales there. It has shipped a large volume of merchandise into Washington over the years, and has exercised continuous and systematic sales activities there. Also, the very nature of this suit arose from the company's activities there. The fact that International Shoe (D) employed salesmen within the state of Washington raised the issue of whether the company, as an employer, was required to make contributions to the state unemployment system. Therefore, the exercise of jurisdiction in this case by the courts of the state of Washington was not improper, and did not infringe International Shoe's (D) due process rights. Judgment affirmed.

■ CONCURRENCE

(Black, J.) Jurisdiction was proper in this case. The U.S. Constitution granted to each state the right to tax and subject to suit any corporation whose activities within a state affect that state's citizens and businesses. Period. This Court should not have the power to invalidate a state's assertion of jurisdiction merely because the members of this Court have a different opinion of what is "fair" or "reasonable."

Analysis:

MINIMUM CONTACTS. FAIR PLAY AND SUBSTANTIAL JUSTICE. REMEMBER THESE WORDS! While *International Shoe* was originally geared to the burgeoning problem of establishing jurisdiction over corporations, which did not really fit within the *Pennoyer* categories, it did not take long at all for the ideas behind *Shoe* to spill over onto individuals. With regard to corporations, however, some guidance was badly needed. Since corporations are considered legal fictions that could not exist outside the state that created them, it was difficult for states to get jurisdiction over foreign corporations. And yet, corporations could obviously operate in more than one state at a time, and could have large impacts on the economy and society of states other than their own. Disputes with a corporation would often arise in a state where that corporation did not legally "exist." Somehow, states needed a way to obtain jurisdiction in these types of situations. Various theories, such as implied consent, were tried, but the time was ripe for change when *International Shoe* came along. *International Shoe* changed the trend in defining the court with jurisdiction away from the court with immediate power over the defendant, to the court where the parties may most conveniently settle their dispute. It also began a trend in defining due process law away from the emphasis on territorial limitations of courts, and towards an emphasis on providing notice and an opportunity to be heard. *International Shoe* uses contacts with the forum in two different ways. First, a defendant may have sufficient contact with the forum to warrant asserting jurisdiction over it for all matters; this is termed "general jurisdiction." Second, a defendant may have sufficient contact with the forum to warrant asserting jurisdiction over it for matters related to its activity with the forum without having sufficient contact with the forum to warrant general jurisdiction. In such a case, the jurisdiction is termed "specific jurisdiction." Whether a corporation is subject to specific or general jurisdiction, however, depends on the nature and number of contacts it has with the forum. Determining what constitutes sufficient business within the state, or what matters are related to activity within it, often are uncertain questions that may blur the distinction between general and specific jurisdiction.

■ **CASE VOCABULARY**

CAPIAS AD RESPONDENDUM: Method of commencing a court action in which the defendant is physically seized by the sheriff, and kept in custody until he is brought before the court.

DISTRAINT: Seizure of property.

Gray v. American Radiator & Standard Sanitary Corp.

(*Victim*) v. (*Manufacturer of Explosive Water Heater*)
22 Ill.2d 432, 176 N.E.2d 761 (1961)

SUPREME COURT OF ILLINOIS DECLARES THAT ILLINOIS COURTS HAVE JURISDICTION OVER CORPORATIONS WHICH CONDUCT NO BUSINESS WHATSOEVER IN ILLINOIS

■ **INSTANT FACTS** An Ohio company made a defective water valve and sold it to a company that used it in manufacturing a water heater in Pennsylvania, which it sold in Illinois, where it blew up.

■ **BLACK LETTER RULE** The *International Shoe* minimum contacts requirement is satisfied even when a corporation conducts no business within a state, so long as the act giving rise to the lawsuit has a "substantial connection" to the state.

■ **PROCEDURAL BASIS**

Appeal from granting of motion to quash service of summons in action for damages for negligence.

■ **FACTS**

The Titan Valve Manufacturing Company ("Titan") (D) was an Ohio company that made valves. It had no personnel in Illinois, and conducted no business there. It sold its completed valves to the American Radiator & Standard Sanitary Corporation ("American Radiator") (D), which incorporated them into its water heaters, which were manufactured in Pennsylvania. American Radiator then sold its water heaters in several states, including Illinois. One of the water heaters sold in Illinois exploded, injuring Phyllis Gray (P), who brought suit against Titan (D) and American Radiator (D) for negligence. American Radiator (D) then filed a cross claim against Titan (D). Titan (D) was served notice in Ohio, under an Illinois statute authorizing long-arm service of process on all out-of-state actors who commit "a tortious act" within the state of Illinois. Titan (D) moved to dismiss, arguing that it had not committed a tortious act within Illinois, and therefore fell outside the reach of the statute. The trial court granted Titan's (D) motion and dismissed both the complaint and the cross claim. Gray (P) appealed directly to the Supreme Court of Illinois.

■ **ISSUE**

Can a state exercise jurisdiction over a corporation which does no business within the state, provided that the act giving rise to the litigation has a substantial connection to the state?

■ **DECISION AND RATIONALE**

(Klingbiel) Yes. A state can exercise jurisdiction over a corporation that does no business within the state, provided that the act giving rise to the suit has a substantial connection to the state. In the context of this case, Illinois can exercise jurisdiction over an Ohio corporation whose only contact with the state was the sale, outside the state, of a product that was incorporated into another product which in turn caused injury in Illinois. Illinois law provides for service on defendants who commit tortious acts within the state, and, since for purposes of this law the actual injury-causing event is what counts as the "tortious act," the law does apply to Titan (D). Nor does this application violate the requirement of due process. Under the rule of *International Shoe,* far fewer contacts are necessary between the defendant and the forum state when the cause of action arises from those contacts, as is the case here. Even single contacts have been held to suffice, so long as that contact has a substantial connection to the state. This is definitely the case here—since the defective product exploded in Illinois, it seems reasonable to expect the maker of that product to answer for it in Illinois. Of course, this might not be the case if the product had been brought into Illinois against Titan's (D) will. However, since Titan (D) presumably contemplated the fact that some of its products would probably wind up in Illinois eventually, and would almost certainly not have objected had it been told point-blank that some of its products *would* wind up there, it is not unjust to subject them to suit there for defects in those products. Titan (D) has benefitted from the laws of Illinois, if indirectly, but that indirectness should not preclude the ultimate consumers of its product from obtaining justice. Considering as well the fact that Illinois has a strong interest in the litigation—that is, the protection of its citizens—and that Illinois is the forum where most witnesses and evidence are likely to be found, it does not infringe Titan's (D) due process rights to subject it to suit in Illinois. Reversed and remanded.

Analysis:

There is definitely something to be said for the argument that the manufacturer of a defective product should be answerable for injuries caused by that product wherever they are caused, as a matter of public policy. So it's understandable that the Supreme Court of Illinois wanted to find a way to hold Titan (D) liable in Illinois. But to base their argument on minimum contacts . . . well, it's what they had to work with, but to say that Titan (D) really had any contact with the state of Illinois is to stretch the word contact beyond its everyday meaning. It certainly shows that *International Shoe* didn't solve all the problems in the area of personal jurisdiction. As *Gray* illustrates, the application of long-arm statutes often entails difficult questions of statutory construction. Long-arm provisions authorizing jurisdiction over a defendant on the basis of the defendant's business within the forum often require that the plaintiff's cause of action "be related to" or "arise from" the business transacted within the state. Under these provisions, jurisdiction will not exist when the cause of action is unrelated to the defendant's contacts with the forum. This case was not reviewed by the U.S. Supreme Court, but has been cited by it several times, with at least lukewarm approval. The Supreme Court definitely picked up on the "stream of commerce" idea, however. This idea, that a corporation which puts a product into the "stream of commerce" (i.e., sells it to someone other than the ultimate consumer), should expect and anticipate that that product might be swept by the current [so to speak] to other states, is examined at length in several very important Supreme Court cases.

■ CASE VOCABULARY

FORUM NON CONVENIENS: Ability of court to decline jurisdiction when it would be unfair to exercise it.

INTER ALIA: Among others.

McGee v. International Life Insurance Co.

(Beneficiary of Policy) v. *(Holder of Policy)*
355 U.S. 220, 78 S.Ct. 199 (1957)

U.S. SUPREME COURT RULES THAT SINGLE BUSINESS TRANSACTION IS ENOUGH TO SATISFY MINIMUM CONTACTS REQUIREMENT

■ **INSTANT FACTS** McGee (P), the beneficiary of a life insurance policy held by International Life (D), a Texas company, brought suit in California when International Life (D) refused to pay.

■ **BLACK LETTER RULE** A state may exercise jurisdiction over a defendant whose contacts with that state consist of only a single act, provided that that act is what gave rise to the claim for which jurisdiction is being sought, and was deliberately directed toward the state.

■ **PROCEDURAL BASIS**

Appeal from Texas court's refusal to enforce California judgment in action to recover proceeds of life insurance policy.

■ **FACTS**

Lowell Franklin, a resident of California, had a life insurance policy with the Empire Mutual Insurance Company, of Arizona. In 1948 International Life Insurance Company (D), of Texas, took over Empire Mutual's policies. International Life (D) sent statements to Franklin in California, and Franklin sent payments to International Life (D) in Texas. When Franklin died in 1950, International Life (D) refused to pay the proceeds of his policy to his designated beneficiary, McGee (P), claiming that Franklin had committed suicide. McGee (P) brought suit in California, under a state law that authorized service of process on out-of-state companies holding insurance contracts with in-state residents. McGee (P) won a judgment against International Life (D) in California, then tried to enforce it in Texas. The Texas courts, however, refused to enforce the judgment, claiming that California's exercise of jurisdiction was improper. McGee (P) appealed the Texas decision to the U.S. Supreme Court.

■ **ISSUE**

Can a state ever exercise jurisdiction over a defendant whose contacts with that state are limited to a single act or contract?

■ **DECISION AND RATIONALE**

Yes. A state can exercise jurisdiction over a defendant whose contacts with that state consist solely of a single act or contract, provided that that act is what gave rise to the claim, and was purposefully undertaken. Due to the fact that business has become increasingly nationalized in recent years, more and more contracts are between actors in different states: This trend has encouraged and necessitated an increasingly wide scope for the exercise of jurisdiction across state lines. California enacted this particular long-arm statute to protect the rights of its citizens against out-of-state insurance companies. Given the nature of the insurance business, it is much more likely that small policy holders would be denied justice if forced to file suit in a foreign jurisdiction, than that insurance companies would be more than slightly inconvenienced by having to defend a suit in California. True, in this particular case International Life (D) claims to have had only the one policy holder in California, and not to have been in the habit of conducting business there. But it did knowingly hold that one policy, and communicated with the policy holder in California, so it shouldn't come as a complete surprise to be required to defend suit there after refusing to pay that policy holder's beneficiary. Also, the inconvenience involved in defending a suit in California cannot be much greater than defending the same suit in Texas, and having to transport all the witnesses and evidence found in California to Texas for the trial. Whatever inconvenience does arise from being subject to suit in California certainly does not amount to a denial of due process. International Life (D) had actual notice of the suit and plenty of time to prepare a defense. Therefore, justice is best served by allowing the California courts to exercise jurisdiction in this case. Reversed.

Analysis:

The *McGee* case represented a rather expansive application of the *International Shoe* guidelines. The Court explicitly approved the idea that minimum contacts could be very minimal indeed, so long as the case came out of those contacts. Although the Court did not use the term, this is now referred to as "specific jurisdiction." That is to say, a defendant does not have extensive contacts with a state, but the nature of the contacts it does have is such as to justify the state's exercise of jurisdiction over cases arising from those contacts, but not over cases unrelated to those contacts. If a defendant's contacts are more extensive, they might give rise to "general jurisdiction," which would enable the state to exercise jurisdiction over any claim involving the defendant, whether or not it was related to the defendant's contacts with the state.

Hanson v. Denckla

(*Not Stated*) v. (*Not Stated*)
357 U.S. 235, 78 S.Ct. 1228 (1958)

SUPREME COURT RULES THAT NOT ALL CONTACTS ARE MINIMUM CONTACTS

■ **INSTANT FACTS** Various claimants to a Delaware trust filed suit against the trustee in Florida, claiming that the trust was invalid under Florida law.

■ **BLACK LETTER RULE** A state may not exercise jurisdiction over a defendant if the defendant's contacts with the state are negligible and non-deliberate, and the claim does not arise from those contacts.

■ **PROCEDURAL BASIS**

Appeal from conflicting judgments in two separate but related actions for final disposition of a trust.

■ **FACTS**

Dora Donner, a resident of Pennsylvania, established a trust with a Delaware bank as trustee. Donner was to collect the income from the trust during her lifetime; after her death the money would go to her beneficiary. She retained the power to change her beneficiary at any time. After establishing the trust, Donner moved to Florida, where she eventually drew up a will naming two of her daughters as her primary heirs. The same day, she named two of her grandchildren—the children of her third daughter, Elizabeth—as the beneficiaries of her trust. However, when Donner died several years later, the two daughters named in her will brought suit in Florida against the trust company (D), claiming that the appointment of beneficiaries had been invalid, and that the trust money should really go to the estate. [That is, to the two of them. How greedy can you get?! They were already getting more than half a million a piece. Are we talking, like, Cinderella here? Did they hate their sister *so much* that they would go to all this trouble to cheat her kids out of their grandmother's inheritance? To get another $200,000 each?] Anyway, while the Florida action was still pending, another action was filed in Delaware to determine the distribution of the trust money. The Florida court then decided that the trust was invalid, and that the money should go to the estate. The sisters tried to introduce this judgment in Delaware, as *res judicata*. The Delaware court held that the Florida court had not had jurisdiction over the trust company, however, and so refused to recognize the validity of that action. The Delaware court resolved that the trust had been valid, and that the grandchildren should get the money. Everybody appealed something, and the U.S. Supreme Court consolidated both actions for review.

■ **ISSUE**

May a state exercise jurisdiction over a non-resident defendant with only sporadic and inadvertent contacts with the state, when those contacts do not give rise to the claim for which jurisdiction is being sought?

■ **DECISION AND RATIONALE**

(Warren) No. A state may not exercise jurisdiction over a non-resident defendant with only sporadic and inadvertent contacts with the state, when those contacts do not give rise to the claim for which jurisdiction is being sought. Although the boundaries of a state's jurisdiction over non-residents have been expanding ever since the decision in *International Shoe*, that does not mean that there are no longer any limits on a state's exercise of personal jurisdiction. There are restrictions on a state's power to exercise jurisdiction over non-residents not just to protect those non-residents from the burden of defending a suit in a distant, inconvenient court, but also to protect other states. In this case, the laws of Delaware allowed the trust to be created, maintained, and administered. Allowing Florida courts using Florida law to invalidate that trust is, in a way, like allowing Florida to overturn Delaware's laws and to legislate for the people of Delaware instead. Without minimum contacts between the trustee (D) and Florida, Florida cannot exercise jurisdiction over the trustee (D). The trustee (D) conducts no business in Florida, has no office there, solicits no business there. The fact that the trustee's (D) client, Mrs. Donner, moved to Florida after the trust had been created does not indicate any desire of the trustee (D) to take advantage of Florida's laws or to start doing business there. Without some action "by which the defendant purposefully avails itself of the privilege of conducting activities within the forum State, thus invoking the benefits and protections of its laws," it cannot be said to have the necessary contacts with that state. The fact that another, independent actor with a relationship to the defendant chose to interact with the forum state does not establish contact between the state and the defendant. Therefore, Mrs. Donner's contacts with Florida did not establish contacts between her trustee (D) and Florida, and Florida thus cannot exercise jurisdiction over the trustee (D). Since the trustee (D) was an essential party to the Florida action, that action is invalid, and the Delaware court was correct in not awarding that judgment res judicata value. The judgment of the Delaware courts is affirmed; that of the Florida courts is reversed.

■ DISSENT

(Black) Florida had a strong interest in overseeing this litigation, and would have been the most convenient forum. Donner lived in Florida, her heirs lived in Florida, her will was being administered in Florida. The trustee (D) chose to carry on business with a resident of Florida. The trust company (D) had sufficient contacts with Florida to justify Florida's exertion of jurisdiction over it, and there was nothing that unfair about subjecting it to suit there. Therefore, Florida's exercise of jurisdiction should have been upheld.

Analysis:

This case sort of put a limit on the expanding boundaries of personal jurisdiction. Where *McGee* had perhaps seemed to indicate that the idea of minimum contacts would continue to expand until it became almost meaningless, *Hanson* tried to reign in this enthusiasm. *Hanson* made clear that some exercises of jurisdiction would be struck down—if not to protect the due process interests of the defendants involved, then to protect the sovereignty of other states. *Hanson* also introduced the idea that a defendant must perform some purposeful, deliberate act in order to associate itself with the forum state. This was to prove a major sticking point between two separate factions of the Court, one of which endorsed the "purposeful availment" idea, and one of which, often led by Brennan, preferred to focus on the relationship between the defendant, the litigation, and the interests of the forum state. The next case, *World-Wide Volkswagen v. Woodson*, begins to demonstrate the depth of the Court's split.

■ CASE VOCABULARY

LEGATEE: Heir designated to receive property in a will.

World-Wide Volkswagen v. Woodson

(Regional Distributor of Defective Car) v. *(Trial Court Judge)*
444 U.S. 286, 100 S.Ct. 559 (1980)

U.S. SUPREME COURT RULES THAT A CORPORATION MUST HAVE PURPOSEFULLY AVAILED ITSELF OF A FORUM IN ORDER TO BE SUBJECT TO JURISDICTION THERE, REGARDLESS OF FAIRNESS OR CONVENIENCE

■ **INSTANT FACTS** A New York family passing through Oklahoma was in a car accident, and tried to bring suit there against the dealer who sold them the car in New York.

■ **BLACK LETTER RULE** In order to be subject to a state's jurisdiction, a defendant must have chosen to have some contact with that state; considerations of fairness, convenience, and the interests of the state in overseeing the litigation are otherwise irrelevant.

■ **PROCEDURAL BASIS**

Writ of Certiorari to the Supreme Court of Oklahoma, for its denial of the defendants' writ of prohibition to restrain the trial court judge from exercising personal jurisdiction over them.

■ **FACTS**

In 1976, the Robinson family—Harry, Kay, and their two kids—purchased a new Audi from Seaway Volkswagen, Inc. ("Seaway") (D), in Massena, New York. A year later, as the Robinsons were en route from their old home in New York to their new home in Arizona, disaster struck. While passing through Oklahoma, another car rear-ended the Robinsons' Audi, rupturing the gas tank and starting a fire that severely injured Kay and both children. Since the driver of the other car was unfortunately not wealthy, the Robinsons brought a product liability suit against the car's manufacturer, Audi NSU Auto Union Aktiengesellschaft ("Audi"), claiming that the gas tank and fuel system had been defective. They filed the action in Oklahoma state court, and named as additional defendants the car's importer, Volkswagen of America, Inc. ("Volkswagen"), its regional distributor, World-Wide Volkswagen Corporation ("World-Wide"), and Seaway, the retail dealer where they had purchased the car. World-Wide (D) and Seaway (D) challenged the Oklahoma court's exercise of jurisdiction, claiming that they did not have the necessary minimum contacts with Oklahoma. Seaway (D) claimed to do business in New York state only, and World-Wide (D) claimed to do business only within the tri-state area of New York, New Jersey, and Connecticut. Neither conducted any business in Oklahoma, employed anyone in Oklahoma, kept office space in Oklahoma, or directed advertising at the Oklahoma market. Both the trial court and the Supreme Court of Oklahoma rejected the claim that World-Wide (D) and Seaway (D) should not be subjected to jurisdiction there, based largely on the theory that they should have foreseen the possibility of litigation there, given the uniquely mobile nature of the product they sold. World-Wide (D) and Seaway (D) next appealed to the U.S. Supreme Court.

■ **ISSUE**

When a particular state would be the most convenient forum for a trial (i.e., all the witnesses are there, the plaintiffs are hospitalized there, the claim arose there, etc.), and the defendant would not find it at all inconvenient to defend itself there, can that state exercise jurisdiction even if the defendant has not deliberately sought contacts with that state?

■ **DECISION AND RATIONALE**

(White) No. A state cannot exercise jurisdiction over a defendant who has not deliberately sought some contact with the state. Minimum contacts must be based on some act committed by the defendant. This is a result, in part, of the requirement, first stated in *International Shoe*, that jurisdiction should not be exercised when it is inconsistent with "traditional notions of fair play and substantial justice." It is fundamentally unfair to hold a defendant responsible for the actions of others, such as the action of the Robinsons in driving their car through Oklahoma. However, the minimum contacts requirement also stems from the idea that each state's jurisdiction is limited, not just to protect defendants, but to protect the interests of other states. It has been becoming less and less difficult for defendants to defend themselves in other states, as technology progresses, but the interests of other states in not having their own sovereignty infringed remains constant, as provided for in the Constitution. Unless a defendant had chosen to avail itself somehow of another state, that state's exercise of jurisdiction might very well conflict with the sovereignty of the state which the defendant did choose. It has been argued that the defendants in this case should have foreseen that their product might wind up in Oklahoma, especially given the mobile nature of automobiles. However, it is not the foreseeability that a given product might travel to a distant forum that is important, but rather the foreseeability that the defendant might be "haled into court there." It is reasonable to believe that neither Seaway (D) nor World-Wide (D) expected to be haled into court in Oklahoma. Since there is no evidence to support the view that either Seaway (D) or World-Wide (D) conducted business in Oklahoma, or intended their products to reach the Oklahoma market, there is basis for the Oklahoma court's exercise of jurisdiction over either defendant. Judgment reversed.

■ **DISSENT**

(Brennan) Yes. A state may exercise jurisdiction over a defendant who has not deliberately sought contacts with that state. Of course, the defendant must have *some* contacts with the state. For instance, in this case, if the Robinsons' car had blown up in Texas the Oklahoma courts would obviously not have jurisdiction over the case. But the fact the defendants did sell the Robinsons the actual car which did reach Oklahoma and did blow up there, should be enough. Perhaps the Court is right to mock the idea of all chattels being treated in this way, but surely an exception should be made for a car, which by its very nature is meant to travel. It would be difficult to believe that the defendants truly believed that none of the cars they sold would ever leave the New York area. It is true that the contacts between Seaway (D) and World-Wide (D) and Oklahoma were not extensive, but given the other factors that must be considered—fairness and convenience—it is certainly reasonable to subject them to Oklahoma's jurisdiction for this case. There is no doubt that Oklahoma is the most efficient forum in which to try the case. The witnesses are there. The evidence is there. The plaintiffs were hospitalized there when they filed suit. And the defendants would only suffer minimal inconvenience, if any, in being required to defend themselves there. The two parent companies, Volkswagen and Audi, will be required to defend the case there one way or another. Expanding that defense to encompass World-Wide (D) and Seaway (D) would not be very difficult. Given these reasons, and Oklahoma's strong interest in the litigation, both Seaway (D) and World-Wide should be held subject to Oklahoma's jurisdiction.

Analysis:

WWVW is the first real indication of a serious split in the Court over what constitutes sufficient minimum contacts. Sometimes, as here, Brennan loses out. Sometimes he wins. And sometimes it's totally unclear if anyone came through the debate alive, let alone with a majority behind them. The split stems from two different views on what the most important concern should be in exercising personal jurisdiction: the due process rights of the defendant, or the interests of the forum state in the litigation. Here, the winning side focused more on the former, and Brennan, on the losing side, focused more on the latter. The great irony of this case, however, lies in the fact that neither side really cared whether or not Oklahoma had jurisdiction over Seaway (D) or World-Wide (D), or whether either of these defendants even stayed in the case—after all, Audi and Volkswagen were still in the case, and they were most likely capable of satisfying any judgment which the Robinsons might be able to recover. What everybody involved really cared about was not whether or not the case would be tried in Oklahoma, but whether the case would be tried in Oklahoma state court or Oklahoma federal court.

Apparently, the relevant federal and state courts must have drawn from significantly different jury pools, since the state court juries had a noticeable tendency to award more money, more often, to plaintiffs, than their federal court counterparts. The Robinsons therefore strategically filed their lawsuit in state court. The defendants, for the same reasons, wanted to be able to remove the action to federal court. (Any action that could have been filed originally in federal court by the plaintiff can be "removed" to federal court by the defendant.) However, the Robinsons, although in the process of moving to Arizona on the fateful day, were still considered residents of New York for diversity purposes. As Seaway (D) and World-Wide (D) were also from New York, the action could not be removed while they remained as defendants in the case, due to a lack of complete diversity. [These concepts will be studied in more detail when you get subject matter jurisdiction, as opposed to personal jurisdiction.] Therefore, if Seaway (D) and World-Wide (D) could be kicked out of the case, then Audi and Volkswagen could remove to federal court and stand a better chance of winning. In short, this is exactly what happened.

■ CASE VOCABULARY

CHATTEL: An item of personal property.

Kulko v. Superior Court

(Ex-Husband) v. *(California Trial Court)*
436 U.S. 84, 98 S.Ct. 1690 (1978)

U.S. SUPREME COURT STRIKES DOWN CALIFORNIA SUPREME COURT'S EXERCISE OF JURISDICTION

■ **INSTANT FACTS** California woman sued New York ex-husband in California for additional child support payments.

■ **BLACK LETTER RULE** A state may not exercise jurisdiction over a defendant who has not purposefully availed himself of the benefits of that state, even if the state has a strong interest in the litigation.

■ **PROCEDURAL BASIS**

Writ of Certiorari for upholding of trial court's exercise of jurisdiction in action to modify child support agreement.

■ **FACTS**

Mr. and Mrs. Kulko separated in New York, and then Mrs. Kulko moved to California. Their two children remained in New York with their father for most of each year, according to the original separation agreement. Then the daughter decided that she wanted to live in California with her mother, and Mr. Kulko (D) bought her a one-way plane ticket to get there. Later, Mrs. Kulko sent the son a one-way ticket without telling Mr. Kulko, and the son also moved to California. Mrs. Kulko then filed for a modification of the child support agreement in a California court. The California court found that it could exercise jurisdiction over Mr. Kulko due to his contacts with California, which consisted of his purchase, in New York, of an airplane ticket to California. Also, the court concluded that he benefitted from California's laws, since his daughter was there and not in New York with him. Mr. Kulko (D) appealed to the U.S. Supreme Court, which understandably found the arguments in favor of jurisdiction to be rather weak.

■ **ISSUE**

Can a state exercise jurisdiction over a defendant who has not purposefully availed himself of the benefits of that state, if the state has a strong interest in the litigation?

■ **DECISION AND RATIONALE**

No. A state may not exercise jurisdiction over a defendant who has not purposefully availed himself of the benefits of that state, even if the state has a strong interest in the litigation. In this case, Mr. Kulko (D) merely agreed to let his daughter go to California and live with her mother. He bought a one-way ticket from New York to California for her, which was a purposeful act, but which can hardly be described as causing an "effect" within the state of California that should warrant his being subject to jurisdiction there. Besides, this "effects" test has traditionally been used in cases where a wrongful act has been committed outside a state but had harmful effects within it. Buying an airplane ticket is hardly a wrongful act. Likewise, the argument that Mr. Kulko (D) is receiving "a benefit" from the laws of California because his daughter now lives there is strained. If he does indeed receive a financial benefit from the fact that his daughter no longer lives with him, this is exactly because she no longer lives with him—NOT because she now lives in California. It is true that California does have a strong interest in seeing that its children receive proper child support, but overall, it would certainly be more reasonable for this case to be tried in New York, since that was the site of the marriage and separation. Therefore, given Mr. Kulko's (D) lack of contacts with California, California should not have exercised jurisdiction in this case.

Analysis:

This decision reinforces the *World-Wide* stance that some purposeful act on the defendant's part is necessary to make him subject to a state's jurisdiction. The fact that this was a case involving child custody and support, however, gives it a slightly different angle. Suits involving domestic relations had enjoyed a special status even under *Pennoyer*, as it was fairly universally recognized that every state should be able to regulate the status of its residents. However, while states had always been able to issue a divorce decree, for example, without jurisdiction over one of the parties, they did not have the power to litigate property or child custody issues without jurisdiction over both parties. Thus, quite a few cases arose involving soon-to-be-ex-spouses bickering over jurisdiction, and courts recognized that special concern had to be taken in these situations. Here, the Supreme Court explicitly acknowledged the public policy involved in its decision, stating that it did fear upholding jurisdiction in this case would discourage parents from cooperating in custody settlements, if by cooperating (*i.e.*, buying a ticket to send a child to the other parent), they could be subjecting themselves to the jurisdiction of the other parent's state. The Court also did consider California's interest in the litigation. It first noted that the state's interest in ensuring the support of children residing in California could be effectively vindicated by using alternative enforcement methods. Even more important, however, the Court emphasized that the state's interest, though substantial and legitimate, did not make California a fair forum. Although the forum state's interest may be considered along with the interest of the plaintiff in choosing the forum, the existence of contacts between the defendant and the forum state remains the essential criterion for jurisdiction.

Burger King Corp. v. Rudzewicz

(Franchise Owner) v. *(Franchisee)*

471 U.S. 462, 105 S.Ct. 2174 (1985)

SUPREME COURT RULES THAT MINIMUM CONTACTS CAN BE A SINGLE CONTRACT

■ **INSTANT FACTS** Rudzewicz (D) contracted with Burger King (D), a Florida corporation, to operate a Burger King restaurant in Michigan, then defaulted on payments, so Burger King (P) sued him in Florida.

■ **BLACK LETTER RULE** Once it has been established that the defendant has minimum contacts with a state, it is up to the defendant to prove that being required to defend a suit there would be "fundamentally unfair."

■ PROCEDURAL BASIS

Appeal from reversal of judgment in action for damages and injunctive relief for breach of contract.

■ FACTS

John Rudzewicz (D) and Brian MacShara, both Michigan residents, entered into a franchise agreement with Burger King Corporation (P), a Florida company. The contract licensed Rudzewicz (D) and MacShara to use Burger King's (P) trademarks and service marks for a period of 20 years, in connection with their operation of a Burger King restaurant in Michigan. The contract provided that the agreement would be governed by Florida law, and called for payment of all franchise fees and royalties to Burger King's (P) Miami headquarters. In connection with establishing the restaurant, MacShara attended a training course at Burger King University in Miami. After operating the restaurant for a while, Rudzewicz (D) and MacShara fell behind in their monthly payments to Burger King (P). Burger King (P) then instituted an action in federal court in Florida, based on diversity jurisdiction. Rudzewicz (D) and MacShara claimed that they did not have sufficient contacts with Florida to be subjected to jurisdiction there. The District Court found that Florida could exercise jurisdiction in this case, based on a long-arm statute which extends jurisdiction to anyone who breaches a contract within the state. The Court of Appeals reversed, however, finding that, although the defendants could be said to have the necessary contacts with Florida, such an exercise of jurisdiction would be fundamentally unfair, and an infringement of due process—and an especially dangerous precedent. Burger King (P) appealed to the U.S. Supreme Court.

■ ISSUE

In asserting jurisdiction against out-of-state defendants, does a state have to show both that the defendant has minimum contacts with the state, and that it would be fair and equitable to require the defendant to defend a suit there?

■ DECISION AND RATIONALE

(Brennan) No. The state does not have to show both that the defendant has minimum contacts with the state, and that it would be fair and equitable to require the defendant to defend a suit there. Once it has been established that the defendant has minimum contacts with a state, there is a presumption that it would be fair to require the defendant to defend a suit there. This presumption can of course be overcome, but it is the defendant who must show that it would be unfair to require him to defend there, and not the state which must show that it would be fair. In deciding the question of fairness, the court may look to and balance the forum state's interest in the litigation, the plaintiff's interest in efficient and convenient relief, the demands and best interests of the federal system as a whole, and the defendant's interest in not having to defend a suit in an extremely remote or disadvantageous forum. In the case at hand, Rudzewicz (D) deliberately and voluntarily entered into a 20-year-long contract with a Florida corporation, governed by Florida law. That contract required that someone associated with the new restaurant attend training in Florida at Burger King University. While Rudzewicz (D) himself did not go, and in fact has never been to Florida at all, it can hardly have come as a complete shock to him to learn that Burger King (P) might sue him there should he breach the agreement. Florida is certainly the most convenient forum for this case, and while this is not the determining factor, it is something to consider. Rudzewicz (D) has not shown that his case would be unfairly prejudiced or harmed by a trial in Florida. Of course he will be somewhat inconvenienced, but doesn't the mere fact of being sued cause some inconvenience in and of itself? We shouldn't therefore prohibit all lawsuits. And undoubtedly Burger King (P) was inconvenienced by not receiving the monthly payments. In short, Rudzewicz's (D) purposeful involvement with a Florida company provides the necessary minimum contacts for Florida to exercise jurisdiction, and he has failed to show that it would be fundamentally unfair to allow Florida to do so. Reversed and remanded.

■ DISSENT

(Stevens) Rudzewicz (D) did no business in Florida. He sold no products there, did not anticipate that any of his products would ever wind up there, maintained no offices there, and had in fact never been there. His principal contact with Burger King (P) was through its Michigan branch office, not its Florida headquarters. There is no reason to believe that Rudzewicz (D) ever anticipated any involvement with the Florida office, and every reason to think that he would have expected to resolve any problems that arose with the Michigan office—including any potential litigation. Also, the typical franchise is at best a very local operation, with far less capital or bargaining power than a huge national corporation like Burger King (P). Therefore, it would be fundamentally unfair to require local franchise operators like Rudzewicz (D) to defend themselves in a forum as distant and unfamiliar as Florida. The judgment of the Court of Appeals dismissing the Florida action should be upheld.

Analysis:

This time, apparently, Brennan's side won. This time it's the majority opinion that stresses the forum state's interest in the litigation, and the dissent that stresses the due process concerns of the defendant. The swing votes must have come over to Brennan's side this time because here, unlike in cases such as *World-Wide Volkswagen,* the defendant had taken some purposeful action to associate himself with the forum state. One interesting question to wonder about, however, is why Rudzewicz (D) took this case all the way up to the Supreme Court. It's not as if, had Burger King (P) been denied the right to sue him in Florida, the case would have ended. Burger King (P) would probably have just turned around and sued him in Michigan. Do you think that having the "home-court" advantage is worth that much effort? Sure, Rudzewicz (D) might have been able to try to portray himself as the virtuous local businessman victimized by a big, out-of-state corporation. But the action was in federal court, and one of the main reasons for establishing a federal court system in the first place was to provide a neutral forum where non-residents could see justice without the interference of local prejudice against out-of-staters.

Asahi Metal Industry Co. v. Superior Court

(Japanese Manufacturer) v. *(California Trial Court)*

480 U.S. 102, 107 S.Ct. 1026 (1987)

SUPREME COURT PLURALITIES FURTHER MUDDY THE WATERS OF PERSONAL JURISDICTION

■ **INSTANT FACTS** Victim of motorcycle accident brought suit in California court against Taiwanese tire-tube maker, who cross-claimed against Japanese manufacturer of the tire tube valve assembly.

■ **BLACK LETTER RULE** The defendant must purposefully avail himself of the forum by more than just putting a product into the stream of commerce with the expectation that it will reach the forum state, however, such conduct is enough to satisfy the minimum contacts requirement. Nonetheless, once it has been established that minimum contacts exist, the fairness requirement must still be met as well, which will be much harder to do in the case of a non-U.S. resident.

■ **PROCEDURAL BASIS**

Writ of Certiorari to the Supreme Court of California for its reversal of the Court of Appeal's writ of mandate directing the Superior Court to quash service of summons on cross-complaint for indemnification in action for damages for negligence.

■ **FACTS**

In September of 1978 Gary Zurcher and his wife, Ruth Ann Moreno, were in a serious motorcycle accident that left Ruth dead and Gary seriously injured. He claimed that the accident had been caused when the rear wheel of his motorcycle suddenly lost air and exploded, sending the motorcycle out of control and into a tractor. Zurcher filed suit in Solano County, California, where the accident had occurred, alleging that the tire, tube, and sealant of his motorcycle were defective. Accordingly, he named as one of the defendants Cheng Shin Rubber Industrial Co., Ltd., the tire tube's Taiwanese manufacturer. Cheng Shin in turn filed a cross-claim—for indemnification in the event it was found liable—against the other defendants, and against Asahi Metal Industry Co., Ltd. (D), the Japanese manufacturer of the tire tube's valve assembly. Zurcher eventually settled out of court with Cheng Shin and all the other defendants, leaving Cheng Shin's cross-claim against Asahi (D) as the sole remaining issue to be tried. Asahi (D) argued that California could not exert jurisdiction over it, since it lacked sufficient contacts with the state. Asahi (D) did not do business in California and did not import any products into California itself. Rather, it sold its valve assemblies to Cheng Shin and various other tire manufacturers. The sales to Cheng Shin took place in Taiwan, and the valve assemblies were shipped to Taiwan. Cheng Shin bought valve assemblies from other manufacturers as well. Sales to Cheng Shin accounted for a very small fraction of Asahi's (D) annual income—usually less than 1–2%. In the years for which data were available, Cheng Shin used anywhere from 100,000 to 500,000 Asahi (D) valve assemblies per year, and sold finished tires all over the world. It is unknown what percentage of its sales are in the U.S., but of those U.S. sales roughly 20 percent are in California. Asahi (D) claimed that it had never contemplated that it might be subject to suit in California because of sales to Cheng Shin in Taiwan, but Cheng Shin claimed that Asahi (D) had been told and definitely knew that its products were being sold in California. The trial court found that Asahi (D), as an international company, could be subjected to California's jurisdiction. The Court of Appeal disagreed, however, and ordered the Superior

Court to quash service of summons on Asahi (D). Unfortunately for Asahi (D), the Supreme Court of California overruled the Court of Appeal, finding that Asahi's (D) intentional act of putting its products into the "stream of commerce" with the awareness that they might wind up in California was enough to justify California's exercise of jurisdiction. Asahi (D) appealed to the U.S. Supreme Court.

■ ISSUE

Is it sufficient, in order to establish minimum contacts with a state, to put a product into the stream of commerce, with the expectation that it will reach the forum state?

■ DECISION AND RATIONALE

(O'Connor, joined by Rehnquist, Powell, and Scalia) No. It is not sufficient, for purposes of establishing that the defendant has minimum contacts with the forum state, to show that the defendant has intentionally placed its products into the stream of commerce—even if the defendant had the expectation in doing so that its products would reach the forum state. Something more, in addition to placing products in the stream of commerce, is necessary to establish minimum contacts between the defendant and the forum state. As the Court decided in *World-Wide Volkswagen*, foreseeability alone is insufficient as a basis for jurisdiction. It is not enough that Asahi (D) might have been able to guess that some one or more of its products might eventually find its way into the state of California. Asahi (D) must have performed some act showing that it deliberately intended to take advantage of that state's market or laws. This does not mean that Asahi (D) could only invoke California's jurisdiction by importing its products directly. Cheng Shin's actions in importing Asahi's (D) products could qualify, provided that Asahi (D) took additional actions indicating its intent, such as, for instance, advertising or marketing its product in California, or deliberately designing its product to conform to regulations or laws unique to California, or providing a means for California users of its products to receive technical help or advice. Since Asahi (D) has done nothing to indicate a deliberate wish on its part to see its products in California or to exploit the California market, it cannot be said to have the requisite minimum contacts with the state. However, in this particular case the minimum contacts analysis is not the only reason why California cannot exercise jurisdiction. There is still the matter of "traditional notions of fair play and substantial justice." Even if minimum contacts existed between Asahi (D) and California, it would be fundamentally unfair to require Asahi (D) to defend itself there. California's interest in this matter—the welfare of its citizens—was put to rest, for the most part, when Zurcher settled. The dispute is between, not just two non-residents of California, but two non-residents of the U.S. Given the rather extreme inconvenience necessitated by defending a suit in a distant forum and a *foreign* legal system, it would be unreasonable and unfair for California to exercise jurisdiction over Asahi (D) in this matter. Reversed and remanded.

■ CONCURRENCE

(Brennan, joined by White, Marshall, and Blackmun, concurring in part and concurring in the judgment) Yes. It is sufficient, for purposes of establishing that the defendant has minimum contacts with the forum state, to show that the defendant has intentionally placed its products into the stream of commerce. The "stream of commerce" referred to here indicates the regular and continuous flow of products from manufacture to consumption, not unanticipated and random single occurrences. Since Asahi's (D) products were regularly and steadily flowing into California, with Asahi's (D) knowledge, Asahi (D) was benefiting from the laws of California and should be held to have the necessary contacts with California to be subject to its jurisdiction. However, the Court is correct in its analysis of the fairness aspect of the test for jurisdiction, as it would be fundamentally unfair and unreasonable to require Asahi (D) to defend this suit in California. Therefore, the Court was correct in overturning the judgment of the California Supreme Court.

■ CONCURRENCE

(Stevens, joined by White and Blackmun, concurring in part and concurring in the judgment) We don't need to decide for this case. It is quite obvious that it would not be fair to require the Japanese defendant to defend itself in California, especially when there are no American parties left in the case. But if we did need to formulate here a test requiring minimum contacts, the Court has not done so correctly. Asahi (D) did have sufficient knowledge that its product was being sold in California and should therefore be held to have had sufficient minimum contacts with that state.

Analysis:

The Court unanimously held in this case that the California state court could not constitutionally exercise jurisdiction over Asahi (D). The Court followed a two-step analysis it had developed in its previous decisions. First, inquiry was made into the sufficiency of Asahi's (D) contacts with the forum state, and then those contacts were examined in light of fairness considerations to determine if the exercise of jurisdiction would be reasonable. Justice O'Connor, in her plurality opinion, understood the teaching of *World-Wide Volkswagen* to be that a manufacturer's contacts must be "more purposefully directed at the forum State than the mere act of placing a product in the stream of commerce." Asahi's (D) mere awareness that the valve assemblies it sold to Cheng Shin eventually would end up in California was not sufficiently purposeful, in her opinion, to establish minimum contacts. The Court divided sharply on this point with three members endorsing the conclusion reached by Justice O'Connor. Given the division of the justices in *Asahi* and the changes in the Court's composition since, the question of what is the appropriate standard to be used to determine whether a manufacturer has established sufficient "minimum contacts" with a forum state has not been fully resolved.

Perkins v. Benguet Consolidated Mining Co.

(*Stockholder*) v. (*Company*)
342 U.S. 437, 72 S.Ct. 413 (1952)

SUPREME COURT RULES THAT DEFENDANT'S CONTACTS WITH A FORUM CAN SERVE AS A BASIS FOR JURISDICTION EVEN IF THE CAUSE OF ACTION ARISES ELSEWHERE

■ **INSTANT FACTS** Stockholder sued Philippine mining company in Ohio, based on that company's president's presence and activities there.

■ **BLACK LETTER RULE** When there are sufficient minimum contacts, a state may assert jurisdiction over a defendant even for causes of action arising outside the jurisdiction.

■ **PROCEDURAL BASIS**

Appeal from granting of motion to quash service of summons in action for damages for failure to issue shares of stock.

■ **FACTS**

During the occupation of the Philippines by the Japanese in World War II, the activities of the Benguet Consolidated Mining Company (D), a Philippine corporation, were suspended. The president of the company, originally from Ohio, returned there. Although the wartime operations of the company were unsurprisingly fairly limited, what activities did occur, occurred in Ohio. The president maintained an office there, with company files, and continued to employ two company secretaries, who worked with him there. Perkins (P), a stockholder of the company, sued the company in Ohio, claiming that the company had failed to issue her stock and had not paid her dividends. Benguet (D) moved to quash service of summons for lack of jurisdiction, since both causes of action arose from actions of the company outside of Ohio. The Ohio courts granted the motion, and Perkins (P) appealed to the U.S. Supreme Court.

■ **ISSUE**

Can a state exercise jurisdiction over a defendant who has minimum contacts with the state for causes of action not arising from those contacts?

■ **DECISION AND RATIONALE**

Yes. A state can exercise jurisdiction over a defendant who has minimum contacts with the state for causes of action not arising from those contacts. It is true that somewhat more extensive contacts are required when the cause of action arises outside of those contacts than from those contacts. However, where, as here, the defendant's contacts with the state are continuous, systematic, and rather extensive, that state can exercise jurisdiction over the defendant regardless of where or how the cause of action arose. Benguet's activities in Ohio were extensive enough to justify that state's exercise of jurisdiction even in this case, where the cause of action is not related to either the state or to the company's activities within it. Of course, Ohio is not *required* to exercise jurisdiction in this case if it does not wish to, but the requirements of federal due process certainly do not prohibit it from doing so. Reversed and remanded.

Analysis:

This case presents an instance of the successful exercise of general jurisdiction. It illustrates the principle whereby the continuous activity of a defendant within the forum may be of such a nature as to subject the defendant to jurisdiction even upon causes of action unrelated to the forum activity. Cases covered by this principle involve highly qualitative evaluations of the particular facts of the case at hand, because the principle requires assessment of the nature, as well as the substantiality, of the defendant's contacts with the forum. The principle provides that a court may assert jurisdiction over a defendant whose continuous activities in the forum are unrelated to the cause of action sued upon when the defendant's contacts are sufficiently substantial and of such a nature as to make the state's assertion of jurisdiction reasonable. The Supreme Court generally has left the states the discretion to assert or forego jurisdiction in these types of cases.

Helicopteros Nacionales de Colombia, S.A. v. Hall

(Helicopter Service) v. (Injured Party)
466 U.S. 408, 104 S.Ct. 1868 (1984)

GENERAL *IN PERSONAM* JURISDICTION REQUIRES SUFFICIENTLY SUBSTANTIAL AND CONTINUOUS MINIMUM CONTACTS WITH THE FORUM STATE

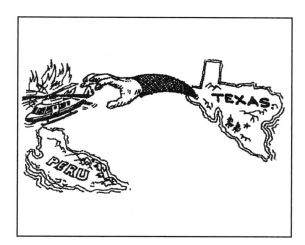

■ **INSTANT FACTS** The representatives of several decedents sued Helicol (D), the owner of a helicopter that crashed in Peru, alleging that Helicol (D) had sufficient contacts with Texas to render it subject to *in personam* jurisdiction in that State.

■ **BLACK LETTER RULE** Personal jurisdiction may be satisfied by sufficient minimum contacts with the forum state so that maintenance of the suit does not offend the traditional notions of fair play and substantial justice.

■ **PROCEDURAL BASIS**

Writ of certiorari reviewing reversal of dismissal of action for damages for wrongful death, due to lack of *in personam* jurisdiction.

■ **FACTS**

In 1976, a helicopter owned by Helicopteros Nacionales De Colombia, S.A. (Helicol) (D), a Colombian corporation, crashed in Peru and resulted in the deaths of four United States citizens. At the time of the crash, the decedents were employed by Consorcio (D), a Peruvian consortium, and WSH (D), a joint venture headquartered in Houston, Texas. Consorcio/WSH (D) had rented the helicopter from Helicol (D) for use on an oil pipeline in Peru. The helicopter had been manufactured by Bell Helicopter Company (D) in Fort Worth, Texas. The survivors and representatives of the decedents, including Hall (P), brought a wrongful-death action in Texas state court against Helicol (D), Consorcio/WSH (D), and Bell Helicopter Company (D). Helicol (D) filed a special appearance and moved to dismiss the actions for lack of personal jurisdiction. Helicol (D) argued that its only contacts with Texas consisted of sending its chief executive officer to Houston to negotiate the rental contract, of accepting checks from Consorcio/WSH (D) drawn on a bank in Houston, and of purchasing helicopters and receiving training from Bell Helicopter (D) in Fort Worth. The motion was denied and the actions were consolidated in a jury trial, resulting in a jury verdict of over $1 million in favor of Hall (P). A Texas appellate court reversed the judgment, holding that *in personam* jurisdiction over Helicol (D) was lacking. The Supreme Court of Texas reversed this judgment, reasoning that it was consistent with the Due Process Clause for the Texas courts to assert *in personam* jurisdiction over Helicol. The Supreme Court granted certiorari.

■ **ISSUE**

Do negotiations and purchasing in the forum state constitute continuous and systematic contacts sufficient to satisfy the requirements for general *in personam* jurisdiction?

■ **DECISION AND RATIONALE**

(Blackmun, J.) No. Negotiations and purchasing in the forum state do not constitute continuous and systematic contacts sufficient to satisfy the requirements for general *in personam* jurisdiction. The Due

Process Clause of the Fourteenth Amendment limits the power of a State to assert *in personam* jurisdiction over a nonresident defendant. Specifically, there must be certain minimum contacts with the forum such that the maintenance of the suit does not offend traditional notions of fair play and substantial justice. When a controversy is related to or arises out of a defendant's contacts with the forum, personal jurisdiction is established. Alternatively, a nonresident may be subjected to *in personam* jurisdiction when there are sufficient contacts between the state and the nonresident. We need not decide whether the controversy at hand arose out of or related to Helicol's (D) contacts with Texas for specific jurisdiction purposes, as Hall (P) did not allege this basis for jurisdiction [Perhaps Hall's next action should be for attorney malpractice!]. Moreover, Helicol's (D) contacts with Texas did not constitute the kind of continuous and systematic general business contacts for general *in personam* jurisdiction. Helicol's (D) contacts with Texas consisted of sending the chief executive officer to Houston for a contract-negotiation session with Consorcio/WSH; accepting checks drawn on a Houston bank; purchasing helicopters, equipment, and training services from Bell Helicopter (D) in Fort Worth; and sending personnel to Fort Worth for training. The one trip to Houston for contract negotiations is certainly not continuous and systematic, and the mere acceptance of checks drawn on a Texas bank account is unilateral conduct and not an appropriate consideration in determining sufficient minimum contacts. Furthermore, the purchases and related training trips were not a sufficient basis for personal jurisdiction. Thus, Helicol's (D) contacts with the State of Texas were insufficient to satisfy the requirements of the Due Process Clause of the Fourteenth Amendment. Reversed.

■ DISSENT

(Brennan, J.) I believe that Helicol's (D) purposeful availment of the benefits and obligations of the State of Texas constitute sufficient minimum contacts to make it fair and reasonable for the State to assert personal jurisdiction over Helicol (D). Furthermore, the undisputed contacts between Helicol (D) and Texas are sufficiently related to the underlying cause of action, and jurisdiction does not offend the traditional notions of fair play and substantial justice. As economic participants in interstate and foreign commerce, Helicol (D) should reasonably expect to be called into Texas for litigation, based on the doctrine of general jurisdiction. Helicol (D) not only purchased equipment in Texas for many years, but it also sent pilots and management personnel to Texas for training. Moreover, negotiations for the contract under which Helicol (D) provided transportation for Consorcio/WSH also took place in Texas. Helicol (D) obtained numerous benefits from these transactions and, thus, it is fair and reasonable for the State to assert jurisdiction. Alternatively, I believe that the wrongful-death claim is sufficiently related to the contacts between Helicol (D) and Texas to warrant specific jurisdiction. Helicol's (D) contacts with Texas were directly related to the negligence that was alleged in Hall's (P) original complaint. I would affirm the judgment of the Supreme Court of Texas.

Analysis:

This opinion marks the first case in which the Supreme Court adopted the distinction between specific jurisdiction and general jurisdiction. Specific jurisdiction is implicated whenever the defendant's contacts with the forum arise out of or relate to the cause of action. Justice Brennan attempted to establish a broad definition of specific jurisdiction, arguing that even a small amount of relatedness satisfies the requirements. However, Justice Blackmun's majority opinion applied a restrictive version of the specific jurisdiction test. Since the helicopter disaster occurred in Peru, and since none of the Texas activities related specifically to the crash, Blackmun concluded that specific jurisdiction was unwarranted. It is easy to see that a broader definition of specific jurisdiction would have rendered Helicol (D) subject to suit in Texas, since the pilots who eventually crashed the helicopter were trained in Fort Worth. Nevertheless, the opinion is more important for its discussion of general jurisdiction. General jurisdiction is appropriate whenever there are sufficient minimum contacts between the State and the nonresident so as not to offend the traditional notions of fair play and substantial justice. Obviously this is a vague standard, and the opinion does little to assist future courts in reaching decisions on general jurisdiction. In the case at hand, Justice Blackmun found that Helicol's (D) contract-negotiation, purchasing and training activities in Texas were not sufficient to satisfy the minimum contacts test. However, Justice Brennan's dissent raises an interesting argument of "purposeful availment." Helicol (D) benefited from participation in interstate and foreign commerce, and it purposefully availed itself of the protections of

Texas in any lawsuit related to these transactions. It seems fair and reasonable that Helicol (D) should be subject to suit in Texas as well.

■ **CASE VOCABULARY**

GENERAL JURISDICTION: Personal jurisdiction based on sufficiently substantial and continuous minimum contacts between a nonresident defendant and the forum state.

PURPOSEFUL AVAILMENT: A proposed test for general jurisdiction, relating to the amount a defendant avails himself of the benefits and protections of the forum state.

SPECIFIC JURISDICTION: Personal jurisdiction based on a cause of action related to or arising out of a defendant's contacts with the forum state.

Pebble Beach Co. v. Caddy

(Pebble Beach Golf Course Owner) v. *(Pebble Beach Bed and Breakfast Owner)*

453 F.3d 1151 (9th Cir. 2006)

NON–INTERACTIVE, PASSIVE WEBSITES DO NOT SPECIFICALLY TARGET FOREIGN JURISDICTIONS

I'm so glad you stumbled upon the website for this bed and breakfast.

Me too. So far this totally beats golfing.

stus.com

■ **INSTANT FACTS** Pebble Beach Co. (P) appealed from the district court's dismissal of its trademark infringement claim against Caddy (D), the owner of the "Pebble Beach" bed and breakfast, for lack of personal jurisdiction over Caddy (D), a resident of England.

■ **BLACK LETTER RULE** Due process is satisfied when (1) the defendant has performed some act or consummated some transaction within the forum or has otherwise purposefully availed himself of the privileges of conducting business in the forum, (2) the claim arises out of or results from these forum-related activities, and (3) the exercise of jurisdiction is reasonable.

■ **PROCEDURAL BASIS**

Appeal by Pebble Beach (P) from a federal district court holding that the court lacked jurisdiction over Caddy (D).

■ **FACTS**

Pebble Beach Co. (P) owns and operates a well known golf course located in California. Caddy (D), a dual citizen of England and the U.S., owns a bed and breakfast in England named the "Pebble Beach," which has a non-interactive website. Pebble Beach (P) sued Caddy (D) for trademark infringement and Caddy (D) moved to dismiss for lack of personal jurisdiction. The federal district court granted the motion and Pebble Beach (P) appealed.

■ **ISSUE**

Did Caddy (D) expressly aim tortious conduct at California such that he was subject to personal jurisdiction in California courts?

■ **DECISION AND RATIONALE**

(Trott, J.) No. Due process is satisfied when (1) the defendant has performed some act or consummated some transaction within the forum or has otherwise purposefully availed himself of the privileges of conducting business in the forum, (2) the claim arises out of or results from these forum-related activities, and (3) the exercise of jurisdiction is reasonable. If any of these requirements is not satisfied, the exercise of jurisdiction would violate the defendant's due process rights. Here, we need go no further than the first prong of the test. Because Caddy's (D) conduct does not meet that requirement, the district court correctly declined to exercise personal jurisdiction over him.

The first aspect of the minimum contacts analysis actually includes two distinct either-or concepts: purposeful availment and purposeful direction. Caddy (D) has done nothing in California to take advantage of its laws or protections that would support a purposeful availment argument. Nor has he committed an intentional act aimed at California. The existence of a non-interactive website and the use of the "Pebble Beach" name were not specifically aimed at California. A passive website does not satisfy the personal jurisdiction requirement, nor does the use of a trademarked name. To satisfy the requirement of purposeful direction, the defendant must do something more than commit a foreign act with foreseeable effects in the forum state. Here, there simply was no individualized targeting of California. We reject any contention that a passive website constitutes express aiming. Where the sole basis for asserting jurisdiction is a non-interactive passive website, the case is no different than those involving print advertisements not directed at the forum state. Caddy (D) did not direct his actions at California nor avail himself of the protections of California law, so he did not have the minimum contacts with California required to satisfy due process. Affirmed.

Analysis:

The court here applies the *"Calder* effects test,"* based on the case of Calder v. Jones. That case involved the actress Shirley Jones's defamation claim against the *National Enquirer* for printing statement regarding her alleged alcoholism. The issue presented was whether the sale of magazines constituted sufficient minimum contacts to permit the exercise of personal jurisdiction over the editor. The Court, in a unanimous opinion written by Justice Rehnquist, held that the California courts did have jurisdiction over the defendant because the editor was aware that the magazine had a significant circulation in California, that the plaintiff resided in California, and that the allegations made in the article would harm her career there. Based on those effects, due process was satisfied.

■ CASE VOCABULARY

AVAILMENT: The act of making use or taking advantage of something for oneself.

Bellino v. Simon

(Memorabilia Seller) v. *(Authentication Expert)*

1999 WL 1059753 (E.D. La. 1999)

PERSONAL JURISDICTION MAY BE EXERCISED OVER A NONRESIDENT DEFENDANT IF (1) THE LONG–ARM STATUTE CONFERS PERSONAL JURISDICTION, AND (2) EXERCISE OF SUCH JURISDICTION COMPORTS WITH THE DUE PROCESS CLAUSE

■ **INSTANT FACTS** A baseball memorabilia seller sued two men in the trade for allegedly defaming the seller, resulting in lost sales and reputation damage.

■ **BLACK LETTER RULE** The exercise of personal jurisdiction over a nonresident defendant satisfies due process when (1) the defendant has purposefully availed himself of the benefits and protections of the forum state by establishing "minimum contacts" with that state; and (2) the exercise of jurisdiction over the defendant comports with "traditional notions of fair play and substantial justice."

■ **FACTS**

Plaintiffs, Forensic Document Services (FDS) and its President, James Bellino (P), filed this action alleging defamation, fraud and deceptive trade practices by Richard Simon (D) and James Spence Jr. (D). None of the parties is a resident of Louisiana, where the action was filed. FDS (P) is a sole proprietorship with its principal place of business in California. Bellino (P) also resides in California. Simon (D), a New York resident, is the president of Richard Simon Sports, Inc., a New York corporation. Spence (D), a Pennsylvania resident, is the Managing Member of James Spence III Vintage Autographs, L.L.C., a limited liability company formed in Pennsylvania. Both Simon (D) and Spence (D) are engaged in the business of buying, selling, and authenticating sports memorabilia and autographs. In the complaint, FDS (P) asserts that defamatory statements made by Simon (D) to the New York City Department of Consumer Affairs caused the suspension of FDS's (P) business from the on-line internet service, eBay. FDS (P) allegedly suffered lost eBay sales in excess of $500,000, and a loss of business reputation. FDS (P) further contends that Simon's (D) and Spence's (D) defamatory remarks to Christopher Aubert, a Louisiana resident, caused Aubert to return two baseballs he had purchased from FDS (P). As a result, FDS (P) allegedly suffered injuries in Louisiana, including a lost sale in the amount of $25,000 and the loss of future business with Aubert. In an effort to learn more about baseballs, Aubert located Simon's (D) website on the Internet. Aubert initiated contact with Simon (D) by e-mail, Simon (D) responded, and the two men apparently exchanged several e-mails discussing an authentication debate underway in the sports memorabilia field. Aubert then invited Simon (D) to call him to discuss the topic further. Simon (D) did so, and during their subsequent telephone conversation, Simon (D) allegedly made defamatory remarks about FDS (P) and Bellino (P). Three additional e-mails contained allegedly defamatory comments as well, and also included invitations for Aubert to call Simon (D) at his home in New York, and a solicitation to purchase a signed photograph by Babe Ruth. Aubert asked Simon (D) to review scans of two baseballs he purchased from FDS (P). After reviewing the scans, Simon (D) responded that he would not buy either ball because they were forgeries. In a subsequent phone call, Simon (D) allegedly made additional defamatory statements about FDS (P). Simon (D) never charged Aubert for his opinion, and he referred him to Spence (D) for a second opinion regarding the authenticity of the two baseballs. When Aubert called Spence (D), he allegedly defamed FDS (P). Thereafter, Spence (D) sent written examination reports to Aubert, indicating that he could not authenticate the baseballs. Although Aubert had an independent examination indicating that the two baseballs were indeed authentic, he returned the baseballs to FDS (P) based on the allegedly defamatory statements of Simon (D) and Spence (D). Aubert stated that he believed the customer/seller relationship between himself and FDS (P) to be "unsalvageable." Nevertheless, Aubert's law firm currently represents FDS (P) in this matter [how very strange!]. Subsequently, Aubert listed the baseballs on eBay, and they sold for $25,000. Simon (D) and Spence (D) move to dismiss this action on the grounds that the Court lacks personal jurisdiction over them. They assert that they do not have minimum contacts with Louisiana, either through specific or general jurisdiction. Finally, Simon (D) and Spence (D) argue that FDS (P) did not actually suffer any injury because Aubert's law firm represents them, and Aubert used the proceeds of the sales of the baseballs to defray FDS's (P) legal expenses.

■ ISSUE

Does the Court lack personal jurisdiction over the defendants such that the action should be dismissed?

■ DECISION AND RATIONALE

(Vance, J.) Yes and No. For the following reasons, the defendant's motion to dismiss is granted as to Mr. Spence (D) and denied as to Mr. Simon (D). FDS (P) asserts that this Court has general jurisdiction over Simon (D) by virtue of his extensive Internet website solicitations and over Spence (D) because of his website in conjunction with his advertising in a national sports memorabilia trade magazine. Further, FDS (P) maintains that specific jurisdiction exists over both defendants because they reached out to Louisiana to commit the intentional torts alleged in the complaint. At issue are e-mail and telephone conversations between Aubert and Spence (D), regarding the authenticity of two baseballs that Aubert had purchased on approval from FDS (P). The exercise of personal jurisdiction over a nonresident defendant satisfies due process when (1) the defendant has purposefully availed himself of the benefits and protections of the forum state by establishing "minimum contacts" with that state; and (2) the exercise of jurisdiction over the defendant comports with "traditional notions of fair play and substantial justice." Simon (D) and Spence (D) argue that the fiduciary shield doctrine precludes the exercise of personal jurisdiction over them because they were at all times acting in their capacities as officers of their respective companies. The doctrine protects corporate officers and employees from personal jurisdiction based on contacts with the forum state made solely in their corporate capacity. However, because it is an equitable, not a constitutional doctrine, some Courts have stated that the doctrine is unnecessary where the state's long-arm statute has been held to extend to the limits of due process. Moreover, a fraud exception has been recognized to the doctrine, thus because FDS (P) alleges that Simon (D) and Spence (D) committed fraud and defamation in Louisiana, the fiduciary shield doctrine does not preclude jurisdiction. The crucial inquiry in determining whether specific jurisdiction exists over a nonresident defendant involves whether the contacts suggest that the nonresident defendant purposefully availed himself of the privilege of conducting activities within the forum state, thus invoking the benefits and protections of its laws. Considerations such as the quality, nature, and extent of the activity in the forum, the foreseeability of consequences within the forum from activities outside it, and the relationship between the cause of action and the contacts, relate to whether it can be said that the defendant's actions constitute "purposeful availment." With regard to Mr. Spence (D), we find that FDS (P) has not established specific contacts sufficient to support personal jurisdiction over this Pennsylvania resident in Louisiana. FDS (P) concedes that Aubert initiated the phone call in which Spence (D) allegedly defamed FDS (P). This telephone call was the only contact between Spence (D) and Aubert related to FDS's (P) defamation claim. We will not exercise personal jurisdiction based on one unsolicited telephone call from the forum state to a nonresident defendant. We now address whether specific jurisdiction exists over Mr. Simon (D). It is uncontested that allegedly defamatory comments made by Simon (D) first occurred during a telephone call made by Aubert. However, this phone call resulted from several e-mail communications which, in a broad sense, Simon (D) initiated through his website. Moreover, it is undisputed that Simon (D) initiated several e-mails relating to FDS's (P) defamation charge. Even assuming that Aubert, a third party, initiated the two telephone calls, Simon (D) affirmatively directed the allegedly tortious e-mails to Louisiana. That allegedly defamatory comments are made over the Internet does not alter the jurisdictional analysis. Accordingly, we conclude that FDS (P) has met its prima facie burden of showing that Simon (D) purposefully established minimum contacts with Louisiana such that he could reasonably anticipate being haled into court here.

When a cause of action does not arise out of a nonresident defendant's purposeful contacts with the forum state, due process requires continuous and systematic contacts between the defendant and the forum before jurisdiction over the defendant can be exercised. Accordingly, we must analyze Spence's (D) contacts with Louisiana to determine if they are sufficient to justify the exercise of general personal jurisdiction. Spence (D) has never owned, leased, rented or controlled any real or personal property in Louisiana; never maintained a business or an office in Louisiana; nor had a mailing address, employees or an agent for service of process in Louisiana. As such, this does not constitute "continuous and systematic" contacts with the forum. While we find that sufficient minimum contacts exist to exercise personal jurisdiction over Simon (D) in Louisiana, he asserts that it would nevertheless offend traditional notions of fair play and substantial justice to compel him to defend this suit in Louisiana because FDS (P) and Bellino (P) are not in Louisiana, and none of the witnesses, except Aubert, are located in Louisiana. Thus, Simon (D) argues, it would be overly burdensome to litigate this action in Louisiana. While we recognize that Louisiana's interest in this dispute is considerably diminished by the fact that the plaintiffs are not Louisiana residents, nevertheless, the effect of the tortious activity was felt here, and Louisiana law applies. Finally, although other witnesses may be located outside the forum state, the principal witness, Aubert, is a Louisiana resident. Simon (D) has not shown that he would suffer a great burden by litigating this case in Louisiana. Weighing all these factors, we are not persuaded that exercising jurisdiction over Simon (D) would violate due process. For the foregoing reasons, we grant defendants' motion to dismiss Mr. Spence (D) from the action but deny the motion to dismiss with regard to Simon (D).

Analysis:

In a diversity action, personal jurisdiction may be exercised over a nonresident defendant if (1) the long-arm statute of the forum state confers personal jurisdiction over that defendant; and (2) exercise of such jurisdiction by the forum state comports with the fourteenth amendment's due process clause. Because Louisiana's long-arm statute extends to the full limits of due process, the Court must determine whether the exercise of jurisdiction satisfies the due process clause. To determine whether specific jurisdiction exists over a nonresident defendant, this Court must examine whether the defendant purposefully directed his activities toward the forum state, or purposefully availed himself of the privilege of conducting activities therein, and whether the cause of action arises out of or relates to those activities. When these conditions exist, the defendant should reasonably anticipate being haled into court in the forum state. The Supreme Court has held that minimum contacts may exist not only when a nonresident defendant defames a plaintiff within the state, but also when the defendant acts outside of the state and the "effects" of the defamation are felt within the state. Under the second prong of the due process analysis, the Court must determine whether the exercise of personal jurisdiction over a nonresident defendant comports with "traditional notions of fair play and substantial justice." The fairness factors considered by the Court include: the defendant's burden, the forum state's interest, the plaintiff's interest in convenient and effective relief, the judicial system's interest in efficient resolution of controversies, and the state's shared interest in furthering fundamental social policies. When minimum contacts have been established, often the interests of the plaintiff and the forum in the exercise of jurisdiction will justify even the serious burdens placed on the alien defendant. The defendant must present a compelling case that conducting the litigation in this court would be so gravely difficult and inconvenient that he would be at a severe disadvantage in comparison to plaintiffs.

■ CASE VOCABULARY

DIVERSITY ACTION: A lawsuit in which the parties are citizens of different states, and the jurisdiction of the federal courts applies.

FIDUCIARY SHIELD DOCTRINE: A doctrine which protects corporate officers and employees from personal jurisdiction based on contacts with the forum state made solely in their corporate capacity.

LONG-ARM STATUTE: State legislation which provides for personal jurisdiction, via substituted service of process, over persons or corporations which are nonresidents of the state and which voluntarily go into the state, directly or by agent, or communicate with persons of the state, in actions concerning claims relating to the performance or execution of those purposes.

PERSONAL JURISDICTION: The power of a court over the person of a defendant, in contrast to the jurisdiction of the court over a defendant's property.

PRIMA FACIE CASE: Sufficient evidence to get the plaintiff past a motion to dismiss.

Pennington v. Fourth National Bank

(*Property Owner*) v. (*Bank*)
243 U.S. 269, 37 S.Ct. 282 (1917)

IN REM JURISDICTION REQUIRES SEIZURE OF PROPERTY WITHIN THE BORDERS OF THE FORUM STATE

■ **INSTANT FACTS** Pennington (P) objected to the exercise of in rem jurisdiction over his personal intangible property.

■ **BLACK LETTER RULE** In rem proceedings require seizure of a res within the forum state's jurisdiction, as well as an opportunity for the owner to be heard.

■ **PROCEDURAL BASIS**

Writ of certiorari reviewing assertion of in rem jurisdiction.

■ **FACTS**

Although the facts are not stated in detail, one can infer that this case involved a court attempting to obtain in rem jurisdiction over Pennington's (P) property. Pennington (P) was, presumably, a nonresident whose intangible property (probably a bank account) was attached by a court. Pennington (P) alleged that his constitutional rights were being violated by the state attaching and proceeding against his property.

■ **ISSUE**

In an in rem proceeding, does due process require jurisdiction over each party claiming title to the property?

■ **DECISION AND RATIONALE**

(Justice Not Named) No. Due process does not require jurisdiction over each party claiming title to the property in an in rem proceeding. The Constitution presents no obstacle to the power of a state court to garnish or attach property in rem. Thus, a court has in rem jurisdiction over all property, whether tangible or intangible, if the following requirements are met: the res is present within the forum state; the res is seized at the commencement of the proceedings; and the owner has an opportunity to be heard.

Analysis:

This case presents the essential bases of in rem jurisdiction. Most importantly, a court must have power over the property, and the property must be within the court's jurisdiction at the time of the suit. In addition, the court must afford the owner with notice and an opportunity to be heard, in order to comply with due process. In the case at hand, Pennington (P) apparently had notice of the proceeding, and the state certainly had power over the bank account which was located within the forum. Contrast these requirements for in rem jurisdiction with the much more stringent requirements for in personam jurisdiction. While service by publication on a nonresident does not furnish a legal basis for in personam judgments, a court need only have power over and attach property in an in rem proceeding in order to comply with due process. Although the personal rights of an individual are certainly at stake in this in rem action, apparently the due process concerns are minimal when the action solely concerns an individual's property.

■ **CASE VOCABULARY**

INCHOATE: Something unfinished or imperfect, such as a claim over property which is not yet ripe.

Harris v. Balk

(Debtor) v. *(Creditor)*
198 U.S. 215, 25 S.Ct. 625 (1905)

FOR JURISDICTIONAL PURPOSES, THE SITUS OF A DEBT IS WHEREVER THE DEBTOR IS LOCATED

■ **INSTANT FACTS** Balk (P) instituted a suit against Harris (D) in North Carolina for payment of a $180 debt, and Harris (D) claimed that the debt had already been satisfied in a prior proceeding in Maryland.

■ **BLACK LETTER RULE** Courts may assert jurisdiction over debts provided personal jurisdiction over the debtor can be attained.

■ PROCEDURAL BASIS

Writ of certiorari reviewing affirmance of judgment for collection of debt.

■ FACTS

This case involves two alleged debts. First, Harris (D) allegedly owed Balk (P) $180. Both Harris (D) and Balk (P) were citizens of North Carolina. Second, Balk (P) allegedly owed $344 to Epstein, a citizen of Maryland. While Harris (D) was visiting Maryland, Epstein instituted a garnishment proceeding against Balk (P), attaching the debt allegedly owed by Harris (D) to Balk (P). Harris (D) was personally served and notice was posted on the courthouse door. Harris (D) consented to the entry of judgment against him and paid $180 to Epstein. Subsequently, Balk (P) instituted the current suit against Harris (D) in North Carolina in order to recover the $180. Although Harris (D) argued that he no longer owed Balk (P) anything, the trial court ruled in favor of Balk (P), refusing to grant full faith and credit to the Maryland judgment. The North Carolina Supreme Court affirmed on grounds that the Maryland court had no jurisdiction over Harris (D), since the situs of the debt was North Carolina and since Harris (D) was only temporarily in Maryland. The Supreme Court granted certiorari.

■ ISSUE

Does the situs of a debt travel with a debtor for jurisdictional purposes?

■ DECISION AND RATIONALE

(Justice Not Named) Yes. The situs of a debt travels with a debtor for jurisdictional purposes. The original situs of the debt is irrelevant. Thus, while temporarily in Maryland, Harris (D) was liable for garnishment even if the debt was incurred in North Carolina. The obligation of a debtor to pay his debt accompanies him wherever he goes. Thus, the obligation to pay can be enforced by courts of a foreign state, such as Maryland, after personal service of process upon a debtor, such as Harris (D). Reversed.

Analysis:

The somewhat tangled fact pattern in this case can be boiled down to one simple issue: Is it possible to obtain jurisdiction over a debt outside of the state in which the debt was incurred? The Supreme Court answered this question in the affirmative, provided personal jurisdiction can be obtained over the debtor. In the case at hand, Harris (D) voluntarily submitted to personal jurisdiction in Maryland by traveling to that state. Thus, Harris' (D) debt could be attached in a proceeding by Epstein to recover from Balk (P), even though Balk (P) himself was not present in Maryland. Notice that the North Carolina court refused to grant full faith and credit to the Maryland judgment. The only legitimate basis for refusing full faith and credit in this context is that Maryland never had jurisdiction over Balk (P). However, as the Supreme Court ruled, full faith and credit should have been given to the judgment, since Harris (D) owed a debt to Balk (P). This ruling makes sense, as a debt is an item of intangible personal property and the typical rules for in rem jurisdiction should not apply. Rather, the court obtained jurisdiction over the debt based on quasi-in-rem jurisdiction, which affects only the interests of particular persons in some property.

■ **CASE VOCABULARY**

GARNISHEE PROCEEDING: A proceeding against a debtor for recovery of the debt.

SITUS: Literally means "location."

VEL NON: Literally means "or not;" Used in the opinion to signify the question of "jurisdiction or not."

Shaffer v. Heitner

(Officer or Director) v. *(Shareholder)*
433 U.S. 186, 97 S.Ct. 2569 (1977)

THE SUPREME COURT EXTENDS THE MINIMUM CONTACTS TEST TO IN REM JURISDICTION

■ **INSTANT FACTS** Heitner (P) brought a shareholder's derivative suit against several officers and directors of Greyhound, a Delaware corporation, gaining in rem jurisdiction by attaching their stock in Greyhound.

■ **BLACK LETTER RULE** Minimum contacts must exist in order for in rem jurisdiction to attach.

■ **PROCEDURAL BASIS**

Writ of certiorari reviewing affirmance of rejection of arguments contesting jurisdiction for shareholder's derivative suit.

■ **FACTS**

Heitner (P), a nonresident of Delaware, owned one share of stock in Greyhound Corp., a business incorporated in Delaware. Heitner (P) filed a shareholder's derivative suit in Delaware state court, naming 28 officers or directors of Greyhound as defendants. Heitner (P) alleged that the officers and directors had breached their fiduciary duties. At the same time the complaint was filed, Heitner (P) filed a motion for sequestration of shares of approximately 82,000 shares of stock owned by 21 of the officers and directors, as allowed by Delaware law. Those 21 defendants entered a special appearance in Delaware, contending that the sequestration procedure violated due process and that the property was incapable of attachment in Delaware. In addition, the 21 defendants asserted that they did not have sufficient minimum contacts to justify Delaware jurisdiction. The Court of Chancery rejected these arguments, and the Delaware Supreme Court affirmed, holding that Delaware had a sufficient interest in the action to justify jurisdiction. The Supreme Court granted certiorari.

■ **ISSUE**

Is in rem jurisdiction subject to a minimum contacts analysis?

■ **DECISION AND RATIONALE**

(Marshall, J.) Yes. In rem jurisdiction is subject to a minimum contacts analysis. Traditionally, courts have ignored the lack of contacts between a defendant and a state in asserting quasi in rem jurisdiction. While the law governing in personam jurisdiction has expanded dramatically in recent years, no such change has occurred in the law governing in rem jurisdiction. In *Mullane v. Central Hanover Bank & Trust Co.* [Reasonable efforts must be made to give property owners actual notice of the action], we noted that, since an adverse judgment in rem directly affects the property owner by divesting him of his rights in property, certain Fourteenth Amendment rights must attach. Since jurisdiction over property involves jurisdiction over a person's interests in the property, the proper standard is the minimum contacts standard elucidated in *International Shoe Co. v. Washington* [Due process requires that minimum contacts exist for in personam jurisdiction]. We recognize that the presence of property in a State may impact this minimum contacts analysis, as a defendant having property in the state would normally have purposefully availed himself of the jurisdiction of the state. However, in this case, we focus on a different type of quasi in rem action, in which the property serving as the basis for state-court jurisdiction is completely unrelated to Heitner's (P) cause of action. Since the assertion of jurisdiction over property is really just an assertion of jurisdiction over the owner of the property, we conclude that all assertions of state-court jurisdiction must be evaluated according to the standards set forth in *International Shoe* and its progeny. In the case at hand, the officers' and directors' holdings in Greyhound do not provide contacts with Delaware sufficient to support Delaware jurisdiction. Indeed, Delaware has a strong interest in supervising the management of a Delaware corporation, but the Delaware Legislature has failed to assert this interest. Moreover, Delaware is not a fair forum for this litigation. As far as the record indicates, the officers and directors had never set foot in Delaware, and they had not purposefully availed themselves of the benefits and protections of that State. It strains reason to suggest that anyone buying securities in a corporation formed in Delaware impliedly consents to Delaware jurisdiction on any cause of action. Reversed.

■ CONCURRENCE

(Powell, J.) While I reserve judgment on whether ownership of property in a State may provide the contacts necessary for jurisdiction, I favor the preservation of the common law concept of quasi in rem jurisdiction in the case of real property.

■ CONCURRENCE

(Stevens, J.) I would find the Delaware sequestration statute unconstitutional, creating an unacceptable risk of judgment without notice. Delaware denies a defendant the opportunity to defend the merits of a suit unless he subjects himself to the jurisdiction of the court. In effect, this creates a duty of inquiry upon every purchaser of securities to know the place of incorporation of the company and the unique requirements of Delaware law. However, I am uneasy with the reach of the opinion, and I concur with Justice Powell that the opinion should not be read so as to invalidate in rem jurisdiction over real property.

■ DISSENT AND CONCURRENCE

(Brennan, J.) While I agree that the minimum-contacts analysis represents a sensible approach to the exertion of state court jurisdiction, I dissent from the ultimate holding of the case. The majority has treated Delaware's statute as a long-arm statute requiring a minimum contacts analysis. However, the Delaware statute expressly denied such an approach. State court jurisdiction is proper only with notice and an applicable long-arm statute, and there was no such statute applicable in this case. Jurisdiction might indeed be in Delaware's best interest, and the problems with other states applying Delaware's laws argues against denying Delaware jurisdiction over this matter. Nothing noted in the majority opinion persuades me that it would be unfair to subject the officers and directors to suit in Delaware. They certainly associated themselves with the State of Delaware, thereby invoking the benefits and protections of its laws.

Analysis:

This is undoubtedly one of the most important of all of the cases pertaining to jurisdiction. In one broad opinion, Justice Marshall overturned the traditional approach to in rem jurisdiction, equating the in rem test with the minimum contacts test for personal jurisdiction. Thus, in rem jurisdiction is appropriate only where a defendant purposefully availed himself to the benefits and protections of the forum state, or where there is sufficient relatedness between the cause of action and the forum state. Arguably, neither were present in this case. Of course, Marshall could have simply chosen to invalidate the sequestration statute, but instead he took this opportunity to alter the constitutional in rem analysis substantially. The opinion makes a number of logically sound conclusions on the way to its revolutionary holding. First, it is indeed true that in rem jurisdiction can affect a person just as much as in personam jurisdiction. Both affect a person's rights in money or property. Second, considerations of fairness dictate requiring some minimum contacts between the forum state and any person whose interests may be adversely affected by litigation. In the case at hand, the only contact between the property at issue and the state of Delaware was the fact that the stock happened to be in a Delaware corporation. If ever there was a case to deny jurisdiction, this seems to be a very strong one. Note that this decision is likely to have the most profound effect on in rem cases where there was no pre-existing legal interest between the plaintiff and the property, and where the suit is unrelated to the property. Otherwise, there may well be sufficient minimum contacts to justify in rem jurisdiction. After this case, it may be questioned whether there is any continued need to distinguish between in rem and in personam jurisdiction. For two reasons, it is important to continue the distinction. First, where a state's long-arm statute does not extend to the full limits of due process, it may remain impossible to obtain in personam jurisdiction over nonresident defendants, even if minimum contacts could be demonstrated to obtain jurisdiction over their property in rem. Second, in some "true" in rem cases, it is impossible to know who the owners of the property are. The traditional rules for in rem jurisdiction continue in force for these cases. It is also important to note the discussion related to the "special appearance" which the officers and directors attempted to make in Delaware. While most states allow limited appearances for the purposes of contesting jurisdiction, Delaware expressly forbade such actions. Thus, by contesting jurisdiction, the officers and directors voluntarily submitted to unlimited jurisdiction of Delaware. In ruling that no such jurisdiction attached in this case, the court may have implicitly invalidated Delaware's harsh law and all others like it.

■ CASE VOCABULARY

SEQUESTRATION STATUTE: A law providing for the attachment of intangible personal property, such as stock, pending a litigation.

SHAREHOLDER'S DERIVATIVE SUIT: A suit by a shareholder raising a corporate cause of action, such as a suit against officers for a breach of fiduciary duty.

SPECIAL APPEARANCE: A submission to the jurisdiction of a court for limited purposes, including the contesting of jurisdiction.

Burnham v. Superior Court

(Prospective Divorcee) v. *(Court)*

495 U.S. 604, 110 S.Ct. 2105 (1990)

TRANSIENT JURISDICTION REMAINS AVAILABLE WITHOUT CONDUCTING A MINIMUM CONTACTS ANALYSIS

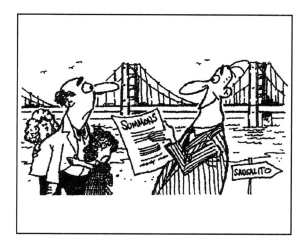

■ **INSTANT FACTS** While visiting California for business and vacation, Dennis Burnham (D) was served with process for a divorce proceeding, and Burnham (D) contends that California jurisdiction violates due process.

■ **BLACK LETTER RULE** Jurisdiction based on physical presence comports with due process, regardless of the defendant's contacts with the forum State.

■ **PROCEDURAL BASIS**

Writ of certiorari reviewing denial of mandamus relief following denial of motion to quash service of process in divorce action.

■ **FACTS**

Francie Burnham (P), a resident of California, brought suit for divorce against her husband, Dennis Burnham (Burnham) (D), in California state court. Mr. Burnham (D) was served with the summons and complaint while voluntarily visiting California for three days. Burnham's (D) presence in California did not relate to the divorce action, as he was initially on business and later traveled to San Francisco to visit his daughters [That's what he gets for trying to do something nice!]. Subsequently, Burnham (D) made a special appearance in California Superior Court, moving to quash the service of process. Burnham (D) argued that the court lacked personal jurisdiction because his only contacts with the state were a few short trips on business and to visit his daughters. The Superior Court denied the motion. Thereafter, the California Court of Appeal denied mandamus relief, holding that physical presence and personal service in the forum state constituted valid grounds for jurisdiction. The Supreme Court granted certiorari.

■ **ISSUE**

Does transient jurisdiction, obtained by a defendant's physical presence in the forum state, violate due process?

■ **DECISION AND RATIONALE**

(Scalia, J.) No. Transient jurisdiction, obtained by a defendant's physical presence in the forum state, does not violate due process. In order to decide whether the assertion of personal jurisdiction comports with due process, we have relied on well-established traditional principles of jurisdiction. Jurisdiction based on physical presence is one of these traditional forms of in personam jurisdiction. On occasion, we have held that deviations from the traditional 19th century rules are permissible, but only with respect to suits arising out of the absent defendant's contacts with the forum state. Thus, in *International Shoe Co. v. Washington* [Minimum contacts are required in order to satisfy the traditional notions of fair play and substantial justice], we established a minimum contacts test for such situations. In the instant action, Burnham (D) contends that the *International Shoe* minimum contacts test should also be applied to a situation where a nonresident defendant is physically present in the forum state. However, we find nothing in *International Shoe* or its progeny requiring an extension to situations of transient jurisdiction. We therefore hold that jurisdiction based on physical presence alone satisfies due process because it is one of the continuing traditions of our legal system and, therefore, is consistent with "traditional notions of fair play and substantial justice." Burnham's (D) argument, that our decision in *Shaffer v. Heitner* [Quasi in rem jurisdiction is subject to the same minimum contacts analysis as is in personam jurisdiction] requires reversal, is likewise unavailing. Burnham (D) misinterprets our statement in *Shaffer* that "all assertions of state-court jurisdiction must be evaluated according to the standards set forth in *International Shoe* and its progeny." The context of this statement reveals that only quasi in rem jurisdiction must be subjected to the minimum contacts analysis. *Shaffer* does not, therefore, compel the conclusion that physically present defendants must be treated identically to absent ones. Where a jurisdictional principal is firmly approved by tradition and still favored, such as the doctrine of jurisdiction by physical presence, due process is not violated by obtaining such jurisdiction. Thus, the California courts could exercise jurisdiction over Burnham (D) based on in-state service of process. Affirmed.

■ **CONCURRENCE**

(White, J.) I concur in the affirmance and in Justice Scalia's conclusion that jurisdiction by personal service is so widely accepted that it should not be struck down as violative of the Fourteenth Amendment Due Process Clause.

■ **CONCURRENCE**

(Brennan, J.) While I concur in the judgment, I do not agree with the unshakable reliance on tradition as supporting all forms of jurisdiction. Unlike Justice Scalia, I would undertake an independent inquiry into the fairness of the prevailing in-state service rule. Justice Scalia's historical approach is foreclosed by our decisions in *International Shoe* and *Shaffer v. Heitner.* Pursuant to *Shaffer*, I believe that all rules of jurisdiction, even ancient ones, must satisfy the contemporary notions of due process elucidated in *International Shoe's* minimum contacts analysis. However, as transient jurisdiction is consistent with the reasonable expectations of a nonresident defendant, it is entitled to a strong presumption that it comports with due process. By visiting the forum State, a nonresident defendant purposefully avails himself of the benefits and protections of the forum State. Moreover, the potential burdens on a transient defendant are slight. Thus, I believe that, as a rule the exercise of personal jurisdiction over a defendant based on his voluntary presence in the forum state will satisfy the requirements of due process.

■ **CONCURRENCE**

(Stevens, J.) I am concerned with the broad reach of Justice Scalia's majority opinion. However, the historical evidence identified by Justice Scalia, the considerations of fairness identified by Justice Brennan, and the common sense displayed by Justice White convince me that this is a very easy case. I agree that the judgment should be affirmed.

Analysis:

This is an extremely important case in ascertaining the correct application of *Shaffer v. Heitner* and *International Shoe.* Although *Shaffer* apparently stated that all jurisdictional issues must now be evaluated by the *International Shoe* minimum contacts test, Justice Scalia's opinion makes it clear that this is not the case. Rather, the traditional notion of jurisdiction based on physical presence can survive even absent sufficient minimum contacts between the defendant and the forum State. While Justice Scalia's unyielding rule has the advantages of certainty and judicial efficiency, his reliance on history should nevertheless be questioned. Indeed, it makes little sense to rely on historical notions of jurisdiction in this case, when prior cases like *Shaffer* and *International Shoe* expressly invalidated other historical approaches. Thus, Justice Brennan's concurrence may present a more sensible approach. Brennan argues that *all* forms of jurisdiction, including jurisdiction based on physical presence, must satisfy the minimum contacts test in order to comport with due process. However, after conducting the minimum contacts analysis as to transient jurisdiction, Brennan seemingly concludes that *every* exercise of personal jurisdiction based on *voluntary* presence comports with due process! Thus, it appears that

Justices Scalia and Brennan reached essentially the same strict rule, although they took different approaches to get there.

■ CASE VOCABULARY

MANDAMUS: A proceeding in some superior court, seeking an order for an inferior court to perform some duty, such as quashing a service of process.

TRANSIENT JURISDICTION: Jurisdiction over a nonresident defendant based on service of process on the defendant while present in the forum State.

Insurance Corp. of Ireland v. Compagnie des Bauxites de Guinee

(*Insurance Company*) v. (*Mining Company*)
456 U.S. 694, 102 S.Ct. 2099 (1982)

CONSENT TO JURISDICTION MAY BE IMPLIED BY FAILURE TO COMPLY WITH JURISDICTIONAL–RELATED DISCOVERY

■ **INSTANT FACTS** Compagnie des Bauxites de Guinee (CBG) (P) sued for the non-payment of insurance benefits, and the insurers failed to comply with the court's discovery order.

■ **BLACK LETTER RULE** The failure to comply with jurisdictional-related discovery may constitute implied consent to jurisdiction.

■ **PROCEDURAL BASIS**

Writ of certiorari reviewing District Court's sanction order for failure to comply with discovery.

■ **FACTS**

Compagnie des Bauxites de Guinee (CBG) (P), a bauxite producer, had purchased business-interruption insurance from the Insurance Corp. of Ireland (D) and other insurers. When a mechanical failure forced a halt in CBG's (P) bauxite production, CBG (P) filed a multi-million dollar claim. However, the insurers refused to pay the claim. CBG (P) then brought suit in federal court in Pennsylvania. Most of the foreign insurance companies made special appearances to contest personal jurisdiction. In order to prove that jurisdiction existed, CBG (P) attempted to use discovery. However, the insurance companies failed to comply with discovery requests and with the court's orders for document production. The District Court then imposed a sanction, pursuant to Rule 37(b)(2)(A) [Court may impose reasonable sanctions for failure to comply with order compelling discovery], consisting of a presumptive finding that the insurers were subject to jurisdiction because of their business contacts with Pennsylvania. The Supreme Court granted certiorari.

■ **ISSUE**

May objections to personal jurisdiction be impliedly waived by failure to comply with a court's discovery orders?

■ **DECISION AND RATIONALE**

(Name of Justice Not Given) Yes. Objections to personal jurisdiction may be impliedly waived by failure to comply with a court's discovery orders. In voluntarily submitting to the jurisdiction of the District Court for the limited purpose of challenging jurisdiction, a defendant agrees to abide by the court's determination on the jurisdictional issue. Thus, the insurers did not have the option of blocking CBG's (P) attempts to prove the insurers had sufficient minimum contacts with Pennsylvania. The insurers' failure to supply the requested information as to their contacts with Pennsylvania supports the presumption that the insurers' jurisdictional defense was invalid. Thus, the sanction was reasonable, as it presumed the facts that CBG (P) was seeking to establish through discovery. Affirmed.

Analysis:

This case presents an extension of the traditional situation of jurisdiction-by-consent under the regime of *Pennoyer v. Neff*. In the case at hand, the insurance companies surely did not voluntarily submit to personal jurisdiction; In fact, they appeared specially in order to contest such jurisdiction. Furthermore, the insurers arguably did not perform acts which directly constituted a waiver of consent. Rather, by failing to comply with the court's discovery order, the insurers were simply liable for the appropriate discovery sanctions pursuant to Rule 37(b)(2)(A). This rule allows a court, in the face of noncompliance with a discovery order, to take the matter sought to be discovered as true. It just so happened that the matter sought to be discovered related to personal jurisdiction. Thus, according to the Supreme Court, the insurance companies indirectly and impliedly consented to a waiver of any objections to personal jurisdiction. If nothing else, this case demonstrates the extremely long reach of consent as a basis for jurisdiction.

■ CASE VOCABULARY

BUSINESS–INTERRUPTION INSURANCE: Insurance which protects a company from suffering losses due to reasonable interruptions in their business dealings.

CHAPTER THREE

Providing Notice and an Opportunity to Be Heard

Mullane v. Central Hanover Bank & Trust Co.

Instant Facts: Central Hanover Bank and Trust Company (P) petitioned for a judicial settlement of a trust and provided notice by publication to all of the beneficiaries.

Black Letter Rule: Notice by publication fails to comply with due process where the names and addresses of the parties are known.

Maryland State Firemen's Association v. Chaves

Instant Facts: A default judgment was entered against a defendant who was served by mail and failed to return the acknowledgment or appear in the action.

Black Letter Rule: A plaintiff must strictly comply with the service provisions, even if the defendant has actual notice of the lawsuit.

National Equipment Rental, Ltd v. Szukhent

Instant Facts: Szukhent (D) was granted a motion to quash a complaint for invalid service, where service was effected on an agent expressly appointed in a lease agreement.

Black Letter Rule: Service upon an expressly-designated agent is proper, even if the agent is not required to deliver notice to the defendant.

Insurance Co. of North America v. S/S "Hellenic Challenger"

Instant Facts: Service of a maritime complaint was made upon a claims adjuster, who was not expressly authorized by the insured to receive service of process.

Black Letter Rule: Service upon a corporation is effective when delivered to anyone so integrated with the organization that he knows what to do with the papers.

State ex rel. Sivnksty v. Duffield

Instant Facts: While incarcerated on criminal charges in a foreign state, Sivnksty (D) was served with process in a civil action and claimed immunity from such service.

Black Letter Rule: Nonresidents confined in jail on criminal charges are not immune from service of process for civil actions.

Wyman v. Newhouse

Instant Facts: Wyman (P) obtained jurisdiction by fraudulently inducing Newhouse (D) to come to Florida and then serving Newhouse (D) with process, and Newhouse (D) collaterally attacked the enforcement of the resulting default judgment.

Black Letter Rule: Service of process procured through trickery renders jurisdiction invalid.

Fuentes v. Shevin

Instant Facts: Margarita Fuentes (P) and other debtors challenge the constitutionality of Florida and Pennsylvania statutes allowing seizure of goods covered by an installment sales contract without providing an opportunity for the debtor to be heard prior to seizure.

Black Letter Rule: In order to comply with procedural due process, notice and an opportunity to be heard must be provided prior to seizure of any protected property interest.

Mitchell v. W.T. Grant Co.

Instant Facts: W.T. Grant Co. (P), who sold goods to Mitchell (D) on an installment sales contract, obtained a writ of sequestration of the goods without providing Mitchell (D) a prior opportunity to be heard.

Black Letter Rule: Statutes allowing for attachment or sequestration without a prior adversarial hearing do not violate procedural due process, if procedural safeguards exist.

North Georgia Finishing, Inc. v. Di–Chem, Inc.

Instant Facts: Pursuant to a Georgia garnishment statute, Di–Chem (P) attached the bank account of North Georgia Finishing (D) without providing pre-attachment notice or an opportunity to be heard.

Black Letter Rule: In order to comply with procedural due process, attachment by garnishment requires a prior adversarial hearing or certain procedural safeguards.

Connecticut v. Doehr

Instant Facts: DiGiovanni (D) attached Doehr's (P) property, pursuant to state statute, without prior notice or hearing, and Doehr (P) claimed the attachment violated due process.

Black Letter Rule: Where the risk of erroneous attachment and the harm to the aggrieved party outweighs the interests of the party seeking attachment, property cannot be attached without notice and a hearing.

Mullane v. Central Hanover Bank & Trust Co.

(Special Guardian) v. *(Common Trustee)*
339 U.S. 306, 70 S.Ct. 652 (1950)

NOTICE BY PUBLICATION IS RARELY "REASONABLY CALCULATED" TO PROVIDE NOTICE WHEN ADDRESSES OF THE PARTIES ARE KNOWN

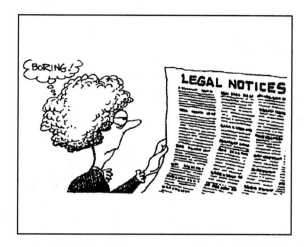

■ **INSTANT FACTS** Central Hanover Bank and Trust Company (P) petitioned for a judicial settlement of a trust and provided notice by publication to all of the beneficiaries.

■ **BLACK LETTER RULE** Notice by publication fails to comply with due process where the names and addresses of the parties are known.

■ **PROCEDURAL BASIS**

Writ of certiorari reviewing affirmance of order overruling due-process objection to service of process in petition for settlement of trust.

■ **FACTS**

Central Hanover Bank and Trust Company (P) established a common trust fund, in which 113 small trusts were pooled into one fund for investment administration. Central Hanover (P) petitioned the Surrogate's Court of New York for judicial settlement of this account as common trustee. If granted, the decree would settle all questions respecting the management of the common fund, terminating all rights of beneficiaries against the trustee for improper management. Pursuant to New York statute, all beneficiaries of this common trust were notified by publication in a local newspaper for four successive weeks. [After all, everyone reads the "legal notices" section of the newspaper, don't they?] Mullane (D), who was appointed special guardian for all beneficiaries not otherwise appearing in the action, entered a special appearance in New York in order to object to the notice. According to Mullane (D), the Trust Company (P) should have provided notice by mail, as the company had actual knowledge of the names and addresses of the beneficiaries. Therefore, Mullane (D) argued that the statutorily-endorsed notice was inadequate to afford due process under the Fourteenth Amendment, and therefore that the court was without jurisdiction to enter a final decree. The Surrogate overruled Mullane's (D) objections, and a final decree accepting the accounts was entered. The Appellate Division of the New York Supreme Court and the Court of Appeals of New York affirmed. The Supreme Court granted certiorari.

■ **ISSUE**

Where the names and addresses of parties are known, does notice by publication comply with due process?

■ **DECISION AND RATIONALE**

(Jackson, J.) No. Where the names and addresses of parties are known, notice by publication does not comply with due process. Due process requires that notice be provided prior to the deprivation of life, liberty or property by adjudication. In the situation at hand, the proceeding had the possibility of depriving the beneficiaries of property, as a decree would cut off their rights to hold the common trustee liable for negligence. Further, we hold that due process requires that this notice be reasonably calculated, under the circumstances, to apprise interested parties of the pendency of the action and afford them and an opportunity to be heard. Personal service of written notice always complies with due process. However, parties residing outside of the forum state do not necessarily have to be provided with written notice, as this would place impossible obstacles in the instant action where the number of interested beneficiaries is numerous. Indeed, in many circumstances, notice by mail complies with due process, even though there is a risk that notice may not actually reach all interested parties. Where a large number of parties share a common interest, it can be assumed that those beneficiaries present will defend the rights of the absent parties. However, in the instant action, Central Hanover (P) only provided notice by publication. Such notice was not reasonably calculated to provide notice to those parties whose names and addresses were known. Notice by publication is certainly not a reliable method of apprising interested parties of the pending adjudication of their rights. The record indicates that, upon the foundation of the common trust, Central Hanover (P) had mailed information to a number of the beneficiaries. Likewise, Central Hanover (P) should have mailed notice of the legal proceeding to all of these beneficiaries, as this would not seriously burden the trust. Thus, the New York statute providing for service by publication in such circumstances is unconstitutional, as it fails to comply with the Fourteenth Amendment. However, with regard to those beneficiaries whose addresses were not known, or whose interests in the trust were uncertain, we hold that notice by publication did comply with due process. Reversed in part.

Analysis:

This case states the essential due process requirements for notice, which typically includes a summons and a copy of the complaint. Whenever legal proceedings affect the life, liberty or property interests of parties, these parties must be provided with notice reasonably calculated under the circumstances to apprise them of the proceedings and give them an opportunity to be heard. There is a wide spectrum of potential notice devices, ranging from personal service (the best form of notice) to notice by publication (the least reliable method). Whenever possible, personal service should be provided, although this may be impossible when the number of parties are numerous or when the parties reside in distant states. In such circumstances, it is easy to see that mailed notice is sufficient, even though some of the parties might not receive the notice. However, courts generally disfavor notice by publication. Indeed, notice by publication is really just a legal fiction, since no reasonable person would regularly read the legal notices of a newspaper (published in a distant state!). Thus, it is interesting that the court allows notice by publication in some situations. However, there really is no other way to provide notice to some parties, such as those parties whose address was not known or easily ascertainable. In addition, as the Court notes, notice by publication is sufficient in some in rem proceedings, since the notice is typically coupled with seizure of property. Even if an interested party failed to read the legal notices in the paper, the seizure of property would certainly afford constructive notice of the proceedings.

■ CASE VOCABULARY

INTER VIVOS TRUST: A trust created by distribution of property to a trustee during the lifetime of the settlor (the entity creating the trust), in which the property is held for the benefit of the beneficiaries.

SURROGATE COURT: A court with jurisdiction over probate matters, including wills and trusts.

TESTAMENTARY TRUST: A trust created by will upon the death of the settlor.

Maryland State Firemen's Association v. Chaves

(Charity) v. *(Rival Charity's President)*
166 F.R.D. 353 (D.C. Md. 1996)

SERVICE BY MAIL REQUIRES STRICT COMPLIANCE WITH STATUTORY PROVISIONS OR A DEFENDANT'S WAIVER OF SERVICE

■ **INSTANT FACTS** A default judgment was entered against a defendant who was served by mail and failed to return the acknowledgment or appear in the action.

■ **BLACK LETTER RULE** A plaintiff must strictly comply with the service provisions, even if the defendant has actual notice of the lawsuit.

■ **PROCEDURAL BASIS**

Motion for Default Judgment for failure to appear.

■ **FACTS**

The Maryland State Firemen's Association ("MSFA") (P) sued John Chaves (D) for illegally soliciting charitable contributions to the Firefighters Association of America ("FFA"). A day after filing the complaint, MSFA (P) allegedly sent a copy of the summons and complaint to Chaves (D) by first class mail. Although Chaves (D) did not return the acknowledgment form, he apparently had actual notice of the lawsuit, since an attorney purporting to represent Chaves (D) called MSFA's (D) attorney to discuss the case one week later. Chaves (D) never answered the complaint, however, and MSFA (P) moved for a default judgment. The clerk initially entered the default, but later the court requested additional information regarding the type of service employed. MSFA (P) responded by detailing the facts and averring that the service was proper.

■ **ISSUE**

Is service by mail proper if the defendant has actual notice but fails to return a waiver or acknowledgment form?

■ **DECISION AND RATIONALE**

(Messitte, J.) No. Even where a defendant has actual notice of a lawsuit, service by mail is not proper if the defendant fails to return a waiver or acknowledgment form. In the instant action, MSFA (P) argues that it complied with both the federal and state provisions for service of process. MSFA (P) is incorrect. The outdated federal statute on which MSFA (P) relies requires a plaintiff to send via first class mail a copy of the summons and complaint, together with two copies of a notice and acknowledgment and a return envelope. The plaintiff must employ an alternate form of service if the written acknowledgment form is not returned within 20. days. Chaves (D) did not return the form, and MSFA (P) never attempted service by another means. Pursuant to the new federal statute, MSFA (P) could have sent Chaves (D) a notice of the action and a request for waiver of service. This would have placed the burden on Chaves (D) to either waive service or pay the costs of the service. However, MSFA (P) did not request a waiver. Finally, MSFA (P) could have served process pursuant to Maryland law by mailing the summons and complaint by registered mail. Because the process was mailed first class, and not certified, MSFA (P) did not comply with this statute either. Thus, although the phone call from Chaves' (D) attorney shows that Chaves (D) apparently had actual notice of the lawsuit, MSFA (P) failed to comply with the service statutes and is not entitled to default judgment. The Clerk's Entry of Default will be set aside and the Motion for Default Judgment will be denied.

Analysis:

The purpose of the service statutes is to ensure that a defendant has adequate notice of a lawsuit and an opportunity to be heard. Where the circumstances indicate that the defendant had actual notice, some jurisdictions relax the service rules. The jurisdiction at issue in this case, however, has adopted a rule of strict compliance. Service by mail is effective only if the defendant returns the written acknowledgment form or consents to a waiver of service. The waiver provision lessens the somewhat harsh rule under the prior federal statute. Apparently the plaintiff can ease his burden merely by sending a request that the defendant waive service. The opinion does not state any requirement that the defendant acknowledge his receipt of the waiver request. If the defendant does not respond or states that he will not waive service, the plaintiff nevertheless must attempt an alternate form of service. The waiver rule simply forces the defendant to pay the cost of the substituted service. This rule makes some sense. It eliminates any incentive for a defendant who has actual knowledge of a lawsuit to attempt to evade service. However, the rule of strict compliance can be questioned. If a plaintiff can provide evidence that the defendant had actual knowledge of the lawsuit, why should the plaintiff not be allowed to obtain a default judgment?

National Equipment Rental, Ltd. v. Szukhent

(*Lessor*) v. (*Lessee*)

375 U.S. 311, 84 S.Ct. 411, 11 L.Ed.2d 354 (1964)

CONTRACTS MAY DESIGNATE AGENTS FOR ACCEPTING SERVICE

Jimmy sent a note to Annie who sent a note to me that I'm being sued!

Would've been nice if Jimmy had just told you to your face.

stus.com

■ **INSTANT FACTS** A farm equipment lessor sued certain lessees for failure to make lease payments, and served the summons and complaint on the agent named in the lease; the defendants argued that such service was inadequate under the Federal Rules of Civil Procedure.

■ **BLACK LETTER RULE** Under well-settled principles of agency law, a contractually designated agent's prompt acceptance and transmittal to the named defendants of a summons and complaint, pursuant to authorization contained in the contract, constitutes adequate service, even when there is no explicit provision in the agreement requiring her to so act.

■ **PROCEDURAL BASIS**

Certiorari to the United States Court of Appeals for the Second Circuit to review a decision in favor of the defendants.

■ **FACTS**

Szukhent (D) and other Michigan residents obtained farm equipment from National Equipment Rental (P) under a lease executed in 1961. The lease consisted of eighteen numbered paragraphs, less than a page and a half in total. The last paragraph, right above the signature lines, designated Florence Weinberg as the lessees' agent for service of process within New York state. The lessees were not familiar with Weinberg.

The lessor sued the lessees in 1962 for failure to make rental payments. It delivered two copies of the summons and complaint to Weinberg, who mailed them the same day to Szukhent (D) and other defaulting lessees. In addition, National Equipment Rental (P) notified the lessees in writing, by certified mail, that Weinberg had been served as their designated agent for acceptance of service, in accordance with the lease agreement. The defendants moved to quash the service, however, and the court granted their motion, reasoning that although Weinberg had in fact mailed the summons and complaint to the defendants, the lease agreement did not require that she do so, such that there was a failure of the agency arrangement. The court of appeals affirmed, and the Supreme Court granted certiorari.

■ **ISSUE**

May a party to a private contract appoint an agent to receive service or process within the meaning of Federal Rule of Civil Procedure 4(e)(2), where the agent is not personally known to the party and the agent has not expressly undertaken the duty to transmit notice to the party?

■ **DECISION AND RATIONALE**

(Stewart, J.) Yes. Under well-settled principles of agency law, a contractually designated agent's prompt acceptance and transmittal to the named defendants of a summons and complaint, pursuant to authorization contained in the contract, constitutes adequate service, even when there is no explicit provision in the agreement requiring her to so act.

The purpose of the lease clause at issue in this case is clear. It was inserted by the plaintiff and agreed to by the defendant to ensure that litigation arising under the lease would take place in New York. The parties to a contract may agree in advance to submit to the jurisdiction of a given court, to permit notice to be served by the opposing party, or even to waive notice altogether. This case would be different if the defendants had not in fact received notice, because then they could argue that the failure to transmit the summons and complaint to them invalidated the agency. But under the circumstances, Weinberg was the defendants' agent authorized by appointment to receive process within the meaning of Federal Rule 4(e)(2).

Moreover, because the defendants did in fact receive timely notice, no due process claim is raised here. Reversed.

■ DISSENT

(Black, J.) New York, not federal, law should determine the outcome here. Upholding the service in this case, contrary to the majority's suggestion, does in fact raise serious due process concerns.

The end result of this decision is not hard to see. Many companies will insert similar clauses in their boilerplate contracts, so that when they want to sue someone, the defendant has to go wherever the big company wants him to go in order to defend himself. The very threat of such a lawsuit can extract payment of alleged claims, even if they are wholly without merit. This fact will not be news to big companies exerting their economic influence to wangle such contracts.

■ DISSENT

(Brennan, J.) I would affirm. I would deny the validity of any appointment that could raise a conflict of interest (though the majority denies one exists here), and I would require that all appointments include an explicit condition that the agent transmit the process forthwith to the principal. Moreover, because the plaintiffs here created the contract, I would not subject the defendants to an inconvenient jurisdiction without proof that they actually consented to be sued in a state that is not their state of residence. It offends common sense to treat a printed form as embodying terms to all of which an individual knowingly assented.

Analysis:

It is not at all uncommon for a contracting company to contractually designate an agent to receive process on its *own* behalf. What troubles the dissent here is that the contracting company designates an agent to receive process on its *customers'* behalf, which is a decidedly different scenario. When the contracting business designates its own agent, it is often referred to as a "process agent" (defined generally as a person authorized to accept service of process on behalf of another) or a "registered" or "resident" agent (defined more specifically as a person authorized to accept service of process for a corporation, in a particular jurisdiction). Some states' corporation laws provide that incorporating within the state gives rise to a constructive designation of the secretary of state as agent for service or process on the corporation.

■ CASE VOCABULARY

AGENCY: A fiduciary relationship created by express or implied contract or by law, in which one party (the *agent*) may act on behalf of another party (the *principal*) and bind that other party by words or actions.

AGENT: One who is authorized to act for or in place of another; a representative.

BOILERPLATE: Ready-made or all-purpose language that will fit in a variety of documents; fixed or standardized contractual language that the proposing party views as relatively nonnegotiable. The term, first recorded in 1893, may have referred to steel plates affixed to boilers. But the modern sense comes from the use of the term to refer to copy set on printing plates (or molds to make the plates) and distributed in that form to newspapers. The copy could not be edited.

MOTION TO QUASH: A party's request that the court nullify process or an act instituted by the other party, as in seeking to nullify a subpoena.

QUASH: To annul or make void.

Insurance Co. of North America v. S/S "Hellenic Challenger"

(Insurance Company) v. *(Vessel)*
88 F.R.D. 545 (S.D.N.Y. 1980)

SERVICE UPON A CORPORATION IS EFFECTIVE EVEN IF MADE UPON SOMEONE NOT EXPRESSLY AUTHORIZED TO RECEIVE PROCESS

■ **INSTANT FACTS** Service of a maritime complaint was made upon a claims adjuster, who was not expressly authorized by the insured to receive service of process.

■ **BLACK LETTER RULE** Service upon a corporation is effective when delivered to anyone so integrated with the organization that he knows what to do with the papers.

■ **PROCEDURAL BASIS**

Motion to set aside default judgment on maritime claim for damages for nondelivery and loss.

■ **FACTS**

This case involves an admiralty and maritime claim for nondelivery and damage relating to pickled sheepskins [What exactly is a pickled sheepskin? A delicacy?] shipped to New York aboard the S/S "Hellenic Challenger" (D). A United States Marshal delivered the summons and complaint to a claims adjuster of the Insurance Co. of North America, the insurer for the Hellenic Challenger (D). The claims adjuster was not expressly authorized by the insured to accept service of process; rather, only the titled officers and claims managers were so authorized. Nevertheless, the claims adjuster had accepted service on at least two previous occasions, as he was the assistant to the expressly-designated claims manager. Because the claims adjuster misplaced the summons and complaint [Oops!], the Hellenic Challenger (D) remained unaware of the lawsuit until its bank informed it that its account had been attached, following a default judgment and writ of execution. The Hellenic Challenger (D) made a motion to set aside the judgment on the basis of improper service.

■ **ISSUE**

Must service of process upon a corporation be delivered to an employee expressly designated to receive service?

■ **DECISION AND RATIONALE**

(Justice Not Stated) No. Service of process upon a corporation does not necessarily have to be made upon an expressly-designated employee. Federal Rule 4(h)(1) has been liberally construed to allow service upon any representative "so integrated with the organization that he will know what to do with the papers." Thus, service is generally sufficient when made upon an individual who stands in such a position to render it fair to imply the authority on his part to receive service. In the case at hand, the service was reasonably calculated to alert the Hellenic Challenger (D) to the initiation of the suit. The claims adjuster was well integrated into the organization and familiar with the formalities associated with service, as he had accepted service on behalf of the Hellenic Challenger (D) on at least two previous occasions. Furthermore, the adjuster had easy access to the claims manager who was officially authorized to accept service. Therefore, the adjuster's loss of the summons and complaint is a mistake in the ordinary course of business and does not merit remedial relief. Motion denied.

Analysis:

This case exemplifies the liberal construction applied to Federal Rule 4(h)(1), authorizing service upon a corporation, partnership or unincorporated association. The Rule specifically states that process must be delivered to "an officer, a managing or general agent, or to any other agent authorized by appointment or by law to receive service...." The court expanded the reach of this Rule, allowing valid service to be made upon anyone so integrated with the organization that he would know what to do with the papers. This interpretation is certainly inconsistent with a strict reading of Rule 4(h)(1). However, it remains true to the primary purpose of the service rules: giving the defendant adequate notice that an action is pending. Perhaps the court could have justified its holding and still stayed within the literal bounds of Rule 4(h)(1) by simply finding that the claims adjuster was a managing or general agent. On the other hand, it is clear that the court desires to broaden the reach of the Rule, and it successfully, if somewhat questionably, accomplishes this goal. It is important to recognize, once again, that service may be proper even if it does not *actually* result in the defendant receiving notice. Any reasonably calculated attempt to give notice appears to be sufficient.

■ CASE VOCABULARY

WRIT OF EXECUTION: A court order pertaining to a debt, allowing the appropriate officer to take property in satisfaction of the debt.

State ex rel. Sivnksty v. Duffield

(*Criminal Defendant*) v. (*Injured Child*)
137 W.Va. 112, 71 S.E.2d 113 (1952)

INCARCERATED NONRESIDENT CRIMINAL DEFENDANTS ARE NOT IMMUNE FROM SERVICE OF PROCESS FOR CIVIL ACTIONS

■ **INSTANT FACTS** While incarcerated on criminal charges in a foreign state, Sivnksty (D) was served with process in a civil action and claimed immunity from such service.

■ **BLACK LETTER RULE** Nonresidents confined in jail on criminal charges are not immune from service of process for civil actions.

■ **PROCEDURAL BASIS**

Petition for writ of prohibition following sustaining of demurrer to plea in abatement on civil tort action.

■ **FACTS**

While vacationing in West Virginia, Sivnksty (D) was arrested on charges of reckless driving after his automobile struck two pedestrians [Not a good way to end one's vacation!]. Sivnksty (D) was incarcerated in county jail, as he was unable to post a bond. While in jail awaiting trial, Sivnksty (D) was served with process in a tort action brought by one of the pedestrians. Subsequently, Sivnksty (D) was found guilty of the crime. He made a special appearance in the civil action and filed a plea in abatement, arguing that the court was without jurisdiction. Sivnksty (D) claimed that he was immune from service since he was a nonresident of the county and a prisoner in county jail at the time of service. The court sustained a demurrer to Sivnksty's (D) pleas in abatement. Then Sivnksty (D) petitioned the Supreme Court of Appeals for West Virginia for a writ of prohibition against the judge of the trial court.

■ **ISSUE**

Is a person confined in jail on a criminal charge immune from process in a civil action?

■ **DECISION AND RATIONALE**

(Riley, J.) No. A person confined in jail on a criminal charge is not immune from process in a civil action. The original purpose for the privilege of immunity from civil process was to protect the court itself from interference with the judicial process. However, when the intended recipient of civil process has been charged with a crime, immunity also furthers the public policy to ensure that a nonresident charged with a crime will not be deterred from appearing before the criminal court by the threat of civil process. Thus, we have held that a nonresident who voluntarily submits himself to jurisdiction, in an answer to an indictment against him, is privileged while attending court from service of process in a civil suit. Nevertheless, in the instant case Sivnksty (D) entered Gilmer County, West Virginia, on his own volition rather than in response to criminal process. At the time of entry, Sivnksty (D) had not yet committed a crime. In such situations, we follow the rule that a person confined in jail on a criminal charge or imprisoned on conviction for such charge is subject to service of civil process if he was voluntarily in the jurisdiction at the time of the arrest and confinement.

■ DISSENT

(Lovins, J.) In the case at hand, I think that whether Sivnksty (D) came into Gilmer County voluntarily or involuntarily is irrelevant. His presence in the county *became* involuntary when he was confined in jail. As a result of this court's holding, Sivnksty (D) will be forced to trial in a county far from his residence. Furthermore, in an age of increased travel by motor vehicles, the majority's holding subjects to civil jurisdiction an unfortunate motorist who is arrested on a real or fanciful criminal charge. This could lead to a widespread abuse of judicial process.

Analysis:

This case demonstrates that immunity from process is limited in some situations. A criminal defendant who allegedly committed a crime while voluntarily in another state, and who is imprisoned pending the criminal trial, is not immune from service of process for civil suits. Of course, in the modern age of extensive long-arm statutes, such immunity would be rather meaningless, since the civil plaintiff could simply serve the nonresident defendant via a long-arm statute. Nevertheless, at the time of this case, Sivnksty (D) certainly appears to suffer some unfairness in the application of the immunity laws. The majority reasons that Sivnksty's (D) voluntary presence in the state removes him from the immunity protections. However, as the dissent notes, Sivnksty's (D) presence became involuntary once he was incarcerated. Perhaps the majority's holding can best be justified by analyzing the public policy behind immunity. Immunity is designed to protect courts and nonculpable persons from the burdens associated with the threat of service of process upon a nonresident. Even criminal defendants are protected when they are not incarcerated, in order to encourage their presence at the criminal indictment or trial. Contrast this with the case at hand, in which Sivnksty (D) was incarcerated and had no choice but to appear at his criminal trial.

■ CASE VOCABULARY

PLEA IN ABATEMENT: A common law plea objecting to jurisdiction without disputing the merits of the claim.

WRIT OF PROHIBITION: Means by which a superior court, such as a court of appeals, restrains an inferior court from determining matters outside of the inferior court's jurisdiction.

Wyman v. Newhouse

(Adulterous Woman) v. *(Adulterous Man)*

93 F.2d 313 (C.C.A.2 1937), cert. denied 303 U.S. 664, 58 S.Ct. 831 (1938)

JURISDICTION IS IMPROPER WHEN SERVICE IS PROCURED BY FRAUDULENT MEANS

■ **INSTANT FACTS** Wyman (P) obtained jurisdiction by fraudulently inducing Newhouse (D) to come to Florida and then serving Newhouse (D) with process, and Newhouse (D) collaterally attacked the enforcement of the resulting default judgment.

■ **BLACK LETTER RULE** Service of process procured through trickery renders jurisdiction invalid.

■ PROCEDURAL BASIS

Appeal from judgment dismissing complaint for damages following default judgment.

■ FACTS

Newhouse (D), a married man and resident of New York, had engaged in meretricious relations with Wyman (P), a married woman. Wyman (P) desired to sue Newhouse (D) for money loaned, money advanced, and seduction under the promise of marriage. Wyman (P) induced Newhouse (D) to travel to Florida in order to serve process upon Newhouse (D). She accomplished this feat by falsely representing that her mother was ill, stating that she was leaving the United States for good to go to her mother, and saying that she could not go without seeing Newhouse (D) one more time. Tricked by her profession of undying love, Newhouse (D) flew to Florida and was met by a deputy sheriff who served him with process in the $500,000 lawsuit. Newhouse (D) ignored the process, and a default judgment was entered against him in Florida. Subsequently, Newhouse (D) collaterally attacked the judgment, alleging that Florida jurisdiction was improper. The Florida court upheld Newhouse's (D) motion to dismiss the complaint, and Wyman (P) appealed.

■ ISSUE

Is service invalid when procured through fraudulent means?

■ DECISION AND RATIONALE

(Manton, J.) Yes. Service is invalid when procured through fraudulent means. In the case at hand, Newhouse (D) was fraudulently induced to enter the jurisdiction of the state of Florida. Any such judgment, procured fraudulently, lacks jurisdiction and is null and void. Furthermore, Newhouse (D) was not required to argue the merits in the original action in Florida. An erroneous judgment may be attacked collaterally. Thus, the complaint was properly dismissed. Affirmed.

Analysis:

This case illustrates two important rules regarding service of process. First, service of process is invalid when a defendant is tricked into appearing in the forum state. However, this opinion fails to state one important requirement for this rule to apply. The forum state (Florida, in this case) must have a statute which makes fraudulent service invalid. Fortunately for Newhouse (D), Florida had such a statute

Fraudulent service renders the court's jurisdiction invalid. Second, a defendant may collaterally attack any default judgment when the rendering court had insufficient jurisdiction. The edited version of this opinion leaves out some important facts in this regard. Following the default judgment, Wyman (P) attempted to enforce the judgment in New York. Because service was improper, Newhouse (D) was allowed to collaterally attack the judgment in the New York enforcement proceeding. Note that a sister state (New York) may only refuse to enforce a judgment if the rendering state (Florida) lacked jurisdiction. Fortunately for Newhouse (D), Florida had a statute making jurisdiction improper when service was fraudulently procured. If Florida did not have such a statute, however, Newhouse (D) would not have succeeded in his collateral attack. Thus, a safer avenue for Newhouse (D) (assuming he did not know the intricacies of Florida law) would have been to make a special appearance in the original action to contest Florida's jurisdiction.

■ **CASE VOCABULARY**

MERETRICIOUS: Pertaining to unlawful sexual activity, such as adultery or prostitution.

Fuentes v. Shevin

(*Debtor*) v. (*Unnamed Party*)

407 U.S. 67, 92 S.Ct. 1983 (1972)

SEIZURE OF A PROTECTED PROPERTY INTEREST MUST BE PRECEDED BY NOTICE AND AN OPPORTUNITY TO BE HEARD

■ **INSTANT FACTS** Margarita Fuentes (P) and other debtors challenge the constitutionality of Florida and Pennsylvania statutes allowing seizure of goods covered by an installment sales contract without providing an opportunity for the debtor to be heard prior to seizure.

■ **BLACK LETTER RULE** In order to comply with procedural due process, notice and an opportunity to be heard must be provided prior to seizure of any protected property interest.

■ **PROCEDURAL BASIS**

Writ of certiorari reviewing affirmance of rejection of constitutional claims concerning replevin of chattels.

■ **FACTS**

In this case, the Supreme Court reviews two separate appellate rulings regarding the constitutionality of state replevin statutes. One ruling involved Margarita Fuentes (P), who had purchased a stove and stereo system under a conditional sales contract. The supplier, Firestone Tire and Rubber Company, was to retain title to the merchandise until Mrs. Fuentes (P) made all of her payments, although Mrs. Fuentes (P) was allowed to possess the items in the interim. After more than a year of progress payments, a dispute developed regarding servicing of the stove. Firestone instituted an action in small claims court for repossession of the items, claiming that Mrs. Fuentes (P) had refused to make her payments. Firestone simultaneously obtained a writ of replevin, pursuant to Florida statute, ordering a sheriff to seize the goods without providing Mrs. Fuentes (P) with a pre-seizure hearing. Thereafter, Mrs. Fuentes (P) instituted the present action in federal district court, challenging the constitutionality of Florida's replevin statute. A similar action was brought in Pennsylvania by four other consumers who had entered into similar conditional sales contracts. In each suit, the district courts rejected the constitutional claims, and three-judge district courts considered the appeal and upheld the constitutionality of the statutes. The Supreme Court granted certiorari to review both appellate rulings.

■ **ISSUE**

Absent extraordinary circumstances, must notice and an opportunity to be heard be provided prior to depriving a party of a protected property interest?

■ **DECISION AND RATIONALE**

(Stewart, J.) Yes. Absent extraordinary circumstances, notice and an opportunity to be heard must be provided *prior* to depriving a party of a protected property interest. Consistent with procedural due process, we have repeatedly held that, prior to depriving a party of a property interest, an opportunity to be heard must be granted at a meaningful time. We now hold that, if notice and a hearing is to serve its full purpose, then the hearing must be granted at a time when the deprivation still can be prevented. Indeed, the Florida statute requires a post-seizure hearing in which the aggrieved party can argue her right to the goods. And in Pennsylvania, the aggrieved party can institute a lawsuit for the return of wrongfully-seized goods. Furthermore, pursuant to both statutes, the creditor seeking replevin must post a bond and may be forced to pay damages for wrongful repossession. However, no later hearing and no damage award can undo the fact that the arbitrary taking that was subject to procedural due process has already occurred. We have never embraced the position that a wrong may be done if it can be undone. Thus, we now hold that, in order to comply with due process, notice and an opportunity to be heard must be provided *prior* to any deprivation of a property interest protected by the Fourteenth Amendment. In the present cases, the Florida and Pennsylvania statutes are unconstitutional, as they provide for the replevin of chattels without the benefit of a hearing. Although Mrs. Fuentes (P) and the Pennsylvania appellants lacked full title to the replevied goods, the Fourteenth Amendment's property protection covers both possession and ownership. There are, however, extraordinary situations that justify postponing notice and opportunity for a hearing. In each such case, the seizure must be directly necessary to secure an important governmental or general public interest, there must be a special need for prompt action, and the statute must be narrowly drawn. For example, the Court has allowed summary seizure of property to collect the internal revenue of the United States, to meet the needs of a national war effort, to protect against the economic disaster of a bank failure, and to protect the public from mislabeled drugs and contaminated food. Since the Florida and Pennsylvania statutes serve no such important interests, and since the facts of the cases at hand are not these unusual situations, we hold that the statutes are unconstitutional. Vacated and remanded.

■ **DISSENT**

(White, J.) I believe that the Florida and Pennsylvania statutes represent fair, constitutionally valid methods of reconciling the conflicting interests of the debtor and creditor in an installment sales contract. Both statutes immobilize the property during the pendency of the action, allowing the aggrieved debtor to reclaim the goods and recover damages if the seizure was invalid. The majority wrongfully ignores the creditor's interest in preventing further use and deterioration of a property in which he has a substantial interest. Finally, the majority's result will have little impact on seizure in the installment sales context. A creditor could withstand attack under the majority's opinion by simply making clear in the original credit documents that they may retake possession without a hearing. Alternatively, they need only give a few days' notice of a hearing, and they need only establish probable cause for the default at the hearing. It is doubtful that such a hearing would result in protections for the debtor substantially different from those the present laws provide.

Analysis:

In this case, the majority presents compelling arguments for providing notice and an opportunity to be heard prior to seizure of goods via a writ of replevin. As we have already seen in *Mullane v. Central Hanover Bank & Trust Co.*, due process requires that notice be provided prior to the deprivation of life, liberty or property by adjudication. The case at hand substantially broadens a party's due process rights, providing an almost universal *opportunity to be heard* prior to the deprivation of property. However, it should be noted that the unconstitutional "seizure" in this case was really only an *attachment,* as the debtor retained an ability to contest the "seizure" after it occurred. Thus, the case stands for the proposition that a pre-attachment opportunity to be heard is consistent with procedural due process. Nevertheless, the dissent raises some good points in questioning the holding. A creditor in an installment sales contract maintains a substantial property interest in the goods until the payments have been made in full. If notice and an opportunity to be heard are necessary prior to attachment, a very real danger exists that the debtor could destroy or conceal the goods, or that the goods would depreciate in value in the interim.

■ **CASE VOCABULARY**

CHATTEL: An item of personal property.

DETINUE: Common law action allowing creditor to recover goods wrongfully detained.

REPLEVIN: Modern action allowing the title holder to repossess goods or chattels from a person who has wrongfully obtained or retained them.

Mitchell v. W.T. Grant Co.

(*Debtor*) v. (*Creditor*)

416 U.S. 600, 94 S.Ct. 1895 (1974)

PROPERTY MAY BE ATTACHED WITHOUT A PRIOR ADVERSARIAL HEARING, PROVIDED PROCEDURAL SAFEGUARDS ARE MET

■ **INSTANT FACTS** W.T. Grant Co. (P), who sold goods to Mitchell (D) on an installment sales contract, obtained a writ of sequestration of the goods without providing Mitchell (D) a prior opportunity to be heard.

■ **BLACK LETTER RULE** Statutes allowing for attachment or sequestration without a prior adversarial hearing do not violate procedural due process, if procedural safeguards exist.

■ **PROCEDURAL BASIS**

Writ of certiorari reviewing affirmance of writ of sequestration of goods on installment sales contract.

■ **FACTS**

Mitchell (D) had purchased goods on an installment sales contract from W.T. Grant Co. (Grant) (P). Asserting that Mitchell (D) was delinquent in payments, Grant (P) sought a writ of sequestration over these goods in order to enforce a vendor's lien. A state trial judge in Louisiana ordered the sequestration, pursuant to a Louisiana sequestration statute. The Supreme Court of Louisiana affirmed the order, and the United States Supreme Court granted certiorari.

■ **ISSUE**

Is sequestration of property, without providing an opportunity to be heard, acceptable provided that certain safeguards are met?

■ **DECISION AND RATIONALE**

(White, J.) Yes. Sequestration of property, without providing an opportunity to be heard, is acceptable provided that certain safeguards are met. The Louisiana sequestration statutes at issue provided that a writ of execution could issue ex parte, but only when the nature of the claim clearly appears from a verified petition. In addition, the statute required the clear showing to be made to a judge. Furthermore, the statute allowed the debtor to seek dissolution of the writ, and then placed the burden on the creditor to prove that the writ was proper. Alternatively, the debtor could regain possession by filing his own bond to protect the creditor against interim damage to the property. In the case at hand, Mitchell (D) claims that the holdings of *Sniadach v. Family Finance Corp.* [prejudgment garnishment procedure violates due process] and *Fuentes v. Shevin* [notice and an opportunity to be heard must be provided *prior* to depriving a party of a protected property interest] are controlling and render the Louisiana statutes unconstitutional. However, *Sniadach* involved a creditor with no prior interest in the property attached, unlike the installment sales contract at issue here. In addition, *Fuentes* was decided against a factual an legal background sufficiently different from that now before us [according to Justice White, at least!]. The Florida and Pennsylvania statutes considered in *Fuentes* were subject to broad factual determinations requiring adversarial input. With respect to the Louisiana statute, on the other hand, the facts relevant to obtaining a writ of sequestration are narrowly confined. Based on the procedural safeguards of the Louisiana statute, there is far less danger here that the seizure will be mistaken. Thus, we hold that the Louisiana sequestration standards are constitutional, and Mitchell was not deprived of procedural due process. Affirmed.

Analysis:

In this case, the Supreme Court reaches the opposite holding of *Fuentes* with regard to the constitutionality of sequestration statutes. Although the Louisiana statute uses terminology of "sequestration" and the statutes in *Fuentes* involved "seizure" or "replevin," all of the statutes involve the same situation. Both cases involved the attachment of property possessed by a debtor in an installment sales contract, and both considered the constitutionality of attachment without a pre-attachment opportunity for the debtor to be heard. Thus, while Justice White attempts to distinguish this case from *Fuentes,* it seems to turn on nearly identical facts and laws. According to most commentators, this case retreats from the strict *Fuentes* holding. While *Fuentes* held that nearly all attachments without a pre-attachment opportunity to be heard violated due process, Justice White's majority opinion in this case holds that a pre-attachment hearing need not be provided if certain procedural safeguards exist. The Louisiana statute is valid because it contains these safeguards. Specifically, the party seeking attachment must first provide, to a judge, clear and specific facts regarding the need for attachment. In addition, a prompt post-attachment hearing must be available to the aggrieved party.

■ CASE VOCABULARY

PENDENTE LITE: Pending the outcome of a lawsuit.

SEQUESTRATION: The process of attaching property pending the outcome of a litigation.

VENDOR'S LIEN: A lien imposed on property for which the possessor has not paid the full consideration.

North Georgia Finishing, Inc. v. Di-Chem, Inc.

(Buyer) v. *(Seller)*

419 U.S. 601, 95 S.Ct. 719 (1975)

PROPERTY MAY NOT BE ATTACHED WITHOUT A PRIOR HEARING UNLESS THE *MITCHELL* PROCEDURAL SAFEGUARDS EXIST

■ **INSTANT FACTS** Pursuant to a Georgia garnishment statute, Di-Chem (P) attached the bank account of North Georgia Finishing (D) without providing pre-attachment notice or an opportunity to be heard.

■ **BLACK LETTER RULE** In order to comply with procedural due process, attachment by garnishment requires a prior adversarial hearing or certain procedural safeguards.

■ **PROCEDURAL BASIS**

Writ of certiorari reviewing order upholding constitutionality of garnishment statute.

■ **FACTS**

Di-Chem, Inc. (P) filed suit against North Georgia Finishing, Inc. (D), alleging that North Georgia (D) owed over $50,000 for the sale of goods. Before North Georgia (D) received the complaint, Di-Chem (P) filed an affidavit and bond in order to garnish North Georgia's (D) bank account. North Georgia (D) challenged the constitutionality of the Georgia garnishment statute, arguing that the statute failed to provide notice and a hearing prior to the garnishment. The Georgia Supreme Court upheld the constitutionality of the statute, and the United States Supreme Court granted certiorari.

■ **ISSUE**

May property be attached without notice and a hearing, and without other procedural safeguards?

■ **DECISION AND RATIONALE**

(White, J.) No. Property may not be attached without notice and a hearing, and without other procedural safeguards protecting the owner's procedural due process rights. The Georgia garnishment statute at issue provided for attachment of property upon filing an affidavit with a court clerk and posting a bond equal to twice the amount alleged to be due. The Georgia Supreme Court upheld this statute in the face of the holding in *Sniadach v. Family Finance Corp.* [prejudgment wage-garnishment procedure violates due process]. The Georgia court noted that *Sniadach* only carved out a narrow exception in favor of wage earners. However, the court apparently overlooked *Fuentes v. Shevin* [notice and an opportunity to be heard must be provided *prior* to depriving a party of a protected property interest]. A writ of garnishment issued by a court clerk without notice or opportunity for an early hearing violates due process, pursuant to *Fuentes.* In addition, the Georgia statute is not saved by the more recent decision in *Mitchell v. W.T. Grant Co.* [statutes allowing for attachment or sequestration without a prior adversarial hearing do not violate procedural due process, if procedural safeguards exist]. The Georgia statute has none of the procedural safeguards present in the Louisiana statute at issue in *Mitchell. For* example, the writ is issuable upon affidavit of the creditor, which need not specify clear proof of the need for attachment. In addition, the Georgia statute does not require the participation of a judge, but rather allows the court clerk to issue the writ. Finally, there is no provision for an early hearing at which the creditor would be required to demonstrate probable cause for the garnishment. Di-Chem's (P) attempts to distinguish *Fuentes* and *Mitchell* from the instant action are likewise ineffective. Although *Fuentes* and *Mitchell* provided due process protections to ordinary consumers damaged by temporary deprivation of household necessities, and although this case involves parties in a commercial sale contract, we are not inclined to distinguish among different kinds of property in applying the Due Process Clause. Reversed and remanded.

Analysis:

This case presents an interesting application of the apparently conflicting holdings in *Fuentes* and *Mitchell*. Notice that Justice White authored this opinion, which was handed down just one year after his opinion in *Mitchell*. Justice White's analysis in this case reveals that the *Mitchell* approach probably prevails over the strict *Fuentes* rule. Even though the Georgia statute clearly violated *Fuentes*, White seems to indicate that the statute would be constitutional if it provided *Mitchell*-like procedural safeguards. It is the absence of these safeguards, and not simply the fact that property is attached without a prior hearing, that renders the Georgia statute unconstitutional. On the other hand, it can be argued that this case expresses no clear preference for either the *Mitchell* or *Fuentes* approaches, and perhaps both continue in effect (to the extent that they can be reconciled) following this case. Even more questionable following these three Supreme Court holdings is the effectiveness of attaching property to gain quasi-in-rem jurisdiction. Recall that a necessary prerequisite to quasi-in-rem jurisdiction is the attachment of the defendant's property. Whether or not such attachment requires a pre-attachment adversarial hearing remains in some doubt following these cases.

■ CASE VOCABULARY

GARNISHMENT: The process of attaching the property or money of another party (debtor) that is being held by a third party in order to satisfy a claim.

Connecticut v. Doehr

(State) v. *(Property Owner)*
501 U.S. 1, 111 S.Ct. 2105 (1991)

SUPREME COURT ADOPTS BALANCING TEST FOR PREJUDGMENT ATTACHMENT OF PROPERTY

■ **INSTANT FACTS** DiGiovanni (D) attached Doehr's (P) property, pursuant to state statute, without prior notice or hearing, and Doehr (P) claimed the attachment violated due process.

■ **BLACK LETTER RULE** Where the risk of erroneous attachment and the harm to the aggrieved party outweighs the interests of the party seeking attachment, property cannot be attached without notice and a hearing.

■ **PROCEDURAL BASIS**

Writ of certiorari reviewing reversal of summary judgment holding that property-attachment statute did not violate due process.

■ **FACTS**

John F. DiGiovanni (D) sued Brian K. Doehr (P) for assault and battery. Pursuant to a Connecticut attachment statute, DiGiovanni (D) submitted an application for a $75,000 attachment of Doehr's (P) home. The suit did not involve Doehr's (P) real estate, and DiGiovanni (D) had no pre-existing interest in the home. A Connecticut Superior Court granted the attachment upon a brief ex-parte affidavit of DiGiovanni (D) showing probable cause [five one-line conclusory assertions!]. Doehr (P) then filed suit in a federal district court, claiming that the statute was unconstitutional under the Due Process Clause. The District Court upheld the statute and granted summary judgment for DiGiovanni (D). The U.S. Court of Appeals reversed, and the Supreme Court granted certiorari.

■ **ISSUE**

May real estate be attached without prior notice or hearing, without extraordinary circumstances, and without a bond-posting requirement?

■ **DECISION AND RATIONALE**

(White, J.) No. Real estate may not be attached without prior notice or hearing, without extraordinary circumstances, and without a bond-posting requirement. In order to determine what process must be afforded by state attachment statutes, we utilize a form of the balancing test adopted in *Mathews v. Eldridge* [threefold inquiry is required in order to determine if government conduct comports with due process]. Our focus is slightly different, as the case at hand involves a prejudgment attachment statute related to private disputes. The relevant inquiries are the following: (1) Consideration of the private interest that will be affected by attachment; (2) Examination of the risk of erroneous deprivation through the statutory procedures and the value of additional alternative safeguards; and (3) The interest of the party seeking the prejudgment remedy. In the case at hand, the private property interests are significant. For a property owner like Doehr (P), attachment may cloud title, impair the ability to alienate the property, taint a credit rating, and even place an existing mortgage in default. Second, there is a substantial risk of erroneous deprivation. The Connecticut statute requires only a minimal showing of probable cause, and it is clear that a judge could make no realistic assessment of the merits of the action based solely on one-sided, conclusory assertions by someone like DiGiovanni (D). Furthermore, the statute does not provide sufficient additional safeguards. While the statute provides Doehr (P) the opportunity for a prompt post-attachment hearing, this would not cure the temporary deprivation of property that already occurred. Third, the interests of DiGiovanni (D) are too minimal to support the prejudgment attachment. There is no indication that Doehr (P) was about to transfer his property or otherwise render his estate unavailable to satisfy a future judgment. Finally, we turn to an analysis of whether due process requires the party seeking attachment to post a bond. We have repeatedly recognized, and continue to recognize, the utility of a bond in protecting the property rights affected by a mistaken prejudgment attachment. The bond entitles an aggrieved party to damages, a remedy not available if a full post-judgment hearing was required. However, we do not hold that a bond excuses the need for a hearing or other safeguards. There are certain harms that bonds cannot undo but that hearings could prevent, such as the aggrieved party's ability to alienate his property. In conclusion, we hold that Connecticut's prejudgment attachment statute violates due process. Affirmed and remanded.

■ CONCURRENCE

(Rehnquist, J.) While I concur in the Court's opinion with regards to the Connecticut statute at issue, I do not join in the final part of the opinion, which considered the necessity for a bond and a hearing. The majority engages in a abstract discussion of hypothetical issues not before it. Furthermore, the discussion is overly vague, failing to consider the important factual differences in various proceedings.

Analysis:

While the majority purports to render a wide-sweeping opinion on the constitutionality of prejudgment attachment statutes, this case is really only an application of the already-existing *Mathews* Test to private lawsuits. The majority conducts the *Mathews* balancing approach, holding that Doehr's (P) interest in having his property free from attachment, plus the large risk of an erroneous attachment, outweighs DiGiovanni's (D) slight interest in attaching the house. However, the holding is limited to the specific facts of this case. If DiGiovanni (D) did have a substantial interest in the attachment—i.e., if there was a large risk of Doehr (P) selling the property while the suit was pending—then the prejudgment attachment would presumably be acceptable. However, the majority notes that the Connecticut statute remains invalid, since even such exigent circumstances would not justify burdening the property owner's rights. Thus, perhaps the third prong of the test is of little consequence. Finally, as Rehnquist's concurrence argued, the majority can be criticized for analyzing a hypothetical situation not in issue in this case. Apparently Justice White really wanted to address the need for a bond and a prejudgment hearing. However, this analysis is likely of little importance, since it is vague and not tied to specific facts.

■ CASE VOCABULARY

DE MINIMIS: A very small matter, with which the law is not concerned.

CHAPTER FOUR

Jurisdiction Over Subject Matter of the Action—The Court's Competency

Lacks v. Lacks

Instant Facts: Two years after a final judgment for divorce was entered, Mrs. Lacks (D) attempted to vacate the judgment on jurisdictional grounds.

Black Letter Rule: In a divorce, a state's residence requirement goes to the merits of the case and does not involve issues of subject matter jurisdiction.

Mas v. Perry

Instant Facts: Mr. Oliver Perry (D), a Louisiana domiciliary, challenges final judgment on grounds that Judy and Jean Paul Mas (Ps), Louisiana residents, failed to prove complete diversity.

Black Letter Rule: For purposes of federal diversity jurisdiction, a party changes domicile only by taking up residence in another state with the intention to remain there, and a wife's domicile is not necessarily deemed to be that of her husband.

A.F.A. Tours v. Whitchurch

Instant Facts: A.F.A. Tours (P) claimed that a former tour guide misappropriated confidential information, but the district court dismissed the claim for failure to satisfy the amount-in-controversy requirement.

Black Letter Rule: The amount-in-controversy requirement for federal diversity jurisdiction is satisfied if the plaintiff makes a good-faith estimate that the value of the claims, including actual and punitive damages and the value of injunctive relief, meets the required amount.

Osborn v. Bank of the United States

Instant Facts: The Bank of the United States (P) sought to enjoin the Ohio state tax auditor from collecting a tax which the Bank (P) alleged was unconstitutional.

Black Letter Rule: Congress has a broad power to confer subject matter jurisdiction over all cases which conceivably involve federal questions.

Louisville & Nashville R. Co. v. Mottley

Instant Facts: Mr. and Mrs. Mottley (P) brought suit in federal court for cancellation of a lifetime free travel pass on the Louisville & Nashville Railroad (D), anticipating that the Railroad's (D) defenses would involve federal questions.

Black Letter Rule: In order to obtain federal question jurisdiction, a plaintiff's cause of action must involve a federal question, rather than anticipating that a defendant's defense will raise a federal question.

T.B. Harms Co. v. Eliscu

Instant Facts: T.B. Harms Co. (P) appeals a dismissal of its complaint for lack of federal jurisdiction, alleging that a dispute involving its rights to a contractual copyright assignment arises under federal copyright law.

Black Letter Rule: A cause of action alleging assignments of copyrights does not arise under the Copyright Act for purposes of federal question jurisdiction.

Merrell Dow Pharmaceuticals v. Thompson

Instant Facts: In a suit for negligence for improperly labeling a prenatal drug, in violation of a federal statute, Merrell Dow Pharmaceuticals (D) attempts to obtain federal-question jurisdiction.

Black Letter Rule: A state-law private action, which alleges a violation of a federal statute, "arises under" the laws of the United States only if Congress intended to provide a federal remedy for the statutory violation.

Grable & Sons Metal Products, Inc. v. Darue Engineering & Manufacturing

Instant Facts: After the IRS seized Grable's (D) property and sold it to Darue (D), Grable (P) brought a quiet title action, claiming that the notice it received was defective, and Darue (D) removed the case to federal court.

Black Letter Rule: The national interest in providing a federal forum for federal tax litigation is sufficiently substantial to support the exercise of federal question jurisdiction over questions presented under federal title law, and would not distort any division of labor between the state and federal courts provided or assumed by Congress.

United Mine Workers of America v. Gibbs

Instant Facts: Paul Gibbs (P) sued the United Mine Workers of America (UMW) (D) on both state and federal claims, and the Supreme Court now reviews the district court's decision to hear both claims.

Black Letter Rule: A federal court may hear a plaintiff's state law claims, based on the doctrine of pendent jurisdiction, whenever one claim arises under federal law and the state and federal claims derive from a common nucleus of operative fact.

Aldinger v. Howard

Instant Facts: Aldinger sued several county officials for federal civil rights violations and attempts to obtain pendent federal jurisdiction over state law claims against county itself.

Black Letter Rule: A federal court may grant pendent party jurisdiction to a state claim against a defendant which is derived from a common nucleus of operative fact with a federal claim against a separate defendant, if the statutory grant of subject-matter jurisdiction did not expressly or implicitly negate such joinder or if judicial efficiency warrants such joinder.

Exxon Mobil Corp. v. Allapattah Services

Instant Facts: A group of Exxon dealers sued Exxon for overcharging them for fuel, but not all of the dealers' claims met the minimum amount-in-controversy requirement for the exercise of federal court diversity jurisdiction.

Black Letter Rule: Where other elements of jurisdiction are present and at least one named plaintiff in the action satisfies the amount-in-controversy requirement, a court may exercise supplemental jurisdiction over the claims of other plaintiffs in the same case or controversy, even if those claims are for less than the jurisdictional amount specified in the statute setting forth the requirements for diversity jurisdiction.

Executive Software North America, Inc. v. U.S. District Court

Instant Facts: A worker who was fired brought federal and state claims for discrimination, and the district court remanded the state law claims.

Black Letter Rule: A court can deny supplemental jurisdiction over pendent state law claims only if one of the exceptions of section 1367(c) is satisfied.

Borough of West Mifflin v. Lancaster

Instant Facts: A jurisdictional issue arose when two people who had been kicked out of a shopping mall sued the mall owners and the local police for violations of their civil rights.

Black Letter Rule: A district court's discretion to remand under § 1441(c) can pertain only to those state law claims which the district court could decline to hear under § 1367.

Lacks v. Lacks

(*Husband*) v. (*Wife*)
41 N.Y.2d 71, 390 N.Y.S.2d 875, 359 N.E.2d 384 (1976)

NEW YORK RESIDENCE IS NOT REQUIRED FOR SUBJECT MATTER JURISDICTION IN STATE COURT

■ **INSTANT FACTS** Two years after a final judgment for divorce was entered, Mrs. Lacks (D) attempted to vacate the judgment on jurisdictional grounds.

■ **BLACK LETTER RULE** In a divorce, a state's residence requirement goes to the merits of the case and does not involve issues of subject matter jurisdiction.

■ **PROCEDURAL BASIS**

Appeal from denial of motion to vacate judgment for divorce.

■ **FACTS**

On August 10, 1965, Mr. Lacks (P) initiated an action for separation from Mrs. Lacks (D) on grounds of cruelty. The Appellate Division reversed a decision dismissing the complaint and ordered a new trial. At the second trial, Mr. Lacks (P) requested a judgment of absolute divorce, which was granted on March 16, 1970, and affirmed on October 26, 1972. When Mrs. Lacks' (D) leave to appeal was denied, the judgment of divorce became final [and Mr. Lacks thought he was finally free!]. However, two years later, Mrs. Lacks (D) moved to vacate the judgment, arguing that Mr. Lacks (P) had not been a New York resident for a full year preceding the divorce action, as required by a New York statute. Thus, Mrs. Lacks (D) contended that the court had been without subject matter jurisdiction to entertain the divorce action.

■ **ISSUE**

Does the failure to meet a state's residence requirement deprive a court of subject matter jurisdiction?

■ **DECISION AND RATIONALE**

(Breitel, J.) No. A state's residence requirement relates to the merits of the case, not to subject matter jurisdiction—the competence of a court to hear the case. New York's residence requirement for divorce cases is a substantive limitation on the cause of action, precluding a court from rendering a judgment on the merits if the requirement is not met. Mr. Lacks' (P) failure to meet the residence requirements could have been raised by Mrs. Lacks (D) at trial or on appeal. However, in this case, Mr. Lacks (P) obtained a *final judgment* for divorce. Despite Mrs. Lacks' (D) characterization of the issue as one related to subject matter jurisdiction, the points she raises relate only to the substantive issues of the cause of action, which are beyond review at this point. Affirmed.

Analysis:

This court does a good job at distinguishing jurisdictional issues from substantive issues. The analysis is straightforward once the court decides that, in a New York divorce action, a party's residence goes to the merits of the case. Failure to meet the residence requirement is, therefore, equivalent to the failure to satisfy other elements of the cause of action. Mrs. Lacks (D) had ample opportunity to contest Mr. Lacks' (P) residence at trial, or to raise this as an issue on appeal. Be sure to notice, when reading the subsequent cases, that residence *is* often an important jurisdictional issue in federal courts. The editors apparently chose this case to show the differences between state and federal courts in the area of subject matter jurisdiction.

■ **CASE VOCABULARY**

RES JUDICATA: Doctrine upholding the finality of a judgment which has been decided on the merits.

SUBJECT MATTER JURISDICTION: The competence of a court to hear a claim based on the general content of the claim.

VACATUR: A process by which a judgment is set aside.

Mas v. Perry

(Tenants) v. *(Landlord)*

489 F.2d 1396 (5th Cir. 1974), *cert. denied* 419 U.S. 842, 95 S.Ct. 74 (1974)

DOMICILE REQUIRES THE INTENTION TO REMAIN IN A CERTAIN STATE AND DOES NOT NECESSARILY CHANGE BASED ON MARRIAGE TO AN ALIEN

■ **INSTANT FACTS** Mr. Oliver Perry (D), a Louisiana domiciliary, challenges final judgment on grounds that Judy and Jean Paul Mas (Ps), Louisiana residents, failed to prove complete diversity.

■ **BLACK LETTER RULE** For purposes of federal diversity jurisdiction, a party changes domicile only by taking up residence in another state with the intention to remain there, and a wife's domicile is not necessarily deemed to be that of her husband.

■ **PROCEDURAL BASIS**

Appeal from final judgment for damages.

■ **FACTS**

Jean Paul and Judy Mas (Ps), who lived and worked in Louisiana, were married at Judy Mas' (P) home in Mississippi. After the marriage, the couple returned to Louisiana to continue their studies and employment at Louisiana State University, and the couple rented an apartment from Oliver H. Perry (D), a citizen of Louisiana. Mr. and Mrs. Mas (Ps) brought a claim against Mr. Perry (D) in federal court when they discovered that Mr. Perry (D) had been watching the couple through two-way mirrors in their bedroom and bathroom. The trial court awarded $5000 in damages to Mr. Mas (P) and $15,000 to Mrs. Mas (P). On appeal, Mr. Perry (D) claims that the federal district court lacked jurisdiction, contending that Mr. and Mrs. Mas (Ps) failed to prove diversity of citizenship among the parties. Mr. Mas (P) was a citizen of France throughout the proceedings. Mr. Perry (D) apparently believed that Mrs. Mas (P) was a domiciliary of Louisiana, or that she acquired French citizenship upon her marriage to Mr. Mas (P). Thus, according to Mr. Perry (D), the parties lacked complete diversity of citizenship, and the federal court had no jurisdiction to entertain the claim.

■ **ISSUE**

(1) Does a party's state citizenship change when she lives in a state without showing an intention to remain in that state? (2) Is a wife's domicile always deemed to be that of her husband?

■ **DECISION AND RATIONALE**

(Ainsworth, J.) (1) No. A person's domicile changes only when that party takes up residence in a different domicile with the intention to remain there. According to *Strawbridge v. Curtiss* [diversity jurisdiction requires that no plaintiff is a citizen of the same state as any defendant], the party invoking federal diversity jurisdiction must prove that, at the time of filing the complaint, complete diversity of citizenship existed. Federal jurisdiction extends to the claim of Mr. Mas (P), a citizen of France, pursuant to 28 U.S.C. § 1332(a)(2). In addition, Mrs. Mas (P) can claim diversity jurisdiction based on § 1332(a)(1), since she had a different domicile than Mr. Perry (D). Prior to her marriage, Mrs. Mas (P) was a domiciliary of Mississippi, where she had her permanent home. Her domicile did not change when she took up residence in Louisiana, as she was only a student/graduate assistant and did not have an intention to remain in that state. Thus, Mrs. Mas should still be considered a Mississippi domiciliary after the marriage, and there is complete diversity. Affirmed. (2) No. Although generally the domicile of a wife is deemed to be that of her husband, this concept does not extend to situations in which the husband is a foreign citizen who resides in the United States. First, such an extension would work absurd results in the case at hand. If Mrs. Mas (P) was considered a domiciliary of France—where her husband was a citizen—then she would not be a citizen of any state in the United States and could not obtain federal jurisdiction pursuant to § 1332(a)(1). In addition, she would not be able to bring the claim pursuant to § 1332(a)(2), since she would not technically be an alien. Second, considerations of judicial efficiency warrant hearing both Mr. Mas' (P) and Mrs. Mas' (P) claims in the same proceeding. Thus, Mrs. Mas (P) remains a Mississippi domiciliary despite her marriage to Mr. Mas (P), a French citizen. For diversity purposes a woman does not have her domicile or State citizenship changed solely by reason of her marriage to an alien. Affirmed.

Analysis:

This opinion contains definitions of domicile and complete diversity [as well as a brief reference to Mr. Perry's (D) *perversity*], and it delineates the requirements for effecting a change of domicile. In this regard, note that domicile is different from residence, and a party's intention to remain in a new domicile is required before a change occurs. This standard is somewhat vague, requiring courts to determine subjective intent without providing guidance as to how long a party must intend to remain in the new domicile. Apparently, Mrs. Mas' (P) intention to remain in Louisiana for a couple of years was insufficient to effect a change in domicile. In addition, note that the domicile of all parties is determined at the time of filing the suit, since otherwise a defendant could avoid diversity jurisdiction simply by taking up residence in the same state as any plaintiff and demonstrating an intention to remain there. Finally, if this case arose today and Mr. Mas was considered a permanent resident alien and Louisiana domiciliary, he would not be able to bring his claim based on a lack of diversity, since a 1988 amendment to § 1332(a) states that "an alien admitted to the United States for permanent residence shall be deemed a citizen of the State in which such alien is domiciled."

■ CASE VOCABULARY

COMPLETE DIVERSITY: The requirement that no party on one side of a litigation be a citizen of the same state as any party on the other side.

DOMICILE: The state of a person's residence, in which the person has the intention of remaining.

A.F.A. Tours v. Whitchurch

(Travel Agency) v. *(Tour Escort)*

937 F.2d 82 (2nd Cir. 1991)

PLAINTIFF EASILY SATISFIES AMOUNT–IN–CONTROVERSY REQUIREMENT THROUGH GOOD–FAITH ESTIMATE OF VALUE OF CLAIM

■ **INSTANT FACTS** A.F.A. Tours (P) claimed that a former tour guide misappropriated confidential information, but the district court dismissed the claim for failure to satisfy the amount-in-controversy requirement.

■ **BLACK LETTER RULE** The amount-in-controversy requirement for federal diversity jurisdiction is satisfied if the plaintiff makes a good-faith estimate that the value of the claims, including actual and punitive damages and the value of injunctive relief, meets the required amount.

■ **PROCEDURAL BASIS**

Appeal from summary judgment dismissing misappropriation action for lack of subject matter jurisdiction.

■ **FACTS**

A.F.A. Tours, Inc., (AFA) (P) operated a travel and tour business, specializing in deluxe tours to destinations in the Australia and the South Pacific. Desmond Whitchurch (D) was employed by AFA (P) as a tour escort for seventeen years. In that position, Whitchurch (D) was privy to confidential information developed by AFA (P), including customer lists, marketing information, and tour information. AFA (P) claimed that Whitchurch (D), upon resigning from AFA (P), misappropriated the confidential information and organized his own tour business in direct competition with AFA (P). AFA (P) sought an injunction against Whitchurch's (D) use of confidential information. Furthermore, AFA (P) claimed damages of at least $50,000 [coincidentally, this is the jurisdictional prerequisite for diversity actions] and sought punitive damages for no less than $250,000. Whitchurch (D) moved for summary judgment based on the merits of the case alone, but the district court raised the jurisdictional issue sua sponte during oral arguments. At arguments, Whitchurch contended that he secured reservations for only two former AFA (P) clients and that AFA's (P) damages could not possibly meet the $50,000 jurisdictional minimum. The federal district court agreed, dismissing the action for failure to meet the amount-in-controversy requirement. AFA (P) appeals the dismissal, contending that the court failed to provide AFA (P) an opportunity to demonstrate that the claim satisfied the jurisdictional amount.

■ **ISSUE**

Will a court grant great latitude to a plaintiff's good-faith estimate of damages, in order to satisfy the amount-in-controversy requirement for federal diversity jurisdiction?

■ **DECISION AND RATIONALE**

(Kearse, J.) Yes. Pursuant to 28 U.S.C.A. § 1332(a), federal diversity jurisdiction requires that the amount in controversy exceed $50,000. As established by the Supreme Court in *St. Paul Mercury Indemnity Co. v. Red Cab Co.* [developing rule for determining whether a plaintiff meets the jurisdictional amount], the sum claimed by the plaintiff in order to satisfy the amount-in-controversy requirement controls, provided it is made in good faith. Dismissal for failure to meet the amount is warranted only where it appears to a legal certainty that the claim is really for less than the jurisdictional amount. In an action for misappropriation of trade secrets, the amount of damages recoverable may be measured either by a plaintiff's losses or by profits unjustly received by the defendant. In addition, the demand for appropriate punitive damages may be included in meeting the amount-in-controversy requirement. Finally, where an injunction is sought, the value of the claim is assessed by measuring the extent of impairment—including both past losses and potential harm—to be prevented by the injunction. These three valuations of AFA's (P) claim could have exceeded $50,000, but the district court did not provide AFA (P) with ample opportunities to prove this. Regardless, even the minimal evidence presented by AFA (P) suggested that the good-faith claims were worth more than $50,000. Whitchurch (D) had led approximately 1,500 people on tours during his tenure with AFA, and tour prices averaged $10,000, with an average profit of 17% per booking. [No wonder Whitchurch (D) wanted to form his own tour business.] Even if Whitchurch's (D) new operation was successful in soliciting repeat business from only 2% of those vacationers, the profit he could siphon from AFA (P) would be $51,000. Furthermore, the record does not foreclose the possibility of punitive damages, and it does not quantify the value of the injunctive relief requested by AFA (P). The district court could not conclude to a legal certainty that the value of AFA's (P) claims would not exceed the $50,000 amount-in-controversy requirement. Reversed.

Analysis:

The St. Paul Mercury good-faith pleading requirement, applied by this court, shifts part of the jurisdictional burden squarely on the shoulders of the defendant. The defendant must prove to a legal certainty that the claim is really for less than the jurisdictional requirement, a difficult showing made almost impossible when injunctive relief and punitive damages are also sought by the plaintiff. On the other hand, in order to avoid dismissal and get the case to trial, a plaintiff must make only a good-faith estimate of the amount of the claim. Compare this with the requirement for proving diversity of citizenship, which places the burden of proof upon the plaintiff and which mandates dismissal if the burden is not met. As this court demonstrated, § 1332(a)'s amount-in-controversy necessitates a very brief showing by the plaintiff, and courts should bend over backwards to allow any reasonable cases to go to trial. In effect, then, a claim with any possible chance of being worth more than $50,000 will go to trial, provided the other requirements for diversity jurisdiction are met. However, plaintiffs should be wary of exaggerating their claim just to get into federal court, since § 1332(b) allows courts to impose costs upon the plaintiff if, at trial, the claim is adjudged to be worth less than $50,000.

■ CASE VOCABULARY

INTER ALIA: Term literally meaning "among other things."

SUA SPONTE: A court raising an issue on its own will, rather than at the request of one of the parties.

Osborn v. Bank of the United States

(State Tax Auditor) v. (Bank)
22 U.S. (9 Wheat.) 738 (1824)

CONGRESS HAS SWEEPING POWERS TO CONFER SUBJECT MATTER JURISDICTION OVER ALL CASES WHICH MAY INVOLVE FEDERAL QUESTIONS

■ **INSTANT FACTS** The Bank of the United States (P) sought to enjoin the Ohio state tax auditor from collecting a tax which the Bank (P) alleged was unconstitutional.

■ **BLACK LETTER RULE** Congress has a broad power to confer subject matter jurisdiction over all cases which conceivably involve federal questions.

■ **PROCEDURAL BASIS**

Appeal from temporary injunction and order to return money.

■ **FACTS**

The Bank of the United States (Bank) (P) sued to enjoin Osborn (D), the state auditor of Ohio, from collecting a tax that the Bank (P) alleged was unconstitutional. After the court granted a temporary injunction, Osborn (D) forcibly entered the bank and took the money. When the court ordered the money returned, state officials appealed on the grounds that the federal court lacked subject matter jurisdiction. However, the congressional act chartering the Bank (P) authorized it to sue or be sued in any Circuit Court of the United States.

■ **ISSUE**

Does Congress have the power to confer subject matter jurisdiction over all cases which conceivably involve federal questions?

■ **DECISION AND RATIONALE**

(Marshall, J.) Yes. Congress has the constitutional power, pursuant to the "arising under" language of Article III, § 2 of the Constitution, to confer subject matter jurisdiction over all cases which conceivably involve federal questions. In the congressional act which chartered the Bank (P), Congress authorized the Bank (P) to sue or be sued in any Circuit Court of the United States, explicitly granting federal jurisdiction over all cases to which the bank was a party. This act is constitutional, as any such lawsuit could conceivably involve a question of federal law and thus "arise under" the Constitution or laws of the United States. Affirmed.

Analysis:

Justice Marshall's opinion is a prime example of an overly broad interpretation of the "arising under" language of the Constitution. As discussed in subsequent cases, Justice Marshall went way too far in reasoning that any suit brought by or against the Bank (P) could conceivably involve a federal question. This is typically a key question to be resolved separately in each case. Perhaps Justice Marshall should

---

have limited the opinion to his reasoning that, in the case at hand, the Bank's (P) suit clearly arose under the Constitution, since the Bank (P) claimed that Ohio's tax was unconstitutional.

Louisville & Nashville R. Co. v. Mottley

(Railroad) v. *(Passengers)*
211 U.S. 149, 29 S.Ct. 42, 53 L.Ed. 126 (1908)

FEDERAL QUESTION JURISDICTION MAY NOT BE OBTAINED BY ANTICIPATING THAT A DEFENDANT WILL RAISE ISSUES OF FEDERAL LAW

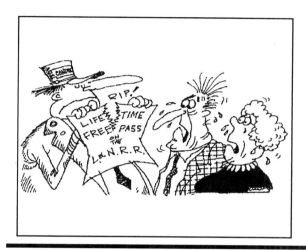

■ **INSTANT FACTS** Mr. and Mrs. Mottley (P) brought suit in federal court for cancellation of a lifetime free travel pass on the Louisville & Nashville Railroad (D), anticipating that the Railroad's (D) defenses would involve federal questions.

■ **BLACK LETTER RULE** In order to obtain federal question jurisdiction, a plaintiff's cause of action must involve a federal question, rather than anticipating that a defendant's defense will raise a federal question.

■ **PROCEDURAL BASIS**

Appeal from decree for relief from breach of contract.

■ **FACTS**

The Mottleys (P), husband and wife, were given a lifetime free ride ticket on the Louisville & Nashville Railroad (D) in exchange for releasing claims for negligence against the Railroad (D). [Apparently they remained confident in the Railroad, even though they were injured by the Railroad's negligence!] After nearly thirty-six years of free rides, the Railroad (D) canceled the free ride ticket and the Mottleys (P) brought suit in federal court. A portion of the Mottleys (P) complaint alleged that the Railroad (D) probably based the cancellation upon a recent act of Congress, which forbade the giving of free transportation. Without even considering the jurisdictional basis, the circuit court judge granted relief for the Mottleys (P), and the Railroad (D) appealed.

■ **ISSUE**

Can a plaintiff obtain federal question jurisdiction by alleging that a defendant will raise certain defenses which arise under the Constitution or the laws of the United States?

■ **DECISION AND RATIONALE**

(Moody, J.) No. A plaintiff cannot obtain subject matter jurisdiction simply by anticipating that the defendant will raise federal questions in its defense. Even if the plaintiff's allegations show that very likely federal questions will arise in the course of litigation, the plaintiff's well-pleaded complaint must itself raise the federal questions in order to obtain subject matter jurisdiction. In the case at hand, it is unnecessary to consider the merits of the Mottleys (P) claim, as the federal court was without jurisdiction. There was no diversity of citizenship, and the only possible grounds for federal jurisdiction were as a suit arising under the Constitution or laws of the United States. However, the Mottleys (P) cause of action did not raise a federal question. Rather, the Mottleys (P) merely anticipated that the Railroad (D) would defend its cancellation based on an act of Congress. Further, the Mottleys (P) contended that, in response to this defense, they would raise constitutional issues. Nevertheless, a well-pleaded complaint by the Mottleys (P) would not have alleged such a defense and made an answer to it before the Railroad (D) even had a chance to answer. And in any case, this is not an acceptable ground for federal question jurisdiction, since the complaint itself must raise the federal questions. Reversed and remanded, with instructions to dismiss for lack of jurisdiction.

Analysis:

This court, in an apparent reaction to Justice Marshall's broad reading of the "arising under" language, decided to significantly curtail federal question jurisdiction. The court's analysis is reasonable, since an alternative holding would allow any plaintiff to obtain federal question jurisdiction simply by alleging that the defendant will raise federal questions in its defense. In effect, the court is telling plaintiffs to mind their own business and state only their own claims, as they will have ample opportunity to contest any defenses later. More importantly, however, it severely limits federal question jurisdiction to causes of action which themselves involve federal questions. This is a fair reading of the "arising under" language. Note that, in an ironic twist, the Mottleys (P) subsequently brought their claim in state court, and the Supreme Court eventually ruled on the merits in favor of the Mottleys (P) three years later.

■ **CASE VOCABULARY**

FEDERAL QUESTION JURISDICTION: Cases that can be heard by the federal courts because the case arises under the federal Constitution, acts of Congress or treaties, and involves interpretation of said laws.

T.B. Harms Co. v. Eliscu

(*Assignee of Copyrights*) v. (*Songwriter*)
339 F.2d 823 (2nd Cir. 1964), *cert. denied* 381 U.S. 915, 85 S.Ct. 1534 (1965)

NOT EVERY COPYRIGHT CASE IS SUBJECT TO FEDERAL QUESTION JURISDICTION

■ **INSTANT FACTS** T.B. Harms Co. (P) appeals a dismissal of its complaint for lack of federal jurisdiction, alleging that a dispute involving its rights to a contractual copyright assignment arises under federal copyright law.

■ **BLACK LETTER RULE** A cause of action alleging assignments of copyrights does not arise under the Copyright Act for purposes of federal question jurisdiction.

■ **PROCEDURAL BASIS**

Appeal from dismissal of complaint for equitable and declaratory relief due to lack of jurisdiction.

■ **FACTS**

Edward Eliscu (D) was a songwriter. T.B. Harms Co. (P) alleged that Eliscu (D) assigned his rights in some copyrights of his songs to Max Dreyfus, and that Harms (P) was a successor to these assigned copyrights. However, Eliscu (D) denied this original assignment, maintaining that he properly renewed the copyrights and assigned then to Ross Jungnickel (D) nearly thirty years after the original alleged assignment. Harms (P) initiated an action in a New York district court for equitable and declaratory relief against Eliscu (D) and Jungnickel (D). Harms (P) predicated federal jurisdiction on 28 U.S.C. § 1338, conceding that no diversity of citizenship existed. The district court granted Eliscu (D) and Jungnickel's (D) motion to dismiss for lack of federal jurisdiction. Harms (P) appeals this dismissal.

■ **ISSUE**

Does a cause of action alleging assignment of a copyright arise under the Copyright Act for purposes of federal jurisdiction?

■ **DECISION AND RATIONALE**

(Friendly, J.) No. An action "arises under" the Copyright Act, for purposes of federal jurisdiction under 28 U.S.C. § 1338, only if the complaint is for a remedy expressly granted by the Act, asserts a claim requiring construction of the Act, or presents a case where a distinctive policy of the Act requires that federal principles control the disposition of the claim. In the case at hand, the crucial issue is whether or not Eliscu (D) assigned his rights in the copyright to Dreyfus—rights to which Harms (P) was a successor. The case does not involve any act or threat of copyright infringement, which would be dealt with under the Copyright Act. Likewise, Harms' (P) claim does not disclose a need for determining the application of the Copyright Act. Finally, there is no distinctive policy of the Copyright Act which requires federal principles to govern this claim. The case involves contractual assignment issues, and the Copyright Act does not create an explicit right of action to enforce or rescind assignments of copyrights. State laws of property and contracts should govern these issues.

Analysis:

This court affirms the Supreme Court's narrow readings of "arising under" language, retreating from Justice Marshall's broad interpretations in *Osborn v. Bank of the United States*. Not every action involving a copyright is subject to federal jurisdiction. Certainly, to grant such jurisdiction could clog the federal courts. State courts typically deal with issues of contractual assignments and breaches of contract, and contract law is almost entirely state-created. Indeed, this case can be analogized to a simple breach of contract case, where a plaintiff alleges that a defendant failed to supply the promised number of banana squashes. Such an action would not be a federal question, and a copyright assignment issue should not be either.

■ CASE VOCABULARY

ASSIGNMENT: A transfer of a person's rights in any type of property.

SUB JUDICE: Before a judge or a court.

Merrell Dow Pharmaceuticals v. Thompson

(*Pharmaceutical Maker*) v. (*Injured Party*)
478 U.S. 804, 106 S.Ct. 3229 (1986)

FEDERAL QUESTION JURISDICTION OVER A STATE CAUSE OF ACTION IS APPROPRIATE ONLY IF THE STATE CLAIM INVOLVES AN ESSENTIAL FEDERAL ELEMENT FOR WHICH CONGRESS INTENDED TO GRANT A FEDERAL REMEDY

■ **INSTANT FACTS** In a suit for negligence for improperly labeling a prenatal drug, in violation of a federal statute, Merrell Dow Pharmaceuticals (D) attempts to obtain federal-question jurisdiction.

■ **BLACK LETTER RULE** A state-law private action, which alleges a violation of a federal statute, "arises under" the laws of the United States only if Congress intended to provide a federal remedy for the statutory violation.

■ **PROCEDURAL BASIS**

Writ of certiorari after reversal of motion for removal to federal court for complaint for damages for negligence.

■ **FACTS**

Mr. and Mrs. Thompson (P) sued Merrell Dow Pharmaceuticals (D) in a state court in Ohio, alleging that their child was born with multiple deformities as a result of Mrs. Thompson (P) ingesting Bendectin, a drug manufactured by Merrell Dow (D), during her pregnancy. Five of the six causes of action clearly involved issues of state law. The other cause of action, for negligence, claimed that Bendectin violated the Federal Food, Drug, and Cosmetic Act (FDCA) because the label did not provide adequate warnings. Merrell Dow (D) filed a petition for removal to federal court, asserting that this cause of action arose under the laws of the United States. The district court granted this petition, denied the Thompsons' (P) motion to remand to state court, and granted Merrell Dow's (D) motion to dismiss on forum non conveniens grounds. However, the Court of Appeals for the Sixth Circuit reversed, holding that the FDCA does not create a private right of action and that the Thompsons' (P) cause of action did not depend necessarily on a question of federal law. The Supreme Court granted certiorari.

■ **ISSUE**

Does a state-law private action, which alleges a violation of a federal statute, "arise under" the laws of the United States if Congress did not intend a private remedy for violations of that federal statute?

■ **DECISION AND RATIONALE**

(Stevens, J.) No. A complaint alleging a violation of a federal statute as an element of a state cause of action, when Congress has determined that there should be no private, federal cause of action for the violation, does not state a claim arising under the laws of the United States. A case may "arise under" the Constitution or laws of the United States, for purposes of 28 U.S.C. § 1331, in two ways. First, and most commonly, federal law itself creates a cause of action. In the case at hand, the Thompsons (P) never asserted that federal law created their negligence cause of action [which would have been erroneous in any event]. Second, a case may arise under federal law where the vindication of a right under state law necessarily turns on some construction of federal law. However, in the instant case, the mere presence of a federal issue as an element of a state tort does not warrant federal jurisdiction. According to the legislative history of the statute, Congress did not intend a private federal remedy for violations of the FDCA. It would undermine congressional intent to conclude that federal-question jurisdiction nevertheless exists in this case solely because the violation of the FDCA is an aid to be a "rebuttable presumption" or a "proximate cause" of the state-created negligence action. Affirmed.

■ DISSENT

(Brennan, J.) There may be federal-question jurisdiction even though both the right asserted and the remedy sought by the plaintiff are state-created. The Thompsons (P) alleged that the violation of the FDCA established Merrell Dow's (D) negligence per se. Thus, as pleaded, the Thompsons' (P) right to relief depended upon a construction of the Constitution or laws of the United States. Although Congress did not create a federal cause of action or federal remedy under the FDCA, it does not follow that Congress precluded federal jurisdiction over state-law claims involving violations of the FDCA. Perhaps Congress intended to pre-empt all private enforcement of FDCA violations, in which case the Thompsons' (P) cause of action could not stand. But if Congress' decision not to provide a private federal remedy does not pre-empt such a state remedy, then it also should not foreclose federal jurisdiction over the state remedy. Finally, federal courts are better able to interpret federal laws, and the necessity of uniformity of decisions warrants federal jurisdiction in the case at hand.

Analysis:

The majority's opinion creates an important caveat to the rule that a state-created cause of action with essential federal elements, which turn on a construction of federal law, mandates federal-question jurisdiction. Pursuant to the opinion, such federal-question jurisdiction is appropriate only if the federal statute intended to create a federal remedy for a violation of the statute. The majority may have gone overboard in further restricting Justice Marshall's liberal construction, in *Osborn v. Bank of the United States*, of the "arising under" language. While federal jurisdiction should not extend over every case in which a federal question is an ingredient of the state action, perhaps jurisdiction should encompass the Thompsons' (P) claim, which alleges that a violation of the FDCA constitutes negligence per se. The majority did not adequately explain why it would flout congressional intent to exercise federal-question jurisdiction simply because the federal statute creates no private federal remedy. Federal courts are, indeed, a more appropriate venue for the interpretation and application of federal laws such as the FDCA. Since the FDCA violation was an essential element of the Thompsons' (P) cause of action, perhaps federal jurisdiction would have been more appropriate.

■ CASE VOCABULARY

FORUM NON CONVENIENS: Grounds for a court discretionarily dismissing a claim which, for matters of convenience, should more appropriately be brought elsewhere.

NEGLIGENCE PER SE: A type of negligence that is presumed whenever a statute is violated.

Grable & Sons Metal Products, Inc. v. Darue Engineering & Manufacturing

(Original Owner of Seized Property) v. *(Purchaser of Seized Property)*

545 U.S. 308, 125 S.Ct. 2363, 162 L.Ed.2d 257 (2005)

EVEN CASES THAT *IMPLICATE* FEDERAL LAW MAY JUSTIFY THE EXERCISE OF FEDERAL COURT JURISDICTION

"Federal question or not federal question, that is the question."

Federal question.

stus.com

■ **INSTANT FACTS** After the IRS seized Grable's (D) property and sold it to Darue (D), Grable (P) brought a quiet title action, claiming that the notice it received was defective, and Darue (D) removed the case to federal court.

■ **BLACK LETTER RULE** The national interest in providing a federal forum for federal tax litigation is sufficiently substantial to support the exercise of federal question jurisdiction over questions presented under federal title law, and would not distort any division of labor between the state and federal courts provided or assumed by Congress.

■ PROCEDURAL BASIS

Supreme Court consideration of the question of federal jurisdiction only, after affirmance of the exercise of jurisdiction by the Sixth Circuit.

■ FACTS

In 1994 the IRS seized real property belonging to Grable & Sons (P) in order to satisfy Grable's (P) tax delinquency. Grable (P) was thereafter notified, by certified mail, that the IRS was selling the seized property to Darue Engineering (D). Grable (P) did not exercise its right to redeem the property, so, after the statutory redemption period had expired, the government gave Darue (D) a quitclaim deed to the property. Five years later, Grable (P) tried to get the property back in a state-court quiet title action, alleging that the notice it had received was deficient because the relevant statute requires personal service, not service by certified mail. Darue (D) removed the case to federal court. Grable (P) tried to get the case remanded back to state court, arguing that it did not raise a federal question, but the district court found that a federal question did exist and granted summary judgment in Darue's (D) favor. The Sixth Circuit affirmed. The Supreme Court granted certiorari on the issue of federal question jurisdiction alone in order to resolve a split in the circuits as to whether the existence of a federal cause of action is a required condition for the exercise of federal question jurisdiction.

■ ISSUE

Does want of a federal cause of action to try claims of title to land obtained at a federal tax sale preclude removal to federal court of a state action with non-diverse parties raising a disputed issue of federal title law?

■ DECISION AND RATIONALE

(Souter, J.) No. The national interest in providing a federal forum for federal tax litigation is sufficiently substantial to support the exercise of federal question jurisdiction over questions presented under federal title law, and would not distort any division of labor between the state and federal courts provided or assumed by Congress. Darue (D) was entitled to remove the quiet title action to federal court if it could have been brought there originally as a civil action arising under the Constitution, laws, or treaties of the United States. The "arising under" language is sometimes read narrowly, but there is another longstanding variety of federal jurisdiction. Federal court jurisdiction lies over state law claims that *implicate* significant federal issues. That is, a state law claim can give rise to federal question jurisdiction if it appears from the complaint that the right to relief depends on the construction or application of federal law. The relevant concern is, does the state law claim necessarily raise a stated federal issue, actually disputed and substantial, that a federal forum may entertain without disturbing any congressionally approved balance of federal and state judicial responsibilities? The answer here is yes. Quiet title actions were the subject of some of the earliest exercises of federal question jurisdiction over state law claims. Although federal law does not provide for quiet title actions, the Government, its buyers, and its delinquents have a clear interest in the availability of a federal forum in tax delinquency cases like this. Moreover, it is the rare quiet title action that actually implicates federal law, so the exercise of jurisdiction here would not threaten the normal currents of litigation. The judgment of the court of appeals upholding the exercise of jurisdiction over Grable's (P) quiet title action is therefore affirmed.

■ **CONCURRENCE**

(Thomas, J.) I would be willing, in an appropriate case, to consider limiting 28 U.S.C. § 1331 jurisdiction to cases in which federal law *creates* the cause of action pleaded on the face of the plaintiff's complaint.

Analysis:

Justice Thomas's concurrence focuses on, and he seems to prefer, the rule announced decades earlier in *American Well Works Co. v. Layne & Bowler Co.*, 241 U.S. 257 (1916). In that case, the Court held that a suit for damages to a business caused by a threat to sue under the patent law was not itself a suit under the patent law. Whether the defendant's act was wrong or not depended on the law of the state where the act was done, the Court explained, not on the patent law, and therefore the suit arose under the law of the state. A suit arises under the law that creates the cause of action, and the fact that the justification for the wrongful acts in that case may have involved the validity and infringement of a patent was no more material to the question of under what law the suit was brought than it would have been in an action of contract.

■ **CASE VOCABULARY**

FEDERAL QUESTION: In litigation, a legal issue involving the interpretation and application of the U.S. Constitution, an act of Congress, or a treaty. Jurisdiction over federal questions rests with the federal courts.

FEDERAL QUESTION JURISDICTION: The exercise of federal-court power over claims arising under the U.S. Constitution, an act of Congress, or a treaty.

QUIET TITLE ACTION: A proceeding to establish a plaintiff's title to land by compelling the adverse claimant to establish a claim or be forever estopped from asserting it.

QUITCLAIM DEED: A deed that conveys a grantor's complete interest or claim in certain real property but that neither warrants nor professes that the title is valid.

PERSONAL SERVICE: Actual delivery of the notice or process to the person to whom it is directed.

REDEEM: The act or an instance of reclaiming or regaining possession by paying a specific price.

REMAND: The act or an instance of sending something (such as a case, claim, or person) back for further action.

REMOVAL: The transfer of an action from state to federal court. In removing a case to federal court, a litigant must timely file the removal papers and must show a valid basis for federal court jurisdiction.

United Mine Workers of America v. Gibbs

(*Mine Workers Union*) v. (*Mine Supervisor*)
383 U.S. 715, 86 S.Ct. 1130 (1966)

FEDERAL COURTS MAY HEAR BOTH STATE AND FEDERAL CLAIMS, PROVIDED THE CLAIMS ARISE FROM A COMMON NUCLEUS OF OPERATIVE FACT

■ **INSTANT FACTS** Paul Gibbs (P) sued the United Mine Workers of America (UMW) (D) on both state and federal claims, and the Supreme Court now reviews the district court's decision to hear both claims.

■ **BLACK LETTER RULE** A federal court may hear a plaintiff's state law claims, based on the doctrine of pendent jurisdiction, whenever one claim arises under federal law and the state and federal claims derive from a common nucleus of operative fact.

■ **PROCEDURAL BASIS**

Writ of certiorari following affirmation of award of damages for interference with an employment contract.

■ **FACTS**

As a result of armed members of the United Mine Workers of America (UMW) (D) forcibly preventing the opening of a mine, Paul Gibbs (P), the mine supervisor, lost his job and was unable to complete a valuable haulage contract. Gibbs (P) brought suit in federal court for both federal and state causes of action, obtaining federal jurisdiction based on the doctrine of pendent jurisdiction. Gibbs (P) claimed that UMW's (D) actions were a secondary boycott, in violation of § 303 of the federal Labor Management Relations Act, and were an unlawful interference with Gibbs' (P) contracts of employment and haulage, in violation of state law. Concluding that UMW (D) violated both federal and state law, the jury awarded Gibbs (P) nearly $200,000 in actual and punitive damages. However, on UMW's (D) motion the court set aside the verdict for damages based on the haulage contract and the federal claim, remitting an award for only the state law claim of interference with Gibbs' (P) employment contract. After the Court of Appeals for the Sixth Circuit affirmed, the Supreme Court granted certiorari to determine whether federal jurisdiction was appropriate.

■ **ISSUE**

Does a federal court have jurisdiction over a plaintiff's state law claims as well as his federal law claims?

■ **DECISION AND RATIONALE**

(Brennan, J.) Yes. A federal court may hear a plaintiff's state law claims, based on the doctrine of pendent jurisdiction, whenever there is a claim arising under federal law and the state and federal claims derive from a common nucleus of operative fact. Thus, pendent jurisdiction exists whenever the state and federal claims are so closely related as to comprise one constitutional case. However, pendent jurisdiction is a doctrine of discretion, based on considerations of judicial economy, convenience and fairness to litigants. A federal court should not exercise pendent jurisdiction if the state issues predominate. Furthermore, pendent jurisdiction is unwarranted if there is a substantial likelihood of a jury confusing the legal theories of the federal and state claims. In the case at issue, the federal district court did not abuse its discretion by taking jurisdiction over Gibbs' state-law claims (P), since his federal claim clearly arose under federal law, and since the scope of Gibbs' (P) state claim implicated the federal doctrine of pre-emption. Although the court eventually set aside the award of damages on the federal claim, dismissal of the pendent state law claims would be warranted only if the federal claims were dismissed *before* trial. Moreover, the danger of confusing the jury was minimized in this case by the district court employing a special verdict form. Reversed.

Analysis:

In utilizing the doctrine of pendent jurisdiction in this case, the Supreme Court employed a little judicial "slight of hand" in order to escape a thorny constitutional issue and achieve some policy goals. Article III, Section 2 of the Constitution extends federal judicial power to only certain types of cases or controversies, including federal questions and diversity of citizenship. The Constitution does not permit federal courts to hear state claims when there is no diversity of citizenship. Justice Brennan, writing for the majority, leaped over this constitutional hurdle by finding that the state claims were really just a part of the overriding federal question, as both the state and federal claims arose from a "common nucleus of operative fact." When the claims are interrelated in this way, pendent jurisdiction allows the court to achieve policy goals. First, pendent jurisdiction is more efficient for courts, since splitting up interrelated state and federal claims into two separate proceedings would waste judicial resources. Second, pendent jurisdiction is beneficial for a plaintiff who could not otherwise afford to litigate the claims separately in both federal and state courts. Third, when claims are interrelated, the lack of pendent jurisdiction would implicate problems with the doctrine of res judicata, which prohibits the litigation of the same claims in separate proceedings. If the state and federal claims were interrelated, and if one claim was decided before the other, then this decision would likely control the resolution of the other issue. Finally, a dismissal of Gibbs' (P) state law claims could cause the statute of limitations to run before he had time to file the complaint in a state court.

■ CASE VOCABULARY

HEGEMONY: The influence or control of one state over other states.

JUDGMENT *N.O.V.* (Judgment *Non Obstante Veredicto*): Literally, a judgment notwithstanding the verdict; a judgment in favor of one party, even though there has been a verdict in favor of the other party.

NUCLEUS: A central part.

Aldinger v. Howard

(*Citizen*) v. (*County Treasurer*)

427 U.S. 1, 96 S.Ct. 2413 (1976)

PENDENT PARTY JURISDICTION IS MORE LIMITED THAN PENDENT CLAIM JURISDICTION, REQUIRING EXPRESS OR IMPLIED CONGRESSIONAL INTENT NOT TO NEGATE SUCH JURISDICTION

■ **INSTANT FACTS** Aldinger sued several county officials for federal civil rights violations and attempts to obtain pendent federal jurisdiction over state law claims against county itself.

■ **BLACK LETTER RULE** A federal court may grant pendent party jurisdiction to a state claim against a defendant which is derived from a common nucleus of operative fact with a federal claim against a separate defendant, if the statutory grant of subject-matter jurisdiction did not expressly or implicitly negate such joinder or if judicial efficiency warrants such joinder.

■ **PROCEDURAL BASIS**

Writ of certiorari to review suit for civil rights violations.

■ **FACTS**

Aldinger (P), a citizen of Washington, brought suit against Howard (D) and several other officers of Spokane County, Washington, for alleged violations of the Civil Rights Act (42 U.S.C. § 1983). Aldinger (P) also sought to join Spokane County as a defendant, but at the time counties were not subject to suit under the Civil Rights Act. Thus, Aldinger (P) sued the county under state law. Although there was no diversity of citizenship between Aldinger (P) and the county, Aldinger (P) argued that the federal court should hear both claims at the same time since the claims arose from a common nucleus of operative fact. The Supreme Court granted certiorari to determine whether such "pendent party" jurisdiction is allowable.

■ **ISSUE**

May a federal court grant "pendent party" jurisdiction to a state claim against a defendant, derived from a common nucleus of operative fact with a federal claim against a separate defendant, where the statute granting jurisdiction does not expressly or implicitly negate such jurisdiction?

■ **DECISION AND RATIONALE**

(Justice Not Stated) Yes. A federal court may grant pendent party jurisdiction to a state claim against a defendant, derived from a common nucleus of operative fact with a federal claim against a separate defendant, if the statutory grant of subject-matter jurisdiction does not negate such joinder. Unlike the *Gibbs* decision [pendent jurisdiction appropriate where state and federal claims arise from a common nucleus of operative fact], a plaintiff who has asserted a federal-jurisdiction claim against one defendant should not necessarily be allowed to join an entirely different defendant on the basis of a state-law claim over which there is no independent basis of federal jurisdiction, simply because the two claims derive from a common nucleus of operative fact. Although the same considerations of judicial efficiency would be served, such addition would run counter to the fact that federal courts have limited jurisdiction. Thus, pendent party jurisdiction is permissible if Congress did not expressly or implicitly negate this jurisdiction within the statute creating the jurisdiction. In the case at hand, the relevant statute [presumably 42 U.S.C. § 1983] excluded municipal corporations, like Spokane County, from the definition of persons covered, evidencing an intent to preclude the exercise of federal-court jurisdiction over them. Nevertheless, pendent party jurisdiction remains possible in some other instances. For example, when the grant of jurisdiction to a federal court is exclusive, the policy of judicial economy may mandate trying the state law claims against one defendant together with the federal claim against another defendant.

Analysis:

The Supreme Court made many seemingly important statements in this case, but did they really say anything? The Court certainly expressed a general uneasiness about allowing pendent party jurisdiction, but it did not provide much guidance in determining when pendent party jurisdiction is allowable. At one stage of the opinion, it appears that such jurisdiction is permissible only when not expressly or implicitly negated by Congress. However, perhaps the mere exclusion of a grant of pendent party jurisdiction from the statute should not be read as Congress negating such jurisdiction. Moreover, the Court took a huge step backwards in retreating from this general rule, acknowledging that other alignments of parties might call for different results. If nothing else, then, the opinion leaves the door open for a plaintiff to argue that considerations of judicial efficiency warrant pendent party jurisdiction in a particular situation.

Exxon Mobil Corp. v. Allapattah Services

(Petroleum Dealers) v. *(Oil Company)*
545 U.S. 546, 125 S.Ct. 2611, 162 L.Ed.2d 502 (2005)

NOT ALL PLAINTIFFS IN A CLASS ACTION LAWSUIT MUST INDIVIDUALLY MEET THE AMOUNT–IN–CONTROVERSY REQUIREMENT

Come on, guys.
Let's follow this big fish
to federal court!

stus.com

■ **INSTANT FACTS** A group of Exxon dealers sued Exxon for overcharging them for fuel, but not all of the dealers' claims met the minimum amount-in-controversy requirement for the exercise of federal court diversity jurisdiction.

■ **BLACK LETTER RULE** Where other elements of jurisdiction are present and at least one named plaintiff in the action satisfies the amount-in-controversy requirement, a court may exercise supplemental jurisdiction over the claims of other plaintiffs in the same case or controversy, even if those claims are for less than the jurisdictional amount specified in the statute setting forth the requirements for diversity jurisdiction.

■ PROCEDURAL BASIS

On certiorari to the Supreme Court to resolve a conflict among the circuit courts of appeals regarding the proper interpretation of 28 U.S.C. § 1367.

■ FACTS

A group of Exxon dealers filed a class action lawsuit alleging that Exxon overcharged them for fuel. Not all class members met the minimum amount-in-controversy requirement for the court's exercise of federal diversity jurisdiction. The federal district court held that 28 U.S.C. § 1367, the supplemental jurisdiction statute, could be extended to include all of the plaintiffs, and the Eleventh Circuit agreed. The Supreme Court granted certiorari to resolve a conflict among the federal circuits as to whether the exercise of such supplemental jurisdiction was proper.

■ ISSUE

May a federal court in a diversity case exercise supplemental jurisdiction over additional plaintiffs whose claims do not satisfy the minimum amount-in-controversy requirement, if their claims are part of the same case or controversy as the claims of the plaintiffs who do allege a sufficient amount in controversy?

■ DECISION AND RATIONALE

(Kennedy, J.) Yes. Where other elements of jurisdiction are present and at least one named plaintiff in the action satisfies the amount-in-controversy requirement, a court may exercise supplemental jurisdiction over the claims of other plaintiffs in the same case or controversy, even if those claims are for less than the jurisdictional amount specified in the statute setting forth the requirements for diversity jurisdiction. Federal district courts may not exercise jurisdiction in the absence of a statutory basis. The statute that applies in this case is 28 U.S.C. § 1367, which contains a broad grant of supplemental jurisdiction over other claims within the same case or controversy, as long as the action is one in which the district courts would have original jurisdiction. The single question before us, then, is whether a diversity case in which the claims of some plaintiffs satisfy the amount-in-controversy requirement, but the claims of other plaintiffs do not, presents a civil action of which the district courts have original jurisdiction. We conclude that the answer must be yes.

We cannot accept the view that each and every claim must individually meet the jurisdictional requirement. This "indivisibility theory" requires that all claims must stand or fall as a single action. The indivisibility theory is easily dismissed as inconsistent with the whole notion of supplemental jurisdiction. Nor is the "contamination theory" viable, because, although it may make sense to apply it in the diversity of citizenship context, it makes no sense with respect to the amount in controversy, which is meant to ensure that a dispute is sufficiently important to warrant federal court attention. We hold that § 1367 authorizes supplemental jurisdiction over all claims by diverse parties arising out of the same Article III case or controversy. Affirmed.

■ DISSENT

(Ginsburg, J.) The Court reads § 1367 as enlarging federal diversity jurisdiction, allowing access to federal courts by co-plaintiffs or class members who do not meet the in-excess-of-$75,000 amount-in-controversy requirement, as long as at least one plaintiff or the named class representative has a jurisdictionally sufficient claim. I disagree with the majority and largely adopt the argument discussed by them as the indivisibility theory.

Analysis:

Section 1367, enacted in 1990, provides federal courts with jurisdiction over claims that are part of the same case or controversy as other claims over which the court has original jurisdiction. Supplemental jurisdiction includes jurisdiction over both ancillary and pendent claims, which were, prior to 1990, treated separately. Ancillary jurisdiction involved a court's jurisdiction to adjudicate claims and proceedings related to a claim that was properly before the court. For example, if a plaintiff brought a lawsuit in federal court based on a federal question (such as a claim under Title VII), the defendant could assert a counterclaim over which the court would not otherwise have jurisdiction (such as a state-law claim for stealing company property). Pendent jurisdiction involved court's jurisdiction to hear and determine a claim over which it would not otherwise have jurisdiction, where the claim arose from the same transaction or occurrence as another claim that was properly before the court. For example, if a plaintiff brought suit in federal court claiming that the defendant, in one transaction, violated both a federal and a state law, the federal court had jurisdiction over the federal claim (under federal-question jurisdiction), and over the state claim that was pendent to the federal claim. Pendent jurisdiction and ancillary jurisdiction have now both been codified as supplemental jurisdiction.

■ CASE VOCABULARY

AMOUNT IN CONTROVERSY: The damages claimed or relief demanded by the injured party in a lawsuit. For a federal court to have diversity jurisdiction, the amount in controversy must exceed $75,000.

ARTICLE III CASE OR CONTROVERSY: The constitutional requirement that, for a federal court to hear a case, the case must involve an actual dispute.

CLASS ACTION: A lawsuit in which the court authorizes a single person or a small group of people to represent the interests of a larger group; specifically, a lawsuit in which the convenience either of the public or of the interested parties requires that the case be settled through litigation by or against only a part of the group of similarly situated persons and in which a person whose interests are or may be affected does not have an opportunity to protect his or her interests by appearing personally or through a personally selected representative, or through a person specially appointed to act as a trustee or guardian. Federal procedure has several prerequisites for maintaining a class action: (1) the class must be so large that individual suits would be impracticable, (2) there must be legal or factual questions common to the class, (3) the claims or defenses of the representative parties must be typical of those of the class, and (4) the representative parties must adequately protect the interests of the class.

DIVERSITY JURISDICTION: A basis for federal-court jurisdiction that exists when (1) a case is between citizens of different states, or between a citizen of a state and an alien, and (2) the matter in controversy exceeds a specific value (now $75,000).

LEGISLATIVE HISTORY: The background and events leading to the enactment of a statute, including hearings, committee reports, and floor debates. Legislative history is sometimes recorded so that it can later be used to aid in interpreting the statute.

Executive Software North America, Inc. v. U.S. District Court

(Employer) v. *(Federal Court)*
24 F.3d 1545 (9th Cir. 1994)

COURTS CAN DENY PENDENT JURISDICTION ONLY FOR THE REASONS EXPRESSLY STATED IN SECTION 1367(c)

■ **INSTANT FACTS** A worker who was fired brought federal and state claims for discrimination, and the district court remanded the state law claims.

■ **BLACK LETTER RULE** A court can deny supplemental jurisdiction over pendent state law claims only if one of the exceptions of section 1367(c) is satisfied.

■ **PROCEDURAL BASIS**

Petition for writ of mandamus to compel district court to retain jurisdiction over pendent state law claims.

■ **FACTS**

Donna Page (P), a black woman, had been employed by Executive Software North America, Inc. ("ESNA") (D). Page (P) refused to comply with ESNA's (D) requirement that all employees study the teachings of the Church of Scientology. As a result, Page (P) contends, ESNA (D) charged Page (P) with a number of errors in her work and eventually fired her. Page (P) filed a complaint in state court, alleging that the termination was a subterfuge for illegal discrimination against non-believers, women and racial minorities. Page's (P) complaint alleged two federal causes of action as well as three state-law causes of action (for unlawful discrimination, wrongful termination and negligent supervision). ESNA (D) removed the action to federal district court. Subsequently, the court issued an order to show cause why the state-law claims should not be remanded to state court. The district court reminded the parties of the requirements for supplemental jurisdiction in *United Mine Workers v. Gibbs* [pendent jurisdiction over state claim is appropriate only if the state and federal claims derive from a common nucleus of operative fact]. In addition, the court noted that federal courts may deny jurisdiction over state law claims in certain situations, even if the *Gibbs* test was satisfied. The district court subsequently remanded the state law claims without providing any reason. ESNA (D) seeks a petition for a writ of mandamus to compel the district court to retain jurisdiction over the state law claims.

■ **ISSUE**

Can a district court look beyond the express exceptions listed in section 1367(c) in declining jurisdiction over pendent state claims?

■ **DECISION AND RATIONALE**

(Nelson, J.) No. A court cannot look beyond the express exceptions listed in section 1367(c) in declining jurisdiction over pendent state law claims. Section 1367 codifies the *Gibbs* test and the exceptions listed in subsequent cases. Where claims are part of a common nucleus of operative fact, federal courts have discretion to decline to exercise supplemental jurisdiction only in the four situations enumerated in section 1367(c). For example, a district court may decline jurisdiction over state law claims if those claims (1) raise a novel or complex issue of State law, (2) "substantially predominate" over the federal claims, or (3) if the district court has dismissed all federal claims. In addition, section 1367(c)(4) permits discretionary remand when "in exceptional circumstances, there are other compelling reasons for declining jurisdiction." This catch-all provision should be construed in the same nature of the other three provisions. The court must conclude that declining jurisdiction best accommodates the values of economy, convenience, fairness, and comity. The court must analyze the specific facts of the case at hand and expressly identify why there are exceptional, compelling reasons for declining jurisdiction. In the instant action, the district court failed to identify these factors. In addition, it appeared to look beyond the statutory exceptions, intimating that it could decline jurisdiction when retention of the state law claims would require the expenditure of substantial time and effort. This was clear error. Courts cannot look beyond the provisions of section 1367(c) in declining jurisdiction over state law claims. Writ of mandamus is granted and the remand order issued by the district court shall be vacated.

■ DISSENT

(Leavy, J.) I disagree with the majority's holding that the district court committed clear error. In my opinion, the ground stated by the district court for denying jurisdiction (i.e., the expenditure of substantial additional judicial time and effort) would be sufficiently compelling. Nothing else in the district court's order indicates that it relied on a ground not authorized by section 1367(c). Courts should be allowed to weigh the values of judicial economy, convenience, fairness, and comity in order to decide whether to exercise pendent jurisdiction over state law claims.

Analysis:

This opinion presents an extensive analysis of the law of supplemental jurisdiction in the wake of the enactment of section 1367. As you will recall, cases following *Gibbs* effectively eliminated pendent jurisdiction over state law claims. Congress aimed to resuscitate pendent jurisdiction by enacting section 1367. Subsection (a) reiterates the basic notion that supplemental jurisdiction is proper as long as the state and federal claims derive from a common nucleus of operative fact. Subsection (c) presents four exceptions to this general notion. The big question is whether these exceptions constitute the exclusive means by which supplemental jurisdiction can be declined. This court thinks so. And in many ways, the court's holding makes sense. By broadly wording section 1367(c)(4), Congress apparently intended to codify any discretionary factors that warrant declining jurisdiction. But the difficult issue lies in interpreting section 1367(c)(4). The majority and dissent differ in how this subsection should be applied. While they agree that the subsection allows district courts to consider economic factors and general fairness, the majority and dissent disagree as to what constitutes "exceptional circumstances" that warrant the denial of supplemental jurisdiction.

■ CASE VOCABULARY

SUA SPONTE: On its own motion; an action that the court takes without a request from either party.

WRIT OF MANDAMUS: An order from a higher court directing a lower court to take some action.

Borough of West Mifflin v. Lancaster

(Municipal Government) v. *(Federal District Court Judge)*

45 F.3d 780 (3rd Cir. 1995)

A DISTRICT COURT HAS ONLY LIMITED AUTHORITY TO REMAND A CASE UNDER 28 U.S.C. § 1441(c)

■ **INSTANT FACTS** A jurisdictional issue arose when two people who had been kicked out of a shopping mall sued the mall owners and the local police for violations of their civil rights.

■ **BLACK LETTER RULE** A district court's discretion to remand under § 1441(c) can pertain only to those state law claims which the district court could decline to hear under § 1367.

■ **PROCEDURAL BASIS**

Appeal to the Third Circuit Court of Appeals of a lower district judge's decision to remand to state court a case that had been removed to federal court.

■ **FACTS**

Allan Lindsey (P) and Randall Coughanour (P) were allegedly "harassed, threatened, and assaulted" by security guards at a mall in West Mifflin Borough. When they requested help from the West Mifflin Police Department (D), they were told that if they ever returned to the mall they would be arrested. For three weeks Lindsey (P) attempted to contact the mall owners to find out why he and his friend had been accosted and banned from the mall, but was unsuccessful in his attempts. On September 27, 1991, Lindsey (P) and Coughanour (P) returned to the mall and were accosted by security guards and arrested. They were subsequently convicted, but a three judge panel of the Superior Court of Pennsylvania vacated the convictions. Lindsey (P) and Coughanour (P) thereafter filed a seven-count complaint in state court against the mall owners and the Borough of West Mifflin (D) alleging abuse and malicious prosecution. Included in the list of claims was an alleged violation of 42 U.S.C. § 1983 [civil rights statute]. Relying on the § 1983 claim, West Mifflin (D) had the case removed to federal court. Lindsey (P) and Coughanour (P) sought remand. A magistrate recommended remand of the entire case, including the federal § 1983 claim, finding that "[t]he issues of state law clearly predominate in this matter." District Judge Lancaster adopted the recommendation and remanded the entire case to state court. West Mifflin (D) appealed.

■ **ISSUE**

Can a district court applying 28 U.S.C. § 1441(c) remand to state court a claim that it is not permitted to decline to hear under § 1367?

■ **DECISION AND RATIONALE**

(Pratt, J.) No. Application of § 1441(c). The dispute on the mandamus application focuses on the effect of 28 U.S.C. § 1441(c), which reads: "Whenever a separate and independent claim or cause of action within the jurisdiction of 1331 of this title is joined with one or more otherwise non-removable claims or causes of action, the entire case may be removed and the district court may determine all issues therein, or, in its discretion, may remand all matters in which State law predominates." A fair reading of the congressional intent behind this statute is that it was designed to restrict removal to only those cases falling within the court's federal question jurisdiction and to bring the remand provisions into harmony with 28 U.S.C. § 1367 [supplemental jurisdiction], thereby avoiding piecemeal litigation. In this case, the district court relied on that portion of the statute which reads "the district court may . . . remand all matters in which State law predominates" to remand the entire case, including the § 1983 claim, to state court. It did so without regard for the requirement that the federal cause of action removed by the municipal defendants had to be "separate and independent" from the state causes of action. Thus, § 1441(c) provides for removal or remand only where the federal question claims are "separate and independent" from the state law claims with which they are joined. However, where there is a single injury for which relief is sought, arising from an interrelated series of events or transactions, there is no separate or independent claim or cause of action under § 1441(c). Suits involving supplemental state claims that derive from a common nucleus of operative fact do not fall within the scope of § 1441(c), since pendent claims are not separate and independent. It is apparent, then, that § 1441(c) grants a district court only a limited authority to remand a case. Indeed, the district court's discretion to remand under § 1441(c) can pertain only to those state law claims which the district court could decline to hear under § 1367. In the present case, Lindsey and Coughanour rely on the same series of events for all counts of their complaint, including the federal § 1983 count; therefore, the federal claim is not separate and independent under § 1441(c), and the district court had no authority to remand the case under that section. Application of § 1367(c). Lindsey (P) and Coughanour (P) insist that, even if the court was not authorized to remand the case under § 1441(c), its action should be sustained under § 1367(c), which gives a district court discretion to decline to hear certain state claims over which it has supplemental jurisdiction. We disagree for two reasons. First, nothing in § 1367(c) authorizes a district court to decline to entertain a claim over which it has original jurisdiction, and, accordingly, that section does not sanction the district court's remand of the entire case, including the civil rights claim, to the state court. Further, § 1367(c) cannot be invoked to affirm even the district court's remand of the state claims to state court. While we agree with Lindsey (P) and Coughanour (P) that the discretion given the trial court under § 1367(c) exists with respect to removed claims as well as claims filed initially in the district court, it is apparent that the district court has not exercised that discretion in this case. Instead, its decision is based solely on § 1441(c). Moreover, the result of an exercise of discretion under § 1367(c) in circumstances like those before the district court would have been two parallel proceedings, one in federal court and one in state court, and a district court cannot exercise its § 1367(c) discretion without taking that fact into account. The district court's § 1441(c) analysis accordingly cannot serve as a surrogate for a § 1367(c) analysis that was never conducted.

As indicated, § 1367(c) is potentially applicable in a removal case involving federal and state claims over which the district court has supplemental jurisdiction. A district court may thus have to exercise its discretion at any time during the course of such a proceeding in light of the circumstances that then exist. Because the district court in this case may have to do just that, we offer the following guidance on the application of § 1367(c). Under *Gibbs,* where the claim over which the district court has original jurisdiction is dismissed before trial, the court must decline to decide the pendent state claims unless considerations of judicial economy, convenience, and fairness to the parties provide an affirmative justification for doing so. Where the original federal jurisdiction claim is proceeding to trial, however, such considerations will normally counsel an exercise of district court jurisdiction over state claims based on the same nucleus of operative facts unless the court can point to some substantial countervailing consideration. In this case, Lindsey (P) and Coughanour (P) maintain that their state claims substantially predominate over their federal claims, and therefore that this case falls within the purview of § 1367(c)(2). That subsection reads: "The district courts may decline to exercise supplemental jurisdiction over a claim under subsection (a) if . . . (2) the claim substantially predominates over the claim or claims over which the district court has original jurisdiction." The district court is in a better position than we are to pass upon this contention. Moreover, even if § 1367(c) does not authorize a refusal to hear the state claims based on the current record, it might provide that authority later in the proceeding. Accordingly, the following observations concerning § 1367(c)(2) are offered by way of guidance. First, the "substantially predominates" standard of § 1367(c)(2) was fashioned as a limited exception to the operation of the doctrine of pendent jurisdiction—a doctrine that seeks to promote judicial economy by litigating in one case all claims that arise out of the same nucleus of operative fact. When a district court exercises its discretion not to hear state claims under § 1367(c)(2), the advantages of a single suit are lost. Thus, § 1367(c)(2)'s authority should only be invoked where there is an important countervailing interest to be served by relegating state claims to the state court. This will normally be the case only where a state claim constitutes the real body of a case, to which the federal claim is only an appendage. In this case, the state issues do not appear to substantially predominate in terms of proof. Nor do they appear to substantially predominate in terms of the comprehensiveness of the remedy sought. The remedy sought based on the state claims is the same remedy sought based on the federal claims: damages for the same set of injuries to the plaintiffs. The difficulty of avoiding duplicative recoveries is a factor tending to weigh against litigating related federal and state claims in different fora. This leaves the issue of whether the state claims can be said to substantially predominate in terms of the scope of the issues raised. While the state claims here outnumber the federal claims, the "substantially predominate" standard is not satisfied simply by a numerical count of the claims. An analysis more sensitive to the relevant interests is required. Here, Lindsey (P) and Coughanour's (P) civil rights claims based on the alleged assault, arrest, and prosecution are nevertheless governed exclusively by federal law. Additionally, the probable cause issue, as well as others, are issues of federal law and concern. There are certainly a complementary set of state law issues arising out of the state claims based on the alleged assault, arrest, and prosecution, but these issues do not appear to substantially predominate over the comparable but distinct federal issues. Further, Lindsey (P) and Coughanour (P) do not suggest that these state issues are more important, complex, or time consuming to resolve, or are in any other way more significant than their federal counterparts. In short, while we do not foreclose the parties from hereafter arguing, and the district court from hereafter considering, the issue posed by § 1367(c)(2), we think it unlikely that either will be able to point to a countervailing interest that would justify bifurcating this case into a federal and a state suit that will essentially duplicate each other. Writ of mandamus granted.

Analysis:

Borough of West Mifflin v. Lancaster is a complicated opinion about a complicated issue of civil procedure—the interplay between supplemental jurisdiction and a district court's power to remove or remand a case in which federal question claims are intertwined with state law claims. To understand the interplay of these two concepts, one must first understand the basics of each. Supplemental jurisdiction, as the prior cases have disclosed, involves the combination of state and federal claims. When a party has only a state claim, it must be brought in state court. However, under 28 U.S.C. § 1367, the supplemental jurisdiction statute, when state law claims arise from a common nucleus of operative fact with those of a federal claim, the law allows a federal court to adjudicate the issues that otherwise would be outside the purview of federal subject matter jurisdiction. Removal, on the other hand, deals with the transfer of a case from one forum to another. In the case of 28 U.S.C. § 1441, the subject of the *West Mifflin* opinion, that transfer is from state court to federal court. Remand, also permitted by § 1441, is, as used here, the transfer of a case from federal district court to state court on the ground that state court is the proper place to adjudicate the claims. So how do these principles, and the statutory provisions in which they are embodied, interact with one another? *West Mifflin* provides the answer. The key lies in the distinction made between the phrases "separate and independent" (found in § 1441(c)), and "common nucleus of operative fact" (found in *United Mine Workers of America v. Gibbs*). Specifically, *West Mifflin* makes it clear that if a federal claim is "separate and independent" from a state claim, then it cannot possibly arise from a "common nucleus of operative fact" shared by the state claim. Similarly, if federal and state claims arise from a "common nucleus of operative fact," then they cannot be "separate and independent" for the purposes of § 1441(c). So why is this distinction important? Because in order for a federal court to be permitted to remand a case or individual claims in a case to state court under § 1441(c), the state and federal claims must be "separate and independent" from one another. Thus, according to *West Mifflin*, if supplemental jurisdiction cannot be declined because federal and state claims arise from a "common nucleus of operative fact," then a federal court cannot remand any of those linked claims to state court, but must hear the entire case. To put it another way, *West Mifflin* limits the power and discretion of a federal court to remand state claims over which it has supplemental jurisdiction.

■ CASE VOCABULARY

BIFURCATE: To divide into two parts.

COMMON NUCLEUS OF OPERATIVE FACT: The standard used for determining whether supplemental jurisdiction should be exercised; if two claims arise from the same "common nucleus of operative fact," or from the same occurrence or controversy, supplemental jurisdiction is appropriate.

FORA: Plural form of the word "forum," or more than one forum.

MANDAMUS: A writ issued by a higher court ordering a lower court to perform a specified act in a certain manner.

REMAND: As used in *West Mifflin*, the transfer of a case that originated in state court but was removed to federal court back to state court.

REMOVAL: As used in *West Mifflin*, the transfer of a case from state court to federal court.

SEPARATE AND INDEPENDENT: Claims that do not arise from the same common nucleus of operative fact, or claims over which supplemental jurisdiction is not appropriate.

CHAPTER FIVE

Venue, Transfer, and Forum Non Conveniens

Reasor–Hill Corp. v. Harrison

Instant Facts: An insecticide-spraying company is suing to collect the debt due for their services from a Missouri land-owner who, in turn, is trying to sue an Arkansas-based insecticide manufacturer for having had his crop ruined by their product.

Black Letter Rule: In a suit for injuries to land, Arkansas can take jurisdiction even if the land is situated in another state.

Bates v. C & S Adjusters, Inc.

Instant Facts: Alleging federal statutory violation, debtor sues a Pennsylvania collection agency in New York court and asserts jurisdiction is proper because their collection notices were forwarded to him in New York.

Black Letter Rule: Venue is proper in the district in which a debtor resides and to which a collection notice was forwarded.

Hoffman v. Blaski

Instant Facts: An Illinois resident brings suit in Texas against a Texas corporation which, in turn, transfers the suit back to the Illinois venue even though the Illinois resident could not have initiated the suit there himself.

Black Letter Rule: A federal court in which suit was properly commenced was not entitled under § 1404(a) to transfer a case to a district in which the plaintiff could not have properly commenced suit.

Piper Aircraft Co. v. Reyno

Instant Facts: The Scottish heirs of plane crash victims in Scotland try to sue for wrongful death in an American court because American courts recognize wrongful death as a cause of action and are known generally to be more favorable to plaintiffs than the courts in Scotland.

Black Letter Rule: The fact of a substantive law being less favorable to plaintiffs in an alternative forum should not be given conclusive or even substantial weight in applying the doctrine of forum non conveniens.

Reasor–Hill Corp. v. Harrison

(Insecticide Manufacturer) v. *(Judge Taking Jurisdiction)*

220 Ark. 521, 249 S.W.2d 994 (1952)

ARKANSAS STATE COURT MAKES RADICAL DECISION TO ACCEPT JURISDICTION IN A SUIT OVER LAND LOCATED IN ANOTHER STATE

■ **INSTANT FACTS** An insecticide-spraying company is suing to collect the debt due for their services from a Missouri land-owner who, in turn, is trying to sue an Arkansas-based insecticide manufacturer for having had his crop ruined by their product.

■ **BLACK LETTER RULE** In a suit for injuries to land, Arkansas can take jurisdiction even if the land is situated in another state.

■ **PROCEDURAL BASIS**

Appeal from overruled motion to dismiss on the basis of lack of jurisdiction.

■ **FACTS**

Planters Flying Service sprayed Barton's cotton crop in Missouri with an insecticide manufactured by Reasor-Hill (P) in Arkansas. Barton refused to pay for the spraying because his crop was damaged. Rather, he attempted to sue Reasor-Hill (P) in an Arkansas court for negligently putting on the market a chemical unsuited to spraying cotton. Reasor-Hill (P) moved to dismiss Barton's cross-complaint in Arkansas because the damaged property is located in Missouri. With the majority of American courts behind them, Reasor-Hill (P) asserts that jurisdiction cannot be established in one state over property located in another. Judge Harrison (D) overruled the motion to dismiss on the ground that a suit in Arkansas is the only way Barton can have a remedy since Reasor-Hill (P) could not be served in Missouri.

■ **ISSUE**

In a suit for injuries to land, is venue proper in one state when the injured land is located in another?

■ **DECISION AND RATIONALE**

(Smith, J.) Yes. In Arkansas, venue is proper in a suit for injuries to land even if the land is located in another state. The leading case on the issue is *Livingston v. Jefferson,* in which Livingston tried to sue Jefferson (yes, *that* Jefferson) in Virginia (where the President lived) for trespass in Louisiana. The suit was dismissed for lack of jurisdiction and has been followed ever since. Three reasons have been given for adherence to *Livingston,* but none of them are persuasive enough in this case. First is the ground that courts are in no position to pass judgement on land outside their jurisdiction. This is a sound argument if the outside jurisdiction is foreign, but not if it is within the states. Every court possesses the laws of every state in their libraries and they have not hesitated to interpret the laws of other states in transitory actions. Second is the argument that since the tort must take place where land is situated, the remedy for damages to that land should be pursued before the defendant leaves the jurisdiction. This applies to foreign tortfeasors who could be detained at a border, but this does not apply to American citizens who have and use the right to travel freely from jurisdiction to jurisdiction. Finally, there is the ground that courts should be loath to subject their own citizens to suits by outsiders, but this does not mean that courts should provide a sanctuary for those who wilfully or wrongfully caused injury to a landowner in our sister states. Hallelujah. There is no reason, therefore, to follow *Livingston* anymore. Rather, Barton should have his day in court. Writ denied.

■ DISSENT

(McFaddin, J.) Just because every court has a library that includes the laws of other states does not mean that every court is prepared to determine those laws. Furthermore, the fact that *Livingston* is more applicable to foreign defendants is inconsistent with the principle of federalism that each state is like a sovereign unto itself. The majority characterizes them as no more than local administrative units. Finally, the desire not to afford citizens sanctuary from damage actions by citizens of other states is a concern for the Legislature rather than the courts. The "ancient landmark," *Livingston*, should be left undisturbed.

Analysis:

The first thing to note about this case is that the venue law is based on a state statute, which is not to be confused with a federal venue statute. Every state makes a statutory provision for the place of trial, usually designated by county. These statutes are varied from state to state but typically make application distinctions between residents and nonresidents and persons and property. Venue rules are said to have developed for the sake of greatest convenience, but states differ as to whom that convenience is geared, plaintiff, defendant, or someone else entirely. Another distinction between types of venue is the one created between "local action" rules and "transitory action" rules. *Reasor-Hill* is an older example of a "transitory action" rule. This means Arkansas treated real property the same way it would treat movable property, as though the out-of-state property was "brought into" the state. This approach has been highly criticized and the majority of states in this country follow the "local action" rule. This means that a state court takes jurisdiction over property that is located locally and pass on jurisdiction on property outside the state. The policy behind this type of rule is rather an assumption that the court in which the fixed property is located must be the best able to deal with the issue in dispute.

■ CASE VOCABULARY

CASE OF FIRST IMPRESSION: Case which presents an entirely novel question of law for the decision of the court; one without precedent.

CROSS-COMPLAINT: Pleading identical to a complaint whereby a defendant sues the plaintiff.

FULL FAITH AND CREDIT CLAUSE: Federal constitutional requirement that public acts, records and judicial proceedings of one state be respected by each of the sister states.

TRANSITORY ACTION: Action that may pass or be changed from one place to another; not local.

WRIT: Mandatory precept issued by the court of justice, requiring some performance or giving authority and commission to have it done.

Bates v. C & S Adjusters, Inc.

(*Debtor*) v. (*Collection Agency*)
980 F.2d 865 (2nd Cir. 1992)

COURT DECLARES VENUE IS PROPER IN, ALTHOUGH NOT NECESSARILY LIMITED TO, THE DISTRICT WHERE A DEBTOR RESIDES IF THAT IS WHERE A SUBSTANTIAL PART OF THE EVENTS GIVING RISE TO THE CLAIM AROSE

■ **INSTANT FACTS** Alleging federal statutory violation, debtor sues a Pennsylvania collection agency in New York court and asserts jurisdiction is proper because their collection notices were forwarded to him in New York.

■ **BLACK LETTER RULE** Venue is proper in the district in which a debtor resides and to which a collection notice was forwarded.

■ **PROCEDURAL BASIS**

Appeal from dismissal of action due to improper venue.

■ **FACTS**

Living in Pennsylvania, Phillip E. Bates (P) incurred a debt to a creditor who referred Bates' (P) account to C & S Adjusters (D), also a Pennsylvania-based business. C & S (D) proceeded to send Bates (P) a collection notice on his account. Unbeknownst (an under-used word if any) to C & S (D), Bates (P) had moved to New York and the collection notice was forwarded to him there. Subsequently, Bates (P) decided to sue C & S (D) for violations of the Fair Debt Collection Practices Act ("FDCPA") and he commenced the action in New York. Although both parties agree that the applicable venue statute is 28 U.S.C § 1391(b)(2), C & S (D) filed to dismiss the suit because New York is an improper venue.

■ **ISSUE**

Within the meaning of the federal venue statute, does venue exist in a district in which the debtor resides and to which a collection notice was forwarded?

■ **DECISION AND RATIONALE**

(Newman, J.) Yes. Venue exists in the district where the debtor resides and to which a collection notice was forwarded, regardless of the collection agency's lack of intent to forward the notice. The applicable federal venue statute allows an action to be brought in "a judicial district in which a substantial part of the events or omissions giving rise to the claim occurred." This language is the result of a 1990 amendment from "the judicial district in which the claim arose." That earlier language was reviewed in the landmark case, *Leroy v. Great Western United Corp.* [holding that a Texas corporation could not bring suit in Texas against Idaho officials just because the effect of the officials' action might be felt in Texas]. *Leroy* considered a number of factors which are relevant to selecting the best venue because the case holding is based on the presumption that only one district can be the place "where the claim arose." This does not apply with equal force to the new version of the statute since there can be more than one district where a "substantial part of the events" occurred. In the instant case, it is also inconsequential that the collection notice was not forwarded to Bates (P) deliberately by the agency but automatically by the trusty U.S. Postal Service. After all, Congress enacted the FDCPA to prevent the harm of abusive debt practices on consumers and that harm does not occur until *receipt* of the collection notice. It is also presumable that C & S (D) should have expected that their notice would get forwarded to New York since they did not mark the envelope "do not forward." (Guilty by sin of omission.) Consequently, receipt of a collection notice is a "substantial part of events giving rise to a claim" and the place where that notice was received constitutes proper venue. Reversed and remanded.

Analysis:

The important thing to note about this case is that it interprets and applies a *federal* venue statute to the action, specifically § 1391 of Title 28 in the U.S. Code. Section 1391 is divided according to category of action—diversity cases, federal question cases, suits against federal agents—but each category provides that venue is proper in the district where a "substantial part of the events or omissions giving rise to the claim occurred." This language is the product of a 1990 amendment from the litigation-breeding phrase "where the claim arose." As you can imagine, there are varying degrees of difficulty in determining where a claim arose which depend on the nature of the claim. For example, if a claim is neither for a physical injury or even for an easily identified injury, it is hard to pinpoint the locus of the damage and the plain language of the phrase fails to clarify matters. The new venue-granting phrase, whose meaning was evolving out of cases like *Bates,* is perhaps no more clear from the plain-meaning point of view but at least it does not seek to narrow down the venue options to a single district. By allowing the courts discretion to pick from a few districts, the statute not only made venue selection more convenient and intuitive, but it also echoed what many courts were already practicing.

■ CASE VOCABULARY

COUNTERCLAIM: Counter demand made by defendant against plaintiff, asserting a cause of action independent from the plaintiff's complaint.

FEDERAL QUESTION CASE: Cases arising under the Constitution, acts of Congress or treaties, and involving their interpretation and action.

Hoffman v. Blaski

(Transferee Judge) v. *(Illinois Resident)*

363 U.S. 335, 80 S.Ct. 1084, 4 L.Ed.2d 1254 (1960)

SUPREME COURT RESOLVES CONFLICT BETWEEN THE CIRCUITS AND INTERPRETS FEDERAL VENUE–TRANSFER POWER IN FAVOR OF PLAINTIFFS

■ **INSTANT FACTS** An Illinois resident brings suit in Texas against a Texas corporation which, in turn, transfers the suit back to the Illinois venue even though the Illinois resident could not have initiated the suit there himself.

■ **BLACK LETTER RULE** A federal court in which suit was properly commenced was not entitled under § 1404(a) to transfer a case to a district in which the plaintiff could *not* have properly commenced suit.

■ **PROCEDURAL BASIS**

Mandamus proceeding for order compelling judge to reverse his order and transfer action from Illinois back to Texas.

■ **FACTS**

Blaski (P) is an Illinois resident who brought a patent infringement action in Texas against Howell, who runs his corporation in Texas. After being served with process, Howell moved to transfer venue to Illinois under § 1404(a) of the federal venue statute. Blaski (P) moved to remand the action back to Texas because, he alleged, the Texas court had no power to transfer to the Illinois court. Blaski (P) argued that since *he* could not have brought the action in Illinois initially, because that is not where Howell resides or does business, the Texas court could not do so either. Judge Hoffman (D) of the Illinois District Court disagreed and denied Blaski's (P) motion for remand. Blaski (P) naturally goes over Hoffman's (D) head, as is done in big business, and petitions for a writ of mandamus in the Seventh Circuit which that court granted. Now that Blaski (P) is where he wants to be, Howell is not. Howell argues that the phrase "where [the action] might have been brought" in § 1404(a) should be broadly construed (in his favor) to extend not only to the time the action is brought but also to the time of the transfer. In other words, Howell might move to Illinois between the time the action is brought and the time it is transferred to Illinois, in which case jurisdiction *would* be proper. Howell even generously promises not to use his power to object to venue if it is transferred to Illinois.

■ **ISSUE**

Can a federal court in which an action was properly brought transfer that action by virtue of its rights under § 1404 to a district in which the plaintiff did not have the right to bring it?

■ **DECISION AND RATIONALE**

(Whittaker, J.) No. Section 1404 does not give a federal court in which an action was properly brought the power to transfer the action to a district in which plaintiff could *not* have properly brought the action. The plain language of the statute clearly states that venue transfer is proper to the place "where the action might have been brought." Obviously, this applies to where it might have been brought by plaintiffs. Therefore, if the plaintiff could not have brought an action in Illinois, the defendant can't motion to transfer into it. To allow the defendant that kind of power would grossly discriminate against plaintiffs. By promising not to object to the transferee venue, defendants would be able to transfer into any district convenient to them. Plaintiffs, on the other hand, would still be statutorily limited in their choices of venue and could not freely motion to transfer because the defendant would still retain the right to object to improper venue. Consequently, "the power of a District Court under § 1404(a) to transfer an action to another district is made to depend not upon the wish or waiver of the defendant but, rather, upon whether the transferee district was one in which the action 'might have been brought' by the plaintiff." Seventh Circuit order affirmed.

■ DISSENT

(Frankfurter, J.) A phrase like "where [an action] might have been brought" may carry more than one meaning. The most appropriate determination of that meaning is one which would allow an action in the forum which is most convenient and just. Not only will there be very few forums where a plaintiff has a "right" to sue, but these are not necessarily the most convenient and just forums for both parties. The "plain meaning" analysis by the majority overlooks this crucial policy consideration. The more sensible approach is to reason that because a defendant has the right to object to venue and move for transfer, the transferee court of his choice should be presumed acceptable unless there are strong considerations otherwise. As to the argument that plaintiffs would be strongly discriminated against by allowing defendants to move venue, this is but a factor in whether there are "strong considerations otherwise" in a particular case. Furthermore, a plaintiff is not always automatically discriminated against just because venue was granted in a place other than his first choice. The majority's view is therefore too restrictive and defies the greater interests of justice.

Analysis:

The pertinent rule in this case is § 1404 of Title 28 in the U.S. Code which allows a defendant to request a change of venue. The statute states that "for the convenience of parties and witnesses, in the interest of justice, a district court may transfer any civil action to any other district or division where it might have been brought." Aside from the possibility of automatic waiver of venue transfer by failing to raise an objection at the proper time, a defendant may object to the plaintiff's chosen venue either if it is improperly chosen or if it is properly chosen but it is not the most convenient and just. When a § 1404 motion to transfer venue on grounds of inconvenience is granted, however, the Supreme Court has stated in *Van Dusen v. Barrack* that the substantive laws of the transferor court carry over to the receiving transferee court. In *Hoffman,* then, Howell would still have been subject to Texas law even if the action was transferred to Illinois. Strategically, there are a number of reasons why this would still be a desirable move for a defendant. The new location could create undue inconvenience to the plaintiff in obtaining witnesses and information or simply the inconvenience of having to fly and establish lodging in a distant location for the duration of a trial. The transfer could also be intended to throw off the plaintiff's attorney, who is probably more familiar with the rules of the court in which he initiated the suit. Finally, the transferee court may be reputed for interpreting the law, even of another state, in a way that is more favorable to defendant's position.

■ CASE VOCABULARY

FORUM NON CONVENIENS: Discretionary doctrine whereby a court which has jurisdiction over a case may decline to exercise it, as there is no substantive reason for the case to be brought there, or if in presenting the case in that court it would create a hardship on the defendants or witnesses.

MANDAMUS PROCEEDING: Proceeding compelled by the court as an absolute duty.

TRANSFEREE FORUM: Forum to which a proceeding is transferred.

Piper Aircraft Co. v. Reyno

(Plane Manufacturer) v. *(Estate Representative)*

454 U.S. 235, 102 S.Ct. 252, 70 L.Ed.2d 419 (1981)

SUPREME COURT ANNOUNCES THAT DISMISSAL FOR FORUM NON CONVENIENS IS NOT AN ABUSE OF JUDICIAL DISCRETION MERELY BECAUSE THE LAW OF THE ALTERNATIVE FORUM IS LESS FAVORABLE TO PLAINTIFFS

■ **INSTANT FACTS** The Scottish heirs of plane crash victims in Scotland try to sue for wrongful death in an American court because American courts recognize wrongful death as a cause of action and are known generally to be more favorable to plaintiffs than the courts in Scotland.

■ **BLACK LETTER RULE** The fact of a substantive law being less favorable to plaintiffs in an alternative forum should not be given conclusive or even substantial weight in applying the doctrine of forum non conveniens.

■ PROCEDURAL BASIS

Appeal from order of the Court of Appeals granting jurisdiction in Pennsylvania District Court.

■ FACTS

A commercial aircraft manufactured in Pennsylvania by Piper (D) crashed in the Scottish highlands. Reports suggested either that the airplane suffered mechanical failure or pilot error. (Legend says only the Lochness monster witnessed it.) At the time of the crash, the plane was registered in Great Britain, operated by a Scottish air taxi service, subject to Scottish air traffic patrol, and full of Scottish residents. Naturally, then, Gaynell Reyno (P), the estate administratrix and legal secretary to the attorney who filed the wrongful death suit on behalf of the Scottish families, brought the action in California state court. Claiming negligence and strict liability, Reyno (P) admits that the choice of forum was determined by the fact that the laws regarding liability, capacity to sue, and damages are more favorable in America than in Scotland. Oddly enough, Piper (D) didn't see this as a boon and moved to transfer the case to a Pennsylvania District Court and subsequently motioned to dismiss it under the doctrine of forum non conveniens. The District Court granted the motion but the Circuit Court overruled it and remanded for trial in Pennsylvania because the plaintiffs would be disadvantaged more by the law in Scotland than the law in Pennsylvania.

■ ISSUE

Should a motion to dismiss for forum non conveniens be denied merely because the substantive law of an alternative forum is less favorable to plaintiffs?

■ DECISION AND RATIONALE

(Marshall, J.) No. In analyzing a motion to dismiss for forum non conveniens, courts should not give dispositive or even substantial weight to the fact that the alternative forum is less favorable to plaintiffs than the one in which the action was initially brought. At present, the doctrine of forum non conveniens is designed to avoid conducting complex exercises in comparative law. Giving substantial weight to such a consideration, however, would render the doctrine effectively moot. On the one hand, if courts give much weight to change in substantive law, they will be forced to interpret the law of foreign jurisdictions to make the determination of which is the more favorable forum. On the other hand, it is clear that plaintiffs initially select the most favorable forum to them so courts won't even have to consider a motion to dismiss for forum non conveniens because any alternative forum will be less favorable to plaintiffs than the one they selected for themselves. Of course, substantial weight may be given to the disadvantaging law of an alternative forum if the remedy would be so clearly inadequate that dismissal would not be "in the interests of justice." This is not the case for the Scottish plaintiffs, though. Other considerations are more important in this case. First, the strong presumption in *Gulf Oil Corp. v. Gilbert* [creating a balancing test of public and private interests between plaintiffs and defendants to determine the appropriateness of a forum non conveniens dismissal] in favor of the plaintiff's choice of forum applies with less force when, as in this case, the plaintiffs are foreign. It is unreasonable to assume that a foreign plaintiff's choice of an American forum is for the sake of convenience. Great deference to a foreign plaintiff would also encourage an onslaught of litigation to be brought in the United States which could and should have been brought in a foreign forum. Second, private policy interests dictate that the result of the District Court should have been upheld. Because witnesses and much relevant evidence are more easily located in Great Britain, there would be fewer evidentiary problems in Scotland. Furthermore, because it is far more convenient to resolve all claims in one trial and because Piper (D) would have a hard time impleading potential third party defendants in the United States, the trial should be held in Scotland. Third, public policy interests recommend toward trial in Scotland because Piper (D) and Hartzell, the other defendant, would have two different sets of law applied to them. Piper (D) would be subject to Pennsylvania law whereas Hartzell would still be subject to Scottish law, with which the Pennsylvania court is understandably unfamiliar. In addition, Scotland has a greater interest in this litigation than does the United States because, apart from Piper (D) and Hartzell, all potential plaintiffs and defendants are either Scottish or English. Finally, the important base consideration is that reversal of a dismissal for forum non conveniens should only be granted if the District Court abused its discretion. In the instant case, it is apparent that the District Court did no such thing, but the Circuit Court simply disagreed with their analysis. Reversed.

Analysis:

Piper represents the current approach to the forum non conveniens doctrine. An underlying tenet of *Piper* is that forum non conveniens doctrine applies only when venue is proper in the initial forum and there is an alternative forum available. In *Piper,* for example, the choice was clearly between the United States and Scotland, both the litigants and the courts were aware of this. The crucial progressive step that *Piper* takes is to establish a balancing test of the conveniences to all parties, without allowing any one factor to be dispositive. The result of such a balancing test is rarely removal to another country. Most courts would not grant such a drastic forum non conveniens motion until all other jurisdictional possibilities have been exhausted. This is an important policy to keep in mind when you remember that a forum non conveniens dismissal is not equivalent or analogous to a § 1404 transfer of venue. Transfer is usually much easier for a court to execute and more predictable for the parties involved since the transferor court's substantive law will be applied regardless of the location of the transferee court. Dismissal is obviously a more final, more difficult decision for a court to make and, therefore, it requires a greater showing of inconvenience than transfer. Once the case is out of the dismissing court's hands, the burden falls on the plaintiffs to re-submit the case in the alternate forum.

■ CASE VOCABULARY

ADMINISTRATRIX: One (female) appointed to handle the affairs of one who has died intestate, or who has left no executor.

CHOICE–OF–LAW RULES: Rule applied in a court to determine whether federal or state law is applicable and/or whether the law of the forum or some other state applies.

FORUM NON CONVENIENS: Discretionary doctrine whereby a court which has jurisdiction over a case may decline to exercise it, as there is no substantive reason for the case to be brought there, or if in presenting the case in that court it would create a hardship on the defendants or witnesses.

IMPLEAD: To bring a third party, who is allegedly liable, into a lawsuit for purposes of indemnity or contribution.

INDEMNITY: The obligation of one person to make good on a loss of another; an assurance to compensate for the damage caused by another.

CHAPTER SIX

Ascertaining the Applicable Law

Swift v. Tyson

Instant Facts: Joseph Swift (P) sued to collect on a note, and the decision hinged on whether New York common law governed the action.

Black Letter Rule: Federal courts must follow only state statutory laws, not state judge-made common law, in cases in which state law applies.

Erie R. Co. v. Tompkins

Instant Facts: Harry Tompkins (P), a pedestrian who was injured when a bar protruding from an Erie Railroad (D) car struck him, sued in federal court and alleged that federal common law should govern the action.

Black Letter Rule: Federal courts are required to apply the substantive common law of the state in which they sit.

Guaranty Trust Co. v. York

Instant Facts: York (P) sued Guaranty Trust Co. (D) in federal district court in order to avoid an application of a state statute of limitations, which would have barred the case in state court.

Black Letter Rule: A federal court with diversity jurisdiction must apply state procedural rules, such as a statute of limitations, if those rules have a substantial effect on the outcome of the litigation.

Byrd v. Blue Ridge Rural Electric Cooperative, Inc.

Instant Facts: Byrd (P) sued Blue Ridge Rural Electric Cooperative (D) for negligence, and a factual determination of the status of Byrd's (P) employment was required in order to determine the appropriate forum.

Black Letter Rule: Federal courts may apply federal rules, even if state rules are outcome-determinative, if federal policy in enacting the rules outweighs state policy.

Hanna v. Plumer

Instant Facts: Hanna (P) sued in Massachusetts district court for negligence following an auto accident, using a substituted service of process rather than in-hand service as required by Massachusetts statute.

Black Letter Rule: Federal rules of civil procedure within the scope of the Rules Enabling Act control over state outcome-determinative rules.

Walker v. Armco Steel Corp.

Instant Facts: A carpenter injured by an alleged faulty nail brought suit in federal court within two years of the injury, but he failed to serve process within the time period required by Oklahoma statute.

Black Letter Rule: Federal rules should not be construed broadly so as to place them in direct conflict with state rules, which would require a federal court to apply the federal rule.

Stewart Organization, Inc. v. Ricoh Corp.

Instant Facts: Relying on a forum selection clause in their dealership agreement, Ricoh (D) attempted to transfer a case from Alabama to New York district court.

Black Letter Rule: A federal rule, established within the limits of the constitution, prevails over conflicting state law provided the federal rule is sufficiently broad to cover the issue.

Gasperini v. Center for Humanities, Inc.

Instant Facts: A federal court applied a state law standard in reviewing whether a jury's verdict was excessive, despite the contrary mandate of the Seventh Amendment.

Black Letter Rule: A state statute governing reexamination of jury awards can be given effect by federal appellate courts without violating the Seventh Amendment's reexamination clause.

Mason v. American Emery Wheel Works

Instant Facts: Whit Mason (P) was injured by an emery wheel constructed by the American Emery Wheel Works (D) and sued this manufacturer, although he was not in privity of contract with the manufacturer.

Black Letter Rule: A federal court may apply recent trends in state law over outdated state common law.

Clearfield Trust Co. v. United States

Instant Facts: A check issued by the United States (P) was fraudulently cashed at a J.C. Penny store and was endorsed by Clearfield Trust (D), who was paid by the United States.

Black Letter Rule: Federal courts may create federal common law in order to serve national interests and fill gaps in federal statutes.

Miree v. Dekalb County

Instant Facts: Miree (P) and several others, who were severely injured when an airplane they were flying took off from an airport operated by DeKalb County (D) and collided with a flock of birds, sued as third-party beneficiaries to a contract between DeKalb County (D) and the FAA.

Black Letter Rule: Federal common law should not be applied when it would serve no significant federal interests.

Boyle v. United Tech Corp.

Instant Facts: Boyle (P) sued United Technologies Corp. (D), a government contractor, for design defects in a helicopter that crashed, resulting in his son's death.

Black Letter Rule: When federal interests significantly conflict with state law liability, federal law preempts state law.

Dice v. Akron, Canton & Youngstown R. Co.

Instant Facts: Dice (P), who sued under the Federal Employers Liability Act in Ohio state court for damages allegedly resulting from a railroad's negligence, maintained that he was fraudulently induced to sign a release of claims by the railroad.

Black Letter Rule: When adjudicating federal claims, state courts must apply federal substantive law as well as federal procedures which are a substantial protection of rights under the federal claim.

Swift v. Tyson

(*Buyer*) v. (*Third-Party Creditor*)

41 U.S. (16 Pet.) 1 (1842)

FEDERAL COURTS DO NOT HAVE TO APPLY STATE COMMON LAW

■ **INSTANT FACTS** Joseph Swift (P) sued to collect on a note, and the decision hinged on whether New York common law governed the action.

■ **BLACK LETTER RULE** Federal courts must follow only state statutory laws, not state judge-made common law, in cases in which state law applies.

■ PROCEDURAL BASIS

Action for payment of debt.

■ FACTS

George Tyson (D) purchased land from Maine land speculators by giving a negotiable instrument to the speculators and receiving a bill of exchange. Tyson (D) did not know at the time that the speculators did not own the land. One of the speculators then delivered Tyson's (D) note to Joseph Swift (P), a Maine banker, to satisfy a pre-existing debt. [Presumably the speculator headed west shortly thereafter, since he was not named in the suit]. Swift (P) sought payment from Tyson (D), but Tyson (D) refused to pay on the grounds that he had been fraudulently induced to purchase the property. Swift (P) then sued Tyson (D) in federal court in New York based on diversity jurisdiction. The principal question of the case was whether New York common law or other newly-developing common law should govern. Pursuant to New York judge-made contract law, the speculator's fraud would provide Tyson (D) with a defense. However, pursuant to the law of negotiable instruments developing in England, Swift (P) would be able to collect on the note as long as he accepted the note without notice of the fraud. In choosing the applicable law, the court could look to the Rules of Decision Act—Section 34 of the Judiciary Act of 1789—which established that the laws of the several states, except where federal law otherwise provides, shall be regarded as rules of decision in civil actions.

■ ISSUE

Does the phrase "laws of several states" require federal courts to follow only state statutory laws and not state judge-made common law, in cases where state law applies?

■ DECISION AND RATIONALE

(Story, J.) Yes. The phrase "laws of several states" in the Rules of Decision Act requires federal courts to follow state statutory law but not state common (judge-made) law. In ordinary language, the phrase "laws" does not encompass the decisions of courts. Likewise, the Supreme Court has consistently presumed that the Rules of Decision Act is limited only to positive statutes of states. In the case at hand, even though New York's common law would provide a defense to Tyson (D), federal courts are not required to apply this law.

Analysis:

The Supreme Court took an extremely narrow view of the phrase "laws of several states." In modern times, it seems clear that state judge-made common law is just as important and valid as state statutory law. Thus, it is difficult to understand Justice Story's logic that, in ordinary language, the decisions of courts do not constitute laws. However, Story's opinion must be placed in its appropriate context. The case was decided at a time where common law was rapidly developing, and Justice Story felt that a federal judge should be able to consult all available authorities (including the newly-developing common law of England and laws of other jurisdictions) in order to make a decision. Story did not want the federal judge's discretion limited by the decisions of some lowly state-court judge in New York. Furthermore, the Court had strong policy reasons for desiring to enforce Tyson's (D) note, since the government was seeking stability in interstate commerce and wanted to encourage businessmen like Swift (P) to trust out-of-state negotiable instruments. Indeed, these policy considerations were substantial enough to allow the *Switt v. Tyson* interpretation of the Rules of Decision Act to stand for nearly one-hundred years, until *Erie R. Co. v. Tompkins.*

■ **CASE VOCABULARY**

BILL OF EXCHANGE: A written order requiring the party to whom the order is addressed to pay a certain amount of money, either on demand or at a fixed future time.

NEGOTIABLE INSTRUMENT: A written promise to pay a certain amount of money, either on demand or at a fixed future time.

Erie R. Co. v. Tompkins

(Railroad) v. *(Injured Pedestrian)*

304 U.S. 64, 58 S.Ct. 817 (1938)

LANDMARK U.S. SUPREME COURT DECISION REQUIRES FEDERAL COURTS TO APPLY STATE SUBSTANTIVE COMMON LAW

■ **INSTANT FACTS** Harry Tompkins (P), a pedestrian who was injured when a bar protruding from an Erie Railroad (D) car struck him, sued in federal court and alleged that federal common law should govern the action.

■ **BLACK LETTER RULE** Federal courts are required to apply the substantive common law of the state in which they sit.

■ **PROCEDURAL BASIS**

Appeal by writ of certiorari from award of damages for negligence.

■ **FACTS**

While walking along a footpath on Erie Railroad Co.'s (D) right of way in Pennsylvania, Harry Tompkins (P) was struck by a bar extending from the side of Erie Railroad's (D) train. Tompkins (P) sued Erie (D) for negligence based on diversity jurisdiction in a New York federal district court. Tompkins (P) argued that, pursuant to Swift (Federal courts must follow only state statutory laws, not state judge-made common law) the "general law" of most states—that a railroad owes a duty of ordinary care to pedestrians such as Tompkins (P)—should govern the case. However, Erie (D) contended that Pennsylvania common law should govern, under which a traveler like Tompkins (P) would be regarded as a trespasser to whom Erie (D) only owed a duty to avoid wanton negligence. The District Court and Court of Appeals sided with Tompkins (P) and applied the general law, awarding Tompkins (P) $30,000 in damages. Supreme Court granted certiorari.

■ **ISSUE**

In the absence of a state statute governing a claim, is a federal court required to apply federal common law?

■ **DECISION AND RATIONALE**

(Brandeis, J.) No. A federal court is required to apply the common law of the state in which it sits rather than federal common law. First, *Swift* was based on a misinterpretation of the Rules of Decision Act, § 34 of the Judiciary Act of 1789. Research into § 34 has revealed that the Rules of Decision Act requires federal courts exercising diversity of citizenship jurisdiction to apply the unwritten common law of the state in which they sit, in addition to the written statutory law. [How convenient for Brandeis that this research had been conducted!] Second, *Swift* has led to discrimination against parties sued in federal courts via diversity jurisdiction. Under *Swift*, a plaintiff of diverse citizenship could choose whether state or federal law would apply by selecting either the state forum or the federal forum. Thus, application of the Swift rule has prevented uniformity of laws throughout the nation. Third, *Swift's* construction of § 34 was itself unconstitutional, allowing federal courts to create federal common law and giving federal courts much more power than the Constitution allows. Congress has no power to declare substantive rules of common law applicable in state actions, and hence Congress could not have delegated this power to federal courts via § 34. Indeed, there is no federal general common law. Thus, Swift's interpretation of § 34 was unconstitutional, although § 34 itself is not unconstitutional. The case is remanded for the lower court to address Tompkins' (P) claim based on Pennsylvania state common law. Reversed.

■ CONCURRENCE

(Reed, J.) The *Swift* doctrine should have been overturned without analyzing the constitutionality of that decision. *Swift* turned on an interpretation of the Rules of Decision Act, in which the phrase "laws of several states" was found to include only state statutory law. The majority in the case at hand should have read this phrase more broadly, to include judge-made law, rather than addressing the constitutionality of *Swift's* interpretation.

■ DISSENT

(Butler, J.) Erie's (D) petition for a writ of certiorari presented only the question of whether Tompkins' (P) claims should have been decided based on Pennsylvania common law and, if so, whether Tompkins (P) was guilty of contributory negligence. No constitutional question was suggested or argued, and the consideration of no constitutional question was necessary in adjudicating this case. Thus, the majority has overstepped their bounds. Moreover, where a constitutional question is forwarded, the procedure established by Congress requires the court to certify the issue to the Attorney General so that the United States might intervene as a party and be heard on the constitutional question. [Apparently the U.S. Supreme Court is incapable of formulating the astute arguments that the Attorney General would raise.] Rather, the judgment below should have been reversed on the grounds of Tompkins' (P) contributory negligence.

Analysis:

This case, announcing the Erie Doctrine, has been called one of the most important cases in American legal history. Indeed, the majority's decision has far-reaching implications for all diversity cases brought in federal courts. Federal courts must now apply the substantive laws of the states in which they sit, whether statutory or judge-made. The holding affirms the concepts of state sovereignty and autonomy. In addition, the holding accomplishes a vital goal, preventing discrimination and encouraging uniformity by eliminating "forum shopping." Under *Swift*, a diverse plaintiff could choose the law most favorable to a claim by selecting either a federal or state forum. The Erie Doctrine results in the same law being applied regardless of forum. Notice that Pennsylvania law was applied in this case, even though the suit was brought in New York district court, since New York's choice of law rules dictate applying the law of the state where the injury occurred.

■ CASE VOCABULARY

GENERAL LAW: An form of federal common law, found by the *Erie* court to be illusory and nonexistent, but previously encompassing such broad-ranging topics as contracts, torts, property, real estate, and remedies.

Guaranty Trust Co. v. York

(*Trustee*) v. (*Note-Holder*)
326 U.S. 99, 65 S.Ct. 1464 (1945)

FEDERAL COURTS MUST APPLY STATE PROCEDURAL RULES IF THOSE RULES ARE OUTCOME–DETERMINATIVE

■ **INSTANT FACTS** York (P) sued Guaranty Trust Co. (D) in federal district court in order to avoid an application of a state statute of limitations, which would have barred the case in state court.

■ **BLACK LETTER RULE** A federal court with diversity jurisdiction must apply state procedural rules, such as a statute of limitations, if those rules have a substantial effect on the outcome of the litigation.

■ **PROCEDURAL BASIS**

Appeal by writ of certiorari from ruling for plaintiff on procedural issue.

■ **FACTS**

York (P) sued Guaranty Trust Co. (D), a trustee, for an alleged breach of fiduciary duty by Guaranty's (D) failure to protect York's (P) interest in a trust. York (P) brought the action in federal court by diversity of citizenship. York's (P) claim involved allegations of fraud and misrepresentation, with relief relying on equitable principles. If brought in state court, the claim would have been barred by the state statute of limitations. Guaranty (D) argued that the state statute of limitations should apply to this action brought in federal court. The Circuit Court of Appeals held that a federal district court, hearing a suit brought in equity, was not required to apply the state statute of limitations. The Supreme Court granted certiorari.

■ **ISSUE**

Is a federal court with diversity jurisdiction required to apply a state statute of limitations?

■ **DECISION AND RATIONALE**

(Frankfurter, J.) Yes. Federal courts with diversity jurisdiction must apply state statutes of limitation if those statutes would have a substantial effect on the outcome of the litigation. Pursuant to the Erie doctrine, federal courts must apply state substantive common law. State law is substantive if it would have a substantial effect upon the eventual outcome of the case. In the case at hand, the statute of limitations would substantially affect the outcome of this case, precluding York (P) from recovering on the claim. Although statutes of limitation are typically considered procedural, and although federal courts generally follow federal rules of procedure, the mere "procedural" or "substantive" label is not controlling. Statutes of limitation can, in fact, be substantive within the bounds of the Erie doctrine. The intent of Erie was to insure that federal courts exercising diversity jurisdiction arrive at the same result that a state court would in the same action. And in this case, the state court would have been required to dismiss the suit for failure to meet the statute of limitations. The federal district court must arrive at the same substantive result, and thus the case must be remanded to the state court for dismissal [Do you ever wonder why the Supreme Court can't just dismiss the suit?] Furthermore, although federal courts sitting in equity may create their own equitable remedies, they cannot do so if this results in denying substantive state law. Reversed.

Analysis:

This case, although purporting to follow the Erie doctrine, actually expanded the Erie doctrine considerably. The Erie decision required a federal court to apply state tort law, since federal courts do not have the authority to create general federal tort law. This case, however, requires federal courts to apply state procedural rules—even if they result in a different outcome than an application of federal procedural rules—whenever the state procedural rules have a substantial effect on the outcome of the litigation. Thus, whenever state and federal procedural rules conflict, the York outcome-determinative test is used to decide if the state law must control. Although it is not specifically stated in the opinion, the obvious conclusion is that the federal statute of limitation, or the more lenient equitable defense of laches, would allow the suit to proceed. This court, as in Erie, wants to prevent forum shopping, discrimination, and non-uniformity in the application of laws that would result if a plaintiff whose statute of limitations had run could simply file in federal court and obtain a more lenient statute of limitations. However, it is important to realize the limits on the outcome-determinative test. A federal court sitting in equity could still, following the York opinion, grant traditional federal equitable remedies such as injunctions, whether or not the same remedy was available in state court.

■ CASE VOCABULARY

EQUITY: A system of justice governed by concerns for fairness rather than by strict rules.

FIDUCIARY DUTY: A high duty to act on another's behalf, usually imposed on a party in control of another's person or property.

Byrd v. Blue Ridge Rural Electric Cooperative, Inc.

(Injured Worker) v. *(Electric Company)*

356 U.S. 525, 78 S.Ct. 893 (1958)

BALANCING TEST ALLOWS FEDERAL COURTS TO APPLY SOME FEDERAL RULES, EVEN WHERE STATE RULES ARE OUTCOME–DETERMINATIVE

■ **INSTANT FACTS** Byrd (P) sued Blue Ridge Rural Electric Cooperative (D) for negligence, and a factual determination of the status of Byrd's (P) employment was required in order to determine the appropriate forum.

■ **BLACK LETTER RULE** Federal courts may apply federal rules, even if state rules are outcome-determinative, if federal policy in enacting the rules outweighs state policy.

■ **FACTS**

Byrd (P) was temporarily employed as a lineman for a construction company that contracted with Blue Ridge Rural Electric Cooperative (D), an electric company. Byrd (P) was injured while connecting power lines, and he sued Blue Ridge (D) in a federal district court in South Carolina based on diversity of citizenship. Blue Ridge (D) defended that, pursuant to South Carolina's Workmen's Compensation Act, Byrd (P) was statutorily required to bring a Workmen's compensation action rather than the civil action at hand. Thus, a factual dispute existed as to whether Byrd (P) should be considered a statutory employee for purposes of Workmen's compensation. Pursuant to South Carolina common law, such a determination could only be decided by the trial judge [well, a jury would probably be *capable* of reaching a conclusion, but state law favored a judge's determination]. However, federal procedural rules would require the issue to go to a jury. The Court of Appeals for the Fourth Circuit reversed a jury verdict for Byrd (P), and Byrd (P) obtained certiorari for a decision as to who should rule on the factual dispute.

■ **ISSUE**

Should state procedural rules that are potentially outcome-determinative always be applied by federal courts?

■ **DECISION AND RATIONALE**

(Brennan, J.) No. State procedural rules that are potentially outcome-determinative should not necessarily be followed in every instance. The factual determination of Byrd's (P) employment status may have been substantially different depending on whether a judge or jury decides the outcome. Nevertheless, York's outcome-determinative test is not the sole test to be applied in this situation. Rather, a balancing test should be used, weighing the state policies behind the rule against countervailing federal policies. Consistent with the Erie doctrine, state procedural rules which affect the outcome of a suit should be applied if they are an integral part of some substantive right [whatever that means!]. In the case at hand, South Carolina common law required the determination of a person's status as a statutory employee to be determined by the judge. However, South Carolina's rationale for the rule was not to further some substantive state policy and was not bound up with the definition of the rights and obligations of the parties. It was simply a procedural practice established by the South Carolina Supreme Court with no strong policy in support. Thus, the balance shifts in favor of countervailing federal policies, including the Seventh Amendment's right to a jury trial. Since the application of South

Carolina common law in this case would deprive Byrd (P) of the right to a jury trial, and since South Carolina does not have sufficient policy goals which justify the denial of this fundamental right, the federal procedure of allowing a jury to decide the issue should be followed. Reversed and remanded.

Analysis:

This case establishes a balancing test which modifies York's outcome-determinative test in some instances. Specifically, when strong federal policies outweigh weak state policies, even an outcome-determinative state law may yield to federal rules. The Supreme Court thus managed to save federal law, including the Federal Rules of Civil Procedure, from partial extinction that federal law faced following York. While this decision seemingly restores a proper balance between applying federal and state law, it proved to be not nearly as easy to apply as a strict York outcome-determinative test. Indeed, courts often experienced difficulties in objectively determining whether state or federal policies were stronger in a given instance. Moreover, a careful reading of the case reveals a fundamental question: Why did the Supreme Court conduct a Rules of Decision analysis, since according to the Supremacy Clause, the Seventh Amendment to the Constitution should *always* prevail over state law? The likely answer is, as stated above, that the Court wanted to modify York's Rules of Decision analysis in order to protect the Federal Rules of Civil Procedure if called into question in the future. Indeed, such a case did arise seven years later, in *Hanna v. Plumer.*

■ CASE VOCABULARY

WORKMEN'S COMPENSATION: System allowing for compensation for an injured employee without the necessity of jury trial and without requiring the employee to prove negligence.

Hanna v. Plumer

(Injured Party) v. *(Deceased Driver)*
380 U.S. 460, 85 S.Ct. 1136 (1965)

THE FEDERAL RULES OF CIVIL PROCEDURE TRIUMPH OVER STATE OUTCOME DETERMINATIVE RULES

■ **INSTANT FACTS** Hanna (P) sued in Massachusetts district court for negligence following an auto accident, using a substituted service of process rather than in-hand service as required by Massachusetts statute.

■ **BLACK LETTER RULE** Federal rules of civil procedure within the scope of the Rules Enabling Act control over state outcome-determinative rules.

■ **PROCEDURAL BASIS**

Appeal by writ of certiorari of summary judgment against plaintiff suing for damages for negligence.

■ **FACTS**

Hanna (P) was injured in an automobile accident with Louise Plumer Osgood (D), who was deceased at the time the complaint was filed. Hanna (P) sued in federal district court in Massachusetts, based on diversity of citizenship. Service was made upon Plumer's (D) executor by leaving copies of the summons and complaint with the executor's wife, in compliance with Rule 4(d)(1) of the federal rules of civil procedure. Plumer's (D) executor contended that such service was improper, as it did not conform to Massachusetts's statutory requirement for personal service upon the executor. The District Court granted Plumer's (D) executor's motion for summary judgment, holding that the Massachusetts statute was outcome-determinative and thus, pursuant to York [federal court must apply outcome-determinative state law], service was improper. The Court of Appeals for the First Circuit affirmed, holding that the Massachusetts statute was substantive and outcome-determinative and must have been followed.

■ **ISSUE**

Where a federal rule of civil procedure conflicts with outcome-determinative state law, must the state law control the issue?

■ **DECISION AND RATIONALE**

(Warren, J.) No. Where a Federal rule of civil procedure conflicts with outcome-determinative state law, the federal Rule may control in certain circumstances. The Rules Enabling Act, 28 U.S.C. § 2072, granted the Supreme Court the authority to prescribe rules of procedure for federal district courts. The Rule at issue, Rule 4(d)(1), was enacted within the limits of the Rules Enabling Act since it regulates procedures of the district courts. Thus, were there no conflicting state procedure, Rule 4(d)(1) would clearly control and service of process would have been proper in the case at hand. Plumer's (D) executor counters that federal district courts must apply outcome-determinative state rules, such as Massachusetts's service statute. However, this argument is flawed for several reasons. As the Court held in Byrd, federal courts may apply federal rules, even if state rules are outcome-determinative, in certain situations. Indeed, at this stage in the proceedings, Massachusetts's rule is outcome-determinative [Hindsight is 20–20]. However, outcome-determination analysis was never intended to serve as a talisman. When the conflict between federal and state law is outcome-determinative, state law should be applied only in reference to the twin aims of the Erie doctrine: discouragement of forum-shopping and avoidance of inequitable administration of the laws. At the time of filing and serving a complaint, a litigant would not forum-shop and choose a federal court simply because Rule 4(d)(1) requires a slightly easier method of service than Massachusetts's rule. Furthermore, this case is fundamentally different from the situations in Erie and York, neither of which dealt with a federal rule of civil procedure conflicting with state law. Erie and York never intended to bottle up federal courts when a constitutional Rule of civil procedure was involved. Congress's exercise of constitutional power in the Rules Enabling Act, and the subsequent establishment of Rule 4(d)(1), do not have to bow to state-created rights and procedures. Rule 4(d)(1) is constitutional, valid, and controls the case at hand. Reversed.

■ CONCURRENCE

(Harlan, J.) Justice Warren's majority opinion minimizes the importance of Erie by condensing the case to two aims. Erie was worried about more than just forum shopping and the inequitable administration of the laws. Rather, Erie's overlying mandate was that there should not be two conflicting systems of law controlling citizens, and Erie recognized that the creation of substantive state law by federal courts—when such law goes beyond constitutional limits—should be avoided. The proper line of approach in determining whether to apply a state or federal rule is to inquire if the choice would substantially affect those primary decisions respecting human conduct that our constitutional system leaves to state regulation [seemingly the court must be omniscient to apply this test!]. If so, the state law should prevail, even in the face of a conflicting federal rule. Thus, federal rules of civil procedure such as Rule 4(d)(1) should not necessarily control in every situation. Nevertheless, as Chief Justice Warren correctly determined, the application of Massachusetts's service rule would not have a substantial effect on the distribution of estates, the state policy which the Massachusetts rule is intended to serve.

Analysis:

Justice Warren established an important analysis for situations in which a federal rule of civil procedure conflicts with state law, requiring the twin aims of Erie to be sacrificed in order for state law to apply to a given situation. Moreover, the majority opinion asserted the strong national interest in establishing and following uniform federal procedural rules in federal courts. In so doing, Warren may have rescued the Rules of Civil Procedure by providing a simple and clear test for determining the validity of federal procedural rules that conflict with state laws. In considering this case, it is important to take a close look at the Rules Enabling Act, 28 U.S.C. § 2072. Indeed, § 2072(a) allows the Supreme Court to establish federal rules of procedure. However, § 2072(b) limits this power, requiring that such rules do not abridge, enlarge or modify any substantive right. Notice that both § 1652, the Rules of Decision Act, and § 2072 require federal courts to use substantive state law. However, the § 2072 test for "substantive" is unclear. Two tests have been proposed for determining if a state law is a "substantive right." Harlan's test maintained that state law is substantive if it is designed to have a substantial impact on the way people conduct themselves outside of court. An alternative test was developed by Ely (Chief Justice Warren's clerk, who probably wrote much of the opinion). This test declared that a state law is substantive if it does something besides regulating efficiency and fairness of a state's litigation process. Thus, Ely's test looks to the purpose of the state law, and Harlan's looks more to the effect of the law. Courts continue to disagree on the interpretation of § 2072(b)'s "substantive right."

■ CASE VOCABULARY

ERGO: Latin word meaning "therefore."

EXECUTOR: A person appointed by a deceased to distribute property according to the decedent's will.

Walker v. Armco Steel Corp.

(*Carpenter*) v. (*Nail Manufacturer*)
446 U.S. 740, 100 S.Ct. 1978 (1980)

FEDERAL RULES MAY NOT BE READ BROADLY SO AS TO BRING THEM IN IMMINENT CONFLICT WITH STATE RULES

■ **INSTANT FACTS** A carpenter injured by an alleged faulty nail brought suit in federal court within two years of the injury, but he failed to serve process within the time period required by Oklahoma statute.

■ **BLACK LETTER RULE** Federal rules should not be construed broadly so as to place them in direct conflict with state rules, which would require a federal court to apply the federal rule.

■ **PROCEDURAL BASIS**

Writ of certiorari from dismissal of complaint for negligence barred by statute of limitations.

■ **FACTS**

Walker (P), a carpenter, was injured while pounding a nail manufactured by Armco Steel (D) when the head of the nail shattered and struck Walker (P) in the eye. Since there was diversity of citizenship, Walker (P) sued Armco (D) for negligence in an Oklahoma district court. Walker (P) filed the complaint within two years of the injury, but service of process was not made on Armco's (P) authorized agent until more than two years and three months after the injury. Armco (P) filed a motion to dismiss on grounds that Oklahoma's 2-year statute of limitations was not met, since Oklahoma law does not deem an action "commenced" until service of process upon on a defendant. Walker (P) countered that Rule 3 of the Federal Rules of Civil Procedure should control this federal-court action. Pursuant to Rule 3, an action is commenced upon filing a complaint with a federal court. The District Court dismissed the complaint as barred by the Oklahoma statute of limitations, and the Court of Appeals for the Tenth Circuit affirmed. The Supreme Court granted certiorari.

■ **ISSUE**

Should a federal rule be construed broadly so as to place it in direct conflict with a state rule, requiring a federal court to apply the federal rule?

■ **DECISION AND RATIONALE**

(Marshall, J.) No. When deciding whether a federal and state rule are in direct conflict, the federal rule should be read based on its plain meaning. Indeed, in cases of direct conflict between a federal rule and a state rule, *Hanna* should be followed [federal rules of civil procedure within the scope of the Rules Enabling Act control over state outcome-determinative rules]. However, in the case at hand, a plain reading of Rule 3 of the Federal Rules of Civil Procedure reveals no conflict with the Oklahoma statute of limitations [the court failed to explain how, exactly, to conduct a "plain" reading]. Rule 3 simply states that a cause of action is commenced upon the filing of a complaint in federal court. The Rule does not state an intention to toll a state statute of limitations, and it certainly does not purport to displace state tolling rules. Thus, Rule 3 and the Oklahoma statute of limitations can exist side by side without conflict, as Rule 3 acts to toll only federal statutes of limitation. Therefore, the *Hanna* analysis does not apply.

Rather, our holding parallels an indistinguishable prior decision, *Ragan v. Merchants Transfer & Warehouse* Co. [Kansas' two-year statute of limitations requires dismissal of action filed within two years, where service was not affected within the requisite period, since the Court could not give the cause of action longer life in federal court than it would have had in the state court without adding something to the cause of action—a violation of Erie]. Furthermore, the failure to apply Oklahoma's statute of limitations would result in an inequitable distribution of law, which the *Erie* and *Hanna* courts sought to prevent. Affirmed.

Analysis:

This case presents the final piece in the somewhat puzzling analysis that a federal court must undergo when the application of a federal rule and state rule would cause disparate results. The first question is whether the federal rule directly conflicts with the state rule. In *Hanna*, Rule 4 providing for substituted service was found to directly clash with the Massachusetts service statute. Without questioning this holding, the *Walker* court finds that a plain reading of Rule 3 does not place it in conflict with the Oklahoma statute of limitations. It is difficult to reconcile these two approaches to interpretation of similar Federal Rules of Civil Procedure. Nevertheless, the second step of the analysis may well have yielded the same result, whether or not the federal and state rules were determined to directly conflict. If Rule 3 *did* directly conflict with the Oklahoma statute, the court would have to look to the Rules Enabling Act, particularly § 2072(b), and determine if Rule 3 abridged a substantive state law. Since the purpose and effect of the Oklahoma statute was to give potential defendants some peace of mind if not served within the required period, this statute was probably substantive, in which case state law would prevail. However, if Rule 3 *did not* directly conflict with the Oklahoma statute, as the Supreme Court found, then a federal court may not circumvent the outcome-determinative state law. To do so, where the Federal Rule does not control the issue, would require a federal court to create federal common law, expressly prohibited since the Erie decision.

■ CASE VOCABULARY

STARE DECISIS: A doctrine requiring courts to adhere to previously-decided case law.

Stewart Organization, Inc. v. Ricoh Corp.

(*Dealer*) v. (*Manufacturer*)

487 U.S. 22, 108 S.Ct. 2239 (1988)

FEDERAL STATUTES, CONSTITUTIONAL AND BROAD ENOUGH TO CONTROL THE ISSUE, CONTROL OVER STATE LAW

■ **INSTANT FACTS** Relying on a forum selection clause in their dealership agreement, Ricoh (D) attempted to transfer a case from Alabama to New York district court.

■ **BLACK LETTER RULE** A federal rule, established within the limits of the constitution, prevails over conflicting state law provided the federal rule is sufficiently broad to cover the issue.

■ **PROCEDURAL BASIS**

Writ of certiorari from reversal of denial of motion to transfer venue in a contractual action.

■ **FACTS**

Stewart Organization (P) entered into a dealership agreement to market the copier products of Ricoh (D). The agreement contained a forum-selection clause, requiring all disputes arising out of the contract to be litigated in Manhattan court. However, when relations soured between the companies, Stewart (P) sued Ricoh (D) in an Alabama district court. Ricoh moved to transfer the case to a New York district court, pursuant to 28 U.S.C. § 1404(a) and in reliance on the forum selection clause. Holding that Alabama law controls the transfer motion, and noting that Alabama looks unfavorably upon contractual forum-selection clauses, the District Court denied the motion. However, the Eleventh Circuit reversed, concluding that the venue question was governed by federal law, under which the forum selection clause was enforceable. The Supreme Court granted certiorari.

■ **ISSUE**

When a constitutional federal rule directly conflicts with state law, does the federal rule prevail?

■ **DECISION AND RATIONALE**

(Marshall, J.) Yes. A simple two-part analysis covers cases in which federal statutes conflict with state law. First, the court must determine whether the statute is sufficiently broad to control the issue before the court. In the case at hand, § 1404(a) is broad enough to cover the issue of whether to transfer the case to a Manhattan court in accordance with the forum selection clause. Section 1404(a) allows a district court, in its discretion, to weigh a number of factors in determining whether transfer is appropriate. The forum selection clause is a significant factor in this analysis, and the district court must analyze the convenience of the forum, the parties' preferences, the fairness of the transfer, and the parties' relative bargaining power in agreeing to the clause. A state policy—such as Alabama's—that focuses on only a subset of these considerations by specifically disfavoring forum selection clauses, cannot co-exist with § 1404(a). Thus, there is a direct conflict between § 1404(a) and the Alabama approach, and we arrive at the second step in the analysis. Section 1404(a) must be applied only if it represents a valid exercise of Congress' authority under the constitution. This is an easy determination, as the constitutional provision for a federal court system carries with it the congressional power to prescribe rules under which these courts operate. Section 1404(a) was a valid exercise of Congress' power under the Necessary and Proper Clause of the Constitution. Remanded for a determination of the forum selection clause on Ricoh's (D) § 1404(a) motion.

Analysis:

Justice Marshall finally manages to consolidate and simplify the analysis for situations where federal statutes conflict with state law. There is really only one step to this analysis, as the constitutional question in all of these cases can be settled by a cursory reference to Congress' power. The more-difficult step has been stated in various ways in cases from *Hanna* to *Walker* to *Stewart*. The previous explanation, that the federal statute must be in direct conflict with a state law, has been changed slightly by Marshall, who now declares that the federal statute must be sufficiently broad to control the issue before the court. These two tests are really saying the same thing. The "issue before the court" is, of course, one for which state law supplies an answer. Thus, state law is necessarily broad enough to control the issue. Furthermore, where a federal rule is also sufficiently broad, there exists a definite conflict between the rule and state law. This new approach perhaps helps explain the questionable earlier ruling in *Walker*, where Rule 3 and an Oklahoma statute appeared to be in direct conflict. Under the new test. Rule 3 was clearly not sufficiently broad enough to control the issue, as it was not in itself a statute of limitations. If Justice Marshall had only reformulated the test in *Walker* perhaps that opinion would have been a bit more clear.

■ **CASE VOCABULARY**

EN BANC: A session (usually of a Court of Appeal) in which all of the members participate in a decision.

INTERLOCUTORY APPEAL: An appeal taken during the course of trial on some decision reached in the case.

Gasperini v. Center for Humanities, Inc.

(Photographer) v. *(Producer)*

518 U.S. 415, 116 S.Ct. 2211 (1996)

STATE LAW STANDARDS FOR REVIEW OF JURY VERDICTS SURVIVE NOTWITHSTANDING THE SEVENTH AMENDMENT

■ **INSTANT FACTS** A federal court applied a state law standard in reviewing whether a jury's verdict was excessive, despite the contrary mandate of the Seventh Amendment.

■ **BLACK LETTER RULE** A state statute governing reexamination of jury awards can be given effect by federal appellate courts without violating the Seventh Amendment's reexamination clause.

■ PROCEDURAL BASIS

Writ of certiorari reviewing vacation of judgment denying motion for new trial for excessiveness of jury verdict.

■ FACTS

William Gasperini (P) was a journalist who photographed events in Central America beginning in 1984. He supplied 300 slides to The Center for Humanities, Inc. ("Center") (D). The Center (D) lost the slides and could not return them to Gasperini (P). Gasperini (P) sued in federal district court, invoking diversity jurisdiction. The Center (D) conceded liability, and the issue of damages was tried before a jury. Gasperini's (P) expert witnesses testified to the "industry standard" and valued a lost slide at $1,500. Accordingly, the jury awarded Gasperini (P) $450,000 in compensatory damages. The Center (D) moved for a new trial, arguing that the verdict was excessive. The district court denied the motion, but the Second Circuit Court of Appeals vacated the judgment. The Second Circuit applied New York law, which required that a state appellate division must determine whether an award deviates materially from what would be reasonable compensation. Based on state holdings, the Second Circuit viewed the award as excessive because other factors (such as the uniqueness of the slides and the photographer's earning level) should be considered. Thus, the Second Circuit set aside the verdict and ordered a new trial, unless Gasperini (P) would accept $100,000. Gasperini (P) contended that the Second Circuit erred in applying New York law. He argued that the Seventh Amendment controls and provides that no fact tried by a jury should be reexamined in a federal court except under federal common law. Federal common law refuses to overturn jury verdicts unless they "shock the conscience." The United States Supreme Court granted certiorari.

■ ISSUE

Can a state statute governing reexamination of jury awards be given effect by federal appellate courts without violating the Seventh Amendment's reexamination clause?

■ DECISION AND RATIONALE

(Ginsburg, J.) Yes. A state statute governing reexamination of jury awards can be given effect by federal appellate courts without violating the Seventh Amendment's reexamination clause. The New York statute's "deviates materially" standard is both procedural and substantive. It is substantive in that the standard controls how much a plaintiff can be awarded, and it is procedural in that it assigns decision-making authority to New York appellate courts. We feel that federal courts can adequately apply the "deviates materially" standard. The standard is "outcome-affective" because failure to apply it would unfairly discriminate against citizens of the forum state or be likely to cause a plaintiff to choose the federal court. In the case at hand, the Second Circuit utilized the "deviates materially" standard. We agree with Gasperini (P) that the Second Circuit did not attend to an essential characteristic of the federal court system when it applied the New York statute. The federal appeals court must overturn a trial judge's decision only if it constitutes an abuse of discretion. It is not clear that the Second Circuit utilized this standard, or that the district court checked the relevant New York decisions demanding more than analysis of the "industry standard" in awarding damages. Accordingly, we vacate the judgment of the Second Circuit and remand the case to the district court so that the trial judge may test the verdict under New York's "deviates materially" standard.

■ DISSENT

(Stevens, J.) While I agree with the majority's reasoning, I would affirm the judgment of the Second Circuit. The district court had the power to consider the propriety of the jury's award, and it erred. Nothing prohibits the reviewing court from correcting the judge's error. I do not agree that the "abuse of discretion" standard is relevant. *Erie* simply requires federal appellate courts to apply the damage control standard state law supplies.

■ DISSENT

(Scalia, J.) The majority holds that a state practice, relating to the division of duties between state judges and juries, must be followed by federal courts. This is contrary to our prior cases. The Seventh Amendment was designed specifically to preclude federal appellate reexamination of facts found by a jury. It puts to rest apprehensions of new trials by appellate courts. Federal appellate courts cannot review the factual issues such as the measure of damages. At common law, reexamination of facts found by a jury could only be undertaken by trial courts. And it is not possible to review the denial of a new trial without engaging in a reexamination of the facts tried by the jury. Changing the standard by which trial judges review jury verdicts does, contrary to the majority's statement, disrupt the federal system and is plainly inconsistent with federal policy. The majority commits the classic *Erie* mistake of regarding whatever changes the outcome as substantive; furthermore, it exaggerates the difference that the state standard will make. Moreover, in my view, the *Erie* question should not even be reached in this case. The Federal Rules of Civil Procedure provide the standard to be applied by a district court in ruling on a motion for new trial. A new trial may be granted for any reason which new trials have been granted in actions in federal courts. This is undeniably a federal standard, and the standard is sufficiently broad to cause a direct collision with state law. Thus, the federal court must apply the Federal Rule.

Analysis:

This complicated case illustrates how courts can shape the determination of whether federal or state law applies. By characterizing the New York statute as "substantive," the majority justifies its tenuous holding that the reviewing appellate court (the Second Circuit) should have applied New York's "deviates materially" standard of review of a jury verdict. The majority further justifies its position by returning to the outdated *York* outcome-determinative test. All in all, the holding seems to be in clear violation of the clear mandate of the Seventh Amendment. But the majority thinks that the holding is not inconsistent with the Seventh Amendment and that the federal and state interests can be accommodated. Justice Scalia's dissent is well-reasoned and merits close attention. The review of jury verdicts does, as Scalia points out, necessarily require a reexamination of the facts of the case. Federal courts are constitutionally forbidden to undertake such factual inquiries. Finally, Scalia makes a good point in mentioning Federal Rule 59. This federal procedural standard limits new trials only based upon federal law, and it certainly appears to be in direct conflict with the New York statute. As we have seen in other cases, federal courts are required to apply federal law in such a situation.

■ CASE VOCABULARY

REMITTITUR: The procedure for reducing an excessive jury verdict.

TALISMAN: Something with apparent magical power.

Mason v. American Emery Wheel Works

(Machine User) v. *(Manufacturer)*

241 F.2d 906 (1st Cir. 1957)

FEDERAL COURTS MAY ANALYZE TRENDS IN STATE LAW AND APPLY THESE TRENDS OVER PREVIOUS CASE AUTHORITY

■ **INSTANT FACTS** Whit Mason (P) was injured by an emery wheel constructed by the American Emery Wheel Works (D) and sued this manufacturer, although he was not in privity of contract with the manufacturer.

■ **BLACK LETTER RULE** A federal court may apply recent trends in state law over outdated state common law.

■ **PROCEDURAL BASIS**

Appeal from dismissal of complaint for damages for negligence.

■ **FACTS**

Whit Mason (P) was injured when an emery wheel disintegrated and exploded in his face. Mason (P) sued The American Emery Wheel Works (D), the original manufacturer of the wheel, in a Rhode island federal district court. American Emery (D) had sold the wheel to the Hoover Company, who attached it to a bench grinding machine and sold it to Miller Falls Company, who then sold the machine to Komp Equipment. Mason's (P) employer, T.H. Pearce Company, purchased the wheel from Komp Equipment. Thus, there was no privity of contract between American Emery (D) and Mason (P). The District Court dismissed the complaint, holding that it was compelled to follow an old Mississippi law (*Ford Motor Co. v. Myers*), which held that a manufacturer was not liable for negligence in manufacture where there is no privity of contract between user and manufacturer. Mason (P) appealed to the First Circuit Court of Appeals.

■ **ISSUE**

Must a federal court apply all state common law, even if that law is outdated?

■ **DECISION AND RATIONALE**

(Magruder, J.) No. A state law that has been undercut by subsequent state court decisions, although not expressly overruled, does not necessarily have to be followed by federal courts. Although the *Erie* doctrine requires federal courts to apply state substantive law, the harsh rule of *Ford v. Myers* is clearly outdated. [Apparently this is outdated because the Court wants it to be outdated!] New trends in Mississippi products liability law point to the inapplicability of the *Ford* decision, which has lost its binding force and has become eroded over time. Recent decisions by the Mississippi Supreme Court indicate a willingness to overturn *Ford*, although an appropriate situation for expressly overruling this precedent has not yet arisen. Nevertheless, we are convinced that the court would accept the more modern doctrine if given the opportunity [Perhaps you didn't know that federal courts were mind-readers.] Order of District Court is vacated and remanded.

■ **CONCURRENCE**

(Hartigan, J.) In the case at hand, it is clear that the Mississippi Supreme Court would overrule *Ford* if given the opportunity. Nevertheless, our holding presents a difficult problem for district court judges who must apply the *Erie* doctrine in situations where conflicting dicta are unclear. The question of how clear dicta must be to prevail over a prior controlling decision is not easily answered.

Analysis:

The *Erie* Doctrine established a seemingly easy framework for analysis, namely that federal courts must apply the relevant state law of the courts in which they sit. However, it is often difficult to ascertain precisely what state law is. This case takes a large and sensible step forward in the workings of the *Erie* Doctrine. If the applicable state law is an outdated precedent which state courts have simply not had the occasion to overrule, federal courts may ignore the law. Rather, based on recent state-court holdings which demonstrate a necessity to, yet do not completely, overrule outdated precedent, federal courts may reasonably predict and apply the trends in the developing body of state law. Nevertheless, as the concurrence mentions, this presents a problem for district court judges, especially in cases where the trend among state court decisions is not as clear-cut as in this case.

■ CASE VOCABULARY

DICTA: Statements made by judges that are not necessarily involved in deciding the case at hand, but that nevertheless carry a certain amount of influence in subsequent decisions.

PRIVITY OF CONTRACT: A relationship between two or more contracting parties, usually carrying with it the right to sue on the contract.

Clearfield Trust Co. v. United States

(*Check Endorser*) v. (*Drawee*)
318 U.S. 363, 63 S.Ct. 573 (1943)

THERE *IS* A FEDERAL COMMON LAW

■ **INSTANT FACTS** A check issued by the United States (P) was fraudulently cashed at a J.C. Penny store and was endorsed by Clearfield Trust (D), who was paid by the United States.

■ **BLACK LETTER RULE** Federal courts may create federal common law in order to serve national interests and fill gaps in federal statutes.

■ **PROCEDURAL BASIS**

Writ of certiorari appealing reversal of decision to dismiss complaint for guaranty of endorsements.

■ **FACTS**

A check issued by the United States (P), for services performed under the Federal Emergency Relief Act of 1935, was stolen and fraudulently cashed by an unknown person at a J.C. Penney store. J.C. Penney endorsed the check to Clearfield Trust (D), and Clearfield Trust (D) in turn endorsed the check, guaranteeing all prior endorsements, and collected the funds from the government. Neither J.C. Penney nor Clearfield Trust (D) suspected forgery. Furthermore, federal officials did not inform either of these endorsers of the forgery until eight months after learning that the intended recipient had not received the check. The United States (P) sued Clearfield Trust (D) in federal court. The District Court applied Pennsylvania law, under which the United States (P) was barred from recovery due to the unreasonable delay in giving notice of the forgery, and dismissed the complaint. The Court of Appeals for the Third Circuit reversed, and the Supreme Court granted certiorari.

■ **ISSUE**

May a federal court create federal common law to issues involving a national interest?

■ **DECISION AND RATIONALE**

(Douglas, J.) Yes. The *Erie* doctrine does not apply in this situation, and the federal court may apply federal common law. The rights and duties of the United States (P) in commercial paper should be governed by federal rather than local law. [This sounds good, but the court does not justify why it is true!] In the instant action, the check was issued for services performed under a federal statute, but the statute failed to cover situations of forgery. With regards to commercial paper issued by the United States (P), there is a strong national interest in applying a uniform body of law. In ascertaining what federal law should govern this action, the Court can look to *United States v. National Exchange Bank* [prompt notice of discovery of forgery is not a condition precedent to suit]. While the Court now holds that the lack of prompt notice may be a defense, Clearfield Trust (D) failed to prove that its injury was caused by the United States' (P) delay. Rather, Clearfield Trust's (D) neglect in accepting the forger's signature occasioned its own loss. Furthermore, Clearfield Trust (D) can still maintain an action against J.C. Penney. Affirmed.

Analysis:

This case clearly overrides the statement in *Erie* that "[t]here is no federal common law." However, the Court gives little justification for going against this established precedent. The case would have made much more sense had it conducted an analysis under § 1652, the Rules of Decision Act. As construed by *Erie*, this Act requires federal courts to apply state common law *except where an Act of Congress (or a federal treaty or the constitution) otherwise provides.* In the case at hand, an Act of Congress (the Federal Emergency Relief Act) authorized the United States (P) to write the check. However, there was a gap in the statute, since it did not address situations in which an endorser forged the signature. In order to establish a cohesive, uniform federal law to cover the situation, the Court fills the statute's gap by creating specialized federal common law. Congress could have filled this gap itself, or Congress could have delegated powers to federal courts to fill gaps in statutes. Although Congress took neither approach, apparently Justice Douglas presumes that federal courts are constitutionally entitled to fill gaps in federal statutes with specialized federal common law. It is interesting to note that this entire controversy, which consumed so much court time and which led to a powerful holding, centered on a check which was worth only $24.20!

■ CASE VOCABULARY

COMMERCIAL PAPER: Any of a number of negotiable instruments, such as a bank check or promissory note, for the payment of money.

Miree v. DeKalb County

(Injured Party) v. *(Airport Operator)*

433 U.S. 25, 97 S.Ct. 2490 (1977)

FEDERAL COMMON LAW SHOULD NOT BE APPLIED WHEN IT WOULD SERVE NO SIGNIFICANT FEDERAL INTERESTS

■ **INSTANT FACTS** Miree (P) and several others, who were severely injured when an airplane they were flying took off from an airport operated by DeKalb County (D) and collided with a flock of birds, sued as third-party beneficiaries to a contract between DeKalb County (D) and the FAA.

■ **BLACK LETTER RULE** Federal common law should not be applied when it would serve no significant federal interests.

■ **PROCEDURAL BASIS**

Writ of certiorari from affirmance of dismissal of complaint for damages for breach of contract.

■ **FACTS**

Several plaintiffs, including Miree (P), brought an action against DeKalb County (D), the owner of an airport, after a fatal air crash shortly following takeoff from the airport. Miree (P) and the others sought to impose liability as third-party beneficiaries to a contract between DeKalb County (D) and the Federal Aviation Administration (FAA). Under this contract, DeKalb County (D) agreed to restrict the uses of land adjacent to the airport to activities compatible with normal airport operations, including takeoff and landing. Miree (P) and the others alleged that DeKalb County (D) breached the contract with the FAA by operating a garbage dump adjacent to the airport, and that the cause of the accident was the ingestion of birds swarming from the dump into the engines of the aircraft. [Apparently the bird's survivors had no standing to assert a claim!] The suit was brought for negligence, nuisance and breach of contract in a Georgia district court, which granted DeKalb County's (D) motions to dismiss each of the claims. All courts agreed that the negligence and nuisance claims were without merit, and the District Court held that Miree (P) and others could not sue on the contracts because of the county's governmental immunity. The Court of Appeals for the Fifth Circuit, sitting en banc, applied federal law and held that Miree (P) and the others had no standing to sue as third-party beneficiaries. Five members of the Court of Appeals dissented, arguing that there was no identifiable federal interest justifying the imposition of federal common law. The Supreme Court granted certiorari.

■ **ISSUE**

Should federal common law be used when its application would serve no significant federal interests?

■ **DECISION AND RATIONALE**

(Rehnquist, J.) No. Federal common law should not be applied where there are no significant interests of the United States at stake. In the case at hand, the relevant inquiry is narrow: Whether Miree (P) and the others had standing to sue DeKalb County (D) as third-party beneficiaries. Indeed, the operations of the United States in connection with FAA grants are of considerable magnitude. However, these operations would not be subjected to uncertainty by variant state-law interpretations of third-party-beneficiary law. This case involves only private parties, paralleling *Bank of American NT & SA v. Parnell* [federal common law should not be applied in litigation among private parties where no substantial national interest is at stake]. Thus, the rule of *Clearfield Trust* [federal courts may create federal common law to fill gaps in federal statutes where national interest is involved] is inapplicable to this issue of third-party-beneficiary standing. Congress clearly has the power to displace variant state laws governing this issue, but it has chosen not to. The federal courts, therefore, should not apply federal common law in this situation, since any federal interest is too speculative to justify the application of federal law to transactions of local concern. Therefore, Georgia law should be used, and we remand to the Court of Appeals for an application of this law. Vacated and remanded.

Analysis:

A comparison of this case with *Clearfield Trust*, in light of the Rules of Decision Act, helps distinguish the two cases. Recall that *Clearfield Trust* arose out of a check written by the United States on the authority granted by an Act of Congress. Thus, where there was a substantial connection between the issue at hand (forgery of the check) and the Act, and where the Act had a gap, federal common law could be used to fill the gap. In the case at hand, however, there is no direct connection between an Act of Congress and the issue of a third-party beneficiaries right to sue under a contract. Indeed, the contract was entered into by the FAA, and the FAA was presumably created by Congress. Nevertheless, implying that this Act contains a gap since it failed to address third-party beneficiaries of contracts involving the FAA is too far of a stretch. Moreover, note that no significant federal interests are involved in this issue of standing, whereas *Clearfield Trust* involved important considerations of commercial paper executed by the federal government.

■ CASE VOCABULARY

THIRD-PARTY BENEFICIARY: A party with rights arising from a contract entered into between two other parties; the beneficiary of the contract may sue to enforce rights under the contract.

Boyle v. United Technologies Corp.

(Deceased Pilot's Father) v. *(Government Contractor)*
487 U.S. 500, 108 S.Ct. 2510, 101 L.Ed.2d 442 (1988)

GOVERNMENT CONTRACTORS ARE IMMUNE FROM STATE LIABILITY IN CARRYING OUT FEDERAL GOVERNMENT INTERESTS

Military contractors get federal immunity.

stus.com

VIRGINIA

■ **INSTANT FACTS** Boyle (P) sued United Technologies Corp. (D), a government contractor, for design defects in a helicopter that crashed, resulting in his son's death.

■ **BLACK LETTER RULE** When federal interests significantly conflict with state law liability, federal law preempts state law.

■ **PROCEDURAL BASIS**

Certiorari to review a decision of the Fourth Circuit Court of Appeals reversing and remanding a judgment for the plaintiff.

■ **FACTS**

Boyle, a Marine helicopter pilot, was killed when his helicopter crashed off the coast of Virginia during a training exercise. Boyle survived the impact but was unable to escape the helicopter and drowned. Boyle's father (P) sued United Technologies Corp. (D), the manufacturer of the helicopter, under Virginia law. The elder Boyle (P) alleged that the defendant defectively repaired a device that later malfunctioned and caused the crash. He further argued that the defendant defectively designed the escape system to open outward rather than inward, which prevented it from opening when submerged in water. The jury returned a verdict for the plaintiff, and the judge denied the defendant's motion for judgment notwithstanding the verdict. On appeal, the Fourth Circuit Court of Appeals reversed and remanded to enter judgment for the defendant. The Fourth Circuit reasoned that the plaintiff had failed to demonstrate that the defendant's negligent repairs, as opposed to those made by the Navy, caused the crash. The Fourth Circuit also concluded that, as a matter of federal law, the defendant could not be held liable for the design defect because of the "military contractor defense," which insulates the defendant as a government contractor.

■ **ISSUE**

Does federal law immunize a government contractor from liability for state law design defect claims?

■ **DECISION AND RATIONALE**

(Scalia, J.) Yes. In the absence of a federal statute, legal issues "so committed by the Constitution and the laws of the United States to federal control" are governed by federal common law, which preempts the application of state law. The obligations and rights of the federal government under its contracts are a matter of federal law. Although this case involves the tort liability of a third party, it arises out of the defendant's performance under a government contract. So, too, is the civil liability of government officials a matter of federal law. While the defendant is an independent contractor, not a federal official, the same interest of achieving a government purpose is involved. The government depends on federal immunity to ensure that its chosen contractors accept government contracts at a price beneficial to the public. The case thus involves sufficient federal interests to invoke federal law.

Federal law, however, preempts state law only when the two significantly conflict and application of state law would considerably undermine federal objectives. Here, the government contract required the escape-hatch mechanism to open outwardly, contractually compelling the defendant to breach the duty of care allegedly owed under state law. It is the defendant's performance of the federal contract that gives rise to state liability, and a significant conflict is evident. This significant conflict is demonstrated by the Federal Tort Claims Act, which establishes the Government's consent to suits based on the negligent or wrongful conduct of its employees to the same extent that private parties would be liable under state law. The Act excludes from such consent, however, any claim based upon a discretionary function of a government employee. Clearly, the exception demonstrates that liability under state law based on the exercise of discretionary functions conflicts with federal interests. Here, the selection of the design for military helicopters is undoubtedly a discretionary function, insulating not only government officials, but also those contractors undertaking a contractual duty to further federal interests as well. The judgment for the plaintiff is vacated, and the case is remanded.

■ DISSENT

(Brennan, J.) Had the defendant built the helicopter for a commercial operation, it certainly would have been liable for any negligent design in the helicopter. Yet, because the design defect occurred during the performance of a government contract, the defendant is relieved of any breach of duty that would otherwise result in liability. Congress has refused to acknowledge such a distinction, and the Court should not step in to legislate where Congress has declined to do so. *Erie Railroad Co. v. Tompkins* firmly established that "[t]here is no federal general common law," and federal courts are not vested with authority to fashion substantive law. Whether or not the Court's rule will further the interests of the national Treasury by eliminating the contractual costs associated with potential tort liability to government contractors, that power properly belongs to Congress.

■ DISSENT

(Stevens, J.) While the judicial process may involve some measure of lawmaking, courts should carefully determine the proper decisionmaker before embarking on the creation of law. Because this case involves the creation of new legal doctrine, it would be better placed in the hands of legislators.

Analysis:

While the Government contractor defense may be seen differently in other contexts, its application to military equipment invokes unique considerations. Generally, the military equipment is not manufactured according to normal economic factors, because the Government is the only purchaser in the market. Because the Government itself is immune from liability for injuries caused by manufacturing defects, there is little incentive for it to heavily factor its liability into its purchase decisions. Presuming, however, that the Government is nonetheless concerned with the safety of its military personnel, it has an interest in securing the safest equipment at the most competitive price, perhaps necessitating contractor immunity to effectively do so.

■ CASE VOCABULARY

DESIGN DEFECT: A product imperfection occurring when the seller or distributor could have reduced or avoided a foreseeable risk of harm by adopting a reasonable alternative design, and when, as a result of not using the alternative, the product is not reasonably safe.

FEDERAL COMMON LAW: The judge-made law of federal courts, excluding the law in all cases governed by state law; specifically, the body of decisional law derived from federal courts adjudicating federal questions and other matters of federal concern, such as the law applying to disputes between two states, as well as foreign-relations law.

JUDGMENT NOTWITHSTANDING THE VERDICT: A judgment entered for one party even though a jury verdict has been rendered for the opposing party.

PREEMPTION: The principle (derived from the Supremacy Clause) that a federal law can supersede or supplant any inconsistent state law or regulation.

Dice v. Akron, Canton & Youngstown R. Co.

(Railroad Employee) v. *(Railroad)*
342 U.S. 359, 72 S.Ct. 312 (1952)

STATE COURTS MUST APPLY SUBSTANTIVE FEDERAL LAW AND SUBSTANTIAL FEDERAL PROCEDURES

■ **INSTANT FACTS** Dice (P), who sued under the Federal Employers Liability Act in Ohio state court for damages allegedly resulting from a railroad's negligence, maintained that he was fraudulently induced to sign a release of claims by the railroad.

■ **BLACK LETTER RULE** When adjudicating federal claims, state courts must apply federal substantive law as well as federal procedures which are a substantial protection of rights under the federal claim.

■ PROCEDURAL BASIS

Writ of certiorari challenging reversal of judgment for damages for negligence.

■ FACTS

Dice (P), a railroad fireman, was injured in the line of duty. Dice (P) brought an action in Ohio state court against Akron, Canton & Youngstown R. Co. (D), claiming negligence under the Federal Employers Liability Act (FELA). Akron (D) claimed that Dice (P) had signed a document releasing Akron (D) in full, but Dice (P) contended he had been fraudulently induced to sign the release without knowledge of its content. At trial, the jury awarded $25,000 to Dice (P), but the trial judge entered a judgment notwithstanding the verdict in favor of Akron (D). An Ohio Court of Appeals reversed the judgment notwithstanding the verdict. The Ohio Supreme Court, relying on Ohio law, found that Dice (P) was negligent in signing the release and was bound by the release. Further, the Court held that the factual issues as to fraud were properly decided by the trial judge rather than the jury. The United States Supreme Court granted certiorari.

■ ISSUE

Should federal law be used to address the substantive and procedural issues in a cause of action arising under a federal Act?

■ DECISION AND RATIONALE

(Black, J.) Yes. When a claim is brought under a federal Act, federal law should be used to address pertinent substantive and procedural issues. First, the validity of releases under FELA should be determined by federal rather than state law. A federal employee's rights under a federally declared standard could be defeated if states were permitted to determine the applicable defenses. Moreover, this application of state law would defeat the uniform application of federal standards. Second, the application of Ohio's harsh law, which holds that the negligence of a worker in signing a release precludes the worker from raising claims of fraudulent inducement, is wholly incongruous with the policy of FELA. The correct federal rule, which should be applied, states that a release is void when an employee is fraudulently induced to sign the release. Third, the judge should not have resolved all factual questions of fraud in this case. Ohio law requires a jury to try the negligence issue but allows the judge to make determinations of fraud. This runs counter to the policy of FELA, since the right to jury trial is a substantial part of the rights accorded by the Act. Reversed and remanded.

■ DISSENT

(Frankfurter, J.) Although we concur with reversal in this case, *we* dissent from the Court's opinion. In all cases in Ohio, the judge is the trier of fact on issues of fraud. The Court should have continued to follow *Minneapolis & St. Louis R. Co. v. Bombolis* [Although federal courts are bound by the Seventh Amendment to provide jury trials, states are not under a similar compulsion when entertaining cases under FELA]. Until today, *Bombolis* has allowed states to choose the fact-finding tribunal in negligence actions arising under the Act. Ohio should be allowed to maintain its traditional division of law and equity courts, and the resulting division of fact-finding authorities. The majority's opinion confuses the administration of justice to require federal practice to be followed in state courts in a single class of cases arising under the Act. Nevertheless, we agree that the federal substantive standards under FELA should have been applied by the Ohio courts, and therefore we concur in the reversal of the case.

Analysis:

As the dissent states, this majority opinion may have gone too far in requiring Ohio courts to apply federal procedures such as the right to jury trial. Typically state courts adjudicating federal claims must apply federal substantive law (the "reverse-*Erie* doctrine"), a policy with which both the majority and dissent concur. However, state courts are generally free to conduct the trials in line with their own procedural standards. Thus, while the substantive law should be identical regardless of forum, a plaintiff generally takes the state court as he finds it as far a procedures are concerned. Apparently the majority is creating a new standard, requiring state courts to apply federal procedures when they are substantial. This holding may be limited only to cases under FELA, as some scholars have noted in attempting to limit the significance of the majority's opinion. Nevertheless, it seems to suggest that Congress has the constitutional power to regulate the mechanics of trial in state court whenever a federal claim is involved.

■ CASE VOCABULARY

JUDGMENT NOTWITHSTANDING THE VERDICT: Procedure by which a judge, re-appraising the evidence of the case, overturns a jury verdict.

RELEASE: A document in which a party dismisses his claims in exchange for something, usually the payment of damages.

CHAPTER SEVEN

The Development of Modern Procedure

Veale v. Warner

Instant Facts: A money lender seeks to collect on the loan he made which the debtor refuses to pay back.

Black Letter Rule: A defendant may not introduce new facts in the rejoinder reply to plaintiff's traverse when he has already demurred to plaintiff's facts as set out in the declaration.

Scott v. Shepherd

Instant Facts: A man throws a lighted squib into a public market place which, after being thrown around by other anxious people ends up hitting another man in the face.

Black Letter Rule: A plaintiff may bring an action in trespass whenever the defendant's unlawful act caused his injuries, directly or consequentially.

Bushel v. Miller

Instant Facts: A porter loses his customer's goods when another porter temporarily removes them from storage and fails to put them back.

Black Letter Rule: Trover cannot lie as a cause of action against a party who removes property from its original location and merely fails to replace it to the same location without converting it to his own use in the interim.

Gordon v. Harper

Instant Facts: While Gordon (P) was leasing his house, Harper (D) seized the furniture in the house and sold it to satisfy a judicial judgment.

Black Letter Rule: A party who neither possesses the goods nor has the right to their possession at the time of their removal cannot bring an action in trover for their loss.

Slade's Case

Instant Facts: A man refuses to buy the grain which he promised to buy before it was harvested.

Black Letter Rule: When an action could have been viably brought on the case or on the contract, a plaintiff may choose whichever action is preferable to him even though it may not be defendant's preference.

Lamine v. Dorrell

Instant Facts: An impostor unlawfully sells part of an estate and the trustee sues to recover the proceeds of the sale.

Black Letter Rule: An action for assumpsit may lie even if the promise upon which it is based was implied rather than actual.

Arguments Proving From Antiquity the Dignity, Power, and Jurisdiction of the Court of Chancery

Instant Facts: When the king asked his Attorney General to certify the difference between his Court of Chancery and King's Bench, a case was presented to him where a individual sought relief from a judgment obtained against him.

Black Letter Rule: The Court of Chancery has the right and power to dispense equitable relief as it finds necessary.

Jones v. Winsor

Instant Facts: Client corporation sues their attorney for keeping money owed to them under the pretense that the money was his fee.

Black Letter Rule: A complaint may not state declarations and facts pertaining to more than one distinct cause of action.

Conaughty v. Nichols

Instant Facts: A person who consigned goods sued the merchant, who failed to pay the consignment share, for breach of contract and conversion.

Black Letter Rule: Pleading rules should be liberally construed to allow the assertion of alternative causes of action.

Garrity v. State Board of Administration

Instant Facts: A valuable fossil is removed from a man's farm and he sues the university that took it for the monetary value of the object.

Black Letter Rule: When a petition states sufficient facts for two possible causes of action against the named defendants, a plaintiff can waive one and proceed only on the other one of his choice.

Veale v. Warner

(*Money Lender*) v. (*Debtor*)

Court of King's Bench, 1.Wms. Saund. 323, 326, Eng.Rep. 463, 468 (1670)

PROCEDURAL TECHNICALITIES DETERMINE THE VERDICTS UNDER THE COMMON LAW PLEADING SYSTEM

■ **INSTANT FACTS** A money lender seeks to collect on the loan he made which the debtor refuses to pay back.

■ **BLACK LETTER RULE** A defendant may not introduce new facts in the rejoinder reply to plaintiff's traverse when he has already demurred to plaintiff's facts as set out in the declaration.

■ PROCEDURAL BASIS

Plaintiff requests injunctive relief to receive money owed to him for breach of contract. Defendant demurs.

■ FACTS

Veale (P) brings an action on a contract to collect 2000£ (English currency) which Warner (D) allegedly borrowed and still owes him. Veale shows the court the required sealed "writing obligatory" and accuses Warner (D) of refusing to pay up. Warner (D) responds with a demurrer that Veale (P) no longer has a valid legal claim against him because prior to this action, an arbitration panel forced Warner (D) to pay Veale (P) the full sum of the debt owed to him at the time, 3169£. Warner (D) claims he has already paid Veale (P) and Veale (P) has already signed a full release of the debt. Veale (P) of course denies that payment was ever made to him and in his "replication" traverses Warner's (D) claim of payment. Nonetheless, Warner (D) replies that he should not have to pay on the debt, regardless of whether or not he has actually paid it, because the contract which formed the debt was not valid to begin with.

■ ISSUE

Can a defendant allege facts in his rejoinder when he has demurred to the plaintiff's declaration?

■ DECISION AND RATIONALE

(Judge Not Stated) No, a defendant cannot introduce new facts in his rejoinder when he has already demurred to plaintiff's facts in the declaration. Consequently, Warner (D) has waived his right to raise the issue that the debt is void because the original contract was invalid because he has demurred to Veale's allegation that there was a valid contract. Warner (D) demurred to the legal validity of the debt based on the fact that he had already received a waiver of it NOT based on the fact that the contract on which the debt was based was internally invalid. Thus, Warner (D) seems to be tricking the court in his pleadings by knowingly pleading a bad rejoinder. Judgment cannot be for Warner (D). Instead, Veale (P) is given leave to discontinue on payment of costs.

Analysis:

Beside being an English case, this is also a case based on the superbly complex common law system of pleadings which current American law no longer utilizes. Nonetheless, the case is an example of early lawyering wizardry with the existing set of laws. The basic process of bringing a case began with a Plaintiff setting forth a claim in his *declaration* and a Defendant either *demurring* or *pleading* his side of the issue. Basically, demurring meant that no factual dispute existed, just a challenge to the legal sufficiency of the claim. Pleading meant actually challenging the Plaintiff's right to have the chosen court hear his case or somehow challenging the facts as alleged by the Plaintiff. In response, a Plaintiff could once again submit a response which could raise new issues and allegations. Defendant would be required to reply to those and the process could go back and forth infinitely until both parties were ready for trial or judgment on the pleadings. As the present case shows, however, a Defendant could not allege new facts in his reply to Plaintiff's *replication* if he had already accepted them by his demurrer. Thus, the fact that the contract between Warner (D) and Veale (P) was a bad one becomes irrelevant once Warner accepts its validity and claims to have paid off his debt on it. Warner's attorney knew what he was doing, though. He knew that on demurrer, the court will consider the whole record before giving judgment to either party. In reviewing the record, if the court sees that the Plaintiff's declaration is substantively bad, they will award judgment for the Defendant. Therefore, despite Warner's (D) bad pleading, he was ultimately the winner of the case because Veale's (P) failure to note his release of the debt pursuant to arbitration was "bad practice."

■ CASE VOCABULARY

PLEA OF DEBT: Common-law action to recover a certain, specified sum of money.

PLEDGES OF PROSECUTION: Plaintiff's insurers who would be responsible for paying the fine against unsuccessful claimants.

PRAY OYER: Method of legally reading a document into the pleadings themselves.

REJOINDER: Defendant's acceptance of plaintiff's reply to defendant's initial responsive pleading.

TRAVERSE: Defendant's denial of plaintiff's allegations in the pleading.

WRITING OBLIGATORY: The technical name in a pleading for a bond of debt.

Scott v. Shepherd

(Injured Victim) v. *(Squib Thrower)*

Court of Common Pleas, 2 Wm.Bl. 892, 92 Eng.Rep. 525 (1773)

BLURRING DISTINCTIONS BETWEEN TRESPASS AND CASE MARKS THE DAWN OF ACTIONS FOR NEGLIGENCE

■ **INSTANT FACTS** A man throws a lighted squib into a public market place which, after being thrown around by other anxious people ends up hitting another man in the face.

■ **BLACK LETTER RULE** A plaintiff may bring an action in trespass whenever the defendant's unlawful act caused his injuries, directly or consequentially.

■ **PROCEDURAL BASIS**

Appeal from a jury verdict for the plaintiff in an action for trespass and assault.

■ **FACTS**

Shepherd (D), a minor, throws a lighted squib made of gunpowder into the market place. The squib lands on Yates' gingerbread stand and Willis picks it up and throws it away to prevent harm. The squib [which is now the subject of a game of "hot potato"] falls on Ryal's market stand. Ryal then immediately picks it up and throws it into another part of the market where it finally lands in Scott's (P) face, blows up and puts out one of his eyes. [Despite Scott's undoubtable desire to let boys be boys] he sues Shepherd (D), as the one responsible for the squib in the first place, in both the trespass and case forms of action. Shepherd (D) pleaded not guilty, but the jury found for Scott (P) and awarded him 100£.

■ **ISSUE**

Is an action in trespass appropriate when a party's injury results indirectly or consequentially from another party's initial wrongful act?

■ **DECISION AND RATIONALE**

(Nares, J.) Yes. A party may bring an action in trespass whenever his injuries were indirectly or consequentially the result of another's wrongful acts. The determinate factor, as in all cases, is that Shepherd's (D) initial act was wrongful on its own. Therefore, Shepherd (D) should be held liable for it in trespass whether the ultimate injury to the victim was caused directly and immediately or after intervening acts. Intervening acts alone cannot remove the wrongfulness of the trespass because they did not exacerbate its effects at all. The lighted squib was already dangerous the moment it was thrown into the market place, not the moment it hit Scott (P) in the face. Therefore, judgment is for Scott (P).

■ **CONCURRENCE**

(Gould, J.) The only difference between trespass and case is pleading the form of action, not in the type of remedy offered the plaintiff. Therefore, trespass is as appropriate as case in this situation. Simply put, the trespass action will be viewed as though Shepherd (D) threw the squib directly into Scott's (P) face, without the intervention of the others [one of the many fictions the courts are willing to rely on].

■ **DISSENT**

(Blackstone, J.) No, trespass is not the appropriate form of action in this case. Trespass may only lie where the injury is the immediate result of the wrongful act. When there are intervening acts, however, the action must be in case. The lawfulness of the original act cannot be determinative because trespass may also lie for injuries caused by lawful acts (as in the famous example of chopping down one's tree and having it accidentally fall onto the neighbor's property and killing the neighbor himself). Thus, the only issue to be raised is whether Scott's (P) injuries were direct and immediate or indirect and consequential. Since Scott's (P) injuries were only consequential, trespass cannot lie against Shepherd (D) but perhaps should lie against Ryal (who could have put the squib out instead of throwing it in Scott's face). Judgment could have been for Scott (P) only if he had brought an action in case rather than trespass.

Analysis:

In addition to highlighting the obvious technicalities of common law pleading requirements, this case is important because of Justice Blackstone's prophetic dissent. An act did not need to be unlawful to cause injury and resultant liability and, at the end of the century, the courts saw a boom in suits over vehicular collisions and pedestrian accidents in which injury was caused by acts that were not unlawful in themselves. The suits expanded both trespass and case to include the tort of negligence. Negligence law, as the name suggests, did not require that the initial act be unlawful, just that it be careless and negligent. Thus, as tort cases grew exponentially, the American courts were more and more lax in allowing a plaintiff to select his cause of action in either trespass or case thereby blurring the lines between both.

■ **CASE VOCABULARY**

CASE (a.k.a. "trespass on the case"): Common law cause of action to recover damages for injury caused by the defendant's wrongful act.

E CONVERSO: Latin for "conversely" or "on the contrary."

IN INFINITUM: Latin for "indefinite" or "continuous."

PER QUOD: Latin for "whereby," as in alleging the consequences of a tortious act.

POSTEA: A common-law device of formally stating the proceedings at trial.

SQUIB: A case filled with gunpowder which is meant to explode when thrown.

SUBJOIN: To add on or attach at the end.

TRESPASS: Common law cause of action to recover damages for *any* injury to one's person or property.

Bushel v. Miller

(*One Who Placed Goods in Storage*) v. (*One Who Removed Goods from Storage*)
Court of King's Bench, 1 Strange 128, 93 Eng.Rep. 428 (1718)

COMMON LAW COURT DEEMS CONVERSION AN ESSENTIAL ELEMENT OF TROVER

■ **INSTANT FACTS** A porter loses his customer's goods when another porter temporarily removes them from storage and fails to put them back.

■ **BLACK LETTER RULE** Trover cannot lie as a cause of action against a party who removes property from its original location and merely fails to replace it to the same location without converting it to his own use in the interim.

■ **PROCEDURAL BASIS**

Suit for monetary damages in trover for conversion of destroyed property.

■ **FACTS**

Bushel (P) is a ship porter who stores items in a shed on the quay before the items are loaded onto the ship. Bushel (P) placed some goods belonging to a customer in his storage compartment on top of a trunk belonging to Miller (D). When Miller (D) came to get his trunk out, he had to take out Bushel's package first, so he placed it about a yard from the door of the shed without returning it back to the shed. When Bushel (P) came back to get the package for his customer, it was not there. [You knew that was coming.] Bushel (P) then paid his customer the value of the goods lost and sued Miller (D) in trover to get the value of the goods that the loss caused him.

■ **ISSUE**

Can trover lie as a cause of action against a party who removes property from their original location and fails to replace them to the same place?

■ **DECISION AND RATIONALE**

(Judge Not Stated) No. Trover cannot lie as a cause of action against a party who merely places goods in a location slightly different from the one in which he found them. Thus, Bushel (P) did have sufficient interest in the lost property to maintain trover after he reimbursed his customer for it. However, Bushel (P) cannot bring trover against Miller (D) because Miller (D) never converted them for his own use. He did not interfere with Bushel's (P) property rights over the goods, which is a prerequisite for an action in trover. If anything, Bushel (P) was somewhat at fault for knowingly placing his goods in a way that interfered with Miller's (D) trunk. Miller (D), therefore, had every right to remove the goods which were in his way. As to Bushel's (P) complaint that Miller (D) failed to replace the goods in the same place, Bushel (P) probably could have established a cause of action in trespass (because it does not require that the trespasser convert the property for his own use). Judgement is for Defendant.

Analysis:

This case exemplifies one of the predominant causes of action in "case" during the eighteenth century. Trover was an action which came to replace the action of detinue, both dealing with the loss and detention of personal property. Detinue was an undesirable action because it required a plaintiff to take back the goods in controversy if the defendant could return them, regardless of the state they were in by the time of trial. Understandably, most plaintiffs preferred just to get the money value of the property instead. Consequently, trover became the action of choice because it was based on the fiction that because defendant took plaintiff's property and will not give it back [which he would have preferred to do instead of paying for it], plaintiff should just be awarded the monetary value of the said property. The problem with trover, however (as Bushel discovered), was that it required the element of conversion. The defendant had to have actually taken the property at issue for his own use. It was not enough if he only handled it but never took it in possession. For whatever reason, the courts were not willing to overlook this element as another aspect of judicial fiction.

■ CASE VOCABULARY

CONVERSION: Unauthorized interference with another's rights of possession and ownership of goods or chattels.

DETINUE: Common law action for the wrongful detention of personal property; an action for the recovery of the item as well as damages for its unlawful detention.

TROVER: Common law action to recover damages against whoever found another's goods rather than to recover the goods themselves.

Gordon v. Harper

(*Landlord*) v. (*Sheriff Seizing Goods*)
Court of Kings Bench, 7 T.R. 9, 101 Eng.Rep. 828 (1796)

COURT DENIES PLAINTIFF AN ACTION IN TROVER EVEN WHILE ADMITTING THAT HE HAS NO OTHER CAUSE OF ACTION

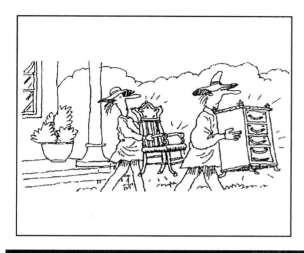

■ **INSTANT FACTS** While Gordon (P) was leasing his house, Harper (D) seized the furniture in the house and sold it to satisfy a judicial judgment.

■ **BLACK LETTER RULE** A party who neither possesses the goods nor has the right to their possession at the time of their removal cannot bring an action in trover for their loss.

■ **PROCEDURAL BASIS**

Action in trover for the seizure and sale of household furniture.

■ **FACTS**

Gordon (P) owns a furnished house and leased it to his tenant for a term that has still not expired at the time of trial. While the tenant was in possession of the house, Harper (D), the Sheriff, came to seize the furniture in the house and sold it [sort of like an eighteenth century repo-man]. It seems that Gordon (P) had purchased the furniture from a man who had a court judgement against him and apparently had no right to have sold the furniture in the first place. [We are spared the seedy details, but the furniture may have been stolen.] When Gordon (P) discovered that the furniture in his house was taken away and sold, even though he was not living in it at the time, he brought a suit in trover against Sheriff Harper (D) for the value of the furniture taken.

■ **ISSUE**

Can a party who neither possessed the goods nor had the right to their possession at the time of their removal bring an action in trover for their loss?

■ **DECISION AND RATIONALE**

(Lord Kenyon, Ch.J.) No. A person who knowingly leases his goods and gives up possession of them for a certain time cannot recover the value of the goods in trover if they are taken during that time. Thus, Gordon (P) only had a reversionary interest in his furniture while he was leasing it to his tenant. Regardless of the nature of the property leased, a party gives up his right to possession when he is leasing it. Trover, therefore, is not a viable cause of action because it is a remedy for an interference with the possessory rights of the plaintiff. If the plaintiff does not have the possessory right, then it is not a right with which one can interfere. [Simple physics is at work here.] Judgement for Defendant.

■ **CONCURRENCE**

(Ashhurst, J.) No. An action in trover can only be brought by someone who had both a right in the property and a right in its possession at the same time.

■ **CONCURRENCE**

(Grose, J.) No. An action in trover can lie only if the plaintiff had actual possession of the goods and a right of possession of the goods. Gordon (P), however, not only did not have actual possession of the furniture but he would have been a trespasser if he took the goods from his tenant himself.

Analysis:

Chief Judge Lord Kenyon cites a case, *Ward v. Macauley*, for which he wrote the opinion and which had essentially the same plot line as this one. In *Ward*, Kenyon stated that plaintiff's chosen cause of action for trespass could not lie in such a case scenario but trover would have. Now in *Gordon*, Kenyon writes that he takes back what he said in the earlier case and trover cannot lie either. The obvious question, then, is what remedy would a landlord have if his furniture was taken while his house was being leased? One option may have been to wait before bringing his suit until the lease ran out and the landlord was again rightfully in possession of his house and the furniture that was supposed to be in it. This would probably be difficult to coordinate with a statute of limitations for such an action. The other option would be to avoid leasing a furnished house. If this seems extreme, then you understand why the common law was in desperate need of reform in this century. The judges were capable of determining which causes of action could not lie but offered no help as to which ones could.

■ **CASE VOCABULARY**

ACTION OF TRESPASS: Action to recover damages for unlawful injury to the plaintiff's person, property or rights.

POSTEA: Formal statement which gives an account of the proceedings at a jury trial.

REVERSIONARY INTEREST: A right to future enjoyment of property which is presently in the possession of another.

REVESTED: Returned the right of present ownership and/or possession.

TROVER: Action for wrongful conversion of another's property; originally, an action against a person who had *found* another's goods and wrongfully converted them to his own use.

Slade's Case

(Slade: Farmer) v. *(Morley: Grain Merchant)*
Court of Exchequer Chamber, 4 Co.Rep. 92b, 76 Eng.Rep. 1074 (1602)

WHEN ACTIONS IN CASE AND ON THE CONTRACT ARE BOTH MAINTAINABLE, PLAINTIFF CAN CHOOSE EITHER

■ **INSTANT FACTS** A man refuses to buy the grain which he promised to buy before it was harvested.

■ **BLACK LETTER RULE** When an action could have been viably brought on the case or on the contract, a plaintiff may choose whichever action is preferable to him even though it may not be defendant's preference.

■ **PROCEDURAL BASIS**

Appeal from a jury verdict for defendant in an action of debt.

■ **FACTS**

Humphrey Morley (D) made a bargain with John Slade (P) that he would buy from Slade (P) a portion of the wheat and rye that Slade (P) grew on his property. Slade (P) promised to grow and harvest the grains for which he was to be paid 16£. When the time came to pay up, Slade (P) had the grain but Morley (D) would not buy it. Thus, Slade (P) brought an action in case on assumpsit to get the money owed him for the grain. Morley (D), however, pleaded "non assumpsit," suggesting that Slade (P) could only bring an action in debt.

■ **ISSUE**

If an action could have been brought either on the case or on the contract, can a plaintiff choose whichever one is preferable to him?

■ **DECISION AND RATIONALE**

(Judge Not Stated) Yes. When two parties enter a bargain and one of them breaches it, the nonbreaching plaintiff may select any cause of action from those available to him. Thus, just because other plaintiffs in Slade's (P) position traditionally bring an action of debt on the contract does not mean Slade (P) cannot bring an action in case, if it applies equally. Assumpsit, an action developed from case, is as much a remedy as "debt" because every "contract executory" includes an assumption of indebtedness to the other party.

Analysis:

Debt was a form of action for breach of contract which could only lie when an agreement had been fully performed by one party who was now entitled to payment for his performance. Case, however, was the chosen cause of action for most plaintiffs because its lengthy history and familiarity made it seem somehow safer. Out of case grew the action of assumpsit, which established a remedy for nonperformance of a promise. However, for a long time assumpsit could only lie if a promise to pay was made explicitly and separately from the initial bargain between the two parties. Thus, for example, not only would Slade (P) and Morley (D) have to have agreed to exchange goods for money but Morley would then separately have to say, "I promise to pay you for this grain you have brought before me." If this seems rather superfluous to you, it did so to many courts as well who, as in *Slade's Case,* agreed to treat the separate promise as a fiction which did not actually have to be stated. Thus, when Morley (D) pleaded "non assumpsit," the court scoffed because his assumption was understood to be implied in the very making of a bargain and the fact that he did not also promise to pay Slade (P) could not deprive Slade (P) of his remedy. It is also interesting to note that the court made sure that Slade (P) recovered as much damages in this action on assumpsit as he would have in an action of debt.

■ CASE VOCABULARY

ACTION OF DEBT: Personal action to recover payment of money owed.

ACTION ON THE CASE: At common law, an action to recover damages that are not the immediate result of a wrongful act but, rather, a later consequence.

ASSUMPSIT: Typical common law cause of action for the recovery of damages against one who failed to perform his contractual obligation.

CLOSE OF LAND: The enclosed portion of land.

CONSIDERATION: The material cause or price which is the inducement to a contract.

CONTRACT EXECUTORY: Contract based on an agreement to perform some act in the future.

NON ASSUMPSIT MODO ET FORMA: A plea to an assumpsit action by which the defendant denies making the promise alleged by the plaintiff.

Lamine v. Dorrell

(*Estate Trustee*) v. (*Impostor Trustee*)

Court of Queen's Bench, 2 Ld.Raym. 1216, 92 Eng.Rep. 303 (1705)

ASSUMPSIT CAN LIE AS A CAUSE OF ACTION EVEN ON AN IMPLIED PROMISE

■ **INSTANT FACTS** An impostor unlawfully sells part of an estate and the trustee sues to recover the proceeds of the sale.

■ **BLACK LETTER RULE** An action for assumpsit may lie even if the promise upon which it is based was implied rather than actual.

■ **PROCEDURAL BASIS**

Motion objecting to plaintiff's bringing an action in an indebitatus assumpsit to which defendant pleaded non assumpsit.

■ **FACTS**

J.S. died intestate but left property in his estate which included some Irish debentures. Before a trustee was appointed to the estate, Dorrell (D) falsely proclaimed himself to be a trustee and sold off the debentures for his own profit. Soon thereafter, Dorrell's (D) administration was repealed and Lamine (P) was officially appointed as trustee. Upon discovering the sale of the debentures, Lamine (P) brought this cause of action in an "indebitatus assumpsit" to recover from Dorrell (D) the money he unlawfully received from their sale. Dorrell (D) motioned the court to throw the case out because an assumpsit action implies the receipt of money for the use of the plaintiff, but Dorrell (D) clearly intended the money for his own use [and he's not too ashamed to admit it]. Therefore, Lamine (P) could only have brought an action for trover or detinue.

■ **ISSUE**

Despite the absence of an actual agreement, can an action for assumpsit lie when premised on an implied agreement?

■ **DECISION AND RATIONALE**

(Powell, J.) Yes. An action for assumpsit may lie even if the agreement to pay the debt is reasonably implied from the facts and not actually stated. Thus, in this case, it is only fair and reasonable to assume that Dorrell (D) sold the debentures with Lamine's (P) consent and received the money from them for Lamine's (P) rather than his own use.

■ **CONCURRENCE**

(Holt, Ch.J.) Yes. The defendant, being the wrongdoer, should be made answerable for the sale even though he did not explicitly make it for the use of Lamine (P). In light of Lamine's (P) probable recovery in this a case, it is also understood that Lamine (P) could not then go and also sue Dorrell (D) in trover or detinue. The actions are in place of one another and not in supplement.

Analysis:

This is a rare example of the bending of the rules in which the English courts were willing to engage for the sake of justice. It is obvious that Dorrell (D) should not have kept the money he made essentially through fraud and theft and the court was not too proud to play favorites when it was this clear who was in the right. Regardless of motive, this type of reform was essential because many contracts and bargains were made on implied assumptions that one party would do something and the other party would pay for it. It was important that the promises to pay could be understood by the courts as implied because many of the agreements were entered into by farmers and merchants who did not know the exacting requirements of the law. For example, note the kind of ingenious theorizing in which Chief Justice Holt engages. He points out that if Lamine (P) was forced to bring his cause of action in trover, Dorrell (D) would not be found guilty because by bringing an action in assumpsit Lamine (P) accepts that the sale of the debentures was lawful and the proceeds owed to him. Trover, however, would require as one of its elements the *un*lawful interference with another's property right. Thus, Lamine's (P) case in trover could be disproved by his own initially chosen cause of action in assumpsit.

■ CASE VOCABULARY

DEBENTURES: Long-term unsecured bond certificate.

DETINUE: Form of action for the physical recovery of wrongfully possessed personal property and for damages for its detention.

INDEBITATUS ASSUMPSIT: An assumpsit cause of action in which plaintiff's declaration alleges that defendant took on a debt and promised to pay it back.

INTESTATE: Dying without providing a valid will to dispose of one's property.

NON ASSUMPSIT: Pleading in which the defendant claims he did not undertake or promise any obligation as set forth in plaintiff's complaint.

TROVER: Common law action to recover damages against whoever found another's goods; now, action for wrongful conversion of another's property.

Arguments Proving From Antiquity the Dignity, Power, and Jurisdiction of the Court of Chancery

(*Not Applicable*)
1 Chan.Rep. (app.) 1, 21 Eng. Rep. 576 (1616)

THE PURPOSE OF CHANCERY COURTS IS TO BRING EQUITY AND JUSTICE TO THOSE WHO ARE UNABLE TO OBTAIN THEM FROM THE COMMON LAW

■ **INSTANT FACTS** When the king asked his Attorney General to certify the difference between his Court of Chancery and King's Bench, a case was presented to him where a individual sought relief from a judgment obtained against him.

■ **BLACK LETTER RULE** The Court of Chancery has the right and power to dispense equitable relief as it finds necessary.

■ **PROCEDURAL BASIS**

None.

■ **FACTS**

The King was presented with a case where "B" (D) sought relief from a judgment in favor of "A" in an action for a debt of £1000 or for possession of "D's" manor.

■ **ISSUE**

May the Chancery Court enjoin the enforcement of a judgment at common law?

■ **DECISION AND RATIONALE**

(Justice Not Stated) Yes. The Court of Chancery has the right and power to dispense equitable relief as it finds necessary. It is the duty to the king to provide equal and indifferent justice. When royal subjects seek relief in equity the Chancery Courts should not abandon or expose them to the strictness of our laws. Accordingly, we approve, ratify and confirm the practice of the Court of Chancery. The Chancellor should not desist from giving the king's subjects relief in equity, notwithstanding any common law proceedings.

Analysis:

The purpose of courts in equity was to achieve justice where the law failed or could not. This argument demonstrates the manner in which equity acted as a check on common law courts. The King (meaning the administration and not necessarily the individual) realized that the strictness of the common law could result in unfair judgments. Accordingly, equity courts were empowered to enjoin individuals from enforcing their common law judgments. Such injunctions, a power held exclusively by courts in equity, were commonly issued in cases of fraud. In many circumstances, common law courts would not hear the defense of fraud; thus, it was up to the Chancellor to grant relief. One can envision the Chancellor as the King's "kind hand." This kindness notwithstanding, the American colonies viewed the equity courts as the King's tool and an enemy of the popular will.

■ CASE VOCABULARY

CHANCERY: The English king's secretarial department, the courts of which dispensed equitable relief in cases where there was no relief at common law or in cases seeking relief from the common law.

EJECTIONE FIRMAE: Common law action to recover possession of land.

Jones v. Winsor

(*Ex-Client*) v. (*Attorney*)
22 S.D. 480, 118 N.W. 716 (1908)

TWO IS NOT BETTER THAN ONE: COURT SAYS MORE THAN ONE CAUSE OF ACTION IS NO CAUSE OF ACTION AT ALL

■ **INSTANT FACTS** Client corporation sues their attorney for keeping money owed to them under the pretense that the money was his fee.

■ **BLACK LETTER RULE** A complaint may not state declarations and facts pertaining to more than one distinct cause of action.

■ **PROCEDURAL BASIS**

Appeal by the defendant from an order of the circuit court overruling his demurrer to the complaint.

■ **FACTS**

Jones (P) hired Winsor (D) as his attorney in efforts to secure an ordinance from the city counsel granting him a license for a railway system. To apply for the license, Jones (P) had to pay $2500 to the city treasurer. So he gave the money, plus another $130, to Winsor (D) to take care of the transfer. When it turned out that Jones (P) was turned down for the license, the treasurer returned the fee to Winsor (D). Winsor (D) [being the reason incarnate why attorneys get such a bad rap] sent Jones (P) back $1250, half of their money, and a bill in the amount of $1250 for "services rendered." Jones (P) believed that he was being charged fraudulently and that he did not owe Winsor (D) more than $250 for his services. Thus, Jones (P) brought this cause of action for the wrongful conversion of property and requested his $1000 back plus costs incurred by the suit itself. Winsor (D) demurred, claiming that Jones' (P) complaint did not state facts sufficient to constitute a cause of action in conversion because Jones (P) does not allege facts to the effect that he owned the property at the time it was converted or at the time he brought the action. Winsor (D) also claims that it is unclear from Jones' (P) complaint whether the action is intended to be for conversion or in assumpsit for money "had and received." Jones (P) replies that it is indeed for money "had and received" and anything else in the complaint may be treated as surplusage.

■ **ISSUE**

May a complaint state facts and allegations pertaining to more than one distinct cause of action?

■ **DECISION AND RATIONALE**

(Corson, J.) No. A complaint may not state facts and allegations of two or more distinct and inconsistent causes of action in one suit. Not only would that be unfair to defendants, who would not know against which counts to defend themselves, but it would generally introduce into the law elements of uncertainty and ambiguity in pleading which would only mislead the courts and opposing parties. [Are these elements missing from the law as we know it?] On demurrer to a complaint, a court must always first establish what the cause of action is of the complaint and then determine if the facts are sufficient to state that cause of action. (Citing, *Supervisors of Kewaunee County v. Decker.*) Since Jones' (P) complaint does not state one distinct cause of action, Winsor's (D) demurrer should be sustained. Judgement is for the defendant, overruling the order of the circuit court.

Analysis:

The citation of this case indicates that it was decided in the United States, as opposed to England, and it was based on several procedural reforms which occurred at the end of the nineteenth century. The previously separate courts of law and equity were brought together. Parties were allowed to testify as their own witnesses. Most importantly, though, Code pleading was introduced to replace the common-law system of civil procedure. The ideology behind this transition was that the substantive law would remain unaltered but the procedural laws would become clearer and more consistent. Nonetheless, Code pleading was not immediately the panacea that it was designed to be. Judges who were trained under the older system were less than thrilled to have to retrain themselves in the new one. As *Jones v. Winsor* illustrates, for example, judges still clung to the common-law doctrine of "theory of the pleading." One of the provisions in the new Field Code, named after one of its most influential commissioners, was that judges should construe the allegations of a pleading liberally with an aim toward justice between the parties. Justice Corson, however, continues to insist that a singular "theory of the case" (a.k.a. "cause of action") is the prerequisite of a successful pleading, regardless of the dictates of justice.

■ CASE VOCABULARY

APPELLANT: Being unsatisfied with a judgment or ruling, the party who makes an appeal from one court to another.

ASSUMPSIT: Action for expectation damages based on breach of express contract alleged in the complaint.

COMPLAINT: The original pleading which initiates an action and sets forth a claim for relief.

DEMURRER: Assertion made that without disputing the facts the pleading does not state a cause of action.

EX CONTRACTU: Referring to those rights and causes of action which arise from a contract, as opposed to a tort, for example.

TORT: Wrong or injury resulting from breach of legal duty, with causal relation between defendant's conduct and resulting damage.

TROVER: Action for wrongful conversion of another's property.

Conaughty v. Nichols

(*Consignor*) v. (*Merchant*)

42 N.Y. 83 (1870)

COURT ALLOWS PLAINTIFF TO ASSERT ALTERNATIVE CAUSES OF ACTION

■ **INSTANT FACTS** A person who consigned goods sued the merchant, who failed to pay the consignment share, for breach of contract and conversion.

■ **BLACK LETTER RULE** Pleading rules should be liberally construed to allow the assertion of alternative causes of action.

■ PROCEDURAL BASIS

Appeal from reversal of nonsuit in action for breach of contract and conversion.

■ FACTS

Conaughty (P) alleged that he had consigned goods for Nichols (D) to sell, and that Nichols (D) sold the goods for $690.82. Conaughty (P) alleged that Nichols (D) refused to pay the $618.43 due to Conaughty (P), and that Nichols (D) converted the money for Nichols's (D) own use. After trial, Conaughty (P) moved to amend the complaint to strike the conversion allegation. The referee denied the motion and nonsuited Conaughty (P) on the ground that the cause of action stated in the complaint was for tort, and the proof established a caused of action upon contract. The General Term reversed, and Nichols (D) appealed.

■ ISSUE

Must a plaintiff be nonsuited for filing a complaint that contains two causes of action?

■ DECISION AND RATIONALE

(Justice Not Stated) No. A plaintiff should not necessarily be nonsuited for filing a complaint that contains two causes of action. Where one of the causes of action is proven at trial, and the other is not necessary, the plaintiff may recover. In this case, Conaughty (P) proved his cause of action based on contract. The cause of action for conversion was unnecessary, but we are of the opinion that this should not be fatal to Conaughty's (P) case under the liberal system introduced by the Code. The facts were fully stated in the complaint, and Nichols (D) was apprised of what he had to defend against. Nichols (D) chose not to move to strike any portion of the complaint or to compel Conaughty (P) to make it more definite. It is probable that Conaughty (P) intended to recover for wrongful conversion. This mistake should have been fatal but for the ample statement of facts that justified a recovery on contract for the amount of Conaughty's (D) demand. Affirmed.

Analysis:

This opinion reflects a liberal approach to pleadings. In modern times a plaintiff may include a number of various causes of action and would never be nonsuited for alleging facts that could support two or more causes of action. Under the old system, as reflected in *Jones v. Windsor*, a complaint could not allege more than one cause of action. The apparent policy rationale was that a plaintiff could not try to confuse a defendant by alleging divergent facts or claims. In addition, a plaintiff could not amend his complaint and change the character of the action at trial. This makes some sense, as the defendant should be allowed to understand and prepare a defense for the causes of action alleged against him. But as long as a defendant is fully apprised of the claims against him, it should not be fatal to allege alternative claims. A defendant has the option, as the opinion notes, for not moving to strike unnecessary causes of action or for requesting a more definite statement of claim.

■ **CASE VOCABULARY**

EX DELICTO: A common law cause of action arising out of a tort.

Garrity v. State Board of Administration

(Farm Owner) v. *(Fossil Taker)*

99 Kan. 695, 162 P. 1167 (1917)

TO WAIVE ONE CAUSE OF ACTION IN FAVOR OF ANOTHER, PLAINTIFF MUST HAVE BEEN ABLE TO BRING BOTH IN THE FIRST PLACE

■ **INSTANT FACTS** A valuable fossil is removed from a man's farm and he sues the university that took it for the monetary value of the object.

■ **BLACK LETTER RULE** When a petition states sufficient facts for two possible causes of action against the named defendants, a plaintiff can waive one and proceed only on the other one of his choice.

■ **PROCEDURAL BASIS**

Appeal from order sustaining defendant's demurrer.

■ **FACTS**

Garrity (P) owns a farm in Wallace county where a large and valuable fossil was discovered. The board of regents of the state university came on the farm and took the fossil and placed it in the university museum. The regents did not ask for Garrity's (P) permission to do this and did not compensate him the $2500 which the fossil was allegedly worth. In his petition, Garrity (P) charges the State Board of Administration (D), who are the successors in interest of the board of regents, with breach of an implied promise to pay on the contract. The Administration (D) demurred after the original petition, claiming that Garrity's only cause of action was in tort and this was already barred by the expiration of a two year statute of limitations. Garrity (P) claimed that he waived the cause of action in tort and was bringing this action on a breach of contract theory. The Administration (D) demurred to the amended petition as well.

■ **ISSUE**

When a petition states a cause of action on more than one theory, can plaintiff choose to waive one of the theories and only bring the suit on the other?

■ **DECISION AND RATIONALE**

(Porter, J.) Yes. If a petition states sufficient facts for more than one cause of action, then plaintiff can waive one and proceed only on the other. Thus, Garrity (P) can waive the cause of action in tort and not be limited by the statute of limitations to bring their cause of action for breach of contract. However, a party can only proceed with the cause of action if it can be maintained against the named defendants. In this case, Garrity cannot bring an action for breach of contract against the Administration (D) because the act which constructed this board to replace the regents only gave them the power "to execute trusts or other obligations now or hereinafter committed to." Thus, the Administration (D) cannot be made liable for torts committed by the regents and Garrity (P) cannot, just by waiving the tort, make the Administration liable by calling the action breach of contract. The judgement is affirmed for defendant.

Analysis:

This is an interesting decision which holds that Garrity's (P) cause of action was in contract for the purpose of statute of limitations but in tort for the purpose of liability. The court does not provide

---

satisfying guidelines as to why they chose to treat the case this way, but a few reasons may have contributed to the outcome. First, historically, governments are presumed to be immune from tort actions unless they expressly waive their immunity. Thus, the court may have thought that Garrity (P) waived the tort action to trick the court into allowing him to sue the government for essentially the same tort just by calling it something different. It seems that if the Administration (D) could have been a liable defendant under either a tort or a contract theory, the court would not have cared which theory Garrity (P) had advanced. Another possible explanation for the outcome is that the court was not really concerned with the theory of the pleading at all but instead wanted to concentrate on careful selection of defendants and could not fathom holding someone liable for an act their predecessors committed six years ago. Courts often make decisions based on unexpressed policy considerations and this is probably an example of that.

■ CASE VOCABULARY

DEMURRER: Assertion made that without disputing the facts, the pleading does not state a cause of action.

TORT: Wrong or injury resulting from breach of legal duty, with causal relation between defendant's conduct and resulting damage.

WRONGFULLY CONVERTED: Wrongful taking or detention, illegal assumption of ownership, or illegal use or misuse of another's property.

CHAPTER EIGHT

Modern Pleading

Dioguardi v. Durning

Instant Facts: A customs collector loses part of a merchant's shipment of medicinal tonics and sells the rest at auction for less than they were worth.

Black Letter Rule: A complaint must state just enough facts to sufficiently notify the opposing party of the claims against him so as to allow him to begin preparing a defense.

Bell Atlantic Corp. v. Twombly

Instant Facts: Telephone and Internet subscribers sued their local telephone companies for allegedly entering into a conspiracy to create monopoly power in their respective markets in violation of § 1 of the Sherman Act.

Black Letter Rule: Federal Rules of Civil Procedure 8(a)(2) requires a "short and plain statement of the claim showing that the pleader is entitled to relief," in order to "give the defendant fair notice of what the . . . claim is and the grounds upon which it rests."

Garcia v. Hilton Hotels International, Inc.

Instant Facts: A hotel employee is fired for bringing women into the hotel for prostitution, but he claims the charge is false and slanderous.

Black Letter Rule: A complaint sufficiently pleads a right to relief when it states enough facts to reasonably assume that the essential elements of the claim can be proven at trial.

Denny v. Carey

Instant Facts: Investors brought suit against First Penn (D) for securities fraud, and the defendants moved to dismiss for failure to plead fraud with sufficient particularity as required by the Federal Rules of Civil Procedure.

Black Letter Rule: Rule 9(b)'s requirement of pleading fraud with particularity must be harmonized with Fed. R. Civ. P. 8's requirement of a short and plain statement of the plaintiff's claim that is simple, concise, and direct.

Tellabs, Inc. v. Makor Issues & Rights, Ltd.

Instant Facts: The plaintiff alleged a violation of the PSLRA by the defendant, and the defendant moved to dismiss for failure to state a claim.

Black Letter Rule: A complaint alleging securities fraud under the Private Securities Litigation Reform Act will survive a motion to dismiss only if a reasonable person would deem the inference of scienter cogent and at least as compelling as any opposing inference one could draw from the facts alleged.

Ziervogel v. Royal Packing Co.

Instant Facts: A woman injured in a car accident tries to bring in evidence at trial of injuries that were not mentioned in her complaint before trial.

Black Letter Rule: A personal injury which is not the necessary or inevitable result of an injury alleged in the petition is a "special damage" which must be specifically pleaded before trial.

Bail v. Cunningham Brothers, Inc.

Instant Facts: A jury awarded judgment for plaintiff in an amount higher than he asked for in his prayer for relief and the defendant requests that the amount be remitted to the lesser one that is in the pleadings.

Black Letter Rule: A claimant is entitled to the amount of relief rendered at trial even if that amount is greater than what was requested in the pleadings.

American Nurses' Association v. Illinois

Instant Facts: District judge dismisses the class action suit of workers charging Illinois with sex discrimination based on facts in the pleadings which fail to state a legal claim and the Association (P) appeals.

Black Letter Rule: A multiple-charge complaint is neither dismissible nor invalid merely because along with stated facts which do state a claim there are a number of stated facts which do not.

Zielinski v. Philadelphia Piers, Inc.

Instant Facts: A man who was hit by a forklift claims that it was owned by large company which denies owning it at the time of the accident.

Black Letter Rule: A general denial will not be valid if any of the allegations being denied have been admitted by both parties as true.

Ingraham v. United States

Instant Facts: Defendants claim the multimillion dollar judgment against them is in excess of a statutory limit set on such judgments but plaintiffs claim that the failure to have brought this up before the judgment was awarded constituted a waiver of this defense.

Black Letter Rule: An affirmative defense will not be saved for appeal unless raised at some point during the pleading or trial stage, before judgment is passed.

Taylor v. United States

Instant Facts: Plaintiff asserts that defendant's failure to raise the issue of an award limitation before judgment effectively waived the right to do so on appeal but the court disagrees.

Black Letter Rule: A defendant does not waive the right to raise on appeal a statutory limitation on damages if he did not raise it in the pleadings.

Beeck v. Aquaslide 'N' Dive Corp.

Instant Facts: Defendant admits manufacturing the defective water slide at issue in the case but a year later moves the court to amend the answer to deny manufacture.

Black Letter Rule: A court does not abuse its discretion by allowing an amendment to an answer which initially admitted responsibility for the manufacture of the product at issue but now seeks to deny manufacturing it.

Worthington v. Wilson

Instant Facts: Plaintiff sues three "unnamed" police officers but by the time he finds out their names and amends his pleadings, the statute of limitations for his claim has run out and his action is dismissed.

Black Letter Rule: Despite the fact that a state rule exists for a certain procedure, a federal court does not borrow that rule unless there is no federal provision concerning the same procedure.

Surowitz v. Hilton Hotels Corp.

Instant Facts: Plaintiff verified and filed a thick and detailed complaint charging fraud but defendants sought to dismiss it because plaintiff did not really understand the complex facts and language in her own pleadings.

Black Letter Rule: A technical violation of the Federal Procedural verification requirement does not alone warrant dismissal of an otherwise meritorious claim.

Hadges v. Yonkers Racing Corp.

Instant Facts: An attorney and his client were sanctioned for submitting factual misrepresentations to a district court.

Black Letter Rule: Rule 11 sanctions require compliance with the 21–day safe harbor, and an attorney may rely on the objectively reasonable representations of his client in avoiding Rule 11 sanctions for submitting false statements to a court.

Dioguardi v. Durning

(*Tonic Importer*) v. (*Customs Collector*)

139 F.2d 774 (C.C.A.2 1944)

FEDERAL SCHEME ABOLISHES CODE PLEADING IN FAVOR OF NOTICE PLEADING AND ABOLISHES REQUIREMENT THAT A "CAUSE OF ACTION" BE STATED

■ **INSTANT FACTS** A customs collector loses part of a merchant's shipment of medicinal tonics and sells the rest at auction for less than they were worth.

■ **BLACK LETTER RULE** A complaint must state just enough facts to sufficiently notify the opposing party of the claims against him so as to allow him to begin preparing a defense.

■ **PROCEDURAL BASIS**

Appeal from judgment dismissing complaint for failure to state facts sufficient to constitute a cause of action.

■ **FACTS**

Dioguardi (P) is an importer of medicinal tonics from Italy, and he is not fluent in English. Without a detailed account as to why, Dioguardi's (P) tonics ended up being placed for sale at public auction, presumably as "unclaimed customs merchandise." In his complaint, Dioguardi (P) states that when Durning (D) sold the tonics at auction, he sold them to another bidder for $10 less than Dioguardi's (P) bidding price of $120. Dioguardi also states that three weeks before the auction sale, two cases with 38 bottles of tonic disappeared. In less than flowing prose, Dioguardi (P) authored his own complaint without the assistance of an attorney and, in it, claimed $5,000 in damages, not including interest and costs. Durning (D) replied with a motion to dismiss the complaint on the ground that it failed to state facts "sufficient to constitute a cause of action." The motion was granted, but after Dioguardi (P) submitted his amended complaint, Durning (D) again moved for dismissal on the same grounds and got it. [If it worked once...]

■ **ISSUE**

Under the Federal Rules of Civil Procedure, must a complaint state facts sufficient to constitute a "cause of action?"

■ **DECISION AND RATIONALE**

(Clark, J.) No. Under the Federal Rules of Civil Procedure, a party need not state in his complaint all the facts sufficient to constitute a cause of action. Pursuant to Rule 8(a), a party need only make a "short and plain statement" which shows that he is entitled to relief. Meaning the only issue for a reviewing court to resolve is whether the opposing party has been sufficiently *notified* about the claim to be able to prepare a defense to it. Thus, despite Dioguardi's obvious problem with the English language, his complaint disclosed enough information to inform Durning (D) that he was being charged with wrongfully converting property in violation of Treasury Regulations and other federal statutes. This is ample notice to a defendant of the type of action brought against him. If Durning (D) truly required more information, he could have easily obtained it through discovery. Judgment for defendant is reversed and remanded for further proceedings. Hopefully, Dioguardi will accept legal assistance to advise him for the duration of his case.

Analysis:

In an unusual display of concern, the court expresses its desire that Dioguardi (P) employ legal assistance for the remand and other proceedings of his case. However, it does seem unlikely that the court would have been as accepting of Dioguardi's (P) confused and ineffective legal arguments if they had been prepared by a paid attorney rather than an innocent immigrant subject to the intricate web of complexities that is the American legal system. As sympathetic as this plaintiff may have been, the court received sharp criticism for its decision in this case as being too liberal. *Dioguardi* offended many judges and legal analysts for its interpretation of the Federal Rules of Civil Procedure as requiring from the complaint little beyond mere "notice." As notice pleading came to replace fact pleading as the norm, the advantages of the new system became clearer. No longer did courts battle over classification distinctions between "ultimate facts" and "conclusions of law." No longer did a party need to take up precious "statute of limitations" time to research and investigate enough facts for an informative pleading. No longer did a meritorious case have to be lost simply because of a technical defect that the opposing party could exploit.

■ CASE VOCABULARY

CONSIGNOR: A person to whom goods are delivered solely for the purpose of shipping or delivering them.

CONVERTED: (Property) wrongfully taken, detained or used by one who has no legal ownership.

INTENDMENTS: The plain and natural meanings of a writing as apparent on its face without special interpretation or analysis.

Bell Atlantic Corp. v. Twombly

(*Local Telephone Companies*) v. (*Telephone and Internet Subscribers*)

550 U.S. 544, 127 S.Ct. 1955, 167 L.Ed.2d 929 (2007)

EVEN SHORT AND PLAIN STATEMENTS REQUIRE SUFFICIENT FACTUAL ALLEGATIONS TO SUPPORT THE CLAIM

■ **INSTANT FACTS** Telephone and Internet subscribers sued their local telephone companies for allegedly entering into a conspiracy to create monopoly power in their respective markets in violation of § 1 of the Sherman Act.

■ **BLACK LETTER RULE** Federal Rules of Civil Procedure 8(a)(2) requires a "short and plain statement of the claim showing that the pleader is entitled to relief," in order to "give the defendant fair notice of what the ... claim is and the grounds upon which it rests."

■ **PROCEDURAL BASIS**

Supreme Court review of a Second Circuit decision reversing the federal district court's dismissal of the complaint.

■ **FACTS**

A group of telephone and Internet subscribers sued their local telephone companies, alleging that the companies were violating antitrust laws by agreeing not to compete with each other and to exclude other potential competitors in their market areas. The plaintiffs further alleged that as a result of this "parallel" conspiracy, each local company benefited from monopoly power in its own market. The district court dismissed the complaint on the pleadings, but the Second Circuit reversed, finding that the plaintiff's allegations satisfied the "short and plain statement" requirement of Rule 8 of the Federal Rules of Civil Procedure. The Supreme Court granted certiorari to address the proper standard for pleading an antitrust conspiracy through allegations of parallel conduct.

■ **ISSUE**

Did the plaintiffs properly allege an antitrust conspiracy claim under § 1 of the Sherman Act?

■ **DECISION AND RATIONALE**

(Souter, J.) No. Federal Rules of Civil Procedure 8(a)(2) requires a "short and plain statement of the claim showing that the pleader is entitled to relief," in order to "give the defendant fair notice of what the ... claim is and the grounds upon which it rests." *Conley v. Gibson*. But the plaintiffs have failed to satisfy that requirement in this case. Although *Conley* suggests that a complaint should not be dismissed unless it appears beyond doubt that the plaintiff can prove no set of facts that would support his entitlement to relief, a better standard is that once a claim has been stated adequately, it may be supported by showing any set of facts consistent with the allegations. *Conley*'s oft-quoted "no set of facts" language does not establish the minimum standard of adequate pleading to govern a complaint's survival.

Although detailed factual allegations are not required, a plaintiff must provide more than labels, conclusions, and a formulaic recitation of the elements of a cause of action. Factual allegations must raise the right to relief about the speculative level, if the allegations are taken as true. Applying these general standards to § 1 requires that the factual allegations must suggest more than parallel behavior; they must suggest that an actual agreement was made. We do not require heightened fact pleading of specifics, but only enough facts to state a claim to relief that is plausible on its face. Because the plaintiffs here have not nudged their claims across the line from conceivable to plausible, their complaint must be dismissed. Reversed.

■ DISSENT

(Stevens, J.) Does a judicial opinion that a charge is not plausible provide a legally acceptable reason for dismissing the complaint? I think not. Although private antitrust litigation can be enormously expensive, and there is a risk that jurors may think that parallel conduct proves that the parties acted pursuant to an agreement when they in fact made similar, independent decisions, those concerns do not justify dismissal of an adequately pleaded complaint.

Analysis:

The defendants moved the court to dismiss the plaintiffs' claims for failure to state a claim under Fed. R. Civ. P. 12(b)(6). Rule 12 (b) provides that "[e]very defense to a claim for relief in any pleading must be asserted in the responsive pleading if one is required." However, the Rule goes on, a party may assert the following defenses by motion, as in this case: "(1) lack of subject-matter jurisdiction; (2) lack of personal jurisdiction; (3) improper venue; (4) insufficient process; (5) insufficient service of process; (6) failure to state a claim upon which relief can be granted; and (7) failure to join a party under Rule 19." A motion asserting one of these defenses generally must be made before the defendant files its answer, unless no responsive pleading is required, in which case it can be raised at trial. "No defense or objection is waived by joining it with one or more other defenses or objections in a responsive pleading or in a motion."

■ CASE VOCABULARY

ANTITRUST LAW: The body of law designed to protect trade and commerce from restraints, monopolies, price-fixing, and price discrimination. The principal federal antitrust laws are the Sherman Act (15 U.S.C.A. §§ 1–7) and the Clayton Act (15 U.S.C.A. §§ 12–27).

CONSPIRACY: An agreement between two or more persons to commit an unlawful act that causes damage to a person or property.

MONOPOLY: Control or advantage obtained by one supplier or producer over the commercial market within a given region; the market condition existing when only one economic entity produces a particular product or provides a particular service. The term is now commonly applied also to situations that approach but do not strictly meet this definition.

SHERMAN ACT: A federal statute, passed in 1890, that prohibits direct or indirect interference with the freely competitive interstate production and distribution of goods. This Act was amended by the Clayton Act in 1914.

Garcia v. Hilton Hotels International, Inc.

(*Object of Slander*) v. (*Slanderers*)

97 F.Supp. 5 (D.P.R. 1951)

UNDER THE NOTICE PLEADING SYSTEM, GENERAL ALLEGATIONS OF LIABILITY DEEMED SUFFICIENT TO OVERCOME SPECIFIC DEFECTS IN THE PLEADING

■ **INSTANT FACTS** A hotel employee is fired for bringing women into the hotel for prostitution, but he claims the charge is false and slanderous.

■ **BLACK LETTER RULE** A complaint sufficiently pleads a right to relief when it states enough facts to reasonably assume that the essential elements of the claim can be proven at trial.

■ **PROCEDURAL BASIS**

Motion to dismiss the complaint for failure to state a claim upon which relief can be granted or, in the alternative, motion to strike for more definite statement.

■ **FACTS**

Garcia (P) was an employee of Hilton Hotels (D) until he was discharged as a result of allegations that he was bringing women into the Hotel for the purpose of prostitution. Consequently, Garcia (P) sued Hilton (D) for falsely and slanderously accusing him of something he did not do. Hilton (D) replied to Garcia's (P) complaint with a motion to dismiss it for failure to state a claim upon which relief can be granted or, in the alternative, to strike certain paragraphs of the complaint or require a more definite statement. As to the grounds for their motion to dismiss, Hilton (D) refers to Garcia's (P) failure to contend in his complaint that the allegedly slanderous statements were published, a necessary element of a defamation cause of action. Hilton (D) further adds that the slanderous statements were conditionally privileged and therefore immune from charges of slander.

■ **ISSUE**

Under the notice pleading system, must a plaintiff plead the right to relief with each element of liability established specifically and completely in the complaint?

■ **DECISION AND RATIONALE**

(Roberts, J.) No. A complaint will be held valid if it is reasonable to conclude from it that the plaintiff *could* make out a case at trial entitling him to some relief, even if he did not explicitly allege every element of his claim. Thus, even though Garcia's (P) cause of action is defectively stated for failing to have alleged the publication of the slanderous remarks, the complaint does state a claim upon which relief can be granted. Despite the conclusive manner in which Garcia (P) states that he was "falsely and slanderously accused," it would be unrealistic for Hilton (D) to claim that they do not understand the claim as implicitly alleging publication. Hilton's (D) other reason for the motion to dismiss Garcia's (P) complaint is the defense of conditional privilege. This fails to show cause for dismissal as well. It is established law that privilege is automatically conclusive as a defense only when it is absolute. However, when privilege is conditional, as it is alleged to be by Hilton (D), it may be lost because, at trial, plaintiff may prove abuse of the privilege or actual malice. Consequently, Hilton's (D) motion to dismiss the complaint is denied. Hilton's (D) alternative motion was to strike paragraphs 5 through 8 of the complaint for a more definite statement. These paragraphs allege that Garcia (P) was further slandered when, in the hearings with the Labor Department for wrongful termination, Hilton (D) again accused Garcia (P) of engaging in prostitution. Garcia's (P) allegations in these paragraphs must be construed under the "Act Authorizing Civil Actions to recover Damages for Libel and Slander." This statute posits that a communication will not be held malicious when made during any proceeding authorized by law. This is essentially a grant of absolute privilege. Thus, the allegations in paragraphs 5 through 8 are covered by absolute privilege and should be stricken from the complaint. Hilton's (D) motion for a more definite statement therefore applies only to paragraph 4 for failing to allege publication of the slanderous comments. Since such omission constitutes vagueness, Hilton (D) is entitled to a more definite statement.

Analysis:

The *Garcia* court has exemplified the compromises available to parties when the state of the pleadings may be less than satisfactory. When courts sense from the pleadings that some type of action may be made out on them, they are loath to quickly dismiss a complaint because it may deprive a plaintiff of his deserved day in court. Instead, the courts will allow plaintiffs to amend the original pleadings. While this seems like a fair alternative, problems may arise when the party moving for dismissal or amendment is actually crossing the line from simple notice pleading requirements and asking for more detailed common law pleadings. Obviously, it is to the moving party's advantage to require as specific a set of pleadings as the court will allow. On the one hand, this may provide that party with strategical knowledge of their opponent's strengths and weaknesses. On the other hand, this may force the opposing party to expose their insufficient knowledge of the facts. In *Garcia*, for example, it would not be surprising if Garcia (P) really did not have any proof of the publication of the slanderous comments prior to trial and that is why he did not plead them. The derivative question is why someone would still bring a lawsuit if they do not have the requisite proof to win. There are a number of possible answers. Perhaps Garcia (P) may have known that he could *not* prove publication and simply hoped that the possibility of a public lawsuit would be so repulsive to Hilton (D) that they would offer him a settlement. Regardless, the court's decision will fish out the strength of his claims before proceeding to trial.

■ CASE VOCABULARY

AFFIRMATIVE DEFENSE: A defense which does not deny a charge but alleges new facts instead; such new facts must be proved by the defendant and constitute a defense.

PRIVILEGE: A right of exemption or immunity generally possessed by a party to another in a certain fiduciary relationship.

REMOVED: Transferred a case from one jurisdiction to another before the case had been finally adjudicated.

Denny v. Carey

(Defrauded Investor) v. *(Financial Company Representative)*
72 F.R.D. 574 (E.D. Pa. 1976)

NOT EVEN FRAUD CASES REQUIRE OVERLY DETAILED FACTUAL SPECIFICITY IN THE PRE-DISCOVERY PHASE

■ **INSTANT FACTS** Investors brought suit against First Penn (D) for securities fraud, and the defendants moved to dismiss for failure to plead fraud with sufficient particularity as required by the Federal Rules of Civil Procedure.

■ **BLACK LETTER RULE** Rule 9(b)'s requirement of pleading fraud with particularity must be harmonized with Fed. R. Civ. P. 8's requirement of a short and plain statement of the plaintiff's claim that is simple, concise, and direct.

■ **PROCEDURAL BASIS**

Federal district court's consideration of the defendants' motion to dismiss.

■ **FACTS**

The plaintiff brought a proposed class action lawsuit against First Pennsylvania Corporation (D) alleging securities fraud. Specifically, the plaintiff alleged that the defendants conspired to conceal the true picture of First Penn's (D) financial condition by improperly including as income certain accruals of interest where the borrower had already defaulted, engaging in "paper" sales of foreclosed properties to avoid showing substantial losses, inadequately accounting for expected uncollectibles, and concealing other defaults. The defendants contended that these conclusory allegations, based only on the plaintiff's "information and belief," failed to state fraud with sufficient particularity under Fed. R. Civ. P. 9(b) and moved to dismiss the case.

■ **ISSUE**

Did the plaintiff plead securities fraud with sufficient particularity to withstand the defendants' motion to dismiss?

■ **DECISION AND RATIONALE**

(Lord, C.J.) Yes. Rule 9(b)'s requirement of pleading fraud with particularity must be harmonized with Fed. R. Civ. P. 8's requirement of a short and plain statement of the plaintiff's claim that is simple, concise, and direct. Since fraud embraces a wide variety of misconduct, Rule 9(b) does require slightly more notice than would be required under Rule 8 in general, but that requirement is met when there is sufficient identification of the circumstances constituting fraud such that the defendant can prepare an adequate answer to the allegations. The complaint here, though not a perfect pleading, satisfies this requirement. Before discovery, any stricter application of Rule 9(b) would be inappropriate, especially when the matters alleged are peculiarly within the knowledge of the defendants. Rule 9(b) does not insulate professionals from claims of fraud where the complaint alleges the fraudulent acts with sufficient particularity.

Analysis:

Fed. R. Civ. P. 9(b) provides that "[i]n alleging fraud or mistake, a party must state with particularity the circumstances constituting fraud or mistake. Malice, intent, knowledge, and other conditions of a person's mind may be alleged generally." Contrast this requirement with Rule 8's general admonition that a pleading must include "(1) a short and plain statement of the grounds for the court's jurisdiction, unless the court already has jurisdiction and the claim needs no new jurisdictional support; (2) a short and plain statement of the claim showing that the pleader is entitled to relief; and (3) a demand for the relief sought, which may include relief in the alternative or different types of relief." Of course, the Rule 8 requirements must be satisfied in a fraud case as well. In *Denny*, the court synchronizes these two rules and holds that in a securities fraud case, the Federal Rules are satisfied when the complaint includes sufficient factual allegations of the fraudulent to enable the defendant to prepare a meaningful defense.

■ CASE VOCABULARY

FRAUD: A knowing misrepresentation of the truth or concealment of a material fact to induce another to act to his or her detriment. Fraud is usually a tort, but in some cases (especially when the conduct is willful) it may be a crime.

ON INFORMATION AND BELIEF: (Of an allegation or assertion) based on secondhand information that the declarant believes to be true.

Tellabs, Inc. v. Makor Issues & Rights, Ltd.

(*Manufacturer*) v. (*Stock Purchasers*)

551 U.S. 308, 127 S.Ct. 2499, 168 L.Ed.2d 179 (2007)

ALL INFERENCES MUST BE CONSIDERED IN DETERMINING WHETHER SCIENTER IS SHOWN

I did it! I'm finally higher than the standard for scienter under the PSLRA!

stus.com

■ **INSTANT FACTS** The plaintiff alleged a violation of the PSLRA by the defendant, and the defendant moved to dismiss for failure to state a claim.

■ **BLACK LETTER RULE** A complaint alleging securities fraud under the Private Securities Litigation Reform Act will survive a motion to dismiss only if a reasonable person would deem the inference of scienter cogent and at least as compelling as any opposing inference one could draw from the facts alleged.

■ PROCEDURAL BASIS

On certiorari to the United States Court of Appeals for the Seventh Circuit.

■ FACTS

The Private Securities Litigation Reform Act requires plaintiffs to state with particularity the circumstances constituting the alleged violation and the facts establishing scienter—i.e., the defendant's intention to deceive, manipulate, or defraud. In particular, the plaintiffs must state with particularity the facts giving rise to a strong inference that the defendant acted with the required state of mind. The defendants in this case brought a motion to dismiss under Fed. R. Civ. P. 12(b)(6), alleging that the plaintiffs did not meet this standard.

■ ISSUE

Did the district court and court of appeals apply the correct analysis in determining whether the plaintiffs alleged a violation of the PSLRA with sufficient particularity to withstand a motion to dismiss?

■ DECISION AND RATIONALE

(Ginsburg, J.) No. A complaint alleging securities fraud under the PSLRA will survive a motion to dismiss only if a reasonable person would deem the inference of scienter cogent and at least as compelling as any opposing inference one could draw from the facts alleged. In determining whether this standard is met, the court must consider more than whether the complaint alleges facts from which a reasonable person could infer that the defendant acted with the required intent. The court must engage in a comparative evaluation, considering not only the inferences urged by the plaintiff, but also any competing inferences rationally drawn from the alleged facts. The strength of an inference cannot be decided in a vacuum. The inquiry is inherently comparative: How likely is it that one conclusion, as compared to others, arises from the underlying facts? Because the lower courts did not have an opportunity to decide the case under this standard, the judgment below is vacated.

■ CONCURRENCE

(Scalia, J., and Alito, J.) The majority's test is flawed. To establish the strong inference required by the PSLRA, the inference of scienter must be more plausible than any opposing inference, not just equal to it.

Analysis:

In the securities context, "scienter" is described as the mental state consisting of an intent to deceive, manipulate, or defraud. The PSLRA requires that, in alleging scienter under the PSLRA, the plaintiff must, "with respect to each act or omission alleged to violate this chapter, state with particularity facts giving rise to a strong inference that the defendant acted with the required state of mind." 15 U.S.C. § 78u–4(b)(2). The plaintiff cannot simply point to a false statement and declare that the defendant "must have known" that the statement was false, based upon his or her position within the company. But at the pleading stage, without the benefit of discovery, plaintiffs often do not have access to witnesses or documents that might prove the defendant's state of mind in making the false statement, so the standard is a difficult one to satisfy.

■ **CASE VOCABULARY**

INFERENCE: A conclusion reached by considering other facts and deducing a logical consequence from them.

SCIENTER: A degree of knowledge that makes a person legally responsible for the consequences of his or her act or omission; the fact of an act's having been done knowingly, especially as a ground for civil damages or criminal punishment.

Ziervogel v. Royal Packing Co.

(*Accident Victim*) v. (*Negligent Driver*)
225 S.W.2d 798 (Mo. App. 1949)

TRADITIONALLY LENIENT NOTICE-PLEADING JURISDICTION FORBIDS EVIDENCE AT TRIAL OF THOSE "SPECIAL DAMAGES" NOT MENTIONED IN THE PLEADINGS

■ **INSTANT FACTS** A woman injured in a car accident tries to bring in evidence at trial of injuries that were not mentioned in her complaint before trial.

■ **BLACK LETTER RULE** A personal injury which is not the necessary or inevitable result of an injury alleged in the petition is a "special damage" which must be specifically pleaded before trial.

■ PROCEDURAL BASIS

Appeal from jury verdict and judgment in favor of plaintiff for $2000. [In 1949, that was a lot of money.]

■ FACTS

Ziervogel (P) was driving her car and was hit by an employee of Royal Packing (D) driving his truck. Ziervogel (P) decided to sue Royal (D) in tort and, in her petition for damages, claimed that she was injured in her neck, back, spine and nervous system as well as "otherwise." During trial, however, Ziervogel's (P) counsel noted during his opening statement and through later admitted evidence the additional injuries of increased blood pressure and hurt shoulder. Royal (D) had notice of these injuries through Ziervogel's (P) statement to her insurer's Claim Agent as well as through her deposition. Nonetheless, Royal (D) moved for a mistrial on the ground that neither the injuries themselves nor the fact that they were a result of the collision was specified in Ziervogel's (P) petition and, therefore, were inadmissible evidence at trial. Royal (D) argued that it is unjust to allow Ziervogel (P) to present evidence of injuries of which Royal (D) did not have lawful notice and for which they did not prepare a defense. The trial court entered judgment for Ziervogel (P) and Royal (D) appealed.

■ ISSUE

May a plaintiff introduce evidence of special damages at trial if these were not pleaded in the petition?

■ DECISION AND RATIONALE

(McCullen, J.) No. One may not introduce evidence of special damages at trial if these were not specifically pleaded in the complaint. Special damages are those which are not the necessary or inevitable result of the injury which is alleged in the complaint. Ziervogel's (P) increased blood pressure and hurting shoulder cannot be seen as the necessary result of the injury to her neck, back and spine which were pleaded in the complaint. Consequently, the mention of increased blood pressure and hurt shoulder was an improper introduction of evidence on special damages missing from the complaint. The fact that Royal (D) was not surprised about the injuries because they had an opportunity to know of them through other means does not relieve Ziervogel (P) of her responsibility to bear the initial burden of pleading. Thus, it was error for the trial court to admit evidence of the special damages. Judgment is overruled.

Analysis:

While it may not be surprising that accident victims can experience the effects of their trauma at different times, and with particularly eviscerating pain right before a lawsuit over the injuries, the decision of the court to exclude them makes a lot of sense. Even in the more lenient jurisdictions which favor notice pleading, it is understandable that a plaintiff should provide notice to the defendant not just of the fact that he is being sued but also of the charges underlying the suit. It cannot be enough to state generally that the plaintiff has suffered physical injury. The injury needs to specified to the degree that a defendant knows he will have to prepare a defense to it in advance of trial. This requirement is short and sweet in the form of Rule 9(g) of the FRCP and states that "when items of special damage are claimed, they shall be specifically stated." The category of exceptions to this rule is made up of injuries which are the necessary or inevitable result of the general injuries which *are* specified.

■ CASE VOCABULARY

SPECIAL DAMAGES: The actual but not necessarily direct or obvious damages resulting from the injury complained of which must be specifically pleaded to be recoverable.

Bail v. Cunningham Brothers, Inc.

(*Injured*) v. (*Tortfeasor*)

452 F.2d 182 (7th Cir. 1971)

IT PAYS TO SETTLE! JURY DAMAGE AWARD ALLOWED TO BE MORE GENEROUS TO VICTIM THAN HIS OWN PRAYER FOR RELIEF

■ **INSTANT FACTS** A jury awarded judgment for plaintiff in an amount higher than he asked for in his prayer for relief and the defendant requests that the amount be remitted to the lesser one that is in the pleadings.

■ **BLACK LETTER RULE** A claimant is entitled to the amount of relief rendered at trial even if that amount is greater than what was requested in the pleadings.

■ **PROCEDURAL BASIS**

Appeal from judgment for plaintiff and request to remit it to a lower amount than awarded.

■ **FACTS**

Bail (P) sued Cunningham (D) and another defendant for personal injuries and asked for $100,000 in the ad damnum clause of the original complaint. On the morning trial was to begin, Bail (P) presented a motion to amend his complaint by increasing the amount requested in the ad damnum clause to $250,000. The trial judge denied the motion because Cunningham (D) had not received proper notice of the amendment and the case proceeded to trial. Ultimately, the jury awarded Bail (P) a judgment of $150,000 and Bail (P) again sought to amend his original complaint in a post-trial motion to the awarded amount. The other named defendant [or his lawyer] was wise enough to settle with Bail (P) for $15,000 during the trial so Bail (P) sought to collect the remaining $135,000 from Cunningham (D). [The amounts are conveniently rounded to the nearest thousand since lawyers are notoriously bad at math, else they'd be doctors!] Cunningham (D) appealed the judgment, arguing that to grant a motion to increase the amount originally sued for after a verdict has been handed down is an abuse of judicial discretion.

■ **ISSUE**

May plaintiffs be awarded and collect a greater amount in damages after trial than they pleaded in the original ad damnum clause?

■ **DECISION AND RATIONALE**

(Pell, J.) Yes. There is substantial federal authority that claimants may be awarded damages in excess of those actually demanded in their pleadings. Although this is a diversity case, federal procedural law is still authoritative. Therefore, Rule 54(C) of the FRCP is applicable as it states that a party shall be granted relief to which it is "entitled" even if the party had not demanded such relief in the pleadings. The new question in this case is whether the fact that Bail (P) attempted to amend his complaint before trial and was denied his motion changes the application of Rule 54(c). Policy dictates that Rule 54(c) applies in the same manner. On oral argument, Cunningham's (D) counsel was aware that the amount requested by Bail (D) was more than trivial but argued for no damages at all. It is unreasonable to believe that if the amended complaint were granted, and the amount requested by Bail (P) were higher, that Cunningham's (D) counsel would have changed their theory of no liability or that a different defense would have been mounted. Thus, the ex post facto change in pleadings did not actually prejudice Cunningham (D) in any real way. At no time during the trial itself was Cunningham (D) prejudiced either since Bail (P) was precluded from arguing for the larger sum he was later awarded. Thus, it is apparent that there was enough in the evidence itself that led the jury to award damages which are neither excessive nor dictated by passion or prejudice. The verdict is affirmed.

Analysis:

The prayer for relief is the final part of a complaint and is considered to be a procedural aspect of pleadings rather than a substantive one. In other words, if the prayer for relief is drafted or selected improperly, the defendant will not have enough on this alone to have the complaint dismissed. It remains common practice to allow an amendment to this section all throughout the pre-trial stage. The court in *Bail,* however, expressed an even more lenient approach to this flexible part of the complaint by allowing its constructive amendment even during the trial. The final disposition in *Bail* is rooted in three apparent policy considerations. First, the court seems to be influenced by the pre-trial failure of the defendant to settle the claim as the first defendant did and avoid wasting the court's time. Second, courts are generally loath to overturn a jury verdict, unless clearly prejudicial or unreasonable, in order to preserve the integrity and security of the jury system. Finally, this court along with many contemporary courts, finds the prayer for relief an unnecessary and ineffectual part of pleadings. While this may give more flexibility to the judge or jury, the prayer serves two important procedural functions. The prayer gives notice to the opposing party of the potential loss they face (and hopefully inspires them to settle if possible) and the prayer allows the court to award correct damages in case of a defendant's default. Therefore, it doesn't look like the prayer will be eliminated anytime soon.

■ CASE VOCABULARY

AD DAMNUM CLAUSE: Technical name for that part of the pleading which contains a statement of the plaintiff's financial loss that is the basis for his requested damages.

DIVERSITY CASE: A case in which the parties come from different, diverse, states and are therefore allowed to remove their lawsuit to a federal court instead of determining which state is the appropriate jurisdiction.

American Nurses' Association v. Illinois

(*Discriminated Employees*) v. (*Discriminatory State Employer*)

783 F.2d 716 (7th Cir. 1986)

THE "IF YOU WRITE THE SAME LETTER ON EVERY ANSWER OF A MULTIPLE CHOICE TEST, AT LEAST ONE IS BOUND TO BE CORRECT" THEORY OF PLEADING: IT ACTUALLY WORKS!!!

■ **INSTANT FACTS** District judge dismisses the class action suit of workers charging Illinois with sex discrimination based on facts in the pleadings which fail to state a legal claim and the Association (P) appeals.

■ **BLACK LETTER RULE** A multiple-charge complaint is neither dismissible nor invalid merely because along with stated facts which do state a claim there are a number of stated facts which do not.

■ **PROCEDURAL BASIS**

Appeal from district court dismissal of the case for failure to state a legal claim.

■ **FACTS**

The American Nurses' Association, "ANA", (P) charges Illinois (D) with wilful sex discrimination in their employment of men and women. The ANA (P) claims that the state (D) pays higher wages to employees (men and women) in predominantly male "job classifications" than to employees [again, men and women] in predominantly female "job classifications." The district court dismissed this complaint, having found that this charge made a "comparable worth" argument which the judiciary has already found not to violate federal antidiscrimination law. The ANA (P) appeals and claims that theirs was not a "comparable worth" argument. Rather, the ANA (P) argues that the state has deliberately segregated and classified jobs by sex so that jobs which require more or less equal skill, effort and responsibility pay more if they are classified as male-type jobs (i.e., lifting boxes of sheets, even if done by a woman, will pay more than laying each one out on a bed because lifting heavy objects is a male-type job).

■ **ISSUE**

Is a multiple-charge complaint dismissible and invalid because along with stated facts which do state a claim there are a number of stated facts which do not?

■ **DECISION AND RATIONALE**

(Posner, J.) No. A complaint should not be dismissed for failure to state a claim merely because invalid claims are interspersed with valid claims. A complaint should be allowed to stand "unless it appears beyond doubt that the plaintiff can prove *no set of facts* in support of his claim." [emphasis added] This is not such a case. This is a case, however, which highlights the merits of brief and simple pleadings. By pleading long and detailed facts and allegations, the ANA (P) got themselves thrown out of court completely. Paragraph 9 of their complaint alleges intentional and wilful discrimination, followed by the seven illustrative factual examples of this which got their complaint dismissed. Within the seven factual statements, five either are completely inscrutable or simply fail to state a legal claim. The complaint hinges on two debatably legal claims of the state's (D) wilful discrimination and departure from the market measure of wages based on gender. While wilfulness is a "classic legal weasel word," it indicates a possible meritorious claim that withstands a motion to dismiss. If this was not readily apparent to the state (D) just by reading the pleadings, their proper course would have been not to move the court to dismiss but to move the ANA (P) for a more definite statement. Thus, the complaint does not fail for merely being confusing or for including invalid claims along with valid ones. Furthermore, the complaint was not required to allege all of the facts logically entailed by the claim. After all, the complaint is not the place to plead evidence. Thus, even though the ANA's (P) claim may not survive summary judgment if discovery does not yield enough evidence to sustain their claim, the pleadings are sufficient to withstand a motion to dismiss. Reversed and remanded.

Analysis:

The appellate court in this case engages in two separate tasks of judicial review. The first, involves admonishing the lower court for a hasty and heavily consequential judicial decision. By dismissing ANA's (P) complaint, the lower court effectively removes any possibility of repleading because the ANA (P) would be precluded from pleading based on any facts which gave rise to the first suit. Thus, due to a "crabbed and literal" reading of the complaint, the lower court would have cost the ANA (P) the chance to litigate those facts which *do* state a claim as a punishment for stating facts which did not. This should remind us that the purpose of federal pleading rules is not to eliminate all imperfectly written complaints, but only those which clearly fail to state any valid legal claim. To treat the rules any other way would deprive indigent and self-represented claimants of their day in court. While the court could have elected to stop at this point in the opinion, it went on to actually review the factual merits of the ANA's (P) claim and to apply the federal antidiscrimination law to it. There would be nothing unusual about this being in an appellate opinion, except that there has been no trial yet to produce a record of facts and law for them to review. Essentially, the court seems to be offering advice through their lengthy opinion to both the parties and the next reviewing court. The parties will know what their strengths are and what weaknesses will have to be accounted for. The lower court will know what elements to look for and what standards to apply to avoid an embarrassing second reversal.

■ CASE VOCABULARY

CLASS ACTION: A consolidated lawsuit brought by a group of people who have common enough characteristics to allow a fair and efficient adjudication in a single proceeding.

COMPARABLE WORTH CASE: Claim of wage discrimination based on an employer's alleged determination of wages based on the impermissible classification of gender.

Zielinski v. Philadelphia Piers, Inc.

(Injured Victim) v. *(Alleged Tortfeasor)*

139 F.Supp. 408 (E.D. Pa. 1956)

ABUSE OF GENERAL DENIAL BACKFIRES WHEN THE COURT EQUATES IT WITH A PRESUMED GENERAL ADMITTANCE

■ **INSTANT FACTS** A man who was hit by a forklift claims that it was owned by large company which denies owning it at the time of the accident.

■ **BLACK LETTER RULE** A general denial will not be valid if any of the allegations being denied have been admitted by both parties as true.

■ FACTS

Zielinski (P) suffered physical injuries on February 9, 1953 when his forklift was struck by another forklift. In his complaint for injuries, filed on April 23, 1953, Zielinski named Philadelphia Piers, Inc. (D) as the defendant because the forklift which collided with his had "PPI" written on its side. Thus, Zielinski (P) presumed an agency relationship existed between Johnson, the driver (who would have no money to go after), and Philadelphia Piers (D) (who would have money) as his employer at the time. After the complaint was served, Philadelphia Piers (D) answered it and referred to themselves as "defendant" within the answer. Furthermore, the complaint was also forwarded to Philadelphia Piers (D) insurance company and they acknowledged responsibility as well. However, at a pretrial conference, information surfaced which made it clear that the business of moving freight on the pier had been sold by Philadelphia Piers (D) to Carload Contractors and Johnson and was switched over to the latter's payroll. In other words, Philadelphia Piers (D) does not believe it shared an agency relationship with Johnson and should, therefore, not be held accountable for any injury caused by him. Thus, Philadelphia Piers (D) generally denied the allegations of Zielinski's (P) complaint. Zielinski (P) responded by filing this motion for a ruling by the court that an agency relationship did exist between Johnson and Philadelphia Piers (D) and that Zielinski (P) was therefore suing the correct defendant.

■ ISSUE

Is a general denial valid when at least some of the allegations being denied have been admitted by both parties as true?

■ DECISION AND RATIONALE

(Van Dusen, J.) No. A general denial is ineffective when at least some of the claims being denied are clearly true and not at issue. In such a circumstance, the defendant must make a more specific answer. Thus, when Zielinski (P) stated in the pleadings that he was hit and injured by a forklift operated by an agent of Philadelphia Piers (D), a general denial is plainly erroneous. It implies not only the intended denial that the forklift was operated by an agent of Philadelphia Piers (D) but also that Zielinski (P) was injured, which cannot be denied because it was previously admitted as a true fact. This finding is supported by two major policy considerations. First, Philadelphia Piers (D) knows that the statute of limitations to file another complaint on a different defendant has already run for Zielinski (P). Thus, dismissing this complaint would effectively deprive him of any opportunity at redress in violation of established principles of equitable estoppel. Second, when an improper and ineffective answer has been filed knowingly after the plaintiff's statute of limitations has run, an allegation of agency will be instructed to the jury as presumptively admitted by both parties for the purpose of the litigation. Therefore, plaintiff's motion to instruct the jury of the agency relationship between Johnson and Philadelphia Piers (D) is granted.

Analysis:

A defendant has three options when answering a complaint. He can either admit, deny, or plead insufficient information to answer at all. The admissions and denials can either be general, referring to every claim in the complaint, or specific, referring to particular claims as admitted and others as denied. A defendant who chooses to deny any of the claims must be very careful to understand everything that is actually being claimed. Otherwise, the defendant will find himself like Philadelphia Piers (D), where he is denying parts that are debatable as to their truth and parts which have clearly been established as truth. As a result of such an ineffective and erroneous denial, defendant may be presumed to admit even those facts which he could have effectively denied. While courts are not especially eager to punish defendants purely for procedural errors and will often allow them to amend the mistakes, there are times when such "punishment" is in the interests of justice. Such is the case in *Zielinski*. The information as to who was the actual employer of the forklift operator was always in the hands of Philadelphia Piers (D). However, by filing their answer in such a sloppy manner, the statute of limitations for Zielinski (P) to file a complaint against another defendant had already run out. Sustaining such behavior would create a devious manipulation tool to future defendants to hold off from making honest answers until it is too late for the plaintiff to do anything about it.

■ CASE VOCABULARY

DEPOSITION: Legally admissible witness testimony taken outside court either in the form of oral questioning or written questionnaire.

EQUITABLE ESTOPPEL: The concept of justice which precludes a party from exercising what he/she would be entitled to if not for some voluntary act of his/her own which would make it unjust to grant him/her those rights.

Ingraham v. United States

(*Patient/Victim*) v. (*Negligent Army Hospital*)
808 F.2d 1075 (5th Cir. 1987)

● SPEAK NOW OR FOREVER HOLD YOUR PEACE: AN AFFIRMATIVE DEFENSE CANNOT BE RAISED FOR THE FIRST TIME ON APPEAL!

■ **INSTANT FACTS** Defendants claim the multi-million dollar judgment against them is in excess of a statutory limit set on such judgments but plaintiffs claim that the failure to have brought this up before the judgment was awarded constituted a waiver of this defense.

■ **BLACK LETTER RULE** An affirmative defense will not be saved for appeal unless raised at some point during the pleading or trial stage, before judgment is passed.

■ **PROCEDURAL BASIS**

Defendants appeal from quantum of judgment awarded plaintiffs.

■ **FACTS**

Ingraham (P) sued the US (D) for severe and permanent injuries to his spinal cord sustained when he was operated on by an Air Force surgeon. The Bondses (P) consolidated with Ingraham (P) when they sued the US (D) for the extensive physical and mental damage suffered by their newborn daughter as a result of an Air Force physician's failure to perform a timely Caesarian section delivery. The court awarded to Ingraham (P) a judgment for $1,264,000 and to the Bondses (P) a judgment for $4,240,555.60. The US (D) appealed both judgments not as to the finding of liability but on the ground that the judgments were in excess of the $500,000 ex delicto recovery cap set by the Legislature of Texas. The Medical Liability and Insurance Improvement Act adopted limitations on damages awarded in actions against health care providers for injuries caused by negligence. Ingraham (P) and the Bondses (P) assert that the statutory limitation is inapposite in this case because it is an affirmative defense under FRCP 8(C) that the US (D) should have but did not raise at any time during the pleadings or trial stages. Failure to raise the defense in a timely manner, claim the plaintiffs, constitutes a waiver of it.

■ **ISSUE**

Can an affirmative defense be raised for the first time in an appeal?

■ **DECISION AND RATIONALE**

(Politz, J.) No. An affirmative defense must be raised at some point before judgment is passed. The initial question, of course, is whether an issue on appeal constitutes an affirmative defense at all. Pertinent to the analysis is the logical relationship between the defense and the cause of action asserted by the plaintiff and the likelihood that the defense would take the plaintiff by surprise. After all, affirmative defenses must be pleaded in a timely manner to prevent an unfair surprise to a plaintiff by raising an unexpected defense. In this case, for example, had Ingraham (P) and the Bondses (P) known of the statutory cap on negligence damages, they would have both attacked the constitutionality of the statute and offered evidence to prove medical damages not subject to the limitation. FRCP 8(C) lists nineteen specific affirmative defenses [which the opinion laboriously enumerates] and the residuary clause names an avoidance as a similar enough action to warrant the same precaution as an affirmative defense. The limitation on damages as a defense is most akin to an avoidance, where the US (D) argues that because of the new statutory limitation, traditional tort precedents should not have their legal effect. Such an argument should have been advanced in the pleadings or at least raised during the trial to allow amendment of the pleadings. Failure to raise the defense prior to judgment constituted its waiver. Judgments affirmed.

Analysis:

Generally, affirmative defenses are those that do not logically or necessarily flow from the claims in the plaintiff's complaint. Usually, this means that the defendant is not just denying plaintiff's allegation but is setting forth facts not mentioned by the plaintiff in his complaint. Thus, a defense that merely denies that plaintiff has proven a certain element of the claim is not an affirmative defense. For example, "You lack the information to prove that I did this" is not an affirmative defense. We expect to hear that from a defendant charged with tortiously beating a motorist. On the other hand, "Yes, everything you say is true but I am immune from suits of this kind" is an affirmative defense that is available only to the few and we would not expect to hear this regularly in an answer. The policy behind the strict enforcement of this rule is understandably the avoidance of unfair surprise. Bringing up a reasonably unexpected argument not only deprives the plaintiff of an opportunity to address it in his case, but the plaintiff may even be deprived of his day in court, if the argument results in a dismissal and the statute of limitations has already run.

■ CASE VOCABULARY

AFFIRMATIVE DEFENSE: A defense not naturally arising out of the plaintiff's charge but unexpectedly challenges plaintiff's legal right to bring the charge.

AVOIDANCE: A type of affirmative defense which alleges new matter not to challenge the pleadings directly but to show cause why they should not be given their ordinary legal effect.

EX DELICTO RECOVERY: A class of recovery founded on tort or other wrongful act, as opposed to that class which arises out of a contractual obligation.

NOVATION: Method of substituting parts of a valid preexisting contract to create a new and binding contract with different parties or slightly different terms.

RESIDUARY CLAUSE: The part of a will, contract or rule after the specifics are enumerated which provides for a method for handling residue of "everything else."

Taylor v. United States

(*Victim's Wife*) v. (*Negligent Army Hospital*)

821 F.2d 1428 (9th Cir. 1987), certiorari denied 485 U.S. 992, 108 S.Ct. 1300, 99 L.Ed.2d 510 (1988)

NOT ALL LAWS ARE CREATED EQUAL: 9TH CIRCUIT DOES NOT FIND LIMITATION ON LIABILITY TO BE AN AFFIRMATIVE DEFENSE

■ **INSTANT FACTS** Plaintiff asserts that defendant's failure to raise the issue of an award limitation before judgment effectively waived the right to do so on appeal but the court disagrees.

■ **BLACK LETTER RULE** A defendant does not waive the right to raise on appeal a statutory limitation on damages if he did not raise it in the pleadings.

■ **PROCEDURAL BASIS**

Appeal from judgment awarding tort damages allegedly in excess of statutory allowance.

■ **FACTS**

Taylor (P) was awarded $500,000 in damages for loss of consortium and emotional distress. Her husband suffered permanent brain damage while receiving medical treatment at an army hospital. The US (D) appealed the judgment on the ground that it exceeded the $250,000 cap on noneconomic injuries from professional negligence under the California Civil Code, as incorporated by the Federal Tort Claims Act. Taylor (P) responded that the US (D) waived the statutory protection by failing to raise the issue before judgment.

■ **ISSUE**

Does a defendant waive the right to raise on appeal a statutory limitation on damages if he did not raise it in the pleadings?

■ **DECISION AND RATIONALE**

No. A defendant may raise a statutory limitation on damages during an appeal even if he failed to raise it in the pleadings. After all, a statutory limitation on liability is not an affirmative defense. Thus, if the Federal Rules do not require plaintiff to plead the extent of damages, defendants should not be required to plead a limitation on them either. To hold otherwise would unrealistically require defendants to anticipate awards in excess of the statutory limitation even when they were not requested by plaintiff. Furthermore, the Federal Rules do not consider a limitation of damages to be an affirmative defense. Specifically, FRCP 8(d) indicates that a defendant's failure to deny the amount of damages in his answer is not automatically deemed an admission. Accordingly, the US (D) was not required to raise the statutory limitation in its answer. Judgement reversed.

Analysis:

This case is difficult to reconcile with *Ingraham v. United States* (holding that an affirmative defense will not be saved for appeal unless raised at some point during the pleading or trial stage, before judgment is passed). They appear clearly contradictory. Perhaps one must look to the specific statute at issue to determine if a defense must be alleged as an affirmative defense. However, there may be an explanation separate from the fact that different circuits decided the cases. In *Taylor*, it appears that the court or jury awarded the $500,000 judgment even though the plaintiff requested less. If that was the case, the policy considerations may merit the holding that the limitation could be raised for the first time on appeal. After all, that means the US (D) did not defend it in its answer because (a) Taylor (P) did not ask for such high damages and (b) because the US (D) assumed that the court was aware of the statutory limitation and would not exceed it.

■ **CASE VOCABULARY**

LOSS OF CONSORTIUM: Loss of the conjugal relationship between husband and wife which includes but is not limited to both material support and such intangibles as companionship and sex.

Beeck v. Aquaslide 'N' Dive Corp.

(Slide Victim) v. *(Alleged Slide Manufacturer)*

562 F.2d 537 (8th Cir. 1977)

AN ADMISSION IN A PLEADING CAN BE CHANGED TO A DENIAL IN THE COURT'S DISCRETION

■ **INSTANT FACTS** Defendant admits manufacturing the defective water slide at issue in the case but a year later moves the court to amend the answer to deny manufacture.

■ **BLACK LETTER RULE** A court does not abuse its discretion by allowing an amendment to an answer which initially admitted responsibility for the manufacture of the product at issue but now seeks to deny manufacturing it.

■ **PROCEDURAL BASIS**

Appeal from trial court's exercise of discretion on procedural matters.

■ **FACTS**

During a company sponsored gathering, Beeck (P) was severely injured at Kimberly Village while using a water slide he claims was negligently manufactured by Aquaslide (D). Kimberly investigated the accident and soon thereafter sent a notice to Aquaslide (D) informing them that one of their Queen Model slides was involved [a kind term for "implicated"]. Aquaslide (D) forwarded this notice to its insurer and an adjuster came out to investigate the slide and question persons who ordered and assembled the slide. The insurance adjuster, as well as investigators for Kimberly Village, indicated that the slide was definitely manufactured by Aquaslide (D). Beeck (P) filed the personal injury complaint which Aquaslide (D) answered, admitting that it "designed, manufactured, assembled and sold" the slide. About six months after the statute of limitations for Beeck's (P) claim had run out (he was on time, though) and a total of one year after the filing of the complaint and answer, the president and owner of Aquaslide (D) himself visited the site of the accident. From his inspection, he determined that the slide was not Aquaslide's (D) product and then moved the court for leave to amend the answer to deny the slide's manufacture. The court granted the motion and Beeck (P) appealed. Then the court granted a separate jury trial to decide the issue of manufacture which Beeck (P) lost and Beeck (P) appealed this too.

■ **ISSUE**

Is it an abuse of trial court discretion to allow an amendment to an answer from admitting to denying responsibility for the manufacture of the product at issue?

■ **DECISION AND RATIONALE**

(Benson, J.) No. A court does not abuse its discretion by allowing an amendment to an answer which initially admitted responsibility for the manufacture of the product at issue but now seeks to deny manufacturing it. There is substantial authority for this decision both in case law and in the Federal Rules. In *Foman v. Davis* the Supreme Court held that, in the absence of bad faith or dilatory motive on the part of the movant, leave to amend is fully within the discretion of the district court. This holding is rooted in FRCP 15(a) which declares that leave to amend should be "freely given when justice so requires." Applying these principles to the case at hand, the trial court did not abuse its discretion by

---

allowing either the amendment or the trial on the issue. The trial court searched the record for evidence of bad faith and rightfully found none. After all, Aquaslide (D) legitimately relied on the findings of separate insurance adjustors until its president made his own belated investigation and arrived at a contrary conclusion. As to Beeck's (P) contention of prejudice because the statute of limitations had already run prior to the motion to amend, it is unfounded. This presumes that the trial court should have known that Beeck (P) would have lost on the issue at trial or at the mini trial on this particular issue. That is an unreasonable expectation. If anything, to prevent the defendant from denying a disputed factual issue would be prejudicial to it more than to Beeck (P). (Aquaslide would be forced into the ludicrous position of arguing that the slide was not manufactured negligently when it did not manufacture the slide at all!) The blame for this gross error should be shared equally. Thus, the district court ruling is affirmed.

Analysis:

The sympathetic reader may be inclined to feel sorry for the poor injured plaintiff who, as a result of the leave to amend, has lost the opportunity to refile his claim against a different defendant because the statute of limitation has run out. The issue of manufacture, however, would have to be resolved by the trier of fact in any case, so Beeck (P) was not really deprived of a fair trial. He was just deprived of a trial on the issue of negligence. This is not necessarily a bad thing because going to trial on all the issues when manufacture was really the essential one would have been a waste of judicial resources. Not to mention, Aquaslide (D) would have been forced to expend much time and money to defend itself against a claim for which it could not have been responsible. While a day in court belongs to everyone who has a legitimate complaint, it should not be afforded at the expense of other parties.

■ CASE VOCABULARY

NEGLIGENCE: Tort term for the failure to use such standard of care as a reasonable person would in the same circumstances.

STRICT LIABILITY: Tort doctrine of imposing liability for any adverse consequences of a product or act, even when it was not negligent (applies to inherently dangerous products).

Worthington v. Wilson

(*Injured Arrestee*) v. (*Arresting Police Officer*)

790 F.Supp. 829 (C.D. Ill. 1992)

IN PROCEDURAL SPARRING BETWEEN STATE AND FEDERAL LAW, FEDERAL PROCEDURE ALWAYS TRUMPS

■ **INSTANT FACTS** Plaintiff sues three "unnamed" police officers but by the time he finds out their names and amends his pleadings, the statute of limitations for his claim has run out and his action is dismissed.

■ **BLACK LETTER RULE** Despite the fact that a state rule exists for a certain procedure, a federal court does not borrow that rule unless there is no federal provision concerning the same procedure.

■ **PROCEDURAL BASIS**

Hearing on motion for sanctions and motion to dismiss amended complaint.

■ **FACTS**

Worthington (P) was arrested by two police officers (D) on February 25, 1989. At that time, Worthington (P) advised the officers (D) that he was nursing an injured hand but they grabbed him, handcuffed him and pulled him up off the ground by the handcuffs. As a result, Worthington (P) suffered broken bones in his hand. Two years later, Worthington (P) filed a complaint against the City and "three unknown named police officers" for deprivation of constitutional rights, in violation of the Civil Rights Act of 1964. Four months later, Worthington (P) filed an amended complaint which actually named the officers as Wilson (D) and Wall (D) but no longer contained a claim against the City. The officers (D) filed a motion to dismiss the complaint on the ground that the statute of limitations had run out. The magistrate judge recommended the dismissal and Worthington (P) appealed. Because the amended complaint was filed after the two-year statute of limitations had run out, the only way the complaint can be found timely is if it relates back to the original complaint. The officers (D) argue that, per FRCP 15(c), relation back is not permitted because there was no "mistake" concerning the proper party. Worthington (P) simply didn't know who the proper party was. Worthington (P) argues that the controlling law is § 2–413 of the Illinois Code of Civil Procedure, not the FRCP. This statute, Worthington (P) posits, does permit relation back in this circumstance because his inability to discover the officers' names was not for want of diligence.

■ **ISSUE**

Does a federal rule of procedure prevail even if there is an existing contradictory state rule governing the same procedure?

■ **DECISION AND RATIONALE**

(Mihm, J.) Yes. Even if a state rule exists for a certain procedure, a federal court does not borrow that rule unless there is no similar federal provision. In this case, FRCP 15(c) addresses the issue of relation back of unknown named defendants addressed in the Illinois Code of Civil Procedure. Thus, not only is the Illinois rule offered by Worthington (P) inapplicable, it is also irrelevant because it is in a conflict between a state and federal procedure rule [the feds always win!]. Worthington (P) is therefore bound by FRCP 15(c). However, there are two versions of this rule. The new standard in the rule allows relation back of a changed name to the original complaint if the new party was given notice within 120 days of the filing of the complaint. As stipulated by the defendants, such notice was in fact given. However, this is sadly of no use to Worthington (P) because the older rule was still in effect at the time he filed the complaint and made the amendments. The old rule required that the new party receive notice before the statute of limitations period expired. Furthermore, this Circuit's cases have indicated that the use of incorrect party names due to lack of knowledge does not constitute a "mistake" for the purpose of a relation back benefit of FRCP 15(c). Thus, regardless of which version of FRCP 15(c) applies for the purpose of timing, Worthington's (P) amended complaint would still not be entitled to relation back. Dismissal affirmed.

Analysis:

The surface decision of this case, that federal procedural law always trumps state procedural, is nothing new or radical. The Supreme Court has said this much itself. The implied crucial issue, then, is arguing that the rule you want applied is not procedural. The law is generally divided into two categories: procedural and substantive. While their names seem relatively self-explanatory, it is not always easy to apply the distinction in practice. As to the issue of relation back, for example, the Supreme Court has never actually declared whether those rules are substantive or procedural. Despite this mystery, relation back has been honed and explained in its actual application. The 1991 amendment, the benefit of which Worthington (P) just missed, particularly allows some leeway in allowing name-correcting amendments. Many states have adopted this new approach. California is especially liberal in allowing a plaintiff to name "John Does" in addition to named defendants and avoid the statute of limitations problem entirely.

■ CASE VOCABULARY

BRIGHT-LINE [RULE]: Legal jargon for a rule that is actually distinct and established in case law, as distinguished from a rule which is not easily discernible from the case law.

RELATION BACK OF AMENDMENTS: An amendment is allowed to relate back to the original pleadings for the purpose of dating them in a timely manner in order to avoid the consequences of an expired statute of limitation.

TOLLING: Privilege of temporarily suspending time for the purpose of avoiding the statute of limitations running out.

Surowitz v. Hilton Hotels Corp.

(Stockholder) v. *(Stock Corporation)*

383 U.S. 363, 86 S.Ct. 845, 15 L.Ed.2d 807 (1966)

JUSTICE TRIUMPHS OVER PROCEDURAL EXACTITUDE AS PLAINTIFF IS ALLOWED TO PROCEED WITH A MERITORIOUS CLAIM DESPITE A PROCEDURAL FLAW IN THE PLEADING

■ **INSTANT FACTS** Plaintiff verified and filed a thick and detailed complaint charging fraud but defendants sought to dismiss it because plaintiff did not really understand the complex facts and language in her own pleadings.

■ **BLACK LETTER RULE** A technical violation of the Federal Procedural verification requirement does not alone warrant dismissal of an otherwise meritorious claim.

■ FACTS

Surowitz (P) is a stockholder of Hilton (D) who brought a class action against Hilton (D) charging that it violated the Securities Act of 1933. Allegedly, Hilton (D) defrauded the stockholders out of millions by illegally cheating and depleting the corporation to enrich the individual defendants. The thickly paginated and detailed complaint was signed by Surowitz's (P) counsel and verified by Surowitz (P) herself. What the complaint does not state, though, is that Surowitz (P) is an elderly Polish immigrant with very little formal education and even less of an English vocabulary. Furthermore, her counsel is also her son-in-law [the brilliant Mr. Brilliant, Harvard Law graduate who "wore a Phi Beta Kappa key" I] Apparently, Brilliant had been investing money for Surowitz (P) and had bought some Hilton (D) stock because they were relatively fool-proof. However, when Surowitz (P) received a letter from Hilton (D) asking to buy a large amount of its own stock, she got concerned and Brilliant got involved. After arriving, at the Hilton's (D) Chicago headquarters, it did not take Brilliant long to discover that Hilton (D) was engaged in a fraudulent scheme. After explaining this to Surowitz (P), Brilliant convinced her to file a suit in her name and explained to her everything he was putting in the complaint before she signed it. Thus, claims Surowitz (P), she knew what the lawsuit was about but she could not have read and understood the complaint as written in English, especially when a lawyer drafted it! Surowitz's (P) minimal English became apparent to Hilton (D) during deposition so they moved the court for dismissal. Hilton (D) claimed that Mrs. Surowitz's (P) affidavit was "false," a "sham," and a "nullity." The district court and appellate court both agreed and, without even requiring Hilton (D) to file an answer, dismissed the case with prejudice. Surowitz (P) appealed it to the Supreme Court.

■ ISSUE

Should an otherwise meritorious case be dismissed when the Federal Procedural Rule 23 verification requirement technically has been violated?

■ DECISION AND RATIONALE

(Black, J.) No. A technical violation of the Federal Procedural verification requirement does not alone warrant dismissal of an otherwise meritorious claim. The Federal Rules of Procedure are promulgated first and foremost to insure that justice is served and that parties receive a fair trial. Uniformity and judicial economy are secondary. Specifically, FRCP 23(b)'s verification requirement that the allegations in the complaint are true to the best of petitioner's knowledge and belief is intended to discourage "strike suits" not bona fide claims. In this case, neither Surowitz (P) nor her counsel sought to do any injury to Hilton (D) or indicated any bad faith. Rather, Surowitz (P) honestly and reasonably relied on the advice of her son-in-law about the complaint she signed and verified. This was neither intended to nor did cause any actual harm to Hilton (D). Furthermore, the serious fraud charges and heavily researched pleading allegations merited an adjudication of the issues. Instead, the lower courts rigidly and erroneously dismissed the complaint without ever even making Hilton (D) answer it. The three years of pleading and appeals it has taken Mrs. Surowitz (P) to be heard is too long. The dismissal is reversed and the case is remanded for trial on the merits.

■ CONCURRENCE

(Harlan, J.) FRCP 23(b) requires that the complaint be "verified by oath." The rule does not state that the verification has to be of the plaintiff shareholder herself. [Thus, even by a technical application of Rule 23(b), the Surowitz (P) complaint should not have been dismissed.]

Analysis:

This decision is famous as an indication of the Court's occasional sacrifice of procedural exactitude for the sake of administering apparent justice. The opinion abounds with lessons that the Federal Rules were designed to be flexible enough to be user-friendly to even the most unsophisticated litigant. Nonetheless, the 1966 Court is archaically sympathetic with the "little old lady" plaintiff. While Rule 23(b) may be flexible as a result of *Surowitz*, the slack is picked up by heightened enforcement of amended Rule 11. Prior to 1983, FRCP 11 employed a subjective standard of good faith to judge attorney conduct. Due to its ultimate ineffectualness, the 1983 amendment replaced the subjective standard with the objective standard of reasonableness. This made attorneys responsible for the facts and law on which their filings are premised and it set mandatory sanctions for violation of the rule. Ironically, Rule 23(b) has now fallen by the litigation wayside and Rule 11 is widely used and abused as the intimidating and evasive tactic of choice.

■ CASE VOCABULARY

CERTIORARI: A common law writ still in practice today which is issued by a higher court to a lower court to see the record for and choose the cases it may wish to hear.

DISMISSAL WITH PREJUDICE: Effectively creates a verdict as though there was trial on the merits and bars the right to bring or maintain the action on the same claim.

SECONDARY ACTION: An action subsequent to or subordinate to the primary law suit.

STRIKE SUITS: Lawsuits brought by parties who have no regard for the truth of their accusations but whose only purpose is to "strike" at a wealthy defendant in hopes that they will prefer to settle the worthless claim rather than go to trial.

Hadges v. Yonkers Racing Corp.

(*Horse Racer*) v. (*Racing Corporation*)
48 F.3d 1320 (2nd Cir. 1995)

RULE 11 ESTABLISHES STRICT GUIDELINES FOR SANCTIONING PARTIES AND ATTORNEYS FOR SUBMITTING MISREPRESENTATIONS TO COURT

■ **INSTANT FACTS** An attorney and his client were sanctioned for submitting factual misrepresentations to a district court.

■ **BLACK LETTER RULE** Rule 11 sanctions require compliance with the 21-day safe harbor, and an attorney may rely on the objectively reasonable representations of his client in avoiding Rule 11 sanctions for submitting false statements to a court.

■ **PROCEDURAL BASIS**

Appeal of imposition of sanctions against attorney and party for submitting misrepresentations to court.

■ **FACTS**

Hadges (P) was a racehorse driver, trainer and owner who was licensed by the New York State Racing Board. His license was suspended on two occasions. Following his second reinstatement in 1989, Hadges (P) was denied the ability to work at a number of racetracks. Hadges (P) sued the Yonkers Racing Corporation ("YRC") (D) in both state and federal court. The federal claim was dismissed and the state court ruled against Hadges (P). Hadges (P) appealed the state decision and filed a Rule 60(b) motion in federal court, requesting that the federal dismissal be vacated. At issue in the federal case was Hadges' (P) ability to work at other racetracks besides Yonkers Raceway. Hadges (P) claimed that other tracks had barred him from working. Hadges (P) and his attorney (William Kunstler) signed statements saying that Hadges (P) had not worked in four years, and they neglected to mention the state appeal. YRC (D) presented evidence that showed Hadges (P) had worked at other racetracks. YRC (D) moved for dismissal of the Rule 60(b) action and requested sanctions against Hadges (P) and Kunstler for misrepresentation and failing to disclose the state court action. Hadges (P) admitted that he had worked at other tracks, but he submitted a "scratch" sheet that showed he was barred by the Racing Board in 1989. YRC (D) established that this sheet was actually from 1987. The district court denied Hadges' (P) Rule 60(b) motion and eventually imposed Rule 11 sanctions against Hadges (P). The court also censured Kunstler for failing to make adequate inquiry as to the truth of Hadges' (P) affidavits and for failing to inform the court of the pending state court action. Kunstler's application to reargue the sanction was denied. Hadges (P) and Kunstler appealed the imposition of the sanctions and the denial to reargue the sanction issues. YRC (D) allegedly failed to comply with the procedural requirements for Rule 11 sanctions. YRC (D) failed to submit the sanction request separately, and it did not serve Hadges (P) and Kunstler with the request 21 days before presenting it to the court.

■ **ISSUE**

(1) In order to obtain Rule 11 sanctions, is it necessary to strictly comply with the procedural requirements? (2) Is an attorney entitled to rely on the objectively reasonable representations of his client when submitting factual statements to the court?

■ DECISION AND RATIONALE

(Justice Not Stated) (1) Yes. In order to obtain Rule 11 sanctions, it is necessary to strictly comply with the procedural requirements. YRC (D) should have served Hadges (P) with the request for sanctions 21 days before presenting it to the court. This would have enabled Hadges (P) to withdraw or appropriately correct his misstatements and avoid sanctions altogether. Hadges (P) did in fact correct his misstatements about the scratching incident and the alleged failure to work for four years. In light of the failure to afford Hadges (P) the 21-day-safe-harbor period provided by revised Rule 11, the sanction of Hadges (P) should be reversed. Like Hadges (P), Kunstler did not receive the benefit of the safe-harbor period. (2) Yes. In addition, under the new version of Rule 11, an attorney is entitled to rely on the objectively reasonable representations of the client when submitting the client's affidavit to the court. Kunstler was required to make an inquiry reasonable under the circumstances to determine whether an objectively reasonable basis for the statements existed. As a reviewing court, we must look at the pretrial proceedings and determine whether they provided evidentiary support for the factual misrepresentations with which the court is concerned. We conclude that the record contained evidentiary support for the claim that Hadges (P) had not worked for four years, and for the claim regarding the scratching incident. Moreover, Hadges (P) was not required to mention the state court proceeding, as the state court opinion was not a decision on the merits and there was no tactical advantage in not mentioning the ruling. For all these reasons, including the failure of YRC (D) to provide Kunstler with the 21-day safe harbor, we reverse the imposition of the censure on Kunstler.

Analysis:

This case raises a number of important issues regarding Rule 11 sanctions. Rule 11's 21-day-safe-harbor provision is especially important, providing parties and their attorneys the opportunity to correct their errors before sanctions are imposed. The case also explains the grounds for sanctioning attorneys for failing to investigate the truthfulness of their client's representations before submitting them to court. Obviously, if an attorney knows that his client's statements are untruthful, the attorney should not submit them to the court. But to what extent must an attorney investigate the truthfulness of the statements? In general, an attorney is entitled to rely on any objectively reasonable statements. The new Rule 11 requires only an inquiry reasonable under the circumstances.

■ CASE VOCABULARY

ANIMUS: Hostility or hatred.

BLACKBALL: A negative vote that blocks some activity.

CHAPTER NINE

Joinder of Claims and Parties: Expanding the Scope of the Civil Action

Harris v. Avery

Instant Facts: Avery (P) sued Harris (D) for slander and false imprisonment after Harris (D) allegedly called Avery (P) a thief and imprisoned Avery (P) for stealing a horse.

Black Letter Rule: Claims arising out of the same transaction may be joined in one lawsuit, pursuant to state codes.

M.K. v. Tenet

Instant Facts: After the plaintiffs amended their complaint to add new claims, the defendants filed a motion to sever.

Black Letter Rule: Federal Rule of Civil Procedure 18 provides for unrestricted joinder of claims against an opposing party.

United States v. Heyward–Robinson Co.

Instant Facts: D'Agostino Excavators (P) brought a claim for a subcontract with Heyward–Robinson Co. (D), Heyward (D) counterclaimed, and D'Agostino (P) counterclaimed back. Heyward (D) disputes the compulsory nature of the counterclaims.

Black Letter Rule: A counterclaim is compulsory if it has some logical relationship to the opposing party's claim.

Lasa Per L'industria Del Marmo Societa Per Azioni v. Alexander

Instant Facts: Several claims arose out of contracts to construct the Memphis City Hall, including cross-claims between the contractor, Southern Builders (D), and one of the subcontractors, Alexander Marble and Tile (D).

Black Letter Rule: A cross-claim is valid as long as it bears some logical relationship with the transaction or occurrence that is the subject matter of the original action or counterclaim.

Ellis Canning Co. v. International Harvester Co.

Instant Facts: Ellis Canning Co. (P) brought a suit for negligence in servicing a tractor against International Harvester Co. (D), even though Ellis (P) had already been compensated for the loss by its insurance company.

Black Letter Rule: Lawsuits must be prosecuted by a real party in interest, one who has an interest in the subject matter of the litigation.

Ryder v. Jefferson Hotel Co.

Instant Facts: The Ryders (P), an allegedly married couple, were roused from their room and verbally insulted by the staff of the Jefferson Hotel (D). The Ryders (P) brought separate tort claims in one action in a South Carolina court.

Black Letter Rule: Separate tort claims by separate parties arising from the same occurrence cannot be joined in one lawsuit.

M.K. v. Tenet (II)

Instant Facts: After the plaintiffs amended their complaint to add new plaintiffs, the defendants opposed the party joinder.

Black Letter Rule: Federal Rule of Civil Procedure 20(a) permits joinder of plaintiffs if all claims arose out of the same transaction or occurrence and share common questions of law or fact.

Tanbro Fabrics Corp. v. Beaunit Mills, Inc.

Instant Facts: Tanbro (P), the buyer of allegedly defective goods, sought to consolidate actions against Beaunit Mills (D), the seller, and Amity (D), the processor.

Black Letter Rule: Separate claims against various parties may be joined if the claims are logically related.

Bank of California Nat. Ass'n v. Superior Court

Instant Facts: Bertha Smedley (P), who claimed entitlement to all of a decedent's estate by contract, sued the executor, Bank of California (D) and the residuary legatee, St. Luke's Hospital (D). These defendants brought a motion to join the other purported beneficiaries to the estate.

Black Letter Rule: Mandatory joinder requires courts to join all necessary and indispensable parties to an action.

Provident Tradesmens Bank & Trust Co. v. Patterson

Instant Facts: In an action arising out of a traffic collision, Provident Tradesmens Bank (P), the administrator of a decedent's estate, sued Lumbermen's Mutual Casualty Company (D), the insurer of the automobile. The Appellate Court dismissed the action for failure to join the insured party.

Black Letter Rule: Where it is not feasible to join a necessary party, the action must be dismissed only if the party is indispensable.

Jeub v. B/G Foods, Inc.

Instant Facts: B/G Foods (D), sued by Jeub (P) for allegedly serving contaminated ham, obtained an order impleading the ham manufacturer, Swift and Company (D), for indemnity purposes.

Black Letter Rule: A party may implead a third party defendant for indemnity even where the state law procedure does not recognize indemnity claims before the party pays more than its share of the loss.

Too Inc. v. Kohl's Dept. Stores

Instant Facts: Windstar Apparel (D) sought leave to implead two former employees allegedly liable for indemnification and contribution to the defendant.

Black Letter Rule: Leave to file a third-party complaint may be granted if the defendant did not deliberately delay the filing of its third-party complaint, impleader would not unduly delay the trial, the third-party defendant would not be prejudiced by the filing, and the third-party complaint states a claim for which relief may be granted.

Hancock Oil Co. v. Independent Distributing Co.

Instant Facts: Hancock Oil (P) leased property from the Hopkinses (D) but was uncertain to whom to pay rent, so Hancock Oil (P) sought to interplead all interested parties and force them to battle over the rents.

Black Letter Rule: The common law of interpleader should be broadly construed to force rival claimants to battle over property.

New York Life Ins. Co. v. Dunlevy

Instant Facts: New York Life (D) sought interpleader of Effie Dunlevy (P) and her father, Joseph Gould (D), to determine who had the right to money from a life insurance policy. Dunlevy (P) never appeared in the interpleader action.

Black Letter Rule: Personal jurisdiction over all claimants is a prerequisite to interpleader actions.

Pan American Fire & Cas. Co. v. Revere

Instant Facts: Pan American Fire & Cas. Co. (P), the insurer of a tractor-trailer which was involved in a collision, brought a motion for interpleader to join all of the various claims and claimants related to the accident.

Black Letter Rule: Federal interpleader rules and statutes should be read broadly so as to grant interpleader whenever possible, although venue and service of process must nevertheless be satisfied.

State Farm Fire & Cas. Co. v. Tashire

Instant Facts: State Farm Fire & Cas. Co. (P) held an insurance policy for the driver of a truck, which collided with a Greyhound bus and caused several injuries. State Farm (P) brought an interpleader action to join all of the potential tortfeasors and resolve all of the claims.

Black Letter Rule: In complex tort situations, the effect of interpleader should not necessarily be to confine the total litigation to a single forum and proceeding.

Smuck v. Hobson

Instant Facts: Smuck (P), a member of the District of Columbia Board of Education, and Hansen, the resigned Superintendent of Schools, along with twenty parents, sought to intervene in order to appeal a judgment in favor of school children suffering from the Board's discriminatory educational practices.

Black Letter Rule: Third parties may intervene after a judgment on the merits, provided the conditions in Federal Rule 24(a) are satisfied.

Harris v. Avery

(Slanderer) v. *(Defamed Individual)*
5 Kan. 146 (1869)

CAUSES OF ACTION ARISING FROM THE SAME TRANSACTION MAY BE JOINED IN ONE LAWSUIT

■ **INSTANT FACTS** Avery (P) sued Harris (D) for slander and false imprisonment after Harris (D) allegedly called Avery (P) a thief and imprisoned Avery (P) for stealing a horse.

■ **BLACK LETTER RULE** Claims arising out of the same transaction may be joined in one lawsuit, pursuant to state codes.

■ **PROCEDURAL BASIS**

Appeal from denial of demurrer to complaint for damages for slander and false imprisonment.

■ **FACTS**

Harris (D) allegedly called Avery (P) a thief, saying Avery (P) had stolen a horse. [Oooh, that's got to hurt!] Harris (D) proceeded to take the horse from Avery (P) and keep it for four or five days, and Harris (D) also imprisoned Avery (P) for four or five days in the county jail. Avery (P) sued Harris (D) for false imprisonment and slander in a state court in Kansas. Harris (D) demurred to the complaint, arguing that several causes of action (slander and false imprisonment) were improperly joined. The state district court overruled the demurrer, and Harris (D) appealed.

■ **ISSUE**

May two causes of action be joined in one lawsuit if they arise from the same transaction?

■ **DECISION AND RATIONALE**

(Valentine, J.) Yes. Two or more causes of action that arise from the same transaction may be joined in one complaint. Pursuant to a Kansas statute, a plaintiff may unite several causes of action if they fall within one of several classes, including actions arising out of the same transaction. We find that Avery's (P) claims for false imprisonment and slander arose out of the same transaction, and thus the claims were properly joined. This represents a departure from common law. At common law, if Harris (D) had arrested Avery (P) without any process—which was in fact the case—then the first cause of action, for false imprisonment, would have to be brought in an action for trespass and the second cause of action, for slander, would have to be brought in an action for trespass on the case. However, our state codes have altered this common law when the two actions arise out of the same transaction. This accomplishes the goal of avoiding multiplicity of suits whenever practicable. Affirmed.

Analysis:

This case represents the modern trend allowing for flexibility in joining several claims. Flexible joinder rules, exemplified by Kansas' statute, encourage judicial efficiency by avoiding a multiplicity of lawsuits. Indeed, it makes sense to try related claims in one action, since the underlying factual issues should only have to be examined one time. Typical state code provisions, such as Kansas', allowed for joinder of claims when they fell into one of several categories, including the following: contracts, injuries to the

---

person, injuries to character, injuries to property, actions to recover real property, actions to recover chattels, or actions arising out of the same transaction. Notice that these codes do not necessarily liberalize all joinder rules. For example, under the codes, a tort action for injury to property could not be joined with a tort action for injury to the person unless they arose out of the same transaction. However, at common law, such actions could be joined if they occurred in the same common law form of action (e.g., trespass or trespass on the case).

■ CASE VOCABULARY

DEMURRER: Motion stating that, even if all of the elements in a complaint are assumed to be true, the complaint nevertheless fails to state a valid claim.

SLANDER: A cause of action for a defamatory false statement concerning another person.

TRESPASS ON THE CASE: Form of action at common law for damages resulting from wrongful immediate force by a defendant.

TROVER: A common law form of action for wrongful conversion of a person's property.

M.K. v. Tenet

(Former Employee) v. *(CIA Director)*
216 F.R.D. 133 (D.D.C. 2002)

PLAINTIFFS MAY JOIN IN ONE ACTION AS MANY CLAIMS AS THEY HAVE AGAINST A DEFENDANT

■ **INSTANT FACTS** After the plaintiffs amended their complaint to add new claims, the defendants filed a motion to sever.

■ **BLACK LETTER RULE** Federal Rule of Civil Procedure 18 provides for unrestricted joinder of claims against an opposing party.

■ **PROCEDURAL BASIS**

Consideration of the defendants' motion to sever.

■ **FACTS**

Six former CIA employees (P) sued Tenet (D) and the Central Intelligence Agency (D) for violating the Privacy Act of 1974 and their constitutional rights by obstructing their access to counsel. In a second amended complaint, the plaintiffs added additional plaintiffs and information concerning existing claims to cure deficiencies in the original complaint. The defendants moved to sever the six existing plaintiffs from the amended claims under Federal Rule of Civil Procedure 21.

■ **ISSUE**

Are the defendants entitled to have the initial claims of the six original plaintiffs severed from the newly asserted claims?

■ **DECISION AND RATIONALE**

(Urbina, J.) No. The defendants argue that the new claims are isolated and unique from the original claims such that they may be severed from them and considered separately. Whether or not the new claims are independent of the original claims, however, joinder is permissible. Federal Rule of Civil Procedure 18 allows unrestricted joinder of all claims a party has against an opposing party. The motion is denied.

Analysis:

Generally, the joinder of all claims one plaintiff has against the same defendant does not prejudice the defendant, even if the claims are sufficiently distinct. By consolidating all claims in one proceeding, the court saves considerable judicial resources by considering all claims before the same jury, on the same docket, and during the same trial. Any potential confusion to the jury can ordinarily be resolved with proper court instruction.

■ **CASE VOCABULARY**

JOINDER: The uniting of parties or claims in a single lawsuit.

SEVERANCE: The separation of claims, by the court, of multiple parties either to permit separate actions on each claim or to allow certain interlocutory orders to become final.

United States v. Heyward-Robinson Co.

(Party to Contract) v. *(Subcontractor)*
430 F.2d 1077 (2nd Cir. 1970)

COUNTERCLAIMS NEED ONLY A LOGICAL RELATIONSHIP TO ORIGINAL CLAIM TO BE CONSIDERED COMPULSORY

■ **INSTANT FACTS** D'Agostino Excavators (P) brought a claim for a subcontract with Heyward-Robinson Co. (D), Heyward (D) counterclaimed, and D'Agostino (P) counterclaimed back. Heyward (D) disputes the compulsory nature of the counterclaims.

■ **BLACK LETTER RULE** A counterclaim is compulsory if it has some logical relationship to the opposing party's claim.

■ **PROCEDURAL BASIS**

Appeal from judgment for damages for breach of contract.

■ **FACTS**

This case involves two subcontracts between D'Agostino Excavators (D'Agostino) (P) and the Heyward-Robinson Company (Heyward) (D). One contract was with the federal government for the construction of naval barracks (the Navy job), and the other contract was for the construction of a private plant for Stelma, Inc. (the Stelma job). D'Agostino (P) sued Heyward (D) under the Miller Act in Connecticut District Court to recover payments due on the Navy job. Heyward (D) counterclaimed for alleged overpayments in the Navy job and the Stelma job. D'Agostino (P) counterclaimed to this counterclaim to recover monies due on the Stelma job. At trial, the jury found that Heyward (D) had breached both subcontracts and that Heyward (D) owed D'Agostino (P) over $63,000 on both jobs. Heyward (D) appealed, contending that the District Court had no jurisdiction over D'Agostino's (P) counterclaims on the Stelma job. Heyward (D) argued that these counterclaims were permissive, not compulsory under Rule 13(a), and that there was no independent basis of federal jurisdiction.

■ **ISSUE**

Should a court broadly interpret the federal rule regarding compulsory counterclaims?

■ **DECISION AND RATIONALE**

(Van Pelt Bryan, J.) Yes. Federal courts should give broad meaning to the language of the federal rule regarding compulsory counterclaims. Rule 13(a) of the Federal Rules of Civil Procedure states that a counterclaim is compulsory "if it arises out of the transaction or occurrence that is the subject matter of the opposing party's claim." In practice the phrase "transaction or occurrence that is the subject matter" has been broadly interpreted to require only a logical relationship between the claims, thereby avoiding a multiplicity of suits. In the case at bar, there was no independent basis for jurisdiction over either Heyward's (D) or D'Agostino's (P) Stelma counterclaims. However, the counterclaims were compulsory within the meaning of Rule 13(a). Both subcontracts were entered into by the same parties for the same type of work to be carried out within the same time frame. Payments on both subcontracts were made on a lump sum basis, and a single insurance policy covered both claims. It would have been impossible for Heyward (D) to litigate the claims against it on the Navy job without reference to the

Stelma job, since payments it made to D'Agostino (P) could not be allocated between the two jobs. Thus, the two claims arose out of the same transaction or occurrence. As such, they are ancillary to D'Agostino's (P) claim and no independent basis of federal jurisdiction is required. Affirmed.

■ CONCURRENCE

(Friendly, J.) Although I reach the same result as the majority, I cannot agree with either of the majority's holdings. First, the Stelma counterclaim should not have been considered a compulsory counterclaim under F.R.Civ.P. 13(a). The determination of whether a counterclaim is compulsory must be made at the pleading stage. The Stelma claim did not have a logical relation to the Navy claim, and the mere fact that the payments were made in lump sums—which was not mentioned in the pleadings—fails to create a logical connection. Nevertheless, I do not believe that permissive counterclaims should require an independent jurisdictional basis. Thus, I concur in the majority's result.

Analysis:

This case brings forth two important concepts regarding counterclaims. When should counterclaims be considered compulsory pursuant to Rule 13(a)? The Rule itself states two requirements. First, the claim must arise out of the transaction or occurrence that is the subject matter of the opposing party's claim. As demonstrated by this court, a broad reading of this section of the Rule requires only some logical relation between the claims, which seems fairly easy to satisfy. Second, and apparently not a factor in this case, the counterclaim cannot require the presence of third parties over whom the court cannot acquire jurisdiction. Once a counterclaim is considered compulsory, it automatically needs no independent jurisdictional basis, since ancillary subject-matter jurisdiction requires the claims to arise from a common nucleus of operative fact. This is essentially identical to Rule 13(a)'s requirement. Another important concept briefly discussed in this opinion is whether permissive counterclaims require an independent jurisdictional basis. Note that, pursuant to Rule 13(b), counterclaims which do not arise out of the transaction or occurrence that is the subject matter of the opposing party's claim *may* be stated in the pleadings—these are permissive counterclaims. The majority simply states that they do require this independent basis, while the concurrence disagrees. On this issue, the majority's stance seems to be supported by the weight of authority, as all claims require some basis of subject matter jurisdiction.

■ CASE VOCABULARY

COUNTERCLAIM: A claim by one party against an adverse party, in response to that adverse party's claim.

LASA Per L'Industria Del Marmo Societa Per Azioni v. Alexander

(*Marble Supplier*) v. (*Subcontractor*)

414 F.2d 143 (6th Cir. 1969)

CROSS–CLAIMS LOGICALLY RELATED TO THE ORIGINAL SUIT MAY BE BROUGHT BY CO–PARTIES

■ **INSTANT FACTS** Several claims arose out of contracts to construct the Memphis City Hall, including cross-claims between the contractor, Southern Builders (D), and one of the subcontractors, Alexander Marble and Tile (D).

■ **BLACK LETTER RULE** A cross-claim is valid as long as it bears some logical relationship with the transaction or occurrence that is the subject matter of the original action or counterclaim.

■ PROCEDURAL BASIS

Appeal from dismissal of cross-claims and third-party complaint for various torts and breaches of contract.

■ FACTS

The following complex web of claims, counterclaims and cross-claims arose out of the construction of the Memphis, Tennessee City Hall. Only those claims relevant to the holding are summarized herein [Of course, if you really want to confuse yourself, examine the summary of claims at the beginning of the opinion]. Southern Builders (D), the principal contractor, subcontracted with Alexander Marble and Tile Co. (Alexander) (D) to install marble, and Alexander (D) subcontracted with LASA Per L'Industria Del Marmo Societa Per Azioni (LASA) (P) to supply it with marble. LASA (P) sued Alexander (D) and Southern Builders (D) in District Court for the balance due on the contract. Alexander (D) and Southern Builders (D) filed counterclaims against LASA (P) for breach of contract. Alexander (D) filed a cross-claim against Southern Builders (D) for money due on that contract and for damages for injuring Alexander's (D) business reputation. In turn, Southern Builders (D) filed a cross-claim against Alexander (D) for breach of contract. Finally, Alexander filed a third-party complaint against A. L. Aydelott and Associates (D), the architect, for negligence in performing the architectural responsibilities. The District Court dismissed the cross-claims between Southern Builders (D) and Alexander (D) and also dismissed the third-party complaint, holding that they did not arise out of the same transaction or occurrence that is the subject matter of the original action. This appeal followed.

■ ISSUE

Is a cross-claim valid if it bears a logical relationship with the transaction or occurrence that is the subject matter of the original action or counterclaim?

■ DECISION AND RATIONALE

(Phillips, J.) Yes. A cross-claim is valid if it bears a logical relationship with the transaction or occurrence that is the subject matter of the original action or counterclaim, pursuant to Rule 13(g) of the Federal Rules of Civil Procedure. A broad reading of the pleadings convinces us that there is a logical relationship between the cross-claims (between Southern Builders (P) and Alexander (P)) and the subject matter of the original complaint and counterclaims. All of the contracts and subcontracts at issue relate to problems arising out of the marble used for the Memphis City Hall, and the question is which party is responsible for these defects. Many of the same factual and legal issues will be presented in the resolution of these various claims, counterclaims and cross-claims. Thus, in line with Rule 13's policy goal of avoiding the multiplicity of litigation, all of the issues should be tried at one time. If a substantial fear of confusing the jury exists, as demonstrated at trial, Rule 42(b) allows the District Judge to order separate trials on the confusing issues. Thus, this case should be remanded in full to the District Court, for proceedings not inconsistent with this opinion. Reversed and remanded.

■ DISSENT

(McAllister, J.) The questions of fact or law involved in the original suit by LASA (P), and the counterclaim for overpayment filed by Alexander (D), are totally different from Alexander's (D) claim against Southern Builders (D). Alexander's (D) cross-claim against Southern Builders (D) does not arise out of the occurrence upon which LASA's (P) suit is based, nor does it arise out of a counterclaim therein, as required by Rule 13(g). Furthermore, the third-party claim by Alexander (D) against Aydelott (D) and the cross-claim by Alexander (D) against Southern Builders (D) were actions in tort, while the original complaint was an action in contract. The facts and evidence that would be raised in each of these cross-claims and the third-party complaint would be entirely different from the facts and evidence in LASA's (P) suit and the related counterclaims. The only claims that arise out of the original transaction or occurrence, for balance due on a contract, are the counterclaims filed by Southern Builders (D) and Alexander (D) against LASA (P) claiming breach of that contract. Opinion should be affirmed.

Analysis:

As this case demonstrates, the policy goal of avoiding multiplicity of litigation often comes at the expense of a thoroughly confusing relationship between the parties and their various claims. The basic issues can, however, be summarized succinctly. Two original defendants, Southern Builders (D) and Alexander (D) wanted to settle their own conflict within the framework of the original lawsuit. Thus, they brought cross-claims, as allowed by Rule 13(g), against each other. For now, ignore the third-party complaint, which will be addressed in a later section of this chapter. While the various claims may be confusing, it seems to make sense to handle all of the various disputes in one lawsuit. Thus, the majority's opinion promotes judicial efficiency. The holding also parallels earlier court decisions in giving a broad reading to "same transaction or occurrence," whether the issue deals with counterclaims (between adverse parties) or cross-claims (between co-parties, such as co-defendants). Even a somewhat stretched logical relationship is sufficient to keep all of the claims in one trial.

■ CASE VOCABULARY

CROSS-CLAIM: Claim between co-parties, such as a claim between two defendants.

THIRD-PARTY COMPLAINT: Claim brought by a defendant against a third-party, who was not a defendant to the original suit.

Ellis Canning Co. v. International Harvester Co.

(Tractor Owner) v. *(Tractor Servicer)*
174 Kan. 357, 255 P.2d 658 (1953)

LAWSUITS MUST BE PROSECUTED BY A REAL PARTY IN INTEREST

■ **INSTANT FACTS** Ellis Canning Co. (P) brought a suit for negligence in servicing a tractor against International Harvester Co. (D), even though Ellis (P) had already been compensated for the loss by its insurance company.

■ **BLACK LETTER RULE** Lawsuits must be prosecuted by a real party in interest, one who has an interest in the subject matter of the litigation.

■ PROCEDURAL BASIS

Appeal from overruling of demurrer to answer to complaint for damages for negligence.

■ FACTS

Ellis Canning Co. (P) alleged that, while servicing Ellis' (P) tractor, International Harvester Co. (D) negligently started a fire resulting in $479 of damage. Ellis (P) admitted that its insurer, The Potomac Insurance Company, had already compensated Ellis (P) for the loss. Thus, Ellis (P) brought this claim to recover money damages for the benefit of its insurance company. [Maybe Ellis failed to realize that the insurance company itself could bring suit!] International Harvester (D) contended that the insurance company, and not Ellis (P), was the real party in interest and, therefore, that Ellis (P) could not bring this suit. The trial court overruled Ellis' (P) demurrer to this answer, and Ellis (P) appealed.

■ ISSUE

Must a lawsuit be brought by a real party in interest?

■ DECISION AND RATIONALE

(Parker, J.) Yes. Every lawsuit must be prosecuted in the name of a real party in interest, pursuant to Kansas statute. In the case at hand, Ellis (P) was no longer directly interested in the subject matter of the litigation, since he had already been paid by The Potomac Insurance Company. Thus, Ellis (P) was not a real party in interest. If the insurer desires to recover the money paid to Ellis (P), then the insurer may, and indeed must, bring the action as the real and only party in interest. Any previous Kansas decisions to the contrary are now overruled by this court. Affirmed.

Analysis:

This case provides a straightforward rule of law. Only parties with an interest in the subject matter of the litigation may maintain a suit. Furthermore, parties who have already been fully compensated for their damages do not have an interest in the subject matter. In modern times, this would be a simple case of subrogation, where the insurer takes over the insured's claim as a real party in interest. Most state courts allow for subrogation, and even where they do not, district courts often follow federal rather than state rules regarding real parties in interest and subrogation. If this case had arisen in federal courts, which utilize a real parties in interest rule (Rule 17) similar to Kansas's, International Harvester (D) could have simply filed a Rule 12(b)(6) motion to dismiss the claim, since Ellis (P) did not have a right to relief.

■ **CASE VOCABULARY**

REAL PARTY IN INTEREST: One who has a direct interest in the subject matter of the litigation.

SERIATIM: Latin word meaning "separately" or "one by one."

Ryder v. Jefferson Hotel Co.

(*Guest*) v. (*Innkeeper*)

121 S.C. 72, 113 S.E. 474 (1922)

PLAINTIFFS ALLEGING SEPARATE TORTS ARISING FROM THE SAME OCCURRENCE CANNOT NECESSARILY JOIN IN ONE LAWSUIT

■ **INSTANT FACTS** The Ryders (P), an allegedly married couple, were roused from their room and verbally insulted by the staff of the Jefferson Hotel (D). The Ryders (P) brought separate tort claims in one action in a South Carolina court.

■ **BLACK LETTER RULE** Separate tort claims by separate parties arising from the same occurrence cannot be joined in one lawsuit.

■ **PROCEDURAL BASIS**

Appeal from order overruling demurrer to complaint for damages for personal torts.

■ **FACTS**

Charles Ryder (P) and Edith Ryder (P), allegedly husband and wife, were guests of the Jefferson Hotel Company (D). According to the complaint, a servant of the Hotel (D) roused the Ryders (P) by rapping upon their door, and the servant insulted Edith Ryder (P). Apparently the couple was expelled under the allegation that they were not husband and wife. As a result, the Ryders (P) were compelled to give up their accommodations and find another lodging place in the middle of the night. The Ryders (P) sued the Jefferson Hotel (D) in South Carolina state court in a joint action for personal torts against Charles (P) and Edith (P). The Hotel (D) demurred to the complaint on the ground that the two causes of action had been improperly joined. The Hotel (D) appeals an order overruling this demurrer.

■ **ISSUE**

May two causes of action that arise from the same occurrence but allege separate torts against separate parties be joined in one suit?

■ **DECISION AND RATIONALE**

(Marion, J.) No. Two causes of action that allege separate torts against separate parties may not be joined in one suit, even if the claims arise from the same occurrence. A South Carolina statute requires joined causes of action to affect all of the parties to the action. In the case at hand, Charles (P) and Edith (P) allege separate torts, for breach of duty growing out of the innkeeper-guest relationship. Although these alleged causes of action arose out of the same transaction or occurrence, the rights invaded are necessarily several. Edith's (P) cause of action does not affect Charles (P), and Charles' (P) action does not affect Edith (P), in the sense contemplated by the South Carolina statute. Neither has a legal interest in the pecuniary recovery of the other, and there is no joint damage to both resulting from the alleged wrong. Thus, the claims must be brought separately. Reversed.

■ **DISSENT**

(Gary, J., and Cothran, J.) The Ryders (P) were expelled from the hotel under the allegation that they were not married. Thus, the injuries to Edith (P) and Charles (P) were joint, similar to an injury to a copartnership. When a copartnership is injured, the partnership can bring an action for injury, even though the injuries to each partner may not be identical. The same should be true in this case, as the alleged tort affected the Ryders' (P) relationship as husband and wife.

Analysis:

This case presents an early and extremely narrow view of permissive joinder of plaintiffs. The Ryders (P) were allegedly injured by a single act, which included a rude rousing from their room and unkind allegations about Edith Ryder (P). However, the Ryders (P) were prohibited from joining as plaintiffs, despite the nearly identical tort claims arising out of this one occurrence. The court narrowly interpreted the South Carolina statute in holding that each spouse's claim did not affect the other spouse. The dissent's stance seems more reasonable, since the unfortunate events occurred because the Hotel (D) felt that the Ryders (P) were not married. Thus, the alleged injuries seem more like injuries to a partnership than injuries to separate individuals. The majority's holding essentially destroys the concept of permissive joinder, allowing joinder only when the parties are united in interest. If the parties are indeed united in interest, then they would be *compelled* to join their claims.

■ CASE VOCABULARY

SEVERAL INJURIES: Injuries that are separate and distinct from one another.

M.K. v. Tenet

(Former Employee) v. *(CIA Director)*
216 F.R.D. 133 (D.D.C. 2002)

Welcome everyone. Thanks to FRCP Rule 20(a), a.k.a. the "More the Merrier" provision, the judge let you join our CIA lawsuit.

stus.com

■ **INSTANT FACTS** After the plaintiffs amended their complaint to add new plaintiffs, the defendants opposed the party joinder.

■ **BLACK LETTER RULE** Federal Rule of Civil Procedure 20(a) permits joinder of plaintiffs if all claims arose out of the same transaction or occurrence and share common questions of law or fact.

■ PROCEDURAL BASIS

Consideration of the defendants' motion opposing the plaintiffs' motion to amend the complaint.

■ FACTS

Six former CIA employees (P) sued Tenet (D) and the Central Intelligence Agency (D) for violating the Privacy Act of 1974 and their constitutional rights by obstructing their access to counsel. In a second amended complaint, the plaintiffs added additional plaintiffs and information concerning existing claims to cure deficiencies in the original complaint. The defendants asked the court to deny the plaintiffs' Rule 20 joinder of the new plaintiffs.

■ ISSUE

May the claims of the new plaintiffs be properly joined in the action against the defendants?

■ DECISION AND RATIONALE

(Urbina, J.) Yes. Under Federal Rule of Civil Procedure 20(a), two requirements must be satisfied to permit the joinder of parties. Under the first prong, a plaintiff asserting a claim against the defendant may be joined in the action if his or her claim "aris[es] out of the same transaction, occurrence, or series of transactions or occurrences." Here, each plaintiff alleges obstruction-of-counsel claims against the defendants based on a policy and practice of denying plaintiffs' counsel access to vital information because of a lack of security clearance. Because such a pattern is prevalent among all plaintiffs' claims, they are logically related and arise out of the same transaction or occurrence. The first prong of Rule 20(a) is satisfied.

Under the second prong, the claims of all plaintiffs against the defendant must share a common question of law or fact. Here, the obstruction-of-counsel claims all relate to an alleged CIA notice restricting counsel's access to crucial information. This notice is sufficient to raise a question of law and fact concerning the effect such a notice has on demonstrating a practice of obstructing the plaintiffs' right to freely discuss their cases with their attorneys, which is common among all plaintiffs' claims. The second prong is met. Furthermore, each plaintiff alleges a common violation under the Privacy Act, presenting another common question of law and fact.

Rule 20 is intended to consolidate related claims to further trial convenience, expedite the final adjudication of claims, and promote judicial efficiency. Against this policy, the joinder of the new parties is appropriate. Motion denied.

Analysis:

Unlike with the joinder of claims, the joinder of new parties presents considerable risks of prejudice to a named defendant. Rather than face the claims of a select group of plaintiffs with common claims, the addition of new parties threaten to inject entirely different claims into the litigation with no relation to the existing claims or the existing plaintiffs. The judicial convenience furthered by the joinder of unrelated claims by existing parties is lost by infusing the trial with multiple unrelated claims by unrelated parties.

■ **CASE VOCABULARY**

PERMISSIVE JOINDER: The optional joinder of parties if (1) their claims or the claims asserted against them are asserted jointly, severally, or in respect of the same transaction or occurrence, and (2) any legal or factual question common to all of them will arise.

Tanbro Fabrics Corp. v. Beaunit Mills, Inc.

(Buyer) v. *(Seller/Manufacturer)*
4 A.D.2d 519, 167 N.Y.S.2d 387 (App. Div. 1957)

PERMISSIVE JOINDER OF PARTIES IS POSSIBLE WHENEVER THE CLAIMS AGAINST EACH PARTY ARE LOGICALLY RELATED

■ **INSTANT FACTS** Tanbro (P), the buyer of allegedly defective goods, sought to consolidate actions against Beaunit Mills (D), the seller, and Amity (D), the processor.

■ **BLACK LETTER RULE** Separate claims against various parties may be joined if the claims are logically related.

■ **PROCEDURAL BASIS**

Appeal from denial of motion to consolidate breach of contract claims for defective goods.

■ **FACTS**

Three lawsuits arose from a dispute about certain manufactured goods. The current action is a suit brought in New York state court by Tanbro Fabrics Corp. (P), a buyer of goods, against Beaunit Mills (D), the seller, and Amity (D), the processor, alleging that certain goods were defective because of yarn slippage caused by one of the two defendants. In one of the earlier actions, Beaunit (D) had sued Tanbro (P) to recover the purchase price of goods sold, and Tanbro (P) counterclaimed for breach of warranty for improper goods. In the other action, Tanbro (P) initiated an action in replevin to recover goods in the hands of the processor, Amity (D). Tanbro (P) moved to consolidate the three actions, and Beaunit (D) and Amity (D) moved to dismiss Tanbro's (P) current complaint on the ground that there were prior actions pending. The court denied Tanbro's (P) motion to consolidate and granted Beaunit's (D) cross-motion to dismiss the complaint. Tanbro (P) appeals.

■ **ISSUE**

May separate claims against various defendants be joined in one action, if those claims are logically related?

■ **DECISION AND RATIONALE**

(Breitel, J.) Yes. Separate claims against various defendants may be joined provided the claims are logically related. Pursuant to New York statute, all parties may be joined in one action if there is asserted against them any right to relief arising out of the same transaction(s) or occurrence(s) and if any question of law or fact common to them would arise in the action. This statute should be read broadly, and any matters that may have conveniently been tried together should be joined. There does not need to be an identity of duty or contract between the parties being joined, as noted by New York courts in *Great Northern Telegraph Company v. Yokohama Specie Bank* [parties owing to plaintiff obligations under separate contracts may be joined]. Rather, the court may grant joinder at its discretion if the claims are logically related, balancing convenience and justice between the parties involved. In the case at hand, the danger of separate trials, leading perhaps to an unjust and illogical result, is well worth avoiding. Thus, Tanbro's (P) motion to consolidate should have been granted, and Beaunit's (D) cross-motion to dismiss should have been denied.

Analysis:

This case demonstrates a more modern "logical relationship" test for permissive joinder of parties. The New York statute, virtually identical to Federal Rule 20, allows joinder of parties when the claims arise out of the same transaction or occurrence and when any questions of law or fact common to the parties will arise in the litigation. In the case at hand, Tanbro's (P) claim against Beaunit (D) arguably did not arise out of the same transaction as the claim against Amity (D), since different contracts were involved. Nevertheless, the court allows joinder of both parties since there is some logical relationship—either one or the other party is allegedly responsible for the defective goods. While the court's reading of the statute may be criticized as overly broad, it certainly is a fair result for Tanbro (P). Consider what could happen if Beaunit (D) and Amity (D) were not joined. At the separate trials, each defendant could simply allege that the other was responsible for the defects. Thus, it is not unfair to require each of the defendants to prove, in one proceeding, that they were not responsible.

■ **CASE VOCABULARY**

A FORTIORI: A Latin phrase meaning "much stronger," used to show that if some weaker assertion is true then some stronger, more obvious conclusion must also be true.

CONSOLIDATION: The joining of two or more claims into a single suit.

REPLEVIN: An action for the recovery of property which is wrongfully in the hands of another party.

Bank of California Nat. Ass'n v. Superior Court

(Executor) v. *(Court)*
16 Cal.2d 516, 106 P.2d 879 (1940)

MANDATORY JOINDER ARISES ONLY WHEN PARTIES ARE NECESSARY AND INDISPENSABLE TO AN ACTION

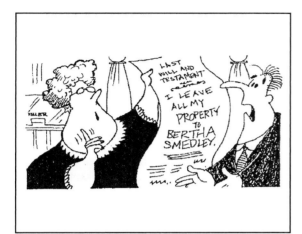

■ **INSTANT FACTS** Bertha Smedley (P), who claimed entitlement to all of a decedent's estate by contract, sued the executor, Bank of California (D) and the residuary legatee, St. Luke's Hospital (D). These defendants brought a motion to join the other purported beneficiaries to the estate.

■ **BLACK LETTER RULE** Mandatory joinder requires courts to join all necessary and indispensable parties to an action.

■ **PROCEDURAL BASIS**

Writ of prohibition to restrain trial, for decree and to quiet title, pending joinder of parties.

■ **FACTS**

Bank of California Nat. Ass'n (Bank) (D) was the executor to an estate valued at about $225,000. The will left individual legacies to a large number of beneficiaries, and St. Luke's Hospital (D) was named residuary legatee, thereby receiving the bulk of the estate. Bertha M. Smedley (P) brought an action to enforce a contract by which the decedent allegedly agreed to leave her entire estate to Smedley (P). [Unfortunately, the decedent was unavailable for comment.] Smedley's (P) complaint named as defendants the Bank (D), St. Luke's (D), and all of the beneficiaries to the will. The complaint prayed for a decree adjudging Smedley (P) as the owner of the entire estate and quieting Smedley's (P) title to the property. However, summons was served only upon the Bank (D) and St. Luke's (D), who made a motion to bring in the other defendants. After the motion was denied, the Bank (D) and St. Luke's (D) applied for a writ of prohibition to restrain the trial until the other defendants were joined.

■ **ISSUE**

Is mandatory joinder appropriate only where the absent parties are necessary and indispensable?

■ **DECISION AND RATIONALE**

(Gibson, J.) Yes. Joinder of absent parties is required only where the parties are both necessary and indispensable to the litigation. Modern California statutes follow the common law of equity courts, requiring a court to bring in parties when a complete determination of the controversy cannot be had without the presence of these parties. In other words, an action may not proceed when necessary and indispensable parties are absent. Parties are "necessary" when they are so interested in the controversy that they should be made parties in order to enable the court to do complete justice. However, necessary parties are not necessarily indispensable. [Thus, they aren't really "necessary" at all!] Parties are "indispensable" only when their rights or duties would be adversely affected by a judgment. For example, where a number of persons have undetermined interests in the same property, and where one person seeks to recover a portion of the property, the others are indispensable since a judgment in favor of one claimant for part of the property would necessarily determine the amount which remains available to the others. In the case at hand, the unserved beneficiaries are not indispensable. Although the validity of the testamentary disposition of the decedent's property affects all of their property interests—making them "necessary" parties—the absent defendants would not be bound by a judgment for or against the Bank (D) and St. Luke's (D). Smedley's (P) action is only against the executor Bank (D) and St. Luke's (D), not against the entire estate. It is independent of the will and the probate proceeding, and any judgment would be binding on the Bank (D) and St. Luke's (D) alone. Indeed, the trial court possesses the discretion to join the unserved "necessary" beneficiaries in order to avoid inconvenience and a multiplicity of suits. Nevertheless, the trial court declined to exercise this discretionary authority, and its determination cannot be attacked on an application for writ of prohibition. The peremptory writ is denied.

Analysis:

This opinion presents a thorough discussion of mandatory joinder in terms of common law and California statutes. Mandatory joinder encompasses all situations in which a court *must* force a plaintiff to expand his or her lawsuit to include (or serve) other defendants. As the opinion explained, a court is not required to join parties as defendants unless those parties are both necessary and indispensable to the litigation. In brief, "necessary" parties are those who *should* be joined if feasible, since they have some interest in the litigation. Thus, joinder of necessary parties avoids a multiplicity of suits and is a matter of convenience. Nevertheless, joinder of necessary parties is not mandatory unless those parties are also "indispensable." Some courts have interpreted "indispensable" parties to mean that the court would have no jurisdiction to proceed without these parties, since their absence would achieve undesirable consequences beyond merely impairing judicial efficiency. This court presents a similar approach, stating that parties are indispensable when the adjudication of the claims would be binding on these parties in future suits (presumably by the doctrines of res judicata and/or collateral estoppel).

■ CASE VOCABULARY

BENEFICIARY: A party entitled to receive property from an estate, trust, life insurance policy, etc.

EXECUTOR: A party appointed to distribute property and otherwise carry out directions of a testator who has an estate.

LEGATEE: A beneficiary entitled to receive property (typically personal property, but potentially real property as well) from an estate.

RESIDUARY LEGATEE: The recipient of the remainder of the estate, after all other beneficiaries receive their share.

Provident Tradesmens Bank & Trust Co. v. Patterson

(*Administrator*) v. (*Unnamed Party*)
390 U.S. 102, 88 S.Ct. 733 (1968)

FEDERAL COURTS DO NOT NECESSARILY HAVE TO DISMISS SUITS WHERE IT IS NOT FEASIBLE TO JOIN A NECESSARY PARTY

■ **INSTANT FACTS** In an action arising out of a traffic collision, Provident Tradesmens Bank (P), the administrator of a decedent's estate, sued Lumbermen's Mutual Casualty Company (D), the insurer of the automobile. The Appellate Court dismissed the action for failure to join the insured party.

■ **BLACK LETTER RULE** Where it is not feasible to join a necessary party, the action must be dismissed only if the party is indispensable.

■ **PROCEDURAL BASIS**

Writ of certiorari from dismissal of action for declaratory judgment.

■ **FACTS**

Donald Cionci, John Lynch, and Thomas Smith died, and John Harris was severely injured, when Cionci negligently drove Edward Dutcher's car, with Lynch and Harris as passengers, over the median line of a highway and collided with a truck driven by Smith. Provident Tradesmens Bank (PTB) (P), the administrator of Lynch's estate, obtained a claim for $50,000 against Cionci's estate. However, the estate was without any funds. Thus, PTB (P) sued Lumbermens Mutual Casualty Company (LMCC) (D), the insurer of Dutcher's automobile, in federal district court for a declaration that the car had been driven with the permission of Dutcher (under which circumstances the insurance policy would cover Cionci's liability). Harris and Smith's administratrix were joined as tort plaintiffs against LMCC (D). The trial court awarded declaratory judgments in favor of PTB (P) and the tort plaintiffs. LMCC (D) appealed on various state law grounds. However, the Court of Appeals for the Third Circuit did not reach the state law issues, reversing the judgments on two other grounds. First, the Appellate Court ruled that Dutcher was an indispensable party to the action who was not joined. Second, since Dutcher could not be joined as a defendant without destroying diversity jurisdiction, the Appellate Court dismissed the action. The United States Supreme Court granted certiorari.

■ **ISSUE**

When it is not feasible to join an indispensable party to an action, must the action be dismissed?

■ **DECISION AND RATIONALE**

(Harlan, J.) No. When it is not feasible to join an indispensable party to an action, the action does not necessarily have to be dismissed. Rule 19 was expressly drafted to avoid such narrow and inflexible reasoning. Dutcher had an interest in preserving the $100,000 of insurance funds available to cover his potential liability. Thus, the possibility existed that an adverse judgment in Dutcher's absence might impede Dutcher's ability to protect his interest, or might lead to a later relitigation by him. Rule 19(a) requires joinder of such a party where feasible. However, it was not feasible to join Dutcher, since Dutcher could not be joined without destroying diversity. In this situation, must a court dismiss the action? Pursuant to Rule 19(b), dismissal is not automatic. Rule 19(b) presents an "equity and good conscience" approach, allowing a court to dismiss such an action if only countervailing interests are not satisfied. However, Rule 19(b)'s balancing approach weighs heavily against the dismissal of this action. First, PTB (P) has an interest in preserving its fully-litigated judgment. Second, LMCC (D) did not have a sufficient interest in the joinder of Dutcher to warrant dismissal. Third, Dutcher would not be substantially prejudiced by the suit continuing without his joinder. Dutcher would only have a need to relitigate the issues if his insurance fund was used to pay judgments against Cionci. Although this is the probable result of the judgment, Dutcher nevertheless is not foreclosed by the lack of joinder since he is not bound by res judicata to a judgment in which he did not participate. Fourth, considerations of judicial efficiency, in which both the courts and the public share an interest, warrant upholding this judgment rather than dismissing it. By the time the case had reached the Appellate Court, considerable judicial resources had already been expended. It would be a great inefficiency to dismiss the suit at this point. Thus, to use familiar terminology, Dutcher was merely a necessary but not indispensable party to this litigation. [The "necessary" and "indispensable" terminology strikes again.] A decision to dismiss a case, pursuant to Rule 19(b), necessitates a finding that the party is indispensable. As the four-prong analysis above describes, Dutcher was not an indispensable party, and the Court of Appeals should not have dismissed the action. The judgment is vacated and remanded to the Court of Appeals. Reversed.

Analysis:

After wading through the intricacies and somewhat verbose opinion of this case, a sensible approach to mandatory joinder surfaces. This approach provides a logical federal substitute to the often clouded state-court holdings regarding "necessary and indispensable" parties. First, Rule 19(a) is used to determine if a party is necessary. If so, the party must be joined if feasible. However, if joinder is not feasible (due to jurisdictional or venue problems), the court does not necessarily have to dismiss the suit. Indeed, the suit must be dismissed only if the absent party is indispensable. This case, along with Rule 19(b), presents a four-part "equity and good conscience" analysis for determining indispensability. In short, the test balances the interests of the plaintiff, the defendants, the absentee, and the public [no easy task!]. Three prongs of the test are easily satisfied, leaving only the considerations of Dutcher's best interests. Clearly, the continuance of the suit without Dutcher's presence is not in Dutcher's best interest, since his insurance funds will be depleted by the judgment. The Court sidesteps this prong, however, noting that Dutcher will not be bound by the judgment. Thus, Rule 19(b)'s analysis is extremely flexible, and a court can basically reach its desired result by minimizing the importance of some prongs and focusing on others.

■ CASE VOCABULARY

LIQUIDATED CLAIM: A payment due to one party, fixed by an agreement of the parties.

Jeub v. B/G Foods, Inc.

(*Diner*) v. (*Restaurant Owner*)
2 F.R.D. 238 (D. Minn. 1942)

IMPLEADER IS POSSIBLE EVEN WHEN SUBSTANTIVE STATE LAW DOES NOT ALLOW ACCELERAT-ED INDEMNITY CLAIMS

■ **INSTANT FACTS** B/G Foods (D), sued by Jeub (P) for allegedly serving contaminated ham, obtained an order impleading the ham manufacturer, Swift and Company (D), for indemnity purposes.

■ **BLACK LETTER RULE** A party may implead a third party defendant for indemnity even where the state law procedure does not recognize indemnity claims before the party pays more than its share of the loss.

■ **PROCEDURAL BASIS**

Motion to vacate ex parte order impleading third party defendant for indemnity for negligence.

■ **FACTS**

Jeub (P) sued B/G Foods (D) in a Minnesota District Court after allegedly eating contaminated ham at one of B/G Foods' (D) restaurants. B/G Foods (D) obtained an ex parte order making Swift and Company (D) a third-party defendant. B/G Foods' (D) third party complaint alleged that the ham was produced by Swift (D) as "Swift Premium Ham" and that Swift (D) would therefore be liable to indemnify and reimburse B/G Foods (D) for any judgment recovered by Jeub (P). Swift (D) brings a motion to vacate the order, arguing that no right of indemnity exists under Minnesota substantive law.

■ **ISSUE**

May a third party defendant be impleaded for indemnity purposes when state law does not allow claims for indemnity before a party pays more than its share of the loss?

■ **DECISION AND RATIONALE**

(Nordbye, J.) Yes. A third party defendant may be impleaded for indemnity purposes, pursuant to Federal Rule 14(a), even though state law does not allow accelerated claims for indemnity. Indeed, the rights of the parties against Swift (D) must be governed by substantive areas of Minnesota law. The invoking of the federal third party procedural practice must not do violence to the substantive rights of the parties. However, an acceleration or expedition of the presentation of such rights does not conflict with Minnesota law. Federal Rule 14(a) allows impleader of a third party defendant for indemnity purposes. If B/G Foods (D) is not allowed to implead Swift (D), it would have to bring a separate action against Swift (D) for the defective ham after the conclusion of this trial. Even if Minnesota law contemplates such a process, this directly conflicts with the purpose and intent of Rule 14(a). The federal impleader rules were designed to enhance judicial efficiency by determining the rights of all parties in one proceeding. The ends of justice will be served by disposition of the entire matter, including B/G Foods' (D) claim for indemnity against Swift (D), in one proceeding. In line with the Minnesota substantive law, any judgment against Swift (D) for indemnity may be stayed until the judgment against B/G Foods (D) is paid or satisfied. The motion to vacate the order making Swift (D) a third party defendant is denied.

Analysis:

This case revisits the *Erie* Doctrine in light of the federal impleader rules. Although Rule 14(a) clearly allows impleader of a third party defendant for indemnity purposes, this rule conflicts with Minnesota's law which does not recognize indemnity claims until a party pays more than its share of a loss. In all likelihood, although it is not specifically stated in the opinion, Swift (D) seeks to avoid impleader based on the Rules Enabling Act, 28 U.S.C. § 2072(b). Recall that this statute permits the adoption of Federal Rules so long as the Rules do not abridge, modify or enlarge a state substantive right. Apparently Swift (D) believes that the Minnesota law is a substantive right, and that Rule 14(a) infringes on this right by allowing impleader for indemnity purposes. The Court presents a sensible approach to recognizing substantive rights under Minnesota law while upholding the purposes of Rule 14(a). Impleader allows the entire matter to be decided in one proceeding, accomplishing the goal of judicial efficiency. At the same time, the substantive aspects of Minnesota law are satisfied by staying any judgment for indemnity against Swift (D) until B/G Foods (D) pays the judgment against it. Without impleader, B/G Foods (D) would first have to pay any judgment and then seek indemnity. The court's holding accomplishes the same result but does so in one proceeding tried by one jury.

■ **CASE VOCABULARY**

EX PARTE: A motion brought by one party and heard outside of the presence of the other parties.

IMPLEADER: The addition of a third party for indemnity purposes.

INDEMNITY: The shifting of a loss onto the party who is responsible for the loss.

THIRD PARTY DEFENDANT: A person or entity that was not a party to the original action.

Too, Inc. v. Kohl's Department Stores, Inc.

(Copyright Holder) v. *(Department Store)*
213 F.R.D. 138 (S.D.N.Y. 2003)

DEFENDANTS MAY BRING THIRD–PARTY COMPLAINTS FOR CONTRIBUTION

My master is using his three wishes to satisfy the requirements for impleading his former employees.

Okay. Too bad for him it's a four part test.

stus.com

■ **INSTANT FACTS** Windstar Apparel (D) sought leave to implead two former employees allegedly liable for indemnification and contribution to the defendant.

■ **BLACK LETTER RULE** Leave to file a third-party complaint may be granted if the defendant did not deliberately delay the filing of its third-party complaint, impleader would not unduly delay the trial, the third-party defendant would not be prejudiced by the filing, and the third-party complaint states a claim for which relief may be granted.

■ **PROCEDURAL BASIS**

Consideration of the defendant's motion for leave to file a third-party complaint.

■ **FACTS**

Windstar Apparel, Inc., (D) produces and sells clothing apparel. DeCaro and Abraham were hired by Windstar (D) and charged with responsibility for its account with Kohl's Department Stores, Inc. (D). Too, Inc. (P) brought copyright infringement, trademark infringement, and unfair competition claims against Windstar Apparel, Inc. (D) and Kohl's (D) resulting from a line of Windstar (D) clothing sold in Kohl's (D) stores. Windstar (D) moved for leave to file a third-party complaint against DeCaro and Abraham for contribution and indemnification, alleging that DeCaro had represented that she designed the clothing at issue and Abraham sold the infringing clothing despite knowledge that they infringed upon the plaintiff's copyright and trademark.

■ **ISSUE**

May the defendant implead its two former employees to seek contribution under Federal Rule of Civil Procedure 14(a)?

■ **DECISION AND RATIONALE**

(Marrero, J.) Yes. Unless a third-party complaint is filed within ten days of serving a party's answer, the defendant must seek leave of court to do so. To obtain such leave, the third-party defendant's liability must depend upon "the outcome of the main claim" or allege the third-party defendant as a contributor to the defendant's liability, to promote judicial efficiency by eliminating a separate cause of action for contribution. If judicial economy would be furthered, the court may grant leave to file a third-party complaint if, in its discretion, it determines that the defendant did not deliberately delay the filing of its third-party complaint, impleader would not unduly delay the trial, the third-party defendant would not be prejudiced by the filing, and the third-party complaint states a claim for which relief may be granted.

Here, the third-party complaint for contribution clearly arises from the same facts on which the plaintiff's claim relies. The third-party defendants' liability arises only if Windstar's (D) liability is established under the plaintiff's complaint. DeCaro and Abraham are material witnesses in the case, and the contribution claim would require a separate repetitive proceeding in the event of a judgment for the plaintiff. Windstar's (D) third-party complaint sufficiently alleges the necessary elements of a claim for contribution and the claim is not "unmeritorious." The third-party defendants would not be prejudiced nor will the proceedings be unduly delayed by the third-party complaint. Any incidental prejudice to DeCaro and Abraham, such as the need to retain counsel, will present itself whether leave is granted or the claim is brought in a subsequent proceeding.

However, the claim for indemnification is without merit. Because state law bars claims for common-law indemnification when the defendant itself is at fault, Windstar (D) may not recover on its indemnification claim. Even if DeCaro and Abraham are found liable for copyright and trademark infringement, Windstar (D), as their employer, maintained sufficient control over the filed copyrights to establish its liability. Because Windstar (D) cannot avoid its liability, its claim for indemnification must fail. Motion granted in part, denied in part.

Analysis:

Impleader is essentially a procedure that allows a defendant to place the blame for a plaintiff's damages on another party. This situation occurs often in breach of contract actions in which the plaintiff has a contractual relationship only with the defendant, but the defendant's actions did not cause the damages. The plaintiff is therefore required to file suit against the defendant to satisfy the privity of contract requirement, and the defendant must then implead the responsible party.

■ CASE VOCABULARY

CONTRIBUTION: The right that gives one of several persons who are liable on a common debt the ability to recover ratably from each of the others when that one person discharges the debt for the benefit of all; the right to demand that another who is jointly responsible for a third party's injury supply part of what is required to compensate the injured party.

IMPLEAD: To bring (someone) into a lawsuit; especially, to bring (a new party) into the action.

IMPLEADER: A procedure by which a third party is brought into a lawsuit, especially by a defendant who seeks to shift liability to someone not sued by the plaintiff.

INDEMNIFICATION: The action of compensating for loss or damage sustained.

INDEMNITY: Reimbursement or compensation for loss, damage, or liability in tort; especially, the right of a party who is secondarily liable to recover from the party who is primarily liable for reimbursement of expenditures paid to a third party for injuries resulting from a violation of a common-law duty.

THIRD–PARTY COMPLAINT: A complaint filed by the defendant against a third party, alleging that the third party may be liable for some or all of the damages that the plaintiff is trying to recover from the defendant.

Hancock Oil Co. v. Independent Distributing Co.

(Tenant) v. *(Alleged Landowner/Trust Beneficiary)*

24 Cal.2d 497 (1944)

THE COMMON LAW REQUIREMENTS FOR INTERPLEADER SHOULD BE BROADLY CONSTRUED

■ **INSTANT FACTS** Hancock Oil (P) leased property from the Hopkinses (D) but was uncertain to whom to pay rent, so Hancock Oil (P) sought to interplead all interested parties and force them to battle over the rents.

■ **BLACK LETTER RULE** The common law of interpleader should be broadly construed to force rival claimants to battle over property.

■ **FACTS**

W.L. Hopkins (D) and Gertrude Ann Hopkins ("the Hopkinses") (D) leased real property to Hancock Oil Company (P). Subsequently, a copartnership named Independent Distributing Co. (IDC) (D) asserted that the Hopkinses (D) held the real property in trust for the copartnership. Hancock Oil (P) brought this action, against IDC, the Hopkinses (D), and four other Hopkinses (D) who were trustees, to determine to whom the rent should be paid. IDC (D) filed an answer alleging that they were the owners of the property, that the Hopkinses (D) were holding the property in trust for IDC (D), and that IDC (D) was therefore entitled to all rents. The Hopkinses (D) demurred to the complaint on the ground of uncertainty. Hancock Oil (P) appeals the court's order sustaining the demurrer without leave to amend.

■ **ISSUE**

May a party who might be exposed to multiple claims force parties to interplead against each other in one proceeding?

■ **DECISION AND RATIONALE**

(Edmonds, J.) Yes. A party who might be exposed to multiple claims arising out of a single obligation may join parties and force them to interplead against each other in one proceeding. At common law a bill of interpleader had four essential elements: (1) the same debt or duty must be claimed by all of the parties; (2) all of the adverse claims must be derived from a common source; (3) the party seeking interpleader must not have an interest in the subject matter; and (4) the party must have incurred no independent liability to any of the claimants. These historical limitations on interpleader have been broadened by California statute, which allows a party facing conflicting claims to bring an action against the conflicting claimants and force them to interplead their claims among themselves. According to the modem statute, interpleader lies even if the adverse claims are not derived from a common source. Interpleader cannot be maintained if the claims are mutually exclusive, but the fact that an identical right is not asserted by each claimant does not preclude the use of interpleader. In the case at hand, Hancock Oil (P) asserted that IDC (D) and the Hopkinses (D) each claim the right to receive rents under the lease. Furthermore, Hancock Oil (P) is a disinterested stakeholder, since the corporation does not care to whom rents should be paid. With regard to the fourth prong of the common law analysis, IDC (D) and the Hopkinses (D) assert that the obligation to pay rent constitutes an independent liability and bars the remedy of interpleader. However, we find no independent liability, as the decision will only determine the liability of the lessees to each of them. Thus, the common law requirements for interpleader are satisfied. Furthermore, the code provision must be liberally construed to allow interpleader, avoiding a multiplicity of suits and preventing vexatious litigation. In the absence of interpleader, Hancock Oil (P) could possibly be faced with having to pay its rent twice. The outdated common law limitation on interpleader in landlord-tenant cases—that a tenant may not question the title of his landlord—upon which the trial court apparently granted the demurrers may be overcome by the benefits of interpleader in this case. The complaint therefore states a cause of action. Reversed.

Analysis:

The court applies the historical common-law background of interpleader to the facts of this case, although the decision focuses on the broad applicability of interpleader as required by California statutes. In brief, the analysis allows for liberal construction of the common law four-prong approach in order to meet the ultimate goal of judicial efficiency. While the opinion can be questioned for failing to convincingly demonstrate how Hancock Oil's (P) complaint satisfied the common law analysis, it nevertheless reaches a just result. Unfortunately, the opinion does not present the "big picture" of an interpleader action. Interpleader is, of course, designed to determine the rights of rival claimants over some property held by the person seeking the interpleader. In this case, the person seeking the interpleader was the tenant, and the rival claimants were landlords or others claiming a right to the rents. Typically, interpleader suits have two stages. First, the court must determine whether interpleader is proper, with a controversy between the stakeholder on one side and the claimants on the other. The first two prongs of the common law analysis are important in this initial stage. If interpleader is granted, the stakeholder may withdraw from the case. Before withdrawing, the stakeholder must typically deposit the money involved in the dispute (e.g., a rent payment in the case at hand), and the remaining claimants are left to battle over who deserves the money. At this point, the final two prongs of the common law analysis are important, since the party bringing the initial action must have no interest in the subject matter and must not have an independent liability to any of the claimants. This allows the claimants to battle over the money without allowing the loser to later bring an action against the original stakeholder.

■ CASE VOCABULARY

CESTUI QUE TRUST: A party with the right to benefit from a trust.

INTERPLEADER: A proceeding to determine the rights of claimants to property held by a disinterested stakeholder.

New York Life Ins. Co. v. Dunlevy

(Life Insurer) v. *(Assignee of Policy)*
241 U.S. 518, 36 S.Ct. 613 (1916)

PERSONAL JURISDICTION OVER ALL RIVAL CLAIMANTS IS REQUIRED FOR INTERPLEADER

■ **INSTANT FACTS** New York Life (D) sought interpleader of Effie Dunlevy (P) and her father, Joseph Gould (D), to determine who had the right to money from a life insurance policy. Dunlevy (P) never appeared in the interpleader action.

■ **BLACK LETTER RULE** Personal jurisdiction over all claimants is a prerequisite to interpleader actions.

■ **PROCEDURAL BASIS**

Writ of certiorari contesting ownership of funds following judgment for assignee of life insurance policy.

■ **FACTS**

This case involves three separate legal actions pertaining to the rights to recover approximately $2500 from a life insurance policy. First, in 1907, Boggs & Buhl (P) had recovered a judgment against Effie Dunlevy (D) in Pennsylvania, where Dunlevy (P) had then resided. Second, in 1910, Dunlevy (P) sued New York Life Insurance Company (D) and her father, Joseph Gould (D), in a California state court to recover the surrender value of a policy on his life which she claimed had been assigned to her. The suit was removed to a federal district court, and a judgment in favor of Dunlevy (P) was granted and affirmed by the Court of Appeals. The third proceeding was an execution on Boggs & Buhl's (P) judgment, in which New York Life (D) and Gould (D) were summoned as garnishees. New York Life (D), acknowledging that it owed approximately $2500 but not knowing whom to pay, asked the court to interplead Dunlevy (D) and Gould (D) for a determination of whom should receive the money. The court granted interpleader and New York Life (D) paid the money to the court, but Dunlevy (D) did not appear. The jury found that no valid assignment of the policy was made to Dunlevy (D), and the fund was paid to Gould (D).

■ **ISSUE**

Is personal jurisdiction over all claimants required before interpleader proceedings can be contested?

■ **DECISION AND RATIONALE**

(McReynolds, J.) Yes. Personal jurisdiction over all rival claimants is a prerequisite to interpleader proceedings. Since Mrs. Dunlevy (D) was originally within the jurisdiction of the court of common pleas of Pittsburgh, this court would have had ample power to inquire whether she held a valid claim against New York Life (D) and to appropriate this claim to discharge the original judgment. Even if she were outside of the state, such disposition of property would have been binding on her. However, the interpleader initiated by New York Life (D) is an altogether different matter, attempting to bring about a final adjudication of her personal rights. Unless the court has personal jurisdiction over her, such a judgment would not be binding on her. Boggs & Buhl (P) maintained that, since Dunlevy (D) was within the jurisdiction of the Pennsylvania court at the time of the initial judgment against her, she remains within the court's jurisdiction for purposes of interpleader. Further, Boggs & Buhl (P) contended, when

New York Life (D) paid the money into court, it was the same in legal effect as if it had been paid to her. We do not agree that a defendant remains in court, subject to whatever orders may be entered, after a final judgment. The interpleader proceedings were not essential concomitants of the original action by Boggs & Buhl (P) in Pennsylvania state court. For purposes of interpleader, therefore, the Pennsylvania court had no jurisdiction over Mrs. Dunlevy (D). The California judgment in favor of Mrs. Dunlevy (D) is, accordingly, affirmed.

Analysis:

This case demonstrates potential jurisdictional problems with interpleader actions. Before a court can validly order interpleader, it must have personal jurisdiction over all of the adverse claimants whose rights to money or property will be adjudicated via interpleader. It is not enough, as this case demonstrates, that the court has in rem jurisdiction over funds in which the claimant holds an ownership interest. In the case at hand, New York Life (D) deposited the approximately $2500 in life insurance funds that Dunlevy (D) had a right to pursuant to the California judgment. Nevertheless, in rem jurisdiction over the funds was insufficient, since the interpleader action required personal jurisdiction over Dunlevy (D) herself. Partially in response to this somewhat narrow decision, Congress passed the Federal Interpleader Act, now codified at 28 U.S.C. §§ 1335, 1397, and 2361. If this interpleader action arose in federal court today, personal jurisdiction over Dunlevy (D) would likely be obtained, since § 1367 permits venue in any judicial district in which a claimant resides and § 2361 permits nationwide service of process.

■ CASE VOCABULARY

GARNISHEE: A person who owes a debt and, thus, property in his possession rightfully belongs to another.

Pan American Fire & Cas. Co. v. Revere

(*Insurer*) v. (*Insured*)

188 F.Supp. 474 (E.D. La. 1960)

FEDERAL INTERPLEADER LAW SHOULD BE BROADLY CONSTRUED

■ **INSTANT FACTS** Pan American Fire & Cas. Co. (P), the insurer of a tractor-trailer which was involved in a collision, brought a motion for interpleader to join all of the various claims and claimants related to the accident.

■ **BLACK LETTER RULE** Federal interpleader rules and statutes should be read broadly so as to grant interpleader whenever possible, although venue and service of process must nevertheless be satisfied.

■ **PROCEDURAL BASIS**

Motion to dismiss interpleader action.

■ **FACTS**

Pan American Fire & Cas. Co. (P) was the insurer of a large tractor-trailer which collided head-on with a school bus, causing several injuries and four deaths. Further injuries occurred when two cars behind the bus collided moments later. Alleging that three suits and numerous other claims had already been made against it, Pan American (P) brought this action in a Louisiana district court for interpleader of all potential claimants. Pan American (P) deposited a bond for $100,000, the full amount of its policy limits. Although Pan American (P) stated that it was merely a disinterested stakeholder, the company nevertheless denied liability toward any and all claimants. [Perhaps only in the world of interpleader can a deposit of money and a complete denial of liability coexist peacefully!] One or more of the claimants brought a motion to dismiss the interpleader action.

■ **ISSUE**

(1) For a federal interpleader action, must the plaintiff be a disinterested stakeholder? (2) May an interpleader action proceed when the claims are independent of one another or not identical? (3) Is interpleader an appropriate method of adjudicating unliquidated tort claims via a jury trial? (4) Does a federal court hearing an interpleader action have authority to enjoin state court proceedings? (5) Must venue and service of process be proper in order to institute an interpleader action?

■ **DECISION AND RATIONALE**

(Wright, J.) (1) No. Interpleader does not have to be instituted by parties who are disinterested stakeholders. This common-law requirement has been considerably relaxed by the Federal Interpleader Act [28 U.S.C. §§ 1335, 1397, 2361] and Rule 22 of the Federal Rules of Civil Procedure. At common law, a difference existed between strict interpleader and bills in the nature of interpleader. While strict interpleader required the plaintiff to be a disinterested stakeholder, bills in the nature of interpleader allowed the stakeholder himself to be a claimant. The Interpleader Act and Rule 22 have eliminated this distinction. Plaintiffs do not necessarily have to be disinterested stakeholders, and thus Pan American (P) may maintain an interpleader action despite its apparently contradictory denial of liability toward any and all plaintiffs. Although modern interpleader is considered an equitable remedy, no special equitable ground must exist for an interpleader action aside from the requirement that the plaintiff be potentially exposed to double or multiple vexation on a single obligation. Rule 22 words this requirement differently, stating that the plaintiff "is or may be exposed to double or multiple *liability*." (Emphasis added.) In this motion, the argument is advanced that, because it has fixed the limits of its liability in its policy, Pan American (P) is not exposed to multiple liability. However, this Rule 22 requirement is not a strict one, and the key words are "may be." Since Pan American (P) "may be" exposed to multiple liability to claims in excess of its policy limits, this Rule 22 requirement is satisfied here. (2) Yes. An interpleader action may proceed even if the claims are independent of each other or not identical. The old doctrine of "mutual exclusiveness" is no longer a bar to the interpleader remedy. All that is required is that the claims be adverse. And in the case at hand, the interest of each claimant is to reduce or defeat recovery altogether of the claim of every other claimant. Therefore, the claims are adverse, and it makes no difference that they are not identical in origin or amount. (3) Yes. Interpleader is an appropriate remedy for adjudicating unliquidated tort claims via a jury trial. It is settled that interpleader is available to an insurer whose policy is insufficient to satisfy contract claims even if those claims have not been reduced to a judgment. However, no federal precedent exists with regard to unliquidated tort claims. Three arguments are suggested for denying the remedy of interpleader to a blameless insurer faced with excessive tort claims: (a) Tort claims are more conjectural than contract claims; (b) The insurer's exposure to tort claims is "remote" until they have been reduced to judgment, since the insurer is not directly liable to the claimants; and (c) tort claims are peculiarly appropriate for jury trial which would have to be denied under the equitable practice of interpleader. With regard to the first objection, while we recognize that it is difficult in tort claims to determine if the aggregate will exceed the policy limits so as to render the claimants adverse, we feel that the case at hand likely will reach this result. The second objection also fails, since the remoteness of the insurer's exposure to claims is irrelevant in light of Rule 22's "may be exposed" and the Interpleader Act's "may claim" language. The third objection presumes that the claims in an interpleader action, being proceedings in equity, must be tried by the judge alone. We disagree, since nothing in Rule 22 or the Interpleader Act opposes a jury trial for questions of liability and damages in this interpleader action. Each claimant in the instant action can, therefore, be given a full opportunity to present his case to a jury. (4) Yes. In most interpleader actions, and especially in the instant action, a federal court may enjoin pending state court proceedings. Of course, interpleader will usually be effective only if all claimants are restricted to a single forum for the assertion of their claims. Thus, a federal court entertaining an interpleader action must have the authority to enjoin all related current or future state court actions. Section 2283 of Title 28 does not present an immovable obstacle to enjoining state court proceedings, since this Section presents exceptions to the general prohibition of federal courts from interfering with state court actions. For example, federal courts may interfere with state court proceedings if expressly authorized by an Act of Congress. For actions brought pursuant to The Interpleader Act, Congress has expressly authorized federal courts to enjoin state court actions related to the interpleaded claims. However, this exception does not apply to non-statutory interpleader actions brought pursuant to Rule 22. Nevertheless, Section 2283 allows federal courts to enjoin state court proceedings when the injunction is necessary in the aid of its jurisdiction. Every indication is that a federal court may, therefore, enjoin state proceedings for the benefit of Rule 22 (non-statutory) interpleader actions. (5) Yes. Venue and service of process must be proper in order to institute and conduct interpleader actions. This can be problematic in the case of Rule 22 interpleader actions. In these actions, the only proper venue for the suit, when the claimants do not all reside in the same state, is the residence of the plaintiff. Furthermore, service of process cannot run beyond the boundaries of the state in which the court sits. On the other hand, in the case of statutory interpleader actions—brought pursuant to the Interpleader Act—venue is appropriate in any district where one claimant resides and process will run throughout the United States. Since these liberal venue and process rules apply only to statutory interpleader, the present action must be brought pursuant to the Interpleader Act unless the non-Louisiana defendant expressly waives any venue objection. In conclusion, the prayer for interpleader will be granted, but Pan American (P) will not be discharged since it is contractually bound to resist the claims. Injunctions will issue to all pending or future state court proceedings, and upon timely motion by any claimant the court will order a jury trial of all of the claims. In the event the aggregate verdicts exceed Pan American's (P) limits of liability, the court reserves the task of apportioning the insurance proceeds in a just manner. The motion to dismiss will be denied.

Analysis:

This case raises a number of important holdings related to federal interpleader actions, as the detailed discussion indicates. The court's approach underlines the fact that interpleader is an equitable remedy, designed to bring justice to the stakeholder and settle all adverse claims while conserving judicial resources. Along these lines, notice how broadly the court construed common law as well as Rule 22 and the Federal Interpleader Act. While the court faced many hurdles to allowing interpleader in the instant case, apparently nothing was going to stop the court from granting the remedy. The court's conclusion, therefore, is not surprising; however, three elements of the conclusion seem somewhat unusual compared to other interpleader actions. First, the court did not discharge Pan American (P) after granting the interpleader. Isn't one purpose of interpleader to allow a stakeholder, such as Pan American (P), to deposit the funds at issue and then let the claimants battle over the funds? Nevertheless, the court noted that Pan American (P) is contractually bound to remain in the action and dispute the claims. Second, in case the aggregate of the jury verdicts turned out to exceed the $100,000 policy limit, the court reserved the right to apportion the insurance proceeds in a just manner. This certainly exemplifies the equitable nature of the remedy. Third, the idea of a court seeking to control the underlying litigation against alleged tortfeasors, rather than simply allocating the fund among successful tort plaintiffs, is unusual. As the Supreme Court noted in the following case, *State Farm Fire & Cas. Co. v. Tashire,* this has occurred only one other time (in a 1964 case).

■ CASE VOCABULARY

VEXATION: An experience of injury or inconvenience caused by the acts of another person.

State Farm Fire & Cas. Co. v. Tashire

(*Insurer*) v. (*Injured Party*)
386 U.S. 523, 87 S.Ct. 1199 (1967)

INTERPLEADER SHOULD NOT ALWAYS BE USED TO LITIGATE A MULTITUDE OF CLAIMS IN A COMPLEX TORT SITUATION

■ **INSTANT FACTS** State Farm Fire & Cas. Co. (P) held an insurance policy for the driver of a truck, which collided with a Greyhound bus and caused several injuries. State Farm (P) brought an interpleader action to join all of the potential tortfeasors and resolve all of the claims.

■ **BLACK LETTER RULE** In complex tort situations, the effect of interpleader should not necessarily be to confine the total litigation to a single forum and proceeding.

■ **PROCEDURAL BASIS**

Writ of certiorari from order dissolving temporary injunction and dismissing interpleader action arising out of complex tort scenario.

■ **FACTS**

A Greyhound bus collided with a pickup truck in California, killing two bus passengers and injuring other passengers as well as the truck driver and its passenger. Four injured passengers filed suit in California state courts seeking over $1 million in damages against Greyhound Lines, Inc.; Nauta, the bus driver; Clark, the truck driver; and Glasgow, the truck passenger. Before these cases came to trial, State Farm Fire & Cas. Co. (P) brought this action for interpleader in an Oregon district court. At the time of the collision, State Farm (P) had a policy covering Clark for bodily injury liability up to $10,000 per person and $20,000 per occurrence. [Apparently Clark never contemplated colliding with a Greyhound bus head-on!] State Farm (P) paid $20,000 into the court and asked the court to require all claimants to establish their claims against Clark and State Farm (P) in the interpleader action and to discharge State Farm (P) from further obligations. State Farm (P) joined Clark, Glasgow, Nauta, Greyhound and all of the prospective claimants. The Oregon District Court issued a temporary injunction requiring all suits against Clark, Glasgow, Nauta, and Greyhound to be litigated in the interpleader proceeding. On interlocutory appeal, the Ninth Circuit reversed on two grounds. First, the Court of Appeals noted that states such as Oregon do not permit a direct action against an insurance company until judgment is obtained against the insured. Thus, State Farm (P) could not seek interpleader until all claims against Clark had been reduced to judgment. Second, the Court of Appeals held that claimants with unliquidated tort claims are not claimants within the Interpleader Act or Rule 22. Thus, the Ninth Circuit dissolved the temporary injunction and dismissed the interpleader action. The Supreme Court granted certiorari.

■ **ISSUE**

(1) Is the "minimal diversity" requirement, as the federal interpleader statute has been construed, constitutional? (2) In the absence of a state law provision for direct actions against an insurance company, must the company wait to file for interpleader until all claims against the insured have been liquidated? (3) Should the effect of interpleader always be to confine the total litigation to a single forum and proceeding?

■ DECISION AND RATIONALE

(Fortas, J.) (1) Yes. The interpleader statute has been uniformly construed to require only minimal diversity, that is, diversity of citizenship between two or more claimants. This seems to conflict with the complete diversity requirement of *Strawbridge v. Curtiss* [Diversity of citizenship requires complete diversity, so no plaintiff may be a citizen of the same state as any defendant]. However, the construction of the interpleader statute is constitutional, as Article III of the Constitution poses no obstacle to the extension of federal diversity jurisdiction, so long as any two adverse parties are not citizens of the same state. (2) No. In the absence of a state law provision for direct actions against an insurance company, the company does not have to wait to file for interpleader until all claims against the insured have been liquidated. Pursuant to the most recent revision of the interpleader statutes, a plaintiff may obtain interpleader whenever two or more claimants *may claim* an interest in the fund which is the subject of the action. This statute is to be liberally construed. If an insurance company were required to await reduction of all claims to judgment, the first claimant to receive such a judgment could appropriate a disproportionate slice of the fund. This race for judgment would result in difficulties for the insurance company and inequities for the claimants. The interpleader statutes were designed to avoid these inequities. (3) No. The effect of interpleader should not necessarily be to confine the total litigation to a single forum and proceeding. In some situations, a court may enjoin the prosecution of all suits against the insurance company and the insured. For example, where a stakeholder is faced with rival claims to the fund, and where the fund itself marks the outer limits of the controversy, interpleader may result in all claims being litigated in one proceeding. However, in the present interpleader action, the court *should not* enjoin the prosecution of the multitude of suits. State Farm's (P) maximum interest in the claim cannot exceed $20,000, and the policy covered claims against Clark only. State Farm (P) should not be allowed to determine that dozens of tort plaintiffs must bring their claims, which may be against a number of other defendants, in a single forum of the company's choosing. State Farm's (P) interest will receive full vindication when this court restrains claimants from seeking to enforce any judgment obtained against Clark outside of the interpleader proceedings. The District Court exceeded the powers granted by the interpleader statutory scheme when it enjoined all tort proceedings against the various potential defendants and required them to be brought within the interpleader action. Unfortunately, interpleader cannot be used to solve all the problems of multiparty litigation arising out of a mass tort. A party, such as State Farm (P), with little interest in the outcome of complex litigation should not strip truly interested parties of substantial rights, such as the choice of forum and the rules of jurisdiction, venue, service of process, removal and change of venue. Upon remand, the injunction is to be modified consistent with this opinion. The judgment of the Court of Appeals is reversed.

■ DISSENT

(Douglas, J.) The prospective litigants should not be considered claimants for purposes of federal interpleader, as state law and the policy itself did not permit an action against the insurer until after a final judgment against the insured.

Analysis:

Justice Fortas' majority opinion presents a sensible approach to interpleader in the context of complex tort litigation. Where several parties are potentially liable for injuries, the insurer of one of the parties should not be allowed to require all of the underlying litigation to be resolved within one interpleader action. It is interesting that the Court does not overrule, or even disagree with, one of the holdings in *Pan American Fire & Cas. Co. v. Revere* [a federal court hearing an interpleader action has broad authority to enjoin state court proceedings and control the underlying litigation against all alleged tortfeasors]. Perhaps the two cases are factually distinguishable, since *Pan American* did not mention that anyone besides the insured was potentially liable. Thus, *Pan American* was possibly a situation in which a number of claimants were battling over just one insurance fund. In the case at hand, the sheer number of potential tort plaintiffs and tortfeasors, and the minimal dollar value of State Farm's (P) policy in comparison to the large damages, militates against similar treatment. It should also be noted that this case, in effect, re-affirmed *Pan American's* holding with regard to unliquidated tort claims. As held in both cases, an insurance company should not be required to wait until tort claims have reached a judgment before initiating an interpleader action.

■ **CASE VOCABULARY**

INTERLOCUTORY APPEAL: An appeal during the course of a judicial proceeding, rather than after a judgment.

Smuck v. Hobson

(*Board Member*) v. (*Class Action Representative*)
132 U.S.App.D.C. 372, 408 F.2d 175 (D.C.Cir. 1969)

IN LIMITED SITUATIONS, THIRD PARTIES MAY INTERVENE AFTER A JUDGMENT ON THE MERITS

■ **INSTANT FACTS** Smuck (P), a member of the District of Columbia Board of Education, and Hansen, the resigned Superintendent of Schools, along with twenty parents, sought to intervene in order to appeal a judgment in favor of school children suffering from the Board's discriminatory educational practices.

■ **BLACK LETTER RULE** Third parties may intervene after a judgment on the merits, provided the conditions in Federal Rule 24(a) are satisfied.

■ PROCEDURAL BASIS

En banc hearing on granting of motions to intervene in order to appeal judgment of equal protection violation.

■ FACTS

Prior to the case at hand, Hobson (D) won a class action suit in federal court on behalf of underprivileged children of District of Columbia schools. The action alleged that the children were being denied their constitutional rights to equal educational opportunities because the schools were operated on a racially and economically discriminatory basis. The Board of Education voted not to appeal, but Hansen, the Superintendent of Schools, and Smuck (P), a dissenting board member, appealed. In addition, Hansen and twenty parents brought motions to intervene in the District Court and the Court of Appeals. The District Court granted the motions to intervene in order to give the Court of Appeals the opportunity to pass on the intervention questions and on the merits of the appeal. The Court of Appeals considered the matter *en banc*.

■ ISSUE

May interested third parties intervene after a judgment on the merits in order to appeal the judgment?

■ DECISION AND RATIONALE

(Bazelon, J.) Yes. Interested third parties may intervene after a judgment on the merits in order to appeal the judgment, provided the requirements of Federal Rule of Civil Procedure Rule 24(a) are satisfied. Rule 24(a) allows intervention of right for third parties who have an interest in the transaction which is the subject of the action, provided the protection of the interest would be impaired if intervention was not allowed, and provided the interest is not adequately represented by existing parties. In the instant action, Hansen resigned following the class action judgment, so he had no standing to appeal. Furthermore, he cannot intervene in the appeal, since a reversal of the action would have no effect on his employment. Smuck (P) likewise has no appealable interest, since he is bound as a member of the Board of Education to follow the Board's decision not to appeal. However, the motion to intervene by the parents deserves closer scrutiny. First, the parents have some interest in the appeal, and this portion of Rule 24(a) is easy to overcome. The parents have an interest in protecting the freedom of the school board to exercise the broadest possible discretion constitutionally permissible in deciding upon educational policies. Second, the parents would be impeded in protecting their interests if not allowed to intervene. Third, the parents' interests are not adequately represented by the Board of Education, since the Board decided not to appeal. The Board's interests do not coincide with the parents' interests, and the parents should thus be allowed to intervene in the appeal in order to protect their interests. The issues on appeal should be limited to those features directly relating to the parents' interests, that is, the features of the judgment which limit the Board's discretion.

Analysis:

This case presents a thorough and insightful analysis of Rule 24(a)'s requirements for intervention of right. Parties may intervene only when they have an interest in the subject matter of the original action which is not adequately represented by the existing parties. And in rare cases, such as the case at hand, parties may intervene even after a judgment. Typically intervention after judgment is not allowed, as Rule 24 states that intervention must be timely. Nevertheless, the court feels compelled to allow the parents to intervene and appeal the decision in the case at hand.

■ **CASE VOCABULARY**

EN BANC: "In the bench"; the full court hearing the matter.

INTERVENTION OF RIGHT: Procedure by which a third party automatically may join an action upon meeting certain statutory prerequisites.

CHAPTER TEN

Class Actions

Castano v. American Tobacco Co.

Instant Facts: The district court certified a class of all persons who had purchased and smoked cigarettes, and the tobacco companies challenged the certification on the ground that the class claims did not predominate and that the class action was not superior to individual actions.

Black Letter Rule: Class actions must meet the predominance and superiority requirements of Rule 23, and predominance cannot be determined in mass tort litigation until some individual trials are litigated.

Hansberry v. Lee

Instant Facts: Hansberry (D), the black purchaser of land that was subject to a racially restrictive sales covenant, sought to avoid a prior class action holding that the covenant was valid.

Black Letter Rule: Granting res judicata effect to a class action judgment, in which the prerequisites and procedures for class action were not satisfied, violates due process.

Phillips Petroleum Co. v. Shutts

Instant Facts: Shutts (P) and several other holders of royalty interests brought a class action against Phillips Petroleum (D) to recover royalty payments. The Kansas court obtained personal jurisdiction over all parties and applied Kansas law to all claims.

Black Letter Rule: In class actions, personal jurisdiction does not require that each class member have minimum contacts with the forum state, but the forum state must have sufficient interests in the claims to assert its state law to all claims.

Amchem Products, Inc. v. Windsor

Instant Facts: To settle asbestos-exposure litigation, the asbestos industry proposed a class action settlement which combined asbestos-sickened plaintiffs with "exposure-only" plaintiffs (who were exposed but have not yet developed any disease).

Black Letter Rule: Class action settlement offers must meet the Rule 23 requirements of "predominance," "superiority," "adequate representation," and "notice" before they may be certified.

Ortiz v. Fibreboard Corp.

Instant Facts: An asbestos manufacturer proposed a settlement which would create a "limited fund" of assets and insurance proceeds for claimants, preserve most of the manufacturer's assets, cap future lawsuits, and exempt 100,000 plaintiffs from the class.

Black Letter Rule: A settlement under Rule 23(b)(1)(B)'s "limited fund" provision must (i) establish a fixed fund which is proven inadequate to satisfy all claims, (ii) apply the fund and the defendant's entire assets for claimants' benefit, (iii) prevent intra-class conflicts of interest and unfair distribution, (iv) include most potential plaintiffs, or provide similar compensation for current and future claimants, and (v) provide a "fair, adequate, and reasonable" settlement under Rule 23(e).

Cooper v. Federal Reserve Bank of Richmond

Instant Facts: Following a class action and appeal in which the Federal Reserve Bank of Richmond (D) was found not to have engaged in a pattern or practice of discrimination, several class members sought to bring individual claims for discrimination.

Black Letter Rule: A general holding adverse to a class does not preclude an individual member of the class from subsequently litigating specific individual claims.

Castano v. American Tobacco Co.

(Class Representative) v. *(Tobacco Company)*

84 F.3d 734 (5th Cir. 1996)

DISTRICT COURTS MUST ANALYZE THE RULE 23 REQUIREMENTS BEFORE CERTIFYING A CLASS, AND MASS TORT CLASS ACTIONS CANNOT BE IMMATURE

■ **INSTANT FACTS** The district court certified a class of all persons who had purchased and smoked cigarettes, and the tobacco companies challenged the certification on the ground that the class claims did not predominate and that the class action was not superior to individual actions.

■ **BLACK LETTER RULE** Class actions must meet the predominance and superiority requirements of Rule 23, and predominance cannot be determined in mass tort litigation until some individual trials are litigated.

■ **PROCEDURAL BASIS**

Appeal of certification of class in action for damages for fraud and intentional tort.

■ **FACTS**

Castano (P), the class representative, sued American Tobacco Co. (D) on two grounds. First, Castano (P) alleged that American Tobacco (D) fraudulently failed to inform consumers that nicotine is addictive. Second, Castano (P) alleged that American Tobacco (D) manipulated the level of nicotine in cigarettes to sustain their addictive nature. The district court defined the class as all nicotine-dependent persons in the United States who have purchased and smoked cigarettes manufactured by American Tobacco (D), and also the estates and relatives of these smokers. American Tobacco (D) appealed the certification order, arguing that the district court abused its discretion in certifying the class. American Tobacco (D) maintained that the court failed to conduct an adequate inquiry into issues of predominance and superiority.

■ **ISSUE**

(1) Prior to certifying a class, must a court consider how variations in state law affect predominance and superiority? (2) Must a court look past the pleadings to consider how the trial on the merits would be conducted? (3) Can a mass tort class action be found "superior" when there is no prior track record of individual trials from which a court can make the predominance and superiority analyses?

■ **DECISION AND RATIONALE**

(Smith, J.) (1) Yes. Prior to certifying a class, a court must consider how variations in state law affect predominance and superiority. Federal Rule 23(b)(3) requires that questions of law or fact common to class members must predominate over any questions affecting individual members, and that the class action must be superior to other methods of adjudication. District courts cannot lightly brush aside these requirements. In multi-state class actions such as this, variations in state law may swamp any common questions and defeat predominance. The district court failed to consider the variations in state law, and it did not determine whether the class action would be manageable in light of these variations. The court simply concluded that any such variations would pale in comparison to the possibility of millions of similar individual trials. In so concluding, the court failed to meet the standard of Rule 23(b)(3). (2) Yes. A court must look past the pleadings to consider how the trial on the merits would be conducted in order to determine whether Rule 23 is satisfied. The district court just assumed that because the common issues would play a part in every trial, they must be significant and predominate over individual questions. However, the claim that American Tobacco (D) fraudulently failed to inform consumers of the addictive nature of nicotine requires proof of individual reliance. Even after the class action, the district court might well decide that each individual's reliance must be proven in separate trials. The court then would be faced with the difficult decision of decertifying the class or continuing even though Rule 23 was not satisfied. (3) No. A mass tort class action cannot be found "superior" when there is no prior track record of individual trials from which a court can make the predominance and superiority analyses. Aggregation of the individual claims makes it more likely that American Tobacco (D) would be found liable, and it strengthens the number of unmeritorious claims. This could force American Tobacco (D) to settle the class action even though many claims are without merit. In general, certification of mass tort classes has been disfavored. Without a prior track record, the district court cannot draw the information necessary to make the predominance and superiority analyses. At this time, no court can determine the very real possibility that the "judicial crisis" of millions of individual trials will ever materialize. In addition, class action may not be superior in cases like this, where the aggregate stakes are in the billions of dollars. Finally, judicial efficiency is lacking in the context of an immature tort. The conflict of law question itself could take decades to work its way through the courts, and even then individual trials on the issue of comparative negligence and damages would be required. For all these reasons, we reverse and remand with instructions for the district court to dismiss the class complaint.

Analysis:

This case illustrates the importance of carefully analyzing the "predominance" and "superiority" requirements of Rule 23(b)(3) prior to certifying a class. Although the opinion chastises the lower court for failing to make these determinations, it is likely that the class would have been decertified regardless. According to this opinion, mass tort class actions can never be certified until a sufficient number of individual trials have been conducted. The Court of Appeals essentially concludes that the class action is "immature." Does this approach make sense? Couldn't the district court determine the superiority of the class action device without the need to waste considerable time and resources litigating individual trials? And even if individual trials are required prior to class certification, doesn't this run counter to the general principles of class action litigation? The class action device is based in public policy, on the ground that it would be better to focus all effort into one trial rather than allow the possibility of thousands or millions of individual trials with disparate results.

■ CASE VOCABULARY

GRAVAMEN: Central basis of a complaint.

SUI GENERIS: The only one of its type.

Hansberry v. Lee

(Buyer) v. *(Covenantor)*

311 U.S. 32, 61 S.Ct. 115 (1940)

● IN A CLASS ACTION SUIT, WHERE A CLASS MEMBER WAS NOT ADEQUATELY REPRESENTED, GIVING RES JUDICATA EFFECT TO THE JUDGMENT VIOLATES DUE PROCESS

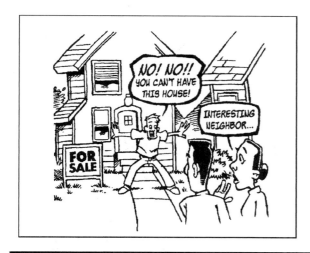

■ **INSTANT FACTS** Hansberry (D), the black purchaser of land that was subject to a racially restrictive sales covenant, sought to avoid a prior class action holding that the covenant was valid.

■ **BLACK LETTER RULE** Granting res judicata effect to a class action judgment, in which the prerequisites and procedures for class action were not satisfied, violates due process.

■ **PROCEDURAL BASIS**

Writ of certiorari from order affirming res judicata effect of prior decree.

● ■ **FACTS**

This class action suit was brought in an Illinois state court to enforce a racially restrictive covenant involving some land in Chicago. The covenant provided that it was not effective unless signed by 95% of the landowners. In the complaint, Lee (P), a white person, sought to enjoin the purchase of some restricted land by Hansberry (D), a black. Lee (P) alleged that the seller had signed the covenant, and that an earlier state court decision had held that the covenant was effective, since 95% of the landowners had signed the agreement. Hansberry (D) and other defendants argued that they were not bound by the res judicata effect of the earlier judgment, since they had not been parties to the suit. Thus, Hansberry (D) and the others argued that their due process rights were being violated. The Illinois Circuit Court and Supreme Court held that the original action was a class suit, and therefore that the holding was binding on all class members, including Hansberry (D) and the sellers. The United States Supreme Court granted certiorari.

■ **ISSUE**

Where the procedural requirements for class action have not been satisfied, is the judgment res judicata and therefore binding on absent parties?

■ **DECISION AND RATIONALE**

(Stone, J.) No. Where the procedure and course of litigation in a class action do not insure the protection of absent parties, a judgment entered in the action is not binding on those absent parties. An alternative holding would violate the due process rights of the absent members. In a typical litigation, notice and an opportunity to be heard are requisite to due process, and a judgment in which a person is not designated as a party does not have a res judicata effect on that person. An exception exists, however, in the class action context [Just when you thought you understood due process, class actions confuse the issue!]. Judgments entered in class or representative suits may bind members of the class or those represented who were not made parties to it. However, there is a failure of due process where the procedure adopted does not fairly insure the protection of the interest of absent parties who are to be bound by it. In the original case at hand, which found the covenant effective, the procedure did not adequately protect the interests of Hansberry (D) and the sellers. First, the restrictive agreement did not purport to create a joint obligation or liability. Rather, the racially restrictive covenant was a series of several obligations of the signers. Second, the signers seeking to enforce the agreement cannot be considered members of the same class as those signers seeking to challenge the validity of the agreement or to resist its performance. The signers such as Lee (P) attempting to enforce the agreement have conflicting interests with the parties such as Hansberry (D) and the sellers attempting to challenge the agreement. Thus, the mere fact that all of the parties had signed the agreement does not make them the same class, and the absent parties in the original litigation were not provided due process protections in asserting their interests. Reversed.

Analysis:

This case presents a different type of due process analysis from the jurisdictional cases encountered early in this book. While due process in the jurisdictional context typically focused on the adequacy of notice and opportunity to be heard, the Supreme Court now focuses on the adequacy of class representation. This makes sense in the class action context, given the potentially sever res judicata effects of a judgment on an absent class member. In effect, the Court is saying that people such as Hansberry (D) and the sellers were not adequately represented in the original litigation. Thus, they are not to be considered members of the original class. Conversely, if they were class members, the Court asserts, then the original judgment would be binding. Note that the "adequacy of representation" argument presents a timing problem, namely, at what point in time should the adequacy of representation be judged? The U.S. Supreme Court apparently assumed that the adequacy of representation in an original action could be analyzed in a later action. The logic of this approach is sound, since a final determination of the adequacy of representation could only be made through subsequent challenges to the res judicata effect of the suit. As Rule 23(c)(3) states, a class action decree should define the members of the class, presumably to aid in future determinations of the judgment's binding effect. The original court hearing the class action cannot predetermine the binding effect of its judgment, since this construction of Rule 23 would arguably be substantive in nature and thus violate the Rules Enabling Act, 28 U.S.C. § 2072.

■ CASE VOCABULARY

CLASS SUIT: An action brought, on behalf of a large number of people, by a representative who is similarly situated and who purports to represent the interests of the absent parties.

Phillips Petroleum Co. v. Shutts

(*Lessee*) v. (*Lessor*)

472 U.S. 797, 105 S.Ct. 2965 (1985)

MINIMUM CONTACTS ARE NOT REQUIRED FOR PERSONAL JURISDICTION IN CLASS ACTIONS, BUT THE FORUM STATE MAY NOT NECESSARILY APPLY ITS OWN LAW TO ALL CLAIMS

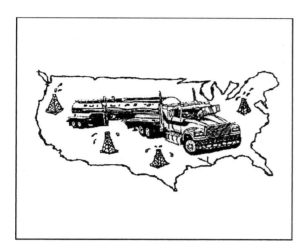

■ **INSTANT FACTS** Shutts (P) and several other holders of royalty interests brought a class action against Phillips Petroleum (D) to recover royalty payments. The Kansas court obtained personal jurisdiction over all parties and applied Kansas law to all claims.

■ **BLACK LETTER RULE** In class actions, personal jurisdiction does not require that each class member have minimum contacts with the forum state, but the forum state must have sufficient interests in the claims to assert its state law to all claims.

■ **PROCEDURAL BASIS**

Writ of certiorari reviewing affirmance of class action judgment in favor of class for damages for contractual violations.

■ **FACTS**

Phillips Petroleum (D) obtained natural gas from leased land in eleven different states. Shutts (P) and several other lessors brought an action against Phillips Petroleum (D) in a Kansas state court, seeking to recover interest on royalty payments due under the leases. The Kansas trial court certified a class consisting of 33,000 royalty owners, and the class representatives provided each class member with notice by mail and with an opportunity to opt out of the class action. [Don't worry, the $100,000 in postage could later be recovered by the representatives!] The final class consisted of 28,100 class members residing in all fifty states and in foreign countries. Nevertheless, the trial court asserted personal jurisdiction and applied only Kansas contract law, finding Phillips Petroleum (D) liable for interest on suspended royalties to all class members. Phillips Petroleum (D) argued that the Due Process Clause prevented the Kansas court from adjudicating the claims of the non-resident class members, and that the Full Faith and Credit Clause prohibited the application of Kansas law to all of the claims. The Kansas Supreme Court affirmed the trial court's ruling, and the U.S. Supreme Court granted certiorari.

■ **ISSUE**

(1) May a court exercise personal jurisdiction over absent class members even if the members do not possess the minimum contacts with the forum which would support personal jurisdiction over a defendant? (2) Does a mailed notice and opt out provision satisfy the notice requirements for due process purposes? (3) May a forum state apply that state's law to every claim in a class action where the state does not have a significant contact and interest in every claim asserted by each member of the class?

■ **DECISION AND RATIONALE**

(Rehnquist, J.) (1) Yes. A court may exercise personal jurisdiction over absent class members even if the members do not possess the minimum contacts with the forum which would support personal jurisdiction over a defendant. As this Court has held in several cases, due process requires that a defendant have sufficient minimum contacts with the forum state in order for a court to obtain personal jurisdiction over a defendant. Phillips Petroleum (D) argues that, likewise, the Kansas courts may not assert personal jurisdiction over class members who neither affirmatively consent to jurisdiction nor have sufficient minimum contacts with Kansas. However, there are significant differences between jurisdiction over a defendant and jurisdiction over a class of plaintiffs. While defendants deserve due process protections from being haled into a distant state with which the defendants have no contacts, plaintiffs in class actions are not haled anywhere to defend themselves upon threat of default judgments. In class actions, both the court and the class representatives protect the interests of absent class members. Moreover, absent class members do not have to hire counsel or appear, are not subject to coercive or punitive remedies, and are not bound by adverse judgments for damages. Thus, the due process rights afforded to defendants, who should not be forced to travel to and appear in distant states with which they have no minimum contacts, do not apply equally to plaintiff class members. (2) Yes. A mailed notice including an opt out provision satisfies the due process requirements to provide notice to all interested litigants. This notice must be reasonably calculated to apprise the interested parties of the pendency of the actions and present them an opportunity to be heard. In the case at hand, the class representatives reasonably used first class mail to notify all 33,000 royalty owners of the pending action. Moreover, this notice provided the parties an opportunity to opt out of the litigation so as to avoid the binding effect of any judgment, allowing such members to bring separate claims. Phillips Petroleum (D) maintains that notice in class actions must provide an "opt in" provision, and that jurisdiction is improper over all distant plaintiffs who do not voluntarily opt in to the litigation. We do not think that the Constitution requires the State to sacrifice the obvious advantages in judicial efficiency resulting from the opt out approach for the protection of the onerous opt in approach. (3) No. Where a forum state does not have a significant contact and interest in every claim asserted by each member of the class, the state may not apply that state's law to every claim in a class action. In the case at hand, the Kansas state court applied Kansas contract law to every claim, notwithstanding that over 99% of the leases and 97% of the plaintiffs had no apparent connection to Kansas. Phillips Petroleum (D) contends that the application of Kansas substantive law in this situation violates the Due Process Clause and the Full Faith and Credit Clause, and we agree. Kansas must have a significant contact to the claims asserted by each member of the plaintiff class, creating sufficient state interests, in order to ensure that the application of Kansas law is not arbitrary or unfair. However, Kansas did not have a sufficient interests in claims unrelated to the state. Moreover, the Kansas laws conflict with laws of jurisdictions such as Texas, in which many class members reside. In addition, there is no indication that the leases contemplated an application of Kansas law to all claims arising out of the leases. Therefore, the application of Kansas law to every claim in this case is sufficiently arbitrary and unfair as to exceed constitutional limits. In conclusion, we affirm the judgment of the Supreme Court of Kansas insofar as it upheld Kansas jurisdiction over all claims, but we reverse its judgment insofar as it held that Kansas law was applicable to all of the transactions. Remanded for further proceedings not inconsistent with this opinion.

Analysis:

Justice Rehnquist presents a thorough and logical analysis of difficult issues in class actions, including requirements for personal jurisdiction and the application of appropriate law. The due process protections afforded to defendants in ordinary civil actions simply do not parallel the protections necessary for plaintiffs in class actions, since class action plaintiffs do not suffer similar hardships and are adequately protected by the court and by the class representatives. Phillips Petroleum's (D) arguments, that every class member must "opt in" to class actions and must have minimum contacts with the forum state, would obliterate class actions involving numerous plaintiffs residing in several different states and countries. Clearly, the efficiencies provided by class actions outweigh the minimal needs to obtain consent or for the forum to have minimum contacts with each class member. In the case at hand, the 33,000 potential class members were treated fairly, as 3,400 opted out of the litigation and an additional 1,500 were excluded because the notice was undeliverable. However, previous Supreme Court decisions regarding personal jurisdiction explicitly stated that *all* assertions of state-court personal jurisdiction must be evaluated on a minimum contacts standard. The instant case alters this requirement, justifying jurisdiction despite a lack of minimum contacts on one of two grounds: either consent to jurisdiction is inferred by the members' failure to opt out, or class action plaintiffs are not entitled to (and do not need) the same due process protections. In all likelihood, the latter interpretation is the most probable.

■ CASE VOCABULARY

PRO FORMA: A required format with which procedures must comply.

RARA AVIS: Literally "a rare bird"; a unique person or thing.

Amchem Products, Inc. v. Windsor

(*Asbestos Manufacturers*) v. (*Class Representatives*)

521 U.S. 591, 117 S.Ct. 2231, 138 L.Ed.2d 689 (1997)

CLASS OF ASBESTOS VICTIMS CANNOT COMBINE ILL PLAINTIFFS WITH PLAINTIFFS WHO WERE EXPOSED BUT ARE NOT YET ILL

■ **INSTANT FACTS** To settle asbestos-exposure litigation, the asbestos industry proposed a class action settlement which combined asbestos-sickened plaintiffs with "exposure-only" plaintiffs (who were exposed but have not yet developed any disease).

■ **BLACK LETTER RULE** Class action settlement offers must meet the *Rule 23* requirements of "predominance," "superiority," "adequate representation," and "notice" before they may be certified.

■ **PROCEDURAL BASIS**

In class action settlement agreement, appeal from appellate decertification order, on writ of certiorari.

■ **FACTS**

All asbestos litigation pending in federal courts was transferred to a single district by a federal advisory committee. The consolidated litigation involved hundreds of thousands of current plaintiffs against 20 asbestos manufacturers, but there was concern there would also be future plaintiffs, who were exposed but had not yet developed symptoms, and had not yet filed suit. In settlement negotiations, the (current) plaintiffs' counsel attempted to represent anticipated future claimants' interests. Then, Amchem (D) and the other asbestos manufacturers ("CCR Defendants") (D) filed a (sham) lawsuit/settlement offer, which certified current and *future* plaintiffs together as a class, to make them accept a stipulated settlement. The suit named 9 lead plaintiffs to represent all people exposed to asbestos manufactured by the CCR Defendants (D), or whose spouses were exposed, but who had not yet filed suit. The settlement stipulated a detailed compensation system, involving capped payments for certain disease categories. Payments were not inflation-adjusted. Additional compensation could be obtained for "extraordinary" claims. However, there was no compensation for lost consortium and some other torts recognized by some states' laws. Also, there was no compensation for mere exposure without actual injury, or "pleural claims" (where asbestos had entered the lungs, but not yet caused any disease), though these claimants could receive compensation upon developing diseases. The CCR Defendants (D) moved to certify the class. The district court certified the class conditionally. Many class members (P) appealed, contending the settlement disadvantaged them unfairly because it (i) did not adjust for inflation, (ii) did not account for changes in medical understanding, (iii) paid low compensation, (iv) did not compensate for certain claims, e.g., medical monitoring. The objectors (P) also claimed inadequate representation, contending counsel representing both current and future claimants had conflicted interests. The Court of Appeals decertified the class, finding (i) individual issues predominated, because class members were exposed to different asbestos products, over different periods, and suffered different symptoms, (ii) the case law governing the members varied, (iii) representation was inadequate due to serious intra-class conflicts, especially the conflict between afflicted plaintiffs (who want higher payouts) and exposure-only plaintiffs (who want inflation adjustment for future injuries and opt-out rights), and (iv) the class action was not superior to individual suits, since it was so large and complex as to be untriable. The CCR Defendants (D) appeal.

■ ISSUE

Must class action settlement offers must meet the *Rule 23* requirements?

■ DECISION AND RATIONALE

(Ginsburg) Yes. Class action settlement offers must meet the *Rule 23* requirements of "predominance," "superiority," "adequate representation," and "notice" before they may be certified. We granted review to decide what role settlement may play in determining the propriety of class certification, under *Rule 23*. *Rule 23(b)(3)* class actions are discretionary, and though they were originally intended to redress injuries which could not be litigated individually, they now provide an increasingly popular form for resolving disputes efficiently. When a district court is confronted with requests for a settlement-only class certification, it need not inquire whether the case, if tried, would present intractable management problems, since there will be no trial. But the district court must consider *Rule 23*'s other requirements to protect absentees. *Rule 23(a)-(b)* considers whether a proposed class has sufficient unity so that absent members can fairly be bound by class representatives' decisions, and that concern persists where settlement, rather than trial, is proposed. Courts lack authority to substitute, in place of *Rule 23*'s requirements, their judgement that the settlement is "fair." We agree the sprawling class certified here does not satisfy *Rule 23*. *Rule 23(b)(3)* requires that common "questions of law or fact . . . predominate over any questions affecting only individual members." Here, the District Court found predominance based on class members' (i) shared experience of asbestos exposure, and (ii) common interest in receiving prompt and fair compensation. However, these findings do not satisfy *Rule 23(b)(3)*. The benefits asbestos victims may obtain from a grand-scale compensation scheme is a matter for legislative consideration, but is irrelevant to the predominance inquiry. The *Rule 23(b)(3)* predominance inquiry tests whether proposed classes are sufficiently cohesive to warrant adjudication by representation; by contrast, the *Rule 23(e)* inquiry protects unnamed class members "from unjust . . . settlements . . . when the representatives become fainthearted before the action is adjudicated." Here, the mere fact that all the plaintiffs were injured by asbestos cannot meet the *23(b)(2)* predominance requirement, since there are many questions peculiar to several categories of class members; particularly, the exposure-only plaintiffs share little in common with each other, or with presently injured plaintiffs, since it is unclear which asbestos-related disease they may contract, if any. While even mass torts arising from a common cause/disaster may conceivably satisfy the predominance requirement, we know of no settlement class as sprawling as this one. The certified class also cannot fairly and adequately protect members' interests, as required by *Rule 23(a)(4)*, since the presently injured plaintiffs want generous immediate payments, which tugs against exposure-only plaintiffs' interest in ensuring an ample, inflation-protected fund for the future. It is irrelevant to *Rule 23(a)(4)* that this is not a "limited fund" case, since the defendants have sufficient assets to pay all claims, because the settlement allocates limited resources (e.g., only a few claimants can opt out). In sum, the settling parties achieved a global compromise with no structural assurance of fair and adequate representation for the diverse individuals affected. The argument is essentially made that a nationwide administrative claims processing regime would provide the most secure, fair, and efficient means of compensating asbestos victims, but Congress has not adopted such a resolution, and *Rule 23* cannot carry this large load. Affirmed.

■ CONCURRENCE

(Breyer) I believe the need for settlement of asbestos litigation is very great, to resolve hundreds of thousands of lawsuits. Second, in determining whether common issues predominate, I would give greater weight to settlement-related issues. Third, I am uncertain that the representation was inadequate, and do not believe it was appropriate for this Court to second-guess the District Court without first having the Court of Appeals consider it. Fourth, I believe the settlement is fair. Fifth, I cannot accept the majority's suggestions that "notice" is inadequate.

Analysis:

The extent of *Amchem*'s holding is disputed. Some believe *Amchem* suggests that certain mass tort claims can never be certified. However, the opinion expressly states that mass tort claims *may* be appropriately certified, but only if they meet stringent requirements. What *Amchem* prohibits is the certification of a class containing both presently-injured plaintiffs and plaintiffs exposed to toxins who have not yet developed symptoms, based on a finding that such plaintiffs intrinsically have conflicted interests. Such classes must be divided into subclasses, each with its own attorneys. However, the stringent requirements may effectively make a class settlement impossible to resolve nationwide asbestos claims.

Ortiz v. Fibreboard Corp.

(*Asbestos Victims*) v. (*Asbestos Manufacturer*)

527 U.S. 815, 119 S.Ct. 2295, 144 L.Ed.2d 715 (1999)

"LIMITED FUND" CLASS ACTION SETTLEMENTS MUST MEET STRICT *RULE 23* REQUIREMENTS

■ **INSTANT FACTS** An asbestos manufacturer proposed a settlement which would create a "limited fund" of assets and insurance proceeds for claimants, preserve most of the manufacturer's assets, cap future lawsuits, and exempt 100,-000 plaintiffs from the class.

■ **BLACK LETTER RULE** A settlement under *Rule 23(b)(1)(B)*'s "limited fund" provision must (i) establish a fixed fund which is proven inadequate to satisfy all claims, (ii) apply the fund and the defendant's entire assets for claimants' benefit, (iii) prevent intra-class conflicts of interest and unfair distribution, (iv) include most potential plaintiffs, or provide similar compensation for current and future claimants, and (v) provide a "fair, adequate, and reasonable" settlement under *Rule 23(e)*.

■ **PROCEDURAL BASIS**

In asbestos class action settlement, appeal from appellate affirmation of class certification and settlement, on writ of certiorari.

■ **FACTS**

Asbestos manufacturer Fibreboard (D) was sued by thousands of asbestos victims. It was unclear whether Fibreboard's (D) insurance policy covered the claims. After Fibreboard (D) settled 45,000 claims, it and its insurers negotiated a "Global Settlement" with plaintiffs' attorneys for its remaining liability. Under the settlement, Fibreboard (D) would establish a "limited fund" of $1.535 billion (composed mostly of insurance proceeds), placed in trust for class members. Individual claimants could sue only after undergoing mandatory alternative dispute resolution, and any suit would be capped at $500K and disallow punitive damages. Some 100,000 litigants, who had settled/pending suits, were excluded from the class. The trial court found the class action met the requirements of *Rule 23(a)* and *Rule 23(b)(1)(B)*'s "limited fund" provision, and provided a "fair, adequate, and reasonable" settlement under *Rule 23(e)*. Dissenting class members (P) appealed. On appeal, the court affirmed the class certification and found the settlement adequate. Certain class members (P) appeal again.

■ **ISSUE**

May a settlement under *Rule 23(b)(1)(B)*'s "limited fund" provision be approved if it provides a "fair, adequate, and reasonable" settlement under *Rule 23(e)*?

■ **DECISION AND RATIONALE**

(Souter) No. A settlement under *Rule 23(b)(1)(B)*'s "limited fund" provision must (i) establish a fixed fund which is proven inadequate to satisfy all claims, (ii) apply the fund and the defendant's entire assets for claimants' benefit, (iii) prevent intra-class conflicts of interest and unfair distribution, (iv) include most potential plaintiffs, or provide similar compensation for current and future claimants, and (v) provide a "fair, adequate, and reasonable" settlement under *Rule 23(e)*. *Rule 23(b)(1)(B)* was enacted for situations where any individual adjudication by a class member would effectively dispose of, or substantially affect, absent class members' interests, to protect class members who have no right to withdraw. One such situation was the "limited fund" class action, which aggregates "claims ... made by numerous persons against a fund insufficient to satisfy all claims." In such cases, equity requires absent parties to be adequately represented, since individual claims satisfied from the single fund would effectively prejudice future/absent claimants' rights. *Rule 23(b)(1)(B)* "limited fund" class actions were intended to have the following characteristics, which justify binding absent class members: (i) there is a fixed fund inadequate to satisfy all claims fully, (ii) the entire fund is set aside for members' benefit, and (iii) the claimants seek recovery under a common theory. However, *Rule 23(b)(1)(B)*'s drafters— Congress and the Advisory Committee—never contemplated it covering "mass accident" cases, so we should be cautious in applying it in such situations, and require that the action have the "limited fund" characteristics listed above. Avoiding overly adventurous use of *Rule 23(b)(1)(B)* is also important because dissenting class members have no inherent right to abstain, and forcing them to be bound by an unwanted settlement may violate their constitutional rights to jury trial and due process. Here, the district court erroneously failed to find the fund was limited, and failed to meet *Amchem*'s requirements. The district court simply accepted the parties' stipulation that the fund was limited, whereas the court should have examined evidence proving the fund's value and insufficiency, in an adversarial proceeding. Here, the "fund" comprised Fibreboard's (D) general assets (worth $235M) and the value of its 2 insurance policies, but the court did not appraise the policies' value, which might have revealed assets sufficient to pay all claims. [Equally likely, pigs might take flight.] Also, the class here was overinclusive, and included claimants with conflicted interests. This class includes myriad claimants with diverse conditions and legal claims, and excludes over 100,000 plaintiffs. While it is uncertain how many plaintiffs may be exempted from a class before it fails to qualify as a mandatory "limited fund" class, there is no question that such a mandatory settlement class will not qualify when, in the very negotiations aimed at a class settlement, class counsel excludes a third of anticipated claimants, many represented by class counsel [i.e., the Court is concerned that too many plaintiffs were excluded from the class, and also that class counsel disadvantaged future claimants' interests by exempting its current clients from being bound by the settlement]. Class exclusions are forgivable upon a showing that the class members ended up with benefits comparable to those received by excluded plaintiffs, but we find the excluded plaintiffs secured better terms. Finally, the class must distribute fund assets fairly among class members; if pro rata distribution is impossible, there must at least be a procedure for resolving how to compensate differently situated claimants. Here, the distribution was unfair. *Amchem* requires that a class including present and future claimants must be subdivided into subclasses, each with separate attorneys. Finally, a limited fund must make [substantially] all the defendant's assets available to claimants, though we leave open the question of whether a class action may allow the defendant to keep some of its assets as an incentive to settle, rather than depleting those assets in defending numerous lawsuits. Here, however, the settlement permits Fibreboard (D) to keep most of its assets, which is hardly in class members' best interest. Reversed and remanded.

■ CONCURRENCE

(Rehnquist) While I agree the District Court's plan resolves asbestos claims more efficiently than the Federal Rules of Civil Procedure, we are not free to devise an ideal system.

■ DISSENT

(Breyer) The proposed settlement is reasonable and thus lawful, because (i) an expedited procedure is necessary to assure asbestos victims receive timely and adequate recovery, (ii) judges must proactively prevent asbestos cases from overloading the courts, (iii) appellate courts should defer to district courts' greater understanding of asbestos litigation's logistical problems, and (iv) courts should recognize that denying class action treatment for asbestos claims will effectively deny victims a fair and timely recovery. Here, it is obvious that the fund is probably insufficient to satisfy all claims, and I find the district court's valuation was reasonable. The district court made numerous factual findings concerning equitable treatment, and the appellate court approved these, so I am inclined to defer. There is no doubt that the settlement made far more money available to victims, so I would uphold it.

Analysis:

Ortiz again strikes down a proposed class settlement for the asbestos problem, on concerns it may be unfair to future claimants. However, there is increasing recognition in the concurrences, dissents, and lower court opinions that resolving asbestos claims through individual suits is inefficient and inherently wasteful, since much of the money which could be used to compensate victims must instead be diverted to maintaining and defending numerous suits across the country.

Cooper v. Federal Reserve Bank of Richmond

(Employee) v. *(Employer)*

467 U.S. 867, 104 S.Ct. 2794 (1984)

GENERAL HOLDINGS IN CLASS ACTIONS DO NOT PRECLUDE SUBSEQUENT SPECIFIC INDIVIDUAL ACTIONS

■ **INSTANT FACTS** Following a class action and appeal in which the Federal Reserve Bank of Richmond (D) was found not to have engaged in a pattern or practice of discrimination, several class members sought to bring individual claims for discrimination.

■ **BLACK LETTER RULE** A general holding adverse to a class does not preclude an individual member of the class from subsequently litigating specific individual claims.

■ **FACTS**

The Equal Employment Opportunity Commission commenced an action against the Federal Reserve Bank of Richmond (Bank) (D), alleging that the Bank violated Title VII of the Civil Rights Act of 1964 by refusing to promote blacks on the basis of race. Four individuals, including Cooper (P), were allowed to intervene. The District Court then certified a class pursuant to Rules 23(b)(2) and (b)(3), including all black employees of the Bank who had been discriminated against. Phyllis Baxter and five other employees (the Baxter petitioners) received notice of the action and made no attempt to opt out of the class. The District Court found that the bank had engaged in a pattern and practice of discrimination only against employees at pay grades 4 or 5, but the Court did not order relief. [Why not?] The Baxter petitioners filed a separate action alleging that each had been denied a promotion because of their race in violation of 42 U.S.C. § 1981. The Bank moved to dismiss on grounds that the Baxter petitioners were employed in a grade other than 4 or 5, and that the District Court's holding that there was no classwide discrimination at these other pay grades was res judicata on Baxter and the others. The District Court denied this motion to dismiss. On appeal, the Fourth Circuit Court of Appeals reversed the judgment on the merits, holding that there was insufficient evidence to establish a pattern or practice of racial discrimination. The Court of Appeals further held that the Baxter petitioners were precluded from bringing their individual claims under the doctrine of res judicata. Thus, the court remanded for dismissal of the Baxter complaint. The Supreme Court granted certiorari.

■ **ISSUE**

Does a general holding adverse to a class preclude an individual member of the class from subsequently litigating specific individual claims?

■ **DECISION AND RATIONALE**

(Stevens, J.) No. A general holding that there has been no pattern and practice of widespread discrimination does not preclude an individual member of a class from subsequently litigating specific individual claims for discrimination. Indeed, the basic principles of res judicata and collateral estoppel apply to class actions. A judgment in favor of the plaintiff class merges any subsequent claim a class member may have into the judgment granting relief. Further, a judgment in favor of the defendant, such as the Appellate Court's judgment for the Bank (D), bars subsequent actions on that claim. Thus, the Court of Appeals was correct in concluding that the Baxter petitioners, as members of the class, are bound by the adverse judgment. However, the court erred in the preclusive effect it attached to that prior adjudication. The judgment only bars the class members from bringing an action against the Bank (D) alleging a *general pattern or practice* of discrimination. It does not bar the members from bringing specific individual claims for discrimination in subsequent litigations. Although the prior holding, that the Bank (D) did not discriminate on a widespread basis, may aid the Bank (D) in the subsequent litigation, it does not preclude the assertion of individual actions. This holding upholds the general purposes of class actions, since otherwise each individual member of the class would be allowed to intervene in the action and assert individual claims. Reversed.

Analysis:

Just when the res judicata effect of class action judgments seemed clear, this case has muddled the issue considerably. As stated in previous cases, a class action decree will be binding on all class members, provided all the requirements and prerequisites for a class action have been satisfied. Thus, the decree in favor of the Bank (D) in this case should be binding on all class members, since there were no allegations of improper class action procedure. Then why are the individual members allowed to subsequently litigate individual claims for discrimination? In all likelihood, it is because the class action complaint sought an extremely broad, general conclusion. The original class action only sought to prove—unsuccessfully, as the Court of Appeals later held—that the Bank (D) was engaged in a widespread pattern and practice of discrimination. The individual litigants including Baxter, on the other hand, sought redress for specific discriminatory actions. Logically, an employer could discriminate against certain employees without engaging in widespread discrimination. Nevertheless, the Bank (D) has gained little from the judgment in its favor, since it must relitigate the issue of discrimination on an individual basis, potentially with all of the class members.

CHAPTER ELEVEN

Pretrial Devices for Obtaining Information: Depositions and Discovery

In re Petition of Sheila Roberts Ford

Instant Facts: Ford (P) sought leave to depose a county sheriff to determine the identity of proper defendants in an unfiled lawsuit.

Black Letter Rule: Pre-complaint discovery may not be used to gather the evidentiary support necessary to file a verified complaint.

Kelly v. Nationwide Mut. Ins. Co.

Instant Facts: Kelly (P), the owner of a tractor in which sugar was allegedly placed in the gas tank, sued its insurer, Nationwide Mutual Insurance Company (D). Nationwide (D) denied the claim and sought discovery, but Kelly (P) failed to completely answer the interrogatories.

Black Letter Rule: Discovery may be used to obtain non-privileged, admissible information related to any issue in the case, provided the information does not relate exclusively to the opponent's case.

Marrese v. American Academy of Orthopaedic Surgeons

Instant Facts: Two doctors, who sued the American Academy of Orthopaedic Surgeons (D) after being denied membership, attempted to obtain confidential information pertaining to the membership discussions, but the Academy (D) refused to comply with the discovery.

Black Letter Rule: A federal court should use its discretionary power to alter discovery or to change the sequence of discovery in order to balance the interests of the parties.

Seattle Times Co. v. Rhinehart

Instant Facts: The Seattle Times (D), which was sued for defamation by Rhinehart (P) on behalf of his religious organization for defamation, appealed a protective order that precluded the Times (D) from publishing certain information obtained via discovery.

Black Letter Rule: A protective order that restricts the dissemination of information obtained by discovery does not necessarily offend the First Amendment.

Cummings v. General Motors Corp.

Instant Facts: Cummings (P) was injured in an automobile accident allegedly due to a design defect in the seatbelt mechanism and passenger seat of the vehicle in which she was riding.

Black Letter Rule: Under Federal Rule of Civil Procedure 26(a), a party must automatically disclose all documents and tangible evidence on which it intends to rely at trial.

Polycast Technology Corp v. Uniroyal

Instant Facts: Deloitte & Touche sought a protective order to prevent Polycast Technology Corp. (P) from deposing a Deloitte employee.

Black Letter Rule: A non-party witness may be deposed when his information is relevant to a claim or defense presented and is likely to supplement other witnesses' deposition testimony.

In re Auction Houses Antitrust Litigation

Instant Facts: Taubman (D) sought additional information concerning documents previously provided by Christie's (D) in discovery, to which Christie's (D) objected as outside its knowledge and control.

Black Letter Rule: Under the Federal Rules of Civil Procedure, a party is obligated to respond to discovery requests with all information available to it.

In re Convergent Technologies Securities Litigation

Instant Facts: The defendants served the plaintiffs with contention interrogatories at the beginning of pretrial discovery.

Black Letter Rule: Contention interrogatories early in litigation are permitted only when they will help clarify or narrow the issues in the case.

Zubulake v. UBS Warburg LLC

Instant Facts: Zubulake (P) sought discovery of archived e-mails from back-up tapes and optical disks.

Black Letter Rule: Discoverable matter includes both paper and electronic documents.

Schlagenhauf v. Holder

Instant Facts: Robert Schlagenhauf (D), a defendant who allegedly caused a collision while driving a bus, objected to an order requiring him to submit to a number of physical and mental examinations.

Black Letter Rule: A physical or mental examination may be ordered when good cause exists, and when a party's physical or mental condition is in controversy.

Battle v. Memorial Hospital at Gulfport

Instant Facts: A magistrate judge prohibited the introduction of the plaintiff's expert's deposition into evidence, while permitting another expert's deposition and precluding that expert from testifying live.

Black Letter Rule: Deposition testimony of an unavailable witness may be introduced at trial when the questioner at the deposition is on the same side of the same issue at both proceedings and has a substantially similar interest in asserting and prevailing on the issue.

Hickman v. Taylor

Instant Facts: Hickman (P) sought to obtain copies of written statements and descriptions of oral interviews acquired by Fortenbaugh, the opposing counsel.

Black Letter Rule: A party is not entitled, without a showing of good cause, to obtain copies of an opposing attorney's notes and memoranda acquired from interviews with witnesses.

Upjohn Co. v. United States

Instant Facts: In response to Upjohn Co.'s (D) internal investigation into potential bribes, the United States (P) sought to obtain information about confidential communications between Upjohn's (D) counsel and employees.

Black Letter Rule: The attorney-client privilege may protect all communications between corporate employees and corporate counsel, and the work-product exemption for oral statements can only be overcome by a strong showing of necessity and unavailability.

Krisa v. Equitable Life Assurance Society

Instant Facts: When an insurer denies its insured's disability claim, the insured sues and demands production of preliminary reports prepared for litigation by experts.

Black Letter Rule: Expert witnesses' reports are discoverable, unless they contain or embody attorney work product.

Cine Forty–Second Street Theatre Corp. v. Allied Artists Pictures Corp.

Instant Facts: In an antitrust action, Cine Forty–Second Street Theatre Corp. (P) continuously failed to adequately respond to interrogatories, and a magistrate recommended that Cine (P) be precluded from entering any evidence related to damages, the subject of the discovery requests.

Black Letter Rule: A party who exhibits gross negligence in responding to discovery requests is subject to the most severe discovery sanctions.

In re Petition of Sheila Roberts Ford

(*Estate Administratrix*)
170 F.R.D. 504 (M.D. Ala. 1997)

RULE 27 DOES NOT AUTHORIZE PRE–COMPLAINT DISCOVERY

It's the chicken. The chicken MUST come first.

Complaint   Rule 27 Deposition   stus.com

■ **INSTANT FACTS** Ford (P) sought leave to depose a county sheriff to determine the identity of proper defendants in an unfiled lawsuit.

■ **BLACK LETTER RULE** Pre-complaint discovery may not be used to gather the evidentiary support necessary to file a verified complaint.

■ **PROCEDURAL BASIS**

Consideration of the plaintiff's petition for pre-complaint discovery.

■ **FACTS**

Ford (P) sought leave to depose a county sheriff under Federal Rule of Civil Procedure 27 to determine who was responsible for the shooting of her father. In her motion, Ford (P) alleged that she expected to be a party to an action involving the shooting of her father as the administratrix of his estate and that the deposition was necessary to determine the proper defendants to the action and the basic facts underlying the suit, including the names, addresses, and descriptions of persons suspected to be proper defendants. The sheriff objected, claiming that the deposition was not authorized under Rule 27.

■ **ISSUE**

May a person depose another for the purpose of preserving testimony in an unfiled lawsuit when there is no danger that the testimony will be lost?

■ **DECISION AND RATIONALE**

(Thompson, C.J.) No. To invoke Rule 27, a party may "perpetuate testimony regarding any matter that may be cognizable in any court of the United States [by] fil[ing] a verified petition." Here, the stated purpose for the deposition was not to perpetuate testimony, but to discover it. There is no risk that the deponent's testimony will be lost or that he will be unavailable for deposition after a suit is commenced. Rule 27 does not allow discovery for the purpose of determining the factual basis for a lawsuit. Although Rule 11 requires a certification of the good-faith belief of the knowledge and information contained therein, a pre-complaint Rule 27 motion is not authorized by the plain language of Rule 27. While Ford (P) is in a difficult position because Rule 11 requires that her complaint be based on evidentiary support, and she cannot obtain such support without pre-complaint discovery, Rule 27 does not authorize the discovery she seeks. Motion denied.

Analysis:

As the court suggests, a plaintiff may find herself in a situation in which it is clear that a claim exists, but the responsible parties are unknown. Rule 11 requires counsel to endorse all pleadings with a certification of good faith, which cannot be met unless the plaintiff has a reasonable basis for asserting her claim. A plaintiff may not simply name as many individuals as she expects may be liable for her injuries, but rather must conduct sufficient pre-complaint investigation to determine with a substantial degree of certainty that the claims against each defendant have merit.

■ CASE VOCABULARY

COMPLAINT: The initial pleading that starts a civil action and states the basis for the court's jurisdiction, the basis for the plaintiff's claim, and the demand for relief.

DISCOVERY: Compulsory disclosure, at a party's request, of information that relates to the litigation.

Kelly v. Nationwide Mut. Ins. Co.

(*Tractor Owner*) v. (*Insurer*)

23 Ohio Op.2d 29, 188 N.E.2d 445 (Com. Pl. 1963)

OPPOSING PARTIES MAY DISCOVER INFORMATION RELATED TO ANY ISSUE IN THE CASE, PROVIDED THE INFORMATION IS ADMISSIBLE AND NON–PRIVILEGED

■ **INSTANT FACTS** Kelly (P), the owner of a tractor in which sugar was allegedly placed in the gas tank, sued its insurer, Nationwide Mutual Insurance Company (D). Nationwide (D) denied the claim and sought discovery, but Kelly (P) failed to completely answer the interrogatories.

■ **BLACK LETTER RULE** Discovery may be used to obtain non-privileged, admissible information related to any issue in the case, provided the information does not relate exclusively to the opponent's case.

■ **PROCEDURAL BASIS**

Motion to compel complete discovery in action for damages via insurance payment.

■ **FACTS**

Kelly (P) sued to recover damages that occurred to Kelly's (P) tractor allegedly as a result of someone putting sugar in the fuel tank. [Quite a sticky situation!] Kelly (P) sued Nationwide Mutual Insurance Company (D), claiming that a Nationwide (D) policy insured the tractor. Nationwide (D) answered with a general denial of the claim, including a contention that no such policy was in effect. In addition, Nationwide (D) attached forty-two interrogatories to the answer. After Kelly (P) failed to completely answer all of the interrogatories, Nationwide (D) moved to require more complete answers.

■ **ISSUE**

May discovery be used to obtain information relevant to any issue in the action, where the information is non-privileged and otherwise admissible at trial?

■ **DECISION AND RATIONALE**

(Pontius, J.) Yes. Pursuant to Ohio law, discovery may be used to obtain information relevant to any issue in the action, provided the information is not privileged and would be otherwise admissible at trial. Older cases in Ohio took a narrow approach, allowing discovery of information pertinent to an issue raised by the pleadings of the party seeking discovery. This Court adopts a somewhat more liberal construction, allowing discovery of any information pertinent to the action as a whole. For example, the mere fact that a defendant does not raise affirmative defenses does not preclude the use of discovery by that defendant. However, such discovery must be relevant to some issue in the action. Moreover, the discovery cannot seek privileged or non-admissible information, cannot seek discovery of the manner in which the opponent's case is to be established, and cannot seek evidence relating exclusively to the opponent's case. Thus, the Ohio law of discovery is not as liberal as the Federal Rules of Civil Procedure. In Ohio, a party may acquire records kept by the opponent in the regular course of business, for example, but may not acquire records amassed by the opponent only after the incident has arisen. As applied to the instant action, only one of Kelly's (P) discovery responses was insufficient.

In interrogatory number 2, Nationwide (D) inquired about the type of business entity that Kelly (P) was engaged in. This basic fact arose prior to the occurrence of the incident in dispute and is, therefore, properly discoverable. Kelly (P) must provide a complete response to this interrogatory. However, with respect to other interrogatories, Nationwide's (D) motion for more complete responses is overruled. Nationwide (D) has no right to obtain information regarding to matters arising after Kelly's (P) alleged claim arose, and Nationwide (D) cannot force Kelly (P) to produce hearsay or mere opinion evidence. Overruled except with reference to interrogatory number 2.

Analysis:

This case raises a number of interesting issues related to the scope of discovery. First, the court easily displaces the old Ohio case law, which allowed discovery only of information directly related to a party's claims. Under this old approach, a defendant would presumably have to raise affirmative defenses (as to which the defendant bears the burden of proof) in order to obtain any discovery. The modern approach is more flexible and more sensible, as it allows a defendant to obtain facts needed to present an adequate defense. Second, the court still maintains a fairly restrictive approach to discovery, especially in comparison to the liberal Federal Rules. It is interesting to note that seven years later Ohio adopted the federal approach. But at the time of this case. Ohio's rules were still very restrictive. Nationwide (D) was not allowed to discovery perhaps the most important information for its defense. Including facts about any events occurring after the alleged sugar-in-the-tank incident. In effect, therefore, Nationwide's (D) ability to formulate a defense to the claims was extremely limited.

■ CASE VOCABULARY

DISCOVERY: The method by which a party obtains information regarding a lawsuit from the opposing party.

GENERAL DENIAL: An answer to a complaint that denies each and every element of all causes of action.

INTERROGATORIES: A form of discovery that requests written responses to an opponent's written questions.

Marrese v. American Academy of Orthopaedic Surgeons

(Doctor) v. (Membership Organization)

726 F.2d 1150 (7th Cir. 1984), reversed on other grounds 470 U.S. 373, 105 S.Ct. 1327 (1985)

JUDGES HAVE BROAD DISCRETIONARY AUTHORITY TO SHAPE THE SCOPE AND SEQUENCE OF DISCOVERY TO PROTECT THE PARTIES

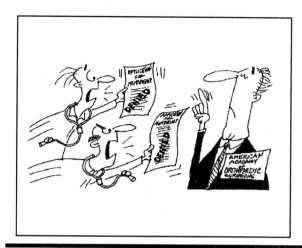

■ **INSTANT FACTS** Two doctors, who sued the American Academy of Orthopaedic Surgeons (D) after being denied membership, attempted to obtain confidential information pertaining to the membership discussions, but the Academy (D) refused to comply with the discovery.

■ **BLACK LETTER RULE** A federal court should use its discretionary power to alter discovery or to change the sequence of discovery in order to balance the interests of the parties.

■ **PROCEDURAL BASIS**

Appeal from order of contempt for failure to comply with discovery order.

■ **FACTS**

Doctors Marrese (P) and Treister (P), two orthopaedic surgeons, initially sued the American Academy of Orthopaedic Surgeons (Academy) (D) in state court alleging that they were refused membership in the Academy (D) without a hearing. After the claim was dismissed for failure to specify a valid state-law claim, the doctors filed suit in federal court, alleging antitrust violations. Marrese (P) and Treister (P) demanded that the Academy (D) produce all documents relating to denials of membership applications between 1970 and 1980. The federal court ordered the Academy (D) to produce the documents, issuing an order protecting the confidentiality of the Academy (D). However, the Academy (D) refused to produce the documents and was held in criminal contempt. The Academy (D) appealed this contempt order.

■ **ISSUE**

(1) When confidentiality of records is important, should a judge use his discretionary power and craft a discovery order maintaining the appropriate level of confidentiality? (2) Should a judge order discovery of nonsensitive information prior to discovery of confidential information?

■ **DECISION AND RATIONALE**

(Posner, J.) (1) Yes. In order to protect the confidentiality of certain persons, a judge should use his discretionary power and issue a discovery order maintaining the appropriate level of confidentiality. Federal Rule 26(c) requires the judge to balance the hardships to the parties in crafting a discovery order. In the case at hand, the members of the Academy (D) had a genuine interest in protecting the confidentiality of their deliberations on membership applications. Membership in the Academy (D) was voluntary, and the involuntary disclosure of deliberations on membership applications would compromise the voluntary character of the organization. Unlimited disclosure of the membership decisions would preclude members from freely discussing the merits of each applicant. Moreover, Marrese (P) intended to utilize the discovery to determine the names of the Academy members (D) and to depose these members in order to determine their motives for denying Marrese's (P) application. On the other side of the coin, however, a failure to grant Marrese (P) any access to the membership files would probably make it impossible for him to prove the antitrust case. In this situation, a judge should use the discretionary powers granted by Rule 26(c) to shape a discovery order reconciling the parties' conflicting needs. For example, the judge could examine all membership files himself *in camera*, or he could order the files of all membership deliberations redacted to remove the names of the deliberating members. If the information pointed to evidence of anticompetitive conduct, Marrese's (P) counsel could request the judge to reveal certain names so the members could be deposed. However, the District Court judge failed to adequately consider the members' confidentiality rights when the judge ordered discovery of all membership files. Since there is ample evidence of predatory discovery attempts by Marrese (P), possibly designed to coerce the Academy (D) to settle the case, the discovery order should be appropriately limited to minimize such devious intent. Reversed for issuance of new discovery order adequately reflecting the competing rights of the parties. (2) Yes. In certain situations, a judge should order discovery of nonsensitive information prior to the discovery of confidential information. Federal Rule 26(d) allows a judge to control the sequence and timing of discovery for the convenience of the parties and in the interests of justice. In the case at hand, Marrese (P) and Treister (P) would have had to conduct additional discovery after examining the confidential membership files. If this additional discovery was less sensitive and less confidential, the judge should have ordered such discovery to be conducted prior to the Academy (D) revealing more confidential information. Perhaps the doctors would have realized, upon conducting the less sensitive discovery, that their case was weak. In this situation, the confidential membership files would never have to be disclosed. Thus, the District Court should have issued an order directing discovery of the confidential files last.

■ DISSENT

(Wood, J.) Although the District Court's discovery order could have been improved, I do not find an abuse of discretion in the District Court's failure to conduct an *in camera* review or to order redaction of the membership files. First, an *in camera* inspection was already conducted in state court, and the state court nevertheless ordered production of all membership files after the review. Thus, an *in camera* review would not likely change the scope of discovery in this case. Second, the Academy (D) maintained its position that disclosure of any membership files, even after redaction by eliminating the names of the members, would overly infringe on the Academy's (D) confidentiality. Thus, a discovery order requiring production of redacted records would not likely avoid the confidentiality problems. The Academy (D) should not now reap a windfall from reversal of the discovery order because the order did not incorporate certain provisions that the Academy (D) still would refuse to accept. Further, I find no abuse of discretion in the court's failure to change the sequence and timing of the discovery. The Academy's (D) interests in confidentiality do not require such delicate treatment. Rather, an order requiring discovery of the less-confidential material first would result in piecemeal discovery and would unnecessarily burden Marrese (P) and Treister (P). Finally, the doctors' discovery does not evidence the slightest predatory motives and does not show an attempt to coerce the Academy (D) into settlement. The doctors deserve the opportunity to develop their case within reasonable limits. Thus, I would affirm the contempt holding, but on remand I would direct the court to review the records in camera and consider redaction before enforcing the discovery order.

Analysis:

This case discusses several options available for a judge when considering a potentially-sensitive discovery order. The basic thrust of the Federal Rules, allowing broad discovery, is restricted somewhat by Rules 26(c) and (d), which require judges to minimize hardship to parties from whom confidential or sensitive discovery is sought. In the case at hand, it does seem that the district court judge failed to adequately consider various options for protecting the privacy of the Academy (D). Why should applicants have a right to review the confidential membership documents of a private organization unless they clearly need the information in order to prove their cases? However, the majority's opinion seems to overlook some valid issues raised by the dissent. First, the majority does not analyze the district court's actions under the appropriate "abuse of discretion" standard. Even if it were possible to create a better discovery order, it is questionable that the district court abused its discretion in the order that it issued. Further, the dissent analyzes the effect of the majority's holding on the Academy (D), who is now relieved of the contempt charges and apparently under no immediate duty to produce the confidential documents.

■ CASE VOCABULARY

IN CAMERA: A review by a judge in the judge's chambers, either with or without the presence of counsel.

REDACTION: The act of striking out certain portions of a document, typically done in order to protect privileges or confidentiality while allowing the remainder of the document to be discovered.

Seattle Times Co. v. Rhinehart

(*Newspaper*) v. (*Leader of Religious Group*)

467 U.S. 20, 104 S.Ct. 2199 (1984)

PROTECTIVE ORDERS MAY LIMIT THE USE OF INFORMATION OBTAINED VIA DISCOVERY

■ **INSTANT FACTS** The Seattle Times (D), which was sued for defamation by Rhinehart (P) on behalf of his religious organization for defamation, appealed a protective order that precluded the Times (D) from publishing certain information obtained via discovery.

■ **BLACK LETTER RULE** A protective order that restricts the dissemination of information obtained by discovery does not necessarily offend the First Amendment.

■ **PROCEDURAL BASIS**

Writ of certiorari considering affirmance of discovery orders in action for defamation and invasion of privacy.

■ **FACTS**

Rhinehart (P), the spiritual leader of the Aquarian Foundation, filed an action in Washington state court against the Seattle Times (D) for alleged defamation and invasion of privacy. Utilizing state discovery rules modeled after the Federal Rules of Civil Procedure, the state court issued a discovery order compelling Rhinehart (P) to identify the Foundation's members and to identify the names and amounts of donations made to the Foundation over a five-year period. The court also issued a protective order prohibiting the Seattle Times (D) from publishing the information gained by the discovery. Both Rhinehart (P) and the Times (D) appealed [The trial court just couldn't make anyone happy!]. The Washington Supreme Court affirmed both orders, holding that the protective order upheld the integrity of the discovery process, an interest sufficient to overcome the Times' (D) claim of First Amendment rights. The U.S. Supreme Court granted certiorari.

■ **ISSUE**

Does a protective order that restricts the dissemination of information obtained via discovery offend the First Amendment?

■ **DECISION AND RATIONALE**

(Powell, J.) No. A protective order that restricts the dissemination of discovered information, but that is limited to the context of pretrial civil discovery and that does not restrict the dissemination of information gained from other sources, does not offend the First Amendment. In order to curtail the potential abuses in broad discovery provisions, the Legislature of the State of Washington has essentially adopted the Federal Rules approach to protective orders in the discovery context. This adoption itself does not require heightened First Amendment scrutiny. In the case at hand, the discovery order entered against Rhinehart (P) was extremely broad, and the Supreme Court of Washington correctly held that the dissemination of the information would result in annoyance, embarrassment, or even oppression of the members and donors to the Aquarian Foundation. The Supreme Court of Washington also correctly held that the trial court did not abuse its discretion in issuing a protective order under these circumstances. Affirmed.

Analysis:

This case demonstrates the extremely broad latitude a court has in drafting protective orders. Whereas previous cases have discussed protective orders that limit the *scope* of discovery, this case demonstrates that protective orders may also limit the *use* of certain information obtained via discovery. Thus, protective orders are a substantial check on the extremely broad approach to discovery embodied in the Federal Rules and in many state codes. As the U.S. Supreme Court held in this case, the need to prevent abuse and protect innocent parties may even justify infringing on a party's First Amendment rights. The protective order allows the Times (D) to discover this essential information for purposes of litigation, and it accomplishes the goal of protecting the confidentiality of parties to the litigation and disinterested third parties. However, newspapers such as the Seattle Times (D) typically enjoy First Amendment protections and can publish almost anything they wish. This case shows that courts may prohibit the publication of certain sensitive information when allowing such publication would undermine the protections granted in the discovery rules.

■ **CASE VOCABULARY**

ABUSE OF DISCRETION: One of the most common standards for appellate review, requiring the reviewing court to uphold any lower court holdings that were not clearly beyond the power of the lower court to grant.

Cummings v. General Motors Corp.

(*Automobile Passenger*) v. (*Automobile Manufacturer*)

365 F.3d 944 (10th Cir. 2004)

AUTOMATIC DISCLOSURE OF EVIDENCE IS NOT REQUIRED MERELY BECAUSE IT IS RELEVANT

■ **INSTANT FACTS** Cummings (P) was injured in an automobile accident allegedly due to a design defect in the seatbelt mechanism and passenger seat of the vehicle in which she was riding.

■ **BLACK LETTER RULE** Under Federal Rule of Civil Procedure 26(a), a party must automatically disclose all documents and tangible evidence on which it intends to rely at trial.

■ PROCEDURAL BASIS

On appeal to review a jury verdict for the defendant and a trial court order denying Rule 60(b) relief.

■ FACTS

Cummings (P) was riding as the front seat passenger in a General Motors (D) automobile in rural Oklahoma. Cummings's (P) young child was seated behind her in a forward-facing child seat. When her husband, the driver, ran a "partially obscured" stop sign, the car came to rest in a field off the road. Cummings (P) suffered a compression fracture to the third vertebra and was paralyzed. Cummings (P) sued General Motors Corp. (D), alleging that her injuries resulted from a design defect in the seatbelt mechanism and front passenger seat. When disputes arose over the sufficiency of General Motors' (D) discovery response, Cummings (P) filed three motions to compel discovery. General Motors (D) responded with a motion for a protective order. A magistrate judge denied the plaintiff's motions to compel discovery and granted the defendant's protective order.

At trial, General Motors (D) offered evidence that no design defect existed and attributed Cummings's (P) injuries to her posture and positioning within the vehicle at impact. Both sides presented considerable evidence concerning the angle at which Cummings's (P) seat was positioned at the time of the accident. At the close of evidence, both the plaintiff and the defendant moved for judgment as a matter of law. In his argument to the court, counsel for the plaintiff contended that regardless of the positioning of the seat, General Motors (D) should have foreseen the possibility that the seat would be reclined, and that if the jury determined that the seat's capability to recline was dangerous, judgment should be entered as a matter of law. The court denied both motions and the jury returned a verdict for General Motors (D). Cummings (P) filed a timely appeal. One month after the verdict, however, Cummings (P) discovered six videos of child safety seat acceleration tests conducted by General Motors (D) that were not produced during discovery. Cummings (P) argued that these videos demonstrated that the front passenger seat could not have reclined to the degree argued by General Motors at trial because of the child seat behind it. Cummings (P) filed a motion for relief under Federal Rule of Civil Procedure 60(b) seven months after the verdict. The court denied the motion as untimely and lacking in support. Cummings (P) appealed.

■ ISSUE

Is Cummings (P) entitled to relief from the judgment due to General Motors's (D) failure to produce evidence during discovery?

■ DECISION AND RATIONALE

(Kelly, Jr., J.) No. Under Federal Rule of Civil Procedure 26(a), a party must make certain mandatory initial disclosures to an opposing party without a formal request. While the failure to disclose information during discovery may constitute misconduct under Rule 60(b)(3) such that an opposing party may be entitled to post-judgment relief, Cummings (P) has not demonstrated General Motors' (D) duty to disclose the videos. Rule 26 does not require a party to disclose evidence that it does not intend to use at trial. Because General Motors (D) did not rely on the videos as evidence, there was no duty of automatic disclosure regardless of their relevance to the facts at issue.

Analysis:

While the videos were not subject to mandatory disclosure under Rule 26 because General Motors (D) did not use them as evidence at trial, they may nonetheless be discoverable under Rule 26 upon a proper discovery request. The relevance of the evidence is immaterial under mandatory disclosure, but highly material in response to a discovery request from the opposing party. If a discovery request seeks immaterial information or documents, a protective order may be appropriate.

■ CASE VOCABULARY

DISCLOSURE: The act or process of making known something that was previously unknown; a revelation of facts.

MOTION TO COMPEL DISCOVERY: A party's request that the court force the party's opponent to respond to the party's discovery request (as to answer interrogatories or produce documents). Often shortened to *motion to compel*.

PROTECTIVE ORDER: A court order prohibiting or restricting a party from engaging in conduct (especially a legal procedure such as discovery) that unduly annoys or burdens the opposing party or a third-party witness.

Polycast Technology Corp. v. Uniroyal, Inc.

(Purchaser) v. (Parent Corporation)

1990 WL 138968 (S.D.N.Y. 1990)

It doesn't matter that we both saw our sister do the same thing, Mommy still wants to depose us both.

■ **INSTANT FACTS** Deloitte & Touche sought a protective order to prevent Polycast Technology Corp. (P) from deposing a Deloitte employee.

■ **BLACK LETTER RULE** A non-party witness may be deposed when his information is relevant to a claim or defense presented and is likely to supplement other witnesses' deposition testimony.

■ PROCEDURAL BASIS

Consideration of a discovery dispute.

■ FACTS

Polycast Technology Corp. (P) purchased Uniroyal Plastics Company, Inc., a wholly owned subsidiary of Uniroyal, Inc. (D). Polycast (P) sued Uniroyal (D), alleging that it made fraudulent misrepresentations that induced the purchase. Both parties received substantial discovery from Deloitte & Touche, the accounting firm providing auditing services to both parties during the sale. First, the deposition of Bowman, Deloitte's engagement partner on the sale audit, was taken. Polycast (D) then sought to take the deposition of Durant, a Deloitte employee who served as on-site manager of the acquired subsidiary after the sale was completed. Deloitte sought a protective order to prevent Durant's deposition as not relevant and duplicative of Bowman's earlier deposition testimony.

■ ISSUE

May a party take deposition testimony from a non-party witness whose testimony will duplicate prior witness testimony but is likely to supplement missing information?

■ DECISION AND RATIONALE

(Francis, Magistrate. J.) Yes. Although Durant's testimony may be largely duplicative of that given by Bowman, his testimony will fill gaps in the Bowman deposition. The plaintiff's claim relates to the stated value of the subsidiary before the transaction and claims of undervalued profits after the sale. Since Durant was present on-site after the acquisition, his testimony is particularly relevant to the accounting methods used to audit post-sale business and fill in gaps in Bowman's testimony due to his inability to recall every detail of the audit. Durant must be produced for deposition. However, because of the highly duplicative nature of his testimony, the deposition must be limited to one full day of examination. The protective order is denied.

Analysis:

A party's interest in exposing information crucial to its claim or defense makes objections based on duplication difficult to sustain. Even if a deponent's testimony will duplicate that of another witness, it is nearly impossible to determine the extent of duplication until the deposition is taken. Often times, the duplication itself may be important evidence, especially when knowledge of certain facts is at issue.

■ CASE VOCABULARY

PROTECTIVE ORDER: A court order prohibiting or restricting a party from engaging in conduct (especially a legal procedure such as discovery) that unduly annoys or burdens the opposing party or a third-party witness.

In re Auction Houses Antitrust Litigation

(*Unidentified Plaintiffs*) v. (*Conspiring Auction Houses*)

196 F.R.D. 444 (S.D.N.Y. 2000)

A CONTRACT MAY FORM THE BASIS OF A DISCOVERY OBLIGATION

■ **INSTANT FACTS** Taubman (D) sought additional information concerning documents previously provided by Christie's (D) in discovery, to which Christie's (D) objected as outside its knowledge and control.

■ **BLACK LETTER RULE** Under the Federal Rules of Civil Procedure, a party is obligated to respond to discovery requests with all information available to it.

■ **PROCEDURAL BASIS**

Trial court consideration of a discovery dispute.

■ **FACTS**

Various plaintiffs sued several defendants alleging a conspiracy to fix the price of auction services for antiques and other collectibles. During discovery, Taubman (D) served Christie's (D), a British corporation, interrogatories seeking clarification and elaboration of handwritten notes from the files of its former chief executive officer, Davidge, who was a British citizen. Previously, Davidge and Christie's (D) had entered into an employment termination agreement whereby Davidge was paid a substantial amount of money, a portion of which remained unpaid pending completion of his contractual duties. Part of those duties involved cooperation with Christie's (D) relating to any ongoing investigations and the provision of any information within his knowledge relating to company business. Christie's (D) had likewise agreed to indemnify Davidge for all defense costs associated with the case in exchange for his cooperation. Nonetheless, Christie's (D) objected to Taubman's (D) interrogatories because they sought information known only by Davidge, who was outside its control.

■ **ISSUE**

Must a party respond to a discovery request with information exclusively in the knowledge and possession of a former employee who is contractually bound to provide it with such information?

■ **DECISION AND RATIONALE**

(Kaplan, J.) Yes. Under the Federal Rules of Civil Procedure, a party is obligated to respond to discovery requests with all relevant information to which it has access. While Christie's (D) may not have knowledge of the matters Taubman (D) requests information on, the responses are available to it by virtue of its contractual agreement with Davidge. Christie's (D) may not avoid its obligation to Taubman (D) merely because it has requested that Davidge provide the information sought. Christie's may threaten to withhold payments remaining on the termination agreement, threaten a breach of contract action, and threaten to terminate its indemnification agreement to obtain the required information. Davidge has accepted the benefits of these agreements, and Christie's (D) must enforce the burdens of the agreements as well.

Many foreign countries have enacted blocking statutes barring their citizens from complying with U.S. discovery requests. When companies face both blocking statutes and U.S. discovery demands, courts often consider the national interests of the nations involved, the nature and extent of the hardship that would be imposed on the company if the two inconsistent obligations were imposed, the good faith or lack thereof of the party resisting the discovery order, and whether a discovery order reasonably can be expected to achieve compliance. Here, there is no compelling United Kingdom government interest at stake or hardship on Christie's (D) by its compliance. While it may face a civil action by Davidge if it threatens to withhold payments or indemnification, it would have a valid defense because of Davidge's prior breach. Christie's (D) good faith must therefore be questioned. Christie's (D) must comply with the discovery order.

Analysis:

Certainly there is nothing about a contractual relationship alone that creates the availability of information known by a contracting party. Likewise, a corporate party has no general access to information known by its former employees, even if it owes them money under a termination agreement. It is the combination of the two, along with the specific terms of the agreement here, that creates the availability of the information. The pressure Christie's (D) could exert over Davidge because of their agreements is the key factor.

■ CASE VOCABULARY

INTERROGATORY: A written question (usually in a set of questions) submitted to an opposing party in a lawsuit as part of discovery.

In re Convergent Technologies Securities Litigation

(*Securities Lawsuit Defendant*)

108 F.R.D. 328 (N.D. Cal. 1985)

DISCOVERY SHOULD BE NARROWLY TAILORED AND COST–EFFECTIVE

■ **INSTANT FACTS** The defendants served the plaintiffs with contention interrogatories at the beginning of pretrial discovery.

■ **BLACK LETTER RULE** Contention interrogatories early in litigation are permitted only when they will help clarify or narrow the issues in the case.

■ **PROCEDURAL BASIS**

Trial court consideration of the defendants' motion to compel discovery.

■ **FACTS**

The plaintiffs sued Convergent Technologies (D) and Burroughs Corporation (D) for various securities laws violations. Before substantial discovery had been conducted, Burroughs (D) filed a set of fifteen interrogatories comprised of fifty-two total questions, many inquiring about the plaintiffs' contentions and facts supporting those contentions. The plaintiffs agreed that the interrogatories should be answered, but they did not agree as to *when* they should be answered. The defendants filed a motion to compel discovery.

■ **ISSUE**

Must a party respond to early contention interrogatories when other discovery is available?

■ **DECISION AND RATIONALE**

(Brazil, Magistrate J.) No. Contention interrogatories come in many forms, but generally involve a request that the opposing party state its contentions, confirm its contentions, or provide factual or evidentiary support for its contentions. While contention interrogatories are a proper form of discovery, they must not be used for an improper purpose or involve unreasonable burden or expense given the needs of the case, the extent of discovery already taken, and the amount in controversy. If alternative means of discovering the information sought are available, a court may properly allow a party to resist its response to interrogatories.

Although contention interrogatories are more appropriate later in pretrial discovery, they are allowable before other discovery has been taken under appropriate conditions. First, the interrogatories must be specific and limited in number. When the early response to the interrogatories will assist in clarifying and narrowing the issues in the case, the responding party must answer them in good faith. When such goals will not in good faith be achieved by early contention interrogatories, however, the responding party is justified in refusing to answer if it provides its basis for its refusal. If objections continue and no resolution of the dispute can be reached, the propounding party must then file a motion to compel discovery and bear the burden of persuasion that early contention interrogatories are appropriate under the circumstances.

Here, the plaintiffs have served Burroughs (D) with a discovery request for the production of documents, which remains outstanding. Burroughs (D) will suffer no harm by suspending the plaintiffs' responses to the contention interrogatories until sixty days after Burroughs (D) has responded to the plaintiffs' request. Burroughs (D) has not shown that early answers to its contention interrogatories will assist in shaping the litigation. Similarly, the plaintiffs' contentions at an early stage in the litigation need not be compelled in order to assist Burroughs (D) in fashioning affirmative defenses. Burroughs (D) has deposed the plaintiffs and already has access to many of their contentions. There is no reason to press early responses to the defendant's contention interrogatories. Motion denied.

Analysis:

Discovery motions are frustrating to many courts. The time spent hearing and deciding such motions uses up judicial resources on matters that are often relatively minor. In addition, as noted by the court in this case, discovery is supposed to be something handled by the parties on their own, without judicial intervention unless absolutely necessary. The federal rules, along with many state court rules, require the parties to a discovery dispute to confer before a motion on the dispute will be heard.

Zubulake v. UBS Warburg LLC

(*Former Employee*) v. (*Employer*)
217 F.R.D. 309 (S.D.N.Y. 2003)

THE EXPENSE AND BURDEN OF CERTAIN DISCOVERY REQUESTS MAY BE SHIFTED TO THE REQUESTING PARTY

■ **INSTANT FACTS** Zubulake (P) sought discovery of archived e-mails from back-up tapes and optical disks.

■ **BLACK LETTER RULE** Discoverable matter includes both paper and electronic documents.

■ **PROCEDURAL BASIS**

Trial court consideration of the plaintiff's motion to compel discovery.

■ **FACTS**

Zubulake (P) sued UBS Warburg LLC (D) and others for gender discrimination and retaliation. In her initial interrogatories, Zubulake (P) requested that UBS (D) produce "[a]ll documents concerning any communication by or between UBS employees concerning Plaintiff," including electronic communications. In response, UBS (D) produced 350 pages of documents, including 100 pages of e-mails. After Zubulake (P) disputed the sufficiency of the response, UBS (D) agreed to retrieve the e-mails of five specifically named individuals, including all responsive e-mails. No additional e-mails were produced and the initial response was asserted to be complete. UBS (D), however, did not search for responsive e-mails on any back-up tapes, claiming that to do so would be cost prohibitive. Zubulake (P) objected to the nonproduction, arguing that the back-up tapes were included in the parties' agreement and that additional responsive e-mails were contained on the back-up tapes. The judge thereafter ordered UBS (D) to produce a witness for deposition to demonstrate UBS's (D) back-up protocol and the cost associated with retrieving archived e-mails. The deposition testimony illustrated that e-mail was an important means of communication at UBS (D) and that federal regulations required that they be archived on back-up tapes or optical disks. Zubulake (P) moved to compel further production.

■ **ISSUE**

Is the plaintiff entitled to discover archived e-mails and other electronic documents when they are relevant to the plaintiff's claims?

■ **DECISION AND RATIONALE**

(Scheindlin, J.) Yes. In discovery, a responding party must bear the expense of complying with discovery requests unless it is determined that the requests present undue burden or expense. When the discovery requests involve the costly retrieval of archived e-mail data, courts have often balanced the need for broad discovery with the heavy costs associated with its retrieval. In so doing, courts consider eight factors to determine whether the cost of retrieval should be shifted to the requesting party, including: (1) the specificity of the discovery requests, (2) the likelihood of discovering critical information, (3) the availability of such information from other sources, (4) the purposes for which the responding party maintains the requested data, (5) the relative benefits to the parties of obtaining the information, (6) the total cost associated with production, (7) the relative ability of each party to control costs and its incentive to do so, and (8) the resources available to each party.

Federal Rule of Civil Procedure 34 requires the disclosure of electronic documents just as it does paper documents, including both currently used electronic documents and those archived on back-up media. Because the e-mails are relevant to Zubulake's (P) claims, she is entitled to discovery of the back-up tapes. UBS (D) clearly has not sufficiently complied with the discovery requests because it does not represent that it has reviewed its back-up tapes, and Zubulake (P) knows additional discoverable e-mails exist because she currently possesses more e-mails than UBS (D) disclosed. Zubulake (P) is entitled to discovery of the archived e-mails.

The e-mails currently in use and those contained on optical disks are readily accessible by UBS (D) such that the burden and expense of reviewing and retrieving is minimal, and cost shifting is inappropriate. For the ninety-four back-up tapes identified, however, UBS (D) must engage in a costly and time-consuming process to access the information and review their contents. Because the back-up tapes are inaccessible, cost shifting may be appropriate. After retrieving a small, defined sample of the information, cost shifting may be ordered based on a consideration of the factors established above.

UBS (D) is ordered to produce all responsive e-mails on its current system and optical disks, as well as responsive e-mails contained on the back-up tapes relating to any five individuals selected by Zubulake (P). After UBS (D) submits its time and expenses associated with the retrieval, the court will consider the contents of the information retrieved to determine the appropriateness of cost shifting.

Analysis:

The court's decision balances the benefit of the requested information to the plaintiff with the burden of its retrieval on the defendant. While the cost of retrieving archived e-mails may be significant, it is the product of the defendant's internal procedures. Certainly, if the defendant itself unreasonably creates a costly procedure it claims results in undue burden, the court will consider such a factor in its balancing approach. By limiting the retrieval to a small number of identified individuals and leaving the question of cost shifting open, the court properly considers the benefits to both parties of resolving the discovery dispute.

Schlagenhauf v. Holder

(*Bus Driver*) v. (*District Court Judge*)
379 U.S. 104, 85 S.Ct. 234 (1964)

PHYSICAL OR MENTAL EXAMINATIONS MAY BE ORDERED FOR ANY PARTY WHOSE CONDITION IS IN CONTROVERSY AND WHEN GOOD CAUSE EXISTS

■ **INSTANT FACTS** Robert Schlagenhauf (D), a defendant who allegedly caused a collision while driving a bus, objected to an order requiring him to submit to a number of physical and mental examinations.

■ **BLACK LETTER RULE** A physical or mental examination may be ordered when good cause exists, and when a party's physical or mental condition is in controversy.

■ **PROCEDURAL BASIS**

Writ of certiorari considering denial of writ of mandamus seeking to set aside order to undergo mental and physical examinations.

■ **FACTS**

An action was brought in district court seeking damages arising from the collision of a tractor-trailer, owned by Contract Carriers (D) and National Lead Company (D), and a Greyhound (D) bus. Robert Schlagenhauf (D) was the driver of the bus at the time of the accident. Numerous cross-claims were filed among the defendants. First, Greyhound (D) cross-claimed against Contract Carriers (D) and National Lead Company (D) for negligence in the operation of the tractor-trailer. Then Contract Carriers (D) and National Lead Company (D) petitioned the District Court for an order directing Schlagenhauf (D) to submit to four mental and/or physical examinations, alleging that the mental and physical condition of Schlagenhauf (D) was "in controversy." National Lead (D) then cross-claimed against Greyhound (D) and Schlagenhauf (D) for damage to its trailer. The District Court ordered Schlagenhauf (D) to submit to nine examinations [Although only four were requested!]. Schlagenhauf (D) applied for a writ of mandamus in the Court of Appeals against Holder (P), the district court judge, seeking to have the examination order set aside. The Court of Appeals denied mandamus, and the Supreme Court granted certiorari.

■ **ISSUE**

(1) May Rule 35 examinations be made on any party, including a defendant to a lawsuit? (2) Do physical or mental examinations require an affirmative showing that the condition sought to be examined is genuinely in controversy and that good cause exists for ordering each examination?

■ **DECISION AND RATIONALE**

(Goldberg, J.) (1) Yes. Rule 35 physical or mental examinations may be made on any party to a lawsuit. On its face, Rule 35 applies to all parties, which would normally include a defendant. However, Schlagenhauf (D) contends that the application of the Rule to him would constitute an unconstitutional invasion of his privacy. Previous cases have held that plaintiffs must submit to physical examinations, as noted in *Sibbach v. Wilson* [plaintiff in negligence action who asserted physical injury as basis for recovery must submit to physical examinations]. However, the application of Rule 35 discovery only to plaintiffs would deprive a plaintiff from obtaining redress for his injuries. Thus, Rule 35 examinations may be conducted on defendants as well. It makes no difference that Schlagenhauf (D) was not a defendant to any cross-claims at the time of the examination order. Schlagenhauf (D) was always a party to the lawsuit, and Rule 35 allows examinations to be conducted on any parties. Insistence that the party seeking examination must file claims against all parties sought to be examined would unnecessarily proliferate cross-claims and would defeat the liberal application of the Federal Rules. (2) Yes. In order to force a physical or mental examination pursuant to Rule 35, the party seeking the discovery must make an affirmative showing that the condition sought to be examined is genuinely in controversy and that good cause exists for ordering each examination. Contract Carriers (D) and National Lead Company (D) failed to make the required showing. The "in controversy" and "good cause" requirements may be automatically satisfied in some situations, such as when a party places his mental or physical condition at issue by asserting the condition either in support of or in defense of a claim. However, Schlagenhauf (D) did not place his conditions at issue. Rather, his condition was sought to be placed in issue by other parties. Nothing in the pleadings affords a basis for the belief that Schlagenhauf (D) was suffering a neurological illness warranting mental examinations. In fact the only allegation made in support of examinations was the contention that Schlagenhauf's (D) eyes and vision were impaired. Thus, if Contract Carriers (D) and National Lead Company (D) had sought to obtain only a visual examination, they might have made the required showing. Nevertheless, there is an insufficient basis for finding that Schlagenhauf's (D) health was in controversy so as to require the battery of tests ordered by the District Court. The judgment of the Court of Appeals denying the writ of mandamus is vacated and remanded.

■ CONCURRENCE AND DISSENT

(Black, J.) In a lawsuit based on a traffic collision, the mental or physical health of the drivers is of the highest relevance. Allegations showed that the tractor-trailer was in plain sight of Schlagenhauf (D), and there was allegedly ample time to avoid the collision. Schlagenhauf's (D) failure to avoid the collision certainly calls into question his mental or physical health, sufficient to put the question "in controversy."

■ DISSENT

(Douglas, J.) Until today, neither Congress nor this Court has required every party to a lawsuit to surrender his right to keep his person inviolate. Of course, *Sibbach* held that a plaintiff must choose between his privacy and his recovery, but this has not been extended to non-voluntary defendants. Furthermore, plaintiff's doctors would naturally go on a fishing expedition in search of anything that would tend to prove that the defendant was unfit to perform certain acts. Any doctor for a fee can discover something wrong with a patient, and a defendant would be at the doctor's mercy, subject to numerous invasive procedures. The doctor's report may either overawe or confuse the jury and prevent a fair trial. Although Congress and this Court can authorize a rule allowing examinations of defendants, such a rule must be carefully drawn in order to prevent blackmail.

Analysis:

This case demonstrates the complexities in dealing with orders that could force a party to surrender his right to bodily autonomy. Even the most basic notions of privacy argue against anyone being forced to submit to an unpleasant, invasive physical or mental examination. These concerns are easily overcome in some cases, such as when a plaintiff puts his conditions at issue in a suit for bodily injuries. However, the case at hand is very different. Schlagenhauf (D) did nothing, other than colliding with a tractor-trailer, which should force him to submit to doctors' examinations. He did not choose to be a party to the lawsuit, and he never defended on the grounds of being mentally or physically fit. In this light, it seems somewhat unfair that Schlagenhauf (D) could be forced to submit to examinations, as the court held in the first part of the opinion. And as Douglas' dissent notes, doctors examining defendants would likely run numerous tests and strive to find anything wrong with a defendant. Contrast this to examinations of plaintiffs, where the defendants do not want to discover any injuries and where the examining physician would not, therefore, subject the plaintiff to similarly invasive treatment. On the other hand, it would present a great hardship to the plaintiff if Schlagenhauf (D) was physically or mentally impaired, and if these impairments caused the accident, if the plaintiff could not independently examine Schlagenhauf (D).

■ CASE VOCABULARY

AFFIANT: A party who makes an affidavit or undergoes a deposition or examination for discovery purposes.

VIS-A-VIS: Literally "face to face"; in relation to another person or thing.

WRIT OF MANDAMUS: An order from a superior jurisdiction commanding an action by an inferior tribunal.

Battle v. Memorial Hospital at Gulfport

(*Patient*) v. (*Hospital*)

228 F.3d 544 (5th Cir. 2000)

A videotaped deposition isn't exactly Hollywood, but the issue is the same--what's my motivation?

stus.com

■ **INSTANT FACTS** A magistrate judge prohibited the introduction of the plaintiff's expert's deposition into evidence, while permitting another expert's deposition and precluding that expert from testifying live.

■ **BLACK LETTER RULE** Deposition testimony of an unavailable witness may be introduced at trial when the questioner at the deposition is on the same side of the same issue at both proceedings and has a substantially similar interest in asserting and prevailing on the issue.

■ **PROCEDURAL BASIS**

On appeal to review a judgment for the defendants.

■ **FACTS**

After several days of unsuccessful treatment for seizures, Battle (P) was finally diagnosed with a form of herpes simplex encephalitis (HSE) and transported to the Tulane Medical Center (D) to be seen by an infectious disease specialist. The test results at Tulane (D) came back negative for HSE, but they were sent to the Whitley lab for further observation by Dr. Lakeman. Nearly a month later, Dr. Lakeman received positive test results for HSE. Battle (P) sued various physicians, Tulane Medical Center (D), and the Memorial Hospital at Gulfport (D) for negligent medical treatment in failing to prescribe Acyclovir upon early suspicion of HSE, resulting in Battle's (P) severe brain and neurological injuries. The court entered summary judgment in favor of Memorial Hospital (D) on the basis of the one-year statute of limitations, allowing trial to proceed against only the individual physicians. Three weeks before trial, the plaintiff informed the defendants that its expert, Dr. Young, would not be available for trial and scheduled a video deposition. The plaintiff then moved for a continuance, which was granted. The case was tried before a magistrate, who prohibited the plaintiff from introducing the deposition of Dr. Lakeland, who served as an expert witness for the plaintiff. Dr. Young's video deposition was admitted into evidence, but the plaintiffs were not allowed to call him for live testimony. Judgment was entered for the defendants.

■ **ISSUE**

May the deposition testimony of an unavailable witness be introduced at trial when the questioner at the deposition is on the same side of the same issue at both proceedings and has a substantially similar interest in asserting and prevailing on the issue?

■ **DECISION AND RATIONALE**

(Parker, J.) Yes. Although Dr. Lakeman was listed as an expert witness, he possessed sufficient knowledge of the facts at issue to consider him an ordinary fact witness. Under Federal Rule of Civil Procedure 32, a party may introduce deposition testimony against any party who was present at the taking of the deposition if the witness is at a distance greater than 100 miles from the place of trial and the deposition is admissible under the rules of evidence. Dr. Lakeman is clearly more than 100 miles away from the place of the trial. The admissibility of the deposition testimony therefore turns on its permissibility under the Federal Rules of Evidence. While hearsay evidence is generally inadmissible, Rule 804 permits the admission of former testimony taken in a deposition if the party against whom the testimony is offered had an opportunity and similar motive to develop the testimony by direct, cross, or redirect examination. To establish similar motive, the questioner at the deposition must not only be on the same side of the same issue at both proceedings, but also have a substantially similar interest in asserting and prevailing on the issue.

Here, Dr. Lakeman's deposition testimony concerned the accuracy of his lab's positive diagnosis of Battle's (P) HSE and Tulane's (D) negative test results, ultimately determining the appropriate timing for administering Acyclovir. The defendants were present at the deposition and permitted to question Lakeman concerning his testimony. Despite claims that their motive was to understand Lakeman's theories rather than subject them to cross-examination, they were on the same side of the same issues during the deposition as they were at trial. The defendants have presented no evidence that Lakeman's testimony is unreliable. Neither is Lakeman's testimony cumulative of the testimony of another plaintiff's expert, which was introduced at trial. Lakeman's testimony elaborated upon that expert's description of the methods used by Tulane (D) and included significantly different information that the jury could find credible. Lakeman's deposition testimony should have been admitted.

With respect to Dr. Young's live testimony, because the video deposition was initially allowed due to Dr. Young's unavailability to testify at trial, requiring the defense to reveal its cross-examination strategy in advance of trial, Dr. Young's live testimony was properly excluded. While live testimony is preferred to deposition testimony at trial, video depositions afford the jury the opportunity to observe the witness's testimony and gauge his attitude by his facial expressions and actions. Balancing the defendants' cross-examination strategy and the plaintiff's need for the testimony, the court properly excluded Dr. Young's live testimony.

The court's evidentiary errors substantially affected the plaintiff's rights at trial. The judgment is therefore vacated and the case remanded.

Analysis:

In the context of deposition testimony in the same proceeding, the similar motive requirement of Rule 804 is almost always satisfied, not because cross-examination at the deposition actually touched upon the same issue for which it is offered at trial, but rather because the opportunity to cross-examine existed. The similar-motive requirement comes into play more often when the former testimony at issue occurred in a different proceeding, which may involve sufficiently different issues to warrant exclusion.

■ CASE VOCABULARY

CONTINUANCE: The adjournment or postponement of a trial or other proceeding to a future date.

DEPOSITION: A witness's out-of-court testimony that is reduced to writing (usually by a court reporter) for later use in court or for discovery purposes.

UNAVAILABILITY: The status or condition of not being accessible, as when a witness is dead, missing, or exempted by court order from testifying. Unavailability is recognized under the Federal Rules of Evidence as an exclusion to the hearsay rule.

Hickman v. Taylor

(Representative of Decedent) v. *(Tugboat Owners)*

329 U.S. 495, 67 S.Ct. 385 (1947)

ABSENT A SHOWING OF NEED, AN ATTORNEY'S WORK PRODUCT IS BEYOND THE SCOPE OF DISCOVERY

■ **INSTANT FACTS** Hickman (P) sought to obtain copies of written statements and descriptions of oral interviews acquired by Fortenbaugh, the opposing counsel.

■ **BLACK LETTER RULE** A party is not entitled, without a showing of good cause, to obtain copies of an opposing attorney's notes and memoranda acquired from interviews with witnesses.

■ **PROCEDURAL BASIS**

Writ of certiorari reviewing reversal of order for contempt and order to respond to discovery request.

■ **FACTS**

This suit arises out of the mysterious sinking of the tugboat "J.M. Taylor," an accident which killed five crew members. Hickman (P), the representative of a deceased crew member, brought suit against the tug owners and the Baltimore & Ohio Railroad, whose cars were being tugged at the time of the accident. The tug owners were represented by Fortenbaugh, an attorney who privately interviewed the survivors and other witnesses prior to the institution of the lawsuit. Hickman (P) submitted interrogatories to the tug owners seeking the production of written statements and other memoranda acquired by Fortenbaugh, as well as detailed accounts of any oral statements made to Fortenbaugh. The tug owners, through Fortenbaugh, declined to answer some interrogatories or produce the documents, claiming that the requests called for privileged matter and constituted an attempt to obtain Fortenbaugh's private files. The District Court, sitting en banc, held that the requested matters were not privileged. Accordingly, the Court ordered the tug owners and Fortenbaugh to answer the interrogatories and produce the documents.

■ **ISSUE**

Are all of an attorney's files related to an incident open to discovery by the opposing party?

■ **DECISION AND RATIONALE**

(Murphy, J.) No. Even with liberal discovery rules, not all of an attorney's files are open to discovery by the opposing party. Rule 26(b) provides necessary limitations on discovery when the inquiry encroaches upon the recognized domains of privilege. In the case at hand, the memoranda, statements and mental impressions in issue and in Fortenbaugh's possession fall outside the scope of the attorney-client privilege. Nevertheless, they are not freely discoverable by Hickman (P). Hickman (P) had an adequate opportunity to seek discovery of the same basic facts, through inquiries and production requests propounded on Fortenbaugh and on the parties to the lawsuit, and through direct interviews with the witnesses themselves. Hickman (P) showed no compelling reason why he should be entitled to the information in Fortenbaugh's files, and he did not indicate that the denial of such production would unduly prejudice the preparation of his case. An attorney's work product may be discovered where

---

relevant and non-privileged facts remain hidden in an attorney's file and where production of those facts is essential to the preparation of the opposing party's case. However, the policy against invading the privacy of an attorney's work product is so essential that the party seeking the production must bear the burden. Hickman (P) failed to make the requisite showing. Further, as to the oral statements made by witnesses to Fortenbaugh, no showing of necessity is sufficient to justify production. It should be noted that procedural irregularities existed in Hickman's (P) discovery requests, although these irregularities are insufficient in themselves to deny production. Hickman was incorrect in propounding Rule 33 interrogatories and seeking the production of documents, and Rule 34 could not have been used to obtain documents from a non-party such as Fortenbaugh. Hickman (P) should have taken Fortenbaugh's deposition under Rule 26 and attempted to force Fortenbaugh to produce the materials by way of a subpoena duces tecum in accordance with Rule 45. Regardless, Hickman (P) would have had no unqualified right to discovery of Fortenbaugh's private files. Affirmed.

■ CONCURRENCE

(Jackson, J.) Hickman (P) has no right to receive a detailed account of any oral statements made to Fortenbaugh. In arguing that such discovery is permissible, Hickman (P) erroneously maintains that the Rules were created to do away with the "battle of wits" between counsel, effectively placing all counsel on equal footing. Discovery was never intended to diminish the adversarial nature of common law trials. Requiring an attorney to recount every statement a witness has uttered would create severe hardship for that attorney. It is almost impossible to accurately record the exact accounts of a witness, and whenever a witness's testimony at trial differed slightly from the attorney's account, the opposing counsel could impeach the witness using the attorney's account. Moreover, in the situation at hand, Hickman (P) gives no reason why he cannot interview the witnesses himself. In addition, Hickman (P) has no right to use the signed statements acquired by Fortenbaugh in the case at hand. Production of such statements is governed by Rule 34, which requires the party seeking discovery to show good cause. Hickman (P) did not make such an application here. Thus, I agree to the affirmance of the Court of Appeals.

Analysis:

This case analyzes the extent to which a party has access to an opposing attorney's "work product," information obtained by counsel in preparation for trial. The literal language of the initial Federal Rules allowed virtually unlimited access to the discovery of such information However, this case creates an exception to the unlimited access approach, requiring the party to show a need for obtaining an opposing counsel's work product. And as the opinion states, this need must be substantial. A party who can question the same witnesses, and obtain much the same information in other ways, has no right to reap the benefits of another party's or another attorney's hard work. This holding is sensible, since an alternative view would discourage attorneys from actively investigating the issues. Notice that this work-product exemption applies only to materials prepared in anticipation of trial. Thus, statements of witnesses taken in the ordinary course of business, outside of a pending litigation, remain open to discovery.

■ CASE VOCABULARY

WORK PRODUCT: Materials prepared and statements obtained in preparation of a lawsuit for trial.

Upjohn Co. v. United States

(Pharmaceutical Manufacturer) v. *(Federal Government)*

449 U.S. 383, 101 S.Ct. 677 (1981)

COMMUNICATIONS BETWEEN COUNSEL AND ALL CORPORATE EMPLOYEES ARE PRIVILEGED, AND THE WORK–PRODUCT EXEMPTION CAN BE OVERCOME ONLY BY A STRONG SHOWING OF NEED

■ **INSTANT FACTS** In response to Upjohn Co.'s (D) internal investigation into potential bribes, the United States (P) sought to obtain information about confidential communications between Upjohn's (D) counsel and employees.

■ **BLACK LETTER RULE** The attorney-client privilege may protect all communications between corporate employees and corporate counsel, and the work-product exemption for oral statements can only be overcome by a strong showing of necessity and unavailability.

■ **PROCEDURAL BASIS**

Writ of certiorari reviewing order upholding enforcement of summons to produce documents.

■ **FACTS**

Upjohn Co. (D) conducted an internal investigation of "questionable payments" allegedly made by Upjohn's (D) foreign subsidiaries to foreign government officials in order to secure government business [a.k.a. "bribes"!]. In the investigation, foreign managers of Upjohn (D) were questioned about possibly illegal payments, and the responses were forwarded to Thomas, Upjohn's (D) general counsel. When the investigation was concluded, Upjohn (D) sent a report to the Securities and Exchange Commission, and the Internal Revenue Service immediately began an investigation to determine the tax consequences of the payments. [Yes, the IRS haunts even corporation's activities in foreign countries!] The IRS issued a summons demanding production of all files relative to the investigation. However, Upjohn (D) refused to produce the documents, contending that they were protected by the attorney-client privilege and the work-product exemption. The United States (P) filed a petition in a Michigan district court seeking enforcement of the summons. The District Court adopted a magistrate's recommendation that the summons should be enforced. Upjohn (D) appealed to the Court of Appeals for the Sixth Circuit, which held that the attorney-client privilege did not apply to the extent the communications were made by officers and agents outside of Upjohn's (D) "control group," since these people were not considered "clients." Further, the Court of Appeals concluded that the work-product doctrine was not applicable to the administrative summonses in this case. The Supreme Court granted certiorari.

■ **ISSUE**

(1) Does the attorney-client privilege protect communications made between a corporation's employees and the corporation's general counsel? (2) May the work-product exemption be overcome, in relation to work based on oral statements, by a mere showing of substantial need and undue hardship?

■ **DECISION AND RATIONALE**

(Rehnquist, J.) (1) Yes. The attorney-client privilege protects communications made between a corporation's employees and the corporation's general counsel. The Court of Appeals adopted a restrictive "control group" test, which protected only those communications made by certain high-level corporate employees. This view overlooks the fact that the attorney-client privilege exists to protect the giving of information to a lawyer to enable him to give sound advice. Even low-level employees can embroil a corporation in serious legal difficulties, and these employees often possess relevant information needed by corporate counsel. The control group test frustrates the purpose of the privilege by discouraging this communication of relevant information, and it makes it difficult for corporate attorneys to formulate sound advice. In the case at hand, the attorney-client privilege protects all communications made between Upjohn (D) employees and Thomas, the general counsel. The Court of Appeals feared that such an extension would create a broad "zone of silence" over corporate affairs. However, application of the privilege here places the opposing party in no worse position than if the communications had never taken place. Further, the privilege only protects the disclosure of communications, not the actual information disclosed. Thus, the United States (P) was free to question the employees who communicated with Thomas, and the IRS possessed a list of these employees and had already interviewed 25 of them. Although it would be more convenient for the Government (P) to obtain the questionnaires and notes sent to Thomas, such considerations of convenience do not overcome the policies served by the attorney-client privilege. (2) No. The work-product doctrine may not be overcome by a mere showing of substantial need and undue hardship, when work based on oral statements and on the mental conclusions of counsel is sought to be discovered. To the extent that the IRS sought discovery of information that was not part of the confidential communications between Upjohn (D) employees and counsel, the attorney-client privilege does not operate. Nevertheless, the work-product doctrine, as described in *Hickman v. Taylor* [a party is not entitled, without a showing of good cause, to obtain copies of an opposing attorney's notes and memoranda acquired from interviews with witnesses] and as codified in Rule 26(b)(3), may protect this information. While the Government (P) concedes that the work product doctrine is applicable to the IRS summonses, it argues that it has made a sufficient showing of necessity to overcome the exemption. We disagree. The notes and memoranda sought by the Government (P) are work product based on oral statements. To the extent they reveal communications, they are, of course, covered by the attorney-client privilege. To the extent they do not reveal communications, they reveal the attorney's mental processes in evaluating the communications. The Magistrate applied the "substantial need" and "without undue hardship" tests articulated in Rule 26(b)(3) to this work product. However, as *Hickman* makes clear, work product obtained from oral statements and through an attorney's mental processes cannot be obtained by a mere showing of substantial need and undue hardship. A far stronger showing of necessity and unavailability by other means must be shown by the Government (P). Reversed and remanded.

Analysis:

While this opinion presents a thorough analysis of the attorney-client privilege and the work-product exemption in the corporate context, it does not, by its own admission, articulate a set of rules controlling these doctrines. Rather, with respect to the work-product exemption for oral statements, it simply applies the high standard stated in *Hickman*. In effect, the holding makes it almost impossible for a party to acquire the work product of an opposing attorney, at least where the work product is tied to oral statements or mental conclusions, whenever any available means exist for the party seeking discovery to obtain the information on its own. Surely the Government (P), armed with a list of Upjohn (D) employees who responded to the questionnaires, could interview the witnesses itself. Further, the employees' attorney-client privilege is waived if the employee voluntarily discloses the information to third parties. Thus, the holding parallels the logical conclusion of *Hickman* that opposing parties should not easily avail themselves of the fruits of another attorney's labor. With regard to the attorney-client privilege, the majority's holding is equally sensible. A corporation is a fictitious entity and, as such, cannot have any direct communications with its counsel. In the corporate setting, therefore, it must be determined which communications are protected by the attorney-client privilege. The Court of Appeals' "control group" test was far too narrow, since corporate counsel often must rely on communications with low-level employees. These communications deserve the same amount of protection as communications with high-level employees, in light of the privilege's purpose to encourage full and frank communication between attorneys and their clients.

■ CASE VOCABULARY

AMICI: A shortened and plural form of "amicus curiae," referring to non-parties with a strong interest in the subject matter of the litigation.

MAGISTRATE: An inferior government judicial officer who may make recommendations to federal courts.

Krisa v. Equitable Life Assurance Society

(*Insured*) v. (*Insurer*)

196 F.R.D. 254 (M.D. Pa. 2000)

EXPERTS' REPORTS ARE DISCOVERABLE

■ **INSTANT FACTS** When an insurer denies its insured's disability claim, the insured sues and demands production of preliminary reports prepared for litigation by experts.

■ **BLACK LETTER RULE** Expert witnesses' reports are discoverable, unless they contain or embody attorney work product.

■ **PROCEDURAL BASIS**

In suit for contract breach, request for production.

■ **FACTS**

Insurer Equitable Life Assurance Society ("Equitable") (D) denied insured Krisa's (P) claim for disability benefits. Krisa (P) sued and demanded Equitable (D) produce preliminary reports created by Equitable's (D) experts, contending expert witnesses' reports are discoverable under *Rule 26(b)(4)*. Equitable (D) objected, contending the reports were work product, privileged under *Rule 26(b)(3)*.

■ **ISSUE**

Are expert witnesses' reports, prepared in anticipation of litigation, discoverable?

■ **DECISION AND RATIONALE**

Yes. Expert witnesses' reports are discoverable, unless they contain or embody attorney work product. Equitable's (D) argument disregards the fact that the protection afforded to work product under *Rule 26(b)(3)* is subject to *Rule 26(b)(4)*, which generally authorizes discovery of testifying expert witnesses. *Rule 23*'s structure and Advisory Committee Notes suggest that documents prepared by expert witnesses are not within the work product doctrine's ambit. The Rules plainly contemplate discovery of not only testifying experts' expected opinions, but also of preliminary or tentative opinions that may conflict with their final opinions. The conclusion that Equitable's (D) witnesses' draft reports are not privileged work product is consistent with the privilege's basic policy considerations. The work product doctrine is based on "the general policy against invading the privacy of an attorney's course of preparation." Here, Equitable (D) admits the experts' draft reports do not contain counsel's mental processes, so production will not invade Equitable's (D) counsel's privacy in developing litigation strategies. Moreover, denying production may deprive Krisa (P) of information that would be material in allowing effective cross-examination of Equitable's (D) experts by depriving him of seeing the evolution of their opinions. Courts are split on whether core attorney work product shared with a party's experts is discoverable, but our Third Circuit holds that it is not. On the one hand, *Rule 26(a)(2)*'s 1993 amendments require parties to disclose automatically an expert's opinions, the basis and reasons therefor, and "the data or other information considered by the witness in forming the opinions." Several courts held this amendment is designed to mandate full disclosure of any materials reviewed by expert witnesses, even if they are opinion work product, finding this "bright-line" interpretation allows effective cross-examination of expert witnesses. However, other courts, including our Court of Appeals, found this interpretation abridges attorneys' work product privilege, without specific authority to do so. Here, Equitable (D) need not produce the few documents which contain or embody core attorney work product. Discovery granted.

Analysis:

Krisa states the minority rule; most courts hold that once attorney work product is supplied to an expert witness, it loses its privileged character and is discoverable from the witness. The majority rule comports more closely with the Advisory Committee's Notes, which explicitly state, "Given this obligation of disclosure, litigants should no longer be able to argue that materials furnished to their experts are privileged . . . ." Still, this interpretation countermands judges' reverence for the inviolability of the work product privilege for lawyers, and some courts are reluctant to embrace it.

■ CASE VOCABULARY

"BRIGHT-LINE" RULE: Rule which is clear and objective (e.g., "red means stop"), as opposed to a standard inviting subjective consideration (e.g. "negligent if failed to exercise *reasonable* care").

Cine Forty-Second Street Theatre Corp. v. Allied Artists Pictures Corp.

(Theater Operator) v. *(Competitor)*

602 F.2d 1062 (2nd Cir. 1979)

A COURT MAY ORDER STRICT SANCTIONS FOR GROSS FAILURE TO COMPLY WITH DISCOVERY REQUESTS

■ **INSTANT FACTS** In an antitrust action, Cine Forty-Second Street Theatre Corp. (P) continuously failed to adequately respond to interrogatories, and a magistrate recommended that Cine (P) be precluded from entering any evidence related to damages, the subject of the discovery requests.

■ **BLACK LETTER RULE** A party who exhibits gross negligence in responding to discovery requests is subject to the most severe discovery sanctions.

■ **PROCEDURAL BASIS**

Interlocutory appeal from order assessing fine for failure to comply with discovery requests.

■ **FACTS**

Cine Forty-Second Street Theatre Corp. (Cine) (P), the operator of a movie theater in New York City, alleged that Allied Artists Pictures Corp. (Allied) (D) and other theater owners entered into a conspiracy to cut off Cine's (P) access to first-run films. Thus, Cine (P) filed an antitrust suit seeking $3,000,000 in damages and an injunction against the alleged anticompetitive practices. In 1975, the eleven defendants served Cine (P) with a set of interrogatories. Cine (P) deferred discovery until it could retain an expert, but it nevertheless filed inadequate responses to these interrogatories four months after the deadline. Three years later, Cine (P) had still failed to retain an expert or adequately respond to the interrogatories. A magistrate ordered Cine (P) to answer the interrogatories, and Cine's (P) response was again late and inadequate. At a formal hearing, the magistrate recommended that the district court preclude Cine (P) from introducing any evidence with respect to damages, the subject matter of the interrogatories. The district court judge "regretfully" concluded that it lacked power to impose this extreme sanction, fining Cine (P) $1000 in costs instead. However, the judge certified this interlocutory appeal, recognizing that he may have misinterpreted the law regarding sanctions for discovery abuses.

■ **ISSUE**

Is a party who exhibits gross negligence in responding to discovery subject to the most severe discovery sanctions?

■ **DECISION AND RATIONALE**

(Kaufman, J.) Yes. A party who exhibits gross negligence in responding to discovery requests is subject to the most severe discovery sanctions. The range of discovery sanctions, specified in Rule 37, serve three purposes. First, sanctions ensure that a party will not be able to profit from a failure to comply with discovery. Second, sanctions may seek to secure compliance with a particular discovery order. Third, and most extreme, sanctions may be imposed as mere penalties, in order to deter similar conduct by other litigants in other lawsuits. If a party makes good faith efforts to comply with discovery requests, the most sever sanctions including dismissal of the complaint should not be employed, as this would amount to a deprivation of a property interest without due process. However, in the case at hand, Cine's (P) failure to respond to discovery was not in good faith and was either a willful failure to comply or at least grossly negligent. In this situation, the full range of discovery sanctions may be marshaled. Cine (P) has, through its own fault, frozen this litigation in the discovery stages for nearly four years. The district court judge declined to adopt the magistrate's suggestion only because the judge misinterpreted the law regarding sanctions. Thus, the district court's order declining to preclude Cine (P) from entering any proof of damages is reversed.

■ CONCURRENCE

(Oakes, J.) If Cine's (P) gross failure to comply with the discovery requests was its own fault, it should be precluded from entering any evidence of damages at trial. If the failure was due to the complexity of the interrogatories, it should have moved for a protective order under Rule 26(c). However, I would be reluctant to impose the shortcomings of Cine's (P) counsel upon Cine (P) absent Cine's (P) knowledge, condonation, compliance or causation.

Analysis:

Sanctions for failure to comply with discovery requests can be very harsh. Because Cine (P) was barred from entering any evidence regarding damages, the most it could hope for at trial would be an injunction. Nevertheless, the holding is a sensible reaction to an almost unbelievable lack of responsibility on the part of Cine (P) and its attorney. The magistrate and district court apparently offered Cine (P) every possible opportunity to comply with the requests. Further, Cine (P) could have moved for a protective order under Rule 26(c) if the discovery requests were oppressive. By completely failing to comply with the discovery requirements, Cine (P) deserved the harsh sanctions it received. However, it is interesting to note the reluctance with which the District Court and Court of Appeals handed out the sanctions. Traditionally, judges were extremely reluctant to apply sanctions to curb abusive discovery practices. This case, and others cited in the opinion, demonstrates that courts are becoming less patient with parties who abuse the discovery practice and are more willing to impose Rule 37 sanctions.

CHAPTER TWELVE

Case Management

Velez v. Awning Windows, Inc.

Instant Facts: Velez (D) was granted partial summary judgment after the court refused to consider an untimely response to the plaintiff's motion, despite several warnings that no further extensions would be granted.

Black Letter Rule: Rule 56(f) relieves a party from the need to timely respond to a motion for summary judgment when the party demonstrates its inability to adduce facts necessary for its response, a plausible belief that further discovery will uncover the necessary facts, and how these facts are expected to affect the summary judgment motion.

Roell v. Withrow

Instant Facts: A prisoner sued prison officials for violations of his civil rights and complained, after the jury reached a defense verdict, that the case should not have been heard by a magistrate judge, because the defendants did not provide express consent.

Black Letter Rule: When a party has signaled consent to the magistrate judge's authority to hear a case through actions rather than words, there is little value in strict insistence on an express consent requirement.

In re Peterson

Instant Facts: The petitioner complained that the court lacked the authority to appoint an auditor to determine the amount due for coal sold and to tax the auditor's fee as costs.

Black Letter Rule: The Seventh Amendment does not prohibit the introduction of new methods for determining what facts are in issue, nor new rules of evidence.

Payne v. S.S. Nabob

Instant Facts: Payne (P), injured during the loading of a ship, attempted to deviate from his pretrial memoranda by introducing new allegations and witnesses at trial.

Black Letter Rule: Parties may be bound by pretrial memoranda, even in the absence of a formal pretrial order.

Nick v. Morgan's Foods, Inc.

Instant Facts: Morgan's Foods, Inc. (D) and its outside counsel were sanctioned for failing to entertain settlement offers during mediation in good faith.

Black Letter Rule: Sanctions are designed to control litigation and preserve the integrity of the judicial process and lie within the sound discretion of the court.

Velez v. Awning Windows, Inc.

(Employee) v. *(Employer)*

375 F.3d 35 (1st Cir. 2004)

THE FAILURE TO MEET COURT DEADLINES IS SANCTIONABLE

■ **INSTANT FACTS** Velez (D) was granted partial summary judgment after the court refused to consider an untimely response to the plaintiff's motion, despite several warnings that no further extensions would be granted.

■ **BLACK LETTER RULE** Rule 56(f) relieves a party from the need to timely respond to a motion for summary judgment when the party demonstrates its inability to adduce facts necessary for its response, a plausible belief that further discovery will uncover the necessary facts, and how these facts are expected to affect the summary judgment motion.

■ **PROCEDURAL BASIS**

On appeal to review a judgment for the plaintiff.

■ **FACTS**

Velez (P) sued Awning Windows, Inc. (D) and Nieves (D) for sexual harassment. After failing to file an answer within the time allotted by the court, the court entered a default judgment for the plaintiff. When Awning Windows (D) demonstrated to the court that Nieves's (D) sudden death impacted its ability to file a timely answer, the court set aside the default judgment, substituted Nieves's (D) estate as a party, and ordered a timely answer to be filed. The defendants complied and filed their answer. After discovery, the plaintiff filed a motion for partial summary judgment on the issue of liability. Having failed to file a timely response after a court extension of the filing deadline, the court held a scheduling conference and established definite deadlines for the submission of various discovery responses, legal memoranda on a hearsay issue, and financial statements, as well as the response to the motion for partial summary judgment. The court warned that the defendants' failure to comply would result in sanctions. The defendants served timely discovery responses, but requested several extensions to submit ordered legal memoranda and a response to the summary judgment motion. A month after the court deadline for responding to the summary judgment motion, the court disregarded the defendants' late response and entered partial summary judgment for the plaintiff. As a sanction for failing to timely file the ordered hearsay memoranda, the court denied the defendants' motion to dismiss the plaintiff's claim for supervisor liability. A jury ultimately awarded the plaintiff $740,000. The defendants appealed.

■ **ISSUE**

Did the court err in granting the plaintiff's motion for partial summary judgment without considering the defendants' late-filed response?

■ **DECISION AND RATIONALE**

(Selya, J.) No. While summary judgments should ordinarily not be granted until parties have an opportunity to conduct the necessary discovery to properly respond, the responding party has a duty to inform the court of the need for additional discovery under Rule 56(f). Rule 56(f) requires the party to file a statement setting forth the party's inability to adduce facts necessary for its response, a plausible belief that further discovery will uncover the necessary facts, and how these facts are expected to affect the summary judgment motion. The defendants' requests for extension do not include these necessary showings. Instead, the defendants blame their inability to respond in a timely fashion on deposition delays and travel obligations of counsel. Such excuses are not sufficient reasons to satisfy Rule 56(f). The defendants had sufficient time to diligently pursue the discovery they now claim is lacking, but failed to do so. The court's entry of summary judgment on the plaintiff's unopposed motion was within its discretion.

Likewise, because the defendants' motion to dismiss did not implicate the court's subject matter jurisdiction, as the defendants contend, the court was free to deny the motion as a sanction for counsel's consistent failure to meet court deadlines. So, too, was the court justified in precluding certain hearsay testimony as a sanction for the defendants' failure to timely submit a memorandum arguing for its admissibility. Courts have the authority to ask counsel for input on legal issues bearing on the case. Failure to comply with such court requests is proper grounds for court sanction. Judgment affirmed.

Analysis:

Rule 56(f) protects a party that may not have been as speedy in taking discovery within the time limits prescribed by the court. Without such relief, summary judgment motions would result in a race between the parties to quickly develop uncontroverted factual bases to support the motion, so that the opposing party is effectively unable to demonstrate general issues of material fact to rebut the motion. Rule 56(f) does not defeat a timely summary judgment motion, but rather suspends the court's decision until both parties have ample time to conduct discovery.

■ CASE VOCABULARY

SANCTIONS: A penalty or coercive measure that results from failure to comply with a rule, law, or order.

Roell v. Withrow

(Prison Official) v. *(Prisoner)*

538 U.S. 580, 123 S.Ct. 1696, 155 L.Ed.2d 775 (2003)

VOLUNTARY PARTICIPATION IN PROCEEDINGS BEFORE A MAGISTRATE JUDGE CONSTITUTES CONSENT TO FORGO A DISTRICT COURT TRIAL

I thought you wanted me to preside over your case.

That was before I lost.

stus.com

■ **INSTANT FACTS** A prisoner sued prison officials for violations of his civil rights and complained, after the jury reached a defense verdict, that the case should not have been heard by a magistrate judge, because the defendants did not provide express consent.

■ **BLACK LETTER RULE** When a party has signaled consent to the magistrate judge's authority to hear a case through actions rather than words, there is little value in strict insistence on an express consent requirement.

■ **PROCEDURAL BASIS**

Certiorari to the United States Court of Appeals for the Fifth Circuit.

■ **FACTS**

Withrow (P), a Texas state prisoner, brought a civil rights action alleging violations of his Eighth Amendment rights resulting from the prison staff's disregard for his medical needs. At a preliminary hearing, the magistrate judge told Withrow (P) that he could choose to have her, rather than a judge, preside over the entire case, and Withrow (P) agreed. The district judge then officially referred the case to the magistrate judge for final disposition, but before hearing whether the defendants had agreed to such an assignment. The case proceeded in front of the magistrate judge and resulted in a judgment for the defendants. When Withrow (P) appealed, the appeals court remanded the case to the district court to determine whether all parties had consented to proceed before a magistrate judge. Only then did Roell (D) and one other defendant formally issue their consent. Upon review, the magistrate judge argued that the defendants' consent was demonstrated by their voluntary participation in the proceedings, without objection. The federal district court found, however, that consent could not be inferred, and the court of appeals agreed. The Supreme Court granted certiorari.

■ **ISSUE**

May the parties' consent to trial before a magistrate judge be inferred from their conduct during the proceedings?

■ **DECISION AND RATIONALE**

(Souter, J.) Yes. When a party has signaled consent to the magistrate judge's authority to hear a case through actions rather than words, there is little value in strict insistence on an express consent requirement. The Federal Magistrate Act expanded the power of magistrate judges by authorizing them to conduct any and all proceedings in jury and non-jury civil matters, as long as they are specially designated by the district court and are acting upon the consent of the parties. Although one federal rule speaks of the parties' election of a magistrate in separate or joint consent forms, other rules speak of consent in general, with no requirement of a formal, written document. A bright line rule requiring express consent in all cases would not be worth the downside of requiring a long and complicated trial where none is needed. The better rule is to accept implied consent where, as here, the litigant or counsel was made aware of the need for consent and the right to refuse it, and still voluntarily appeared to try the case before the magistrate judge. Inferring consent under these circumstances checks the risk of gamesmanship by depriving parties of the luxury of waiting for the outcome before denying the magistrate's authority. Roell's (D) and the other defendant's appearance before the magistrate judge after being told of their right to trial by a district judge supplies the consent necessary to obtain rightful jurisdiction. Reversed.

Analysis:

The Federal Magistrates Act instituted a system of magistrate judges to replace the former "United States commissioners," a system that had been in place since the nineteenth century. Commissioners were first authorized to arrest and imprison criminal offenders, and Congress later extended their duties to include enforcement of the Fugitive Slave Act of 1850, the Civil Rights Act of 1866, and the Chinese Exclusion Act of 1888, to name just a few of their diverse responsibilities. In the mid-twentieth century, the operation of the U.S. commissioner system varied greatly from one district to the next. Most commissioners were part-time judicial officers, but they were not required to be attorneys. After the Judicial Conference recommended reform, a Senate Judiciary subcommittee opened hearings that led to the Federal Magistrates Act of 1968. The Act instituted a salary schedule and required all magistrates to be members of the bar. Subsequent legislation expanded the magistrates' trial authority, especially in civil cases.

■ CASE VOCABULARY

UNITED STATES MAGISTRATE JUDGE: A federal judicial officer who hears civil and criminal pretrial matters and who may conduct civil trials or criminal misdemeanor trials.

In re Peterson

(Petitioner for Writ of Mandamus and/or Prohibition)
253 U.S. 300, 40 S.Ct. 543, 64 L.Ed. 919 (1920)

COURTS ARE FREE TO USE NON-COURT PERSONNEL TO AID THEM IN THEIR DUTIES

You had to hire an auditor to help you with your case? Schmuck.

So much for my peers respecting me once I became a judge.

stus.com

■ **INSTANT FACTS** The petitioner complained that the court lacked the authority to appoint an auditor to determine the amount due for coal sold and to tax the auditor's fee as costs.

■ **BLACK LETTER RULE** The Seventh Amendment does not prohibit the introduction of new methods for determining what facts are in issue, nor new rules of evidence.

■ **PROCEDURAL BASIS**

Petition for a writ of mandamus or writ of prohibition to the District Court for the Southern District of New York.

■ **FACTS**

Peterson (P) challenged the authority of the court to appoint an auditor to conduct a preliminary hearing to determine amounts due for coal sold, and to tax the auditor's expenses as costs. He also claimed that the appointment of the auditor violated his right to a jury trial under the Seventh Amendment.

■ **ISSUE**

Did the court have the authority to appoint the auditor to determine the amounts due for coal sold and to tax the auditor's fee as costs?

■ **DECISION AND RATIONALE**

(Brandeis, J.) Yes. The Seventh Amendment does not prohibit the introduction of new methods for determining what facts are in issue, nor new rules of evidence. The office of auditor was apparently invented in Massachusetts in 1818. No congressional act has specifically authorized the adoption of the practice in federal courts. But an auditor simplifies the issues in a case, such that his role is essentially the same as that of a pleading. There is no constitutional obstacle to the appointment of an auditor. Courts, in the absence of a legislative prohibition to the contrary, have the authority to provide themselves with the appropriate instruments for the performance of their duties, including the appointment of persons to aid judges in the progress of a case. Nor is there any statute or rule of court excluding auditors' fees from the items taxable as costs. Motion denied.

Analysis:

The petitioner in this case moved the court for a writ of mandamus, or, in the alternative, a writ of prohibition. A writ of mandamus is issued by a superior court to compel a lower court or a government officer to perform its mandatory or purely ministerial duties correctly. A writ of prohibition, by contrast, is an extraordinary writ issued by an appellate court to prevent a lower court from exceeding its jurisdiction, or to prevent a non-judicial officer or entity from exercising a power. A writ of prohibition is a kind of common law injunction that prevents an unlawful assumption of jurisdiction. It arrests the proceedings of any tribunal exercising judicial functions in a manner or by means not within its discretion. In the present case, however, the court denied both types of writ.

Payne v. S.S. Nabob

(*Injured Party*) v. (*Ship*)
302 F.2d 803 (3rd Cir. 1962)

EVEN WITHOUT A PRETRIAL ORDER, PARTIES MAY BE BOUND BY THEIR PRETRIAL MEMORANDA

■ **INSTANT FACTS** Payne (P), injured during the loading of a ship, attempted to deviate from his pretrial memoranda by introducing new allegations and witnesses at trial.

■ **BLACK LETTER RULE** Parties may be bound by pretrial memoranda, even in the absence of a formal pretrial order.

■ PROCEDURAL BASIS

Appeal from denial of motion for continuance of personal injury action and from sustaining of objections to opening argument.

■ FACTS

Payne (P) brought a personal injury admiralty action, apparently alleging that the S.S. Nabob (D) was unseaworthy. In his opening argument, Payne's (P) attorney alleged that the ship's employees improperly handled the loading. This issue was outside of the scope of Payne's (P) pretrial memorandum, which stated that he was relying on the condition of a winch to prove his claim. Thus, the trial court sustained an objection to this argument. In addition, the court refused to allow two witnesses, who were not listed on the pretrial memorandum, to testify. Payne (P) moved for a continuance, but it was denied. Payne (P) appeals on grounds that the pretrial memorandum was merely preparatory to the pretrial conference and was not, therefore, binding on the parties.

■ ISSUE

May parties be bound by statements included in their pretrial memoranda?

■ DECISION AND RATIONALE

(McLaughlin, J.) Yes. Parties may be bound by statements, including contentions of fact and witness lists, contained in their pretrial memoranda. Even if a pretrial order is not entered by the judge, pretrial steps can produce binding results. In the case at hand, the judge issued a pretrial report, which referenced the pretrial memoranda of Payne (P) and other parties. This report fulfilled the letter and spirit of Federal Rule of Civil Procedure Rule 16 with regard to pretrial orders. Further, the judge did not abuse his discretion in denying the continuance. Payne (P) had ample opportunity to alter his pretrial memoranda by, for example, changing his contentions or modifying his witness list. However, he failed to do so. If the judge had allowed a continuance of the trial, he would have repudiated the efficiency rationale of the entire pretrial system. Affirmed.

Analysis:

This case takes an extremely broad reading of Rule 16, accomplishing the goal of judicial efficiency by imposing a binding effect of pretrial memoranda on parties. Note that Rule 16(e) specifically requires a judge to enter a binding pretrial order following a pretrial conference. Such orders typically include the parties' contentions, as well as exhibit lists and witness lists. However, in the case at hand, the judge failed to draft a pretrial order. In spite of this shortcoming, the appellate court reaches a sensible result in granting a binding effect to the judge's pretrial report. If the report had been labeled an "order," then there would be no question of its binding effect. Indeed, as the opinion notes, allowing a party to deviate substantially from pretrial memoranda would eviscerate the important policy goals of pretrial procedure. Further, since Payne (P) had an adequate opportunity to amend his pretrial memorandum prior to trial, he cannot claim any substantial unfairness in the judge's decision to deny the continuance. Although judges are usually inclined to assist parties by providing continuances when necessary, the facts of this case clearly do not warrant a continuance.

■ **CASE VOCABULARY**

CONTINUANCE: The postponement of a trial, usually upon motion by one of the parties.

Nick v. Morgan's Foods, Inc.

(Employee) v. *(Employer)*

270 F.3d 590 (8th Cir. 2001)

A PARTY MAY BE SANCTIONED FOR ITS ATTORNEY'S TRANSGRESSIONS

The mediation was voluntary and nonbinding, but my sanctions for failing to comply with local rules are quite involuntary and binding.

stus.com

■ **INSTANT FACTS** Morgan's Foods, Inc. (D) and its outside counsel were sanctioned for failing to entertain settlement offers during mediation in good faith.

■ **BLACK LETTER RULE** Sanctions are designed to control litigation and preserve the integrity of the judicial process and lie within the sound discretion of the court.

■ **PROCEDURAL BASIS**

On appeal to review an order for sanctions.

■ **FACTS**

Nick (P) sued Morgan's Foods, Inc. (D) in federal court for sexual harassment. Morgan's (D) was represented by outside counsel, Seibel, but all business decisions were made by inside counsel, Craig. After the parties consented to voluntary mediation, the court issued an order requiring mediation to be conducted in compliance with local rules. Local rules required (1) that no later than seven days before the scheduled mediation, the parties must submit a memorandum stating a summary of the disputed facts and each party's position on liability and damages; (2) that all parties with authority to settle be present at all mediation conferences; and (3) that settlement be entertained in good faith. Failure to meet a deadline is grounds for sanctions.

Morgan's (D) outside counsel and a corporate representative with no knowledge of the facts and limited authority to settle were present at the mediation conference. Moreover, Morgan's (D) failed to file the memorandum of disputed facts and position seven days before the conference and summarily rejected two settlement offers extended by Nick (P), without making a counteroffer. The district court ordered Morgan's (D) to show cause why sanctions should not be imposed. Morgan's (D) responded that the guidelines were nonbinding and compliance would have been a waste of time and money. Nick (P) then moved for sanctions and attorneys' fees. Morgan's (D) and its outside counsel were ordered to pay monetary sanctions to the court and to Nick (P). Morgan's (D) moved the court to reconsider, which motion was denied and resulted in additional sanctions for filing a frivolous motion.

■ **ISSUE**

Is a federal court authorized to sanction a party and its attorney for failure to engage in mandatory nonbinding mediation in good faith?

■ **DECISION AND RATIONALE**

(McMillan, J.) Yes. Sanctions are designed to control litigation and preserve the integrity of the judicial process and lie within the sound discretion of the court. Under Federal Rule of Civil Procedure 16, courts have the explicit authority to require pretrial conferences to facilitate settlement of a case. Likewise, local rules empower the court to order civil cases to mediation and establish the procedural requirements expected of the parties to ensure meaningful settlement opportunities. The failure to follow these requirements and to participate in good faith are proper grounds for sanctions. Rule 16 is not limited to the payment of reasonable expenses associated with a pretrial conference, but also authorizes other sanctions deemed appropriate. Sanctions payable to the clerk of court are properly within the court's discretion.

Whether or not the sanctions against a party are a product of its attorney's actions, a party may be held responsible for its attorney's conduct. If the attorney's conduct significantly prejudices the party's interests, the party may have a claim for malpractice, and the party's sanction must be tailored to the severity of the violation. Here, the amount of the sanction against Morgan's (D) was proportionate to the costs it would have incurred by its counsel's preparation of the required memorandum and by sending a corporate representative with authority to negotiate settlements. Affirmed.

Analysis:

As a practical matter, it makes little sense to empower a court to order nonbinding mediation but strip the court of the authority to order the parties' meaningful participation. Nonetheless, sanctions are not appropriate as a matter of course merely because a party declines a settlement offer. Instead, so long as the party participates in good faith and considers the offers presented, the party's duty of participation is satisfied, even if it never intends to accept any offer presented at mediation.

■ CASE VOCABULARY

GOOD FAITH: A state of mind consisting in (1) honesty in belief or purpose, (2) faithfulness to one's duty or obligation, (3) observance of reasonable commercial standards of fair dealing in a given trade or business, or (4) absence of intent to defraud or seek unconscionable advantage.

MEDIATION: A method of nonbinding dispute resolution involving a neutral third party who tries to help the disputing parties reach a mutually agreeable solution.

SANCTIONS: A penalty or coercive measure that results from failure to comply with a rule, law, or order.

CHAPTER THIRTEEN

Adjudication Without Trial or by Special Proceeding

Lundeen v. Cordner

Instant Facts: France Cordon (D), the wife of the decedent Joseph Cordon, sought summary judgment against a claim for payment of life insurance proceeds by former beneficiaries to Joseph's policy, presenting evidence that Joseph had changed his beneficiaries.

Black Letter Rule: When faced with evidence showing no factual dispute exists, the party opposing summary judgment must present some evidence to the contrary.

Cross v. United States

Instant Facts: The United States (P) challenged certain educational deductions taken by Professor Cross (D) on his tax return, alleging that some of the expenses were vacation-related, but the trial court granted summary judgment in Cross's (D) favor.

Black Letter Rule: A party opposing summary judgment is entitled to cross-examine witnesses and parties at trial where there state of mind is at issue.

Adickes v. S.H. Kress & Co.

Instant Facts: Adickes (P), a white teacher who was denied service in a restaurant owned by S.H. Kress & Co. (D), sued Kress (D) and the policeman who arrested her.

Black Letter Rule: Evidence supporting a motion for summary judgment must establish the absence of a genuine issue, when viewed in a light most favorable to the opposing party.

Celotex Corp. v. Catrett

Instant Facts: Charged with several claims for asbestos poisoning that lead to the death of Mr. Catrett, Celotex (D) moved for summary judgment on the grounds that Mrs. Catrett (P) failed to produce evidence to support the claims.

Black Letter Rule: In a summary judgment motion, a moving party may meet its burden of persuasion by demonstrating that the nonmoving party failed to supply sufficient evidence of a genuine dispute of material fact.

Anderson v. Liberty Lobby, Inc.

Instant Facts: Liberty Lobby (P), a right wing organization, sued The Investigator magazine and its publisher, Jack Anderson (D), for libel. Anderson (D) moved for summary judgment, but the Court of Appeals failed to consider the higher evidentiary standard required for libel suits by public figures.

Black Letter Rule: The determination of whether a factual dispute must go to a jury should be guided in light of the substantive evidentiary standards that apply to the claims at issue.

Matsushita Electric Industrial Co. v. Zenith Radio Corp.

Instant Facts: When Zenith Radio Corp. (P) sued Matsushita Electric (D) and other Japanese firms for alleged price fixing, the Appellate Court reversed a summary judgment on grounds that evidence created a genuine issue for trial.

Black Letter Rule: A judge may draw an inference from the absence of a plausible motive upon a motion for summary judgment.

Link v. Wabash R. Co.

Instant Facts: A party appeals the dismissal of his action based upon his attorney's failure to appear at a pretrial conference.

Black Letter Rule: Rule 41 empowers courts to dismiss actions without providing a prior adversary hearing.

Coulas v. Smith

Instant Facts: Coulas (D), who answered complaints yet failed to appear at trial, appealed the denial of his motion to set aside the subsequent adverse judgment.

Black Letter Rule: When a case is called for trial and is at issue, the failure of a defendant to appear does not warrant a default judgment against him.

Lundeen v. Cordner

(Ex–Wife) v. *(Purported Beneficiary)*
354 F.2d 401 (8th Cir. 1966)

A PARTY OPPOSING A SUMMARY JUDGMENT MOTION MUST MAKE SOME SHOWING OF FACTUAL DISPUTE

■ **INSTANT FACTS** France Cordon (D), the wife of the decedent Joseph Cordon, sought summary judgment against a claim for payment of life insurance proceeds by former beneficiaries to Joseph's policy, presenting evidence that Joseph had changed his beneficiaries.

■ **BLACK LETTER RULE** When faced with evidence showing no factual dispute exists, the party opposing summary judgment must present some evidence to the contrary.

■ **PROCEDURAL BASIS**

Appeal from summary judgment against plaintiff suing for life insurance proceeds.

■ **FACTS**

Mrs. Lundeen (P) brought an action as guardian and on behalf of her two children, Maureen and Michael Cordner, to recover the proceeds of a life insurance policy on her deceased ex-husband, Joseph Cordner. Joseph had originally designated Maureen and Michael as beneficiaries to his life insurance policy, which he possessed through his employer, Socony Mobil Oil Company. After divorcing Lundeen (P), Joseph married France Jeanne Cordner (D). Alleging that Joseph had done everything in his power to change the beneficiaries, and that she was a new beneficiary to the policy, France Cordner (D) intervened in the action. Further, Northwestern National Bank of Minneapolis (D) was interpleaded as a trustee under the will and as another purported beneficiary. France Cordner (D) moved for summary judgment, presenting affidavits and exhibits supporting her position that Joseph changed the beneficiary designation. One of these affidavits was written by Mr. Burks, an employee of Socony through whom Joseph allegedly conducted the change of beneficiaries. In response to the motion for summary judgment, Mrs. Lundeen (P) merely submitted her own counter-affidavit averring that Joseph was interested in the future financial welfare of Maureen and Michael. The trial court granted the motion for summary judgment, and Mrs. Lundeen (P) appeals on the ground that there remains a genuine issue of material fact.

■ **ISSUE**

Where evidence by a party moving for summary judgment shows that no factual dispute exists, must the opposing party demonstrate that a factual issue does exist?

■ **DECISION AND RATIONALE**

(Gibson, J.) Yes. Where evidence by a party moving for summary judgment shows that no factual dispute exists, the opposing party must demonstrate that a factual issue does exist. In support of the summary judgment motion, France Cordner (D) submitted extensive evidence indicating that Joseph had done everything in his power to change the beneficiaries designated by his life insurance. France (D) submitted two affidavits by Mr. Burks that described Joseph's attempts to modify his policy. According to the affidavits, Joseph completed a form of beneficiary designation and left the forms with

Burks for transmittal. Burks sent the form to Socony's home office, and the office in turn indicated that it was processing the papers. Furthermore, Mr. Burks first affidavit stated that Joseph intended to leave one-fourth of the insurance proceeds to France Cordner (D) and the balance to Northwestern in trust for the purposes set forth in his will. Additional correspondence indicated that the company had sent Joseph's forms to Socony's insurance department. In order for France Cordner (D) to succeed on her motion, the wording of Joseph's change of beneficiary must show that no dispute exists as to his intentions. Given the facts at hand, Joseph's intentions are clear. Mr. Burks was a non-interested third party who executed the change forms in the regular course of his duties. There is no indication that Burks was biased or mistaken as to the facts. Further, there is no showing that a trial would produce any different results, since Mr. Burks is in Singapore, far beyond the subpoena powers of the trial court. Thus, in order to counter Burks' affidavits, Mrs. Lundeen (P) would have to rely on a deposition. However, Lundeen (P) failed to take Burks' deposition prior to the motion for summary judgment, and she failed to move for a delay in this hearing in order to secure the deposition. In order to counter the evidence supporting the summary judgment motion, Lundeen (P) must assume some initiative in showing that some factual dispute actually exists. However, she made no such showing. She did not attempt to show that Burks' affidavits were untrustworthy, alleging only that Burks' credibility is an issue for the trial court to decide. If this were true, then the granting of summary judgment would be virtually impossible when it is based in any way upon an affidavit. Rather than attempting to undermine Burks' credibility in response to this motion, Lundeen (P) only submitted a counter-affidavit to the effect that Joseph was interested in the future financial welfare of Michael and Maureen. This allegation does not conflict with the factual allegations in the evidence submitted by France Cordner (D). Thus, Lundeen (P) failed to respond to the adequate and substantial showing of France (D). Affirmed.

Analysis:

Although a party moving for summary judgment bears a high burden of proof, this case demonstrates that it is not impossible to prove that no factual dispute exists. At first glance, the requirement to prove that there is no factual dispute seems analogous to the logically impossible task of proving a negative. However, this is not the case. A party seeking summary judgment must only present sufficient evidence to show that the facts are well-settled. In the case at hand, France Cordner (D) made this showing by presenting weighty evidence of her deceased husband's actions. The burden then shifts to the opposing party to make only a minor showing that there is still some factual dispute, and Mrs. Lundeen's (P) efforts in this regard were abysmall Lundeen (P) apparently believed that she could get the case to trial only by stating (with little or no supporting evidence) that France's (D) allegations were wrong. As this case demonstrates, a party opposing summary judgment must show some factual controversy, such as some evidence that Mr. Burks should not be believed or that her husband actually had expressed contradictory intent. If Lundeen (P) intended to attack Burks' veracity, she should have submitted affidavits casting doubt on Burks. Since she made no such effort, and since she failed to show any contradictory intent of her ex-husband, the court's decision seems reasonable.

■ CASE VOCABULARY

DIRECTED VERDICT: A verdict entered against the party who bears the burden of proof but who has failed to present a prima facie case sufficient to bring the action to the jury.

GRAVAMEN: The material, essential part of a claim.

Cross v. United States

(Income Tax Filer) v. *(Government)*
336 F.2d 431 (2nd Cir. 1964)

WHERE FACTS RESIDE SOLELY IN THE MIND OF A PARTY, SUMMARY JUDGMENT IS INAPPROPRIATE AND THE PARTY SHOULD BE SUBJECT TO CROSS–EXAMINATION AT TRIAL

■ **INSTANT FACTS** The United States (P) challenged certain educational deductions taken by Professor Cross (D) on his tax return, alleging that some of the expenses were vacation-related, but the trial court granted summary judgment in Cross's (D) favor.

■ **BLACK LETTER RULE** A party opposing summary judgment is entitled to cross-examine witnesses and parties at trial where there state of mind is at issue.

■ **PROCEDURAL BASIS**

Appeal from summary judgment against United States in income tax refund suit.

■ **FACTS**

The United States (P) brought this action against Professor Ephraim Cross (D) for an alleged improper deduction on Cross's (D) income taxes. Cross (D) claimed that he was entitled to a deduction for travel expenses incurred in conjunction with a summer vacation [with his wife and poodle!] to Europe and the Mediterranean, justifying the deduction as an educational venture for the purpose of improving his skills as a teacher of romance languages. Cross (D) moved for a summary judgment, submitting affidavits of several professors that testified to the educational nature of the journey. The Government (P) opposes this judgment on two levels. First, it claims that at least part of Cross's (D) expenses were purely recreational and, hence, not deductible. Second, the Government (P) claims a right to cross-examine Cross (D) as to the nature of his expenses and a right to cross-examine the witnesses.

■ **ISSUE**

Should a party opposing summary judgment be entitled an opportunity to cross-examine witnesses and parties at trial in order to test their credibility?

■ **DECISION AND RATIONALE**

(Moore, J.) Yes. A party opposing summary judgment should be entitled an opportunity to cross-examine witnesses and parties at trial in order to test their credibility. This is especially true in the case at hand, where the disputed questions of fact turn exclusively on the credibility of Cross's (D) witnesses and Cross (D) himself. Before travel expenses can be deductible, there must be a factual determination of what parts, if any, are to be attributed to vacation travel or to educational advancement. Many of the facts related to Cross's (D) vacation remain largely within his own knowledge, and the Government (P) should have the opportunity to test his credibility on cross-examination. At trial, the trier of fact will have to ascertain what portions of the trip were educational and which were purely recreational [the 21-day cruise across the Atlantic with his wife and poodle probably did not enhance his intellectual capacity as a professor!]. Reversed and remanded for trial.

Analysis:

With respect to the issue of testing a witness' credibility, this case reaches the opposite result of *Lundeen v. Cordner* [summary judgment proper even where veracity of affiants may be in dispute]. In this respect, the holding seems to reach an incorrect result. Indeed, whenever witness affidavits are used by a party moving for summary judgment, the credibility of the witnesses could be called into question. Allowing a case to proceed to trial in every instance would effectively undermine the purpose of summary judgments, i.e., to avoid useless trials. Thus, the need for cross-examination of witnesses at trial should be grounds for denying summary judgment only where the opposing party gives some evidence calling their credibility into question. In the case at hand, the Government (P) apparently did not enter any such evidence, and it did not provide evidence showing that the deductions were improper. As Rule 56(e) of the Federal Rules of Civil Procedure states, an adverse party may not rest upon the mere denials of the moving party's pleadings. Nevertheless, the holding seems fair. The Government (P) could oppose Cross's (D) deductions only by examining Cross (D) as to the nature of his travel. Since only Cross (D) knew the precise amount of money expended for recreational and educational purposes on the trip, the Government (P) should be allowed to obtain this information.

■ CASE VOCABULARY

DEDUCTION: A sum of money subtracted from a person's income when computing income taxes.

DE MINIMIS: A legally insignificant amount of something.

Adickes v. S.H. Kress & Co.

(Customer) v. *(Restaurant Owner)*
398 U.S. 144, 90 S.Ct. 1598 (1970)

THE PARTY MOVING FOR SUMMARY JUDGMENT BEARS A HEAVY BURDEN OF ESTABLISHING NO FACTUAL DISPUTE

■ **INSTANT FACTS** Adickes (P), a white teacher who was denied service in a restaurant owned by S.H. Kress & Co. (D), sued Kress (D) and the policeman who arrested her.

■ **BLACK LETTER RULE** Evidence supporting a motion for summary judgment must establish the absence of a genuine issue, when viewed in a light most favorable to the opposing party.

■ PROCEDURAL BASIS

Writ of certiorari from summary judgment against claim for damages for equal protection and civil rights violations.

■ FACTS

Adickes (P) was a white female teacher at a school for black children. When Adickes (P) entered a restaurant owned by S.H. Kress & Co. (D), she was denied service because she was a white person in the company of blacks. A policeman in the store then arrested Adickes (P) on a charge of vagrancy. [Yes, the charge was unfounded and ridiculous!]. Adickes (P) sued for damages, alleging that the denial of service plus the arrest constituted a conspiracy between Kress (D) and the police to violate Adickes's (P) constitutional right to equal protection. Kress (D) moved for summary judgment, producing affidavits from the store manager, the chief of police, and the arresting officers denying any pre-arranged conspiracy. In response, Adickes (P) simply restated her complaint and offered an unsworn statement by a Kress (D) employee that the policeman had been in the store prior to the refusal of service. The District Court granted the summary judgment, the Court of Appeals affirmed, and the Supreme Court granted certiorari.

■ ISSUE

Must evidence be presented in opposition to a summary judgment motion where the evidence supporting the motion fails to establish absence of a genuine issue?

■ DECISION AND RATIONALE

(Judge Not Stated) No. In response to a summary judgment motion, evidence does not have to be presented when evidence supporting the motion fails to establish the absence of a genuine issue. On its motion for summary judgment, Kress (D) had the initial burden of demonstrating that there was no policeman in the store. If a policeman were present, it would be open to a jury to infer from the circumstances whether the policeman and Kress (D) had a "meeting of the minds" and had formulated a conspiracy to deny service. Kress (D) did not meet this initial burden. This could have been accomplished, for example, by submitting affidavits from the policemen denying their presence in the store at the time in question. If Kress (D) had produced this evidence, then Adickes (P) would have been required to do more than simply restate a contrary allegation of her complaint. On summary judgment, the inferences to be drawn from the underlying facts in the moving party's materials must be viewed in a light most favorable to the party opposing the motion. Kress's (D) evidence, viewed in a light most favorable to Adickes (P), fails to show the absence of a genuine issue of fact in dispute. Thus, Kress's (D) failure to show that there was no policeman in the store requires reversal. Reversed.

Analysis:

This case demonstrates the heavy burden borne by a party moving for summary judgment. As the court noted, all inferences from the moving party's motion must be drawn in a light most favorable to the opposing party. Thus, even though Kress (D) submitted affidavits from the policemen and the store manager denying any conspiracy, this was insufficient to establish that there was no factual dispute. In effect, Kress (D) supported the summary judgment motion simply by denying the conspiracy. However, the Court's reasoning must be critically examined. The Court reasons that affidavits declaring that the policeman was not in the store would be sufficient to demonstrate that no conspiracy existed. This conclusion seems flawed. Couldn't Kress (D) and the police have reached a conspiracy without the police officer being present in the store? For example, if a conspiracy existed, Kress (D) could have denied service to Adickes (P) and telephoned the police to arrest the "vagrant." Nevertheless, the central theme of the heavy burden borne by the moving party is adequately conveyed.

■ **CASE VOCABULARY**

VAGRANCY: A general term describing such arguably criminal activities as failing to seek employment or loitering in public without any visible means of support or with the intent to solicit funds.

Celotex Corp. v. Catrett

(Product Manufacturer) v. *(Wife of Decedent)*
477 U.S. 317, 106 S.Ct. 2548 (1986)

SUMMARY JUDGMENT MAY BE APPROPRIATE EVEN IF THE MOVING PARTY FAILS TO PRODUCE EVIDENCE DEMONSTRATING A LACK OF A FACTUAL DISPUTE

■ **INSTANT FACTS** Charged with several claims for asbestos poisoning that lead to the death of Mr. Catrett, Celotex (D) moved for summary judgment on the grounds that Mrs. Catrett (P) failed to produce evidence to support the claims.

■ **BLACK LETTER RULE** In a summary judgment motion, a moving party may meet its burden of persuasion by demonstrating that the nonmoving party failed to supply sufficient evidence of a genuine dispute of material fact.

■ **PROCEDURAL BASIS**

Writ of certiorari reviewing reversal of granting of summary judgment against a party claiming damages for negligence, breach of warranty and strict liability.

■ **FACTS**

Mrs. Catrett (P) sued Celotex Corp. (D) and others for negligence, breach of warranty, and strict liability, alleging that her husband's death was caused by exposure to products containing asbestos manufactured by Celotex (D) and the other defendants. Celotex (D) moved for summary judgment on the grounds that Catrett (P) failed to produce any evidence that any Celotex (D) product caused the injuries. In response, Catrett (P) produced three documents which she claimed demonstrated that a genuine factual dispute existed. Celotex (D) argued that the three documents, including the husband's deposition and two letters, were inadmissible hearsay. The District Court granted Celotex's (D) motion for summary judgment because there was no showing that Mr. Catrett was exposed to Celotex's (D) product. The Court of Appeals reversed since Celotex (D) made no effort to adduce any evidence, in the form of affidavits or otherwise, in support of its motion for summary judgment. The Supreme Court granted certiorari.

■ **ISSUE**

Must a party moving for summary judgment supply evidence or affidavits showing the absence of a genuine dispute about a material fact?

■ **DECISION AND RATIONALE**

(Rehnquist, J.) No. A party moving for summary judgment does not necessarily bear the burden of supplying evidence or affidavits showing the absence of a genuine dispute about a material fact. The plain language of Rule 56(c) of the Federal Rules of Civil Procedure mandates the entry of summary judgment, after adequate time for discovery, against a party who fails to establish the existence of an element essential to that party's case, and on which that party will bear the burden of proof at trial. The Court of Appeals misconstrued the holding in *Adickes v. S.H. Kress & Co.* [the party moving for summary judgment must establish the absence of a genuine issue, when viewed in a light most favorable to the opposing party]. This holding should not be construed to mean that the burden is always on the moving party to produce evidence showing the absence of a material fact in dispute.

Rather, a summary judgment motion may properly be made in reliance solely on the pleadings, depositions, answers to interrogatories, and admissions on file. Thus, the moving party does not have to submit supporting evidence, as the plain language of Rules 56(a) and (b) indicate. The moving party only bears the initial responsibility of informing the court of the basis for its motion. This responsibility may be met by showing the court that there is an absence of evidence to support the nonmoving party's case. The amendment to Rule 56(e), precluding a party opposing summary judgment from referring only to its pleadings, was intended to broaden the scope of summary judgment motions. However, the Court of Appeal's reasoning tends to make summary judgments more difficult to obtain. In the case at hand, the parties had an adequate opportunity to conduct discovery and establish the evidence needed to prove their cases. The Court of Appeals declined to address whether Catrett (P) had made an adequate showing to carry her burden of proof at trial. For this reason, and based on the foregoing analysis, the judgment of the Court of Appeals is reversed for such a determination. Reversed and remanded.

■ CONCURRENCE

(White, J.) I agree that a moving party must not always support a summary judgment motion with evidence or affidavits showing the absence of a genuine dispute of a material fact. However, the movant may not simply discharge his burden by asserting that the opposing party has no evidence to prove his or her case. The case should be reversed for the Court of Appeals to consider whether Catrett (P) revealed enough evidence to defeat the motion for summary judgment.

■ DISSENT

(Brennan, J.) The Court has not clearly explained what is required of a moving party seeking summary judgment on the ground that the nonmoving party cannot prove its case. I believe that Celotex (D) has failed to meet its burden of production. The burden on the party seeking summary judgment has two components. First, the party bears the initial burden of production, which shifts to the nonmoving party if satisfied by the moving party. Second, the moving party bears the ultimate burden of persuasion. The decision as to whether the moving party has discharged its initial burden of production depends upon which party will bear the burden of persuasion on the challenged claim at trial. If the moving party will bear the burden of persuasion, it must support its motion with credible evidence that would entitle it to a directed verdict if not controverted at trial. On the other hand, if the burden of persuasion at trial would be on the nonmoving party, then the party moving for summary judgment may satisfy its burden of production in two ways. First, it may submit affirmative evidence that negates an essential element of the nonmoving party's claim. Second, it may demonstrate that the nonmoving party's evidence itself is insufficient to establish an essential element of the nonmoving party's claim. However, the moving party in this scenario may not simply assert a conclusory statement that the nonmoving party's evidence is insufficient. Rather, it must affirmatively show the absence of evidence in the record to support a judgment for the nonmoving party. Based on the facts of this case, Celotex (D) failed to discharge its initial burden of production. Thus, summary judgment is improper.

Analysis:

The majority, led by Justice Rehnquist, clearly desired to expand the scope of summary judgment motions following the restrictive holding in *Adickes v. S.H. Kress & Co.* They accomplished this goal by significantly reducing the burden borne by the party moving for summary judgment. As a result of this holding, a moving party meets its burden by simply alerting the court that the nonmoving party has failed to establish evidence sufficient to prove its claims. Indeed, this holding furthers the general goals of the Federal Rules of Civil Procedure, which were designed to secure speedy and inexpensive determinations of controversies. However, the majority may have been too willing to grant summary judgment. As Justice Brennan's well-reasoned dissent mentions, the Court failed to establish what is required of a moving party. While the Court stated that a moving party cannot simply assert that the nonmoving party has no evidence to prove its case, this seems to be exactly what Celotex (D) did. The dissent presents a more reasoned analysis, predicated on which party will bear the burden of persuasion on the challenged claim at trial. If the moving party will bear the burden of persuasion, then it must produce credible evidence over and above what Celotex (D) produced. However, with respect to the asbestos poisoning. Catrett (D) clearly would bear the burden of persuasion. In this instance, Celotex (D) would only have to demonstrate that Catrett's (D) evidence was insufficient to meet its burden of persuasion. Nevertheless, according to the portions of the opinion reprinted in the book, it seems that Celotex (D) failed to make even this minimal showing.

■ CASE VOCABULARY

BURDEN OF PERSUASION: A party's obligation to establish evidence sufficient to convince the trier of fact that each element of the party's claim or defense is correct.

BURDEN OF PRODUCTION: A party's obligation to produce evidence sufficient to avoid an adverse ruling on an issue, even if this falls short of persuasion.

Anderson v. Liberty Lobby, Inc.

(Publisher) v. *(Organization)*

477 U.S. 242, 106 S.Ct. 2505 (1986)

MOTIONS FOR SUMMARY JUDGMENT MUST CONSIDER THE APPLICABLE STANDARD OF PROOF APPLIED TO THE OPPOSING PARTY'S CLAIMS

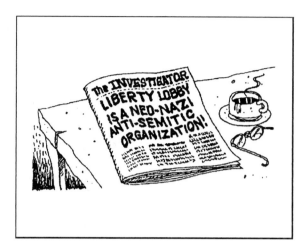

■ **INSTANT FACTS** Liberty Lobby (P), a right wing organization, sued *The Investigator* magazine and its publisher, Jack Anderson (D), for libel. Anderson (D) moved for summary judgment, but the Court of Appeals failed to consider the higher evidentiary standard required for libel suits by public figures.

■ **BLACK LETTER RULE** The determination of whether a factual dispute must go to a jury should be guided in light of the substantive evidentiary standards that apply to the claims at issue.

■ **PROCEDURAL BASIS**

Writ of certiorari considering reversal of summary judgment against claim for libel.

■ **FACTS**

Liberty Lobby (P), a right wing organization, filed a libel suit against *The Investigator* magazine, its president, and its publisher, Jack Anderson (D), for articles that portrayed Liberty Lobby (P) as fascist and racist [Liberty Lobby did not want to be *that* far to the right!]. Anderson (D) moved for summary judgment on the ground that Liberty Lobby (P) could not prove by clear and convincing evidence—the standard for libel suits brought by public figures—that Anderson (D) acted with actual malice. In support of his motion, Anderson (D) submitted affidavits from the columnist who wrote the articles documenting the research that the columnist made prior to the articles. Liberty Lobby (P) responded by noting numerous inaccuracies in the articles. The District Court granted the motion for summary judgment, but the Court of Appeals for the District of Columbia Circuit reversed as to some of the allegedly defamatory statements, holding that a jury could reasonably conclude that the allegations were made with actual malice. The Court of Appeals gave no weight to the heightened "clear and convincing evidence" standard in the case. The Supreme Court granted certiorari.

■ **ISSUE**

Must the determination of whether a factual dispute requires submission to a jury be guided by the substantive evidentiary standards that apply to the case?

■ **DECISION AND RATIONALE**

(White, J.) Yes. The determination of whether a factual dispute requires submission to a jury must be guided by the substantive evidentiary standards that apply to the case. Summary judgment can be granted only when there is no genuine issue of material fact. In order for a material fact to be genuine, and hence to preclude summary judgment, the evidence must be such that a reasonable jury could return a verdict for the nonmoving party. This standard mirrors the standard for a directed verdict under Federal Rules of Civil Procedure 50(a). In every case, there is a preliminary question for the judge, not whether there is literally no evidence, but whether there is any evidence upon which a jury could find a verdict for the party upon whom the onus of proof is imposed. Thus, the inquiry involved in ruling on a motion for summary judgment or a directed verdict necessarily implicates the substantive evidentiary standard of proof that would apply at the trial on the merits. In the case at hand, the *New York Times v. Sullivan* [libel suits brought by public figures requires proof of actual malice by clear and convincing evidence] evidentiary standard governs. Thus, the judge must determine whether the evidence in the record could support a reasonable jury finding either that the plaintiff has shown actual malice by clear and convincing evidence or that the plaintiff has not. Credibility determinations, the weighing of evidence, and the drawing of legitimate inferences from the facts remain questions for the jury. Because the Court of Appeals did not apply this standard in reviewing the District Court's grant of summary judgment, we vacate its decision and remand the case for further proceedings. Vacated and remanded.

■ DISSENT

(Brennan, J.) While the Court instructs the judge to consider heightened evidentiary standards, the Court fails to explain what this means. It appears that the Court is contradicting itself, requiring, on one hand, the judge to bear in mind the quantum of proof required but forbidding, on the other hand, the judge from weighing the evidence himself. If indeed a judge can only determine the quality of evidence by weighing the evidence, as logic would dictate, then I am fearful that this new rule would transform summary judgments into full blown trials on the merits. A party moving for summary judgment, aware that the judge will be assessing the quantum of evidence, would bring forth all of the evidence he could muster in support of his case. In my view, when a party presents evidence which either directly or by permissible inference supports all of the elements of his claim, the party has made a prima facie case and the summary judgment motion must fail.

■ DISSENT

(Rehnquist, J.) The Court's decision will be of little practical effect, since the Court upholds our previous rulings requiring credibility determinations to be made by the jury. If the application of evidentiary standards makes no difference in cases involving credibility determinations, in what sort of case does the difference in standards make a difference in outcome?

Analysis:

This case demonstrates the logical tangles inherent in summary judgment procedures. Justice White's majority opinion seems to arrive at a logical holding. By the terms of Rule 56(c), summary judgment is inappropriate whenever a dispute about a material fact is genuine. It makes sense that a dispute is genuine if the evidence is such that a reasonable jury could return a verdict for the nonmoving party. However, the court enters a logical morass by forcing judges to determine whether a jury could return such a verdict. On one hand, as Brennan's dissent mentions, the judge is not allowed to weight the evidence himself—this is a function for the jury. However, it certainly seems that the judge *must* weigh the evidence in order to determine whether the dispute is genuine, i.e., whether a jury could return a verdict for the nonmoving party. And if a judge must determine the sufficiency of the evidence, both the majority and dissent agree that this must be done in light of the applicable evidentiary standard of proof.

■ CASE VOCABULARY

ONUS: Another term for burden, such as a burden of proof.

QUANTUM: A Latin term meaning "how much," typically referring to a certain amount of evidence.

Matsushita Electric Industrial Co. v. Zenith Radio Corp.

(*Japanese Manufacturer*) v. (*American Manufacturer*)
475 U.S. 574, 106 S.Ct. 1348 (1986)

ONE MAY DRAW REASONABLE INFERENCES ON SUMMARY JUDGMENT UNLESS TWO COMPETING INFERENCES ARE EQUALLY PLAUSIBLE

■ **INSTANT FACTS** When Zenith Radio Corp. (P) sued Matsushita Electric (D) and other Japanese firms for alleged price fixing, the Appellate Court reversed a summary judgment on grounds that evidence created a genuine issue for trial.

■ **BLACK LETTER RULE** A judge may draw an inference from the absence of a plausible motive upon a motion for summary judgment.

■ **PROCEDURAL BASIS**

Writ of certiorari considering reversal of summary judgment against party suing for antitrust violations.

■ **FACTS**

Zenith Radio Corp. (P) and other American television manufacturers alleged that Matsushita Electric Industrial Co. (D) and other Japanese manufacturers conspired to fix prices in an effort to monopolize the American market. The trial court granted Matsushita's (D) motion for summary judgment, but the Third Circuit Reversed, arguing that direct evidence of the conspiracy created a genuine issue for trial. The Supreme Court granted certiorari.

■ **ISSUE**

May a judge draw an inference from the absence of a plausible motive upon a motion for summary judgment.

■ **DECISION AND RATIONALE**

(Judge Not Stated) Yes. When ruling on a summary judgment motion, a judge may consider the absence of a plausible motive to engage in the conduct at issue. In the case at hand, the Court of Appeals failed to consider that Matsushita (D) had no rational economic motive to engage in predatory pricing. If Matsushita (D) and the other Japanese firms had no motive to conspire, then the conduct does not give rise to an inference of conspiracy. Evidence in this case supported the inference that the Japanese firms did not have any rational motive to fix prices. In light of this absence of motive, neither Matsushita's (D) pricing practices, nor their agreements respecting prices in the Japanese or American markets, suffice to create a genuine issue for trial. Thus, summary judgment is proper. Reversed.

Analysis:

Once again, this case demonstrates the increasing willingness of the Supreme Court to liberalize the use of summary judgment. The Court holds that the judge considering a motion for summary judgment may consider the inferences to be drawn from the evidence. Upon finding that there was no rational basis for the Japanese firms to conspire, the court makes the inference that there was no conspiracy. Thus, the decision between competing inferences is not always for the jury. If one of the inferences—

e.g., that there was no conspiracy—is more plausible than the alternative, then the court may grant summary judgment. In a portion of the opinion not reproduced in the casebook, the Court held that only when a trier of fact is confronted with two equally plausible, competing inferences should summary judgment be denied. In light of this standard, the Court clearly reached a correct decision, since there is really only one rational inference from the fact that Matsushita (D) and the others had no motive to conspire—namely, that they did not conspire.

■ **CASE VOCABULARY**

PRICE FIXING: A violation of antitrust law in which several firms conspire to artificially set the prices of their products.

Link v. Wabash R. Co.

(*Injured Party*) v. (*Railroad*)
370 U.S. 626, 82 S.Ct. 1386 (1962)

RULE 41 DISMISSAL MAY BE MADE AT THE COURT'S DISCRETION WITHOUT NOTICE TO THE AGGRIEVED PARTY

■ **INSTANT FACTS** A party appeals the dismissal of his action based upon his attorney's failure to appear at a pretrial conference.

■ **BLACK LETTER RULE** Rule 41 empowers courts to dismiss actions without providing a prior adversary hearing.

■ **PROCEDURAL BASIS**

Writ of certiorari reviewing order affirming dismissal of negligence action for failure to prosecute.

■ **FACTS**

Link (P) and his attorney failed to attend a pretrial conference. The trial had been continued two times and was set for a date six years after the action had been commenced. The court *sua sponte* dismissed Link's (P) negligence action. Link (P) appealed on the ground that the dismissal was an overly harsh penalty for the misdeeds of Link's (P) attorney. The Seventh Circuit affirmed and the Supreme Court granted certiorari.

■ **ISSUE**

May a court dismiss a complaint for failure to prosecute even without affording notice of its intention to do so or providing an adversary hearing before acting?

■ **DECISION AND RATIONALE**

(Harlan, J.) Yes. A court may dismiss a complaint for failure to prosecute even without affording notice of its intention to do so or providing an adversary hearing before acting. Rule 41(b) allows a court to dismiss a complaint with prejudice because of the plaintiff's failure to prosecute. This sanction is necessary to prevent undue delays in the disposition of pending cases and to avoid congestion in the calendars of the District Courts. There is no merit to Link's (P) claim that dismissal of his claim because of his counsel's unexcused conduct imposes an unjust penalty on Link (P). Link (P) voluntarily chose this attorney, and he cannot now avoid the consequences of the acts or omissions of this freely selected agent. Any other notion would run contrary to our system of representative litigation, in which each party is deemed bound by the acts of his lawyer and is considered to have notice of all facts. Affirmed.

■ **DISSENT**

(Black, J.) It is unfair to impose such a harsh penalty as dismissal with prejudice upon Link (P) for the misconduct of his attorney. Numerous other sanctions are available that could have penalized Link's (P) attorney without barring forever Link's (P) right to recovery for his injuries.

Analysis:

This case summarizes the pros and cons of Rule 41 dismissal for failure to prosecute. Without question, at some point a case should be dismissed if a party and his attorney fail to take any steps to prosecute. The real issue is whether a party should be punished if his incompetent attorney forgets to attend a pretrial conference and/or forgets to take other steps to bring a case to trial. Justice Harlan's majority opinion certainly does appear somewhat harsh. A litigant who blindly trusts his attorney to follow the proper steps may suffer the ultimate penalty of being forever barred from recovering for his injuries. Should a plaintiff be required to closely monitor his attorney's actions? On one hand, this is an onerous burden for someone who probably has no idea about the procedural requirements of bringing a case to trial.

■ CASE VOCABULARY

DILATORINESS: Tending to cause delay; tardiness.

NON PROSEQUITUR: A judgment against a plaintiff for not taking required steps in an action.

NONSUIT: A termination of an action not based on the merits of the case.

WITH PREJUDICE: A binding action taken by a court, typically in the form of a dismissal, that does not allow the foreclosed party from taking any further steps.

Coulas v. Smith

(*Absent Defendant*) v. (*Present Claimant*)

96 Ariz. 325, 395 P.2d 527 (1964)

A DEFAULT JUDGMENT MAY NOT BE ENTERED AGAINST A DEFENDANT WHO HAS ANSWERED A COMPLAINT AND YET FAILS TO APPEAR AT TRIAL

■ **INSTANT FACTS** Coulas (D), who answered complaints yet failed to appear at trial, appealed the denial of his motion to set aside the subsequent adverse judgment.

■ **BLACK LETTER RULE** When a case is called for trial and is at issue, the failure of a defendant to appear does not warrant a default judgment against him.

■ **PROCEDURAL BASIS**

Appeal from denial of motion to set aside and vacate judgment for damages on open account and promissory note.

■ **FACTS**

Smith (P) filed a complaint against Coulas (D) and Bray (D) for money due on an open account and a promissory note. Coulas (D) and Bray (D) each answered the complaint and asserted various counterclaims and cross-claims. Each party responded to the applicable counterclaims and cross-claims. Although the original trial date was set for October 10, counsel for Smith (P) and Bray (D) stipulated at a hearing to continue the trial until December 10. Counsel for Coulas (D) were not present at this hearing, even though they were notified by the clerk, and Coulas (D) now denies ever receiving notice of the new trial date. Consequently, Coulas (D) did not appear at the trial, and judgments were entered against Coulas (D) on each applicable claim. [Shouldn't he have known something had changed when he showed up for trial on October 10?] Nearly two years later, Coulas (D) filed a motion to set aside and vacate the judgment, claiming the "default" judgment was void since he did not receive 3 days' notice. The trial court denied the motion, and Coulas (D) now appeals.

■ **ISSUE**

Is a default judgment proper once an answer on the merits has been filed by a defendant who subsequently fails to appear at trial?

■ **DECISION AND RATIONALE**

(Udall, J.) No. Once an answer on the merits has been filed and the case is at issue, default judgment may not be entered against a defendant who fails to appear at trial. Thus, in the case at hand, the judgment entered against Coulas (D) was not a default judgment. Rule 55 of the Arizona Rules of Civil Procedure [modeled after Rule 55 of the Federal Rules] allows for entry of default judgment only when a party has failed to plead or otherwise defend in the action. However, Coulas (D) *did* indeed defend in the action by answering the claims against him. If he had not answered the claims, then he would have been entitled to a 3-day notice prior to entry of default judgment, pursuant to Rule 55(b). However, in the situation at hand, the case was at issue at the time of trial and Smith (P) and Bray (D) bore the burden of proof with respect to their claims against Coulas (D). Thus, each of these parties were still required to prove their cases against Coulas (D), even though Coulas (D) was not represented at trial.

Both Smith (P) and Bray (D) met their burdens of proof. Coulas's (D) contention that he did not receive notice of the new trial date is not substantiated, since parties are presumed to have received notice by the clerk. In addition, if Coulas (D) did not receive notice of the new date, he certainly would have learned of the change when he appeared for trial on October 10. Moreover, Coulas (D) is precluded from attacking a judgment more than six months after it was entered. Affirmed.

Analysis:

This case is notable, first and foremost, for the incompetence demonstrated by Coulas (D) and his counsel. Certainly Coulas (D) is not a party for whom the court should have much sympathy. Although he answered the complaints and cross-claims, he did nothing else to warrant lenient treatment by the court. Even if Coulas (D) did indeed fail to receive notice of the continued trial date, he certainly should have known that the date had been changed if he appeared for the original October 10 trial. In all likelihood, either Coulas (D) or his attorney completely dropped the bail, failing to appear at the motion in which the trial date was continued, and failing to appear at either the October 10 or December 10 trial date. His efforts to vacate the adverse judgment, made nearly two years after the original trial, demonstrate a considerable lack of competence. Nevertheless, the irony of the holding bears some attention. If Coulas (D) had appeared in the action but failed to answer any of the pleadings, he would have been entitled to a 3-day notice prior to a default judgment. This appearance could have been a simple challenge on a procedural ground or an exchange of letters concerning settlement of the action. However, by answering the claims, he placed the case at issue and was required to appear at trial. The moral of this story is that a party should not file an answer unless that party is prepared to go to trial.

■ CASE VOCABULARY

AT ISSUE: The state of a case in which adverse parties have stated conflicting positions, such as when a defendant answers a complaint by denying the allegations.

CHAPTER FOURTEEN

Trial

Beacon Theatres, Inc. v. Westover

Instant Facts: Beacon Theatres (D) sought a jury determination of antitrust claims raised in response to equitable claims for declaratory judgment and injunction brought by Fox West Coast Theatres (P), the owner of an exclusive right to show first-run movies.

Black Letter Rule: A court may not deny a jury determination of factual issues through a prior determination of equitable claims.

Dairy Queen, Inc. v. Wood

Instant Facts: Dairy Queen (D) sought an injunction and damages for breach of contract when a licensee and franchise owner, Wood (P), failed to comply with the payment scheme. Wood (P) was denied a jury trial on grounds that the action was purely equitable.

Black Letter Rule: An action seeking money damages, even phrased in equitable terms, cannot be considered purely equitable.

Ross v. Bernhard

Instant Facts: Shareholders of a corporation, who brought a derivative suit against the board of directors, demanded a jury trial despite the traditionally equitable nature of the proceeding.

Black Letter Rule: A court may overcome procedural impediments, which traditionally precluded a jury trial, in order to grant a jury trial.

Curtis v. Loether

Instant Facts: Curtis (P), who sued for damages and injunctive relief for alleged discrimination in violation of Title VIII, challenges the Court of Appeals' grant of jury trial to this statutory action.

Black Letter Rule: The Seventh Amendment provides a right to jury trial for actions based on a statute that creates legal rights and remedies.

Katchen v. Landy

Instant Facts: Katchen (P), the holder of preferential payments received from a now-insolvent corporation, sought to have other bankruptcy claims adjudicated by a jury.

Black Letter Rule: Where a statutory scheme provides for prompt trial without jury intervention, a party's equitable claims may be tried prior to their legal claims, even if this will be dispositive of the legal issues.

Tull v. United States

Instant Facts: Tull (D), sued by the Government for alleged violations of the Clean Water Act, was denied a jury trial and appealed the decision.

Black Letter Rule: A statute may provide for jury trial by codifying common-law actions and also allow a judge to impose a remedy once liability is established.

Atlas Roofing Co. v. Occupational Safety & Health Review Commission

Instant Facts: Atlas Roofing Co. (D) objected to an administrative agency determining the facts of a suit in which Atlas (D) was cited for violations of the Occupational Safety and Health Act.

Black Letter Rule: Congress may assign the fact-finding function of adjudication of cases involving public rights to an administrative agency rather than to a jury.

Granfinanciera, S.A. v. Nordberg

Instant Facts: Granfinanciera (D), sued by a bankruptcy trustee to recover allegedly fraudulent transfers, was denied a jury trial on grounds that such actions were merely adjudications of public rights.

Black Letter Rule: The "public right" exception does not allow Congress to reclassify traditionally legal claims in order to deny the right to jury trial.

Chauffeurs, Teamsters and Helpers Local 391 v. Terry

Instant Facts: Several employees sued their union, the Chauffeurs, Teamsters and Helpers Local 391 (D), for alleged violations of the Union's duty of fair representation. Against the Union's protest that the claim was equitable in nature, the District Court and Appellate Court granted a right to jury trial.

Black Letter Rule: An action for breach of fair representation, although analogous to equitable claims at common law, carries a right to jury trial.

Markman v. Westview Instruments, Inc.

Instant Facts: A patent holder sued a corporation, alleging a violation of his patent for a dry-cleaning inventory tracking system.

Black Letter Rule: The construction of a patent is a legal question to be decided by a judge rather than by a jury.

Colgrove v. Battin

Instant Facts: A party to a civil action challenges a local district court rule that allows six-member juries in civil trials.

Black Letter Rule: Courts may adopt rules limiting juries to six members in civil trials without violating the Seventh Amendment.

Flowers v. Flowers

Instant Facts: Attorneys for Billie Flowers (P), a mother who occasionally consumed alcohol to excess, moved for a new trial on grounds that a prospective juror, who demonstrated a reprehension for all drinking, should have been dismissed.

Black Letter Rule: A prospective juror who demonstrates bias or prejudice towards the litigants or subject matter of the action should be excluded from the jury pool.

Edmonson v. Leesville Concrete Company, Inc.

Instant Facts: Thaddeus Edmonson (P), injured when a truck owned by Leesville Concrete (D) smashed into him, appealed a judgment after Leesville (D) used two peremptory challenges to exclude black jurors.

Black Letter Rule: Peremptory challenges may not be used to exclude jurors on account of their race.

Galloway v. United States

Instant Facts: Galloway (P) sought benefits resulting from his total mental disability, presenting evidence of his insanity for several periods but demonstrating no evidence for a several-year interval.

Black Letter Rule: A directed verdict is proper where juries would have to make inferences and bridge large gaps in testimony, and this verdict does not violate the Seventh Amendment.

Neely v. Martin K. Eby Construction Co.

Instant Facts: Neely (D) brought an action for wrongful death, alleging negligence on the part of a construction company, and obtained a jury verdict that was overturned on appeal.

Black Letter Rule: An appellate court may reverse the denial of a judgment notwithstanding the verdict, and the court does not have to order a new trial.

Denman v. Spain

Instant Facts: Betty Denman (P) sued the executrix of the estate of Joseph Ross, who allegedly caused an accident on a foggy day by negligently operating his vehicle.

Black Letter Rule: A judgment n.o.v. may be entered against a party who fails to meet her burden of proof.

Rogers v. Missouri Pacific R. Co.

Instant Facts: Rogers (P), a railroad worker assigned to burn off vegetation alongside a railroad, sued Missouri Pacific (D) for injuries resulting in the course of his duties.

Black Letter Rule: A statutory action must go to the jury if the evidence is sufficient to meet the statutory burden of proof.

Reeves v. Sanderson Plumbing Products, Inc.

Instant Facts: A fired employee sued under the ADEA and argued that the employer's allegations that he failed to keep accurate attendance records were just a cover-up up for age discrimination.

Black Letter Rule: A discrimination plaintiff's case may be sufficient to submit to the jury if it consists of a prima facie case of discrimination and sufficient evidence that the defendant's proffered explanation for its action was merely a pretext for discrimination, without the need for additional, independent evidence of discrimination.

Baltimore & Carolina Line, Inc. v. Redman

Instant Facts: In reviewing the denial of Baltimore & Carolina's (D) motion for directed verdict, the appellate court reversed the denial but ordered a new trial rather than entering a judgment for Baltimore & Carolina (D).

Black Letter Rule: When reversing the denial of a directed verdict, an appellate court does not necessarily have to order a new trial, but it may enter a judgment in favor of the party who brought the original directed verdict.

Kennedy v. Southern California Edison Co.

Instant Facts: After a jury found against him, a husband who had brought a wrongful death action against a nuclear power plant owner for the death of his wife from radiation exposure appealed, arguing that the trial court had erroneously refused to instruct the jury according to the husband's proposed jury instruction on the burden of proof for causation.

Black Letter Rule: Where a trial court is presented with a proposed jury instruction that raises an important issue of law or directs the court's attention to a point on which an instruction to the jury would be appropriate, the court is not relieved from the responsibility of giving a proper instruction simply because the proposed instruction does not completely comply with the relevant law.

Nunley v. Pettway Oil Co.

Instant Facts: In Nunley's (P) action for damages resulting from a truck falling off a grease rack in a gas station, the judge opined to the jury that Nunley was a licensee rather than an invitee.

Black Letter Rule: Judges must refrain from providing their opinions to the jury with regard to ultimate facts of the case.

Securities and Exchange Commission v. Koenig

Instant Facts: The SEC penalized the CFO of Waste Management, and he appealed from the decision, arguing that the judge should not have been allowed to ask questions of the witnesses that were submitted by the jury.

Black Letter Rule: Just as questions from the bench can provide insight that helps lawyers make a stronger case, so too can questions from the jury help lawyers tailor their presentations.

Nollenberger v. United Air Lines, Inc.

Instant Facts: In a wrongful death action, a jury returned a general verdict for Nollenberger (P) accompanied by answers to special interrogatories, but Nollenberger (P) argued that the award was inconsistent with the answers.

Black Letter Rule: After a jury has returned a general verdict and answered special interrogatories, the court may not submit additional interrogatories but may recalculate the damage award based on the answers.

Roberts v. Ross

Instant Facts: In an action for payment of an agency fee, the trial judge accepted counsel's proposed findings of fact and conclusions of law as his own in entering a verdict.

Black Letter Rule: A trial judge in a non-jury trial should formulate his own findings of fact and conclusions of law in entering a judgment.

Ginsberg v. Williams

Instant Facts: After a jury verdict for Williams (D), the trial judge granted a new trial based on "the interests of justice," and Williams (D) sought a writ of prohibition since this was a non-enumerated reason for new trial.

Black Letter Rule: A state trial judge may grant a new trial only for reasons enumerated by the applicable state rules.

Magnani v. Trogi

Instant Facts: After the jury returned a verdict for Magnani (P) for $19,000 on one or both of her causes of action, the trial court granted Trogi's (D) motion for new trial based on the incomplete nature of the jury verdict.

Black Letter Rule: A trial judge may grant a new trial where a jury verdict is incoherent or not sufficiently detailed.

Robb v. John C. Hickey, Inc.

Instant Facts: In an action based on negligence and contributory negligence, the jury held that the decedent, represented by Robb (P), was partially negligent but nevertheless suggested $2000 in damages for Robb (P), in conflict with the stated law. Both parties contested the verdict.

Black Letter Rule: A judge may mold an incoherent jury verdict to coincide with the substance of the jury's declaration only if the verdict clearly expresses the intent of the jury.

Duk v. MGM Grand Hotel, Inc.

Instant Facts: Hotel security staff took an unruly Duk (P) into custody on the premises; Duk (P) suffered a heart attack while in hotel custody and later sued the hotel, but the jury returned inconsistent verdicts, so both parties appealed.

Black Letter Rule: Where the jury is still available, a district court's decision to resubmit an inconsistent verdict for clarification is within its discretion.

Hukle v. Kimble

Instant Facts: Following a quotient verdict in favor of Hukle (P) for damages, Kimble (D) appeals the denial of his motion for retrial on grounds of jury misconduct.

Black Letter Rule: The use of quotient verdicts may constitute jury misconduct.

McDonough Power Equipment, Inc. v. Greenwood

Instant Facts: In an action for damages caused by a power mower, Greenwood (P) moved for a new trial on the basis of newly-discovered information that a juror had incorrectly answered a question on voir dire.

Black Letter Rule: A mistaken response on voir dire constitutes juror misconduct only if the question was material and if a correct response would have provided a valid basis for challenging for cause.

Aetna Casualty & Surety Co. v. Yeatts

Instant Facts: In response to an adverse jury verdict on its action for declaratory relief, Aetna Casualty (D) moved for a new trial or judgment n.o.v., but the judge denied both motions.

Black Letter Rule: Trial judges may grant or deny new trials under circumstances which would prevent judgments n.o.v. or directed verdicts.

Fisch v. Manger

Instant Facts: Following a jury verdict in his favor for $3000, Fisch (P) objected to the court's use of additur, by which the decision to deny Fisch's (P) motion for new trial was made conditional on Manger's (D) acceptance of an increased damages award.

Black Letter Rule: A court may employ the practice of additur without violating the constitutional right to a jury trial.

Powers v. Allstate Ins. Co.

Instant Facts: In response to an excessive award of $5000 of damages to Powers (P), the Wisconsin Supreme Court is asked to review the amount at which remittitur is set.

Black Letter Rule: The trial or appellate court can set the reasonable amount for remittitur.

Doutre v. Niec

Instant Facts: Doutre (P) sued Niec (D) for injuries suffered in the course of a hair bleach and color treatment, and both parties appeal to a judgment for a new trial on the issue of liability alone.

Black Letter Rule: The issue of liability should not be retried without a reconsideration of the amount of damages.

Hulson v. Atchison, Topeka & Santa Fe Ry.

Instant Facts: Hulson (P) and Christensen (P), injured while working in a postal railroad car, sought relief under Rule 60(b) from failure to timely file motions for new trial and for judgment n.o.v.

Black Letter Rule: Relief from judgment under Rule 60(b)(1) is allowed only in exceptional circumstances, and these must be specifically noted in the motion for relief.

Briones v. Riviera Hotel & Casino

Instant Facts: When his wrongful termination suit was dismissed for failure to respond to his former employer's motion to dismiss, an employee moved to set aside the judgment dismissing the case, asserting that his failure to respond had constituted excusable neglect under Rule 60(b)(1) of the Federal Rules of Civil Procedure.

Black Letter Rule: Under certain circumstances, the negligent failure to file a response to a motion to dismiss can be excusable sufficient to justify the setting aside of a judgment under Rule 60(b)(1) of the Federal Rules of Civil Procedure.

Patrick v. Sedwick

Instant Facts: A doctor appealed a judgment of damages for medical malpractice alleging that a new medical treatment, discovered after a judgment of liability had been entered in the case, that would benefit the suing patient's injuries should have been taken into account to reduce the damages owed.

Black Letter Rule: In order to constitute valid grounds for granting a motion for a new trial, "newly discovered" evidence must have been in existence at the time of the trial of the case under review.

Marcelli v. Walker

Instant Facts: After a voluntary consent to dismiss his cause of action was entered, Marcelli (P) attempted to reopen the case, but the court denied his request.

Black Letter Rule: The elements of a Rule 60(d) cause of action include (1) a judgment that, in equity and good conscience, ought not be enforced; (2) a good defense to the cause of action on which the judgment is founded; (3) fraud, accident, or mistake that prevented the movant from obtaining the benefit of a defense to the underlying judgment; (4) the absence of fault or negligence on the movant's part; and (5) the absence of an adequate remedy at law.

Beacon Theatres, Inc. v. Westover

(Movie Exhibitor) v. (District Court Judge)

359 U.S. 500, 79 S.Ct. 948 (1959)

A PRIOR DETERMINATION OF EQUITABLE CLAIMS MAY NOT BE USED TO DEPRIVE A RIGHT TO JURY TRIAL ON LEGAL ISSUES

■ **INSTANT FACTS** Beacon Theatres (D) sought a jury determination of antitrust claims raised in response to equitable claims for declaratory judgment and injunction brought by Fox West Coast Theatres (P), the owner of an exclusive right to show first-run movies.

■ **BLACK LETTER RULE** A court may not deny a jury determination of factual issues through a prior determination of equitable claims.

■ **PROCEDURAL BASIS**

Writ of certiorari reviewing refusal of writ of mandamus seeking vacatur of order precluding jury trial on claims for declaratory judgment and injunction and counterclaims for treble damages for antitrust violations.

■ **FACTS**

Fox West Coast Theatres (Fox) (P), the operator of a movie theater in San Bernardino, contracted with movie distributors to have the exclusive right to show "first run" pictures in the San Bernardino competitive area. In addition, the contracts provided for a "clearance" period in which only Fox could exhibit these pictures. Beacon Theatres, Inc. (D) constructed a drive-in theater 11 miles from San Bernardino, and thereafter Beacon (D) notified Fox (P) that it considered its exclusive-rights contract to violate the antitrust laws. Fox (P) brought an action for declaratory relief against Beacon (D), seeking a declaration that the clearance contract was not in violation of antitrust laws. Further, pending the outcome of the litigation, Fox (P) sought an injunction to prevent Beacon (D) from instituting any action under the antitrust laws against Fox (P) and its distributors. Beacon (D) answered this complaint and counterclaimed against Fox (P) for the alleged conspiracy in violation of antitrust laws. Beacon (D) sought treble damages for Fox's (P) alleged violation, and Beacon (D) demanded a jury trial of the factual issues as provided by Federal Rule of Civil Procedure 38(b). However, the District Court viewed Fox's (P) action as essentially equitable. Thus, the Court directed the issues to be tried before the court prior to a jury determination of the validity of the antitrust allegations. Beacon (D) then sought by mandamus to require the district judge to vacate this order. The Court of Appeals for the Ninth Circuit refused the writ, holding that the district judge acted within his proper discretion in denying Beacon's (D) request for a jury trial. The Supreme Court granted certiorari.

■ **ISSUE**

May a district court deny the right to a jury trial for factual issues through a prior determination of equitable claims?

■ **DECISION AND RATIONALE**

(Black, J.) No. A district court may not deny the right to a jury trial for factual issues through a prior determination of equitable claims. In the case at hand, a common issue between Fox's (P) claim for declaratory relief and Beacon's (D) counterclaims for antitrust violations was the reasonableness of the clearances granted to Fox (P). Thus, the effect of the District Court's order requiring the court, rather than a jury, to determine these issues would be to limit Beacon's (D) opportunity to fully try before a jury every issue which has a bearing upon its antitrust claims, since a determination of the clearance issue by the judge might operate by res judicata or collateral estoppel to conclude the parties with respect to the antitrust claims. Beacon (D) would have been entitled to a jury trial in a treble damage antitrust suit against Fox (P), and it cannot be deprived of that right merely because Fox (P) took advantage of the availability of declaratory relief to sue Beacon (D) first. The Court of Appeals reasoned that Fox (P) brought an equitable claim for injunctive relief, and a party who is entitled to maintain a suit in equity for an injunction may have all the issues in his suit determined by the judge regardless of whether legal rights are involved. Indeed, certain cases have traditionally justified equity to take jurisdiction and settle the case in one suit. However, under the modern Declaratory Judgment Act and the Federal Rules, this cannot justify denying Beacon (D) a trial by jury of all the issues in the antitrust controversy. Under the Federal Rules, a court may try both legal and equitable causes in the same action. If Fox (P) properly demonstrated that Beacon (D) had threatened or had brought other suits, these suits could be temporarily enjoined pending the outcome of this litigation. In this way, the issues could be settled in one suit giving Beacon (D) a full jury trial of every antitrust issue. By contrast, the Court of Appeals' decision would compel Beacon (D) to split his antitrust case, trying part to a judge and part to a jury. Such a result, which subordinates the antitrust claims that Beacon (D) was required to bring under the Federal Rules, is not permissible. The plan of the Federal Rules is to retain a distinction between jury and nonjury issues, but the liberal joinder provisions of the Rules cause us to reconsider the traditional role of equity courts to decide all issues. In order to protect Fox (P), the court must use its discretion in order to decide whether the legal or equitable issues should be tried first. However, the constitutional right to jury trial must be protected. We cannot anticipate any circumstances in which the right to a jury trial of legal issues should be lost through a prior determination of equitable claims. Reversed.

■ DISSENT

(Stewart, J.) The availability of an action for declaratory judgment should not deprive a court of equity of the power to act. Rather, when declaratory relief is sought, the right to trial by jury depends on the basic context in which the issues are presented. In the case at hand, if Fox (P) had merely asked for a judgment declaring that Fox's (P) business dealings did not render it liable to Beacon (D) under antitrust laws, then this would have been a simple "juxtaposition of parties" and Beacon (D) could have demanded a jury trial. However, the complaint presented issues cognizable solely in equity, going beyond a mere defense to legal actions. The availability of a declaratory judgment did not, therefore, confer Beacon (D) a right to jury trial with respect to these equitable issues. The majority departs from long-settled principles in holding that, because it is possible to assert a counterclaim involving legal issues, the original claim for equitable relief must be tried by a jury. Pursuant to Rule 42(b), a trial judge retains the power to determine whether equitable claims should be heard prior to legal claims. Thus, the District Court's order requiring the equitable claims to be decided first, by the court, was valid and the petition for writ of mandamus should have been dismissed.

Analysis:

In order to fully understand the rationale of this case, it is important to recognize the distinction between legal and equitable claims and the relation to a right to jury trial. Traditionally, claims brought in equity (such as injunctions) could be determined exclusively by the court, so no right to a jury trial attached. However, modern causes of actions complicate this notion, since parties now bring both legal and equitable claims in the same case. If the claim is primarily equitable, the "clean-up" doctrine allows courts sitting in equity to decide any incidental legal issues that arise in the course of the litigation. This case presents a more complicated scenario, in which purely (or at least primarily) equitable claims are opposed by purely legal counterclaims. Should the party bringing the original equitable claim be entitled to a non-jury determination, or should the opposing party be entitled to a jury trial? According to the majority, the constitutional right to a jury trial supersedes any rights in equity to avoid trial by jury. While the majority acknowledges that courts retain the discretion to bifurcate the separate determinations, deciding some equitable claims prior to legal claims, it opines that this should never operate to deny the right to jury trial on factual issues. Indeed, it is nearly impossible to imagine a case, in which legal counterclaims are entered in opposition to equitable claims, where the equitable claims should be tried first, since any original determination of the equitable claims would surely involve a factual determination of certain legal issues. In terms of the case at hand, any resolution of Fox's (P) claims for declaratory relief and injunction necessarily would require an analysis of the underlying antitrust issues raised by Beacon's (D) counterclaims. It makes sense to allow Beacon (D) to submit the factual issues to a jury. Further, it is unlikely that this would cause any great prejudice to Fox (P), as the majority notes. Nevertheless, the dissent raises some interesting points. It certainly appears that the majority is undermining Rule 42(b)'s grant of discretion to a trial judge, since the situations in which an equitable claim could be tried first are probably nonexistent.

■ CASE VOCABULARY

BILL OF PEACE: Common law equitable remedy filed by a party with rights that could be controverted by other persons.

QUIA TIMET: Equitable bill filed by a party seeking judicial assistance because he fears some future injury.

Dairy Queen, Inc. v. Wood

(Trademark Holder) v. *(Licensee)*

369 U.S. 469, 82 S.Ct. 894 (1962)

A JURY TRIAL CANNOT BE AVOIDED BY CASTING LEGAL ISSUES IN TERMS OF EQUITABLE RELIEF

■ **INSTANT FACTS** Dairy Queen (D) sought an injunction and damages for breach of contract when a licensee and franchise owner, Wood (P), failed to comply with the payment scheme. Wood (P) was denied a jury trial on grounds that the action was purely equitable.

■ **BLACK LETTER RULE** An action seeking money damages, even phrased in equitable terms, cannot be considered purely equitable.

■ **PROCEDURAL BASIS**

Writ of certiorari reviewing dismissal of writ of mandamus seeking vacatur of order to strike demand for jury trial for claims seeking injunctions and an accounting for breach of contract.

■ **FACTS**

This suit arose out of a licensing agreement between Dairy Queen, Inc. (P) and Wood (D), under which Wood (D) agreed to pay for the use of Dairy Queen's (P) trademark in certain parts of Pennsylvania. When Wood (D) allegedly defaulted on the contract's payment provisions, Dairy Queen (P) wrote a letter claiming that Wood (D) had materially breached the contract. However, Wood (D) continued to use the trademark, and Dairy Queen (P) brought an action for breach of contract seeking the following: temporary and permanent injunctions against Wood's (D) use of the trademark; an accounting to determine the amount owed by Wood (D) and a judgment for that amount; and a temporary injunction pending an accounting to prevent Wood's (D) collection from any Dairy Queen stores. The Eastern District of Pennsylvania granted Dairy Queen's (P) motion to strike Wood's (D) demand for a jury trial on the grounds that either the action was purely equitable or that the legal issues were incidental to the equitable issues. Wood (D) sought a writ of mandamus for vacatur of this order, but the Third Circuit denied the writ. The Supreme Court granted certiorari.

■ **ISSUE**

Can an action seeking money damages be considered purely equitable?

■ **DECISION AND RATIONALE**

(Judge Not Stated) No. An action seeking money damages cannot be considered purely equitable, for which no right to jury trial exists. Dairy Queen's (P) request for damages can be considered either an action for debt allegedly due under a contract or an action for damages based on trademark infringement. Both of these actions are cognizable by a court of law, and hence a jury trial for them is appropriate. The mere fact that Dairy Queen (P) cast their claim in terms of an accounting rather than an action for debt cannot alter Wood's (D) constitutional right to trial by jury. As we pointed out in *Beacon Theatres v. Westover* [a court may not deny a jury determination of factual issues through a prior determination of equitable claims], the prerequisite to a suit for equitable accounting is the absence of an adequate remedy at law. In order to maintain such a suit on a cause of action cognizable at law, such as this one, Dairy Queen (P) must be able to show that the accounts are so complicated that only a court of equity can satisfactorily unravel them. However, Rule 53(b) gives district courts the power to appoint masters to assist the jury in the exceptional cases where the legal issues are too complicated for the jury to handle alone. In the case at hand, the jury could determine the recovery under the breach of contract or trademark infringement claims with the proper assistance. Furthermore, even if the legal claims in this case are considered purely incidental to the equitable claims, *Beacon Theatres* requires that any legal issues be submitted to a jury. Reversed.

Analysis:

This case continues the *Beacon Theatres* trend towards a liberal application of the right to jury trial. Even when claims are raised which appear purely equitable, a court may scrutinize the claims for any potential legal aspects. Thus, a party is precluded from making their claims purely equitable simply by phrasing the prayer for relief in terms of equitable remedies. This makes sense. If Dairy Queen (P) was seeking damages for any of Wood's (D) actions, then the claims should be treated as legal and a right to jury trial should attach. Dairy Queen (P) cannot maintain that the legal issues are merely incidental to the equitable ones, since *Beacon Theatres* clearly held that any legal issues should be submitted to a jury, even where the equitable issues predominate. It is interesting to note the Court's reference to the potentially complicated nature of the claims. Apparently, if claims are sufficiently complicated so as to hinder a jury from reaching a conclusion, then the claims may be treated as equitable and no right to a jury trial will attach. However, this scenario would probably arise very infrequently. The Court notes that judges should go out of their way, e.g. by appointing masters to assist the jury, in order to maintain the important right to jury trial.

■ CASE VOCABULARY

ACCOUNTING: An equitable action to provide details of an account, typically in order to recover profits improperly taken.

Ross v. Bernhard

(*Corporate Shareholder*) v. (*Not Stated*)
396 U.S. 531, 90 S.Ct. 733 (1970)

TRADITIONALLY EQUITABLE PROCEEDINGS FALL TO THE REVISED RULES, LIBERALLY ALLOWING JURY TRIALS

■ **INSTANT FACTS** Shareholders of a corporation, who brought a derivative suit against the board of directors, demanded a jury trial despite the traditionally equitable nature of the proceeding.

■ **BLACK LETTER RULE** A court may overcome procedural impediments, which traditionally precluded a jury trial, in order to grant a jury trial.

■ **PROCEDURAL BASIS**

Writ of certiorari reviewing reversal of grant of jury trial in shareholder's derivative action for damages.

■ **FACTS**

Ross (P) and other shareholders (P) brought a derivative suit against the directors of an investment company and the brokers, alleging that the company had been charged excessive brokerage fees. The trial court granted the shareholders' (P) demand for jury trial. However, the Second Circuit Court of Appeals set aside this grant, since at common law a derivative action was purely an equitable proceeding warranting no right to a jury trial. The Supreme Court granted certiorari.

■ **ISSUE**

May a court overcome procedural impediments and grant a jury trial for a traditionally equitable proceeding?

■ **DECISION AND RATIONALE**

(Justice Not Stated) Yes. In some situations, a court may overcome procedural impediments and grant a jury trial for a traditionally equitable proceeding. Stockholders derivative suits were traditionally equitable in nature. A derivative suit involves two components. First, stockholders must have the right to sue on behalf of their corporation for a claim that the corporation had refused to proceed with. Second, the merits of the corporation's claim itself must be considered. In the case at hand, the corporation has a legal claim against its directors and third parties, including the company's brokers. Because the heart of the action is a corporate claim that presents a legal issue, the right to jury trial is not forfeited merely because the stockholder's right to sue must first be adjudicated as an equitable issue triable to the court. The modern Rules provide for only one form of action, departing from the traditional division of legal and equitable claims. The Rules intended to destroy purely procedural impediments to the presentation of any issue. In the derivative suit context, the original hurdle requiring a court to determine whether the stockholders can bring the action is purely procedural. After passing upon this right to sue, the claim for damages becomes triable with the aid of a jury. Reversed.

■ **DISSENT**

(Stewart, J.) There is no constitutional right to trial by jury for shareholder's derivative lawsuits which, the court concedes, could traditionally be brought only in equity. The Court's reliance on *Beacon*

Theatres v. Westover [a court may not deny a jury determination of factual issues through a prior determination of equitable claims] and *Dairy Queen v. Wood* [an action seeking money damages, even phrased in equitable terms, cannot be considered purely equitable] is misplaced. The present case does not involve traditionally equitable claims by one party and traditionally legal claims by the other. Nor is it a suit in which Ross (P) is asserting a combination of legal and equitable claims. Rather, it is purely an equitable cause of action, and the historical significance of this action should not be cavalierly dismissed.

Analysis:

Once again, the Supreme Court takes great strides to preserve the important right to trial by jury. The majority demonstrates a willingness to depart from long-established distinctions of law and equity, justifying its position by reference to the modern Federal Rules. According to the majority, the revised Rules intended to eliminate all procedural impediments to jury trial by recognizing only one form of action, a "civil action." Thus, the court finds that the equitable nature of a derivative proceeding is purely a "procedural impediment" which can be easily overcome, allowing a jury to decide the more important legal issues. However, Justice Stewart's dissent astutely notes the shortcomings of the majority's approach. By dividing the traditionally-equitable shareholder's derivative suit into two components (a procedural hurdle and a legal claim), the Court is able to sidetrack the traditional nature of an equitable proceeding. Indeed, as Stewart mentions, in nearly every equitable cause of action there exists some hidden legal claim.

■ CASE VOCABULARY

DERIVATIVE SUIT: A lawsuit brought by corporate shareholders on behalf of the corporation, raising claims that the corporation could have, but declined to, bring to trial.

Curtis v. Loether

(Prospective Tenant) v. *(Prospective Landlord)*

415 U.S. 189, 94 S.Ct. 1005 (1974)

THE SEVENTH AMENDMENT RIGHT TO JURY TRIAL APPLIES TO STATUTORY ACTIONS ENFORCING LEGAL RIGHTS TO DAMAGES

■ **INSTANT FACTS** Curtis (P), who sued for damages and injunctive relief for alleged discrimination in violation of Title VIII, challenges the Court of Appeals' grant of jury trial to this statutory action.

■ **BLACK LETTER RULE** The Seventh Amendment provides a right to jury trial for actions based on a statute that creates legal rights and remedies.

■ **PROCEDURAL BASIS**

Writ of certiorari reviewing reversal of denial of jury trial for action for damages and injunctive relief for discrimination claims based on Title VIII.

■ **FACTS**

Curtis (P), a black woman, brought an action under Section 812 of the Civil Rights Act of 1968 to redress violations of Title VIII (the fair housing provisions of the Act). Alleging that Loether (D) refused to rent an apartment to Curtis (P) because of her race, Curtis (P) sought injunctive relief as well as compensatory and punitive damages. The District Court granted a preliminary injunction, enjoining Loether (D) from renting the apartment to anyone else pending a trial on the merits [pretty steep penalty before trial!]. The injunction was subsequently dissolved with Curtis's (P) consent, and the case went to trial on the issues of damages. Although Loether (D) made a demand for a jury trial, the District Court denied the request. At a trial on the merits, the District Judge awarded $250 in punitive damages to Curtis (P). The Court of Appeals reversed on the jury issue, and the Supreme Court granted certiorari.

■ **ISSUE**

Does the Seventh Amendment's right to jury trial apply to actions based on a statute that creates legal rights and remedies?

■ **DECISION AND RATIONALE**

(Marshall, J.) Yes. The Seventh Amendment's right to jury trial applies to actions enforcing statutory rights, and a jury trial is available if the statute creates legal rights and remedies enforceable in an action for damages in the courts of law. Curtis's (P) damages action under § 812 is an action to enforce legal rights within the meaning of the Seventh Amendment and, hence, a jury trial must be available. Curtis (P) argues that the Seventh Amendment is inapplicable to causes of action created by Congress. However, we have often found the Seventh Amendment applicable to causes of action based on statutes. Curtis (P) relies upon *NLRB v. Jones & Laughlin Steel Corp.* [Jury trial not available in NLRB unfair labor practice proceeding, because case involved a statutory proceeding and not a suit at common law]. This case is distinguishable, as *Jones & Laughlin* merely held that the Seventh Amendment is generally applicable in administrative proceedings, where jury trials would be incompatible with the concept of administrative adjudication. Further, *Katchen v. Landy* [where a statutory scheme provides for prompt trial without jury intervention, a party's equitable claims may be tried prior to their legal claims, even if this will be dispositive of the legal issues] can be distinguished, since a jury trial in bankruptcy proceedings would dismember the statutory scheme of the Bankruptcy Act. In the case at hand, Congress expressly provided for the enforcement of statutory rights under Title VIII in an ordinary civil action in the district courts. Even though certain Title VII cases have been characterized as "equitable," there is no basis for characterizing the award of damages under Title VIII as equitable relief. While we realize that jury trials may prejudice a victim of discrimination, we feel that the trial judge's power to direct a verdict, to grant a judgment notwithstanding the verdict, or to grant a new trial, protects victims against this risk. Any considerations of prejudice are insufficient to overcome the clear command of the Seventh Amendment. Affirmed.

Analysis:

This is the first case in this chapter that specifically addresses the seemingly narrow language of the Seventh Amendment. By a plain reading of the Amendment, it appears that the right to jury trials extends only to suits at common law. However, the Court easily overcomes this obstacle, noting that the constitutional right to jury trials for causes of action based on statutes is "a matter too obvious to be doubted." The Court then takes this liberal reading of the Seventh Amendment one step further. Although the Court recognizes that a victim of discrimination could be deprived of a well-deserved verdict based on jury prejudice, it states that "these considerations are insufficient to overcome the clear command of the Seventh Amendment." Where does the Seventh Amendment state this command? Surely not in the text of the Amendment, which refers only to suits at common law. Thus, this opinion may be criticized for an overly broad reading of the Seventh Amendment.

■ CASE VOCABULARY

ADMINISTRATIVE PROCEEDINGS: Actions before certain governmental bodies that implement particular legislation, as opposed to judicial proceedings before a court.

JUDGMENT NOTWITHSTANDING THE VERDICT: A judgment entered by court order even though a prior verdict was entered in favor of the opponent.

Katchen v. Landy

(Claimant) v. *(Bankruptcy Trustee)*
382 U.S. 323, 86 S.Ct. 467 (1966)

EQUITABLE ISSUES MAY BE TRIED PRIOR TO LEGAL ISSUES WHERE A SPECIFIC STATUTORY SCHEME SO PROVIDES

■ **INSTANT FACTS** Katchen (P), the holder of preferential payments received from a now-insolvent corporation, sought to have other bankruptcy claims adjudicated by a jury.

■ **BLACK LETTER RULE** Where a statutory scheme provides for prompt trial without jury intervention, a party's equitable claims may be tried prior to their legal claims, even if this will be dispositive of the legal issues.

■ **PROCEDURAL BASIS**

Writ of certiorari reviewing affirmance of non-jury judgment for preferences and bankruptcy claims.

■ **FACTS**

Katchen (P) filed two claims in bankruptcy for sums due from an insolvent corporation. The bankruptcy trustee asserted that certain payments from the corporation to Katchen (P) were voidable preferences and, as such, could be recouped by the trustee in summary bankruptcy proceedings. Katchen (P) argued that a creditor who has received a preference can hold the property and force the trustee to recover the preference by a plenary action. In such a plenary action, the creditor could demand a jury trial. Katchen (P) maintained that the right to a jury trial is the same when a creditor files a claim and the trustee objects to the claim and demands surrender of the preference. Judgment was entered for the trustee on the preferences, and it was ordered that Katchen's (P) claims remain unpaid until after the judgment had been satisfied. The Tenth Circuit affirmed, and the Supreme Court granted certiorari.

■ **ISSUE**

May the right to jury trial be foreclosed by a specific statutory scheme contemplating a prompt trial without the intervention of a jury?

■ **DECISION AND RATIONALE**

(Judge Not Stated) Yes. The right to a jury trial may be foreclosed by a specific statutory scheme contemplating a prompt trial without the intervention of a jury. In the case at hand, the Bankruptcy Act governs the resolution of Katchen's (P) disputes. The Bankruptcy Act does confer summary jurisdiction allowing a court to compel a claimant to surrender preferences. Further, the Act converts any creditor's legal claim into an equitable claim for a pro rata share of the res. Thus, proceedings of bankruptcy courts are inherently proceedings in equity, and there is no Seventh Amendment right to a jury trial for determination of objections to claims. Katchen (P) argues that the determination of whether he received a preference may be presented either as equitable issues in bankruptcy court or as legal issues in a plenary suit. Consequently, according to Katchen (P), *Beacon Theatres v. Westover* [a court may not deny a jury determination of factual issues through a prior determination of equitable claims] and *Dairy Queen v. Wood* [an action seeking money damages, even phrased in equitable terms, cannot be considered purely equitable] require a bankruptcy court to stay its own proceedings and direct the bankruptcy trustee to commence a plenary suit so as to preserve Katchen's (P) right to a jury trial. However, this would require the suspension of bankruptcy proceedings whenever a preference was at issue, causing great delay and expense in an otherwise summary procedure. This result is unwarranted, as neither *Beacon Theatres* nor *Dairy Queen* involved a specific statutory scheme contemplating the prompt trial of a disputed claim without the intervention of a jury. As both *Beacon Theatres* and *Dairy Queen* recognized, there are situations in which a Court may resolve the equitable claim first even though the results might be dispositive of the issues involved in the legal claim.

Analysis:

This case presents an example of the unique situation that the Court in *Beacon Theatres* mentioned could infrequently occur, but that they could not anticipate—namely, a situation calling for the resolution of equitable issues first, without a jury trial, even though their resolution might be dispositive of legal issues. Katchen (P) is stuck in a difficult position. On one hand, Katchen (P) could have held the preferential payments as an adverse claimant, forcing the bankruptcy trustee to bring a plenary action for which jury trial is appropriate. On the other hand, because Katchen (P) still has additional claims against the insolvent corporation, he desired to file the claims in the bankruptcy proceeding. By filing these claims, Katchen (P) thought he would be able to maintain his right to jury trial, since he possessed preference payments for which a jury trial is appropriate. However, the unique statutory scheme governing bankruptcy proceedings warrants a different result. The Court reaches a sensible conclusion in holding that claimants should not be allowed to delay the otherwise summary nature of bankruptcy proceedings by demanding jury trials for their claims. Nevertheless, the holding may be questioned as unnecessarily infringing upon Katchen's (P) constitutional right to a jury trial. If he simply held the preferences and did not file a claim, the bankruptcy trustee would have to go after the money in a plenary proceeding tried by a jury. Why should the result change substantially simply because Katchen (P) desires to pursue his legally-acceptable right to recover other payments?

■ CASE VOCABULARY

PLENARY ACTION: A complete trial on the merits, rather than a summary proceeding.

PREFERENCE PAYMENT: The payment of money from an insolvent entity to a creditor, operating to the detriment of other creditors.

RES: The subject matter of an action, in this case referring to the total amount of funds out of which the creditors are to be paid in the bankruptcy proceeding.

Tull v. United States

(*Landowner*) v. (*Government*)
481 U.S. 412, 107 S.Ct. 1831 (1987)

A JURY MAY DETERMINE LIABILITY UNDER STATUTES CODIFYING COMMON-LAW RIGHTS, AND A JUDGE MAY IMPOSE A REMEDY

■ **INSTANT FACTS** Tull (D), sued by the Government for alleged violations of the Clean Water Act, was denied a jury trial and appealed the decision.

■ **BLACK LETTER RULE** A statute may provide for jury trial by codifying common-law actions and also allow a judge to impose a remedy once liability is established.

■ **PROCEDURAL BASIS**

Writ of certiorari reviewing denial of demand for jury trial and reviewing judgment for civil penalties for statutory violation.

■ **FACTS**

The United States (P) brought an action against Tull (D) for violations of the Clean Water Act, alleging that Tull (D) dumped fill on wetlands in Virginia. The Government sought injunctive relief and civil penalties of over $22 million, pursuant to Section 1319 of the Act. However, when the complaint was filed, Tull (D) had sold most of its property [apparently the dump was full and Tull no longer had a use for the property!] and an injunction was proper only for a small portion of the land. The District Court denied Tull's (D) demand for a jury trial and concluded that Tull (D) had illegally filled in wetland areas, awarding a $325,000 judgment for the Government. The Court of Appeals rejected Tull's (D) argument that, under the Seventh Amendment, he was entitled to a jury trial. The Supreme Court granted certiorari.

■ **ISSUE**

(1) Do liability statutes that codify common-law rights fall within the scope of the Seventh Amendment?
(2) Can Congress authorize judges to impose a remedy when liability is determined by a jury?

■ **DECISION AND RATIONALE**

(Brennan, J.) (1) Yes. Liability statutes that codify common-law rights fall within the scope of the Seventh Amendment. Previous holdings have construed the Seventh Amendment to require a jury trial on the merits in those actions that are analogous to "suits at common law." The Government's claims under the Clean Water Act are analogous to common law actions for public nuisance and actions in debt, based on the nature of the actions and the remedies sought. At common law, civil penalties could only be enforced in courts of law. Section 1319(d) of the Clean Water Act authorizes punishment for violations, and this reflects more than a concern to provide equitable relief. The Government contends that this suit for penalties is similar to a suit for disgorgement of improper profits, traditionally considered an equitable remedy. However, Section 1319(d) clearly is not limited to a restoration of the status quo; rather, it allows for punitive fines for violations of the Act. Furthermore, the Government's contention that a court in equity was nevertheless entitled to provide monetary awards is to no avail in the present case. While a court in equity may provide restitution as an adjunct to monetary relief, a court in equity may not enforce civil penalties, and a potential penalty of $22 million hardly can be considered incidental to the modest injunctive relief in this case. Moreover, even when an equitable claim is joined with a legal claim, the right to jury trial on the legal claim remains intact. Thus, in the case at hand, Tull (D) was entitled to a jury trial with respect to the issue of liability. (2) Yes. Congress can authorize judges to impose a remedy, such as civil penalties, when liability is determined by a jury. The legislative history of the Clean Water Act shows that Congress intended trial judges to perform the discretionary calculations necessary to award civil penalties after liability is found. The Seventh Amendment is silent on the question whether a jury must determine the remedy in a trial in which it must determine liability. However, we do not believe that a jury role is necessary to preserve the substance of the common-law right of trial by jury. The assessment of a civil penalty is not one of the most fundamental elements of trial by jury. Thus, Congress' assignment of trial judges to determine the amount of civil penalties does not infringe on the constitutional right to jury trial. In conclusion, the Seventh Amendment requires that Tull's (D) demand for jury trial be granted to determine his liability, but the trial court should determine the amount of the penalty. Reversed and remanded for further proceedings consistent with this opinion.

■ CONCURRENCE AND DISSENT

(Scalia, J.) While I agree with the first parts of the opinion, I disagree with the holding that judges may impose a remedy when liability is determined by a jury. In my view, the right to jury trial on whether a civil penalty is assessable also involves a right to jury trial on what that amount should be. I can recall no precedent for judgment of civil liability by jury but assessment of amount by the court. In the case at hand, the Government obtained the benefits of a civil rather than criminal proceeding, and it must accept the disadvantages of a receiving a damages award calculated by twelve private citizens. I would reverse and remand for a jury trial on both issues.

Analysis:

This Supreme Court decision revisits the conflict between law and equity. At first glance, this case seems comparable to *Curtis v. Loether* [the Seventh Amendment provides a right to jury trial for actions based on a statute that creates legal rights and remedies], and it is curious why the Court did not simply conclude that the Clean Water Act created legal remedies (civil penalties). If this were the case, then the jury could decide on both the issues of liability and the scope of the remedies. However, the Court chose to conduct an extensive examination of the remedies provided by the Clean Water Act, analogizing the claims to various common law actions for which jury trial was appropriate. Perhaps there is a marked difference between the civil penalties available under the Clean Water Act and the damages available under Title VIII of the Civil Rights Act, considered in *Curtis*, that requires the Court to fully examine whether the Clean Water Act's remedies are legal in nature. Nevertheless, the result is the same in both cases: a jury may determine the issue of liability.

Atlas Roofing Co. v. Occupational Safety & Health Review Commission

(Roofing Company) v. *(Administrative Commission)*
430 U.S. 442, 97 S.Ct. 1261 (1977)

ADMINISTRATIVE AGENCIES MAY HANDLE THE ADJUDICATION OF PUBLIC RIGHTS

■ **INSTANT FACTS** Atlas Roofing Co. (D) objected to an administrative agency determining the facts of a suit in which Atlas (D) was cited for violations of the Occupational Safety and Health Act.

■ **BLACK LETTER RULE** Congress may assign the fact-finding function of adjudication of cases involving public rights to an administrative agency rather than to a jury.

■ **PROCEDURAL BASIS**

Writ of certiorari considering affirmance of administrative enforcement of claims alleging violations of federal act.

■ **FACTS**

Atlas Roofing Co. (D) was cited for violations of the Occupational Safety and Health Act (OSHA) and was fined after hearings before administrative law judges of the Occupational Safety and Health Review Commission (OSHRC) (P). Two Courts of Appeals upheld the Commission's orders, rejecting Atlas's (D) claim that such adjudication violated the Seventh Amendment. The Supreme Court granted certiorari.

■ **ISSUE**

Does the Seventh Amendment prohibit Congress from assigning the fact-finding function of an adjudication to an administrative forum?

■ **DECISION AND RATIONALE**

(White, J.) No. The Seventh Amendment imposes no bar on Congress from assigning the fact-finding function of adjudication to an administrative forum rather than to a jury. Fact-finding was never the exclusive province of the jury under the English or American legal systems at the time the Seventh Amendment was drafted. The determination of whether a case would be tried with or without a jury did not depend on the extent of fact-finding. Rather, the decision turned on whether courts of law supplied an adequate remedy. For example, suits for damages for breach of contract involved issues to be determined by a jury. However, the Seventh Amendment was never intended to establish the jury as the exclusive mechanism for fact-finding in civil cases. Congress may, therefore, require that facts related to certain cases be determined by an administrative agency rather than by a jury. Contrary to Atlas's (D) allegations, this does not allow Congress to utterly destroy the right to jury trial by always providing for administrative resolution of complaints. Rather, Congress may only require such administrative adjudication in situations involving public rights. Private tort, contract, property, and other cases are not implicated by this holding. Affirmed.

Analysis:

This case presents the "public right" exception to the Seventh Amendment's right to jury trial. The Supreme Court here limits the broad scope of the Seventh Amendment. Although the right to a jury trial remains an important aspect of American jurisprudence, the Court upholds the Congressional intent to provide for administrative fact-finding of certain issues related to public rights. In essence, the holding demonstrates that the right to a jury trial depends in part on the forum in which an action is to be resolved. Certainly, administrative adjudication of some cases accomplishes the goal of judicial efficiency, since governmental agencies are likely much better skilled at resolving violations of their own provisions. On the other hand, it is easy to sympathize with Atlas (D). Atlas (D) was cited for violations of OSHA, and the claims were adjudicated by the OSHRC, a branch of the federal government. This branch is likely more inclined to recognize violations of the Act under its control than a jury of twelve citizens would be. On its face, the case only upholds the fact-finding function of OSHRC, apparently leaving some room for jury determination of the penalties. However, the OSHRC imposed fines upon Atlas (D), and the Courts of Appeals upheld these orders. Thus, the OSHRC was empowered to do much more than simply determine the facts of the case. It was given the ultimate authority to fine companies for violations, completely supplanting the role of a jury. The Court's decision simply underscores the distinction between public and private rights. While public rights may be fully adjudicated by a governmental agency, private rights remain under the control of juries.

■ **CASE VOCABULARY**

PUBLIC RIGHTS: Rights created by statutes within the power of Congress to enact.

Granfinanciera, S.A. v. Nordberg

(Transferee) v. *(Bankruptcy Trustee)*

492 U.S. 33, 109 S.Ct. 2782 (1989)

CONGRESS MAY NOT RECLASSIFY A PRE–EXISTING LEGAL CAUSE OF ACTION AS A "PUBLIC RIGHT" IN ORDER TO AVOID JURY TRIAL

■ **INSTANT FACTS** Granfinanciera (D), sued by a bankruptcy trustee to recover allegedly fraudulent transfers, was denied a jury trial on grounds that such actions were merely adjudications of public rights.

■ **BLACK LETTER RULE** The "public right" exception does not allow Congress to reclassify traditionally legal claims in order to deny the right to jury trial.

■ FACTS

Nordberg (P), the bankruptcy trustee for a corporate debtor, filed a claim against Granfinanciera, S.A. (D) to recover funds that were allegedly fraudulently transferred from the debtor. The District Court denied Granfinanciera's (D) request for a jury trial on the ground that bankruptcy courts, like administrative agencies, were outside the Seventh Amendment. The Eleventh Circuit affirmed, arguing that the applicable statute did not provide for jury trials and that actions to recover fraudulent conveyances were equitable in nature. The Supreme Court granted certiorari.

■ ISSUE

Is the "public right" exception applicable to actions for the recovery of fraudulent conveyances?

■ DECISION AND RATIONALE

(Brennan, J.) No. The "public right" exception, allowing Congress to assign the resolution of a claim to an administrative agency, does not apply to actions for the recovery of fraudulent conveyances. In order to determine if a jury trial is necessary, three stages of analysis are necessary. First, the statutory action must be compared to common law actions brought prior to the merger of law and equity. Second, it must be determined whether the remedy is legal or equitable. If these factors indicate that a party is entitled to a jury trial, then we must decide whether Congress may assign the resolution of the complaint to an administrative body. In the case at hand, an action to recover a fraudulent conveyance requires a jury trial. Furthermore, the public right exception is inapplicable. As we stated in *Atlas Roofing Co. v. Occupational Safety & Health Review Commission* [Congress may assign the fact-finding function of adjudication of cases involving public rights to an administrative agency rather than to a jury], Congress may only deny jury trials in actions at law where public rights are litigated. In the case at hand, a fraudulent conveyance seems more accurately characterized as a private rather than a public right. Fraudulent conveyance actions nearly resemble state-law contract claims. Thus, Congress has no power to require their adjudication in a non-Article III Tribunal.

Analysis:

This case presents a much-needed explanation of the "public right" exception enunciated in *Atlas Roofing.* Congress has a broad power to create administrative agencies for the adjudication of public rights—i.e., cases in which the Government sues to enforce rights created by statute. However, Congress may not use this power to simply reclassify cases involving private rights, resulting in a denial of the right to jury trial. According to a footnote not reproduced in this opinion, Justice Brennan raised an interesting issue that connects this case with *Ross v. Bernhard* and its progeny. Recall that *Ross* identified three prongs to consider in determining if a case is legal in nature (and thus if a jury trial is mandated): the pre-merger custom with reference to such questions; the remedy sought; and the practical abilities and limitations of juries. Cases subsequent to *Ross* abandoned this three-prong approach, focusing primarily on the nature of the remedy sought. Perhaps the "public rights" exception is now replacing the third prong of this test, because public rights are more easily adjudicated by administrative agencies than by ordinary jurors.

■ CASE VOCABULARY

ARTICLE III TRIBUNAL: Any of the judicial bodies established in Article III of the Constitution, including the Supreme Court and inferior courts.

Chauffeurs, Teamsters and Helpers Local 391 v. Terry

(*Labor Union*) v. (*Employee*)
494 U.S. 558, 110 S.Ct. 1339 (1990)

THE SUPREME COURT CONTINUES TO EXPAND THE SEVENTH AMENDMENT RIGHT TO JURY TRIAL

■ **INSTANT FACTS** Several employees sued their union, the Chauffeurs, Teamsters and Helpers Local 391 (D), for alleged violations of the Union's duty of fair representation. Against the Union's protest that the claim was equitable in nature, the District Court and Appellate Court granted a right to jury trial.

■ **BLACK LETTER RULE** An action for breach of fair representation, although analogous to equitable claims at common law, carries a right to jury trial.

■ **PROCEDURAL BASIS**

Writ of certiorari considering affirmance of denial of motion to strike demand for jury trial in action for back pay for breach of duty of fair representation.

■ **FACTS**

McLean Trucking Company and the Chauffeurs, Teamsters and Helpers Local 391 (Union) (D) were parties to a collective-bargaining agreement. Terry (P) and 26 other plaintiffs were employed by McLean as truck drivers and were all members of the Union (D). Terry (P) and the others filed a grievance with the Union (D), but the Union (D) declined to refer the charges to a grievance committee. Terry (P) and the other employees then filed an action in District Court, alleging that the Union (D) had violated its duty of fair representation. The complaint sought compensatory damages for lost wages and health benefits. The Union (D) moved to strike Terry's (P) request for a jury trial on the ground that no right to a jury trial exists in a duty of fair representation suit. The District Court denied this motion to strike, and the Fourth Circuit affirmed upon an interlocutory appeal. The Supreme Court granted certiorari to resolve a circuit conflict on the issue.

■ **ISSUE**

Does an employee seeking an award of back pay from a union's alleged breach of fair representation have a right to trial by jury?

■ **DECISION AND RATIONALE**

(Marshall, J.) Yes. An employee seeking an award of back pay from a union's alleged breach of fair representation does have a right to trial by jury. In order to determine whether a particular action involves legal rights, and hence whether a jury trial is allowed, we conduct a two-step inquiry. First, we compare the statutory action to the 18th-century actions brought in England prior to the merger of law and equity. Second, we examine the remedy sought and determine whether it is legal or equitable in nature. This second inquiry is more important. With respect to the first part of the analysis, there was no such thing as an action for breach of a union's duty of fair representation in 18th-century England; in fact, collective bargaining was unlawful. However, we are persuaded by the Union's (D) analogy between a duty of fair representation action and an action by a trust beneficiary against a trustee for breach of legal duty. Both the union and a trustee has broad discretion in determining how to dispose of claims brought by employees or trustees. We disagree with Terry's (P) analogy to an attorney malpractice action, since a client controls the significant decisions concerning his representation in the attorney-client setting, whereas an individual employee has no such control over a union. Nevertheless, we are not convinced that Terry's (P) claim is wholly equitable. While a duty of fair representation claim is analogous to a common-law equitable action against a trustee, Terry (P) must also prove that the Union (D) breached the collective bargaining agreement. This latter element is comparable to a breach of contract claim, which is a legal issue. Thus, the first part of the analysis does not resolve the issue of whether Terry (P) is entitled to a jury trial. In conducting the second part of the analysis, we note that the only remedy sought by Terry (P) is an award of back pay and benefits. Although this is an award for compensatory damages, we have not held that any award of monetary relief must necessarily be legal in nature. Furthermore, the Union (D) argues that back pay relief must be considered equitable, because the Court has labeled back pay awards under Title VII as equitable. Nevertheless, Congress specifically characterized back pay under Title VII as a form of equitable relief, and Congress made no similar pronouncement regarding the duty of fair representation. We therefore hold that the remedy of back pay is legal in nature, as it is not a form of restitutionary relief but rather an action for the payment of money and benefits. All in all, considering both elements of the Seventh Amendment inquiry, we conclude that Terry (P) is entitled to a jury trial. Affirmed.

■ CONCURRENCE

(Brennan, J.) I agree that Terry (P) and the other employees seek a remedy that is legal in nature and, hence, that the Seventh Amendment mandates a jury trial. However, I believe that the historical inquiry conducted by the Court can and should be simplified. In expounding the historical test, this Court has repeatedly discounted the significance of the analogous form of action at English common law. I think it is time we dispense with it altogether. Trial judges, who neither have the training nor time necessary to adequately conduct this historical inquiry, should not be required to expend vast judicial resources trying to match a modem claim against an antiquated one. Of course, courts will still be required to examine the nature of the remedies sought and to determine whether they are legal or equitable in nature.

■ CONCURRENCE

(Stevens, J.) I believe that the Court has made this case unnecessarily difficult by exaggerating the importance of finding a precise common-law analogy. Duty of fair representation suits are ordinary civil actions similar to contract and malpractice disputes. There is no ground for excluding these actions from the right to jury trial.

■ DISSENT

(Kennedy, J.) The Court initially determined that the duty of fair representation action is more similar to cases tried in equity than cases tried in courts of law. Thus, our inquiry should end and there should be no right to jury trial. However, the majority overcomes the equitable nature of the claim by noting that Terry (P) must prove a breach of the collective-bargaining agreement as one element of the claim. I disagree with Justice Marshall's reliance on previous cases to reach this conclusion. Having determined that the duty of fair representation claim is equitable in nature, the cases relied upon by Marshall are inapplicable. Absent certain procedural justifications, we have never parsed legal elements out of equitable claims. The Court also rules that Terry (P) and the other employees have a right to jury trial because they seek money damages. However, we have consistently held that an award of monetary relief must not necessarily be legal in nature. I believe that the injunctive and monetary remedies available make the duty of fair representation suit analogous to an equitable action. I also disagree with the concurrences by Justices Brennan and Stevens, calling for an abandonment of the historical test. Our entire constitutional experience teaches that history must inform the judicial inquiry, and thus we should continue to look to 18th-century England for a resolution of the legal vs. equitable dispute.

Analysis:

This case demonstrates that the majority of the Supreme Court remains committed to an expanded view of the Seventh Amendment right to jury trial. Although the Court recognized the equitable nature of Terry's (P) claim, the majority takes great strides to find that the cause of action was legal in character. Further, the opinion underscores the importance of the two-pronged approach to determining the Seventh Amendment right. Justices Brennan and Stevens, in their concurring opinions, raised valid points about the difficulties courts face in attempting to find analogies between modern causes of action and English common-law claims. While the majority seems unwilling to abandon this historical analysis, it is interesting that the court essentially sidesteps the issue when the result—that the "duty of fair representation" claim parallels a common-law equitable action—argues against the right to jury trial. Thus, perhaps the Court would have been better off abandoning the historical approach altogether. After all, the second prong of the test—whether the remedy is legal or equitable in nature—seems to always decide the issue. On the other hand, the three dissenting justices also raise some valid points in favor of maintaining a strict historical approach to Seventh Amendment issues.

■ CASE VOCABULARY

COLLECTIVE-BARGAINING AGREEMENT: A labor agreement entered into between employers and a union representing employees.

EQUIPOISE: A point of equal distribution between two opposing claims or sides.

Markman v. Westview Instruments, Inc.

(Patent Holder) v. *(Alleged Patent Infringer)*

517 U.S. 370, 116 S.Ct. 1384 (1996)

U.S. SUPREME COURT HOLDS THAT THE INTERPRETATION OF A PATENT IS A QUESTION OF LAW FOR THE TRIAL JUDGE RATHER THAN A QUESTION OF FACT FOR A JURY

■ **INSTANT FACTS** A patent holder sued a corporation, alleging a violation of his patent for a dry-cleaning inventory tracking system.

■ **BLACK LETTER RULE** The construction of a patent is a legal question to be decided by a judge rather than by a jury.

■ **PROCEDURAL BASIS**

Appeal, following a grant of certiorari by the U.S. Supreme Court, of a decision of the U.S. Court of Appeals for the Federal Circuit affirming a federal trial court's decision to overturn a jury verdict and direct a verdict as a matter of law on a suit for patent infringement.

■ **FACTS**

Herbert Markman ("Markman") (P) had been granted a patent for a system that could monitor and report the status, location, and movement of clothing in a dry-cleaning business. The system was made up of a keyboard and data processor that generated written records for each dry-cleaning transaction, including a barcode that could be read by an optical scanner operated by employees who could then log the process of the clothing through the entire dry-cleaning process. Westview Instruments, Inc. ("Westview") (D) put out its own product that included a keyboard and processor and listed charges for dry-cleaning services on bar-coded tickets that could be read by portable optical scanners. Markman (P) sued, asserting that Westview (D) had infringed on his patent grant, emphasizing that the language of his patent claim stated that his product could be used to "maintain an inventory total." Westview (D) countered by arguing that there was no infringement of the patent grant because its system functioned merely to record an inventory of receivables by tracking invoices and transaction totals, rather than to record an inventory of articles of clothing. Markman (P) had an expert witness testify as to the meaning of the language of his patent claim. The case was tried before a jury which found an infringement of Markman's (P) patent by Westview (D). Following the jury's verdict, Westview (D) moved for a judgment as a matter of law in its favor. The trial judge granted Westview's (D) motion, concluding from his own construction of the language of the patent claim that there was no infringement of the patent because Westview's (D) system was not able to track an inventory of articles of clothing throughout the cleaning process and generate reports about the status and location of particular items. Markman (P) appealed, arguing that it was error for the trial judge to substitute his construction of the language of the patent claim for the construction the jury had adopted. The U.S. Court of Appeals for the Federal Circuit affirmed the trial judge, holding that the interpretation of the patent claim language was the responsibility of the judge and not the jury and that this was consistent with the Seventh Amendment's right to a jury trial. Markman (P) appealed and the U.S. Supreme Court granted certiorari.

■ **ISSUE**

Is the construction of a patent a legal question to be decided by a judge, rather than a factual question to be decided by a jury?

■ DECISION AND RATIONALE

(Souter, J.) Yes. Sometimes, the answer to a question of whether a judge or a jury must decide an issue at trial is easy because of clear historical evidence showing that the issue was decided by the jury at English common law. Where, as here, the historical evidence provides no answer, we must make a judgment as to whether a jury's decision of the issue is necessary to preserve the substance of the common-law right of trial by jury. To make this judgment, we look to precedent and consider both the relative interpretive skills of judges and juries and the statutory policies that ought to be furthered by our decision. Here, since legal precedent provides no conclusive answer, we must decide the question solely as a matter of the sound administration of justice. We find that judges are better suited than juries to find the meaning of the terms of a patent. Patent claims have become highly technical due to special rules relating to their form and scope that have developed in the government's Patent Office. A judge, from his training and discipline, is more likely to be right in giving a proper interpretation to patent instruments than a jury can be expected to be. Markman (P) argues that a jury should decide a question of meaning peculiar to a trade or profession simply because the question is a subject of testimony requiring credibility determinations, which are a strong point of a jury. While in theory, there could be a case where a simple credibility judgment would be enough to choose between experts whose testimony was equally consistent with a patent's internal logic, our own experience with document construction leads us to doubt that trial courts will run into many such cases. In general, we expect that any credibility determinations would be subsumed within a sophisticated analysis of the whole patent document, required by the standard construction rule that a term can be defined only in a way that comports with the instrument as a whole. Thus, in these cases, a jury's abilities to evaluate demeanor or reflect community standards are much less significant than a judge's trained ability to evaluate testimony in relation to the overall structure of the patent. Affirmed.

Analysis:

In determining whether an issue must be decided by a jury under the Seventh Amendment, the Supreme Court has typically looked to determine whether that issue was left to the decision of a jury under English common law. Here, explaining that English common law provides no answer to the issue of the construction of a patent claim, the Court relies on functional considerations and unanimously finds that judges are better suited than juries to find the meaning of language used in a patent claim. Patent claims are generally interpreted as they would be understood by those skilled in the art, trade, or profession with which the patent is concerned. Typically, expert testimony by such people is used as support for an interpretation of a patent claim. Markman's (P) argument is that the jury should be the decision maker in judging the credibility of the experts. Emphasizing their own experience with the complexities of document interpretation, the justices reject the notion that the case depends solely upon a credibility contest between expert witnesses. In the Court's view, the decision maker must review expert testimony within the context of the interpretation of the entire patent document, a task the Court concludes is handled better by judges rather than juries.

■ CASE VOCABULARY

CLAIM: In patent law, an explanation of what a proposed invention can do, which defines the extent of the patent for that invention, if and when it is granted by the federal government.

GRANT: A written authorization by the federal government of a right to use and sell a patented invention.

INFRINGEMENT: An unauthorized use or sale of an invention protected by a claim of patent.

PATENT: A grant by the federal government of an exclusive right to make, use, sell, and license an invention.

Colgrove v. Battin

(Not Stated) v. (Not Stated)

413 U.S. 149, 93 S.Ct. 2448 (1973)

SIX-MEMBER CIVIL JURIES DO NOT VIOLATE THE SEVENTH AMENDMENT

■ **INSTANT FACTS** A party to a civil action challenges a local district court rule that allows six-member juries in civil trials.

■ **BLACK LETTER RULE** Courts may adopt rules limiting juries to six members in civil trials without violating the Seventh Amendment.

■ **PROCEDURAL BASIS**

Writ of certiorari reviewing local district court rule that provided for juries of six in civil trials.

■ **FACTS**

Colgrove (P) brought an action in a federal district court in Montana. A local rule of the court provided for a six-member jury in all civil trials. Colgrove (P) sought mandamus to compel a federal district judge to impanel a twelve-member jury. He argued that the local rule violated the Seventh Amendment, the Rules Enabling Act, and Federal Rule 48. The Ninth Circuit denied mandamus, and the Supreme Court granted certiorari.

■ **ISSUE**

Does a jury of six people satisfy the Seventh Amendment's guarantee of trial by jury in civil cases?

■ **DECISION AND RATIONALE**

(Justice Not Stated). Yes. A jury of six people satisfies the Seventh Amendment's guarantee of trial by jury in civil cases. The Seventh Amendment was adopted not to preserve jury characteristics at common law but rather to prevent the civil jury itself from being abolished unless protected by express words. In referring to the "common law," the Framers of the Seventh Amendment were concerned with preserving the right to jury trial in civil cases where it existed at common law, rather than the various incidents of trial by jury. We reject the notion that the reliability of the jury as a factfinder is a function of its size. Studies have shown that there is no discernible difference between the results reached by two different-sized juries. Further, the Montana local rule does not violate the Enabling Act, since Congress did not intend to go beyond the Seventh Amendment in saying that the rules "shall preserve the right of trial by jury as at common law. . . ." Finally, the local rule is not in conflict with Federal Rule 48, which is concerned only with numbers stipulated by the parties. Affirmed.

Analysis:

The Court here rules that a jury of six does not violate the Seventh Amendment. This ruling for civil cases is consistent with its previous holding for criminal cases in *Williams v. Florida* [U.S. Supreme Court case concluding that both the states and the federal government can constitutionally use a jury with six, rather than twelve members in criminal cases]. The Court's reading of the Seventh Amendment certainly can be questioned. When the Framers declared an intent to preserve the right of trial by jury "where it existed at common law," why shouldn't this be considered an intent to preserve the traditional number of jurors as well? Regardless, the case shows how much power the Supreme Court has in interpreting the Constitution. Furthermore, the Court's analysis of the Enabling Act and Rule 48 is sound. At the time of this case, Federal Rule 48 allowed parties to stipulate that the jury could consist of any number less than twelve. In 1991, the Rule was amended to require at least six members. Later efforts to require a twelve-person jury were rejected.

Flowers v. Flowers

(Wife) v. *(Husband)*
397 S.W.2d 121 (Tex. Civ. App. 1965)

CHALLENGES FOR CAUSE ALLOW THE DISMISSAL OF POTENTIAL JURORS WHO DEMONSTRATE BIAS OR PREJUDICE

■ **INSTANT FACTS** Attorneys for Billie Flowers (P), a mother who occasionally consumed alcohol to excess, moved for a new trial on grounds that a prospective juror, who demonstrated a reprehension for all drinking, should have been dismissed.

■ **BLACK LETTER RULE** A prospective juror who demonstrates bias or prejudice towards the litigants or subject matter of the action should be excluded from the jury pool.

■ **PROCEDURAL BASIS**

Appeal from overruling of challenge to juror for cause.

■ **FACTS**

Billie Charlene Flowers (P) and R.A. Flowers (D) were involved in a child custody dispute. On voir dire examination, the prospective jurors were told that Billie (P) drank alcoholic beverages socially and on occasion had consumed to excess. [Of course, the jurors in this small community already knew these facts!] One of the potential jurors, Mrs. Schmidt, responded on voir dire that she did not approve of any alcoholic beverage consumption. However, when asked the leading question of whether she would hold Billie's (P) consumption against her at trial, Mrs. Schmidt responded "not especially." The court overruled Billie's (P) attorney's challenge to Mrs. Schmidt for cause. Subsequently, evidence revealed that Mrs. Philpot, a panelist who sat next to Mrs. Schmidt, had heard Mrs. Schmidt make derogatory statements about Billie (P). Nevertheless, at Billie's (P) motion for mistrial and motion for new trial, the court refused to hear Mrs. Philpot's testimony. Billie Flowers (P) appealed.

■ **ISSUE**

Should a party who shows bias or prejudice be dismissed from the jury pool?

■ **DECISION AND RATIONALE**

(Chapman, J.) Yes. A party who demonstrates bias or prejudice should be dismissed from the jury pool. Texas statute and case law provides that a prospective juror may be disqualified whenever that person has a bias or prejudice towards either party or the subject matter of the litigation. Mrs. Schmidt's statements indicate bias and prejudice, indicating that she could not have acted with impartiality. Thus, she should have been disqualified as a matter of law. Even if her statements did not clearly show prejudice or bias, the trial judge abused his discretion in refusing Billie's (P) attorney's challenge for cause. Mrs. Schmidt's answer to the leading question should be disregarded, and the remainder of the record shows bias and prejudice on the part of Mrs. Schmidt toward Billie's (P) alcoholic consumption. Reversed and remanded for a new trial.

Analysis:

This case illustrates some of the problems involved in removing a juror for cause. While a partial juror, who demonstrates bias or prejudice to the litigants or the subject matter of the case, clearly should be dismissed, the determination is not always easy to make. Indeed, Mrs. Schmidt expressed a great reprehension towards anyone who consumed alcoholic beverages. However, she opined that she could still remain an impartial juror. The judge apparently based his decision not to dismiss Mrs. Schmidt on this latter revelation. Nevertheless, the remainder of her voir dire examination seems to reveal a clear slant against Billie Flowers (P) and her drinking habits, and it is curious that she was not dismissed initially. Perhaps the judge realized that most potential jurors in this small town would have some prejudice to the facts of this case, and he felt that Mrs. Schmidt's honest answers revealed qualities suitable for jury service. The judge certainly faced a difficult task, as he could only rely on the voir dire examination and could not read the minds of potential jurors. At any event, however, the judge should have questioned Mrs. Schmidt more extensively. This may have uncovered some of her other biases and prejudices that she revealed to Mrs. Philpot after the voir dire concluded.

■ CASE VOCABULARY

CHALLENGE FOR CAUSE: A challenge to a prospective juror's competence to serve based on partiality such as bias or prejudice.

VOIR DIRE: The process of examining prospective jurors for their qualification and of selecting a jury.

Edmonson v. Leesville Concrete Company, Inc.

(Construction Worker) v. *(Truck Owner)*

500 U.S. 614, 111 S.Ct. 2077 (1991)

RACE-BASED EXCLUSION OF JURORS VIOLATES EQUAL PROTECTION RIGHTS OF THE CHALLENGED JURORS

■ **INSTANT FACTS** Thaddeus Edmonson (P), injured when a truck owned by Leesville Concrete (D) smashed into him, appealed a judgment after Leesville (D) used two peremptory challenges to exclude black jurors.

■ **BLACK LETTER RULE** Peremptory challenges may not be used to exclude jurors on account of their race.

■ **PROCEDURAL BASIS**

Writ of certiorari reviewing affirmance of judgment for damages for negligence.

■ **FACTS**

Thaddeus Donald Edmonson (P), a construction worker, sued the Leesville Concrete Company (D) in district court for negligence after one of the company's trucks pinned Edmonson (P) against some construction equipment. Edmonson (P) asserted his Seventh Amendment right to jury trial. At voir dire, Leesville (D) invoked two of its three peremptory challenges to remove black persons from the prospective jury. Edmonson (P), a black man, requested that the District Court require Leesville (D) to articulate a race-neutral explanation for the peremptory challenges. [Yes, peremptory challenges used to require no reason whatsoever.] The District Court denied the request on the ground that the cited case, *Batson v. Kentucky* [peremptory challenges cannot be used to excuse black jurors solely on the basis of race], does not apply to civil proceedings. The jury, including eleven whites and one black, found Edmonson (P) 80% contributorily negligent and returned a partial damages verdict for Edmonson (P). Edmonson (P) appealed [apparently feeling that his meager $18,000 award was racially-motivated]. An en banc panel of the Court of Appeals affirmed the judgment, and the Supreme Court granted certiorari.

■ **ISSUE**

May peremptory challenges be used to exclude jurors on account of their race?

■ **DECISION AND RATIONALE**

(Kennedy, J.) No. Peremptory challenges may not be used to exclude jurors on account of their race. Our *Batson* decision made clear that a prosecutor's race-based peremptory challenge violates the equal protection rights of those people excluded from jury service. Indeed, these constitutional guarantees of equal protection apply in general only to action by the government, and racial discrimination violates the Constitution only when it may be attributed to state action. However, the entire process of jury selection retains an element of state action. A trial judge exercises substantial control over voir dire in the federal system. Further, the objective of jury selection is to determine representation on a governmental body. The fact that the government delegates some portion of the jury-selection process to private litigants does not change the governmental character of the power exercised. When private litigants participate in the selection of jurors, they serve an important governmental function and operate with its substantial assistance. The injury caused by racial discrimination in jury selection is made more severe because the government permits it to occur within the courthouse itself. It only remains to consider whether a prima facie case of racial discrimination has been established in the instant action, requiring Leesville (D) to offer race-neutral explanations for its exclusion of black jurors. We leave it to the trial courts to answer this question. Reversed and remanded.

■ DISSENT

(O'Connor, J.) The decision to strike a juror is entirely up to the litigant and is not encouraged by the judge in any manner. The judge does little more than acquiesce in the decision by excusing the juror. The government only establishes the requirements for jury service, leaving to the private litigant the decision to use peremptory challenges for any reason. Thus, the government is not responsible for everything that occurs in a courtroom, including private challenges by a litigant. No state action is involved in these challenges, and hence the Fifth Amendment's Due Process Clause [and Equal Protection Clause] are not applicable.

Analysis:

This case essentially changes the entire nature of peremptory challenges in civil proceedings. By definition, peremptory challenges to prospective jurors may be made for *any* reason. However, *Batson* had already undermined this basic concept by precluding the use of such challenges to eliminate potential black jurors in criminal proceedings. Nevertheless, in that case, the state-action requirement for equal protection violations was clearly satisfied, since a government prosecutor was engaging in the discriminatory behavior. In the case at hand, conversely, only private litigants are involved in striking certain black jurors. Regardless, the Court desired to eliminate such discriminatory treatment using the only vehicle it saw possible, the equal protection clause. In doing so, the Court quite possibly stretched the concept of state-action beyond its logical extreme. As the strong dissent by three justices accurately noted, peremptory challenges in civil suits involve only the actions of private litigants. The government engages in absolutely no "action" whatsoever. Furthermore, private litigants are not engaging in a governmental function by conducting voir dire, rather, they are simply attempting to win their case for their client. Although racial discrimination at any level is a terrible thing, the Constitution does not necessarily provide recourse for all such discrimination. Nevertheless, the holding stands, essentially redefining the traditional concept of peremptory challenges. Peremptory challenges have now become only a more-flexible form of challenges for cause.

■ CASE VOCABULARY

OPPROBRIOUS: Shameful or disgraceful.

PEREMPTORY CHALLENGES: Challenges used to exclude potential jurors without stating the reason for such exclusion.

PETIT JURY: The jury for a civil or criminal trial, as distinguished from a grand jury.

Galloway v. United States

(Alleged Beneficiary) v. *(Government)*
319 U.S. 372, 63 S.Ct. 1077 (1943)

THE SUPREME COURT EXPANDS THE USE OF DIRECTED VERDICTS TO CASES REQUIRING LARGE INFERENTIAL LEAPS

■ **INSTANT FACTS** Galloway (P) sought benefits resulting from his total mental disability, presenting evidence of his insanity for several periods but demonstrating no evidence for a several-year interval.

■ **BLACK LETTER RULE** A directed verdict is proper where juries would have to make inferences and bridge large gaps in testimony, and this verdict does not violate the Seventh Amendment.

■ **PROCEDURAL BASIS**

Writ of certiorari reviewing affirmance of directed verdict against claims for insurance benefits.

■ **FACTS**

Galloway (P) sought benefits for total and permanent disability he claims existed in 1919, when his policy of yearly renewable term insurance lapsed for nonpayment, and extending to the time of this case. Galloway (P) claimed that the strain of military service in France during 1918 began a mental breakdown that resulted in total disability by 1919. In support of this claim, Galloway (P) presented evidence from witnesses who had served with him in France that testified to Galloway's (P) disturbed mind. However, Galloway (P) presented little or no evidence of whether his insanity continued between 1922 and 1930. Evidence revealed that Galloway (P) was medically diagnosed as psychotic in 1930, 1931 and 1934. Further, an expert witness testified that Galloway (P) was born with an inherent disability and that his service in France brought about permanent and total disability. At the close of all the evidence, the Government (D) moved for a directed verdict. The District Court granted this verdict, and the Circuit Court of Appeals affirmed, holding the evidence legally insufficient to sustain a verdict for Galloway (P). Galloway (P) sought certiorari on grounds that the directed verdict was erroneous and deprived him of his Seventh Amendment right to trial by jury.

■ **ISSUE**

(1) Is inference capable of bridging large gaps in evidence, rendering a directed verdict improper? (2) Does a directed verdict unconstitutionally deny a party his Seventh Amendment right to jury trial?

■ **DECISION AND RATIONALE**

(Rutledge, J.) (1) No. Inference is not capable of bridging large gaps in evidence. In the case at hand, Galloway (P) presented evidence demonstrating his total mental disability some time before 1930. However, the evidence failed to show total disability as of 1919. Inference is incapable of bridging the large gap of eight years for which little or no evidence of disability was presented. Apparently Galloway (P) deliberately chose to present no evidence concerning this large interval, relying on the jury to bridge the gap. Perhaps the inference would have been more plausible if Galloway's (P) evidence of insanity as of 1919 was stronger. Nevertheless, in no case has such a large leap been made, and there is nothing to show Galloway's (P) total or permanent disability continuously from 1919 to the present. (2)

No. A directed verdict does not unconstitutionally deny a party his Seventh Amendment right to jury trial. Repeated decisions have held that federal courts do have the power to direct verdicts where evidence is insufficient to support a claim. Furthermore, Galloway's (P) argument from history is unconvincing. Even in 1791, a litigant could challenge his opponent's evidence by demurrer or a motion for new trial. However, the Seventh Amendment did not exclude any other challenges. Furthermore, federal courts are not tied to the exact procedural details of jury trial according to common law in 1791. The Amendment was only designed to preserve the basic institution of jury trial, not the great mass of procedural details. Finally, Galloway's (P) objection appears directed at the standards of proof judges have required for submission to the jury. We hold that mere speculation must not be allowed to substitute for probative facts. One whose burden is to show continuing and total disability for nearly twenty years must produce substantial evidence in support. Galloway (P) did not provide such evidence, and accordingly the judgment is affirmed.

■ **DISSENT**

(Black, J.) This decision continues the trend to wearing away an essential guarantee of the Seventh Amendment. The Court comes dangerously close to weighing the credibility of Galloway's (P) witnesses and rejecting the testimony because the majority does not believe it. The invention of the directed verdict, occurring long after the adoption of the Seventh Amendment, creates the potential for judicial control of the jury which had not previously existed. Initially, a directed verdict was possible only if there was no evidence, given the admission of all facts and reasonable inferences. The standard was later replaced by the substantial evidence rule, which permitted directed verdicts even though there was far more evidence than a plaintiff would have needed to withstand a demurrer at common law. I believe that a directed verdict should be granted only if, without weighing the credibility of witnesses, there is no room whatsoever for honest difference of opinion over the factual issue at controversy. In the case at hand, there is room for such difference of opinion. Galloway (P) presented testimony from which reasonable men could conclude that he was insane from 1919 to the time of the trial. The mere fact that there was no testimony for a period of several years does not create a presumption against Galloway (P) so strong that his case must be excluded from the jury entirely. This case illustrates the injustice resulting from judges directing verdicts instead of allowing them to go to trial and then, if necessary, allow a new trial. We should at least authorize a new trial for the instant action.

Analysis:

As this case demonstrates, judges now have a tremendous amount of power in entering verdicts against parties when the evidence appears unsatisfactory to prove the claims. Justice Black's dissent notes that courts have traditionally applied one of two tests for directed verdicts. The first, known as the "scintilla" test, requires a judge to deny the motion if there is *any* evidence on which the jury might possibly render a verdict for the nonmoving party. In comparison, the "substantial evidence" test allows a judge to direct a verdict unless there is substantial evidence suggesting that the jury might decide for the nonmovant. The dissent supports a return to the scintilla test in order to take some power away from judges and give credence to the Seventh Amendment. This case demonstrates the potential problems with the substantial evidence test. Indeed, Galloway (P) failed to produce evidence of his insanity for a period of several years. However, Galloway (P) did present evidence of total disability in 1919 and in 1930. If he was totally mentally disabled in 1919, and again in 1930, couldn't a reasonable jury conclude that he was insane in the interim? Apparently the majority believes that the answer is No, and thus the Court refuses to allow this case to go to a jury.

■ **CASE VOCABULARY**

DIRECTED VERDICT: A verdict entered by the court against a party who fails to establish a prima facie case to meet the burden of proof.

IN TOTO: Completely; as a whole.

Neely v. Martin K. Eby Construction Co.

(*Daughter of Decedent*) v. (*Construction Company*)
386 U.S. 317, 87 S.Ct. 1072 (1967)

■ **INSTANT FACTS** Neely (D) brought an action for wrongful death, alleging negligence on the part of a construction company, and obtained a jury verdict that was overturned on appeal.

■ **BLACK LETTER RULE** An appellate court may reverse the denial of a judgment notwithstanding the verdict, and the court does not have to order a new trial.

■ **PROCEDURAL BASIS**

Writ of certiorari reviewing reversal of denial of motion for judgment notwithstanding the verdict for damages for negligence.

■ **FACTS**

Neely (P) brought a wrongful death action against Martin K. Eby Construction Co. (Eby) (D), claiming that Eby (D) negligently constructed and maintained a missile silo, proximately causing the death of Neely's (P) father, who fell from a platform while working at the silo. At the close of Neely's (P) case, Eby (D) brought a motion for directed verdict. This motion was denied by the trial court. After the jury returned a $25,000 verdict for Neely (P), the court entered judgment for Neely (P) and denied Ely's (D) motions for judgment notwithstanding the verdict (j.n.o.v.) or a new trial. On appeal, the Tenth Circuit Court of Appeals found the evidence insufficient to establish negligence. Accordingly, the Appellate Court reversed the District Court's ruling on Ely's (D) motion for j.n.o.v. Neely (P) appealed to the Supreme Court, arguing that she had no opportunity to raise a claim for a new trial. Thus, according to Neely (P), the Appellate Court could not dismiss the case without violating the Seventh Amendment.

■ **ISSUE**

May an appellate court reverse the denial of a judgment notwithstanding the verdict without ordering a new trial?

■ **DECISION AND RATIONALE**

(White, J.) Yes. An appellate court may reverse the denial of a judgment notwithstanding the verdict without ordering a new trial. A judgment n.o.v. entered by an appellate court does not impinge upon the Seventh Amendment any more than a judgment n.o.v. entered by the trial court. In the case at hand, the appeal was from the original verdict entered by the jury in favor of Neely (P). Rule 50(d) provides an adequate opportunity for Neely (P) to present her grounds for a new trial in the event her verdict is set aside by the appellate court. However, Neely (P) suggested no grounds for a new trial in the event her judgment was reversed, and she failed to petition for a rehearing in the Court of Appeals. Indeed, where an appellee presents no new trial issues in her brief or petition for rehearing, the court of appeals may nevertheless order a new trial or refer the question to the district court. However, Neely (P) never suggested that the record was insufficient to present any new trial issues or that any other reason required a remand to the District Court. Affirmed.

Analysis:

At first glance, this holding seems unfair to Neely (P). After obtaining a judgment in the District Court, and after having Ely's (D) motions for a j.n.o.v. and new trial denied, Neely (P) certainly must have felt like she would be victorious. However, the ensuing events in the Court of Appeals, and perhaps some attorney incompetence, soon changed this. It is important to note the precise status of the case as it entered the Court of Appeals. Because the District Court denied Ely's (D) motions for j.n.o.v. and a new trial, the appeal essentially related to the jury verdict (although it was phrased in terms of an appeal on the District Court's denial of the j.n.o.v.). Of course, a court of appeals has full discretion to reverse a lower court's verdict, and this should have come as no surprise to Neely (P). However, Neely's (P) attorney acted incompetently in not following Rule 50(d)'s provisions. When Ely (D) appealed the denial of the j.n.o.v., Neely (P) should have either asserted grounds entitling her to a new trial or petitioned for rehearing. While Rule 50(d) *allows* the appellate court to grant a new trial if it reverses the denial of the j.n.o.v., the court is certainly not *required* to grant a new trial. A competent attorney would have the foresight to recognize that the original verdict could be overturned by the court of appeals and, therefore, to act accordingly in preserving his client's ability to obtain a new trial.

■ CASE VOCABULARY

JUDGMENT NOTWITHSTANDING THE VERDICT (JUDGMENT NON OBSTANTE VEREDICTO) (J.N.O.V.): A judgment entered for one party even though a judgment was originally entered in favor of the other party.

Denman v. Spain

(Injured Passenger) v. (Executrix)
242 Miss. 431, 135 So.2d 195 (1961)

A DIRECTED VERDICT IS PROPER WHEN THE PARTY BEARING THE BURDEN OF PROOF FAILS TO MEET THAT BURDEN

■ **INSTANT FACTS** Betty Denman (P) sued the executrix of the estate of Joseph Ross, who allegedly caused an accident on a foggy day by negligently operating his vehicle.

■ **BLACK LETTER RULE** A judgment n.o.v. may be entered against a party who fails to meet her burden of proof.

■ **PROCEDURAL BASIS**

Appeal from sustaining of judgment n.o.v. for defendant in action for damages for negligence.

■ **FACTS**

Betty Denman (P) sued the executrix (Spain (D)) of the estate of Joseph Ross for injuries sustained in an auto accident. Betty (P) was riding in a Ford which collided with a Plymouth driven by Ross. Betty (P) alleged that her injuries allegedly resulted from the negligence of Ross in operating his vehicle. Three people, including Ross and Eva Denman, Betty's (P) grandmother, were killed in the accident. Betty (P) and a passenger in Ross's vehicle had no recollection of how the collision occurred. Evidence demonstrated that the accident occurred at dusk on a rainy, foggy day. Two witnesses, who were driving along the same stretch of road, testified on behalf of Betty (P). First, John Barnett testified that Ross had passed him, traveling at seventy miles per hour [on a foggy day!] some three-fourths of a mile from the place of the accident. Second, Hal Buckley testified that Ross passed him about two hundred yards from the place of the accident, traveling at seventy-five or eighty miles per hour, and that he saw Ross's car until the time of the accident. In addition, Betty (P) offered several pictures of the accident scene. The issue was submitted to the jury on this evidence submitted by Betty (P), with Spain (D) offering no evidence on behalf of Ross [who was, unfortunately, unavailable for comment!]. The jury returned a verdict and judgment for Betty (P) for $5000, but the court sustained Spain's (D) motion for a judgment non obstante veredicto. Betty Denman (P) now appeals the sustaining of that motion.

■ **ISSUE**

Is a judgment n.o.v. proper for a defendant where the plaintiff fails to prove her case by a preponderance of the evidence?

■ **DECISION AND RATIONALE**

(Lee, J.) Yes. A judgment n.o.v. is proper for a defendant where the plaintiff fails to prove her case by a preponderance of the evidence. In this action, Betty Denman (P) failed to meet this required evidentiary standard. The photographs only depict a terrible accident scene and do not depict a reasonable or plausible explanation why the accident occurred, or who was responsible for it. Furthermore, Barnett's testimony is inadmissible, since his knowledge of the Plymouth's speed was based on what he saw nearly a mile south of the accident. Buckley's testimony, while admissible, does not indicate the place in the road where the vehicles collided. There was no showing of the speed of the Ford, or as to which car

---

was on the wrong side of the road. Thus, the tragedy is completely shrouded in mystery. Betty Denman (P) bore the burden of proving Ross's negligence by a preponderance of the evidence, and several possible conclusions may be made about who was at fault. Verdicts cannot be based on possibilities, and there is no reasonable evidence on which a jury can say that Betty (P) demonstrated Ross's negligence by a preponderance of the evidence. Affirmed.

Analysis:

This case focuses on the evidentiary burden that a civil plaintiff must meet in order to obtain a jury verdict. Inasmuch as a judgment n.o.v. is proper only where a plaintiff has failed to meet this standard, the case also demonstrates the standard required for a judgment n.o.v., i.e., a demonstration that the opposing side has failed to meet her burden. In nearly every civil cause of action, the party bringing the action must prove her case by a preponderance of the evidence. As this case adequately demonstrates, the preponderance of evidence standard does *not* entail simply providing more evidence than the opposing side. Rather, it requires the party to show that the fact sought to be proved *was more probable than not*. While Betty Denman (P) provided some evidence supporting her side, Spain (D) presented absolutely no evidence to dismiss Ross's negligence. Spain (D) most likely realized that Betty (P) would have a difficult time proving her case, since no eyewitness information or empirical data existed demonstrating the precise cause of the accident, and in any case the defendant does not have to prove that he was not negligent. Nevertheless, even though Betty (P) submitted only circumstantial evidence of Ross's negligence, perhaps this evidence should have been sufficient to allow the case to go to a jury. Unfortunately for Betty (P), the appellate court answered this question in the negative, and Betty (P) received no compensation for her injuries in this extremely unfortunate, tragic occurrence.

■ CASE VOCABULARY

PREPONDERANCE OF THE EVIDENCE: The typical evidentiary standard in civil actions, requiring the party bringing a claim to show that the fact sought to be proved is more probable than not.

Rogers v. Missouri Pacific R. Co.

(Railroad Laborer) v. *(Railroad)*
352 U.S. 500, 77 S.Ct. 443 (1957)

BURDENS OF PROOF MAY BE DETERMINED FROM THE STATUTE ON WHICH A CAUSE OF ACTION IS BASED

■ **INSTANT FACTS** Rogers (P), a railroad worker assigned to burn off vegetation alongside a railroad, sued Missouri Pacific (D) for injuries resulting in the course of his duties.

■ **BLACK LETTER RULE** A statutory action must go to the jury if the evidence is sufficient to meet the statutory burden of proof.

■ **PROCEDURAL BASIS**

Writ of certiorari reviewing reversal of judgment for damages for negligence under the Federal Employers' Liability Act.

■ **FACTS**

Rogers (P) was a laborer working along a portion of Missouri Pacific R. Co.'s (D) tracks. Rogers' (P) foreman assigned Rogers (P) to the task of burning weeds and vegetation growing alongside the tracks. Although Rogers (P) testified that it was customary to burn off such vegetation with a flame thrower operated from a car running on the tracks, Rogers (P) was instructed to bum the weeds with a crude hand torch. While engaged in this task, Rogers (P) properly ceased work when a train passed by. However, the train fanned some of the flames Rogers (P) had already created, causing Rogers (P) to retreat backwards and fall into a culvert, suffering serious injuries. Rogers (P) sued under the Federal Employers' Liability Act (FELA), and a jury in the Circuit Court of St. Louis awarded damages for Rogers (P). However, the Supreme Court of Missouri reversed on the ground that Rogers's (P) evidence did not support the finding of Missouri Pacific's (D) liability. The Supreme Court granted certiorari.

■ **ISSUE**

In a statutory action, must a case go to the jury if the evidence is sufficient to meet the statutory burden of proof?

■ **DECISION AND RATIONALE**

(Brennan, J.) Yes. In a statutory action, a case must go to the jury if the evidence is sufficient to meet the statutory burden of proof. FELA, the applicable statute in the instant action, imposes liability upon an employer for injury or death due in whole *or in part* to its negligence. Apparently the Missouri Supreme Court felt that Rogers's (P) conduct was at least as probable a cause for his mishap as any negligence of Missouri Pacific (D) and that in such case there was no case for the jury. This is not the applicable test of a jury case. If a reasonable jury could conclude from Rogers's (P) evidence that the injury was at least partially caused by Missouri Pacific (D), then the case requires submission to the jury. Alternatively, the Missouri Supreme Court could have based its reversal upon a finding that Rogers's (P) conduct was the sole cause of the injury. While this would not require jury submission, it is clear from the evidence that there existed some uncertainty as to the party at fault. No witness testified on behalf of Missouri Pacific (D) that Rogers was acting contrary to his assigned duties. All in all, we think that the evidence was sufficient to support the jury finding for Rogers (P). The testimony that the burning of vegetation was ordinarily done with flame throwers from cars on the tract supplied ample support for a jury finding that Missouri Pacific's (D) negligence played a part in Rogers's (P) injury.

Analysis:

This case deals only with the evidentiary standard in a certain statutory action, and not specifically with a judgment n.o.v. or directed verdict. Nevertheless, the standard for reversing a jury verdict is the same as the standard to grant a judgment n.o.v. or directed verdict, namely, that the party bearing the burden of proof failed to produce evidence sufficient to send the case to the jury. In terms of FELA, this would be possible only if Rogers (P) submitted no evidence from which a reasonable jury could conclude that Missouri Pacific (D) was at least partially responsible for the injuries. Note that the burden of proof in this case is, therefore, different from the typical preponderance of the evidence standard expressed in *Denman v. Spain* [preponderance of evidence standard not satisfied if plaintiff fails to prove that it was more probable than not that defendant caused the injuries]. Of course, if this case were based on *Denman*'s preponderance of the evidence standard, it may well be that Rogers (P) failed to produce enough evidence to take the case to trial. These cases may also be reconciled on another ground. Perhaps the Supreme Court of Mississippi was using the more stringent "substantial evidence" test in *Denman*, while the U.S. Supreme Court chose to apply a looser "scintilla" test in the case at hand. Regardless, despite the judicial efficiencies achieved by directing a verdict or granting a judgment n.o.v., fairness dictates that a plaintiff with any possibility of proving his case should have the opportunity to submit it to a jury.

■ CASE VOCABULARY

BALLAST: Gravel placed beneath railroad ties.

CULVERT: A drain crossing under some avenue of transportation.

Reeves v. Sanderson Plumbing Products, Inc.

(Fired Employee) v. *(Former Employer)*

530 U.S. 133, 120 S.Ct. 2097, 147 L.Ed.2d 105 (2000)

THE COURT MUST CONSIDER ALL REASONABLE INFERENCES IN THE DISCRIMINATION PLAINTIFF'S CASE

■ **INSTANT FACTS:** A fired employee sued under the ADEA and argued that the employer's allegations that he failed to keep accurate attendance records were just a cover-up up for age discrimination.

■ **BLACK LETTER RULE** A discrimination plaintiff's case may be sufficient to submit to the jury if it consists of a prima facie case of discrimination and sufficient evidence that the defendant's proffered explanation for its action was merely a pretext for discrimination, without the need for additional, independent evidence of discrimination.

■ **PROCEDURAL BASIS**

Certiorari to the United States Court of Appeals for the Fifth Circuit.

■ **FACTS**

Fifty-seven-year-old Reeves (P) had been employed by Sanderson Plumbing (D) for forty years as an attendance monitor in the "Hinge Room." Sanderson (D) believed that production was down in the Hinge Room and that employees were leaving work early or were often absent, but that these facts were not recorded in Reeves's (P) attendance records. Reeves's (P) supervisor recommended that he be fired, and the company terminated him. Reeves (P) filed suit, alleging that he had been fired on the basis of his age in violation of the Age Discrimination in Employment Act (ADEA). Reeves (P) argued that Sanderson's (D) proffered explanation for his discharge—the allegedly erroneous attendance records—was merely a pretext for discrimination. He introduced at trial evidence that he had kept accurate attendance records, and that his supervisor had previously demonstrated age-based animus toward him. The jury returned a verdict in Reeves's (P) favor, but the Court of Appeals for the Fifth Circuit reversed, holding that he had not introduced sufficient evidence that Sanderson's (D) action was based on age discrimination.

■ **ISSUE**

Is the defendant employer entitled to judgment as a matter of law when the discrimination plaintiff's case consists exclusively of a prima facie case of discrimination and sufficient evidence for the trier of fact to disbelieve the employer's legitimate, nondiscriminatory explanation for its action?

■ **DECISION AND RATIONALE**

(O'Connor, J.) No. A discrimination plaintiff's case may be sufficient to submit to the jury if it consists of a prima facie case of discrimination and sufficient evidence that the defendant's proffered explanation for its action was merely a pretext for discrimination, without the need for additional, independent evidence of discrimination. Under the ADEA, it is unlawful for an employer to discharge an employee because of such individual's age. In order for liability to be found, the plaintiff's age must have actually played a role in the decision-making process and had a determinative influence in the outcome. First, the plaintiff must establish a prima facie case of discrimination, and then the burden shifts to the defendant to present evidence supporting a legitimate, nondiscriminatory reason for the job action. Reeves (P) met his burden here by making his prima facie case, such that the burden then shifted to Sanderson (D), which also met its burden by offering admissible evidence sufficient for the trier of fact to conclude that Reeves (P) was fired due to his failure to maintain accurate attendance records. Once the employer produces sufficient evidence of a nondiscriminatory basis for its action, however, the plaintiff must be afforded an opportunity to prove, by a preponderance of the evidence, that he was the victim of intentional discrimination by showing that the employer's explanation is unworthy of credence. Here, Reeves (P) made a substantial showing that Sanderson's (D) explanation was false. He amply demonstrated that he had properly maintained the attendance records, and that his supervisor was "ageist"—he told Reeves (P), for instance, that he was "too damn old to do [his] job." Proof that the defendant's explanation is unworthy of credence is probative of intentional discrimination, and indeed may be quite persuasive. In appropriate cases, evidence of pretext may suffice to make the plaintiff's case, without the need for additional, independent evidence of discrimination. The district court was correct in submitting the case to the jury, and the court of appeals erred in overturning the jury's verdict and holding that more was required of the plaintiff. Reversed.

Analysis:

Twenty-seven years after the Supreme Court established the *McDonnell Douglas* burden-shifting analysis for employment discrimination cases, the Court unanimously rejected the notion that a plaintiff must establish "pretext-plus" to prevail at trial. In *Reeves v. Sanderson Plumbing Products, Inc.*, the Supreme Court held that a case may go to the jury if the plaintiff establishes nothing more than a prima facie case of discrimination and that the employer's proffered nondiscriminatory reason for his discharge is false. Basically, *Reeves* makes it more difficult for the court to take a case from the jury, and for the employer to achieve summary judgment in its favor.

■ CASE VOCABULARY

MCDONNELL DOUGLAS TEST: The principle for applying a shifting burden of proof in employment discrimination cases, essentially requiring the plaintiff to come forward with evidence of discrimination and the defendant to come forward with evidence showing that the employment action complained of was taken for nondiscriminatory reasons. Under this test, the plaintiff is first required to establish a prima facie case of discrimination, as by showing that the plaintiff is a member of a protected group and suffered an adverse employment action. If the plaintiff satisfies that burden, then the defendant must articulate a legitimate, nondiscriminatory reason for the employment action complained of. If the defendant satisfies that burden, then the plaintiff must prove that the defendant's stated reason is just a pretext for discrimination and that discrimination was the real reason for the employment action.

PREPONDERANCE OF THE EVIDENCE: The greater weight of the evidence, not necessarily established by the greater number of witnesses testifying to a fact but by evidence that has the most convincing force; superior evidentiary weight that, though not sufficient to free the mind wholly from all reasonable doubt, is still sufficient to incline a fair and impartial mind to one side of the issue rather than the other. This is the burden of proof in most civil trials, in which the jury is instructed to find for the party that, on the whole, has the stronger evidence, however slight the edge may be.

PRETEXT: A false or weak reason or motive advanced to hide the actual or strong reason or motive.

PRIMA FACIE CASE: The establishment of a legally required rebuttable presumption; a party's production of enough evidence to allow the fact-trier to infer the fact at issue and rule in the party's favor.

Baltimore & Carolina Line, Inc. v. Redman

(*Railroad*) v. (*Injured Party*)
295 U.S. 654, 55 S.Ct. 890 (1935)

WHEN REVERSING THE DENIAL OF A DIRECTED VERDICT, AN APPELLATE COURT MAY ENTER A JUDGMENT IN FAVOR OF THE PARTY WHO BROUGHT THE ORIGINAL DIRECTED VERDICT

■ **INSTANT FACTS** In reviewing the denial of Baltimore & Carolina's (D) motion for directed verdict, the appellate court reversed the denial but ordered a new trial rather than entering a judgment for Baltimore & Carolina (D).

■ **BLACK LETTER RULE** When reversing the denial of a directed verdict, an appellate court does not necessarily have to order a new trial, but it may enter a judgment in favor of the party who brought the original directed verdict.

■ PROCEDURAL BASIS

Writ of certiorari reviewing reversal of denial of motion for directed verdict in action for damages for negligence.

■ FACTS

Redman (P) brought an action against Baltimore & Carolina Line, Inc. (D) in federal court to recover damages for personal injuries allegedly caused by Baltimore & Carolina's (D) negligence. At the conclusion of evidence, Baltimore & Carolina (D) moved for a dismissal of the complaint and for a directed verdict, arguing that the evidence was insufficient to support a verdict for Redman (P). The court reserved its decision on both motions, without objection by either party, pending the jury's verdict. The jury subsequently returned a verdict for Redman (P). Then the court denied Baltimore & Carolina's (D) motions, holding that Redman's (P) evidence was sufficient. Baltimore & Carolina (D) appealed to the Circuit Court of Appeals, which held the evidence insufficient and ordered a new trial. Baltimore & Carolina (D) urged that the complaint should have been dismissed. The Supreme Court granted certiorari.

■ ISSUE

When reversing the denial of a directed verdict, must an appellate court order a new trial?

■ DECISION AND RATIONALE

(Van Devanter, J.) No. When reversing the denial of a directed verdict, an appellate court does not necessarily have to order a new trial. Rather, the appellate court may enter a judgment in favor of the party who brought the original directed verdict. In the case at hand, we agree with the Court of Appeals' decision to reverse the denial of the directed verdict motion brought by Baltimore & Carolina (D). However, we disagree with the outcome of the Appellate Court's decision. The Court of Appeals based its decision to order a new trial on our decision in *Slocum v. New York Life Insurance Company* [once a trial court had denied a defendant's directed verdict motion and allowed the case to go to the jury, the court could not order a judgment contrary to the jury verdict, but rather the court must order a new trial]. The factual situation of the case at hand differs significantly from that presented in *Slocum.* In the case at hand, the trial court expressly reserved its rulings on Baltimore & Carolina's (D) motions for directed verdict or dismissal of the complaint. At common law, there was a well-established practice of reserving such questions of law pending a jury verdict. This practice existed prior to the adoption of the Seventh Amendment, and therefore it must be regarded as part of the common-law rules protected by that amendment. Thus, the Court of Appeals could have, and should have, entered a judgment in favor of Baltimore & Carolina (D) when it held Redman's (P) evidence insufficient. Affirmed as modified.

Analysis:

This somewhat tangled holding is made even more confusing by the constant references to directed verdicts. In essence, by reserving a ruling on the directed verdict motion until after the jury verdict, the court transformed the motion into a motion for judgment notwithstanding the verdict. Thus, the original jury verdict was taken conditionally. The trial court could have overturned this verdict by entering a judgment n.o.v. However, the trial court erroneously (as the Court of Appeals held) denied the judgment n.o.v. By appealing this denial, Baltimore & Carolina (D) basically renewed a motion for judgment n.o.v. Thus, the holding of the case relates to an appellate court's duties when considering the denial of a judgment n.o.v. And according to the Supreme Court, an appellate court that disagrees with the denial of the judgment as a matter of law may grant the judgment, in favor of the original moving party, rather than ordering a new trial.

Kennedy v. Southern California Edison Co.

(Husband) v. *(Nuclear Power Plant Owner)*

219 F.3d 988 (9th Cir. 2000)

FAILURE TO INSTRUCT A JURY ON AN IMPORTANT ISSUE RAISED BY A PROPOSED JURY INSTRUCTION THAT WAS IMPROPER CAN BE REVERSIBLE ERROR

■ **INSTANT FACTS** After a jury found against him, a husband who had brought a wrongful death action against a nuclear power plant owner for the death of his wife from radiation exposure appealed, arguing that the trial court had erroneously refused to instruct the jury according to the husband's proposed jury instruction on the burden of proof for causation.

■ **BLACK LETTER RULE** Where a trial court is presented with a proposed jury instruction that raises an important issue of law or directs the court's attention to a point on which an instruction to the jury would be appropriate, the court is not relieved from the responsibility of giving a proper instruction simply because the proposed instruction does not completely comply with the relevant law.

■ **PROCEDURAL BASIS**

Appeal of a trial court judgment finding no liability in a wrongful death action.

■ **FACTS**

Joe Kennedy ("Kennedy") (P) brought a wrongful death action against Southern California Edison Co. ("Power Co.") (D) for the death of his wife from cancer, which he alleged had been caused by exposure to radiation from nuclear rods manufactured at Power Co.'s (D) nuclear plant. Prior to Kennedy's (P) lawsuit, a 1997 California Supreme Court opinion had held that a trial judge must instruct a jury that a plaintiff may meet the burden of proving that exposure to a product was a substantial factor in causing a person's cancer by showing that in reasonable medical probability the exposure was a substantial factor contributing to the person's risk of developing cancer. At the close of the trial of Kennedy's (P) lawsuit, Kennedy (P) proposed that the judge instruct the jury that radiation from Power Co.'s (D) nuclear plant need only have contributed to his wife's risk of developing cancer in order to be held to have been the cause of her death. The trial judge refused to give Kennedy's (P) proposed instruction and also did not give the instruction required by the 1997 California Supreme Court case. The jury found in favor of Power Co. (D) and Kennedy (P) appealed.

■ **ISSUE**

Where a trial court is presented with a proposed jury instruction that raises an important issue of law or directs the court's attention to a point on which an instruction to the jury would be appropriate, is the court relieved from the responsibility of giving a proper instruction simply because the proposed instruction does not completely comply with the relevant law?

■ **DECISION AND RATIONALE**

(Hawkins, J.) No. The trial court properly refused to give the jury instruction proposed by Kennedy (P). Kennedy's (P) suggested instruction would have permitted a finding that exposure caused the illness if the exposure merely contributed to the risk of cancer and not, as required by the 1997 California

---

Supreme Court decision, if the exposure was a substantial factor in contributing to the risk of cancer. Nevertheless, while ordinarily, a trial court does not err in refusing to give incorrect or misleading jury instructions, it may have an obligation to correctly instruct the jury after being presented with an improper proposed instruction that nonetheless directs its attention to an important issue. We hold that when a trial court is presented with an applicable instruction that raises an important point of law or directs the court's attention to a point on which instruction of the jury would be important, the court is not relieved from the responsibility of giving a proper instruction simply because the party making the request has proposed an instruction that does not completely comply with the relevant law. Here, the trial court's failure to give a proper instruction was not harmless error. An error in jury instructions relating to the parties' respective burdens of proof ordinarily requires reversal. We remand the case for a new trial. Reversed.

Analysis:

Most of the federal courts of appeals that have considered the issue have taken the approach of the court here and ruled that, if an incorrect proposed instruction is submitted to the trial judge which raises an important issue of law involved in the case, it becomes the court's duty to frame a proper instruction on the issue raised. Other circuits, however, have refused to find an error by the trial judge where the party making the improper request does not object to the absence of an instruction on the issue, on the grounds that any claim that the trial judge should have been aware of the propriety of instructing on the issue, is too speculative to constitute error. While sometimes it may be appropriate to place the burden of requesting jury instructions on the parties, rather than on the trial judge, a court must still charge the jury on the broad fundamental rules of law applicable to the facts in the case, even where the parties have not filed instruction requests under Rule 51 of the Federal Rules of Civil Procedure. Here, the California Supreme Court had recently established a clear rule on the issue of causation. It seems reasonable to charge the trial judge with the responsibility for knowing this new rule and instructing the jury on such a critical point of law, even if the parties did not properly raise it in their requests for jury instruction.

■ CASE VOCABULARY

HARMLESS ERROR: A minor error at a trial which was not prejudicial to the substantial rights of the party affected by the error and does not justify an appellate court in disturbing the trial court's judgment.

JURY INSTRUCTION: A statement made by the trial judge to the jurors informing them of the specific law they should apply to the facts of the case to reach their decision.

Nunley v. Pettway Oil Co.

(*Injured Party*) v. (*Landowner*)
346 F.2d 95 (6th Cir. 1965)

A JUDGE MAY NOT COMMENT TO THE JURY AS TO HIS OPINION ON A QUESTION OF FACT

■ **INSTANT FACTS** In Nunley's (P) action for damages resulting from a truck falling off a grease rack in a gas station, the judge opined to the jury that Nunley was a licensee rather than an invitee.

■ **BLACK LETTER RULE** Judges must refrain from providing their opinions to the jury with regard to ultimate facts of the case.

■ PROCEDURAL BASIS

Appeal of judgment for defendant in action for damages for negligence.

■ FACTS

Nunley (P) brought an action against Pettway Oil Co. (D) for injuries received when a truck fell off a grease rack in a gas station. During their initial deliberations, the jurors were unable to agree on whether Nunley (P) was a licensee or an invitee. The trial judge then called the jury into the courtroom and attempted to help them reach a decision. Although the judge noted that the jury was under no obligation to accept his statements, he commented that, in his opinion, Nunley (P) was a licensee and not an invitee. The jury subsequently entered a judgment for Pettway Oil (D) after concluding that Nunley (P) was a licensee rather than an invitee at the time of the accident. [What a surprise!] Nunley (P) appeals on the ground that the court had improperly commented to the jury on the licensee-invitee question.

■ ISSUE

May a judge give the jury his opinion as to an ultimate fact of a case?

■ DECISION AND RATIONALE

No. A judge may not give to the jury his opinion as to an ultimate fact of a case. Indeed, the District Judge has a right to comment on the evidence, as held in *Quercia v. United States* [the privilege of the judge to comment on the facts has its inherent limitations]. The *Quercia* Court noted that a judge may analyze and dissect the evidence, but he may not distort it or add to it. A judge who abuses his discretion in expressing an opinion cannot cure this error by stating that the opinion is not binding on the jury. His definite assertion of fact, made with all the persuasiveness of judicial utterance, must be withdrawn in order to avoid error. In the case at hand, the judge's comment as to the licensee-invitee question of fact amounted to an instructed verdict as to Pettway Oil (D). Reversed.

Analysis:

Common sense dictates that a judge, holding a position of esteem and power in the eyes of the jury, should not provide his opinion as to the ultimate facts of a case. While the judge can explain the law to the jury, and while he can analyze the evidence in order to aid the jury, he cannot give his personal opinion pertaining to an important fact. Naturally, if this were allowed, it would essentially undermine the role of a jury. Why would a jury who was confused on a complex factual distinction (such as that between a licensee and invitee) possibly go against the knowledgeable judge's pronouncement. A skilled judge would utilize other tactics to avoid having to assert his opinion. For example, a judge must ensure that jury instructions are sufficiently clear to avoid any problem. And even if the jury remains confused, a judge should take the role of a teacher and explain the issue to the jury without reaching his own conclusion.

■ CASE VOCABULARY

INSTRUCTED VERDICT: Another term for a directed verdict.

INVITEE: A person who enters the land of another for the economic benefit of the owner or both parties, and to whom a landowner owes a higher duty of care than a licensee.

LICENSEE: A person who enters the land of another for his own purposes, but who has a right to do so based on the permission of the landowner.

Securities and Exchange Commission v. Koenig

(*Federal Agency*) v. (*Company Official*)
557 F.3d 736 (7th Cir. 2009)

EVEN THE JURORS CAN SOMETIMES QUESTION THE WITNESSES

Yes, jurors can ask questions.

But my entire trial strategy is confusing the jury.

stus.com

■ **INSTANT FACTS** The SEC penalized the CFO of Waste Management, and he appealed from the decision, arguing that the judge should not have been allowed to ask questions of the witnesses that were submitted by the jury.

■ **BLACK LETTER RULE** Just as questions from the bench can provide insight that helps lawyers make a stronger case, so too can questions from the jury help lawyers tailor their presentations.

■ **PROCEDURAL BASIS**

Appeal to the federal circuit court from a federal district court decision imposing civil penalties on the defendant.

■ **FACTS**

Waste Management, Inc. grew at an average annual rate of twenty-six percent between 1979 and 1991. When the rate of growth declined, CFO Koenig (D) decided to improve appearances by devising accounting strategies that a jury found to be fraudulent. The judge imposed a $2.1 civil penalty and ordered Koenig (D) to pay back bonuses paid to him in the years for which he had misstated profits, since the amount of the bonuses was tied to company profitability. The court also enjoined Koenig (P) from ever again serving as a top official of a public company. Koenig (D) appealed.

■ **ISSUE**

Did the trial court improperly manage Koenig's (D) trial by allowing the judge to ask the witnesses questions submitted by the jury during the course of the trial?

■ **DECISION AND RATIONALE**

(Easterbrook, C.J.) No. Just as questions from the bench can provide insight that helps lawyers make a stronger case, so too can questions from the jury help lawyers tailor their presentations. Here, the SEC had made a motion in limine to exclude certain evidence relating to Koenig's (D) motive, but the court denied the motion, and as a result the trial dragged on for twelve weeks. Research shows that a jury cannot comprehend a trial that lasts more than twenty days. The jury understandably had questions as the lengthy trial progressed, and the judge passed some of them along to the witnesses, to be answered in court. Koenig (D) argued that allowing the jurors to participate in this fashion was error. Although the judge failed to ask the witnesses some of the jurors' questions, allowing the questions was not error. The litigation was not taken over by the jurors. Affirmed.

■ **CASE VOCABULARY**

MOTION IN LIMINE: A pretrial request that certain inadmissible evidence not be referred to or offered at trial. Typically, a party makes this motion when it believes that mere mention of the evidence during trial would be highly prejudicial and could not be remedied by an instruction to disregard. If, after the motion is granted, the opposing party mentions or attempts to offer the evidence in the jury's presence, a mistrial may be ordered. A ruling on a motion in limine does not always preserve evidentiary error for appellate purposes. To raise such an error on appeal, a party may be required to formally object when the evidence is actually admitted or excluded during trial.

Nollenberger v. United Air Lines, Inc.

(Representative of Decedent) v. *(Airline)*

216 F.Supp. 734 (S.D. Cal. 1963), vacated 335 F.2d 379 (9th Cir.), cert. dismissed 379 U.S. 951, 85 S.Ct. 452 (1964)

A COURT MAY NOT SUBMIT ADDITIONAL INTERROGATORIES FOLLOWING A JURY'S VERDICT AND SPECIAL ANSWERS, BUT IT MAY RECALCULATE THE DAMAGE AWARD IN THE FACE OF INCONSISTENCY

■ **INSTANT FACTS** In a wrongful death action, a jury returned a general verdict for Nollenberger (P) accompanied by answers to special interrogatories, but Nollenberger (P) argued that the award was inconsistent with the answers.

■ **BLACK LETTER RULE** After a jury has returned a general verdict and answered special interrogatories, the court may not submit additional interrogatories but may recalculate the damage award based on the answers.

■ **PROCEDURAL BASIS**

Review of jury verdict in wrongful death action.

■ **FACTS**

In a wrongful death action brought by Nollenberger (P), the jury rendered a general verdict accompanied by answers to interrogatories, pursuant to Federal Rule 49(b). The general verdict awarded over $114,000 in damages to Nollenberger (P). However, Nollenberger (P) alleges that the answers to the interrogatories are inconsistent with the general verdict. Thus, Nollenberger (P) requests that the court either submit additional interrogatories to the jury, calculate the amount of damages on the basis of the answers to the interrogatories given, or grant a new trial.

■ **ISSUE**

May a court submit additional interrogatories after a jury has returned its verdict answering the special interrogatories and returning a general verdict?

■ **DECISION AND RATIONALE**

(Hall, J.) No. A court may not submit additional interrogatories after a jury has returned its verdict answering the special interrogatories and returning a general verdict. The special interrogatories answered by the jury are not harmonious or reconcilable with the general verdict of $114,655. In these circumstances, Rule 49(b) permits the Court to choose from three alternatives, including re-submitting the matter to the jury for further consideration. However, the Rule does not permit the court to submit additional interrogatories after the jury has returned its verdict. If this were the intention of the Rule, it would have so provided. Although the Rule allows a court to grant a new trial under these circumstances, the Court must first attempt to make calculations from the special interrogatories and enter a judgment thereon. I calculate the damages at $171,702, and a judgment shall be entered for that amount.

Analysis:

This case illustrates a district court judge taking control, perhaps to an inordinate degree, over a jury verdict. The general holding of the case is sound, since Rule 49(b) does not specifically allow a court to submit additional interrogatories to the jury after it has rendered its verdict. Furthermore, Judge Hall's conclusion that the general verdict was unreconcilable with the answers to the special interrogatories might be correct. However, the language of Rule 49(b) *does not require* a judge to make calculations from the special interrogatories rather than granting a new trial. Judge Hall may have asserted too much control over the verdict in recalculating the damages award. Moreover, as the Court of Appeals subsequently noted in overturning Judge Hall's judgment, nothing compels a jury to calculate damage awards based on a fixed mathematical formula. The jury could have included factors extending beyond the eleven special interrogatories in arriving at the $114,655 figure. Thus, according to the Court of Appeals, no definite conflict existed between the answers and the general verdict.

■ **CASE VOCABULARY**

GENERAL VERDICT: A decision returned by a jury that simply announces which party wins and fixes an amount of damages, if applicable.

Roberts v. Ross

(*Agent*) v. (*Seller*)
344 F.2d 747 (3rd Cir. 1965)

IN A NON–JURY TRIAL, A JUDGE SHOULD SPECIFICALLY STATE HIS OWN CONCLUSIONS OF LAW AND FINDINGS OF FACT IN RENDERING A VERDICT

■ **INSTANT FACTS** In an action for payment of an agency fee, the trial judge accepted counsel's proposed findings of fact and conclusions of law as his own in entering a verdict.

■ **BLACK LETTER RULE** A trial judge in a non-jury trial should formulate his own findings of fact and conclusions of law in entering a judgment.

■ **PROCEDURAL BASIS**

Appeal from non-jury verdict for defendant in action for damages for breach of contract.

■ **FACTS**

Herbert Roberts (P) sued Norman Ross (D) to recover over $3000, alleging that Ross (D) promised to pay Roberts (P) for services rendered in providing a buyer for Ross's (P) house. The trial judge entered an order stating that he had found for Ross (D), and he directed counsel for Ross (D) to prepare proposed findings of fact, conclusions of law and draft of judgment. Over Roberts's (P) objections to these documents, the judge signed all of the documents without change. [Maybe he was late for a golf date!] The findings of fact and conclusions of law stated that, as a matter of law, Roberts (P) failed to prove by a preponderance of the evidence that the sale was procured through the agency of Roberts (P), and in any event that the promise violated the Statute of Frauds. Roberts (P) appealed from this judgment that dismissed his complaint.

■ **ISSUE**

Should a trial judge formulate his own findings of fact and conclusions of law in entering a judgment?

■ **DECISION AND RATIONALE**

(Maris, J.) Yes. In an action tried without a jury, a trial judge should formulate his own findings of fact and conclusions of law in entering a judgment. In the appeal of the instant action, Ross (D) argues that the trial judge expressly found that Ross (D) never agreed to pay Roberts (P) a commission for selling his property. This is the crucial aspect of the case, but the judge's conclusion is so inadequate as to afford this court no indication of the legal standard under which the evidence was considered. Rule 52(a) requires the trier of facts to find the facts specially and state his conclusions of law with clarity, sufficient to indicate the bases of the trial judge's decision. In the case at hand, the trial judge failed to meet this requirement. We strongly disapprove of the practice employed by this judge, who accepted Ross's (D) findings of fact and conclusions of law without articulating the judge's own reasoning process. Although a trial judge may invite counsel for both parties to submit proposed findings and conclusions, the judge should formulate his own findings and conclusions and articulate them at the time of announcing the decision, either in an opinion or a separate document. The practice of simply accepting a party's findings and conclusions does not serve the purposes of Rule 52(a). We therefore direct the court below to follow the practice of specifically enumerating his findings of fact and conclusions of law.

Analysis:

This case expresses the minimum standards required for a judge in announcing his verdict in a non-jury action. Pursuant to Rule 52(a), a judge must clearly state his findings of fact and conclusions of law. However, the Rule itself does not state that a judge cannot utilize findings and conclusions prepared *by counsel* for this purpose. In a situation where the party's proposed conclusions and findings are exactly what the judge had in mind, it does not seem to violate Rule 52(a) for the judge to simply sign and affirm these conclusions and findings. In the case at hand, while the appellate court clearly voices its disapproval of the trial judge's tactics in this case, the opinion is somewhat contradictory. On one hand, the appellate court says that the judge's tactic of adopting Ross's (D) findings of fact and conclusions of law was inadequate because these documents were not sufficient to indicate the bases of the judge's decision. Thus, presumably, a trial judge could employ this practice if the documents provided by counsel *did* exactly indicate the bases of his decision. However, the appellate court later voices disapproval for this entire practice, directing the judge to formulate his own findings and conclusions.

■ **CASE VOCABULARY**

EX POST FACTO: Literally "after the fact."

VERBATIM: Literally "word for word."

Ginsberg v. Williams

(*Injured Party*) v. (*Motorist*)
270 Minn. 474, 135 N.W.2d 213 (1965)

WHEN STATE RULES SPECIFICALLY ENUMERATE THE GROUNDS FOR A NEW TRIAL, A JUDGE MAY NOT GRANT A NEW TRIAL FOR A NON–ENUMERATE REASON

■ **INSTANT FACTS** After a jury verdict for Williams (D), the trial judge granted a new trial based on "the interests of justice," and Williams (D) sought a writ of prohibition since this was a non-enumerated reason for new trial.

■ **BLACK LETTER RULE** A state trial judge may grant a new trial only for reasons enumerated by the applicable state rules.

■ **PROCEDURAL BASIS**

Writ of prohibition seeking to restrain enforcement of new trial following verdict for defendant in action for damages for negligence.

■ **FACTS**

Ginsberg (P) sued Williams (D) for damages for injuries received in an automobile accident. In response to a jury verdict for Williams (D), Ginsberg (P) moved for a new trial. The trial judge granted the motion "in the interests of justice." Williams (D) sought a writ of prohibition to restrain enforcement of the ruling, arguing that the trial court is only permitted to grant a new trial for one of the grounds enumerated in the Minnesota Rules of Civil Procedure, and that "the interests of justice" was not one of these grounds.

■ **ISSUE**

When a rule of procedure allows for new trial only in enumerated circumstances, may a judge grant a new trial for a non-enumerated reason?

■ **DECISION AND RATIONALE**

(Justice Not Stated) No. When a rule of procedure allows for new trial only in enumerated circumstances, a judge may not grant a new trial for a non-enumerated reason. Rule 59.01 of the Minnesota Rules of Civil Procedure specifies a comprehensive set of reasons for a new trial. These reasons, ranging from irregularities denying a fair trial to insufficiency of the evidence, grant broad discretion to the trial court. However, the "interests of justice" is not listed as a reason. Thus, the granting of a new trial "in the interests of justice" involves a trial judge's arbitrary exercise of power over which appellate review is not available. It is difficult to conceive how such a general ground would add anything to the enumerated grounds unless it is desirable to restore the common-law power of granting a new trial when the judge is personally dissatisfied with the verdict. Accordingly, Williams's (D) writ is granted.

Analysis:

In enumerating the possible grounds for a new trial, the Minnesota Rules take a restrictive approach to a judge's power in granting new trials. Contrast this with Federal Rules 59 and 61, which empower a judge to grant a new trial when this is consistent with "substantial justice." For example, at a nonjury trial, a judge may grant a new trial for any of the reasons for which rehearings have been granted in suits in equity. Thus, the Federal Rules apparently allow trial judges to grant a new trial based on common-law powers whenever the judge is personally dissatisfied with the verdict. According to the opinion of the Minnesota Supreme Court in this case, such is clearly not the standard in Minnesota. It may be argued that the Minnesota Rules were more carefully considered than the Federal Rules, since they prohibit the arbitrary assertion of power by a trial judge. On the other hand, the reasons enumerated in the Minnesota Rules may be overly restrictive, and perhaps a judge should have a broad power to grant new trial with regard to any errors that effect the result in the case but would not necessarily lead to reversal on appeal.

■ CASE VOCABULARY

WRIT OF PROHIBITION: Process by which a superior court restrains an inferior court from exercising powers exceeding the inferior court's scope.

Magnani v. Trogi

(*Administratrix*) v. (*Unspecified Party*)
70 Ill.App.2d 216, 218 N.E.2d 21 (1966)

A COURT MAY GRANT A NEW TRIAL IN RESPONSE TO INCOHERENT JURY VERDICTS

■ **INSTANT FACTS** After the jury returned a verdict for Magnani (P) for $19,000 on one or both of her causes of action, the trial court granted Trogi's (D) motion for new trial based on the incomplete nature of the jury verdict.

■ **BLACK LETTER RULE** A trial judge may grant a new trial where a jury verdict is incoherent or not sufficiently detailed.

■ PROCEDURAL BASIS

Appeal from order granting motion for new trial, vacating judgment, and denying motion for judgment notwithstanding the verdict, in action for damages for wrongful death and for reimbursement of medical and funeral expenses.

■ FACTS

Magnani (P) sued Trogi (D) based on two causes of action. The first cause of action sought recovery of $30,000, as administratrix, for the wrongful death of her husband. The second cause of action sought reimbursement, in her individual capacity, for medical and funeral expenses incurred as the result of the injury and death to her husband. While the first cause of action would require any recovery to be distributed to the widow and the next of kin, there would be no apportionment under the second cause of action. Neither party tendered separate forms of verdict for each of these counts. The jury returned a general verdict in favor of Magnani (P) for $19,000. Trogi (D) filed for a new trial, arguing that there was no way to determine what cause of action formed the basis for the jury verdict. The trial judge vacated the verdict and judgment, granted this motion for new trial, and denied Trogi's (D) motion for judgment notwithstanding the verdict. Magnani (P) appealed.

■ ISSUE

Where an incoherent jury verdict could be construed in two ways, each providing for different distribution of the award, may a trial judge grant a new trial?

■ DECISION AND RATIONALE

(Coryn, J.) Yes. Where an incoherent jury verdict could be construed in two ways, each providing for different distribution of the award, a trial judge may grant a new trial. In the case at hand, the general jury verdict did not detail whether the damages award was based on the first or second cause of action or on both of them. It might be that the verdict was based on the wrongful death action and non-liability as to the medical expense cause of action. However, the jury verdict gives no indication of the jury's determination as to what portion of the $19,000 it attributed to damages for wrongful death and what portion, if any, it attributed to damages for medical and funeral expenses. In this situation, it was not an abuse of discretion for the trial judge to grant a new trial. A trial court is generally allowed great latitude in granting a new trial, in order to permit the judge to correct errors that he or the jury might have made during the course of the trial. In the case at hand, Trogi (D) did not waive his right to complain of the form of verdict simply because Trogi (D) did not object to the giving of this form to the jury. Thus, the order of the trial court, granting Trogi's (D) motion for new trial, vacating the verdict and judgment, and denying Trogi's (D) motion for judgment notwithstanding the verdict, is affirmed.

■ DISSENT

(Stouder, J.) Although a trial judge has broad latitude in granting a new trial, this rule has limitations. A judge is not allowed to set aside a verdict simply because he does not agree with it. In the case at hand, the trial judge granted a new trial because he found that the forms of verdict submitted to the jury were improper. I am unable to find that Trogi (D) made any objection to the forms of verdict at any time prior to his post-trial motion. Thus, Trogi's (D) motion for a new trial should have been denied.

Analysis:

This case analyzes the scope of a state court judge's discretion to grant a new trial. In general, as the majority notes, judges are allowed broad discretion to grant new trials in order to correct errors that they or the jury made during the course of the trial. However, in the case at hand, it is questionable whether the jury or judge actually made any such errors. The jury simply returned a verdict based on the form submitted to it. Unfortunately, this form did not compel the jury to specify which cause of action, if any, it based its damages award upon. Nevertheless, this error was caused by attorney incompetence in not preparing two separate verdict forms. Trogi (D) clearly had the opportunity to submit different forms, forcing the jury to explain whether damages were being awarded for the wrongful death action, for the reimbursement action, or for both. The dissent therefore raises a valid point. Perhaps Trogi (D) should not have been allowed to bring a post-trial motion for new trial when he himself caused the incoherent jury verdict. All in all, however, the case further illustrates a trial judge's broad discretion in granting a new trial based on any major deficiencies in the form or substance of the jury verdict.

Robb v. John C. Hickey, Inc.

(*Representative of Decedent*) v. (*Unspecified Party*)

19 N.J.Misc. 455, 20 A.2d 707 (1941)

A JUDGE MAY MOLD AN INCOHERENT JURY VERDICT ONLY WHERE THE VERDICT CLEARLY EXPRESSES THE INTENT OF THE JURY

■ **INSTANT FACTS** In an action based on negligence and contributory negligence, the jury held that the decedent, represented by Robb (P), was partially negligent but nevertheless suggested $2000 in damages for Robb (P), in conflict with the stated law. Both parties contested the verdict.

■ **BLACK LETTER RULE** A judge may mold an incoherent jury verdict to coincide with the substance of the jury's declaration only if the verdict clearly expresses the intent of the jury.

■ **PROCEDURAL BASIS**

Review of motions to set aside or mold a jury verdict for damages for comparatory negligence.

■ **FACTS**

Robb (P) sued John C. Hickey, Inc. (D) for negligence on behalf of a decedent. The jury was instructed to rule for Hickey (D) if any contributory negligence on the part of the decedent was shown. The jury verdict stated that the jury found negligence on the part of both parties. Nevertheless, the jury concluded that Hickey (D) was more negligent than the decedent, so it recommended an award of $2000 in favor of Robb (P). [Apparently the jury wanted to formulate its own legal standard!] Both Robb (P) and Hickey (D) are dissatisfied with the verdict. [In trying to be fair, the jury upset both parties!] Robb (P) contends that the verdict is ambiguous, inconsistent, and contrary to the charge of the court. Thus, Robb (P) moves to set aside the verdict. Hickey (D) moves for the court to mold the verdict into one in favor of Hickey (D), arguing that this was the true intent of the jury.

■ **ISSUE**

Where a self-contradictory jury verdict fails to clearly indicate the intent of the jury, may a judge mold the verdict to coincide with the substance of the jury's declaration?

■ **DECISION AND RATIONALE**

(Leyden, J.) No. Where a self-contradictory jury verdict fails to clearly indicate the intent of the jury, a judge may not mold the verdict to coincide with the substance of the jury's declaration. The verdict recommended by the jury in the case at hand was self-contradictory, since it noted that the decedent was negligent but nevertheless recommended an award of $2000 in favor of the decedent and Robb (P), suing on the decedent's behalf. This verdict was defective in substance and in form. When a jury's informal verdict is incoherent, a court may mold this verdict only where the real purpose and intent of the jury clearly, sufficiently and convincingly appears. However, the jury's informal verdict in this case was uncertain and ambiguous. Thus, Hickey's (D) motion to mold the verdict is denied, and a new trial will be granted.

Analysis:

What should a judge do when a jury verdict is self-contradictory or fails to accurately apply the legal standards stated in the jury instructions? This is a difficult issue for the trial judge. In some situations, as this opinion notes, a judge may mold a jury verdict into a correct statement of law. However, this option is only available where the purpose and intent of the jury clearly, sufficiently and convincingly appears in the verdict. In the case at hand, the jury appears to have reached legally contradictory conclusions. On one hand, the jury found that the decedent was contributorily negligent. Based on the jury instructions and on the applicable law of contributory negligence, a verdict should have been entered for Hickey (D). However, the jury apparently misconstrued the law and proceeded to weigh the relative degrees of negligence of the two parties, finding that Hickey (D) should pay $2000 because it was more negligent.

■ CASE VOCABULARY

DEHORS: Term meaning "unconnected with."

Duk v. MGM Grand Hotel, Inc.

(*Injured Hotel Patron*) v. (*Casino Hotel*)

320 F.3d 1052 (9th Cir. 2003)

JURORS SHOULD BE ALLOWED TO RECONCILE INCONSISTENT VERDICTS

The judge says we need to return a new verdict because our first try proves we're morons.

■ **INSTANT FACTS** Hotel security staff took an unruly Duk (P) into custody on the premises; Duk (P) suffered a heart attack while in hotel custody and later sued the hotel, but the jury returned inconsistent verdicts, so both parties appealed.

■ **BLACK LETTER RULE** Where the jury is still available, a district court's decision to resubmit an inconsistent verdict for clarification is within its discretion.

■ **PROCEDURAL BASIS**

Appeal by the plaintiff from a defense verdict after the second trial, and cross-appeal by the defendant from the district court's decision to resubmit the first verdict to the jury for clarification.

■ **FACTS**

Duk (P) became boisterous after a night of drinking and gambling at the MGM Grand Hotel (D), and security guards asked him to leave. When he refused, Duk (P) was detained at the hotel until the police could arrive and take him to jail. Duk's (P) wife contacted the hotel and told them her husband was an insulin-dependent diabetic. After about twenty minutes in detention, Duk (P) complained of lung and chest pain. The security guards called for an ambulance and the medics examined Duk (P), but apparently they failed to tell the medics he was having chest pain. More than two hours later, Duk (P) was taken to jail. When he was released the next morning, Duk (P) went to the hospital, where it was discovered that he had suffered a heart attack and sustained severe damage to his heart, ultimately requiring a transplant. Duk (P) sued the hotel and the case was tried to a jury.

The jury was instructed, pursuant to Nevada's comparative negligence law, that if Duk (P) was more than fifty percent at fault, he should not be awarded damages. Nonetheless, the jury returned a verdict finding Duk (P) sixty-five percent negligent, but awarding him $3.3 million in damages. The court returned the verdict form to the jury and reinstructed the jurors, and they returned a second verdict assigning forty-nine percent of the negligence to Duk (P), and leaving the damages award intact. MGM Grand (D) moved for a new trial based on the inconsistency of the verdicts, and the court granted the motion. At the second trial, the jury entered a verdict for the defendant. Duk (P) appealed, arguing that the second verdict from the first trial was legitimate and that a new trial should not have been granted. MGM Grand (D) cross-appealed, arguing that the case should have been disposed of after the first verdict, wherein Duk (P) was found more than fifty percent negligent; in the alternative, the defendant argued, the new trial was properly ordered.

■ **ISSUE**

Did the trial court properly resubmit the case to the jury for a second verdict after the first trial?

■ **DECISION AND RATIONALE**

(Hawkins, J.) Yes. Where the jury is still available, a district court's decision to resubmit an inconsistent verdict for clarification is within its discretion. If the district court judge does not push the jury in one

---

direction or another, resubmission is the most sensible solution. In *Larson v. Neimi*, 9 F.3d 1397 (9th Cir. 1993), for instance, we applied this principle, holding that it was proper to resubmit the special verdict to the jury where it had found the defendant had qualified immunity, but awarded the plaintiff damages nonetheless. The jury's second verdict found that the defendant did not have qualified immunity, and still awarded the plaintiff damages. Although resubmission opens the door to the possibility that the jury will reach an improper "compromise" verdict, we have to trust the jury system. Rarely is a court entitled to disregard a jury verdict that is supported by substantial evidence. But allowing a jury to reconcile inconsistencies is only possible if the jury is allowed to resume its deliberations. In this case, it is quite plausible that the jury changed the apportionment of liability because it redeliberated and changed its mind or clarified its thinking. It cannot be said that the jury was seeking a predetermined result. The trial court has a duty to reconcile the verdicts on any reasonable theory consistent with the evidence. Because it is possible to explain the inconsistency here in a way that comports with the law, the district court's decision to disregard the second verdict and order a new trial was an abuse of discretion. The trial court did not abuse its discretion, however, in ordering resubmission of the first verdict. We order reinstatement of the second verdict and entry of judgment in favor of the plaintiff.

Analysis:

This case involves consideration of the plaintiff's comparative negligence. The court explained to the jury that if Duk (P) was more than fifty percent at fault for his own injuries, he could not recover at all. Not all states' comparative negligence laws are like Nevada's. Some states apply "pure comparative negligence"—the principle that liability for negligence is apportioned according to the percentage of fault that the factfinder assigns to each party, and the plaintiff's percentage of fault reduces the amount of recoverable damages but does not bar recovery. "Modified comparative negligence," by contrast, is the principle that liability for negligence is apportioned in accordance with the percentage of fault that the factfinder assigns to each party, and the plaintiff's recovery is reduced by the percentage of negligence assigned to the plaintiff—but the plaintiff's recovery is barred completely if the plaintiff was more at fault than the defendant(s).

■ CASE VOCABULARY

COMPARATIVE NEGLIGENCE: A plaintiff's own negligence that proportionally reduces the damages recoverable from a defendant.

CONTRIBUTORY NEGLIGENCE: A plaintiff's own negligence that played a part in causing the plaintiff's injury and that is significant enough (in a few jurisdictions) to bar the plaintiff from recovering damages. In most jurisdictions, this defense has been superseded by comparative negligence.

Hukle v. Kimble

(*Elevator Employee*) v. (*Driver*)

172 Kan. 630, 243 P.2d 225 (1952)

QUOTIENT VERDICTS MAY CONSTITUTE JURY MISCONDUCT

■ **INSTANT FACTS** Following a quotient verdict in favor of Hukle (P) for damages, Kimble (D) appeals the denial of his motion for retrial on grounds of jury misconduct.

■ **BLACK LETTER RULE** The use of quotient verdicts may constitute jury misconduct.

■ **PROCEDURAL BASIS**

Appeal from denial of motion for new trial following quotient verdict for damages for negligence.

■ **FACTS**

Hukle (P) brought an action for damages sustained when he was pinned between a truck driven by Kimble (D) and a pillar. Using a quotient verdict, the jury arrived at an award of over $5000 for Hukle (P). Kimble (D) moved for a new trial on the grounds that the quotient verdict amounted to jury misconduct. Kimble (D) now appeals the denial of this motion.

■ **ISSUE**

Does the use of a quotient verdict constitute jury misconduct?

■ **DECISION AND RATIONALE**

(Smith, J.) Yes. The use of a quotient verdict constitutes jury misconduct. On a hearing of the motion for new trial, various jury members testified that the foreman suggested the use of a quotient verdict. Before the verdict was taken, there had been some discussion and the foreman opined that there should be a judgment for Hukle (P). Apparently all jurors felt that the quotient verdict would arrive at a fair measure of damages, and each juror attested to the fairness of the verdict after it was reached. Nevertheless, the use of the quotient verdict constitutes jury misconduct. Accordingly, the trial court erred in overruling Kimble's (D) motion for new trial.

Analysis:

This puzzling holding undermines a seemingly efficient and fair approach to the determination of a damage award. After all, if every juror agrees on the issue of liability, then the measure of damages must be determined somehow. Why not allow the jurors to independently write down what they feel is an appropriate damages figure and simply average the amounts? The answer is straightforward but was not mentioned in this opinion. Quotient verdicts, such as the one at issue in this case, make sense *only* *after* the jury reaches unanimous consent on the issue of liability. The facts of this case do not demonstrate that each member of the jury agreed on liability. Thus, perhaps some jurors wrote "no damages" as the recommended amount, feeling that Kimble (D) was not liable. However, when these zero amounts are averaged with other damage figures, the resulting quotient verdict makes it appear that unanimous consent was reached as to liability. In the case at hand, all jurors agreed that the quotient verdict was fair. But maybe some jurors felt that there was no liability and were afraid to contest the mathematical derivation. Perhaps quotient verdicts do not constitute jury misconduct per se. If used after liability is determined, or merely as a basis for further deliberation, quotient verdicts have some advantages and probably would not constitute jury misconduct but rather would exemplify an efficient approach for jury deliberations.

■ CASE VOCABULARY

QUOTIENT VERDICT: A damages award calculated by each juror writing down what he thinks is an appropriate amount and then averaging the figures.

McDonough Power Equipment, Inc. v. Greenwood

(Lawnmower Manufacturer) v. *(Injured Party)*

464 U.S. 548, 104 S.Ct. 845 (1984)

MISTAKEN VOIR DIRE ANSWERS CONSTITUTE JUROR MISCONDUCT ONLY IF CORRECT ANSWERS WOULD CONSTITUTE A VALID BASIS FOR DISMISSING THE JUROR FOR CAUSE

■ **INSTANT FACTS** In an action for damages caused by a power mower, Greenwood (P) moved for a new trial on the basis of newly-discovered information that a juror had incorrectly answered a question on voir dire.

■ **BLACK LETTER RULE** A mistaken response on voir dire constitutes juror misconduct only if the question was material and if a correct response would have provided a valid basis for challenging for cause.

■ **PROCEDURAL BASIS**

Writ of certiorari reviewing reversal of denial of motion for new trial on the basis of juror misconduct in action for damages for negligence.

■ **FACTS**

Greenwood (P) sued McDonough Power Equipment, Inc. (D) for injuries allegedly suffered in an accident involving a power mower manufactured by McDonough (D). Following a jury verdict for McDonough (D), Greenwood (P) moved for a new trial, claiming based on newly discovered information that the foreman had dishonestly answered a question on voir dire. This foreman initially answered in the negative when asked if he or any member of his family had sustained any severe injury. However, Greenwood's (P) attorney later discovered that the foreman's son had suffered a broken leg by the explosion of a truck tire. Without these details, the District Court denied Greenwood's (P) motion for new trial. The Tenth Circuit ruled that the juror's failure to honestly respond to the question on voir dire constituted juror misconduct requiring a new trial. The Supreme Court granted certiorari.

■ **ISSUE**

Does a mistaken response on voir dire necessarily mandate a new trial?

■ **DECISION AND RATIONALE**

No. A mistaken or inaccurate response on voir dire does not necessarily mandate a new trial. To invalidate the result of a 3-week trial because of a juror's mistaken, though honest, response to a question is to insist on something closer to perfection than our judicial system can be expected to give. In order to obtain a new trial as a result of a mistaken answer on voir dire, the moving party must first demonstrate that the juror failed to honestly answer a material question. Further, the party must show that a correct response would have provided a valid basis for a challenge for cause. This standard was not met in the case at hand. Reversed.

■ **CONCURRENCE**

(Blackmun, J.) Although we concur in the judgment, the Court's holding should not be understood to foreclose the normal avenue of relief available to a party who is asserting that he did not have the benefit of an impartial jury.

■ CONCURRENCE

(Brennan, J.) Although we concur in the result of this case, a different legal test should have been used. The proper focus when ruling on a motion for new trial in this situation should be on the bias of the juror and the resulting prejudice to the litigant. In order to be awarded a new trial, the litigant should be required to show that the juror incorrectly responded to a material question on voir dire *and* that the juror was biased against the litigant. Bias may be established if facts conclusively dictate a presumption of bias, or if it is more probable than not that the juror was actually biased.

Analysis:

The majority raises a good point regarding motions for new trial in light of erroneous jury answers on voir dire. A mistaken answer should not ordinarily overturn the hard work of a long trial, wasting judicial resources. The main focus of the majority opinion and concurrences is the legal standard by which new trials should be granted in these situations. All of the justices agree that the mistakenly-answered question must have been material. In the case at hand, an action for serious injuries, the issue of whether a juror or family member had ever sustained a serious injury was undoubtedly material. Pursuant to the majority's approach, new trial is appropriate only if a correct response would have provided a valid basis for a challenge for cause. Although the excerpt does not specifically analyze the case at hand, the Court's holding suggests that even if the foreman had correctly disclosed the nature of his son's previous injury, this would be insufficient to dismiss the juror for cause. Probably Greenwood (P) would not have desired to dismiss this juror, since the juror would likely be sympathetic to an injured person like Greenwood (P). Greenwood's (P) contention of jury misconduct seems tenuous at best. And according to the standard set forth in Justice Brennan's concurrence, it is unlikely that the juror had any bias against Greenwood (P). In sum, this case reveals a wise, conservative approach to overturning valid jury verdicts on the mere basis that a question was incorrectly answered on voir dire.

Aetna Casualty & Surety Co. v. Yeatts

(*Insurer*) v. (*Doctor*)
122 F.2d 350 (4th Cir. 1941)

A TRIAL COURT HAS BROAD DISCRETION TO GRANT OR DENY NEW TRIALS BASED ON SUFFI-CIENCY OF THE EVIDENCE

■ **INSTANT FACTS** In response to an adverse jury verdict on its action for declaratory relief, Aetna Casualty (D) moved for a new trial or judgment n.o.v., but the judge denied both motions.

■ **BLACK LETTER RULE** Trial judges may grant or deny new trials under circumstances which would prevent judgments n.o.v. or directed verdicts.

■ **PROCEDURAL BASIS**

Appeal from denial of motion for new trial and motion for judgment n.o.v. in action for declaratory judgment regarding insurance benefits.

■ **FACTS**

Aetna Casualty & Surety Co. (P) sought a declaratory judgment stating that Yeatts (the insured) (D) was engaged in the performance of a criminal abortion at the time of his acts, the liability for which Aetna (P) was not obliged to cover. The jury rendered a verdict in support of Yeatts (D). The sufficiency of the evidence was not challenged before the verdict. Aetna (P) moved for a judgment non obstante veredicto and a new trial, on the ground that the verdict was contrary to the credible evidence in the case. The court denied these motions, and Aetna (P) appeals.

■ **ISSUE**

(1) May a trial court grant a motion for new trial under circumstances insufficient to direct a verdict or grant a judgment n.o.v.? (2) Is a trial judge's decision to deny a new trial not reviewable upon appeal, save the most exceptional circumstances?

■ **DECISION AND RATIONALE**

(Parker, J.) (1) Yes. A trial court may grant a motion for new trial under circumstances insufficient to direct a verdict or grant a judgment n.o.v. A trial judge may not direct a verdict against a party where there is substantial evidence in support of that party's case. Nevertheless, the judge may set aside a verdict supported by substantial evidence where he is of the opinion that the verdict is contradictory to the clear weight of the evidence, or is based upon evidence which is false, or will result in a miscarriage of justice. The judge must prevent a miscarriage of justice, even if the evidence is sufficient to preclude the direction of a verdict. (2) Yes. A trial judge's decision to deny a new trial is not reviewable upon appeal, save the most exceptional circumstances. The granting or refusing of a new trial is a matter resting in the sole discretion of a trial judge. In the case at hand, while the trial judge might very properly have granted the motion for new trial, we cannot say that his denial of the motion amounted to an abuse of discretion on his part. Further, there are not present any special circumstances which would subject his action to review by this court. Affirmed.

Analysis:

This case demonstrates a trial judge's considerable power with respect to granting new trials. When sufficiency of the evidence is an issue, the overlap between new trials and directed verdicts or judgments n.o.v. can be somewhat confusing. All of these potential judicial tools are based on legal insufficiency of the evidence, but the difference is one of degree. As this case demonstrates, a new trial may be granted even though the amount of insufficiency fails short of the standard required to support a directed verdict or judgment n.o.v. In other words, perhaps the evidence was sufficient enough that reasonable jurors could have reached a certain verdict, but the verdict remains manifestly against the weight of the evidence. In this situation, a judge may prevent the miscarriage of justice by granting a new trial, which is much less severe than directing a verdict or entering a judgment n.o.v. that contradicts the jury verdict.

Fisch v. Manger

(*Injured Party*) v. (*Allegedly Negligent Party*)

24 N.J. 66, 130 A.2d 815 (1957)

A JUDGE MAY CONSTITUTIONALLY ALTER THE AMOUNT OF A JURY VERDICT AND DEMAND THAT A PARTY ACCEPT THE NEW AMOUNT RATHER THAN GRANT A NEW TRIAL

■ **INSTANT FACTS** Following a jury verdict in his favor for $3000, Fisch (P) objected to the court's use of additur, by which the decision to deny Fisch's (P) motion for new trial was made conditional on Manger's (D) acceptance of an increased damages award.

■ **BLACK LETTER RULE** A court may employ the practice of additur without violating the constitutional right to a jury trial.

■ FACTS

Fisch (P) sued Manger (D) for injuries in an automobile accident. After the jury returned a verdict for Fisch (P) for $3000, Fisch (P) applied for a new trial because of the inadequacy of the verdict. The trial judge ordered that the motion for new trial would be denied if Manger (D) consented that the damages be increased to $7500 [a procedure known as "additur"]. Manger (D) consented, and a judgment for this amount was entered. Fisch (P) now appeals the inadequacy of the increased amount of damages, contending that the trial court had no legal power to condition the grant of new trial upon Manger's (D) failure to consent to a proposed increase in the damages amount [even though the increase inured to Fisch's benefit!]. Fisch (P) further contends that, in any event, the increase to $7500 was grossly inadequate and should be set aside.

■ ISSUE

May a trial court constitutionally employ the practice of additur?

■ DECISION AND RATIONALE

(Jacobs, J.) Yes. A trial court may constitutionally apply the practice of additur. Under this procedure, a trial judge may make his denial of a motion for new trial conditional on the other party's acceptance of an increased award of damages. Fisch (P) contends that the court had no legal power to condition the grant of a new trial upon Manger's (D) failure to consent to the $4500 increase in the jury verdict. Stated another way, Fisch (P) did not feel that Manger (D) should be allowed to escape a new trial by agreeing to increase the damage award. Courts have historically applied the practices of additur and remittitur, although some federal courts have held that additur is prohibited by the Seventh Amendment. However, the Seventh Amendment differs somewhat from our constitutional provision regarding jury trial, and thus the Seventh Amendment has no application to these proceedings. The highly desirable practices of remittitur and additur have been recognized in New Jersey. They violate none of our constitutional provisions and, if properly invoked, serve the laudable purpose of avoiding a further trial where substantial justice may be attained on the basis of the original trial. Nevertheless, we agree with Fisch's (P) second contention, namely that the prescribed increase to $7500 was grossly inadequate. The trial judge apparently had a mistaken notion of the evidence, leading to a scanty sum of $7500 being offered to Manger (D) as an alternative to a new trial. We thus believe that the trial court's action should not be permitted to stand. The issue of liability was clearly decided against Manger (D), but we remand for a new trial on the issue of damages. Reversed, with direction for a new trial on the issue of damages.

■ CONCURRENCE

(In Result) (Heher, J.) The power to conditionally increase a jury verdict through additur does not follow from the power to conditionally decrease it through remittitur. In the case of additur, no jury has ever passed on the increased amount of damages, and the practice has no precedent in common law. Where an inadequate verdict is increased by the court there is a bald addition of something which in no sense can be said to be included in the jury's verdict. This contravenes the essence of the common-law right of jury trial.

Analysis:

At first glance, the practices of remittitur and additur appear to be a beneficial settlement-like tool employed by trial judges. As discussed in earlier chapters, judges have broad authority to encourage settlement in order to conserve judicial resources and efficiently resolve a dispute. However, additur and remittitur involve something not implicated by simple settlement negotiations—the right to jury trial. The right to trial by jury, as provided by the Seventh Amendment and analogous state constitutions, allows a party to have many of its issues, including the amount of damages, decided by a jury rather than a judge. Does a judge's attempt at modifying a jury verdict, used as a tool to coerce acceptance of the verdict and avoid a new trial, necessarily impinge on the right to jury trial? The majority clearly feels that the efficiency justifications and the long history of the process of remittitur justify an acceptance of the process of additur as well. Nevertheless, the concurrence raises a point that bears mention. While remittitur involves decreasing an amount already decided by a jury, additur involves a judge going over and above the jury's determination of damages. While these two practices are logically distinguishable, in reality they both appear laudable and useful.

■ CASE VOCABULARY

ADDITUR: The practice of entering an order denying a party's application for new trial on condition that the other party consent to a specified increase in the jury's award of damages.

REMITTITUR: The practice of entering an order denying a party's application for new trial on condition that the other party consent to a specified reduction in the jury's award of damages.

Powers v. Allstate Ins. Co.

(*Insured*) v. (*Insurer*)
10 Wis.2d 78, 102 N.W.2d 393 (1960)

THE AMOUNT FOR REMITTITUR CAN BE SET BY THE COURT

■ **INSTANT FACTS** In response to an excessive award of $5000 of damages to Powers (P), the Wisconsin Supreme Court is asked to review the amount at which remittitur is set.

■ **BLACK LETTER RULE** The trial or appellate court can set the reasonable amount for remittitur.

■ **PROCEDURAL BASIS**

Review of remittitur of judgment for damages for injuries.

■ **FACTS**

Powers (P) received a jury award for permanent injuries in the amount of $5000. The award was excessive and called for remittitur. The Wisconsin Supreme Court was asked to consider what standard should determine the amount to which the damages should be reduced.

■ **ISSUE**

May remittitur be set at a reasonable amount as determined by a trial or appellate court?

■ **DECISION AND RATIONALE**

(Justice Not Stated) Yes. Remittitur may be set as a reasonable amount as determined by a trial or appellate court. This holding overrules our prior decision in *Heimlich v. Tabor* [remittitur amount must be set at the lowest amount that a reasonable jury could have awarded]. The *Heimlich* rule tends to limit the effectiveness of the remittitur practice. Pursuant to this rule, a plaintiff would be likely to refuse the remittitur amount and elect a new trial.

Analysis:

This case focuses on a practical and important aspect of the use of remittitur and additur. If these practices are to be truly effective, then the revised amount of damages must be set at a level appealing to the party called upon to accept the revised figure. In the case of remittitur, a defendant brings a motion for new trial based on an inordinate amount of damages awarded to the plaintiff. The plaintiff can avoid the new trial only by agreeing to a lower amount of damages, as set by the court. In the case at hand, it is likely that Powers (P) would have opted for a new trial if the damages were remitted to a low amount, such as $300. However, using the *Heimlich* rule, a court might have been required to set the amount this low; at least, at the lowest amount a reasonable jury could have awarded. The revised approach adopted by this court allows the judge to utilize his discretion, with a knowledge of the nuances and desires of each party, to set a fair amount which the plaintiff would happily accept in order to avoid the risk and expense of new trial.

Doutre v. Niec

(*Client*) v. (*Beautician*)
2 Mich.App. 88, 138 N.W.2d 501 (1965)

THE ISSUE OF LIABILITY SHOULD NOT BE RETRIED WITHOUT ALSO RESUBMITTING THE AMOUNT OF DAMAGES

■ **INSTANT FACTS** Doutre (P) sued Niec (D) for injuries suffered in the course of a hair bleach and color treatment, and both parties appeal to a judgment for a new trial on the issue of liability alone.

■ **BLACK LETTER RULE** The issue of liability should not be retried without a reconsideration of the amount of damages.

■ **PROCEDURAL BASIS**

Appeal from grant of partial new trial on issue of liability following a jury verdict for damages for negligence.

■ **FACTS**

Doutre (P) sued Niec (D), the operator of a beauty shop, after Doutre (P) was given a bleach and color treatment without a pretreatment patch test. Doutre (P) received head and facial injuries and sued for damages. At trial, Niec (D) was not allowed to testify as to the standard of care of beauty shops in the area. [Perhaps all beauticians in the area recklessly disregarded the safety of their patients!] The jury awarded $10,000 to Doutre (P). Niec (D) moved for a new trial, and the court granted a partial new trial limited to the question of liability only. Both parties appeal the order for partial new trial. Doutre (P) alleges that the court was correct in ruling that the testimony on the standard of care was not admissible. Niec (D) alleges that the new trial should not have been limited to the issue of liability because questions of liability and damages are closely intertwined.

■ **ISSUE**

May a court separate the issue of liability from the issue of damages and grant a partial new trial on the issue of liability alone?

■ **DECISION AND RATIONALE**

(Kavanagh, J.) No. A court may not separate the issue of liability from the issue of damages and grant a partial new trial on the issue of liability alone. The questions of liability and damages are so closely intertwined that they may not usually be separated. Our cases have allowed retrial of the issue of damages where liability is clear. However, no compelling reason exists to extend this rule to a retrial of liability alone. Any liability was determined pursuant to a trial in which an admitted error pertaining to liability was committed. Thus, justice requires that the jury which determines liability should have the responsibility for measuring damages. Further, there is no merit in Doutre's (P) contention that evidence regarding standard of care in the industry was rightfully excluded. The trial court's order for a new trial shall be extended to both the issue of damages and of liability.

Analysis:

This case reveals that partial new trials are generally not favored. Judges granting partial new trials must take great care to ensure that the issues not being retried are separable from those actually being retried. However, the opinion notes that the issue of damages alone may be retried when liability is clearly established. Why, then, cannot the question of liability be retried when the measure of damages is clear? The answer is simple. There can be no damages without liability. If a new jury must reconsider the question of liability, the very basis for a tort lawsuit, then they should take an entirely fresh look at all of the issues. The amount of damages is inextricably intertwined with whether or not liability is established. Conversely, an infinite variety of damages awards are possible once liability is established. Thus, a second jury could easily focus on the appropriate amount of damages after having been told that one party was liable. But telling a second jury that the amount of damages is set already decides, to a large degree, the question of liability, since damages are only granted when one party is liable. Perhaps this problem could have been remedied in this case by informing the second jury that they are under no duty to find liability, but if they do find liability then the amount of damages must be $10,000. Nevertheless, this approach fails to account for the very nature of liability, which is not simply a yes or no question. Rather, liability may be placed on a continuum, with a larger amount of damages being awarded for a greater degree of liability. A new jury should have the power to place liability at any reasonable point on the continuum.

Hulson v. Atchison, Topeka & Santa Fe Ry.

(Injured Postal Worker) v. *(Railroad)*

289 F.2d 726 (7th Cir. 1961), cert. denied 368 U.S. 835, 82 S.Ct. 61 (1961)

RULE 60(b)(1) RELIEF IS ALLOWED ONLY IN EXCEPTIONAL CIRCUMSTANCES

■ **INSTANT FACTS** Hulson (P) and Christensen (P), injured while working in a postal railroad car, sought relief under Rule 60(b) from failure to timely file motions for new trial and for judgment n.o.v.

■ **BLACK LETTER RULE** Relief from judgment under Rule 60(b)(1) is allowed only in exceptional circumstances, and these must be specifically noted in the motion for relief.

■ **PROCEDURAL BASIS**

Appeal from judgment, from order denying directed verdict, from order extending time period for filing motions, and from order striking motions for judgment n.o.v. and new trial in action for damages for negligence.

■ **FACTS**

Edward Hulson (P) and Walter Christensen (P) were employed by the United States Post Office as postal transportation clerks, working on the inside of a Atchison, Topeka & Santa Fe (Railroad) (D) railroad car [which did double duty as a post office and mail carrier!]. Hulson (P) and Christensen (P) were injured while inside a train car when the Railroad (D) was engaged in a switching operation. Hulson (P) and Christensen (P) brought suit in Illinois state court, and the Railroad (D) removed the action to Illinois federal court. Following the denial of Hulson (P) and Christensen's (P) motion for directed verdict, the jury rendered a verdict in favor of the defendant. Ten days later, Hulson (P) and Christensen (P) filed a motion requesting that they be granted a reasonable time to amend their motion for new trial. However, at this time, Hulson (P) and Christensen (P) had not yet filed a motion for new trial. Upon a hearing, the court granted Hulson (P) and Christensen (P) ten additional days to file a motion for new trial or for judgment n.o.v. Within this time period, Hulson (P) and Christensen (P) filed their first motions for new trial or judgment n.o.v. The trial court subsequently granted the Railroad's (D) motion to strike these motions. Further, the court held that it could not grant relief requested by Hulson (P) and Christensen (P) under Rule 60(b). Hulson (P) and Christensen (P) now appeal four separate judgments or orders: the judgment on the verdict, the order denying the motion for directed verdict, the order extending for ten days the period to file for new trial or judgment n.o.v., and the order striking Hulson (P) and Christensen's (P) motion for new trial or judgment n.o.v. The Railroad (D) moved to dismiss each of these appeals.

■ **ISSUE**

Must a showing of exceptional circumstances be made in order to obtain relief under Rule 60(b) from a judgment or order?

■ **DECISION AND RATIONALE**

(Hastings, J.) Yes. A showing of exceptional circumstances must be made in order to obtain relief under Rule 60(b) from a judgment or order. With regard to the first three issues on appeal, we hold that

Hulson (P) and Christensen (P) failed to comply with the requisite time restraints. Pursuant to Rule 73(a), Hulson (P) and Christensen (P) were entitled to appeal the verdict within 30 days. They did not appeal until almost four months after the verdict. Furthermore, under Rule 50(b) Hulson (P) and Christensen (P) were required to bring a motion for judgment n.o.v. within 10 days of the verdict. However, they brought this motion 20 days after. Rule 59 (b), (d) and (e) prohibit a trial court from granting a motion for new trial made after the expiration of 10 days after entry of judgment. Further, Rule 6(b) prohibits a trial court from extending the time restraints imposed by the above rules. Thus, the Railroad's (D) motion to dismiss the first three paragraphs of the appeal must be sustained for lack of jurisdiction. With respect to the Rule 60(b) motion, Hulson (P) and Christensen (P) admit that they misunderstood the time restraints but allege that the Railroad (D) waived their failure to comply with the rules by agreeing to a 10-day extension to file the motion for judgment n.o.v. or new trial. However, ignorance of the rules resulting in an agreement for an unauthorized extension of time cannot serve to furnish grounds for relief under Rule 60(b). Hulson (P) and Christensen (P) made no showing of exceptional circumstances, such as "mistake, inadvertence, or excusable neglect," which would allow a court to grant relief from judgment under Rule 60(b). Accordingly, the trial court did not err in denying the motion for relief under Rule 60(b). Dismissed in part and affirmed in part.

Analysis:

This case exemplifies a party seeking to take advantage of Rule 60(b)'s broad remedial powers in order to rectify obvious oversights and shortcomings of counsel. Further, the case touches on the time limits imposed by other Federal Rules. The opinion makes clear that, absent a showing of "mistake, inadvertence, or excusable neglect" or any other extraordinary circumstances, a court cannot extend the time for moving for a new trial or a judgment n.o.v. For the sake of analysis, we shall focus only on the motion for new trial. Rule 59(b) requires a motion for new trial to be served within 10 days of the entry of judgment. Thus, the trial court was apparently mistaken in allowing Hulson (P) and Christensen (P) ten more days to file their motion for new trial. Nevertheless, Rule 60(b) allows the court to entertain a motion for new trial which was untimely under Rule 59(b) *if the request complies with the requirements of Rule 60(b).* In the case at hand, Hulson (P) and Christensen (P) made no showing of exceptional circumstances calling for Rule 60(b) extraordinary relief.

Briones v. Riviera Hotel & Casino

(Employee) v. *(Employer)*
116 F.3d 379 (9th Cir. 1997)

COURT FINDS LITIGANT'S NEGLIGENCE COULD POTENTIALLY BE EXCUSABLE, JUSTIFYING A MOTION TO SET ASIDE A JUDGMENT

■ **INSTANT FACTS** When his wrongful termination suit was dismissed for failure to respond to his former employer's motion to dismiss, an employee moved to set aside the judgment dismissing the case, asserting that his failure to respond had constituted excusable neglect under Rule 60(b)(1) of the Federal Rules of Civil Procedure.

■ **BLACK LETTER RULE** Under certain circumstances, the negligent failure to file a response to a motion to dismiss can be excusable sufficient to justify the setting aside of a judgment under Rule 60(b)(1) of the Federal Rules of Civil Procedure.

■ **PROCEDURAL BASIS**

Appeal of a trial court's denial of a motion to set aside a judgment under Rule 60(b)(1) of the Federal Rules of Civil Procedure.

■ **FACTS**

Briones (P) sued his former employer, Riviera Hotel & Casino ("Riviera") (D) for wrongly firing him. Riviera (D) filed a motion to dismiss the case with the trial court and Briones (P), acting pro se, failed to respond to the motion. The trial court granted the motion to dismiss and entered judgment against Briones (P). Briones (P) then filed a motion to set aside the judgment, pursuant to Fed. R. Civ. P. 60(b)(1), asserting that his failure to respond to the motion to dismiss resulted from excusable neglect. Briones (P) claimed that the trial court had failed to warn him of the possibility of dismissal and that Briones (P), himself, who spoke very little English, had failed to notify his translator/typist of the deadline for filing opposition to the motion to dismiss. The trial court denied the motion and Briones (P) appealed.

■ **ISSUE**

Can the failure to file a response to a motion to dismiss constitute "excusable neglect" sufficient to justify the setting aside of a judgment under Rule 60(b)(1) of the Federal Rules of Civil Procedure?

■ **DECISION AND RATIONALE**

(Per Curiam) Yes. At the time the trial court denied the motion by Briones (P) to set aside the judgment against him, the applicable cases appeared to establish an automatic rule that a motion under Rule 60(b) could not be used to cure a failure to comply with the rules of procedure. Since that time, however, the U.S. Supreme Court, has ruled in the context of a bankruptcy case that, while ignorance of the rules or mistakes in construing the rules do not *usually* constitute excusable neglect, for purposes of Rule 60(b), the term "excusable neglect" does encompass certain situations in which the failure to comply with a filing deadline is attributable to negligence. In *Pioneer Inv. Servs. Co. v. Brunswick Assocs. Ltd. Partnership* [U.S. Supreme Court case analyzing the circumstances under which missing a filing deadline constitutes excusable neglect], the Supreme Court indicated that several factors must be considered in deciding if neglect was excusable, including: the danger of prejudice to the opposing party; the length of the delay and its impact on the judicial proceedings; the reason for the delay; and whether the moving party acted in good faith. We hold that the Supreme Court's standard in *Pioneer* should control for purposes of Rule 60(b). Accordingly, we remand this case to the trial court to reconsider whether or not Briones' (P) negligence was excusable under all of the facts and circumstances. Vacated and remanded.

Analysis:

Following the U.S. Supreme Court's approach in *Pioneer*, the appeals court here adopts an equitable test for determining whether a party's negligence in missing a court filing deadline can be excused sufficient to justify the setting aside of a motion to dismiss based on that failure to file under Rule 60(b)(1) of the Federal Rules of Civil Procedure. The test balances prejudice to the opposing party against the reason for the failure to file and the good faith of the negligent party. The court's test represents a more flexible approach to the notion of excusable neglect than a per se rule concluding that a negligent failure to file a response to a motion cannot ever constitute grounds for setting aside a judgment of dismissal.

■ CASE VOCABULARY

PRO SE: Appearing on your own behalf before a court, without an attorney.

Patrick v. Sedwick

(Patient) v. *(Doctor)*

413 P.2d 169 (Alaska 1966)

ALASKA SUPREME COURT RULES THAT "NEWLY DISCOVERED" EVIDENCE MUST HAVE BEEN IN EXISTENCE AT THE TIME OF TRIAL IN ORDER TO BE USED AS GROUNDS FOR A MOTION FOR A NEW TRIAL

■ **INSTANT FACTS** A doctor appealed a judgment of damages for medical malpractice alleging that a new medical treatment, discovered after a judgment of liability had been entered in the case, that would benefit the suing patient's injuries should have been taken into account to reduce the damages owed.

■ **BLACK LETTER RULE** In order to constitute valid grounds for granting a motion for a new trial, "newly discovered" evidence must have been in existence at the time of the trial of the case under review.

■ **PROCEDURAL BASIS**

Appeal of a trial court's denial of a motion for a new trial on the basis of newly discovered evidence.

■ **FACTS**

Patrick (P) sued her doctor, Dr. Sedwick (D) for medical malpractice, claiming permanent physical injuries from an operation. In February 1962, the trial judge rendered findings on the issue of liability. Dr. Sedwick (D) appealed those findings prior to any determination of damages by the trial court. Two years later an appellate court ruled for Patrick (P) on the issue of liability and directed the trial court to determine damages. In January 1965, the trial court set the amount of damages owed and entered judgment. Subsequently, Dr. Sedwick (D) moved for a new trial on the ground that in 1963, a doctor had developed a new treatment that would have helped Patrick's (P) injuries. Dr. Sedwick (D) argued that this should have reduced the damages he owed. The trial court denied the motion and Dr. Sedwick (D) appealed.

■ **ISSUE**

In order to constitute valid grounds for granting a motion for a new trial, must "newly discovered" evidence have been in existence at the time of the trial of the case under review?

■ **DECISION AND RATIONALE**

(Rabinowitz, J.) Yes. A motion for a new trial on the grounds of newly discovered evidence can be granted only if the evidence discovered: (1) would probably change the result on a new trial; (2) has been discovered since the trial; (3) could not have been discovered prior to trial by due diligence; (4) is material; (5) is not cumulative or impeaching; and (6) relates to facts that were in existence at the time of trial. Here, the new medical treatment that might help Patrick's (P) injuries was not discovered until *after* the case was tried. Thus, the new medical technique was not in existence at the time the trial took place and does not qualify as newly discovered evidence. Affirmed.

Analysis:

Rule 60(b)(2) of the Federal Rules of Civil Procedure permits relief from judgment on grounds of newly discovered evidence. As the court here notes, interpreting a state rule similar to the federal rule, the granting of such a motion depends upon whether or not the newly discovered evidence relates to facts that were in existence at the time of trial. If the discovered evidence was not in existence at the time of trial, courts will generally not grant a new trial on that basis. In certain cases, where a scientific discovery following a trial has been the new evidence at issue in a motion for a new trial, courts have granted new trial motions, reasoning that the scientific discovery at issue always existed, but was simply not measurable by man until "discovered" by scientists.

■ **CASE VOCABULARY**

CUMULATIVE: Evidence that would be used to prove something that has already been shown by other evidence.

IMPEACHING: Evidence used merely to call into question whether a witness is telling the truth.

Marcelli v. Walker

(*Construction Company Principal*) v. (*Insurance Company Representative*)

2009 WL 415998 (6th Cir 2009)

THREE STRIKES AND YOU'RE OUT (OF COURT)

■ **INSTANT FACTS** After a voluntary consent to dismiss his cause of action was entered, Marcelli (P) attempted to reopen the case, but the court denied his request.

■ **BLACK LETTER RULE** The elements of a Rule 60(d) cause of action include (1) a judgment that, in equity and good conscience, ought not be enforced; (2) a good defense to the cause of action on which the judgment is founded; (3) fraud, accident, or mistake that prevented the movant from obtaining the benefit of a defense to the underlying judgment; (4) the absence of fault or negligence on the movant's part; and (5) the absence of an adequate remedy at law.

■ **PROCEDURAL BASIS**

Appeal from the district court's denial of the plaintiff's motion to reopen a closed case.

■ **FACTS**

A dispute arose over an indemnification agreement connected to municipal construction projects. The circuit court ruled against Marcelli (P) and awarded damages. The state supreme court denied review, and Marcelli (P) filed a second suit in the circuit court, asking the court to set aside the first judgment. The circuit court granted summary judgment against Marcelli (P) on the ground of res judicata and the court of appeals affirmed. Marcelli (P) then filed a federal court action against several defendants, alleging fraud, conspiracy, legal malpractice, and violations of the Racketeer Influenced and Corrupt Organizations Act, as well as violations of his due process and equal protection rights. The federal district court ordered Marcelli (P) to provide a "Case Statement to assure compliance" with Rule 11 of the Federal Rules of Civil Procedure. Counsel for Marcelli (P) filed a Response in Lieu of Case Statement, informing the court that though counsel had originally believed that the plaintiff's case satisfied Rule 11, discussions with defense counsel revealed that it did not, so the parties had agreed to voluntarily dismiss the case. Thereafter, the court dismissed Marcelli's federal (P) case. Sixteen months later, however, Marcelli (P) filed a request to reopen the case, arguing that his attorney had acted without his consent. The court denied Marcelli's (P) request. Marcelli (P) then requested to proceed "In Forma Pauperis," and the court denied that request as well, finding that Marcelli (P) had failed to present an actionable claim, so any appeal would be frivolous. Marcelli (P) appealed and sought relief under Federal Rule of Procedure 60(d).

■ **ISSUE**

Did the district court abuse its discretion by denying the plaintiff's motion to reopen his case after it had been voluntarily dismissed?

■ **DECISION AND RATIONALE**

(Cole, J.) No. The elements of a Rule 60(d) cause of action include (1) a judgment that, in equity and good conscience, ought not be enforced; (2) a good defense to the cause of action on which the judgment is founded; (3) fraud, accident, or mistake that prevented the movant from obtaining the benefit of a defense to the underlying judgment; (4) the absence of fault or negligence on the movant's part; and (5) the absence of an adequate remedy at law. Rule 60(d) of the Federal Rules of Civil Procedure provides a savings clause that allows judgments to be attacked without regard to the passage of time, but only if the circumstances are sufficiently gross to demand a departure from rigid adherence to the doctrine of res judicata. Otherwise, Rule 60(b) is generally the exclusive avenue for seeking relief from a final judgment. A Rule 60(d) motion will be granted only in cases of unusual and exceptional circumstances. Marcelli's (P) effort to reopen his case fails to meet this standard. Indeed, he has not filed an independent action under Rule 60(d), nor has he presented good cause for the stipulated dismissal to be overturned. He also had more than adequate opportunity to be heard on his claims. The district court therefore did not abuse its discretion.

Analysis:

This case references the important legal doctrine of res judicata. "Res judicata" refers to the way in which one judgment will have a binding effect on another. Res judicata precludes the litigation in a later suit not only of matters that were litigated in an earlier action, but also of those that could or should have been litigated, or were necessarily decided as a result of the court's judgment. This doctrine has also been called "true res judicata." The preclusion only of matters that have actually been decided is usually called "collateral estoppel." Some prefer the use of the terms "claim preclusion" and "issue preclusion" for these two doctrines. Collateral estoppel, or issue preclusion, is defined as the binding effect of a judgment as to matters actually litigated and determined in one action on later controversies between the parties.

■ CASE VOCABULARY

APPEAL IN FORMA PAUPERIS: An appeal by an indigent party, for whom court costs are waived.

IN FORMA PAUPERIS: [Latin, "in the manner of a pauper."] In the manner of an indigent who is permitted to disregard filing fees and court costs (e.g., when suing, a poor person is generally entitled to proceed *in forma pauperis*). For instance, in many jurisdictions, an indigent divorce petitioner's filing fees and court costs are waived.

RES JUDICATA: [Latin, "a thing adjudicated."] An issue that has been definitively settled by judicial decision; an affirmative defense barring the same parties from litigating a second lawsuit on the same claim, or any other claim arising from the same transaction or series of transactions and that could have been—but was not—raised in the first suit. The three essential elements are (1) an earlier decision on the issue, (2) a final judgment on the merits, and (3) the involvement of the same parties, or parties in privity with the original parties.

RULE 11: In federal practice, the procedural rule requiring the attorney of record or the party (if not represented by an attorney) to sign all pleadings, motions, and other papers filed with the court and—by this signing—to represent that the paper is filed in good faith after an inquiry that is reasonable under the circumstances. This rule provides for the imposition of sanctions, upon a party's or the court's own motion, if an attorney or party violates the conditions stated in the rule.

CHAPTER FIFTEEN

Securing and Enforcing Judgments

Griggs v. Miller

Instant Facts: W.A. Brookshire (D) owed nearly $19,000 in judgments, and he challenged the sheriff's execution sale of his entire tract of land.

Black Letter Rule: In levying on an execution, sheriffs should make reasonable efforts to obtain fair sales prices, and should parcel any property prior to sale where practicable.

Reeves v. Crownshield

Instant Facts: Reeves (D), a judgment debtor, appeals the constitutionality of his imprisonment for failure to obey a court order to pay his debt.

Black Letter Rule: A party may constitutionally be imprisoned for failure to heed a court order to pay a judgment.

Griggs v. Miller

(*Land Purchaser*) v. (*Land Owner*)
374 S.W.2d 119 (Mo. 1963)

SHERIFFS HAVE A DUTY TO MAKE A GOOD FAITH EFFORT TO OBTAIN THE MARKET VALUE OF ITEMS SOLD AT EXECUTION SALES

■ **INSTANT FACTS** W.A. Brookshire (D) owed nearly $19,000 in judgments, and he challenged the sheriff's execution sale of his entire tract of land.

■ **BLACK LETTER RULE** In levying on an execution, sheriffs should make reasonable efforts to obtain fair sales prices, and should parcel any property prior to sale where practicable.

■ **PROCEDURAL BASIS**

Appeal from judgment and decree disallowing claim to set aside execution sale.

■ **FACTS**

Bill Griggs (P) purchased the land of W.A. Brookshire (D) at an execution sale. Although the land was valued at approximately $46,000, Griggs (P) was able to purchase it for $20,600. [The bidding was apparently not very competitive!] When Brookshire (D) failed to deliver possession of the property, Griggs (P) sued for ejectment and damages. Brookshire (D) counterclaimed, seeking to set aside the sheriff's execution sale. Brookshire (D) argued that the sheriff should have levied on only a portion of the 320 acre estate in order to satisfy the nearly $19,000 of prior judgments that Brookshire (D) had to pay. However, despite Brookshire's (D) requests to the contrary, the sheriff levied against all 320 acres, apparently finding this easier than parceling out the land. Brookshire (D) lost at trial, was ordered to pay $2483 in damages, and was incarcerated pending his appeal of the judgment. Miller was appointed trustee of the Estate of W.A. Brookshire for purposes of this appeal.

■ **ISSUE**

In levying against property in order to enforce a judgment, should a sheriff attempt to recover the market value of the land?

■ **DECISION AND RATIONALE**

(Boling, J.) Yes. In levying against property in order to enforce a judgment, a sheriff should attempt, whenever possible, to recover the market value of the land. A sheriff conducting an execution sale is an agent of both the property owner and the judgment creditor. His duty is to protect the interests of both, which did not occur in the case at hand. While the sheriff could have offered Brookshire's (D) land for sale in parcels, his failure to do so resulted in a sale for much less than the actual value of the property. Pursuant to Missouri statutes, a judgment debtor has a right to elect what portion of his estate is sold in order to pay the judgments. Brookshire (D) attempted to exercise this right by sending a letter to the sheriff limiting the execution sale to only the northeast 40 acres of land. The sheriff's failure to follow these instructions, or at least the failure to parcel the property and sell something less than the entire tract of land, requires setting aside the execution sale. Thus, the decree will be reversed, provided Brookshire (D) repays the $20,600 he received from the execution sale, plus interest from the date of the sale. In addition, costs are assessed against Brookshire (D). Reversed.

Analysis:

This case presents a good overview of the basic components of an execution. Essentially, an execution is a court-issued document which instructs a sheriff to seize or assert dominion over the property of the judgment debtor. The execution may authorize the sheriff to levy against real property, personal property, or even income of the judgment debtor. Furthermore, if the judgment creditor is owed money, the sheriff has the authority to sell any property at an execution sale. Any proceeds up to the amount of the judgment are transferred to the judgment creditor, and the remainder is returned to the judgment debtor. However, a judgment debtor often gets the short end of the deal, as the property often sells for far below market price. In the instant action, Brookshire (D) suffered this fate at the hands of an inconsiderate sheriff. The sheriff should have attempted to parcel the land and, hopefully, receive a higher selling price. However, the court's logic can be questioned, since there is no guarantee that the sheriff would have received any more money had he parceled out the land prior to the sale. Perhaps a sale of anything less than the entire parcel would not have returned sufficient funds to pay the $19,000 in judgments. Nevertheless, at the very least, the sheriff should have advertised the sale and attempted to receive a higher selling price.

■ CASE VOCABULARY

LEVY: The act of collecting on an execution.

SUPERSEDEAS BOND: A bond executed by someone who wants to contest an execution, from which the other party can get paid if the challenge is unsuccessful.

Reeves v. Crownshield

(*Judgment Debtor*) v. (*Judgment Creditor*)

274 N.Y. 74, 8 N.E.2d 283 (1937)

IMPRISONMENT IS A VALID SANCTION FOR REFUSAL TO PAY A JUDGMENT DEBT

■ **INSTANT FACTS** Reeves (D), a judgment debtor, appeals the constitutionality of his imprisonment for failure to obey a court order to pay his debt.

■ **BLACK LETTER RULE** A party may constitutionally be imprisoned for failure to heed a court order to pay a judgment.

■ **PROCEDURAL BASIS**

Appeal from order for contempt, fine, and incarceration for failure to pay a debt.

■ **FACTS**

Crownshield (P) apparently brought an action against Reeves (D) to collect on a judgment for approximately $400. A judgment debtor examination of Reeves (D) revealed that he earned $230 per month, that he paid $48 per month in rent, and that he had no other financial obligations. The court ordered that Reeves (D) pay $20 per month until the judgment was satisfied, but he refused. Pursuant to New York statute, Reeves (D) was held in contempt, fined $20, and imprisoned. Reeves (D) appealed on constitutional grounds, arguing that imprisonment for a debt was barred by the due process clauses of the state and federal constitutions.

■ **ISSUE**

Is it unconstitutional to hold a party in contempt and incarcerate the party for failure to pay a judgment?

■ **DECISION AND RATIONALE**

(Finch, J.). No. It is not unconstitutional to hold a party in contempt and incarcerate the party for failure to pay a judgment. In the case at hand, Reeves (D) does not argue that the $20 payment is unjust, inequitable or harsh. He merely contends that courts are powerless to make him pay. Indeed, without contempt sanctions, courts would have no ability to compel judgment debtors to pay their debts. However, there can be no doubt that imprisonment for failure to obey a court order, which order is made with due regard to the needs of the debtor and his family, is not violative of due process. Although courts cannot garnish the wages of a federal employee, once the wages are paid they become part of the employees general income. Courts are free to execute against such general income to the same extent that courts can execute against any property purchased with the income. Affirmed.

Analysis:

This case accurately sets out the law of civil contempt. First, it is important to note that incarceration is an appropriate remedy for civil contempt. This incarceration is utilized to coerce the judgment debtor into paying on the judgment, not to punish the individual (as in the case of criminal contempt). As the opinion points out, court orders would be meaningless and unenforceable without some contempt sanctions. Notice that the court must examine the unique situation of each debtor, so that only those willfully in violation of the court order—and not those simply too poor to pay—are sent to prison.

■ CASE VOCABULARY

GARNISHMENT: Process in which money or goods, which are controlled by a third person but which are due the defendant, are attached by the plaintiff to satisfy a debt.

CHAPTER SIXTEEN

Appellate Review

Liberty Mutual Insurance Co. v. Wetzel

Instant Facts: Liberty Mutual Insurance Co. (D) appealed the grant of partial summary judgment against it, and the Supreme Court now considers the jurisdiction of the appellate court.

Black Letter Rule: A grant of partial summary judgment on the issue of liability is an interlocutory order and is not appealable.

Jetco Electronic Industries, Inc. v. Gardiner

Instant Facts: ETL (D) brings a motion to dismiss the appeal of an order dismissing an action in ETL's (D) favor, arguing that the decision was not a final judgment.

Black Letter Rule: Courts may employ a flexible approach to the final judgment rule where justice so warrants.

Sears, Roebuck & Co. v. Mackey

Instant Facts: Mackey (P) challenges Rule 54(b), which allowed a District Court to render final (and therefore appealable) judgments on certain claims.

Black Letter Rule: Rule 54(b) does not make an unauthorized extension of 28 U.S.C. § 1291 by allowing a district court to declare that certain claims in a multi-claim suit are final.

Cold Metal Process Co. v. United Engineering & Foundry Co.

Instant Facts: Cold Metal Process Co. (P) presumably petitioned for review of an appellate court's jurisdiction over a claim, when the related counterclaim remained in the district court.

Black Letter Rule: A final judgment may be entered on a claim even if a related counterclaim remains at issue in the litigation.

Will v. Hallock

Instant Facts: U.S. Customs Agents argued that the case against them should have been dismissed once the case against the government was dismissed, but the court denied their motion and they appealed.

Black Letter Rule: The requirements for a collateral order appeal are that an order (1) conclusively determine the disputed question, (2) resolve an important issue completely separate from the merits of the action, and (3) be effectively unreviewable on appeal from the final judgment.

Gillespie v. United States Steel Corp.

Instant Facts: Mrs. Gillespie (P) brought suit on behalf of her deceased son for the events leading to his death, and the appellate court reached the merits on the appeal of the dismissal of certain causes of action.

Black Letter Rule: In the appropriate circumstances, an appellate court may hear an appeal even though the district judge fails to expressly certify the issue for appeal.

LaBuy v. Howes Leather Co.

Instant Facts: Parties to an antitrust action sought a writ of mandamus to reverse an order of LaBuy (P), the District Court judge, referring the case to a Master.

Black Letter Rule: In extraordinary circumstances, appellate courts may review an interlocutory order via mandamus.

Atlantic City Elec. Co. v. General Elec. Co.

Instant Facts: General Electric Co. (D) applies for leave to file an interlocutory appeal from the district court's order sustaining Atlantic City Electric Co.'s (P) objections to interrogatories.

Black Letter Rule: Discretionary appeals should be allowed only where a party would otherwise have no ability to protect its rights via a later appeal.

J.F. White Contracting Co. v. New England Tank Industries of New Hampshire, Inc.

Instant Facts: White (D) appeals a judgment on grounds that the lower court committed error, and White (D) attempts to introduce evidence not entered at trial.

Black Letter Rule: Appellate courts may only consider issues which were actually raised at trial, and harmless errors by the trial court do not constitute grounds for vacating a judgment.

Electrical Fittings Corp. v. Thomas & Betts Co.

Instant Facts: Electrical Fittings Corp. (D) attempted to appeal a judgment entered in its favor because the decree stated that the claim against EFC (D) had some validity.

Black Letter Rule: A party may appeal a favorable judgment that contains unfavorable conclusions of law or fact provided those conclusions were necessary to support the judgment.

International Ore & Fertilizer Corp. v. SGS Control Services

Instant Facts: After the trial court entered judgment for the plaintiff on a negligent misrepresentation claim but dismissed its contract claim, the defendant appealed the negligent misrepresentation judgment.

Black Letter Rule: A party may urge on appeal any matter appearing in the appellate record without filing a cross-appeal, even if the trial court's reasoning is challenged in the process.

Corcoran v. City of Chicago

Instant Facts: John Corcoran (P) argued that an appellate court has no authority to determine whether a verdict is supported by the evidence presented at trial.

Black Letter Rule: An appellate court may set aside a verdict on the grounds that findings of fact are not supported by evidence.

Pullman–Standard v. Swint

Instant Facts: Pullman–Standard (D) contends that the Court of Appeals incorrectly avoided the "clearly erroneous" standard when reviewing the District Court's determination that the company did not discriminate.

Black Letter Rule: A Court of Appeals is bound by the "clearly erroneous" standard whenever reviewing questions of fact.

Inwood Labs, Inc. v. Ives Labs, Inc.

Instant Facts: The Court of Appeals, conducting an independent review of the factual issues, found Inwood Labs (D) violated Ives Labs' (P) patent.

Black Letter Rule: Appellate courts are bound by the "clearly erroneous" standard when reviewing lower court's findings of fact.

Bose Corp. v. Consumers Union of United States, Inc.

Instant Facts: In reviewing a defamation action, the Court of Appeals conducted a de novo review of the determination of "actual malice," rather than following Rule 52(a)'s "clearly erroneous" standard.

Black Letter Rule: The "clearly erroneous" standard does not apply when reviewing the constitutional facts surrounding a determination of actual malice in a defamation action.

Dick v. New York Life Ins. Co.

Instant Facts: The facts of this case are not provided in the text.

Black Letter Rule: The U.S. Supreme Court should exercise its discretionary power of certiorari only in cases of general importance or to secure uniformity of decision.

Harris v. Pennsylvania R. Co.

Instant Facts: In a FELA action, the Supreme Court is faced with defending its procedure for denying certiorari.

Black Letter Rule: The Supreme Court's discretion is limited by the "rule of four," requiring four of nine judges to vote to grant certiorari.

Liberty Mutual Insurance Co. v. Wetzel

(Employer) v. (Employee)

424 U.S. 737, 96 S.Ct. 1202 (1976)

THE SUPREME COURT REAFFIRMS THE FINAL JUDGMENT RULE

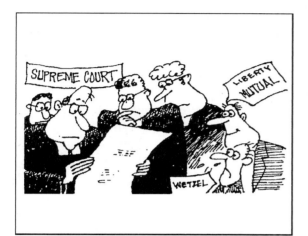

■ **INSTANT FACTS** Liberty Mutual Insurance Co. (D) appealed the grant of partial summary judgment against it, and the Supreme Court now considers the jurisdiction of the appellate court.

■ **BLACK LETTER RULE** A grant of partial summary judgment on the issue of liability is an interlocutory order and is not appealable.

■ PROCEDURAL BASIS

Writ of certiorari reviewing jurisdiction of Court of Appeals following affirmance of partial summary judgment finding liability for violations of the Civil Rights Act.

■ FACTS

Wetzel (P) sued Liberty Mutual Insurance Co. (D) in federal district court, alleging that Liberty Mutual's employee insurance benefits and maternity leave provisions violated Title VII of the Civil Rights Act of 1964. Wetzel (P) sought a declaratory judgment, an injunction, and damages. The District Court granted Wetzel (P) partial summary judgment on the issue of liability, holding that the policies did indeed violate Title VII. However, the judgment did not provide any of the relief sought by Wetzel (P). Liberty Mutual (D) appealed this grant of partial summary judgment. The Third Circuit Court of Appeals held that it had jurisdiction and affirmed the judgment. The Supreme Court granted certiorari, and the Supreme Court now analyzes the jurisdiction of the Court of Appeals.

■ ISSUE

Does a Court of Appeals have jurisdiction to review the granting of partial summary judgment.

■ DECISION AND RATIONALE

(Rehnquist, J.) No. A Court of Appeals does not have jurisdiction to review the granting of partial summary judgment. Such orders are interlocutory in nature, and thus are not final judgments within the meaning of 28 U.S.C. § 1291. Moreover, § 1292 is not applicable as a basis for jurisdiction in the instant action. If the District Court had granted injunctive relief, this interlocutory order would have been appealable under § 1292(a)(1). However, the District Court granted no relief whatsoever when it decided on the issue of Liberty Mutual's (D) liability. In addition, Rule 54(b) does not apply to cases like this, which are actions on a single claim, and the requirements of § 1292(b) are not satisfied. Were we to allow the Court of Appeals to exercise jurisdiction over cases like this, we would condone the procedure whereby any district court could render an interlocutory decision on liability which would be immediately appealable. Although Congress has provided for exceptions to the "final judgment" rule, none are applicable in the case at hand. Vacated and remanded, with instructions to dismiss Liberty Mutual's (D) appeal.

Analysis:

As a general rule, only final decisions are appealable to higher federal courts. While there are numerous exceptions, which are addressed throughout this chapter, this case involves a straightforward application of the final judgment rule. The only difficult task is defining what exactly constitutes a final judgment. According to many commentators, a final judgment is one rendered after all possible issues have been determined by a trial court. Stated differently, a final judgment ends the litigation on the merits and leaves nothing for the court to do but execute the judgment. Thus, a decision addressing only liability but not considering possible remedies, as in this case, is not a final judgment. Consider briefly the rationale for the final judgment rule. Trial courts make several decisions, ranging from minor orders to grants of summary judgment, throughout the course of the trial. It would obviously cause a substantial disruption in the trial process if each decision were appealable. On the other hand, if one of these decisions is erroneous, it appears to be a tremendous waste of judicial resources to litigate the case to conclusion only to have the entire case reversed on appeal and retried. As the Supreme Court mentions in this opinion, Congress has attempted to reconcile these two arguments by providing limited exceptions to the final judgment rule.

■ CASE VOCABULARY

INTERLOCUTORY: An order occurring during a proceeding which is not final and does not ultimately resolve the issues in dispute.

Jetco Electronic Industries, Inc. v. Gardiner

(*Not Stated*) v. (*Not Stated*)
473 F.2d 1228 (5th Cir. 1973)

A FLEXIBLE APPROACH SHOULD BE TAKEN WHEN DEALING WITH THE FINAL JUDGMENT RULE

■ **INSTANT FACTS** ETL (D) brings a motion to dismiss the appeal of an order dismissing an action in ETL's (D) favor, arguing that the decision was not a final judgment.

■ **BLACK LETTER RULE** Courts may employ a flexible approach to the final judgment rule where justice so warrants.

■ **PROCEDURAL BASIS**

Motion to dismiss appeal, on grounds of lack of appellate jurisdiction, of order dismissing action for lack of personal jurisdiction and for failure to state a claim.

■ **FACTS**

Jetco Electronic Industries, Inc. (P) sued ETL (D), Gardiner (D), and Gardiner Electronics (D). ETL (D) moved to dismiss for lack of personal jurisdiction and for failure to state a claim. The trial court granted this motion, and Jetco (P) appealed. Subsequently, the trial court disposed of the claims against Gardiner (D) and Gardiner Electronics (D). ETL (D) brought a motion to dismiss the appeal, arguing that the original grant of ETL's (D) motion to dismiss was not a final judgment and, thus, was not appealable.

■ **ISSUE**

Is appellate jurisdiction proper even if the matter appealed was not a final judgment at the time the appeal was filed?

■ **DECISION AND RATIONALE**

(Justice Not Stated) Yes. Appellate jurisdiction may be proper even if the matter appealed was not a final judgment at the time the appeal was filed. The final judgment rule is flexible. Practical, not technical, considerations govern its application. Indeed, in the case at hand the original grant of ETL's (D) motion to dismiss was not a final judgment when it was made, since it said nothing about Jetco's (P) rights against the other defendants. Similarly, the order dismissing the claims against Gardiner (D) and Gardiner Electronics (D) was not a final judgment when it was issued. However, both of these orders, taken together, do constitute a final judgment. We therefore adopt a flexible approach to the final judgment rule and hold that the order dismissing ETL's (D) case is within our appellate jurisdiction.

Analysis:

What would a rule be without exceptions? This case exemplifies one of the many exceptions to the final judgment rule, demonstrating that courts have the flexibility to sidestep the strict mandate of the rule where justice requires. Certainly, at the time it was entered, the order granting ETL's (D) motion to dismiss was not "final" with respect to the entire action. Thus, the appellate court may well have been without jurisdiction when this case originally reached it. Nevertheless, it makes sense to allow the court to consider all of the orders taken together. At the time of hearing this appeal, the trial court had finally resolved all of the issues in dispute, and the entire case or any issues therein were appealable. It should be noted, however, that this holding conveys a slightly different approach to the final judgment rule than *Liberty Mutual* [a grant of partial summary judgment on the issue of liability is an interlocutory order and is not appealable]. Whereas *Liberty Mutual* treated appellate jurisdiction as essentially a question of subject matter, this court takes a different approach. If appellate jurisdiction were strictly a subject matter issue, then the original appeal would seemingly have to be dismissed, since jurisdiction was lacking at the time the appeal was taken. Clearly, this case exemplifies a more flexible approach.

Sears, Roebuck & Co. v. Mackey

(Retailer) v. *(Patent Holder)*

351 U.S. 427, 76 S.Ct. 895 (1956)

SUPREME COURT UPHOLDS THE VALIDITY OF AMENDED RULE 54(B), ALLOWING A DISTRICT COURT TO DECLARE THAT CERTAIN CLAIMS ARE FINAL AND APPEALABLE

■ **INSTANT FACTS** Mackey (P) challenges Rule 54(b), which allowed a District Court to render final (and therefore appealable) judgments on certain claims.

■ **BLACK LETTER RULE** Rule 54(b) does not make an unauthorized extension of 28 U.S.C. § 1291 by allowing a district court to declare that certain claims in a multi-claim suit are final.

■ PROCEDURAL BASIS

Writ of certiorari reviewing order upholding appellate jurisdiction over antitrust claim.

■ FACTS

Mackey (P) brought claims against Sears, Roebuck & Co. (D) for breach of contract, unfair competition, and violations of the Sherman Antitrust Act. The District Court dismissed only the antitrust claims, and Sears (D) appealed the dismissal. Apparently Mackey (P) challenged the appeal on the basis of the "final decision" rule and argued that Rule 54(b) [final judgment may be entered for one or more claims in a multiple-claim suit] made an unauthorized extension of 28 U.S.C. § 1291 [courts of appeal have jurisdiction over appeals from all final decisions]. The Seventh Circuit Court of Appeals upheld its jurisdiction, and the Supreme Court granted certiorari.

■ ISSUE

In a suit involving multiple claims, may an appeal be taken as to one or more, but less than all, of the claims?

■ DECISION AND RATIONALE

Yes. In a suit involving multiple claims, an appeal may be taken as to one or more, but less than all, of the claims. Federal Rule 54(b) was adopted in order to ameliorate the harsh effects of the standard that all claims had to be finally decided before an appeal could be made as to any of them. Pursuant to Rule 54(b), a district court may render final decisions for one or more claims, and hence make them appealable, provided the court makes an express determination that there is no just reason for delay and an express direction for the entry of judgment. With respect to the instant action, it is clear that the antitrust claims can be decided independently from the other claims, and thus the District Court did not abuse its discretion in certifying that there was no reason for delay. Rule 54(b) does not make an unauthorized extension of § 1291. Rather, Rule 54(b) recognizes the requirement of a "final decision" under § 1291, and the Rule leaves the decision of what claims are appealable to the discretion of the district court. Rule 54(b) provides for the release of more decisions to the appellate court and preserves the federal policy against piecemeal appeals more effectively than the former Rule 54(b).

Analysis:

In 1948, the Federal Rules Advisory Committee amended Rule 54(b) in order to better meet the goals of judicial efficiency and to avoid piecemeal disposition of cases. The old Rule did not include the "final judgment" language, but instead it allowed a court to enter judgment on any claim in a multi-claim litigation. Considerable confusion ensued with respect to these partial judgments and the "final decision" rule of § 1291. Consequently, Rule 54(b) was amended to require the district courts to make express findings and declarations regarding the final nature of the judgments, so that their appealability could not be questioned. While it may seem strange that a rule allowing for appeals of certain parts of a case actually enhances judicial efficiency or prevents piecemeal litigation, the Committee apparently felt that the ambiguities surrounding the former rule were the source of many problems. It is important to note that the District Court must determine that there is no just reason for delaying the final decision of certain claims. If two or more claims cannot be decided independently from each other, they may not be severed for purposes of final judgment and appeal. One final concept arising out of this case deals with the relationship between the Federal Rules and the U.S. Code, as described in 28 U.S.C. § 2072. Notice that the Rules of Civil Procedure cannot abridge, enlarge or modify any substantive right (such as § 1291); however, pursuant to § 2072(c), the Rules may define when a ruling of a district court is final. That is precisely the function of Rule 54(b).

Cold Metal Process Co. v. United Engineering & Foundry Co.

(*Not Stated*) v. (*Not Stated*)
351 U.S. 445, 76 S.Ct. 904 (1956)

CLAIMS MAY BE APPEALED EVEN WHILE RELATED COUNTERCLAIMS REMAIN IN LITIGATION

■ **INSTANT FACTS** Cold Metal Process Co. (P) presumably petitioned for review of an appellate court's jurisdiction over a claim, when the related counterclaim remained in the district court.

■ **BLACK LETTER RULE** A final judgment may be entered on a claim even if a related counterclaim remains at issue in the litigation.

■ **PROCEDURAL BASIS**

Writ of certiorari reviewing jurisdiction of appellate court over claim.

■ **FACTS**

Although the facts are omitted from this portion of the opinion, it can be inferred that Cold Metal Process Co. (P) challenged the jurisdiction of an appellate court. Apparently the district court rendered a final judgment on a claim, effectively certifying the claim for appeal under Rule 54(b) [final judgment may be entered for one or more claims in a multiple-claim suit]. However, the district court had not yet reached a decision or rendered a final judgment on the related counterclaim. Thus, the claim itself was subject to appeal while the counterclaim remained in the original litigation. The Supreme Court granted certiorari.

■ **ISSUE**

In a multi-claim lawsuit, may a judgment on a claim be considered "final" even though a counterclaim arising out of the same transaction has not been decided?

■ **DECISION AND RATIONALE**

Yes. In a multi-claim lawsuit, a judgment on a claim may be considered "final" even though a counterclaim arising out of the same transaction has not been decided. The former doctrine of finality, as related to multiple-claim litigation, provided that only pieces entirely separate from the remainder of the litigation could be appealed before the completion of the entire litigation. This is no longer the exclusive standard for determining finality under 28 U.S.C. § 1291 [courts of appeal have jurisdiction over appeals from all final decisions]. Thus, an appeal by a defendant is appropriate under § 1291 and Rule 54(b) even though a related counterclaim still exists.

■ **DISSENT**

(Frankfurter, J.) The court fails to indicate what standards the courts are to apply in determining when a decision is final and, hence, appealable under § 1291. The district courts must utilize their discretion, which can only be overturned by the appellate court finding an abuse of discretion. However, the statute itself limits the jurisdiction of the appellate courts, and thus the appellate courts seem to possess a duty of independent judgment broader than the usual "abuse of discretion" review. It should be noted that § 1291 is aimed at preventing piecemeal appeals. In the case at hand, the counterclaim is based in substantial part on the transactions involved in the main litigation. Consistent with the purpose of § 1291, this counterclaim is not appealable.

Analysis:

This case is somewhat difficult to reconstruct, especially since the textbook editors only provide a small piece of the dissent and none of the majority opinion. In brief, the case announces a further relaxation of the final judgment rule, in light of § 1291 and Rule 54(b). Apparently final judgments may be rendered on claims, and thus these claims may be appealed, even if the counterclaims remain. Of course, Rule 54(b) still requires the district court to make an express determination that there is no reason for a delay of the final judgment on the claim. It would seem that, in most cases, the mere existence of a counterclaim would be a compelling reason to delay final judgment on the related claim.

■ CASE VOCABULARY

ABUSE OF DISCRETION STANDARD: A strict standard of appellate review, allowing an appellate court to overturn a lower court's decision only if the lower court clearly exceeded its authority or committed a major error.

Will v. Hallock

(*Customs Agent*) v. (*Owner of Seized Computers*)

546 U.S. 345, 126 S.Ct. 952, 163 L.Ed.2d 836 (2006)

THE FINAL JUDGMENT RULE APPLIES IN ALL BUT EXCEPTIONAL CASES

Sorry, the final judgment rule applies in all but exceptional cases.

stus.com

INSTANT FACTS U.S. Customs Agents argued that the case against them should have been dismissed once the case against the government was dismissed, but the court denied their motion and they appealed.

BLACK LETTER RULE The requirements for a collateral order appeal are that an order (1) conclusively determine the disputed question, (2) resolve an important issue completely separate from the merits of the action, and (3) be effectively unreviewable on appeal from the final judgment.

■ **PROCEDURAL BASIS**

Certiorari to the United States Court of Appeals for the Second Circuit.

■ **FACTS**

U.S. Customs Agents, acting on a warrant, seized computer equipment from the plaintiff's home. No charges were brought, and the equipment was returned, albeit in a very damaged condition. The plaintiff brought suit against the United States under the Federal Tort Claims Act, and while that suit was pending, she brought a second suit against the agents, alleging negligence. After the suit against the United States was dismissed, the agents moved for dismissal of the case against them, arguing that the action was barred by a federal statute, 28 U.S.C. § 2676 (the "judgment bar" urged by the defendants), once the first case was dismissed. The trial court denied the agents' motion and they appealed, despite the lack of a final judgment on the merits. On appeal, the Second Circuit held that the collateral order doctrine justified the appeal, even though there had been no final judgment.

■ **ISSUE**

Did the court properly consider the appeal in this case despite the lack of a final judgment on the merits?

■ **DECISION AND RATIONALE**

(Souter, J.) No. The requirements for a collateral order appeal are that an order (1) conclusively determine the disputed question, (2) resolve an important issue completely separate from the merits of the action, and (3) be effectively unreviewable on appeal from the final judgment. There is only a small class of collaterally appealable orders, and the requirements are stringent. An order rejecting immunity, for instance, may be immediately appealable. If, through rigorous application of the final judgment requirement, the value of the interests that would be lost supersedes the value of applying the general rule, a collateral order appeal may be allowed. Honoring the separation of powers, preserving the efficiency of government, respecting a state's dignitary interests, and mitigating the government's advantage over an individual are examples of such interests. Does the claim of the customs agents in this case serve such a weighty public objective? There is no such public interest at stake simply because the "judgment bar" is said to be applicable. The judgment bar at issue in this case is no more important than the typical defense of claim preclusion, and it justifies no immediate appeal of right. The judgment of the court of appeals is vacated and the case is remanded with instructions to dismiss the appeal for lack of jurisdiction.

Analysis:

Section 2676 of Title 28 of the United States Code provides that "[t]he judgment in an action under section 1346 (b) of this title [against the United States or its agents acting within the scope of their office] shall constitute a complete bar to any action by the claimant, by reason of the same subject matter, against the employee of the government whose act or omission gave rise to the claim." Here, the claim against the government was dismissed. The trial court held that the bar of § 2676 did not apply, however, and refused to dismiss the case against the agents. According to the Supreme Court, the judgment bar of the statute was not the kind of interest that would justify an exception to the application of the final judgment rule.

■ CASE VOCABULARY

COLLATERAL ORDER DOCTRINE: A doctrine allowing appeal from an interlocutory order that conclusively determines an issue wholly separate from the merits of the action and effectively unreviewable on appeal from a final judgment. Also termed *Cohen* doctrine.

FINAL JUDGMENT RULE: The principle that a party may appeal only from a district court's final decision that ends the litigation on the merits. Under this rule, a party must raise all claims of error in a single appeal.

Gillespie v. United States Steel Corp.

(*Administratrix*) v. (*Boat Manufacturer*)
379 U.S. 148, 85 S.Ct. 308 (1964)

APPELLATE JURISDICTION OVER INTERLOCUTORY ISSUES MAY EXIST EVEN WHERE THE DISTRICT COURT FAILS TO CERTIFY THE ISSUE

■ **INSTANT FACTS** Mrs. Gillespie (P) brought suit on behalf of her deceased son for the events leading to his death, and the appellate court reached the merits on the appeal of the dismissal of certain causes of action.

■ **BLACK LETTER RULE** In the appropriate circumstances, an appellate court may hear an appeal even though the district judge fails to expressly certify the issue for appeal.

■ **PROCEDURAL BASIS**

Writ of certiorari reviewing appellate court's actions in reaching the merits on interlocutory appeal of dismissal of state-law causes of action for wrongful death.

■ **FACTS**

Mrs. Gillespie (P), the mother of David Gillespie, brought an action in federal court to recover damages for David's death. David fell and was drowned while working on a ship owned by United States Steel Corp. (D). Mrs. Gillespie (P) claimed a right to recover under the Jones Act and under various Ohio laws. Upon motion of U.S. Steel (D), the District Court struck all parts of the complaint referring to the Ohio laws. Mrs. Gillespie (P) filed an immediate appeal to the Court of Appeals, and U.S. Steel (D) moved to dismiss on grounds that the District Court's order was not a final judgment. Mrs. Gillespie (P) then filed a petition for mandamus in the Court of Appeals, seeking a writ commanding the District Judge to vacate his order. The Court of Appeals heard the appeal on the merits and ruled for U.S. Steel (D), holding that the court was allowed to decide on the merits because U.S. Steel (D) suffered no prejudice from the decision in its favor. The Supreme Court granted certiorari, with both Mrs. Gillespie (P) and U.S. Steel (D) urging the Court not to dismiss the case.

■ **ISSUE**

May an appellate court hear an interlocutory appeal even if the district court fails to certify the issue for immediate appeal?

■ **DECISION AND RATIONALE**

(Black, J.) Yes. An appellate court may hear an interlocutory appeal even if the district court fails to certify the issue for immediate appeal under 28 U.S.C. 1292(b). In the case at hand, even though the Court of Appeals handled the case in a piecemeal fashion, the cost of trying the case was not made greater by the Court hearing the appeal on its merits. The issues on appeal, presented by Mrs. Gillespie (P), were fundamental to the further conduct of the case. If the District Judge had certified the case to the Court of Appeals under section 1292(b), the appeal unquestionably would have been proper. And even though there was no lower court certification of the issue for appeal, we hold that the Court of Appeals properly implemented Congress's policy considerations by treating the issue as appealable.

■ DISSENT

(Harlan, J.) This case presents an example of the problems that occur when a lawsuit is handled in a piecemeal fashion. The majority sanctioned the loose practices of the Court of Appeals, and the majority's justifications are unavailing. First, the District Court did not certify the case under 1292(b), and the Court of Appeals cannot take this discretionary action on its own. Second, Mrs. Gillespie would have been able to raise her challenge on appeal. Finally, the fact that the parties may incur lesser costs as a result of the Court of Appeals' actions does not justify the abandonment of the final judgment rule.

Analysis:

The Supreme Court takes a loose, policy-based approach to the issue of appealability in this case, supplanting the final judgment rule and the statutory prescriptions of the U.S. Code with its own ideas of fairness and justice. The holding essentially allows Courts of Appeal to take unlimited discretion over hearing appeals, doing away with the safeguards of 1292(b), which require both the district judge and the appellate court to certify a case for interlocutory appeal. Commentators warn that this case should not be read too broadly, however, since the Supreme Court subsequently refused to extend this holding beyond its limited facts in *Coopers & Lybrand v. Livesay.* But even narrowly applying the holding to the facts reveals some questionable logical reasoning. For example, the Court of Appeals justified its hearing the appeal on the merits, in the face of an opposition by U.S. Steel (D), by stating that U.S. Steel (D) would not be prejudiced since the Court was holding in its favor. Does this mean that the appellate court would have been unjustified in hearing on the merits if it decided *against* U.S. Steel (D)? The Supreme Court's majority opinion also stretches logic when it notes that the issue would have been appealable had the District Judge certified it for appeal. As Justice Harlan's dissent points out, this point is moot, since the District Judge *did not* certify the case, as required by the express language of section 1292(b).

■ CASE VOCABULARY

ADMINISTRATRIX: The female personal representative of a deceased party, who oversees the settling and distribution of the decedent's estate.

LaBuy v. Howes Leather Co.

(District Court Judge) v. *(Antitrust Litigation Party)*

352 U.S. 249, 77 S.Ct. 309 (1957)

MANDAMUS IS AVAILABLE FOR APPELLATE REVIEW OF INTERLOCUTORY ORDERS

■ **INSTANT FACTS** Parties to an antitrust action sought a writ of mandamus to reverse an order of LaBuy (P), the District Court judge, referring the case to a Master.

■ **BLACK LETTER RULE** In extraordinary circumstances, appellate courts may review an interlocutory order via mandamus.

■ PROCEDURAL BASIS

Writ of certiorari reviewing order granting writ of mandamus.

■ FACTS

LaBuy (P), a District Court Judge, was presiding over a burdensome and complex antitrust litigation. Fearing that he had no time to try the six-week case, LaBuy (P) referred the entire case to a Master to take evidence and make findings of fact and conclusions of law. LaBuy (P) based this referral on Rule 53(b) [allowing for references to masters in exceptional circumstances]. Howes Leather Co. (D) and other parties to the litigation filed an action in the Court of Appeals, seeking a writ of mandamus ordering LaBuy (P) to vacate the reference to the Master. LaBuy (P) challenged this action on the grounds that Courts of Appeal have no power to issue such a writ. A unanimous Court of Appeals held that it did, indeed, have the power [what a surprise!]. The Supreme Court granted certiorari.

■ ISSUE

Does an appellate court possess the discretionary power to issue a writ of mandamus as a means of reviewing an interlocutory order?

■ DECISION AND RATIONALE

(Clark, J.) Yes. An appellate court possesses the discretionary power to issue a writ of mandamus as a means of reviewing an interlocutory order. Appellate courts are empowered to issue writs of mandamus pursuant to 28 U.S.C. § 1651(a) [stating that the Supreme Court and all courts created by Congress may issue writs], and the extraordinary writ of mandamus is appropriate when exceptional circumstances exist. In the case at hand, LaBuy (P) contends that appellate courts may not issue writs of mandamus to review interlocutory orders except in those cases where the review of the case on appeal after final judgment would be frustrated. We disagree. Since the Court of Appeals could at some stage of the antitrust proceedings entertain appeals in these cases, it has power to issue writs of mandamus reaching them, provided exceptional circumstances exist. We hold that exceptional circumstances do exist in the present case. LaBuy (P) abused his power under Rule 53(b) by referring the case to the Master, as this was essentially an abdication of his judicial role. The use of masters is to aid judges in the performance of specific duties, not to displace the court. Moreover, the mere congestion of LaBuy's (P) calendar was not such an exceptional circumstance as to warrant a reference to a master. Affirmed.

■ DISSENT

(Brennan, J.) In hearing this action and granting the writ of mandamus, this court has seriously undermined the long-standing statutory policy against piecemeal appeals. The All Writs Act, § 1651(a), does not confer an independent appellate power in the Courts of Appeals to review interlocutory orders.

Analysis:

This case details the elements underlying a review of an interlocutory court order via mandamus. It should be noted that mandamus is procedurally different from all other means of review, because it is technically an original proceeding entered in the appellate court against the trial judge. Thus, the writ of mandamus is used to confine trial judges to the lawful exercise of their powers. As the opinion stated, mandamus is an extraordinary type of review, used only in exceptional circumstances. In the case at hand, the Supreme Court held that exceptional circumstances did exist, as LaBuy (P) completely abdicated his judicial functions by depriving the parties of a trial before a District Court judge. Although the Court never hesitated in allowing the writ of mandamus in this case, subsequent Supreme Court decisions narrowed the availability of this avenue of review. In modern times, mandamus is available only when the issue goes to the jurisdiction of the court, or when the district judge's order is seen as a clear abuse of discretion.

■ CASE VOCABULARY

AD HOC: For a certain or special purpose.

SUA SPONTE: On his own motion; typically refers to a judge or court performing an action on their own volition.

VEL NON: Used to mean "or not," such as in the phrase "liability vel non."

WRIT OF MANDAMUS: Writ issued by a superior court to an inferior court, typically in response to a judge's abuse of discretion.

Atlantic City Elec. Co. v. General Elec. Co.

(Electricity Supplier) v. *(Electric Company)*

337 F.2d 844 (2nd Cir. 1964)

LEAVE TO FILE A DISCRETIONARY INTERLOCUTORY APPEAL IS GRANTED ONLY IN EXTREME SITUATIONS

■ **INSTANT FACTS** General Electric Co. (D) applies for leave to file an interlocutory appeal from the district court's order sustaining Atlantic City Electric Co.'s (P) objections to interrogatories.

■ **BLACK LETTER RULE** Discretionary appeals should be allowed only where a party would otherwise have no ability to protect its rights via a later appeal.

■ **PROCEDURAL BASIS**

Application for leave to appeal order sustaining objection to interrogatories.

■ **FACTS**

General Electric Company ("GE") (D) propounded interrogatories upon Atlantic City Electric Company ("ACE") (P) in pretrial discovery. ACE objected to the interrogatories, which were designed to discover whether ACE had shifted their alleged damages on to their consumers. The District Court sustained the objections, precluding GE's discovery attempt. However, the District Court also certified its order for appeal pursuant to 28 U.S.C. 1292(b). Thus, GE now applies to the Second Circuit for leave to appeal the order sustaining the objections.

■ **ISSUE**

Should interlocutory discretionary appeals be permitted where the party seeking the appeal would have a full opportunity to contest the issue following the trial?

■ **DECISION AND RATIONALE**

(Per Curiam) No. Discretionary appeals should not be permitted where the party seeking the appeal would have a full opportunity to contest the issue following the trial. In the case *sub judice*, it is not appropriate to review the order sustaining the objections prior to a final judgment. To do otherwise would delay the already extensive pre-trial proceedings. Moreover, GE's rights and defenses are not prejudiced by denying the interlocutory appeal. If GE loses at trial, it will have a full opportunity to appeal any alleged errors at trial, including the order currently at issue. We find that the ultimate disposition of the issues would be delayed rather than advanced by granting the leave to appeal. Application denied.

Analysis:

This case details some of the factors considered by an appellate court when deciding whether to grant leave to file an interlocutory appeal. As the case demonstrates, the appellate court has ultimate discretion to grant or deny the leave to file, and its decision can have a major impact on the parties to the litigation. Notice that there are actually two levels of discretion required for a Section 1292(b) appeal—the district court must first certify the issue for appeal, and then the appellate court must grant leave for the appeal. The express statutory language states that the appeal should be allowed only where an immediate appeal would materially advance the ultimate termination of the litigation. The Second Circuit in this case has taken a fairly strict approach to granting Section 1292(b) leaves. As a result, GE is forced to proceed to trial without some important evidence, and its only recourse in case it loses is to go to the expense of filing an appeal. However, the Court raises some compelling points regarding the leniency with which appellate courts should view Section 1292(b) motions. While the denial of leave for interlocutory appeals may result in some hardship for the parties, the widespread granting of such leave could cause major congestion problems at the trial level and delay trials even further. For this reason, the language of 1292(b) imposes fairly strict limits on this statutory exception to the "final judgment" rule.

■ CASE VOCABULARY

SUB JUDICE: Under judicial consideration.

J.F. White Contracting Co. v. New England Tank Industries of New Hampshire, Inc.

(*Contractor*) v. (*Landowner*)
393 F.2d 449 (1st Cir. 1968)

APPELLATE COURTS MAY ONLY CONSIDER ERRORS WHICH WERE NOT HARMLESS AND ISSUES WHICH WERE ACTUALLY RAISED AT TRIAL

■ **INSTANT FACTS** White (D) appeals a judgment on grounds that the lower court committed error, and White (D) attempts to introduce evidence not entered at trial.

■ **BLACK LETTER RULE** Appellate courts may only consider issues which were actually raised at trial, and harmless errors by the trial court do not constitute grounds for vacating a judgment.

■ **PROCEDURAL BASIS**

Appeal from judgment for damages for defective workmanship.

■ **FACTS**

New England Tank Industries of New Hampshire, Inc. ("Tank") (P) hired J.F. White Contracting Co. ("White") (D) to construct oil tanker dock facilities. The dock consisted of four metal cylinders filled with sand and gravel, connected by catwalks. Tank (P) sued White (D) for defective workmanship, including the fact that one of the cells was "out of round." A jury awarded $20,000 to Tank (P), and White (D) appealed on two grounds. First, White (D) argued that recovery was barred by a contract provision which stipulated that invoice approval by Tank's (P) engineers was binding on both parties, although White (D) had failed to raise this issue at trial. Second, White (D) contended that it was error to allow the "out-of-roundness" issue to the jury, since there was insufficient evidence presented to the jury to make the determination.

■ **ISSUE**

(1) Is an issue subject to review on appeal when the issue was not raised at trial? (2) Is an error subject to review on appeal when it does not affect the substantial rights of the parties?

■ **DECISION AND RATIONALE**

(Coffin, J.) (1) No. An issue is not subject to review on appeal when the issue was not raised at trial. White (D) attempts to raise the issue of the contractual provision, dealing with invoice approval, for the first time on appeal. We cannot consider such an issue which has neither been pleaded as an affirmative defense nor considered in the district court. (2) No. An error is not subject to review when it does not affect the substantial rights of the parties. In the case at hand, it was error for the district court to submit the out-of-roundness issue to the jury, as there was insufficient evidence for the jury to make a rational determination of the extent of damage. However, we are not persuaded that there was not even a remote possibility that this error affected the verdict or the substantial rights of the parties. The court properly instructed the jury to consider only evidence of value and cost of repairs when rendering a damage award, and there is no reason to suspect that the jury even considered the out-of-roundness issue. Affirmed.

Analysis:

While the first holding of this court, that only issues raised at trial are subject to appeal, is fairly straightforward, the holding dealing with harmless errors warrants close attention. As noted in Federal Rule of Civil Procedure 61, not every error made by a trial court is grounds for vacating the judgment on appeal. Only errors which affect the "substantial rights of the parties" may be considered on appeal. Of course, this phrase is wide open for interpretation, and indeed a central function of appellate courts is to determine if such substantial errors occurred. In the instant action, the appellate court's determination is somewhat questionable. The appellate court reasoned that the substantial rights of White (D) were not affected by the erroneous submission of the "out-of-roundness" issue to the jury. However, even if this evidence was not specifically considered by the jury when awarding damages, it probably entered the subconscious mind of the jurors in determining White's (D) degree of negligence.

Electrical Fittings Corp. v. Thomas & Betts Co.

(Corporation) v. *(Patent Holder)*
307 U.S. 241, 59 S.Ct. 860 (1939)

SUPREME COURT UPHOLDS VICTORIOUS PARTY'S RIGHT TO APPEAL

■ **INSTANT FACTS** Electrical Fittings Corp. (D) attempted to appeal a judgment entered in its favor because the decree stated that the claim against EFC (D) had some validity.

■ **BLACK LETTER RULE** A party may appeal a favorable judgment that contains unfavorable conclusions of law or fact provided those conclusions were necessary to support the judgment.

■ **PROCEDURAL BASIS**

Writ of certiorari reviewing dismissal of appeal of decree adjudging patent claim valid but dismissing for failure to prove infringement.

■ **FACTS**

Thomas & Betts Co. (P) sued Electrical Fittings Corp. ("EFC") (D) for patent infringement. The district court entered a decree adjudging one of Thomas & Betts's (P) claims as valid, but dismissing the bill for failure to prove infringement. EFC (D) appealed the portion of the decree which adjudged the one claim as valid. The court of appeals dismissed on the ground that, because the litigation terminated in its favor, EFC (D) was not entitled to appeal the decree. The Supreme Court granted certiorari.

■ **ISSUE**

May an appellate court entertain an appeal by the party who won at trial?

■ **DECISION AND RATIONALE**

(Roberts, J.) Yes. An appellate court may, in some circumstances, entertain an appeal by the party who won at trial. Indeed, a party may not appeal a favorable judgment for the purpose of reviewing certain findings which were not necessary to support the decree. However, where a decree stands as an adjudication of one of the issues litigated, the decree may be appealed from, even by the victorious party. The district court adjudicated the validity of the patent infringement claim, and its decree is subject to appeal by EFC (D). Reversed and remanded.

Analysis:

This case presents an unusual situation—a party appealing from a favorable judgment. But given the facts of the case, it is easy to see why EFC (D) would want to appeal the decree, since the trial court expressly held that there was some validity to Thomas & Betts's (P) patent infringement claim against EFC (D). Courts have generally held that only parties aggrieved by a judgment can appeal from it. And a party can only be aggrieved by those findings of law or fact that were actually necessary for a decree, since unnecessary findings cannot be the basis for collateral estoppel. In other words, EFC (D) could not appeal the decree if they would not be bound by it in subsequent suits. Such a rule is reasonable, as it protects the rights of the parties while avoiding needless appeals.

■ CASE VOCABULARY

BILL: A common law pleading setting forth a party's claims, analogous to a modern-day complaint.

DISCLAIMER: Act by which a patent holder releases certain features or specifications from the scope of the patent when they are deemed to be non-patentable.

International Ore & Fertilizer Corp. v. SGS Control Services, Inc.

(Shipper) v. *(Vendor)*

38 F.3d 1279 (2d Cir. 1994)

APPELLATE COURTS HAVE DISCRETION TO DISPENSE WITH THE CROSS APPEAL REQUIREMENT

■ **INSTANT FACTS** After the trial court entered judgment for the plaintiff on a negligent misrepresentation claim but dismissed its contract claim, the defendant appealed the negligent misrepresentation judgment.

■ **BLACK LETTER RULE** A party may urge on appeal any matter appearing in the appellate record without filing a cross-appeal, even if the trial court's reasoning is challenged in the process.

■ **PROCEDURAL BASIS**

Appeal to consider a judgment entered against the defendant.

■ **FACTS**

International Ore & Fertilizer Corp. (D) agreed to transport fertilizer for SGS Control Services, Inc. (P) to a buyer in New Zealand. Due to a failure to sufficiently clean the ship, the cargo became contaminated in transit and the buyer refused the delivery. The plaintiff sued the defendant for breach of contract and negligent misrepresentation of the condition of its ship. After hearing evidence, the trial judge rejected the contract claim, but awarded the plaintiff judgment on its negligent misrepresentation claim. The defendant appealed the judgment as to the negligent misrepresentation claim. On appeal, the court concluded that the negligent misrepresentation claim should have been dismissed, but that the contract claim should have been upheld. The defendant objected because the contract claim was not before the court on a cross-appeal by the plaintiff.

■ **ISSUE**

May a party attack a trial court judgment without filing a cross-appeal to preserve the issue on appeal?

■ **DECISION AND RATIONALE**

(Undisclosed judge.) Yes. Generally, when a party fails to file a cross-appeal, the party may not oppose a trial court's adverse decision in an appeal by an adverse party. However, a party may urge any matter appearing in the appellate record without filing a cross-appeal, even if the trial court's reasoning is challenged in the process. The court has discretion to dispense with the strict cross-appeal requirement when the party's challenge is based on the record. The court may, therefore, uphold the breach of contract claim. However, a party who fails to cross-appeal may not enlarge its rights under the judgment by seeking larger damages or equitable relief. Reversed.

Analysis:

By way of further explanation of the court's holding, the court ruled in the plaintiff's favor on its tort cause of action for negligent misrepresentation, but found that the defendant did not breach its contract with the plaintiff. In the process, the court reduced the plaintiff's recovery by fifty percent because of its contributory negligence. Because the plaintiff neglected to file a cross-appeal on the amount of damages awarded, it was not entitled to challenge the reduction of damages, although the appellate court determined that the defendant breached the contract, which would ordinarily entitle the plaintiff to its full damages.

■ **CASE VOCABULARY**

CROSS–APPEAL: An appeal by the appellee, usually heard at the same time as the appellant's appeal.

Corcoran v. City of Chicago

(*Injured party*) v. (*Government*)

373 Ill. 567, 27 N.E.2d 451 (1940)

APPELLATE COURTS MAY ANALYZE THE SUFFICIENCY OF FACTS AND MAY OVERTURN ORDERS DENYING NEW TRIALS

■ **INSTANT FACTS** John Corcoran (P) argued that an appellate court has no authority to determine whether a verdict is supported by the evidence presented at trial.

■ **BLACK LETTER RULE** An appellate court may set aside a verdict on the grounds that findings of fact are not supported by evidence.

■ **PROCEDURAL BASIS**

Appeal from reversal of overruling of motion for new trial in action for damages for personal injuries.

■ **FACTS**

John Corcoran (P) [No, this was not O.J.'s attorney!] sued the City of Chicago (D) for negligently permitting certain streets to remain unsafe for travel, resulting in personal injuries for Corcoran (P). The jury awarded $5000 for Corcoran (P), and the judge overruled a motion for new trial. On appeal, the appellate court found that the verdict was against the manifest weight of the evidence and reversed the judgment. An Illinois statute allowed appellate courts to review judgments which appear against the weight of the evidence. Corcoran (P) appealed, arguing that the statute unconstitutionally denied him the right to trial by jury.

■ **ISSUE**

May an appellate court set aside a verdict on the grounds the findings of fact were not supported by the evidence?

■ **DECISION AND RATIONALE**

(Murphy, J.) Yes. An appellate court may set aside a verdict on the grounds that the findings of fact were not supported by the evidence. Prior to the enactment of the Illinois statute, only trial courts could rule on motions for new trial, pursuant to the old maxim that "the judges respond to the law, the jury to the facts." However, in modern times appellate judges have as much power as trial courts to set aside a verdict if the facts do not support the verdict. Thus, the appellate court in the instant action was empowered to set aside the verdict. Affirmed.

Analysis:

Contrary to popular belief, appellate courts often are as involved with the facts of a given case as with the law at issue. While appellate courts cannot receive new evidence concerning the facts, they can analyze the facts and determine if the facts were sufficient to warrant a particular jury verdict. As this court held, such authority does not deny a party's constitutional right to trial by jury. Although the court did not go into detail on the constitutional issue, apparently the fact that the party initially had the opportunity to present the facts to a jury satisfies the party's constitutional right.

Pullman-Standard v. Swint

(Manufacturer) v. *(Employee)*
456 U.S. 273, 102 S.Ct. 1781 (1982)

THE "CLEARLY ERRONEOUS" STANDARD APPLIES WHENEVER APPELLATE COURTS REVIEW FINDINGS OF FACT

■ **INSTANT FACTS** Pullman-Standard (D) contends that the Court of Appeals incorrectly avoided the "clearly erroneous" standard when reviewing the District Court's determination that the company did not discriminate.

■ **BLACK LETTER RULE** A Court of Appeals is bound by the "clearly erroneous" standard whenever reviewing questions of fact.

■ **PROCEDURAL BASIS**

Writ of certiorari reviewing reversal of finding of intentional discrimination in violation of Civil Rights Act.

■ **FACTS**

Swint (P) and other black employees of Pullman-Standard (D), a manufacturer of railway freight cars, brought suit against the company for alleged violations of Title VII of the Civil Rights Act of 1964. The District Court held that the purported violations at issue, dealing with the company's seniority system, were not the result of an intention to discriminate and, therefore, were not violations of the Act. The Court of Appeals reversed, finding that Pullman-Standard (D) did intentionally discriminate. The Supreme Court granted certiorari.

■ **ISSUE**

Is a Court of Appeals bound by the "clearly erroneous" standard of Rule 52(a) of the Federal Rules in reviewing a question of fact?

■ **DECISION AND RATIONALE**

(White, J.) Yes. A Court of Appeals is bound by the "clearly erroneous" standard of Rule 52(a) in reviewing a question of fact. In the case at hand, Pullman-Standard (D) submits that the Court of Appeals erroneously made an independent determination of the discriminatory purpose behind the seniority system and ignored the "clearly erroneous" standard. We agree. We find that the question of the discriminatory intent was a pure question of fact, and therefore that the Appellate Court could only overturn this factual determination if it was clearly erroneous. Discriminatory intent here means actual motive, not a legal presumption to be drawn from some factual showing. Thus, the Court of Appeals applied the incorrect standard. And even if the Court of Appeals believed that a question of law was involved, it should have remanded to the District Court for fact-finding. Reversed and remanded.

■ **DISSENT**

(Marshall, J.) In some cases, such as the case at hand, remand is inappropriate where the facts on the record are susceptible to only one reasonable interpretation. The findings made by the District Court were entirely based on documentary evidence, and therefore the Court of Appeals could easily reach its own conclusions. I believe that the Court of Appeals correctly determined that a finding of discriminatory intent was compelled by the documentary evidence.

Analysis:

This seemingly straightforward holding is complicated by a number of issues. On its face, the case simply stands for the proposition that a Court of Appeals must apply the "clearly erroneous" standard when analyzing questions of fact. The case gets complicated when it tackles the appropriate approach to questions of law. If the Court of Appeals believed that the issue of discrimination involved a question of law, then, according to the majority, it was required to remand to the District Court for further factfinding. This makes some sense, as factfinding is one of the central tasks of a trial court. However, the dissent reveals that, at least on some occasions, remand is inappropriate. Where the lower court's findings are based on purely documentary evidence, then apparently appellate courts can make an independent determination of the issue.

■ CASE VOCABULARY

BONA FIDES: Good faith.

Inwood Labs, Inc. v. Ives Labs, Inc.

(*Laboratory*) v. (*Patent Holder*)

456 U.S. 844, 102 S.Ct. 2182 (1982)

DEFERENCE SHOULD BE GIVEN TO THE TRIAL JUDGE'S FACTUAL DETERMINATIONS UNLESS CLEARLY ERRONEOUS

■ **INSTANT FACTS** The Court of Appeals, conducting an independent review of the factual issues, found Inwood Labs (D) violated Ives Labs' (P) patent.

■ **BLACK LETTER RULE** Appellate courts are bound by the "clearly erroneous" standard when reviewing lower court's findings of fact.

■ PROCEDURAL BASIS

Writ of certiorari reviewing reversal of finding that no patent infringement existed.

■ FACTS

Ives Labs (P) sued Inwood Labs (D) for patent infringement. The District Court ruled that Ives (P) failed to make the necessary factual showings and entered judgment for Inwood (D). The Court of Appeals, conducting an independent review of the evidence, found that Inwood (D) did infringe on the patent. The Supreme Court granted certiorari.

■ ISSUE

May an appellate court substitute its own interpretation of the evidence for that of the trial court?

■ DECISION AND RATIONALE

(Name of Justice Not Given) No. An appellate court may not substitute its own interpretation of the evidence for that of the trial court. Rather, the appellate court is bound by the clearly erroneous standard, and must accept the trial court's findings unless left with the definite and firm conviction that a mistake has been committed. Reversed.

Analysis:

This case essentially repeats the holding of previous holdings, although it presents a couple of sentences which further explain the "clearly erroneous" standard. Basically, trial court judges have a unique opportunity to evaluate the evidence and get a firsthand view of the credibility of the witnesses. Thus, their judgments should not be reversed unless it is obvious that they made some serious error. It is important to remember that this standard only applies to actions tried without a jury.

Bose Corp. v. Consumers Union of United States, Inc.

(*Loudspeaker Manufacturer*) v. (*Consumer Publication*)

466 U.S. 485, 104 S.Ct. 1949 (1984)

THE "CLEARLY ERRONEOUS" STANDARD MAY BE ALTERED WHEN CONSTITUTIONAL PROTECTIONS ARE AT ISSUE

■ **INSTANT FACTS** In reviewing a defamation action, the Court of Appeals conducted a *de novo* review of the determination of "actual malice," rather than following Rule 52(a)'s "clearly erroneous" standard.

■ **BLACK LETTER RULE** The "clearly erroneous" standard does not apply when reviewing the constitutional facts surrounding a determination of actual malice in a defamation action.

■ **PROCEDURAL BASIS**

Writ of certiorari reviewing reversal of finding of actual malice in defamation action.

■ **FACTS**

Bose Corp. (P) sued the Consumers Union (D) for defamation after Consumers Union (D) allegedly published disparaging statements about a loudspeaker system manufactured by Bose (P). Utilizing the "actual malice" standard of *New York Times Co. v. Sullivan* [a public figure suing for defamation must prove that the statements were made with actual malice], the District Court found that clear and convincing evidence of defamation existed, and the Court ruled for Bose (P). On appeal, the Court of Appeals ruled that it was not governed by the "clearly erroneous" standard of Rule 52(a). Rather, the Appellate Court conducted a *de novo* review of the record because the case raised First Amendment concerns that required an independent review of the trial judge's findings, and the Appellate Court reversed the District Court's holding. The Supreme Court granted certiorari.

■ **ISSUE**

Is an appellate court bound by the Rule 52(a) "clearly erroneous" standard when a case raises First Amendment concerns?

■ **DECISION AND RATIONALE**

(Stevens, J.) No. An appellate court is not necessarily bound by the Rule 52(a) "clearly erroneous" standard when a case raises First Amendment concerns. As we held in *New York Times*, appellate courts must conduct a complete examination of the trial record to measure the judgment by the constitutional protection afforded by the First Amendment. This conflicts to some degree with Rule 52(a), but the conflict is not very significant. Rule 52(a) does not forbid an independent examination by the appellate court, and does not inhibit an appellate court's power to correct errors of law, even where the law is mixed with factual determinations. Thus, we hold that the question, whether the evidence in the record in a defamation case is clear and convincing enough to render the speech unprotected by the First Amendment, is not merely a question for the trier of fact. Upon a *de novo* review of this case, we hold that the record contains no clear and convincing evidence that Consumers Union (D) made the allegedly disparaging remarks with actual malice. Affirmed.

■ DISSENT

(Rehnquist, J.) When making a determination of actual malice pursuant to the *New York Times* standard, the dispositive facts—actual knowledge of misrepresentation or subjective reckless disregard for the truth—merely involve factual determinations about the mens rea of the party who made the statement. Appellate courts are not prepared to make these purely factual determinations. I believe that the constitutional requirement of "actual malice" in defamation actions requires a "clearly erroneous" standard of review.

Analysis:

This case reaches the important conclusion that the "clearly erroneous" standard of review does not necessarily apply to all reviews of factual findings. There is little question that the determination of "actual malice" is a factual finding. However, Justice Stevens ruled that a court is not bound by the "clearly erroneous" standard in defamation actions, since a finding of actual malice implicates First Amendment concerns. Indeed, a person's fundamental right to free speech can be limited when actual malice is found, and First Amendment rights should not be limited unless there is a compelling need. But is the existence of constitutional issues sufficient to alter an express Federal Rule that limits any appellate court to the "clearly erroneous" standard when reviewing factual determinations? Does this mean that Rule 52(a)'s requirement can be altered whenever constitutional protections are at issue? The Court's holding seems more limited, and it most likely applies only to defamation actions.

■ CASE VOCABULARY

MENS REA: A term, typically utilized in criminal actions, referring to the various states of mind of the actor.

Dick v. New York Life Ins. Co.

(*Not Stated*) v. (*Insurance Company*)

359 U.S. 437, 79 S.Ct. 921 (1959)

JUSTICE FRANKFURTER RECOMMENDS SUPREME COURT REVIEW ONLY IN EXTREMELY LIMITED SITUATIONS

■ **INSTANT FACTS** The facts of this case are not provided in the text.

■ **BLACK LETTER RULE** The U.S. Supreme Court should exercise its discretionary power of certiorari only in cases of general importance or to secure uniformity of decision.

■ FACTS

The facts of this case are not provided in the text.

■ ISSUE

Should the U.S. Supreme Court exercise its discretionary power of certiorari only in cases of general importance or to secure uniformity of decision?

■ DECISION AND RATIONALE

The majority opinion is not provided in the text.

■ DISSENT

(Frankfurter, J.) Yes. The U.S. Supreme Court should exercise its discretionary power of certiorari only in cases of general importance or to secure uniformity of decision. The Court should not review questions of fact or examine evidence unless the questions of fact are interwoven with questions of law, and even then review should be made only in limited situations. In general, no litigant is entitled to more than two chances. The intermediate appellate courts were created to give litigants their second chance, and were designed to be equal in dignity to the Supreme Courts of the several States. The decisions of these courts should be final except in the most necessary of situations where Supreme Court review is warranted.

Analysis:

Although it is nearly impossible to decipher what is happening in this case from the limited excerpt printed in the text, it is important to note that not all Supreme Court justices necessarily agree on what the proper scope of Supreme Court review should entail. Justice Frankfurter, in this dissent, clearly argues for a limited role of certiorari. Where a case is not of grave importance or a Supreme Court decision is not necessary to secure uniformity of laws throughout the nation, Frankfurter argues that the appellate court's decision should be final. This is a fairly compelling argument, although a look at any law school case book demonstrates how little weight many appellate decisions actually carry.

Harris v. Pennsylvania R. Co.

(*Not Stated*) v. (*Railroad Company*)
361 U.S. 15, 80 S.Ct. 22 (1959)

THE SUPREME COURT AGAIN DEFENDS ITS DISCRETIONARY POWER TO CONTROL ITS CALENDAR VIA CERTIORARI

■ **INSTANT FACTS** In a FELA action, the Supreme Court is faced with defending its procedure for denying certiorari.

■ **BLACK LETTER RULE** The Supreme Court's discretion is limited by the "rule of four," requiring four of nine judges to vote to grant certiorari.

■ FACTS

Although the facts of this case are not set out in detail, it can be inferred that this case arises under FELA (Federal Employer's Liability Act). This was one of 33 FELA cases in which the Supreme Court had granted certiorari between 1949 and 1959, although only 12 of the cases were actually argued, briefed and disposed of with full opinions by the Court. Apparently some party made the claim that the Supreme Court should not have granted certiorari to all of these cases, and that the Court was wasting its time.

■ ISSUE

Is the Supreme Court too liberal in granting certiorari and certifying cases for review?

■ DECISION AND RATIONALE

The majority opinion is not provided in the text.

■ CONCURRENCE

(Douglas, J.) No. The Supreme Court is not too liberal in granting certiorari and certifying cases for review. It is incorrect to claim that the FELA cases waste inordinate amounts of the Supreme Court's time, as we have only heard slightly more than one case per year in the ten years at issue. Further, the Supreme Court does not possess too much discretion over what cases it desires to review. The "rule of four," by which at least four justices must agree that a case is deserving of review before certiorari is granted, operates to temper the otherwise vast amount of discretion granted by Congress.

Analysis:

The brief excerpt from this case addresses many issues, but the most important issue is the scope of the Supreme Court's discretion with respect to granting certiorari. Obviously the Court should not have unlimited discretion to review cases, because this could lead to a seriously overburdened and therefore ineffective Court. Justice Douglas seems to believe that the "rule of four" operates effectively to restrict the number of cases the Court hears. While the requirement for four votes may limit the number of cases to some extent, many commentators have nevertheless criticized the Court for hearing too many actions.

■ CASE VOCABULARY

FELA: Federal Employer's Liability Act.

CHAPTER SEVENTEEN

The Binding Effect of Prior Decisions: Res Judicata and Collateral Estoppel

Rush v. City of Maple Heights

Instant Facts: One judge limited Rush's recovery from the City for her injuries from an accident to $100, and another judge ordered the County to pay more.

Black Letter Rule: Whether or not injuries to both person and property resulting from the same wrongful act are to be treated as injuries to separate rights or as separate items of damage, a plaintiff may maintain only one action to enforce his rights existing at the time such action is commenced.

Mathews v. New York Racing Association, Inc.

Instant Facts: Mathews alleged certain facts in an assault suit against the Association, and then alleged the same facts in a second suit for false arrest.

Black Letter Rule: The doctrine of res judicata operates as a bar to subsequent suits involving the same parties, or those in privity with them, based on a claim which has once reached a judgment on the merits.

Federated Department Stores, Inc. v. Moitie

Instant Facts: The Ninth Circuit did not apply res judicata to actions that were dismissed on the basis of an opinion that had later been effectively overruled.

Black Letter Rule: The doctrine of res judicata is a rule of fundamental and substantial justice, of public policy and private peace, which should be cordially regarded and enforced by the courts.

Jones v. Morris Plan Bank of Portsmouth

Instant Facts: The Bank won a judgment against Jones for two missed car payments, and tried to sue Jones again after he sold the automobile without consent.

Black Letter Rule: If a transaction is represented by one single and indivisible contract and the breach of that contract gives rise to one single cause of action, it cannot be split into distinct parts, with separate actions maintained for each.

Mitchell v. Federal Intermediate Credit Bank

Instant Facts: Mitchell used the proceeds from the sale of his potato crop as security for two loans, then claimed the bank kept the proceeds for itself.

Black Letter Rule: A party cannot split a cause of action and use one portion of it for defense in one suit and then use the remainder for offense in a subsequent suit.

Linderman Machine Co. v. Hillenbrand Co.

Instant Facts: Hillenbrand (D), after winning a suit brought against it by Linderman (P), sued the latter for recovery of expenses incurred due to Linderman's (P) fraud.

Black Letter Rule: When a party is sued, a judgment in that suit is not conclusive as to an affirmative cause of action which the party may have asserted against the other in a cross-complaint.

Cromwell v. County of Sac

Instant Facts: County of Sac (D) ("County") sought to estop Cromwell's (P) action against County (D) for bonds issued by the latter, based on an earlier decision rendered in County's favor.

Black Letter Rule: Estoppel of a judgment in one cause of action to an action arising out of another cause of action applies when the issue in question was actually litigated and determined in the first action.

Russell v. Place

Instant Facts: In a patent infringement action against Place (D), Russell (P) sought to estop re-litigation of the novelty of the product based on a previous judgment for the same patent between the same parties.

Black Letter Rule: Collateral estoppel applies only if the precise issue in question has been litigated and determined in the former suit.

Rios v. Davis

Instant Facts: Rios (P) brought an action against Davis (D) for injuries suffered in automobile accident between Rios (P), Davis (D), and Popular Dry Goods Company ("Popular").

Black Letter Rule: A finding of fact which is not material or essential to the judgment of a suit between two parties is not binding on the parties in a later suit.

Commissioner of Internal Revenue v. Sunnen

Instant Facts: The Commissioner of Internal Revenue (P) assessed taxes against Sunnen (D) on the ground that the royalties which Sunnen's (D) wife received from Sunnen's (D) corporation were Sunnen's (D) own taxable income.

Black Letter Rule: Collateral estoppel may only be applied in situations where the issue raised in the second suit is identical to the issue in the first suit and the controlling law and facts remain the same.

Hanover Logansport, Inc. v. Robert C. Anderson, Inc.

Instant Facts: Hanover Logansport, Inc. (P) ("Hanover") having entered a settlement agreement with Robert C. Anderson, Inc. (D) ("Anderson") for breach of a lease contract, contends that the agreement precludes a claim for recovery of further damages against Hanover (P) by Anderson (D).

Black Letter Rule: The preclusive effect of a consent judgment should depend upon the intent of the parties entering into the consent judgment.

Housing Authority for La Salle County v. Young Men's Christian Ass'n of Ottawa

Instant Facts: Housing Authority for La Salle County (P) ("county") sought an injunction against Young Men's Christian Ass'n of Ottawa (D) ("YMCA") preventing the YMCA from building a parking structure on a property owned by the YMCA.

Black Letter Rule: Under the doctrine of res judicata, a default judgment has the same preclusive effect as any other judgment.

Holmberg v. State, Division of Risk Management

Instant Facts: State employee attempts to use subsequent decision on disability to reverse an earlier decision by a state workers' compensation board.

Black Letter Rule: Res judicata can be used only against parties or those in privity, and a final judgment retains its res judicata effects pending resolution of an appeal of the judgment.

Bernhard v. Bank of America Nat. Trust & Sav. Ass'n

Instant Facts: Bernhard (P), administratrix of the estate of Mrs. Slather, sued Bank of America (D) for allegedly allowing an unauthorized withdrawal from Mrs. Sather's account during her life.

Black Letter Rule: A party may assert res judicata even though he was not a party, or in privy with a party in the earlier litigation.

Blonder–Tongue Laboratories, Inc. v. University of Illinois Foundation

Instant Facts: A university foundation sued for the infringement of its alleged patent for a radio antenna, even though a prior lawsuit had determined that the foundation did not own the patent.

Black Letter Rule: Nonmutual collateral estoppel may be applied defensively against a party who had a full and fair opportunity to litigate the issue in a prior proceeding.

Parklane Hosiery Co. v. Shore

Instant Facts: Shore (P), a stockholder in Parklane Hosiery Co. (D) ("Parklane") brought a class action against the latter alleging that Parklane (D) had issued a materially false and misleading proxy statement in connection with a merger.

Black Letter Rule: Trial courts have broad discretion to apply the doctrine of offensive collateral estoppel, even in cases where the defendant will be deprived of a jury trial.

Martin v. Wilks

Instant Facts: Pursuant to consent judgments between the City of Birmingham ("City") and the Jefferson County Personnel Board ("Board") with black firefighters, the white firefighters filed a suit against the City and the Board alleging reverse discrimination.

Black Letter Rule: A party seeking a judgment binding on another cannot obligate the latter to intervene in the action without mandatorily joining that person in the action.

Taylor v. Sturgell

Instant Facts: After on antique aircraft enthusiast's Freedom of Information lawsuit proved unsuccessful, Taylor (P), a friend and fellow enthusiast, brought suit seeking the same information, and the court similarly denied his request based on the judgment in the first case; Taylor (P) appealed.

Black Letter Rule: The rule against nonparty preclusion is subject only to certain recognized exceptions: (1) a nonparty may agree to be bound by a judgment, (2) certain substantive relationships may justify preclusion (e.g., privity), (3) a nonparty's interests may have been adequately represented in the prior litigation (e.g., class actions and suits by trustees or guardians), (4) a nonparty may have assumed control over the earlier lawsuit, (5) a nonparty may have colluded to avoid the preclusive effect of an earlier judgment by litigating through a proxy, or (6) special statutory schemes (such as bankruptcy) may apply.

Hart v. American Airlines, Inc.

Instant Facts: In a New York action, American Airlines attempts to resist preclusive effect from being given to the issue of liability for an airline crash that was previously decided in Texas.

Black Letter Rule: Offensive nonmutual estoppel can be utilized by courts that are part of different judicial systems from the rendering court.

Thompson v. Thompson

Instant Facts: A father sought to utilize a federal act to resolve two conflicting state child custody decrees.

Black Letter Rule: The PKPA precludes a state court from maintaining the ability to reopen child custody proceedings.

Allen v. McCurry

Instant Facts: McCurry (P), having been found guilty of drug possession, later sued Allen (D) and other police officers for alleged violations of McCurry's (P) constitutional rights against unlawful search and seizure.

Black Letter Rule: Federal courts must give preclusive effect to state court judgments even where federal civil rights are at issue.

Semtek International, Inc. v. Lockheed Martin, Corp.

Instant Facts: After a California federal court dismissed the plaintiff's action on the basis of the state statute of limitations, a Maryland state court dismissed a subsequent suit brought by the plaintiff on the same grounds.

Black Letter Rule: The law of the state in which the federal court sits governs the claim-preclusive effect of a judgment on the merits in a federal diversity action.

Rush v. City of Maple Heights

(Motorcycle Rider) v. *(City)*

167 Ohio St. 221, 147 N.E.2d 599 (1958)

A PLAINTIFF MAY MAINTAIN ONLY ONE ACTION TO ENFORCE HIS OR HER RIGHTS EXISTING AT THE TIME SUCH ACTION IS COMMENCED

■ **INSTANT FACTS** One judge limited Rush's recovery from the City for her injuries from an accident to $100, and another judge ordered the County to pay more.

■ **BLACK LETTER RULE** Whether or not injuries to both person and property resulting from the same wrongful act are to be treated as injuries to separate rights or as separate items of damage, a plaintiff may maintain only one action to enforce his rights existing at the time such action is commenced.

■ **PROCEDURAL BASIS**

Appeal from judgment in negligence action for damages.

■ **FACTS**

Rush (P) was injured in a motorcycle accident. She (P) sued the City of Maple Heights (D) in the Municipal Court of Cleveland. Rush (P) claimed the City (D) was negligent in maintaining the street and this negligence was the proximate cause of her (P's) damages. The trial court ruled for Rush (P), and damages were fixed at $100. The City (P) appealed, but the judgment was affirmed by the Ohio Court of Appeals and Supreme Court. Rush (P) also brought this action in the Court of Common Pleas of Cuyahoga. Rush (P) sought recovery for personal injuries she suffered in the same accident. She (P) moved to set trial on the issue of damages alone. The court granted this motion on the ground that the issue of negligence was res judicata because of the Municipal Court action. The Cuyahoga court entered judgment on a verdict for $12,000 for Rush (P). The Court of Appeals affirmed.

■ **ISSUE**

Can a plaintiff maintain more than one action for injuries to his or her rights resulting from one accident?

■ **DECISION AND RATIONALE**

(Herbert, J.) No. Whether or not injuries to both person and property resulting from the same wrongful act are to be treated as injuries to separate rights or as separate items of damage, a plaintiff may maintain only one action to enforce his rights existing at the time such action is commenced. The rule presented in *Vasu v. Kohlers* [recovery or denial of recovery of compensation for damages to property is no bar to subsequent action for personal injury from same wrongful act unless an adverse judgment in first action would affect issue in second action] should not be followed because it is in conflict with the great weight of authority in this country. Generally, injuries to person and property amount to several effects of a single, wrongful act. A single tort can be the basis of but one action. Otherwise, multiple suits will arise, leading to significant delays and costs for all parties concerned. Allowing more than one action to arise from a single tort would allow, as Lord Coleridge stated in his dissent in *Brunsden v. Humphrey*, a man to bring two actions "if besides his arm and leg being injured, his trousers, which contain his leg, and his coat-sleeve, which contains his arm, have been torn." Judgment reversed, and final judgment for the City (D).

■ CONCURRENCE

(Stewart, J.) The discussion in *Vasu* as to whether a single or double cause of action arises from one tort nor the language of the syllabus of the lower court in *Vasu* were necessary to decide this case. Neither are appropriate to the question presented in this case.

■ DISSENT

(Zimmerman, J.) Without changing conditions to compel upsetting prior decisions of this court, established law should remain undisturbed. There should be some kind of stability that the lower courts and other members of the legal profession can rely on.

Analysis:

The limits on the scope of claim preclusion have developed greatly since the turn of the century. As the Restatement (Second) of Judgments explains, the courts used to associate the word "claim" with a plaintiff's single theory of recovery. This meant that a plaintiff would have as many claims as there were theories of substantive law that he could use to gain relief from the defendant. Thus, a plaintiff could raise several claims from just one injury-causing act or event. For instance, some courts would hold that a denial of relief in a claim for bodily injury did not preclude relief for injury to property. Also, some courts believed that a plaintiff had an amount of claims equal to the amount of his primary rights that were violated. Other courts would find that if certain evidence were used in an earlier claim, then a second action on the same evidence was precluded. At times, this evidence test was used as the sole test; at other times, courts used it as just one test out of many. Today, the courts generally see claims in factual terms and make the underlying transaction the basis of the litigation. In other words, the scope of claim preclusion was tied to the transaction as far as litigation was concerned, and not the number of theories, the number of primary rights, or the body of evidence.

■ CASE VOCABULARY

VEXATIOUS: Distressing, troubling.

Mathews v. New York Racing Association, Inc.

(Gambler) v. *(Racetrack Operator)*

193 F.Supp. 293 (S.D.N.Y. 1961)

PLAINTIFFS CANNOT SPLINTER THEIR CLAIMS INTO MULTIPLE SUITS AND TRY THEM PIECEMEAL AT THEIR CONVENIENCE

■ **INSTANT FACTS** Mathews alleged certain facts in an assault suit against the Association, and then alleged the same facts in a second suit for false arrest.

■ **BLACK LETTER RULE** The doctrine of res judicata operates as a bar to subsequent suits involving the same parties, or those in privity with them, based on a claim which has once reached a judgment on the merits.

■ **PROCEDURAL BASIS**

Motion for summary judgment in false arrest action for damages and injunctive relief.

■ **FACTS**

New York Racing Association, Inc. (Association) (D) operates Jamaica Race Track. The Association employs Thoroughbred Protective Association Inc. (Thoroughbred) (D), a private detective agency, to provide security. Matthews (P) sued the Association and Thoroughbred (D), claiming that on April 4, 1958, he (P) was "assaulted," "kidnapped," "falsely arrested," and "falsely imprisoned" by Thoroughbred (D) employees. In addition, he (P) claims that the Association and Thoroughbred (D) charged him with disorderly conduct and maliciously caused him to be prosecuted and convicted in the Magistrate's Court of the City of New York on April 10, 1958. In this action, Matthews (P) is asking for money damages and an injunction restraining the Association and Thoroughbred (D) from interfering with his attendance at the racetracks, from printing libelous statements about him (P), and from acting against peace officers. The Association and Thoroughbred (D) moved for summary judgment under Federal Rule of Civil Procedure 56(b). The Association and Thoroughbred (D) argue that on June 30, 1960, Matthews (P) sued three individual employees of Thoroughbred and the Association (D), alleging he (P) had been assaulted by Thoroughbred's (D) private investigators at Jamaica Race Track on April 4, 1958. Matthews (P) also prayed for monetary and injunctive relief in that earlier action.

■ **ISSUE**

Can one party in a dispute sue another party to the same dispute again after a judgment on the merits of the case has already been reached?

■ **DECISION AND RATIONALE**

(MacMahon, J.) No. The doctrine of res judicata operates as a bar to subsequent suits involving the same parties, or those in privity with them, based on a claim which has once reached a judgment on the merits. The classic situation involving this issue is where a second claim between the same parties is based on the same operative facts as the earlier one. The issues tried in the first claim and any other issues which could have been dealt with there are forever barred by the first judgment. The term "claim" refers to a group of facts limited to a single occurrence or transaction without particular reference to the resulting legal rights. In other words, it is the facts surrounding the occurrence which make up a claim, and not the legal theory upon which the plaintiff relies. Here, Matthews' (P) ejection from the racetrack and his (P) trial for disorderly conduct happened within a matter of days. Matthews' (P) earlier claim of assault and his present claim for false arrest are both based on the actions of the Thoroughbred (D) employees. Moreover, Matthews' (P) previous claim of libel and his present claim for malicious prosecution are both based on the statements of those same employees. Clearly, the doctrine of respondeat superior would have to be applied when determining the liability of the Association and Thoroughbred (D) and their (D) employees. If the agents of the Association and Thoroughbred (Ds) committed no actionable wrong against Matthews (P), then neither did those corporations (D). Essentially, Matthews (P) is asserting the same facts as the basis of liability in each suit. A plaintiff cannot be permitted to splinter his or her claim into a multiplicity of suits and try them at his or her convenience. Such a person does not get another day in court after the first lawsuit is over by presenting the same facts with a new reason as to why he or she should be entitled to recovery. Because of this, Matthews (P) is estopped, both directly and collaterally, from maintaining this action.

Analysis:

The courts in both *Mathews* and *Rush* determined the scope of preclusion according to the "transaction approach." This method is often praised for its flexibility, allowing courts to adjust their findings based on the particular facts of the case. This flexibility, however, does impose certain disadvantages. A party, in failing to raise certain parts of his or her action, could end up forfeiting those parts because a judge may interpret the claim much more broadly than the litigant had anticipated. To protect against this outcome, a plaintiff may likely raise every last possible allegation connected to his or her case, and thus advance claims that he or she would otherwise have not brought to court.

■ CASE VOCABULARY

LIBELOUS: Defamatory, attacking.

PRO SE: "For one's own behalf"; term used to describe individual who represents himself or herself in court, without the aid of a lawyer.

Federated Department Stores, Inc. v. Moitie

(*Large Retail Corporation*) v. (*One of the Original Plaintiffs*)
452 U.S. 394, 101 S.Ct. 2424, 69 L.Ed.2d 103 (1981)

NO PRINCIPLE OR LAW OF EQUITY ALLOWS A FEDERAL COURT TO REJECT RES JUDICATA PRINCIPLES

■ **INSTANT FACTS** The Ninth Circuit did not apply res judicata to actions that were dismissed on the basis of an opinion that had later been effectively overruled.

■ **BLACK LETTER RULE** The doctrine of res judicata is a rule of fundamental and substantial justice, of public policy and private peace, which should be cordially regarded and enforced by the courts.

■ **PROCEDURAL BASIS**

Appeal from judgment in antitrust action.

■ **FACTS**

Moitie and Brown (P) and five others filed separate antitrust actions against Federated Department Stores, Inc. (Federated) (D). Their separate actions were consolidated in the District Court and were then dismissed. The grounds for dismissal were that Moitie and Brown and the others (Ps) failed to allege an "injury" to their "business or property" as required by the Clayton Act. Moitie and Brown (Ps) refiled their actions in state court, while the other five (Ps) appealed to the Ninth Circuit. Moitie's and Brown's (P) actions were removed to federal court and then dismissed on res judicata grounds. The other five appeals were reversed and remanded to the District Court to be reconsidered in light of a recent Supreme Court opinion. When Moitie's and Brown's (P) refiled actions reached the Ninth Circuit on appeal, the Court opted not to apply res judicata. It noted that while a strict application of res judicata would preclude the second action, an exception should be made to that doctrine when the dismissal rested on a case that had been effectively overruled.

■ **ISSUE**

Can a court waive the use of res judicata when such use would lead to the dismissal of a case which had been effectively overruled?

■ **DECISION AND RATIONALE**

(Justice Not Named) No. The doctrine of res judicata is a rule of fundamental and substantial justice, of public policy and private peace, which should be cordially regarded and enforced by the courts. The Court of Appeals rested its opinion on what it considered to be "simple justice." "Simple justice," however, is achieved when a complex body of law, developed over a period of years, is *evenhandedly applied.* The doctrine of res judicata serves vital public interests beyond one judge's ad hoc determination of the equities of a case. There is no principle of law or equity which sanctions the rejection by a federal court of the salutary principle of res judicata. Judgment of Ninth Circuit reversed.

Analysis:

Despite the seemingly monumental scope of the language in this case, there are a number of scenarios in which prior judgments are not found to preclude a current action. Indeed, these situations arise out of considerations of "justice and fairness." For example, courts have not generally considered prior judgments obtained through the use of fraud to be binding. In addition, courts have found that a judgment will have no preclusive effect when the first court should have been prevented from hearing the action by a clear and fundamental problem of jurisdiction. Also, while federal courts can and do grant preclusion pending appeal of an underlying judgment, the state courts are governed by varying rules for such situations.

■ **CASE VOCABULARY**

SALUTARY: Producing a remedy or benefit.

Jones v. Morris Plan Bank of Portsmouth

(Car Buyer) v. *(Loan Provider)*
168 Va. 284, 191 S.E. 608 (1937)

A SINGLE CAUSE OF ACTION STEMMING FROM A BREACH OF A SINGLE, INDIVISIBLE CONTRACT CANNOT BE SPLIT INTO SEPARATE, DISTINCT CAUSES OF ACTION

■ **INSTANT FACTS** The Bank won a judgment against Jones for two missed car payments, and tried to sue Jones again after he sold the automobile without consent.

■ **BLACK LETTER RULE** If a transaction is represented by one single and indivisible contract and the breach of that contract gives rise to one single cause of action, it cannot be split into distinct parts, with separate actions maintained for each.

■ **PROCEDURAL BASIS**

Action to recover on a note.

■ **FACTS**

Jones (P) agreed to purchase an automobile from a dealer for $595. He (P) paid $245 of the purchase price by trading in a used car. After the dealer assessed a finance charge of $78.40, a balance of $428.40 remained. Jones (P) was to pay this sum in 12 monthly installments of $35.70 each. A note indicating this debt contained the following provision: "The whole amount of this note (less any payments made hereon) becomes immediately due and payable in the event of nonpayment at maturity of any installment thereof." This note was secured by the usual conditional sales contract, which stated that the dealer would retain title to the car until Jones (P) paid the entire purchase price. The sales contract eventually passed to the Morris Plan Bank of Portsmouth (Bank) (D). The Bank (D) sued to recover the May and June installments after Jones (P) failed to pay. Judgment was obtained against Jones (P), and he (P) satisfied the judgment. After Jones (P) failed to pay the July installment, the Bank (D) sued to recover that installment, as well. For this action, Jones (P) filed a plea of res adjudicata, whereupon the Bank (D) took a nonsuit. The Bank (D) then took possession of the automobile without Jones' (P) consent and sold it, applying the proceeds to the note. Jones (P) then filed this action for conversion to recover damages for the loss of the automobile. Jones (P) claimed that when the Bank (D) sued to recover only two overdue installments, it (D) waived its right to recover the balance of payments under the note. The Bank (D) argued that the subject of the alleged conversion, namely the title of the automobile, had not yet passed to Jones (P) because the purchase price had not yet been fully paid. The Bank (D) also claims that the note and the sales contract were divisible, and thus it (D) was not bound to sue for all installments in one action.

■ **ISSUE**

Can one breach of a single, indivisible contract result in two different causes of action?

■ **DECISION AND RATIONALE**

(Gregory, J.) No. If a transaction is represented by one single and indivisible contract and the breach of that contract gives rise to one single cause of action, it cannot be split into distinct parts, with separate actions maintained for each. If, however, a contract is divisible, and more than one cause of action arises, then each action may be pursued separately. Here, the note and conditional sales contract constituted one whole, single contract. The sole purpose of the conditional sales contract was to retain the title of the automobile in the seller until the note was entirely paid. That contract ended only when that payment condition was performed. One of the main tests to determine whether causes of action are truly separate or all part of one demand is the identity of facts necessary to maintain the action. If the same evidence will support all actions, then only one cause of action exists. Here, all the installments were due. The evidence required to maintain the action for two installments was the same as the evidence that would have been required for an action for all installments. Thus, any installments not embraced in the Bank's (D) first cause of action are barred. This, in turn, means that when the Bank (D) lost the rights to institute an action for the remaining installments, the title to the automobile passed to Jones (P). Jones (P) was the owner of the automobile when the Bank's (D) agent sold the automobile. Judgment reversed and remanded.

Analysis:

Defining the scope of a prior judgment in a dispute involving continuing or renewed conduct is still an especially difficult task. Section 24 of the Restatement (Second) of Judgments offers several suggestions for what may be relevant in determining whether a particular fact pattern constitutes a single transaction. These include "whether the facts are related in time, space, origin or motivation, whether they form a convenient trial unit, and whether their treatment as a unit conforms to the parties' expectations or business understanding or usage." In addition, a general rule is that claim preclusion would not prevent a second suit when the conduct involved in the first suit is continuing. Still, issue preclusion may apply to questions of status or issues of fact that were resolved in that first suit. Further, subsequent actions on one's particular conduct are considered precluded when the first suit was initiated to establish general rules of the legality of the conduct.

Mitchell v. Federal Intermediate Credit Bank

(*Potato Farmer*) v. (*Bank*)

165 S.C. 457, 164 S.E. 136 (1932)

A PARTY CANNOT USE PART OF A CONTRACT AS A SHIELD IN ONE ACTION AND THEN ANOTHER PART OF THE SAME CONTRACT AS A SWORD IN ANOTHER

■ **INSTANT FACTS** Mitchell used the proceeds from the sale of his potato crop as security for two loans, then claimed the bank kept the proceeds for itself.

■ **BLACK LETTER RULE** A party cannot split a cause of action and use one portion of it for defense in one suit and then use the remainder for offense in a subsequent suit.

■ **PROCEDURAL BASIS**

Appeal from judgment in action for accounting.

■ **FACTS**

Mitchell (P) brought this action for an accounting against Federal Intermediate Credit Bank (Bank) (D). Mitchell (P) claimed that, at the urging of the Bank's (P's) agent, he (P) sold his potato crop and used the proceeds as security for two notes for loans from the Bank (D). These loans equaled $9,000, but Mitchell (P) claimed that the proceeds actually amounted to $18,000. Mitchell (P) claimed he never received any of these proceeds, and that the Bank (D) did receive the proceeds. Previously, the Bank (D) had pursued an action on these notes. Mitchell (P) had pleaded these same facts in his (P's) earlier answer, but had not counterclaimed or asked for relief. Mitchell (P) had prevailed in the first case. Here, the Bank (D) claimed that Mitchell's (P) claim was merged in the earlier judgment. The trial court upheld the Bank's (D) contention and barred Mitchell's (P) more recent claim.

■ **ISSUE**

Is a party barred from pleading a set of facts, facts that he or she pleaded as a defense to an earlier complaint, as the basis of a later complaint of his or her own?

■ **DECISION AND RATIONALE**

(Stabler, J.) Yes. A party cannot split a cause of action and use one portion of it for defense in one suit and then use the remainder for offense in a subsequent suit. In both actions, Mitchell (P) pleaded that the amount of the potato crop proceeds that the Bank (D) received exceeded the amount paid to Mitchell (P). To support his (P's) position, Mitchell (P) relies on *Kirven v. Chemical Co.* [Kirven was allowed to pursue an action against Chemical Co. for deleterious effect of fertilizer on crop because issue had not been litigated and determined in previous action by Company]. A different situation from *Kirven*, however, presents itself here. In *O'Connor v. Varney* [Varney was not entitled to recover in first action on contract to build additions to O'Connor's house because Varney's intentional neglect of project amounted to more than he sued for], the court wrote that a party "may allege specific breaches of the contract declared upon, and rely on them in defense. But, if he intends to claim . . . more than the amount of for which he is sued, he must not rely on the contract in defense, *but must bring a cross action* . . . He cannot use the same defense, first as a shield, and then as a sword." (italics added) The situation in *O'Connor* would seem to be exactly the situation in the present case. When the Bank (D) sued Mitchell (P) on the two notes, he (P) had the option to position his (P) current claim either as a defense to the Bank's (D) action, or as a means of obtaining a judgment against the Bank (D). The transaction at issue here is the same one which served as the basis of Mitchell's (P) earlier defense. Mitchell (P) could have recovered in the previous action. Instead, he (P) chose to split his cause of action in two, with part of it as an earlier defense, and the rest as a later complaint. This tactic cannot be allowed under applicable principles of law. Judgment affirmed.

Analysis:

Today, Federal Rule of Civil Procedure 13(a) and other compulsory-counterclaim rules have essentially replaced rules of preclusion in several contexts. Generally, Rule 13(a) bars a plaintiff from raising counterclaims in subsequent litigation in federal court if he or she chose not to raise it in the beginning. Usually, the wide scope of this compulsory-counterclaim preclusion makes considerations of whether and how defense preclusion might apply irrelevant. Such questions of defense preclusion do matter, however, in the many state jurisdictions where compulsory-counterclaim rules are *not* in effect. In addition, those state rules often include their own express exceptions. Indeed, under Rule 13(a), parties do not have to include claims that are already pending in another suit, and some courts have found the Rule to be inapplicable where the action was terminated by default, settlement, or dismissed on a party's motion.

■ CASE VOCABULARY

PRO TANTO: "For so much"; used to describe partial payment made on a claim.

Linderman Machine Co. v. Hillenbrand Co.

(Seller) v. (Buyer)
75 Ind.App. 111, 127 N.E. 813 (1920)

A JUDGMENT IS CONCLUSIVE AS TO ALL OF A DEFENDANT'S DEFENSES WHETHER PLEADED OR NOT

■ **INSTANT FACTS** Hillenbrand (D), after winning a suit brought against it by Linderman (P), sued the latter for recovery of expenses incurred due to Linderman's (P) fraud.

■ **BLACK LETTER RULE** When a party is sued, a judgment in that suit is not conclusive as to an affirmative cause of action which the party may have asserted against the other in a cross-complaint.

■ **PROCEDURAL BASIS**

Contract action for recovery of damages.

■ **FACTS**

Linderman (P) sued Hillenbrand (D) for the purchase price of a machine sold to the latter. Hillenbrand (D) defended, alleging that the contract for purchase of the machine was fraudulently obtained and that the machine did not perform as represented by Linderman (P). The trail court ruled in favor of Hillenbrand (D). Hillenbrand (now P) subsequently brought an action against Linderman (now D) to recover for the expenses incurred as a result of Linderman's (D) fraud, and for the cost of installing the machine. Linderman (D) answered that the action was barred by a judgment in the original case.

■ **ISSUE**

When a party is sued, is a judgment in the suit conclusive as to an affirmative cause of action which the party may have asserted against the other in a cross-complaint?

■ **DECISION AND RATIONALE**

(Justice Not Stated) No. When a party is sued, a judgment in that suit is not conclusive as to an affirmative cause of action which the party may have asserted against the other in a cross-complaint. A party, when sued, must interpose all the defenses that he has, and whether or not pleaded, a judgment in the suit is conclusive as to the defenses. A defendant may bring an affirmative cause of action against the plaintiff in a cross-complaint, but he is not compelled to do so, and on his failure to do so, his affirmative rights will not be adjudged. In Linderman's (P) action there was no issue regarding the cost of installation of the machine, thus res judicata does not operate here to prohibit the action by Hillenbrand (P) against Linderman (D).

Analysis:

This case deals with the application of res judicata to defenses. Under res judicata once a claim is ruled on, the party is not allowed to sue on the same claim again. This rule stems from the policy making court judgments conclusive and final. However, note that it is sometimes very difficult to determine what a "claim" is in the above case the original claim was for the recovery of the purchase price of a machine. The defense was that the contract for purchase was obtained by fraud. Thus the court ruled for the defendants who later brought their own claim against the plaintiff for recovery of expenses for the installation of the machine. Note that the claim for recovery of expenses is not a defense. It is an affirmative cause of action. Thus, the defendant is not precluded from bringing a later action for this claim. This case also indicates that res judicata is an estoppel from asserting new defenses once a claim is over. Res judicata operates as a bar against all defenses, even those that the defendant has failed to assert in the original action. This simply means that the defendant can not re-open a case which is already decided based on a new defense that it could have pleaded at the time of trial.

■ CASE VOCABULARY

CROSS-COMPLAINT: A complaint filed by the defendant against the plaintiff in the same claim or transaction for which the plaintiff has brought an action against the defendant.

RES JUDICATA: Means "the thing has been decided"; a doctrine by which a final judgment by the court of competent jurisdiction is conclusive upon the same cause of action.

Cromwell v. County of Sac

(Bond Holder) v. *(Bond Issuer)*
94 U.S. (4 Otto) 351, 24 L.Ed. 195 (1876)

COLLATERAL ESTOPPEL OPERATES BETWEEN PLAINTIFFS AND DEFENDANTS AND THEIR PRIVIES TO ESTOP RE–LITIGATION OF ISSUES UPON WHICH A FINAL JUDGMENT HAS BEEN RENDERED IN A PREVIOUS SUIT

■ **INSTANT FACTS** County of Sac (D) ("County") sought to estop Cromwell's (P) action against County (D) for bonds issued by the latter, based on an earlier decision rendered in County's favor.

■ **BLACK LETTER RULE** Estoppel of a judgment in one cause of action to an action arising out of another cause of action applies when the issue in question was actually litigated and determined in the first action.

■ **PROCEDURAL BASIS**

Appeal to the Supreme Court of the United States on Writ of Certiorari from error in the Circuit Court in Iowa.

■ **FACTS**

Cromwell (P) brought an action against the County of Sac ("County") (D) on four bonds and four coupons issued to Cromwell (P) by the County (D). In an earlier similar action by Samuel Smith against the County (D) for the same bonds, the court ruled in favor of the County (D). The latter sought to estop the present action in reliance on the judgment rendered in the earlier action and by proof that the earlier action was instituted for the sole benefit of Cromwell (P), who was at all times holder of the bonds.

■ **ISSUE**

Does estoppel of a judgment in one cause of action to an action arising out of another cause of action apply when the issue in question was actually litigated and determined in the first action?

■ **DECISION AND RATIONALE**

(Field, J.) Yes. Estoppel of a judgment in one cause of action to an action arising out of another cause of action applies when the issue in question was actually litigated and determined in the first action. However, a party ought not to be precluded from contesting, in a later action, other issues arising out of the same cause of action. The findings in the Samuel Smith case indicate that Smith had become, before maturity, the holder of 25 coupons attached to the bonds issued by the County. However, there was no finding that he had ever given any value for them. The judgment for the County was affirmed because it was found that the bonds were void against the County in the hands of parties who acquired them before maturity without paying value for them. However, the bonds, as negotiable instruments, would be valid against the County if the holder had paid value for them before their maturity. The facts of the previous case can not preclude the present plaintiff from showing that he has paid value for the bonds. The fact that a party did not pay value for one bond is not presumptive or conclusive of the fact that he did not pay value for another bond. (Reversed and Remanded.)

Analysis:

So far we have seen that res judicata (also known as claim preclusion) bars a party from re-asserting a claim on which final judgment was rendered. This case stands for another policy oriented rule which is known as collateral estoppel or issue preclusion. Under collateral estoppel, a right, a fact, or an issue which is directly determined in a court, can not be re-litigated in a subsequent suit between the same parties or their "privies" even if the later suit is based on a different cause of action. Again, this doctrine gives finality to matters that have been determined by a competent court, and enhances judicial efficiency. Thus, remember, while under res judicata a whole claim or cause of action is barred, under collateral estoppel only the issues which have already been determined are estopped from re-litigation. Collateral estoppel has several requirements: 1) The later suit must involve the same issue as the previous suit, 2) The issue must have been actually litigated, 3) the judgment in the previous action must have been final, valid, and on the merits, and 4) the determination of the issue in question must have been necessary to the court's judgment.

■ CASE VOCABULARY

BONA FIDE PURCHASER: One who pays a valuable consideration, has no notice of the outstanding rights of others and who acts in good faith concerning the purchase.

COLLATERAL ESTOPPEL: The doctrine recognizing that the determination of facts litigated between two parties in a proceeding is binding on those parties in all future proceedings against each other. Collateral estoppel is also known as issue preclusion.

Russell v. Place

(Patent Holder) v. *(Alleged Patent Infringer)*
94 U.S. (4 Otto) 606, 24 L.Ed. 214 (1876)

A JUDGMENT OF A COURT OF COMPETENT JURISDICTION, UPON A QUESTION DIRECTLY INVOLVED IN ONE SUIT, IS CONCLUSIVE AS TO THAT QUESTION IN ANOTHER SUIT BETWEEN THE SAME PARTIES

■ **INSTANT FACTS** In a patent infringement action against Place (D), Russell (P) sought to estop re-litigation of the novelty of the product based on a previous judgment for the same patent between the same parties.

■ **BLACK LETTER RULE** Collateral estoppel applies only if the precise issue in question has been litigated and determined in the former suit.

■ **PROCEDURAL BASIS**

Appeal on writ of certiorari in patent infringement action.

■ **FACTS**

Russell (P) invented a product for which a patent was issued. The patent being defective, Russell (P) amended it and was issued a new patent. Russell (P) then sued Place (D) for patent infringement for the manufacture and use of Russell's (P) invention. The court rendered a judgment in favor of Russell (P) for damages. Subsequently, Russell (P) brought another action against Place (D) alleging further manufacture and use of Russell's (P) products. The latter sought to use the previous court's judgment on the issue of patent infringement. The Circuit Court of Appeals rejected Russell's (P) argument. The latter appeals.

■ **ISSUE**

Does collateral estoppel apply only where the precise issue in question has been litigated and determined in the former suit?

■ **DECISION AND RATIONALE**

(Field, J.) Yes. Collateral estoppel applies only if the precise issue in question has been litigated and determined in the former suit. If it appears that several distinct matters may have been litigated, upon one or more of which the judgment may have been passed, without indicating which of them was thus litigated, and upon which the judgment was rendered, the uncertainty must be removed by extrinsic evidence showing the precise point involved and determined. In this case, the judgment in the previous action does not indicate the nature of the infringement. The patent contains two claims for two different processes: one is for use of fat liquor in the treatment of leather and the other for a process of treating bark tanned lamb or sheep skin. In does not appear from the record of the judgment in the previous action, which of the two claims the plaintiff's recovery was based on. A recovery for the infringement of one claim of the patent is not conclusive of an infringement of the other claims and there is no extrinsic evidence offered to resolve the uncertainty. Thus, the record does lack certainty and does not preclude the defendants from challenging the validity of the patent or contesting the infringement. (Affirmed.)

Analysis:

As we saw in the previous case, one of the requirements of collateral estoppel is that the precise issue in the case must have been litigated and determined in the previous suit between the parties. Whereas in this case, in which the record of judgment is not clear as to which issue was the basis of the court's judgment, then parties may rely on extrinsic evidence to prove what the precise issue in question was. However, where this is not proven, parties are precluded from the benefit of collateral estoppel, and all doubts will be resolved against the party asserting collateral estoppel.

■ **CASE VOCABULARY**

COLLATERAL ESTOPPEL: The doctrine recognizing that the determination of facts litigated between two parties in a proceeding is binding on those parties in all future proceedings against each other. Collateral estoppel is also known as issue preclusion.

Rios v. Davis

(Injured Driver) v. *(Negligent Driver)*

373 S.W.2d 386 (Tex. Civ. App. 1963)

IN ORDER FOR COLLATERAL ESTOPPEL TO APPLY, THE DETERMINATION OF AN ISSUE MUST HAVE BEEN ESSENTIAL TO THE JUDGMENT RENDERED IN THE PREVIOUS CASE

■ **INSTANT FACTS** Rios (P) brought an action against Davis (D) for injuries suffered in automobile accident between Rios (P), Davis (D), and Popular Dry Goods Company ("Popular").

■ **BLACK LETTER RULE** A finding of fact which is not material or essential to the judgment of a suit between two parties is not binding on the parties in a later suit.

■ **PROCEDURAL BASIS**

Appeal in action in negligence for recovery of damages.

■ **FACTS**

Rios (P), Davis (D), and Popular Dry Goods ("Popular") got into an automobile accident. Popular sued Davis (D) to recover for the damages suffered. Davis (D) contended that both Popular and Rios (P) were negligent, and joined Rios (P) as a third party defendant. The jury returned a verdict, finding Davis (D) negligent and both Popular and Rios (P) proximately negligent. The jury also denied recovery to all parties. Subsequently, Rios (P) brought suit against Davis (D). The latter defended on the ground that Rios (P) was contributorily negligent, and urged the application of res judicata and collateral estoppel based on the judgment in the previous suit between Davis (D) and Popular. The District Court ruled in favor of Davis (D). Rios (P) appeals.

■ **ISSUE**

Is a finding of fact which is not material or essential to the judgment of a suit between two parties binding on the parties in a later suit?

■ **DECISION AND RATIONALE**

(Collings, J.) No. A finding of fact which is not material or essential to the judgment of a suit between two parties is not binding on the parties in a later suit. In the previous action, the sole basis for the judgment as between Rios (P) and Davis (D) was the findings concerning the negligence of Davis (D). Rios' (P) negligence was not essential to the judgment. If Rios' (P) negligence was in fact the basis of that judgment, the result would have been different. However, since the judgment was in favor of Rios (P), he had no opportunity to appeal from the finding that he was guilty of negligence even if such finding had been without any support whatever in the evidence. It is the judgment and not the conclusions of fact filed by a trial court, which constitutes the estoppel. A finding of fact which does not become the basis of the judgment rendered is not conclusive against either party to the suit. (Reversed and Remanded.)

Analysis:

So far we have seen that in order for collateral estoppel to apply, the precise issue in question in a suit must have been litigated and determined in the previous suit between the parties. Another requirement of collateral estoppel is that the issue must have been necessary and essential to the judgment of the previous suit. Thus, if the issue is not essential to the outcome of the case, collateral estoppel does not apply to the issue. Notice another way that the court looks at this problem: In the previous judgment in the instant case, Rios and the truck driver both were found negligent, however, the final judgment was in their favor and against Davis. The court in the instant case indicated that since the judgment was in favor of Rios, he did not have the opportunity to appeal the issue of his negligence. Additionally, if the issue of his negligence was essential to the outcome of the case, the judgment would not have been in his favor. Thus, not having been essential to the outcome, collateral estoppel could not apply to the issue.

■ CASE VOCABULARY

THIRD PARTY DEFENDANT: The defendant that is not named by the plaintiff in the original complaint, but who is joined in that action by the original defendant.

Commissioner of Internal Revenue v. Sunnen

(IRS) v. (Taxpayer)

333 U.S. 591, 68 S.Ct. 715, 92 L.Ed. 898 (1948)

COLLATERAL ESTOPPEL IS DESIGNED TO PREVENT REPETITIOUS LAWSUITS OVER MATTERS WHICH HAVE BEEN ONCE DECIDED AND WHICH HAVE REMAINED STATIC FACTUALLY AND LEGALLY

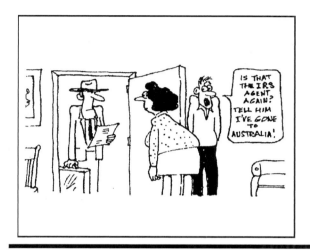

■ **INSTANT FACTS** The Commissioner of Internal Revenue (P) assessed taxes against Sunnen (D) on the ground that the royalties which Sunnen's (D) wife received from Sunnen's (D) corporation were Sunnen's (D) own taxable income.

■ **BLACK LETTER RULE** Collateral estoppel may only be applied in situations where the issue raised in the second suit is identical to the issue in the first suit and the controlling law and facts remain the same.

■ **PROCEDURAL BASIS**

Certiorari by the United States Supreme Court to the 8th Circuit Court of Appeals in action for recovery of taxes.

■ **FACTS**

Through a series of agreements, Sunnen (D) assigned rights to 10% royalties from his corporation to his wife for no consideration. Sunnen's (D) wife reported the royalties on her income tax returns and paid the taxes on it. In 1935, the Board of Tax Appeals held that based on a 1928 agreement, Sunnen's (D) wife, and not Sunnen (D) himself, was liable for taxes between 1929–1931. The Commissioner (P) then contended that the income from royalties from 1937–1941 was taxable to Sunnen (D) himself, and assessed tax against Sunnen (D). The Tax Court, applying the decision of the Board through res judicata held that with the exception of 1937 taxes, all taxes from 1937 to 1941 were assessable against Sunnen (D). The Court of Appeals for the 8th Circuit affirmed the Tax Court's application of res judicata to the 1937 taxes, and reversed the Tax Court's decision with respect to taxes between 1938–1941 on the ground that the royalty payments were not income to Sunnen (D). The Supreme Court of the United States granted certiorari.

■ **ISSUE**

May collateral estoppel only be applied in situations where the issue in the second suit is identical to the issue in the first suit and the controlling law and facts remain unchanged?

■ **DECISION AND RATIONALE**

(Murphy, J.) Yes. Collateral estoppel may only be applied in situations where the issue raised in the second suit is identical to the issue in the first suit and the controlling law and facts remain the same. The doctrine of collateral estoppel is applicable to annual income taxes. Each year is the origin of a new liability based on a separate cause of action. Thus, a claim which has been litigated for a particular tax year is res judicata as to any subsequent claim for the same tax year and that same claim. In a similar or different suit in a different year, the principles of collateral estoppel apply. However, collateral estoppel can not be applied where a later modification of certain significant facts or controlling legal principles may make the determination of an issue in a prior suit erroneous, or inapplicable. Thus, the supervening decisions of the Supreme Court of the United States or state courts can not be ignored in determining whether the application of collateral estoppel is proper. In this case, collateral estoppel does not apply to the royalties which were not involved in the earlier suit. With respect to the 1937 taxes, however, which were the subject of the earlier suit, the Commissioner contends that legal principles have developed in intervening decisions which make the Board's conclusion with respect to the tax in that year erroneous. This Court is in agreement with the Commissioner. The principles developed in *Helvering v. Clifford* and *Helvering v. Horst* [which amplified the concept that an assignor is taxable if he retains control over the assigned property or power to defeat the the receipt of income by the assignee] are directly applicable to the income tax liability of an assignee. The principles extended by those cases have developed sufficient change in the legal principles as to render collateral estoppel inapplicable in the instant case. A proper application of the legal principles later developed may create a different result in the instant case. (Reversed and Remanded.)

■ DISSENT

(Frankfurter, J. and Jackson, J.) The judgment of the Tax Court should be affirmed because it is based on substantial evidence and is consistent with the law.

Analysis:

So far, we have seen that in order for collateral estoppel to be applicable, the issue in the second case, must be the same exact issue as the one in the previous case. Also, collateral estoppel requires the same issue to have been litigated and determined. This case illustrates the meaning of the word "issue". The same issue means that all the significant facts and legal principles remain unchanged. In this case, the legal principles which applied in the first case had changed substantially. Thus, the issues were not the same. Note that the court's decision has a broader perspective than the rights of the parties in the action. The court is more concerned with the inequality, which will result if collateral estoppel applies to situations where legal principles and rights of parties have been changed. For example, in this case, there would be an inequality in taxation between taxpayers in the same class.

■ CASE VOCABULARY

COLLATERAL ESTOPPEL: The doctrine recognizing that the determination of facts litigated between two parties in a proceeding is binding on those parties in all future proceedings against each other. Collateral estoppel is also known as issue preclusion.

RES JUDICATA: Means "the thing has been decided," a doctrine by which a final judgment by the court of competent jurisdiction is conclusive upon the same cause of action.

Hanover Logansport, Inc. v. Robert C. Anderson, Inc.

(*Lessor*) v. (*Lessee*)

512 N.E.2d 465 (Ind. App. 1987)

CLAIM AND ISSUE PRECLUSION ONLY APPLY TO JUDGMENTS WHICH ARE VALID, FINAL, AND ON THE MERITS

■ **INSTANT FACTS** Hanover Logansport, Inc. (P) ("Hanover") having entered a settlement agreement with Robert C. Anderson, Inc. (D) ("Anderson") for breach of a lease contract, contends that the agreement precludes a claim for recovery of further damages against Hanover (P) by Anderson (D).

■ **BLACK LETTER RULE** The preclusive effect of a consent judgment should depend upon the intent of the parties entering into the consent judgment.

■ **PROCEDURAL BASIS**

Appeal in contract action for recovery of damages.

■ **FACTS**

Anderson (D) entered into an agreement with Hanover Logansport ("Hanover") (P) to lease a parcel of property from Hanover (P). Anderson (D) filed suit against Hanover (P) for breach of the lease, upon the latter's failure to deliver the premises on the agreed date. Before the trial, Hanover (P) agreed to deliver the property. Anderson (D) accepted this offer only as mitigation of damages and not as settlement of the damages that Anderson (D) incurred as a result of the breach of the contract. Subsequently, Anderson (D) and Hanover (P) filed a stipulation of their settlement, and recorded it in the judgment record book of the county. Hanover (P) filed a motion to dismiss Anderson's (D) earlier suit. The trial court denied the motion. Hanover (P) appeals on the ground that the settlement between Hanover (P) and Anderson (D), and the latter's acceptance of the real estate, precluded any further litigation based on the same claim. Anderson (D) defends on the ground that both Hanover (P) and the trial court were aware that the recorded judgment did not dispose of the whole claim, and that Hanover's (P) offer was accepted only for the purpose of mitigation of damages, and not for damages arising out of Hanover's (P) breach of contract.

■ **ISSUE**

Should the preclusive effect of a consent judgment depend upon the intent of the parties entering the consent judgment?

■ **DECISION AND RATIONALE**

(Staton, J.) Yes. The preclusive effect of a consent judgment should depend upon the intent of the parties entering into the consent judgment. A consent judgment is both an agreement between the parties settling the underlying claim, and an entry of judgment on the pending claim or action. Thus, consent judgments are seen by some courts as an agreement, or a contract, the preclusive effects of which depends on the intent of the parties. Proponents of this view are of the opinion that any harsher view of consent judgments would discourage parties from entering into such agreements in fear that they will "miss" something, and will never have the chance to bring an action against the other party for the same claim. Other courts however, view consent judgments as one which possesses the same force as a judgment by a court with regards to collateral estoppel and res judicata. This court agrees that consent judgments should be viewed as contracts, and holds that the preclusive effect of the judgment must be measured by the intent of the parties. However, it must be clear that both parties have agreed to reserve an issue or a claim from the consent judgment, and the judgment must clearly state the issues that are reserved. Additionally, the issue reserved must appear on the plaintiff's original complaint. In this case, Anderson (D) did not include a claim for damages for delay in tendering the real estate in its complaint. Thus, it is precluded from reserving this claim in the consent judgment. Hanover's (P) motion to dismiss should be granted. (Reversed and Remanded.)

Analysis:

Claim and issue preclusion apply to cases where the judgment is final, valid, and on the merits of the case. This is known as the "quality" of the judgment. In this case, the court determines that a consent judgment should be viewed as a contract, and that they do not act automatically preclude a future action based on the same claim. The preclusive effect of the consent judgment depends on the intent of the parties as to what issues and claims they indeed settled upon. This view allows parties to reserve certain issues for future litigation. However, such reservation is only effective where both parties consent to it and the claim which is reserved appears on the plaintiff's original complaint.

■ CASE VOCABULARY

CONSENT JUDGMENT: The stipulation of the parties that judgment may be entered.

Housing Authority for La Salle County v. Young Men's Christian Ass'n of Ottawa

(Party Seeking Injunction) v. *(Title Owner of Property)*

101 Ill.2d 246, 461 N.E.2d 959 (1984)

WHERE A COURT HAS ENTERED A DEFAULT JUDGMENT ON A CLAIM, RES JUDICATA APPLIES TO BAR LATER LITIGATION OF THE SAME CLAIM

■ **INSTANT FACTS** Housing Authority for La Salle County (P) ("county") sought an injunction against Young Men's Christian Ass'n of Ottawa (D) ("YMCA") preventing the YMCA from building a parking structure on a property owned by the YMCA.

■ **BLACK LETTER RULE** Under the doctrine of res judicata, a default judgment has the same preclusive effect as any other judgment.

■ **PROCEDURAL BASIS**

Action for injunction.

■ **FACTS**

In 1932, the federal government brought a condemnation action concerning certain parcels of property, and properly summoned the owners of the properties in order to compensate them for the condemnation. There was a conflict as to ownership of one parcel of property between Ella Deenis, and the First Trust Company of Ottawa. Deenis' failure to appear after being properly served resulted in a default judgment in favor of the Trust Company as the proper owners of the property. The government paid the latter compensation for the condemnation. A second suit arose between the county (P), Deenis' successor in interest, and the YMCA (D), the successor in interest of the Trust Company, where the county (P) sought to enjoin the YMCA (D) from constructing a parking lot on the property in question. The YMCA (D) asserted that the earlier suit between the Trust Company and Deenis operated as collateral estoppel with respect to the title in the property. The court decided that the principles of res judicata and not collateral estoppel applied to preclude another claim regarding the title to the property. The county defended on the ground that at the time of the default judgment, Deenis did not have an incentive to litigate the title issue and consequently allowing the preclusion of the later claim would be inequitable.

■ **ISSUE**

Under the doctrine of res judicata, does a default judgment have the same preclusive effect as any other judgment?

■ **DECISION AND RATIONALE**

(Justice Not Stated) Yes. Under the doctrine of res judicata, a default judgment has the same preclusive effect as any other judgment. When Deenis defaulted and the court entered a judgment finding the Trust Company to be the owner of the property, the title dispute was resolved and the doctrine of res judicata applied to bar any litigation of that claim. While default judgments have limited preclusive effect under the doctrine of collateral estoppel, such judgments are always res judicata on the ultimate claim or demand presented in the initial complaint. Contrary to the county's (P) argument, while lack of incentive to litigate may be relevant in application of collateral estoppel, it is not relevant in the application of res judicata.

Analysis:

The basic thrust of this court's opinion is that a default judgment on a particular claim is enough to bar the later re-litigation of the same claim under the doctrine of res judicata. However, notice that the same may not be true when it comes to collateral estoppel. Remember that collateral estoppel applies only where the same issue in dispute has been litigated. Where a court has entered a default judgment, it means that it has entered a judgment procedurally, without litigating the merits of the case. In turn, this means that the issue has not been litigated. Thus, where the court has entered a default judgment, a later litigation of the same issue may not necessarily be barred under collateral estoppel.

■ CASE VOCABULARY

DEFAULT JUDGMENT: A judgment entered against a defendant due to his failure to respond to the plaintiff's action or to appear at the trial.

INJUNCTION: A judicial remedy afforded for the purpose of requiring a party to refrain from doing or continuing to do a particular act or activity.

Holmberg v. State, Division of Risk Management

(*State Employee*) v. (*State Agency*)

796 P.2d 823 (Alaska 1990)

FINAL JUDGMENTS RETAIN RES JUDICATA EFFECTS PENDING RESOLUTION OF APPEAL

■ **INSTANT FACTS** State employee attempts to use subsequent decision on disability to reverse an earlier decision by a state workers' compensation board.

■ **BLACK LETTER RULE** Res judicata can be used only against parties or those in privity, and a final judgment retains its res judicata effects pending resolution of an appeal of the judgment.

■ **PROCEDURAL BASIS**

Appeal challenging order affirming decision by state workers' compensation board for disability benefits.

■ **FACTS**

Karen Holmberg (P) had been employed by the State of Alaska, Division of Risk Management ("Risk Management") (D) since 1979. She had a history of back injuries. In February 1988, the Alaska Workers' Compensation Board ("AWCB") denied Holmberg's (P) claim for permanent disability benefits. Holmberg (P) appealed this decision. While the appeal was pending, Holmberg (P) sought disability benefits from the Public Employees Retirement System ("PERS"). The State Division of Retirement and Benefits, which administers PERS, awarded non-occupational disability benefits, but her claim for occupational disability benefits was denied. Holmberg (P) appealed, and in April 1988 the Public Employees Retirement Board ("PERB") reversed the decision, finding that Holmberg (P) was permanently and totally disabled as a result of accidents at work. Holmberg (P) then sued Risk Management (D) in superior court. She argued that the AWCB decision should be reversed because of the preclusive effect of the later PERB decision. The superior court affirmed the AWCB decision, and Holmberg (P) appeals.

■ **ISSUE**

(1) Must collateral estoppel be asserted against a party or one in privity with a party to the first action?
(2) Does a final judgment retain its res judicata effects pending resolution of an appeal of the judgment?

■ **DECISION AND RATIONALE**

(Moore, J.) (1) Yes. Collateral estoppel must be asserted against a party or one in privity with a party to the first action. In general, a judgment rendered against one state agency is binding on another agency of the same state unless there are important differences in the authority of the representative agencies. Holmberg (P) argues that the State Division of Risk Management (D) is in privity with the State Division of Retirement and Benefits. However, the PERB judgment was not entered against the State Division of Retirement and Benefits. Retirement and Benefits is merely charged with administrative responsibility for PERS. When Retirement and Benefits appears before PERB, it represents the interests of PERS, not the state. The PERB decision was rendered against PERS. PERS is not a state agency, but an independent retirement plan. Therefore, PERS is not in privity with the State Division of Risk Management (D). Collateral estoppel does not apply. (2) Yes. A final judgment retains its res judicata effects pending resolution of the appeal of the judgment. In the instant action, even if the state and PERS were in privity, the PERB decision would not preclude any issues raised in the earlier AWCB proceeding because the PERB decision was not the first final judgment addressing the issue. The AWCB judgment was final and binding even though Holmberg (P) appealed the decision. Conversely, in the PERB proceedings, res judicata could likely have been asserted *against* Holmberg (P). She was a party to both the AWCB and PERB decisions, and the issues were identical. However, Retirement and Benefits did not assert collateral estoppel. Affirmed.

Analysis:

This fact-intensive case illustrates some of the fundamental principles of res judicata. It is essential to remember that res judicata may be asserted only against a party or one in privity with a party to an earlier decision. The first key issue of this holding is whether the state was in privity with a party to the PERB decision. Here the opinion gets a bit tricky. Although a state agency (Retirement and Benefits) is in charge of administering PERS, it is not actually a party to any PERS proceeding. In these circumstances, it makes sense not to grant a preclusive effect against the state for PERS decisions. After all, res judicata is fair only if the party to be precluded had a full opportunity to litigate a claim in a prior proceeding. Because the state only administers PERS, it theoretically would not care if Holmberg (P) won or lost in the PERS proceeding. The second important concept of this opinion deals with the finality of judgments. Once a judgment is rendered and appealed, the original judgment is final for purposes of res judicata until the appeal is resolved. If this were not true, then any person who lost an issue could simply appeal and refile an identical case against the same party in another court.

■ CASE VOCABULARY

PRIVITY: A relationship or identity of legal interest between two persons.

Bernhard v. Bank of America Nat. Trust & Sav. Ass'n

(Beneficiaries) v. *(Bank)*
19 Cal.2d 807, 122 P.2d 892 (1942)

THE SUPREME COURT OF CALIFORNIA REJECTS MUTUALITY AS A REQUIREMENT OF RES JUDICATA

■ **INSTANT FACTS** Bernhard (P), administratrix of the estate of Mrs. Sather, sued Bank of America (D) for allegedly allowing an unauthorized withdrawal from Mrs. Sather's account during her life.

■ **BLACK LETTER RULE** A party may assert res judicata even though he was not a party, or in privy with a party in the earlier litigation.

■ **PROCEDURAL BASIS**

Appeal in action for recovery of unauthorized withdrawal of funds.

■ **FACTS**

Mrs. Clara Sather, living with Mr. and Mrs. Cook, asked the latter to transfer her account from the Security First National Bank of Los Angeles to the First National Bank of San Dimas. The account was opened in the name of "Clara Sather by Charles Cook." Thereafter the bank in Los Angeles transferred $4,155.68 to the new account in San Dimas. Subsequently, Mr. Cook withdrew the whole amount and transferred it to a new account in the name of himself and his wife. After the death of Mrs. Sather, Mr. Cook became the executor of the estate. After having administered the estate for a few years, Mr. Cook resigned, filing an account with the probate court, but making no mention of the money which he withdrew from Mrs. Sather's account. Helen Bernhard (P), and other beneficiaries of the estate, objected to the accounting, and the probate court determined that the money in that account was given as a gift to Mr. Cook during Mrs. Sather's life. Later, Bernhard (P), as the administratrix of the estate instituted an action against Bank of America (D), the successor of the San Dimas Bank, to recover the $4,155.68 on the ground that Mrs. Sather had never authorized the withdrawal by Mr. Cook. Bank of America (D) defended on the ground that this fact was res judicata by virtue of the finding of the probate court that the withdrawal was a gift to Mr. Cook. The trial court decided in favor of Bank of America (D). Bernhard (P) appeals, contending that res judicata should not be asserted by someone who was not a party to the previous action because there is no mutuality of estoppel.

■ **ISSUE**

May a party assert res judicata, even though he was not a party or in privy with a party in the earlier litigation?

■ **DECISION AND RATIONALE**

(Traynor, J.) Yes. A party may assert res judicata even though he was not a party, or in privy with a party in the earlier litigation. Many courts have stated that res judicata may only be asserted when there is privity and mutuality of estoppel, thus allowing only parties to the former judgment or their privies to take advantage of or be bound by res judicata. The estoppel is mutual if the one taking advantage of the earlier judgment would have been bound by it had it gone against him. Res judicata may not be asserted against a party who was not bound by the earlier judgment in which the matter in question was decided. However, there is no reason for requiring that the party asserting the estoppel must have been a party to the earlier action. Most courts have abandoned the mutuality requirement where the liability of the defendant asserting res judicata is dependent or derived from the liability of one who was exonerated in the earlier suit brought by the same plaintiff upon the same facts. Examples of such derivative liability are master and servant, principal and agent, and indemnitor and indemnitee. The validity of a plea of res judicata depends on three factors: 1) was the issue decided in the earlier litigation identical to the issue in question, 2) was there a final judgment rendered on the issue presented in the previous action and 3) was the party against whom the plea is asserted a party or in privity with a party to the earlier litigation? In the instant case, the issue of ownership of money is identical with the issue determined by the probate court. Additionally, the probate court determined the issue on the merits. Also, Bernhard (P) can be considered in privity with parties in the earlier litigation because Bernhard (P) brings this action as the administratrix of the estate of Mrs. Sather, thus, representing the same persons and interests that were represented in the probate court proceedings. (Affirmed.)

Analysis:

Traditionally, a plea of res judicata was allowed by a party (and against a party) who was a party, or in privity with a party in the earlier action. Additionally, courts imposed a mutuality requirement for a plea of res judicata. Estoppel under this doctrine is mutual if the party asserting the estoppel would have been bound by the earlier judgment had the judgment gone against him. Thus, in many instances, a party in a later suit could not assert a plea of res judicata because the party lacked mutuality. Many courts now look at mutuality from a different perspective. The court first looks at the party who is asserting the estoppel. There is no reason according to many modern decisions, including the instant case, for the party asserting the estoppel to have been a party to the earlier litigation. Then the courts look at the party against whom the estoppel is asserted. The requirement of due process requires such a party to have been a party or in privity with a party in the earlier litigation. This will allow the party an opportunity to litigate the issue and to present his/her case.

■ CASE VOCABULARY

MUTUALITY OF ESTOPPEL: The doctrine which prohibits one party from raising an issue or a matter as to which the other party is estopped. The estoppel is mutual if the one taking advantage of the earlier adjudication would have been bound by it, had it gone against him.

PRIVITY: A relationship between parties out of which some mutuality of interest arises. The doctrine of res judicata is said to apply not only to one who was a party to the litigation in question, but also to those in privity with him because their mutual or subsequent interests can be considered so related to the interest of the actual party litigant that it is proper to hold them bound by the judgment as well.

Blonder-Tongue Laboratories, Inc. v. University of Illinois Foundation

(Antenna Manufacturer) v. *(Purported Patent Holder)*
402 U.S. 313, 91 S.Ct. 1434 (1971)

SUPREME COURT ALLOWS DEFENSIVE NONMUTUAL USE OF COLLATERAL ESTOPPEL

■ **INSTANT FACTS** A university foundation sued for the infringement of its alleged patent for a radio antenna, even though a prior lawsuit had determined that the foundation did not own the patent.

■ **BLACK LETTER RULE** Nonmutual collateral estoppel may be applied defensively against a party who had a full and fair opportunity to litigate the issue in a prior proceeding.

■ **PROCEDURAL BASIS**

Writ of certiorari reviewing viability of nonmutual defensive collateral estoppel.

■ **FACTS**

The University of Illinois Foundation (P) purportedly owned a patent for a radio and television antenna. The Foundation (P) sued an antenna manufacturer for patent infringement, and the trial court held the Foundation's (P) patent invalid. The Foundation (P) then sued Blonder-Tongue Laboratories, Inc. (D) for infringement of the same patent. Blonder-Tongue (D) asserted that the Foundation (P) was collaterally estopped, based on the former judgment, from asserting that it held a valid patent. The Supreme Court granted certiorari to determine whether to allow nonmutual use of collateral estoppel.

■ **ISSUE**

Where a party has had a full and fair opportunity to litigate an issue, may the judgment be used defensively against that party by a third party?

■ **DECISION AND RATIONALE**

(Justice Not Stated) Yes. Where a party has had a full and fair opportunity to litigate an issue, the judgment may be used defensively against that party by a third party. We abandon the mutuality requirement, at least to the extent that it forecloses a plea of estoppel by one facing a charge of infringement of a patent that has once been declared invalid. Thus, we abrogate the *Triplett v. Lowell* rule [a holding that a patent was invalid does not preclude a patent holder from asserting the validity of the patent in subsequent litigation against different defendants]. It is no longer tenable to afford a litigate more than one full and fair opportunity for judicial resolution of the same issue. Nonmutual defensive estoppel will save judicial resources, and it will save costs for both the alleged patent holder and the new defendant. Of course, litigants who never appeared in a prior action may not be collaterally estopped. Due process requires that they have a chance to litigate the issue, even though existing adjudications of the same issue stand squarely against their position. However, we are not dealing with an "offensive" use of estoppel, and we do not have any due process problems in the instant action. Although the Foundation (P) argues that the burden on the courts from relitigation of patents once held invalid is *de minimis*, we feel that our abrogation of *Triplett* will save some judicial time.

Analysis:

This case represents the U.S. Supreme Court's first endorsement of nonmutual estoppel, a principle that had been allowed in certain situations in various federal and state courts. On its face, the holding is limited to the narrow factual situation at hand—a purported patent holder who attempts to switch adversaries and relitigate the validity of a patent that has previously been declared invalid. However, lower courts have cited this case as persuasive authority for allowing nonmutual estoppel in a variety of situations. It makes sense to preclude the party from taking a second bite at the same apple. As long as the party had a full opportunity to litigate the issue in the former lawsuit, due process concerns are not implicated by nonmutual use of collateral estoppel. In addition, nonmutual estoppel saves money for the courts and for all parties.

■ **CASE VOCABULARY**

ABROGATE: To overturn or invalidate.

DE MINIMIS: A shortened form of "de minimis non curat lex," the law does not concern itself with small matters; a phrase meaning that something is very small and insignificant.

MUTUALITY OF ESTOPPEL: The principle that collateral estoppel can be asserted only by persons who were parties or privies to an original action.

Parklane Hosiery Co. v. Shore

(*Corporation*) v. (*Shareholder*)

439 U.S. 322, 99 S.Ct. 645, 58 L.Ed.2d 552 (1979)

THE SUPREME COURT OF THE UNITED STATES GIVES COURTS BROAD DISCRETION IN DETERMINING WHEN AND WHERE OFFENSIVE COLLATERAL ESTOPPEL SHOULD BE APPLIED

■ **INSTANT FACTS** Shore (P), a stockholder in Parklane Hosiery Co. (D) ("Parklane") brought a class action against the latter alleging that Parklane (D) had issued a materially false and misleading proxy statement in connection with a merger.

■ **BLACK LETTER RULE** Trial courts have broad discretion to apply the doctrine of offensive collateral estoppel, even in cases where the defendant will be deprived of a jury trial.

■ **PROCEDURAL BASIS**

Certiorari to the United States Court of Appeals for the Second Circuit in stockholder class action suit.

■ **FACTS**

Shore (P), a stockholder, brought a class action suit against Parklane (D) alleging that the latter had issued a materially false and misleading proxy statement in connection with a merger. Before, the instant case reached trial, the SEC filed suit against Parklane (D) based on the same allegations as Shore (P). In that action, the District Court ruled in favor of the SEC, and entered a declaratory judgment to that effect. The Court of Appeals for the Second Circuit affirmed. Subsequently, Shore (P) moved for summary judgment, asserting that Parklane (D) was collaterally estopped from litigating the same issues which had been resolved against it in the suit by the SEC. The District Court denied the motion on the ground that the estoppel would deny Parklane (D) its Seventh Amendment Right to a jury trial. The Court of Appeals for the Second Circuit reversed. The Supreme Court of the United States granted certiorari.

■ **ISSUE**

1) Can a party be precluded from re-litigating facts resolved adversely to the party in prior equitable proceedings where the court determines that the party has had full and fair opportunity to litigate the facts? 2) Would the use of offensive collateral estoppel violate such party's Seventh Amendment right to a jury trial?

■ **DECISION AND RATIONALE**

(Stewart, J.) (1) Yes. A party can be precluded from re-litigating facts resolved adversely to the party in prior equitable proceedings where a court has determined that the party has had a fair and full opportunity to litigate the facts. This case involves offensive collateral estoppel, where a plaintiff is seeking to estop a defendant from re-litigating the issues which the defendant previously litigated and lost in an earlier action. This court resolved that the *Blonder-Tongue* case involved defensive collateral estoppel. Contrary to defensive collateral estoppel, offensive collateral estoppel does not promote judicial economy. Since the plaintiff will be able to rely on a previous judgment against a defendant but will not be bound by that judgment if the defendant wins, the plaintiff has every incentive to wait before bringing an action against the defendant, in the hope that the first action by another plaintiff will result in a favorable judgment. Also, offensive collateral estoppel may be unfair to the defendant if the defendant had little incentive to defend vigorously in the first action. However, the preferable approach is not to rule out offensive collateral estoppel altogether, but to allow judges broad discretion to determine when it should be applied. Thus, where a plaintiff could have easily joined the earlier action, where for other reasons the application of offensive collateral estoppel would be unfair to the defendant, a trial judge should not allow its use to the plaintiff. In this case, the use of offensive collateral estoppel should be allowed because the plaintiff most probably could not have joined in the injunctive action brought by the SEC. Also, there is no unfairness to Parklane (D) because the latter had every incentive to litigate the SEC lawsuit fully and vigorously in light of the gravity of the charges and the foreseeability of private lawsuits which could follow. Additionally, there are no procedural opportunities in this action that were not available in the SEC action. (2) No. The use of offensive collateral estoppel would not violate the party's Seventh Amendment right to a jury trial. Parklane (D) argues that the Seventh Amendment should be interpreted based on its scope in 1791, and that since the common law at that time permitted collateral estoppel only where there was mutuality, collateral estoppel can not be applied where there is no mutuality. There is no persuasive reason however, why the meaning of the Seventh Amendment should depend on the existence of mutuality. A litigant who has lost in an equity action is equally deprived of a jury trial whether he is estopped from re-litigating the same facts and issues against the same or a different party. In either case, there are no more factual issues to be decided by the jury because the facts were already resolved in the previous action. The development of collateral estoppel is not repugnant to the Seventh Amendment simply because they did not exist in 1791. (Affirmed.)

■ DISSENT

(Rehnquist, J.) The contents of the Seventh Amendment right to jury trial should be judged based on historical standards. If a jury would have been impaneled in a particular case in 1791, the Seventh Amendment requires a jury trial today. No one can doubt that at common law, as it existed in 1791, Parklane would have been entitled to a jury trial to determine whether the proxy statement was false and misleading as alleged. The development of non-mutual collateral estoppel is a substantial departure from the common law and its use in this case completely deprives Parklane of its right to have a jury determine contested issues of fact.

Analysis:

Remember that traditionally, collateral estoppel could be used by a party only if that party was bound by the earlier judgment. That is, I could use collateral estoppel against you if and only if you could use collateral estoppel against me. However, in this case, the party seeking to assert collateral estoppel against the other party was not even involved in the earlier action. We did encounter the same scenario in the *Blonder* case. However, the collateral estoppel in that case was called defensive collateral estoppel. This means that the defendant in that case, was asserting collateral estoppel against a party who was a plaintiff in the earlier action. In this case however, we are encountered with offensive collateral estoppel, where the plaintiff in the instant action is asserting the judgment of the court against the defendant in the earlier action. Note that in both cases the party asserting the estoppel was not involved in the earlier action. That is why we call the doctrine "non-mutual" collateral estoppel.

■ CASE VOCABULARY

IN PERSONAM: "Into or against the person"; in pleading, the term refers to an action against a person or persons founded on personal liability, and requiring jurisdiction over the person sought to be held liable.

NON-MUTUAL COLLATERAL ESTOPPEL: Where a party who is not bound by an earlier judgment may use the judgment against a party who is bound by the judgment.

OFFENSIVE COLLATERAL ESTOPPEL: Offensive collateral estoppel refers to a situation where a plaintiff is seeking to estop a defendant from re-litigating the issues which the defendant previously litigated and lost in an earlier action.

Martin v. Wilks

(City) v. *(Firefighters)*
490 U.S. 755, 109 S.Ct. 2180, 104 L.Ed.2d 835 (1989)

A PARTY SEEKING A JUDGMENT BINDING ON ANOTHER CANNOT OBLIGATE THE LATTER TO INTERVENE IN A SUIT TO WHICH THAT PERSON IS NOT A PARTY

■ **INSTANT FACTS** Pursuant to consent judgments between the City of Birmingham ("City") and the Jefferson County Personnel Board ("Board") with black firefighters, the white firefighters filed a suit against the City and the Board alleging reverse discrimination.

■ **BLACK LETTER RULE** A party seeking a judgment binding on another cannot obligate the latter to intervene in the action without mandatorily joining that person in the action.

■ **PROCEDURAL BASIS**

Certiorari to the United States Court of Appeals for the Eleventh District in discrimination suit.

■ **FACTS**

The City of Birmingham ("City") and the Jefferson County Personnel Board ("Board") entered into a consent judgment with black firefighters for discrimination in hiring and promotion of the latter. Subsequently, white firefighters ("Martin") (P) brought an action against the City and the Board (D), alleging that the promotions were in violation of federal law because they were based on race. The City and the Board (D) defended on the ground that the consent judgment precluded the current suit. The District Court, holding in favor of the City and the Board (D), declared that the consent judgment was a defense to the reverse discrimination alleged by the white firefighters (P). The Court of Appeals reversed on the ground that the consent judgment did not preclude the current suit because the white firefighters (P) were not parties to the previous judgment. In the Supreme Court, the City and the Board (D) argued that the white firefighters could have intervened in the first suit.

■ **ISSUE**

May a party seeking a judgment binding another obligate the latter to intervene in the action without mandatorily joining that party in the action?

■ **DECISION AND RATIONALE**

(Rehnquist, C.J.) No. A party seeking a judgment binding on another cannot obligate the latter to intervene in the action without mandatorily joining that person in the action. Generally, one is not bound by a judgment in which he was not a party, or was not made a party by service of process. The City and the Board (D) argue that because the white firefighters (P) failed to voluntarily intervene in the earlier action, their suit is impermissible, especially in light of their knowledge that the consent judgment would affect them. This court, however, is in agreement with Justice Brandeis' view in *Chase National Bank v. Norwalk*, that a person entitled to a hearing does not have the burden of voluntary intervention in a suit in which he is not a party. The drafters of the Federal Rules of Civil Procedure have determined that the concern for finality and completion of a judgment is better served by mandatory joinder procedure and not by permissive intervention. FRCP 19(a) provides for mandatory joinder in circumstances where a judgment rendered in the absence of a person may impose a risk of incurring inconsistent obligations in a party. Joinder as a party, rather than knowledge of a lawsuit and an opportunity to intervene, is the method by which potential parties are subjected to the jurisdiction of the court and bound by a judgment or decree. The parties in a suit know better the nature and scope of the relief sought in the action, and at whose expense the relief might be granted. Thus, the burden should be on these parties to bring additional parties where such a step is indicated, rather than potential additional parties to intervene upon gaining knowledge of the suit. The City and the Board (D) argue that mandatory joinder will be burdensome because the potential claimants may be numerous and difficult to identify, and that if they are not joined, there is potential for inconsistent judgments. Such difficulties, although possible, are not alleviated by allowing voluntary intervention. Again, plaintiffs who seek the aid of the courts to alter existing employment opportunities, or the employer who might be subject to conflicting decrees, are best able to bear the burden of designating those who would be adversely affected if the plaintiffs prevail. (Affirmed.)

■ DISSENT

(Stevens, J., Brennan, J., Marshall, J., Blackmun, J.) While the consent decree in this case could not deprive the white firefighters of their contractual rights, such as seniority or other legal rights, there is no reason why the consent judgment might not produce changes in conditions at the white firefighters' place of employment that may have a serious effect on their opportunities for employment or promotion. The fact that one of the effects of the decree is to curtail the opportunities of nonparties does not mean that the nonparties have been deprived of legal rights or that they have standing to appeal from that decree without becoming parties. A person who can foresee that a lawsuit is likely to have an impact on his interests may pay a heavy price if he elects to sit on the sidelines instead of intervening in the action. In this case, the District Court, after conducting a trial and carefully considering the firefighters' arguments, concluded that the effort of the City and the Board to eradicate discrimination through a consent decree was lawful. Thus, the firefighters have already had their day in court and have failed to carry their burden.

Analysis:

Note, this case was subsequently overruled by an act of Congress which prohibits challenges to employment consent decrees by individuals who had actual notice and reasonable opportunity to intervene, or those whose interest were adequately represented. In this case, we see that the court distinguishes between a voluntary intervention and mandatory joinder. As the word itself suggests, voluntary intervention is "voluntary"; a party whose interests are at stake may choose to join in the action. Mandatory joinder, on the other hand, is when a party to the case seeks to join other parties as plaintiffs or defendants. The decision of the court in this case indicates that even if a party's rights may be affected, the party is not obligated to intervene. However, when a party in a case wants to make the judgment binding on a nonparty, that party must join the nonparty in the action under the mandatory joinder rules of the Federal Rules of Civil Procedure.

■ CASE VOCABULARY

INTERVENTION: A proceeding permitting a person to enter into a lawsuit already in progress. This term refers to admission of a person not an original party to the suit, so that the person can protect some right or interest which is allegedly affected by the proceeding.

JOINDER: Uniting of several causes of action or parties in a single suit. Mandatory joinder refers to the mandatory joining of certain parties which are required for the just adjudication of a controversy.

Taylor v. Sturgell

(Antique Aircraft Enthusiast) v. (FAA Administrator)
553 U.S. 880, 128 S.Ct. 2161, 171 L.Ed.2d 155 (2008)

NONPARTIES ARE RARELY BOUND BY EARLIER JUDGMENTS IN SIMILAR CASES

■ **INSTANT FACTS** After an antique aircraft enthusiast's Freedom of Information lawsuit proved unsuccessful, Taylor (P), a friend and fellow enthusiast, brought suit seeking the same information, and the court similarly denied his request based on the judgment in the first case; Taylor (P) appealed.

■ **BLACK LETTER RULE** The rule against nonparty preclusion is subject only to certain recognized exceptions: (1) a nonparty may agree to be bound by a judgment, (2) certain substantive relationships may justify preclusion (e.g., privity), (3) a nonparty's interests may have been adequately represented in the prior litigation (e.g., class actions and suits by trustees or guardians), (4) a nonparty may have assumed control over the earlier lawsuit, (5) a nonparty may have colluded to avoid the preclusive effect of an earlier judgment by litigating through a proxy, or (6) special statutory schemes (such as bankruptcy) may apply.

■ **PROCEDURAL BASIS**

Certiorari to the United States Court of Appeals for the District of Columbia.

■ **FACTS**

Taylor (P), a vintage aircraft enthusiast, filed a lawsuit under the Freedom of Information Act, seeking documents relating to a vintage airplane. Herrick, a friend of Taylor's (P), had previously filed an unsuccessful suit seeking the same documents. The court denied Taylor's (P) request, concluding that Taylor's (P) interests had been virtually represented by Herrick, despite the fact that there was no evidence that Taylor (P) controlled, financed, participated in, or even had notice of Herrick's lawsuit.

Different federal circuit courts had applied different standards to determine whether a unity of interests existed such that a judgment in one case had preclusive effect in another. In this case, the Court of Appeals for the District of Columbia rejected the tests applied in other circuits and devised its own five-factor test. Under the D.C. test, the first two factors—identity of interest and adequacy of representation—were *necessary*, but not *sufficient*, for virtual representation. In addition, the court concluded, one of three additional factors must be established: either a close relationship between the present party and his or her putative representative, or substantial participation by the present party in the first case, or tactical maneuvering on the part of the present party to avoid preclusion by the prior judgment. Applying that test to Taylor's(P) case, the court concluded that the necessary conditions for "virtual representation" were met. Taylor (P) appealed, and the Supreme Court granted certiorari to resolve the disagreement among the circuits over the permissibility and scope of preclusion based on so-called virtual representation.

■ **ISSUE**

Did the District of Columbia Court of Appeals apply the correct test to determine whether Taylor's (P) lawsuit was precluded by the earlier judgment in his friend Herrick's case?

■ DECISION AND RATIONALE

(Ginsburg, J.) No. The rule against nonparty preclusion is subject only to certain recognized exceptions: (1) a nonparty may agree to be bound by a judgment, (2) certain substantive relationships may justify preclusion (e.g., privity), (3) a nonparty's interests may have been adequately represented in the prior litigation (e.g., class actions and suits by trustees or guardians), (4) a nonparty may have assumed control over the earlier lawsuit, (5) a nonparty may have colluded to avoid the preclusive effect of an earlier judgment by litigating through a proxy, or (6) special statutory schemes (such as bankruptcy) may apply. Beyond these established exceptions, some courts recognize a "virtual representation" exception. We find none of the reasons in support of such an exception persuasive.

First, we must once again emphasize the importance of the general rule that a litigant is not bound by a judgment to which he or she was not a party. Second, "adequate representation," to suffice as "virtual representation," requires that (1) the interests of the nonparty and her representative are aligned; and (2) either the party understood herself to be acting in a representative capacity, or the original court took care to protect the interest of the nonparty. Adequate representation sometimes also requires actual notice of the original suit to the persons alleged to have been represented. Third, a balancing approach to nonparty preclusion, like that applied by the appellate court, would create more headaches than it relieves. Preclusion doctrine is intended to reduce the courts' burden, not increase it. The doctrine of stare decisis already allows courts to swiftly dispose of repetitive lawsuits. Human tendency as well will generally prevent a litigant from bringing an identical claim to one that has already proven to be fruitless.

Turning to Taylor's (P) case, there is nothing in the record to suggest that Taylor (P) agreed to be bound by Herrick's litigation, that they have any legal relationship, that Taylor (P) controlled Herrick's lawsuit, or that Taylor (P) was adequately represented by Herrick. Nor did Herrick bring suit as a representative or agent of Taylor (P). As to the argument that Herrick and Taylor (P) have colluded to avoid the preclusive effect of the first judgment (or that Taylor (P) was the agent of Herrick), we have never enunciated a clear standard, but courts should be cautious before finding collusion. A remand is appropriate for further determination as to whether Taylor (P) was acting as Herrick's agent in bringing the second lawsuit—an issue on which the defendant will bear the burden of proof. Vacated and remanded.

Analysis:

Virtual representation generally refers to the bringing of an action on behalf of an unnamed party or parties, as in a class action, where a number of people have similar interests to the named party, and upon whom the court's judgment will be binding. It can also refer to representation by a guardian ad litems or trustees, for instance, who represent the interests of others more than themselves. In the present case, the defendants argued that once Herrick's claims proved unsuccessful, he engaged his friend to try again on his behalf, essentially tricking the court into giving them another shot at the defendants. The court was unpersuaded that this case presented a proper scenario for application of an exception to the rule against nonparty preclusion, but it gave the defendants one more chance, on remand, to show that Taylor (P) and Herrick colluded to avoid the preclusive effect of the judgment in Herrick's case.

■ CASE VOCABULARY

ADEQUATE REPRESENTATION: A close alignment of interests between actual parties and potential parties in a lawsuit, so that the interests of potential parties are sufficiently protected by the actual parties. The concept of adequate representation is often used in procedural contexts. For example, if a case is to be certified as a class action, there must be adequate representation by the named plaintiffs of all the potential class members. And if a nonparty is to intervene in a lawsuit, there must not already be adequate representation of the nonparty by an existing party.

STARE DECISIS: [Latin, "to stand by things decided."] The doctrine of precedent, under which it is necessary for a court to follow earlier judicial decisions when the same points arise again in litigation.

VIRTUAL REPRESENTATION: A party's maintenance of an action on behalf of others with a similar interest, as a class representative does in a class action.

VIRTUAL–REPRESENTATION DOCTRINE: The principle that a judgment may bind a person who is not a party to the litigation if one of the parties is so closely aligned with the nonparty's interests that the nonparty has been adequately represented by the party in court. Under this doctrine, for instance, a judgment in a case naming only the husband as a party can be binding on his wife as well.

Hart v. American Airlines, Inc.

(*Passenger*) v. (*Airline*)

61 Misc.2d 41, 304 N.Y.S.2d 810 (1969)

NEW YORK APPLIES OFFENSIVE NONMUTUAL ESTOPPEL TO A JUDGMENT FROM A SEPARATE JUDICIAL SYSTEM

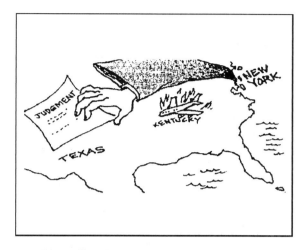

■ **INSTANT FACTS** In a New York action, American Airlines attempts to resist preclusive effect from being given to the issue of liability for an airline crash that was previously decided in Texas.

■ **BLACK LETTER RULE** Offensive nonmutual estoppel can be utilized by courts that are part of different judicial systems from the rendering court.

■ **PROCEDURAL BASIS**

Cross-motion for summary judgment on issue of liability for damages arising out of airline crash.

■ **FACTS**

Hart (P), Landano (P), Kirchstein (P), and other plaintiffs brought actions against American Airlines, Inc. (D) arising out of the crash in Kentucky of an American Airlines (D) airplane that was flying from New York to Kentucky. The crash resulted in the death of 58 out of the 62 persons aboard. Comparable actions had been brought in various state and federal courts. The first action to be tried to conclusion was brought in federal district court in Texas, resulting in a verdict against American Airlines (D) that was affirmed on appeal. It is undisputed that the issue of American Airlines' (D) liability in the current action is identical to the issue determined in the Texas action. American Airlines (D) moves for a joint trial, and Landano (P) and Kirchstein (P) cross-move for summary judgment on the issue of liability. Landano (P) and Kirchstein (P) argue that the Texas decision is conclusive on the issue of American Airlines' (D) liability in this action. American Airlines (D) raises several arguments in opposition, including the Full Faith and Credit Clause of the Constitution and the doctrine of mutuality.

■ **ISSUE**

May offensive nonmutual estoppel be utilized in a court that is part of a judicial system different from the court that rendered the prior judgment?

■ **DECISION AND RATIONALE**

(Frank, J.) Yes. Offensive nonmutual estoppel may be utilized in a court that is part of a judicial system different from the court that rendered the prior judgment. Landano (P) and Kirchstein (P) do not dispute that they were not parties to the Texas action. Nevertheless, the issue of American Airlines' (D) liability is identical in both actions. In addition, American Airlines (D) had a full and fair opportunity to contest the decision in the 19-day trial and appeal of the Texas action. Thus, the requirements for collateral estoppel are met. American Airlines (D) contends that the Full Faith and Credit Clause prevents the Texas decision from having preclusive effect. However, this Clause is implicated only when a judgment of another court is sought to be enforced in a different jurisdiction. In our case, Landano (P) and Kirchstein (P) do not seek to enforce the Texas decision, but rather to utilize the issue decided against the airline. American Airlines (D) further argues that mutuality is required to apply collateral estoppel.

This contention completely ignores the New York Supreme Court's holding in *DeWitt, Inc. v. Hall* [The doctrine of mutuality is a dead letter]. Next, American Airlines (D) contends that the Texas issue was submitted under Kentucky substantive law rather than New York law. This argument ignores the fact that the New York court is obliged to decide this case under Kentucky law as well. Finally, American Airlines (D) argues that the Texas judgment should not be given preclusive effect because that action involved only a single claimant and because the jury's decision was rendered without any awareness that the jury would determine the obligation of American Airlines (D) to many other persons not before it. However, the negligence of American Airlines (D) in no way depends upon the number of claims which may ultimately be asserted against it. Accordingly, Landano (P) and Kirchstein's (P) cross motion for summary judgment is granted and American Airlines' (D) motion for a joint trial is denied.

Analysis:

This case reaffirms the doctrine of offensive nonmutual estoppel, and it applies the doctrine to preclude an issue in a jurisdiction different from the court that originally rendered the judgment. It makes sense that American Airlines (D) should be precluded from relitigating the identical issue that was decided in Texas, because American Airlines (D) had a full opportunity to contest the issue in Texas. As the opinion notes, a party who has had his day in court should not be permitted to litigate the same question anew. In addition, this avoids the condition where one fact-finder could, on the same set of facts, find a party liable while another exonerates him, leading to inconsistent results which are a blemish on a judicial system.

■ CASE VOCABULARY

MUTUALITY: The doctrine requiring a party asserting collateral estoppel to have been a party to the prior action.

Thompson v. Thompson

(Father) v. (Mother)
484 U.S. 174, 108 S.Ct. 513 (1988)

THE RES JUDICATA EFFECT OF A MODIFIABLE CHILD CUSTODY DECREE SHOULD BE ASSERTED IN STATE COURT AND NOT IN FEDERAL COURT

■ **INSTANT FACTS** A father sought to utilize a federal act to resolve two conflicting state child custody decrees.

■ **BLACK LETTER RULE** The PKPA precludes a state court from maintaining the ability to reopen child custody proceedings.

■ **PROCEDURAL BASIS**

Writ of certiorari reviewing order affirming motion to dismiss federal court action to determine which of two conflicting state custody decrees was valid.

■ **FACTS**

In July 1978, Susan Thompson (D) filed a petition in California state court seeking marital dissolution and sole custody of her son, Matthew. The court initially awarded joint custody to Susan (D) and her husband, David (P). The joint custody arrangement became infeasible once Susan (D) desired to move to Louisiana for a new job. The court then entered an order awarding Susan (D) sole custody once she left for Louisiana, but it reserved the right to change the custody determination once the court investigator submitted his report. Susan (P) moved to Louisiana and filed a petition in Louisiana state court for enforcement of the California custody decree. In April 1981 the Louisiana state court granted the petition and awarded Susan (P) sole custody. In June 1981, however, the California court changed its original order, after receiving the investigator's report, and awarded sole custody to David (P). David (P) then filed a petition in California federal court to have the Louisiana decree declared invalid and the California decree valid pursuant to the federal Parental Kidnaping Prevention Act ("PKPA"). The PKPA requires States to enforce child custody determinations entered by a court of a sister State provided certain conditions are met. David (P) did not attempt to enforce the California decree in Louisiana. Susan (D) moved to dismiss for lack of subject-matter and personal jurisdiction, arguing that the PKPA does not create a new federal cause of action. The District Court granted the motion, the Ninth Circuit Court of Appeals affirmed, and the Supreme Court granted certiorari.

■ **ISSUE**

Is the ability to reopen child custody disputes entitled to preclusive effect?

■ **DECISION AND RATIONALE**

(Marshall, J.) Yes. The ability to reopen child custody disputes is entitled to preclusive effect, unless the PKPA conditions are satisfied. Furthermore, the PKPA does not provide a federal cause of action to determine which of two conflicting state custody decrees is valid. The PKPA was created because of an anomaly in applying the Full Faith and Credit Clause to custody disputes. The full faith and credit doctrine obliges States only to accord the same force to judgments as would be accorded by the courts of the rendering State. Because courts entering custody orders generally retain the power to modify them, courts in other States were no less entitled to change the terms of custody according to their own views of the child's best interest. For those reasons, a parent who lost a custody battle in one State had an incentive to kidnap the child and move to another State to relitigate the issue. Thus, the context of the PKPA suggests that Congress was seeking to remedy the inapplicability of the Full Faith and Credit Clause to custody determinations. The PKPA was not drafted in order to create a federal cause of action to resolve conflicting custody determinations between two states. The states themselves must enforce the provisions of the PKPA and refuse to give the sister state the ability to reopen the custody dispute. Affirmed.

Analysis:

This case sheds an interesting light on the Full Faith and Credit Clause and indirectly raises some collateral estoppel issues. In order for either the full faith and credit doctrine or the collateral estoppel doctrine to operate, the prior judgment must be considered "final." The problem with most child custody judgments, as the opinion notes, is that they are rarely "final." Rather, they are subject to modification in the best interests of the child. As a result, custody determinations were not enforceable and could not necessarily be given preclusive effect in other states, creating the kidnaping crisis. In the case at hand, Louisiana initially honored California's decision regarding Matthew's sole custody. This was probably based upon the PKPA, because the California judgment was not "final" for purposes of collateral estoppel. Once the California court changed its determination, all David Thompson (P) had to do was file an action in Louisiana to enforce the California decree. However, he apparently thought that the PKPA entitled him to bring a federal action in California. Assuming the statute of limitations had not yet run, David (P) probably could have initiated an action in Louisiana based upon the PKPA. This would sidestep the California court's ability to reopen the custody dispute.

■ **CASE VOCABULARY**

INTRACTABLE: Difficult to manage.

NUGATORY: Futile or invalid.

Allen v. McCurry

(*Police Officer*) v. (*Drug Dealer*)

449 U.S. 90, 101 S.Ct. 411, 66 L.Ed.2d 308 (1980)

CONGRESS REQUIRES ALL FEDERAL COURTS TO GIVE PRECLUSIVE EFFECT TO STATE COURT JUDGMENTS WHENEVER A STATE COURT ITSELF WOULD DO SO

■ **INSTANT FACTS** McCurry (P), having been found guilty of drug possession, later sued Allen (D) and other police officers for alleged violations of McCurry's (P) constitutional rights against unlawful search and seizure.

■ **BLACK LETTER RULE** Federal courts must give preclusive effect to state court judgments even where federal civil rights are at issue.

■ PROCEDURAL BASIS

Certiorari to the United States Court of Appeals for the Eighth Circuit in action for violation of the Fourth Amendment and Civil Rights Act § 1983.

■ FACTS

McCurry (P) was charged with possession of heroin in a state-court proceeding. The trial judge excluded some of the evidence, holding that it was seized through illegal police search. The jury, nonetheless, found McCurry (P) guilty of the charge. Subsequently, McCurry (P) filed a civil action for damages in federal court based on 28 U.S.C. § 1983 and alleged violations of Fourth Amendment rights against unlawful search and seizure against Allen (D) and other police officers. The District Court granted Allen's (D) motion for summary judgment on the ground that the Fourth Amendment issue had already been raised in the state-court proceedings. The Court of Appeals reversed, holding that the rules of issue preclusion should not apply due to the special role of federal courts in protecting the civil rights of individuals. The Supreme Court of the United States granted certiorari to the Court of Appeals.

■ ISSUE

Must federal courts give preclusive effect to state court judgments even where federal civil rights are at issue?

■ DECISION AND RATIONALE

(Stewart, J.) Yes. Federal courts must give preclusive effect to state court judgments even where federal civil rights are at issue. Congress has specifically required all federal courts to give preclusive effect to state-court judgments whenever the courts of the state from which the judgments emerged would do so. Nothing in the language of § 1983 indicates the congressional intent to contravene the common law rules of preclusion. Neither does the legislative history of the law indicate such an intent. Through this legislation Congress added to the jurisdiction of federal courts. It did not, however, subtract from the jurisdiction of state courts. This law was intended as a remedy in three situations: (a) where state substantive law was facially unconstitutional, (b) where state procedural law was inadequate to allow full litigation of a constitutional claim, and (c) where state procedural law, though adequate in theory, was inadequate in practice. The law thus, allows federal courts to step in where state courts are unwilling or unable to protect federal rights of individuals. This view of § 1983 would allow an exception to res judicata and collateral estoppel where state law did not provide fair procedures for the litigation of constitutional claims, or where a state court failed or even acknowledged the existence of the principle on which the litigant based his claims. Thus, it would support the general exception to collateral estoppel which prohibits application of the doctrine where the party against whom an earlier court decision is asserted did not have a full and fair opportunity to litigate the claim or the issue decided by the first court. There is however, no reason to believe that Congress intended to provide a person claiming a federal right violation, an unrestricted opportunity to re-litigate an issue already decided in state court simply because the issue arose in state proceedings. (Reversed and Remanded.)

■ DISSENT

(Blackmun, Brennan, Marshall, JJ.) In this case McCurry (P) should be allowed to litigate his claim. First, at the time § 1983 was passed, a nonparty's ability to invoke collateral estoppel did not exist. Also, no preclusive effect could arise out of criminal proceedings which could affect subsequent civil liability because of the narrow definition of issue and claim. Also, the process and remedy of deciding in a state criminal proceeding to exclude or admit evidence is not equal to a § 1983 proceeding. In the civil suit, the defendant simply wants money damages. However, in the criminal trial, exclusion of evidence may lead to criminal conviction and to the determination of guilt or innocence of the defendant which is a separate issue from damages.

Analysis:

This case involves the effect of collateral estoppel and res judicata on state-court judgments in a federal court. The result is very much like the *Parker* case. As long as an individual has had the full and fair opportunity to litigate the issues and the claims against him, then the earlier judgment can be used against him. This is true even if the earlier judgment emerged from a state court and is then used by a federal court.

Semtek International, Inc. v. Lockheed Martin Corp.

(Plaintiff) v. *(Defendant)*

531 U.S. 497, 121 S.Ct. 1021, 149 L.Ed.2d 32 (2001)

A CLAIM DISMISSED AS TIME–BARRED MAY BE BROUGHT IN ANOTHER JURISDICTION WITH A LONGER STATUTORY PERIOD

■ **INSTANT FACTS** After a California federal court dismissed the plaintiff's action on the basis of the state statute of limitations, a Maryland state court dismissed a subsequent suit brought by the plaintiff on the same grounds.

■ **BLACK LETTER RULE** The law of the state in which the federal court sits governs the claim-preclusive effect of a judgment on the merits in a federal diversity action.

■ **PROCEDURAL BASIS**

Certiorari to review a decision of the Maryland Court of Special Appeals affirming a trial court dismissal of the plaintiff's action.

■ **FACTS**

Semtek International, Inc. (P) sued Lockheed Martin Corp. (D) in California state court for breach of contract and various torts. Lockheed Martin (D) removed the case to California federal court on the basis of diversity of citizenship and successfully moved for dismissal of the action with prejudice on the merits as barred by the state-law statute of limitations. The Ninth Circuit Court of Appeals affirmed. Thereafter, Semtek (P) refiled its case against Lockheed Martin (D) in Maryland state court within the Maryland statute of limitations. On the defendant's motion, the Maryland court dismissed the complaint on the basis of res judicata, reasoning that the decision of the California federal court was on the merits and precluded the subsequent suit. After a Maryland court of appeals affirmed, Semtek (P) sought a writ of certiorari.

■ **ISSUE**

Is the claim-preclusive effect of a federal judgment dismissing a diversity action on statute-of-limitations grounds determined by the law of the state in which the federal court sits?

■ **DECISION AND RATIONALE**

(Scalia, J.) Yes. Under Federal Rule of Civil Procedure 41(b), a court order dismissing a plaintiff's complaint "operates as an adjudication on the merits" unless otherwise specified. While an adjudication on the merits generally has a claim-preclusive effect on the relitigation of those claims, not all adjudications on the merits are barred by res judicata. "On the merits" is generally understood as a determination of the substance of the claim. While traditionally judgments on the merits have invoked the doctrines of res judicata and claim preclusion, no longer do all adjudications on the merits have a claim-preclusive effect under Rule 41(b). In this instance, Rule 41(b) governs the internal procedures of the California federal court, declaring its decision on the merits by default. To hold this procedural declaration binding upon the plaintiff's substantive state-law rights to pursue its claims in another jurisdiction would violate the principles of the Rules Enabling Act, which specifically preserves a party's substantive rights. Further, any claim-preclusive effect of the federal court judgment on the plaintiff's state-law rights would give rise to conflicting decisions based on the forum in which the decision is rendered. For instance, under California state law, a party may not recover a desired remedy after the expiration of the state statute of limitations. Yet, the claims remain viable for consideration in an appropriate foreign jurisdiction. If a defendant in a diversity action could defeat the law of the state by merely removing the action to federal court for a decision on the merits under state law, the result of the action would be determined not by the law of the state, but by the forum in which the law is applied. Accordingly, the reasonable understanding of the default language of Rule 41(b) is that "adjudication on the merits" is the opposite of "dismissal without prejudice" as discussed in Rule 41(a). Although a dismissal with prejudice may, under certain circumstances, bar a party from relitigating his claims in other courts, the default provisions of Rule 41(b) should be construed only to preclude relitigation of the claims in the same court in which the adjudication on the merits was decided. Rule 41(b) does not determine the claim-preclusive effect of the California federal court judgment in the Maryland state court.

Since Rule 41(b) does not control the preclusive effect of the federal court judgment, the Court must fashion a rule to be applied. In *Dupasseur v. Rochereau*, the Court applied a since-repealed statute to determine that the law of the state in which the federal court sits properly determines the claim-preclusive effect of a federal diversity judgment. Although *Dupasseur* does not apply to this matter given its reliance upon a repealed statute, its reasoning continues to be appropriate in diversity actions. Because state law governs the substantive rights involved in a federal diversity action, state law should similarly govern the claim-preclusive effect of a federal court judgment applying state law. As mentioned, any uniform federal rule would create forum shopping and promote removal, when available, for a tactical advantage. Only when federal interests directly conflict with the state-law interests will the federal interests prevail.

Here, because the California federal court granted dismissal on the merits only because state law so required, California state law governs the issue of claim preclusion. Because California does not forbid the plaintiff from bringing its claims in another jurisdiction, the Maryland court erred in dismissing the plaintiff's claims. Reversed.

Analysis:

Semtek is controversial, in part, because it endeavors to apply state procedural law in a federal diversity case. Under *Erie v. Tompkins* and its progeny, a federal court sitting in diversity generally applies the substantive law of the state in which the action arose and the procedural rules of the federal court, most notably the Federal Rules of Civil Procedure. The problem encountered in *Semtek*, however, is that the Federal Rules of Civil Procedure fail to discuss the claim-preclusive effect of federal diversity judgments. With no procedural rule to enforce, the Court created federal common law to resolve the issue.

■ CASE VOCABULARY

CLAIM PRECLUSION: "[T]he principal distinction between claim preclusion and issue preclusion is . . . that the former forecloses litigation of matters that have never been litigated. This makes it important to know the dimensions of the 'claim' that is foreclosed by bringing the first action, but unfortunately no precise definition is possible." Charles Alan Wright, *The Law of Federal Courts* § 100A, at 723 (5th ed. 1994).

RES JUDICATA: An issue that has been definitely settled by judicial decision. An affirmative defense barring the same parties from litigating a second lawsuit on the same claim, or any other claim arising from the same transaction or series of transactions and that could have been—but was not—raised in the first suit. The three essential elements are (1) an earlier decision on the same issue, (2) a final judgment on the merits, and (3) the involvement of the same parties in privity with the original parties.

STATUTE OF LIMITATIONS: A law that bars claims after a specified period; specifically, a statute establishing a time limit for suing in a civil case, based on the date when the claim accrued (as when the injury occurred or was discovered). The purpose of such a statute is to require diligent prosecution of known claims, thereby providing finality and predictability in legal affairs and ensuring that claims will be resolved while evidence is reasonably available and fresh.

CHAPTER EIGHTEEN

Alternative Dispute Resolution

Delta Air Lines, Inc. v. August

Instant Facts: August (D) filed a suit against Delta Air Lines (P) ("Delta") for $20,000 in back pay, and lost her case after having refused Delta's (P) formal settlement offer for $450.

Black Letter Rule: FRCP 68 does not apply to a case in which judgment is entered against a plaintiff-offeree and in favor of the defendant-offeror.

Marek v. Chesny

Instant Facts: Chesny (D), having filed suit against Marek (P), a police officer for the death of Chesny's (D) son, and having won a judgment, filed a request for attorney's fees.

Black Letter Rule: FRCP does not require that a defendant's offer itemize the respective amounts being tendered for settlement of the underlying claim and for costs.

In Re African–American Slave Descendants Litigation

Instant Facts: Descendants of former slaves sought the appointment of a mediator to resolve pending claims.

Black Letter Rule: Alternative dispute resolution may be ordered when authorized by local rule, applicable statute, the Federal Rules of Civil Procedure, or the court's inherent power.

Delta Air Lines, Inc. v. August

(*Employer*) v. (*Employee*)
450 U.S. 346, 101 S.Ct. 1146, 67 L.Ed.2d 287 (1981)

FEDERAL RULE OF CIVIL PROCEDURE 68 DIRECTS THAT A PLAINTIFF WHO REJECTS A FORMAL SETTLEMENT OFFER MUST PAY POST–OFFER COSTS IF THE JUDGMENT FINALLY OBTAINED BY THE OFFEREE IS NOT MORE FAVORABLE THAN THE OFFER

■ **INSTANT FACTS** August (D) filed a suit against Delta Air Lines (P) ("Delta") for $20,000 in back pay, and lost her case after having refused Delta's (P) formal settlement offer for $450.

■ **BLACK LETTER RULE** FRCP 68 does not apply to a case in which judgment is entered against a plaintiff-offeree and in favor of the defendant-offeror.

■ **PROCEDURAL BASIS**

Certiorari to the Court of Appeals for the Seventh Circuit in action for application of FRCP 68.

■ **FACTS**

August (D), having filed a suit against Delta (P) to recover $20,000 in back pay, rejected Delta's (P) formal offer of settlement for $450. The trial court ruled in favor of Delta (P). Under Federal Rule of Civil Procedure 68 ("FRCP 68"), a plaintiff who rejects a formal settlement offer must pay litigation costs if the plaintiff-offeree gets a lower judgment than the settlement offer. The trial court, however, held that FRCP was not applicable in this case because Delta's (P) offer was not a reasonable, good-faith attempt to settle the case. The Court of Appeal for the Seventh Circuit affirmed. The Supreme Court of the United States granted certiorari.

■ **ISSUE**

Does FRCP 68 apply to a case in which judgment is entered against a plaintiff-offeree and in favor of the defendant-offeror?

■ **DECISION AND RATIONALE**

(Stevens, J.) No. FRCP 68 does not apply to a case in which judgment is entered against a plaintiff-offeree and in favor of the defendant-offeror. This court's interpretation of FRCP 68 is consistent with its plain language and purpose of the rule, which is to encourage settlement of litigation. While potential defeat of a claim is an incentive to settlement, this rule has the additional incentive in cases where there is a strong probability that the plaintiff will obtain a judgment but the amount is uncertain. Under this rule, the plaintiff will lose the benefit of winning if the recovery after litigation is less than the offer. Since the losing party often bears the cost of litigation, this rule would provide little incentive if it were applied when a plaintiff loses completely. Delta (P), on the other hand, argues that FRCP 68 does provide such an incentive because it operates to deprive the trial judge of the discretion vested to him under FRCP 54 (d) to allow a prevailing plaintiff to recover costs of litigation. According to Delta (P), FRCP is mandatory, and a district judge must assess costs against a plaintiff who rejects a settlement offer and then either fails to obtain a judgment or recovers less than the offer. Based on this reasoning, any defendant, by making a meaningless offer, would eliminate the trial judge's discretion in imposing costs of litigation. This court can not reasonably conclude that the drafters of FRCP 54(d) grant the trial judge discretion which can be easily taken away by a meaningless settlement offer of a defendant. This court believes that FRCP 54(d) allows the trial judge to retain discretion in imposing costs of litigation where a defendant wins, or when the judgment in favor of plaintiff is greater than the settlement offer. Thus, FRCP 68 only applies where the plaintiff gets a judgment less than the settlement offer. (Affirmed on different grounds.)

■ DISSENT

(Rehnquist, J.) The Court maintains that its holding "is dictated by the plain language, the purpose, and the history of Rule 68." Though it reaches the same result as the Court of Appeals, the majority indicates the lower court was entirely in error in even reaching the question of whether Delta's (D) offer was reasonable because Rule 68 does not apply where the judgment is entered *against* the plaintiff-offeree and *in favor of* the defendant-offeror. This totally ignores the common sense maxim that the greater includes the lesser. In my view the only conditions for bringing the Rule into play are those contained in the provisions of the Rule itself. Therefore, the best and shortest response to the Court of Appeals' suggestion that a Rule 68 offer must be "reasonable" and made in good "faith" is that Rule 68 simply does not incorporate any such requirement; it deprives a court of its discretion under Rule 54 to disallow costs to the prevailing party with the word "must." This has never been interpreted to mean "may." To import the requirement that a offer be "reasonable" or made in "good faith" rewrites the Rule and places a court in the tenuous position of evaluating such nebulous concepts. According to the Court, a plaintiff-offeree must *win* in the trial court in order to "obtain" a "judgment" within the meaning of the Rule. This conclusion is anomalous. "Judgment" is defined in Rule 54(a) to mean a "decree and any order from which an appeal lies." August (P) unquestionably "obtained" an "order from which an appeal lies" when the District Court entered its judgment. Rule 68, when construed to include a traditional "take nothing" judgment, as well as a judgment in favor of the plaintiff but less than the amount of the offer, thus fits with the remaining parts of the Federal Rules of Civil Procedure pertaining to judgments and orders in a manner in which the drafters of the Rule surely must have intended. The event that triggered operation of the original Rule 68 was the plaintiff's failure to obtain a judgment more favorable than that offered. The operation of the Rule was not intended to change when this part of the Rule was amended in 1948 to its present form. Under the Courts interpretation, a plaintiff who refuses an offer and then has a "take nothing" judgment is better off than a plaintiff who refuses an offer and then obtains a favorable judgment that is less than the offer. This result is illogical.

Analysis:

According to FRCP 54(d), the trial judge has discretion to deny costs to the prevailing party. FRCP 68, on the other hand, directs that a plaintiff who rejects a formal settlement offer must pay costs of litigation, if the final judgment is not more than the settlement offer. This case deals with the scenario where the plaintiff has received a judgment against it and can not recover at all. The Supreme Court in this case is attempting to reach a decision which is in accordance with the other relevant rules of the FRCP. Thus, the Court compromises by indicating that FRCP 68 only applies to situations where the plaintiff does recover, however, the recovery is less than the amount of the formal settlement offer. According to this reasoning, FRCP 68 does not apply where the defendant wins a judgment in its favor, or where the plaintiff wins a greater amount than the settlement offer.

■ CASE VOCABULARY

SETTLEMENT: A compromise achieved by the adverse parties in a civil suit before final judgment, whereby they agree between themselves upon their respective rights and obligations, thus eliminating the necessity of judicial resolution of the controversy.

Marek v. Chesny

(*Police Officers*) v. (*Administrator of Estate of Decedent*)
473 U.S. 1, 105 S.Ct. 3012, 87 L.Ed.2d 1 (1985)

ACCORDING TO THE SUPREME COURT, THE TERM "COSTS" UNDER FRCP 68 INCLUDES ATTORNEY'S FEES

■ **INSTANT FACTS** Chesny (D), having filed suit against Marek (P), a police officer for the death of Chesny's (D) son, and having won a judgment, filed a request for attorney's fees.

■ **BLACK LETTER RULE** FRCP does not require that a defendant's offer itemize the respective amounts being tendered for settlement of the underlying claim and for costs.

■ **PROCEDURAL BASIS**

Certiorari to the Court of Appeals in action for recovery of attorney's fees under FRCP 68.

■ **FACTS**

Chesny (D) filed suit under 42 U.S.C. § 1983 and state tort law against Marek (P) and other police officers who had shot and killed Chesny's (D) son. Prior to the trial, the police officers (P) made an offer of settlement for $100,000, which Chesny (D) refused. At trial, Chesny (D) was awarded $5,000 on the state-law claim, $52,000 for the 1983 violation, and $3,000 in punitive damages. Chesny (D) then filed a request for attorney's fees for work performed subsequent to the settlement offer under § 1983 which allows a prevailing party under this section to recover attorney's fees as a part of the costs. The District Court declined the request pursuant to FRCP 68. The Court of Appeals reversed. The Supreme Court of the Unites States granted certiorari.

■ **ISSUE**

Does FRCP 68 require that a defendant's offer itemize the respective amounts being tendered for settlement of the underlying claim and for costs?

■ **DECISION AND RATIONALE**

(Burger, J.) No. FRCP does not require that a defendant's offer itemize the respective amounts being tendered for settlement of the underlying claim and for costs. Whether or not a settlement offer recites that costs are included or specifies an amount for costs, the offer allows a judgment to be entered against the defendant both for damages caused by the unlawful conduct and for costs. In FRCP 68, the term "costs" refers to all costs properly awardable under relevant substantive statute. Thus, where the relevant statute defines costs to include attorney's fees, the fees are to be included as costs for the purposes of FRCP 68. In this case therefore, since Section 1983 expressly includes attorney's fees as "costs" available to a prevailing plaintiff, those fees are subject to the cost-shifting provision of FRCP 68.

■ **DISSENT**

(Brennan, Marshall, Blackmun, JJ.) The question in this case is whether the term "costs" under FRCP 68 refers to traditional costs such as court fees, printing expenses, and the like, or instead includes attorney's fees. The court today holds that a prevailing civil rights litigant entitled to fees under that statute is per se barred from receiving any fees for work after rejecting a settlement offer based on FRCP 68. The Court's reasoning is inconsistent with the structure and history of the Federal Rules and with the attorney's fees statutes enacted by Congress. Also, the Court's interpretation will undermine the purposes behind the attorney's fees provisions of the civil rights laws.

Analysis:

Note that in this case, the Supreme Court is attempting to strike a compromise between a civil rights statute allowing attorney's fees to a prevailing plaintiff, and FRCP 68 which holds a plaintiff liable for costs when the plaintiff receives a judgment which is less than the settlement offer. The court does so by defining the term "costs," as it appears in FRCP 68, to include attorney's fees. In this case, the Chesny prevailed. However, the amount of the judgment that he received was less than the settlement offer. Under FRCP 68, Chesny would not be able to recover the costs of litigation. Chesny, however, is relying on a statute which specifically allows him to recover attorney's fees as the prevailing party. The Court, however, in reaching a compromise, defines costs to include attorney's fees, and holds that even though the statute may allow the recovery of such fees, FRCP limits recovery by looking at the amount of the settlement and the amount recovered by the plaintiff in the court's judgment.

In re African–American Slave Descendants' Litigation

(Descendants of Slaves)
272 F.Supp.2d 755 (N.D. Ill. 2003)

COURTS MAY ORDER MANDATORY NONBINDING MEDIATION

Daddy has the power to order me to mediate, but nobody can force me to compromise.

stus.com

■ **INSTANT FACTS** Descendants of former slaves sought the appointment of a mediator to resolve pending claims.

■ **BLACK LETTER RULE** Alternative dispute resolution may be ordered when authorized by local rule, applicable statute, the Federal Rules of Civil Procedure, or the court's inherent power.

■ **PROCEDURAL BASIS**

Consideration of the plaintiffs' motion to request the appointment of a mediator.

■ **FACTS**

Former slaves and the descendents of former slaves filed suit against various corporate defendants who allegedly benefited from the slave trade, claiming a property interest in the fruits of their ancestors' unpaid labor. At an initial status conference, the plaintiffs indicated their intention to request the appointment of a special master. Two months after the expiration of the deadline for such a request, the plaintiffs filed a motion to appoint a mediator.

■ **ISSUE**

May the court order mandatory nonbinding mediation when one of the parties refuses to consent to alternative dispute resolution?

■ **DECISION AND RATIONALE**

(Norgle, J.) Yes. Courts often rely upon alternative dispute resolution to minimize the cost and burden of complex litigation to the parties and the court system. The Alternative Dispute Resolution Act demands that a federal court require civil litigants to consider alternative dispute resolution as a means of reaching a compromise. Even when the parties refuse to consent to mediation, a court may nonetheless order mandatory mediation when local rules, an applicable statute, the Federal Rules of Civil Procedure, or the court's inherent power so authorize. Here, local rules provide for voluntary mediation in specified cases, but confer no authority to compel mandatory mediation. Similarly, the Alternative Dispute Resolution Act, while stressing the importance of mediation and other alternative dispute resolution methods, requires authority under local rules to compel mandatory mediation. Neither does Federal Rule of Civil Procedure 16(c)(9), authorizing the court to take appropriate action relating to settlement and special procedures to resolve the litigation, specifically authorize compelled mediation when the parties are unwilling to consent. However, under the court's inherent power to enhance the court process by expeditiously and reasonably disposing of pending cases, the court may order nonbinding mediation even without the parties' consent. But because of the vastly differing views of the case at issue, nonbinding mediation in this case will not expedite resolution and would serve only to expose the parties to additional burden and cost, without a substantial likelihood of settling the matter. Motion denied.

Analysis:

From a practical standpoint, a court that wants the parties to submit to nonbinding mediation may nearly always rationalize its decision on the basis of its inherent powers. While this court considered mediation a meaningless effort to bring the two sides together on important issues, other courts may see such an opportunity as meaningful and properly exercise their discretion. Furthermore, because such mediation is nonbinding, any settlement will nearly always be voluntary, eliminating challenges to the court's order on appeal.

■ **CASE VOCABULARY**

ALTERNATIVE DISPUTE RESOLUTION: A procedure for settling a dispute by means other than litigation, such as arbitration, mediation, or mini-trial.

MEDIATION: A method of nonbinding dispute resolution involving a neutral third party who tries to help the disputing parties reach a mutually agreeable solution.